MODERN AND CONTEMPORARY
MACEDONIA

HISTORY – ECONOMY – SOCIETY – CULTURE

VOLUME I

MACEDONIA UNDER OTTOMAN RULE

EDITED BY: IOANNIS KOLIOPOULOS – IOANNIS HASSIOTIS

PAPAZISSIS PUBLISHERS – PARATIRITIS PUBLISHING HOUSE

© Papazissis Publishers - Paratiritis Publishing house

ISBN 960-260-724-6

Papazissis Publishers and Paratiritis Publishing house wish to express their gratitude to the Institute for Balkan Studies, the Society for Macedonian Studies, the Folklore Museum of Thessaloniki,the Benakis Museum, the Folklore Archive of the University of Thessaloniki, the Municipal Library of Thessaloniki, the Museum of Macedonian Struggle, the History Centre of Thessaloniki, Mr. Ioannis Mazarakis-Ainian, Mr. Vassilis Tzanakaris and all those who contributed to this publication

CONTENS

A WORD ABOUT OUR CONTRIBUTORS

Ioannis D. Psaras

Born in Thessaloniki in 1946. He graduated from the Faculty of Arts of the University of Thessaloniki in 1969, whence he also obtained a post-graduate degree (1976) and a Doctorate (1985), and where he is now Assistant Professor of Modern History in the Department of History and Archaeology. He has worked in archives and libraries both in Greece and abroad (especially Venice). He is a member of the principal scholarly historic societies; and his studies refer to the relationships between the worlds of Greece and Europe in the 15th to the 19th centuries, and to Venetian rule in Greece.

Vassilis K. Gounaris

Born in Switzerland in 1961, he graduated from the Faculty of Arts (Department of History) of the University of Thessaloniki in 1983. In 1985 he obtained a post-graduate degree from the same Faculty, and in 1988 a Doctorate from St Antony's College, Oxford, where he had studied on a scholarship from the Ismene Fitch Charitable Trust. Since 1990 he has been a consultant historian for the Museum of the Macedonian Struggle. His specialty is the economic and social history of modern Macedonia.

Charalampos Papastathis

Born in Thessaloniki in 1940. A graduate of the University of Thessaloniki Law School, he is an expert on ecclesiastical law and the history of law. Today he is Professor of Ecclesiastical Law at the Faculty of Law of the University of Thessaloniki. He has also served as General Secretary of Religious Affairs in the Ministry of Education and Religious Affairs (1987-1988).

Father Andreas Nanakis

Born in Herakleion in 1957. He was ordained by Timothy, Bishop of Crete. He studied Theology and History at the University of Thessaloniki and at the Instituto Orientale in Rome. In 1988 he obtained a Doctorate from the Faculty of Theology of the University of Thessaloniki, where since 1989 he has been a lecturer. His interest is in the field of modern ecclesiastical history.

Christos Patrinelis

Born in Kiato, in the Prefecture of Corinth, in 1929, he has been Professor of Modern Greek History at the Faculty of Arts of the University of Thessaloniki since 1973. Before that (1959-1973) he worked at the "Centre for Research on Mediaeval and Modern Hellenism" at the Academy of Athens. His research and publications are chiefly in the field of the History of Education and the Church, as well as on demographic matters in the period 1453-1821.

Athanasios Karathanasis

Born in Volos in 1946. Graduated from the Faculty of Arts of the University of Thessaloniki in 1969, whence he obtained a Doctorate in 1975. He taught Modern Greek Philology at the University of Athens, first as Lecturer (1983) and then as Assistant Professor (1987-1989). Since 1989 he has been Associate Professor of the History of Hellenism at the Pastoral Department of the University of Thessaloniki, and since 1974 has been a consultant at the Institute for Balkan Studies. His work is chiefly in the field of the intellectual and educational movements in Turkish-occupied Greece, especially in the period between the 17th and the early 19th centuries.

Nikos Nikonanos

Born in Thessaloniki in 1935, he studied Classical Byzantine Architecture at the city's Aristotelian University. From 1965 to 1984 he worked as an Inspector of Antiquities in Macedonia, Thessaly, the northern Sporades and Mount Athos; today he is Professor of Art History in the School of Architecture at the University of Thessaloniki. His particular field of study is the art and architecture of Macedonia and Thessaly.

Plutarchos Theocharides

Born in Thessaloniki in 1946, he studied architecture at the University of Thessaloniki before specializing in the restoration of monuments at the University of Rome. He works at the 10th Inspectorate of Byzantine Antiquities, and is particularly interested in the history of Athonite architecture.

Miltiades D. Polubiou

Born in Nea Moudania (Chalcidice) in 1946, he graduated in architecture from the University of Thessaloniki, where he continued with post-graduate studies in the Department of History and Archaeology at the Faculty of Arts. Since 1977 he has been employed by the Archaelogical Service, and works on the restoration of monuments in Chalcidice and Mount Athos. His principal field of research is in post-Byzantine ecclesiastical architecture.

Kalliopi Theocharidou

Born in Thessaloniki in 1950, she studied architecture at the city's Aristotelian University, and continued her studies with post-graduate work in the restoration of monuments and historic buildings at York University (England). She obtained a Doctorate in the history of architecture from the Metsovion Polytechnic School in Athens, and did post-doctoral work on Byzantine Architecture at the Centre for Byzantine Studies at Dumbarton Oaks, Washington. She works at the 9th Inspectorate of Byzantine Antiquities, where her special field of study is Byzantine architecture in Thessaloniki and post-Byzantine architecture in Macedonia.

Nikolaos Moutsopoulos

Born in Athens in 1927, where he studied Architecture at the Metsovion Polytechnical School, graduating in 1953. He did post-graduate work at the Sorbonne, studied theology at the University of Thessaloniki, and obtained a Doctorate in 1956. In 1958 he became a Professor in the Department of Architecture of the University of Thessaloniki's Polytechnic School. His principal fields of study are Byzantine architecture, mediaeval fortifications and traditional architecture. He has served as president of the International Institute of Towers and Fortifications (IBI), and is a member of numerous scholarly societies and institutes. He has published work on various topics within his field, and has carried out excavations in southwest Euboia (watch towers), Prespa (basilica of Aghios Achilleios, church of Aghion Apostolon), Kastoria (the Longa fort), Florina (the Setina fort), Rentina, and elsewhere. He is the President of the Comite International d'Architecture Vernaculaire (UNESCO - I.CO.MO.S), and a corresponding member of the Academy of Athens, the Rontiana Academy of Naples, and the Bulgarian Academy of Sciences.

Efthymia Georgiadou-Kountoura

Born in Florina in 1944. She graduated from the Department of History and Archaeology of the Faculty of Arts at the University of Thessaloniki, and continued with post-graduate work in Art History and Museology in Paris. In 1975 she returned to the University of Thessaloniki, first as assistant, in 1984 as lecturer, and now as Assistant Professor. Her particular field of study is Greek painting in the 19th and early 20th centuries, and with secular art in Macedonia and Thrace during the period of the Turkish occupation.

Eleonora Skouteri-Didaskalou

Studied archaeology at the University of Thessaloniki (1965-1970), and did post-gradute work in social anthropology at University College, London (1974-1976). She teaches social anthropology and folklore at the University of Thessaloniki (Department of History and Archaeology). Her chief field of study is the theory and history of social anthropology and folklore, with particular reference to single sex social relationships and to the traditional culture and daily life of northern Greece.

Ioannis A. Papadrianos

Born in Drepano (near Nafplion) in 1913. He graduated from the University of Thessaloniki (Faculty of Arts) in 1955, and in 1985 obtained a Doctorate from the same Faculty. He specialized in Slavic studies and the history of the Balkan peoples at the Universities of Moscow and Belgrade. From 1968-1987 he worked as a consultant at the Institute for Balkan Studies; since 1988 he has been at the Department of History and Archaeology at the University of Thessaloniki, first as lecturer and since 1992 as Assistant Professor of Balkan History. His published work is in the field of Helleno-Serbian relations from the 15th to the early 20th centuries, and on the activity of Greek emigrants to southeastern Europe.

Ioannis K. Hassiotis

Born in Volos in 1936. He studied at the University of Thessaloniki (Faculty of Arts), otaining his doctoral degree in 1966. He has been on the staff of the Faculty since 1961, and today is Professor of Modern History in the Department of History and Archaeology. He has worked in archives and libraries in Greece, Italy, Spain, Great Britain, Germany, Austria, the USA, and elsewhere. His published work deals with the history of the Greek Diaspora, the revolutionary movements on the Greek mainland during the period of the Turkish occupation, Hispano-Hellenic and Armeno-Hellenic relationships, and various aspects of the Eastern Question in the 19th and 20th centuries.

Artemis Xanthopoulou-Kyriakou

Born in Serres in 1941. She graduated from the University of Thessaloniki (Faculty of Arts) in 1964, obtained her Doctorate from the same Faculty in 1978, where since 1966 she has been on the staff, as assistant, assistant lecturer (1979), lecturer (1985), and since 1985 Assistant Professor of Modern Greek History in the Department of History and Archaeology. She has worked in libraries and archives in Greece, France and Great Britain. Her principal fields of study deal with the history of the Greek colonies in northern Italy in the late 18th and early 19th centuries, the activity of Kosmas Aitolos during the 1821-1822 Revolution in Macedonia, and the migrations of the Greek inhabitants of the Black Sea provinces to the Caucasus in the 19th century.

Ioannis S. Koliopoulos

Professor of Modern Greek History at the University of Thessaloniki (Department of History and Archaeology). He studied Modern History at New York City University (B.A.), and at London University (M.A., Ph.D.) His principal publications are: "Greece and the British Connection 1935-1941" (Oxford 1977), and "Brigands with a Cause: Brigandage and Irredentism in ModernGreece, 1821-1912" (Oxford 1987).

Vassileios Kontis

Born in Argyrokastro. Professor of Modern History at the University of Thessaloniki. His principal field of study is modern political and diplomatic history, with particular reference to Helleno-Albanian relations in the 19th and the first decades of the 20th century.

Giannis D. Stephanides

Born in Thessaloniki in 1961. In 1984 he graduated from the Law School of the University of Thessaloniki, and went on to study at the London School of Economics, where he obtained the degrees of Master of European Studies (1986) and Doctor of International History (1989). He has studied American and British policy in Greece and the Eastern Mediterranean during the Korean War, and has also published work on contemporary Greek history. Today he works as historical consultant at the Institute for Balkan Studies.

Theano Tsiovaridou

Studied political and economic sciences at the University of Thessaloniki, and obtained a doctoral degree from the School of Political and Economic Sciences of the University of Paris. From 1966-1969 she worked with the O.C.D.E. Since 1974 she has been on the staff of the Thessaloniki School of Economics, as assistant lecturer and (1983) Assistant Professor. She has published many studies on the economic development of Northern Greece and the economic history of Macedonia.

Miltiades Papanikolaou

Studied Archaeology and Modern Greek Philology at the University of Thessaloniki (Faculty of Arts), and was awarded a scholarship to study History of Art at the University of Munich. In 1978 he obtained a doctoral degree from the University of Thessaloniki (Faculty of Arts), and in 1981 was appointed assistant lecturer on the staff of the Faculty of Arts of the University of Athens; today he is Professor of History of Art at the University of Thessaloniki. He is joint author of many studies and articles in Greek and foreign periodicals.

Tolis Kazantzis (1938-1991)

Born in Thessaloniki, where he studied law at the University of Thessaloniki's Law School, he may be described as the Macedonian writer who best embodied the historic memory of post-war Thessaloniki in his narratives. In 1966 he received the National Award for Fictional Biography. His texts (short stories, novellas, novels, and translations) were originally published in the periodical "Diagonios" (1958-1983), and later in independent volumes or in other periodicals over the last decade. The bulk of his research has been published in "Prose Literature in Thessaloniki, 1912-1983" (1991). His essay in the second volume of "Modern and Contemporary Macedonia", the manuscript of which he managed to deliver only a short time before his untimely death, constitutes his most extensive evaluation of the intellectual (and, in general, cultural) history of Macedonia from the mid 19th century until the present.

Evaggelos Kophos

Born in Edessa in 1934, he has degrees from the Universities of Ohio and Georgetown, and a Doctorate from the University of London. His specialty is Modern Balkan History. He is a contributor to the Institute for Balkan Studies and the Greek Foreign Defense Policy Foundation, and is a consultant on Balkan affairs for the Ministry of Foreign Affairs. He has written a number of books and articles on modern political and diplomatic history, especially on the historical and political dimensions of the Macedonian Question.

Eirini Th. Lagani

Born in Athens in 1956, she graduated from the Athens Law School (Department of Political Sciences and Public Law), and obtained a doctoral degree in the History of Contemporary International Relationsfrom the Sorbonne (Paris I, Pantheon - Sorbonne). She has taught History of Contemporary Greek Foreign Policy at the Athens Law School (Department of Politics) and at the School of Public Administration, as well as Contemporary Balkan Relations at the University of Sydney, Australia (NSU). She is lecturer in history in the Faculty of Law of the Democritos University of Thrace.

Editiors-in-chief: Ioannis Koliopoulos, Ioannis Hassiotis, Yiannis Stefanidis
Lay Out: Klearchos Tsaousidis
Production Editor: Dimitra Assimakopoulou
Translation: Yiannis Stefanidis, John Solman, Jeoffrey Cox, Giorgos Magazis
Pagination: Anna Apokoroniotaki
Montage: Andreas Ziogas
Sources: Xanthippi Kotzagiorgi
Index: Maria Athanassiadou

Phototypesetting-Printing-Bookbinding: "Paratiritis" Publishing house S.A.
   15, Al. Stavrou Str., Thessaloniki, Greece, GR-546 44
   Tel. (003031) 927685, 938427, Fax. 935922, Telex. 410749
Separations: a = α, 1, I. Dragoumi Str., Thessaloniki, Tel. (031) 511220, 546565
Distribution: – Athens: "Paratiritis", 39, Didotou Str., Tel. (01) 3600658, 3608527
                        "Papazissis", 2, Nikitara Str., Tel. (01) 3609150, 3606402
            – Thessaloniki: "Paratiritis", 30, Grigoriou E Str. Tel. (031) 310506

Photos-slides: Giorgos Poupis, Nontas Stylianidis, Giorgos Giakoumidis

FOREWORD BY THE PUBLISHERS

"Modern and Contemporary Macedonia - from the Turkish occupation to the present" is the fruit of an editorial effort which began in 1986.

We were induced to publish this book by the realization that Greek literature on this subject is far from exhaustive: while coverage of ancient Macedonia is good, there is very little on modern (and less on contemporary) Macedonia.

Our decison was greeted with enthusiasm by Ioannis Koliopoulos and Ioannis Hassiotis, Professors of History at the University of Thessaloniki, who also agreed to supervise and co-ordinate this undertaking. Twenty-eight historians, economists, architects, sociologists, writers, and professors, most from the Aristotelian University, undertook to produce original texts in order to create a coherent work on the history, the economy, the society and the culture of modern and contemporary Macedonia. A vast number of archives and collections were sifted, while our photographers literally combed northern Greece to obtain photographs of the places and buildings mentioned in the text.

Now, six years later, we present with pride to the reading public a work of a thousand pages and a thousand photographs and drawings, published in English and in Greek, with texts full of overpowering detail which deflect any attempt at perversion of the historic truth.

In this troubled region, where neighbours tear each other apart, our country is the only one with no designs on any other; nor however does it tolerate perfidy. Our positions are founded on right and on history, on knowledge and memory; and we would point out that the very essence of human existence is the struggle of memory against oblivion. A nation's historical memory should be ever vigilant, especially now that the Macedonian issue has again come to the fore in such painful fashion.

And since we should not deceive ourselves into believing that a final solution can be reached in the near future, we must prepare ourselves for a long struggle. The best armour is a knowledge of history. Declarations and high oratory are of little service to the truth if there is no collective consciousness of the historical truth.

In their desire to further and promote this consciousness, the publishers have decided to publish semi-annual reports on the most recent developments in Macedonia: these supplements will guarantee that our two-volume work is always be up to date.

In the hope that other Greek publishers and scholars will combine their efforts to keep the Greek and foreign reader informed on the critical issues so inimical to peace and progress in our region, we submit this work to the readers and scholars who are our ultimate judges.

The publishers

Victor Papazissis
Petros Papassarantopoulos

Modern Macedonia

Ioannis S. Koliopoulos

Certain definitions are required with respect to the geographical area and the historical period, which provide the context for the particular chapters of the present work.

The term 'Macedonia' is used in its conventional meaning, as established by 19th century diplomacy, and refers to the geographical area then comprising the three administrative regions of European Turkey, the *vilayets* of Thessaloniki, Monastir, and Skopje. This area includes regions which had never been part of the Hellenic kingdom of Macedon, which extended up to the large lakes of the area, Prespa and Ohrid. To the north of these lakes, as it is known, lived tribes hostile to the Macedonians, the Paeones and the Dardans, which were at times subjugated by Macedonian kings but had never been incorporated culturally into the ancient Greek world. This Macedonia of diplomacy or 'Greater' Macedonia, as it is often called, was divided after the Balkan Wars (1912-1913) between Greece, on the one hand, which took her southern regions, namely the greatest part of the *vilayet* of Thessaloniki and part of the *vilayet* of Monastir, and Bulgaria, Serbia and Albania on the other, which took the northern parts. This territorial division was decided on the battlefield, first in the war of the Balkan allies against Turkey and then in the war of former allies and adversaries against Bulgaria, and was confirmed by the treaty of Bucharest (1913).

The period or, more precisely, the beginning of the present narrative and analysis is also conventional. As starting point the final capitulation of the city of Thessaloniki to the Ottoman Turks (1430) was adopted, because it marked the completion of the conquest of Macedonia, as the fall of Constantinople, a little later, has come to signify the official end of the Byzantine Empire. As in the case of the fall of the *Vasileuousa* ('the Reigning City'), the fall of Thessaloniki drew the curtain over the drama enacted over several decades, during which the provinces of Macedonia, one after the other, fell into Turkish hands. However, this date is also suitable as a starting point because with the fall of the most important, from every aspect, city of Macedonia, the whole region was brought under single rule and administration. Single rule and administrative integra-

tion created the necessary conditions for certain developments which are identified with the dawn of Modern Age. Moreover, the withdrawal of the Venetians, the last vestiges of Western presence, from Thessaloniki increased the existing distance between Orthodox and Catholics and favoured all those elements that shaped the Greek-Orthodox identity of those who remained within the jurisdiction of the Ecumenical Patriarchate.

The Turkish rule and administration and the religious authority of the Ecumenical Patriarchate were the two basic factors that, along with the impact which the policies and interventions of the Great Powers had on the Ottoman Empire, determined the fortunes of the enslaved peoples and ethnic groups of Macedonia. The division between secular authority, on one hand, and the spiritual one, on the other, led to the formation of new leading social and political groups as well as new criteria and points of reference for determining the identity of those subjected. For four centuries, until modern Western ideas of social and political organization, the new principles of self-determination of human communities in particular, penetrated the country, the secular authority of the Ottomans and the spiritual authority of the Ecumenical Patriarchate moulded the communities on the basis of religion which tended to blunt and limit the role of other cultural elements defining common identity, such as language, which in the West favoured the early growth of ethnicity. The Greek, Slav, Vlach and Albanian-speaking Christian Orthodox of Macedonia, all constituted part of the Orthodox *Oecoumeni*; they identified themselves with the Ecumenical Patriarchate, they were regarded as members of the same community and differentiated themselves from the heterodox communities of the empire, Muslims and Jews, as well as from Western Christia-nity.

The dynamic advance of national ideals during the tumultuous period of the French Revolution and the Napoleonic wars inaugurated a new era in the history of Macedonia which coincides with the vigorous appearance of the Greeks in the arena of modern nations. Modern Greek nationalism, immediately after the formation of an independent Greek state in the south of the

A map of Macedonia in Roman times, drawn by Muscovite Ivan Petrov in his illustrated **Macedonia.**
The region is divided into four **nomoi.**

Balkans, had a catalytic effect on the Orthodox community of Macedonia.

The Greek Revolution of 1821 was a major landmark in the history of Macedonia. By opening a breach between the enslaved Christians and the ruling Turks, the revolution irrevocably connected Mace-donia with the fortunes of the Modern Greek nation and its struggle for liberation. This connection was achieved first with the revolt of the Greeks of Macedonia in 1822 and its bloody supression, which brought the first wave of refugees to the liberated southern parts of Greece. These refugees, and those who followed after each revolt of Macedonian Greeks throughout the 19th century, provided the links connecting the independent national centre with the enslaved Macedonia.

The connection was also achieved by the ever- increas-ing penetration of Modern Greek national ideology through schools, cultural associations and the patriotic organizations in Macedonia as well as through the gradual incorporation of wider social groups within the system of Greek national aspirations. Linguistic groups of the same cultural community, the Greek Orthodox Oecoumeni, accepted the ideological influence of the Greek national centre from the south and were firmly tied in with its destiny. Until serious contestants for the succession to Ottoman rule in Macedonia appeared –the Bulgarians, from the last quarter of the 19th century onwards– the Greeks had succeeded in attaching the best part of the Christian Orthodox population of the country to their national objectives.

The Greek War of Independence and, in particular, the latent and inevitable antagonism between the new

Othrodoxy was a fundamental factor in determing the identity of the enslaved people of Macedonia. Mount Athos served as a major centre of the Patriarchate's religious authrority. The **Megisti Lavra** *monastery (photograph) was the earliest established on Athos.*

Greek national centre and the traditional one, the Ecumenical Patriarchate, afforded the Bulgarians with a precedent their autocephalous Church served as a vehicle for their developing into a modern nation. The delayed appearance of Bulgarian nationalism on Balkan stage caused the gradual transformation of the Greek national claims towards more realistic boundaries, on the one hand, and, on the other, the attachment of the traditional centre of the Greek-Orthodox to the aspirations of the independent national Greek centre.

The contest between Greeks and Bulgarians for the allegiance of the Christian Slavophones of the bilingual zone of Macedonia developed into a ruthless armed struggle, which raged from the beginning of the 20th century to the Young Turk revolution, in 1908. That was the Macedonian Struggle (1904-1908), the period of Greek and Bulgarian guerilla band activity in pursuit of their respective national objectives in the area. These guerilla bands consisted of volunteers from Greece and Bulgaria, but chiefly of local Slav-speaking Christians who sided with one or another depending on their national proclivities and other circumstances.

The Balkan Wars (1912-1913) called a halt to Greek-Bulgarian antagonism with the distribution of the three Turkish *vilayets*, which international diplomacy had named 'Macedonia', among Greece, Serbia, Albania and Bulgaria. The First World War consolidated the territorial *status quo* of the Balkan Wars and the terms of the Peace Treaties radically changed the ethnological composition of the area. The Neuilly Greek-Bulgarian Convention for mutual emigration (1919), which was repeatedly extended, made it possible for tens of thousands of Slavs of Greece to emigrate to Bulgaria as it did for as many Greeks of Bulgaria. Furthermore, under the terms of the Lausanne Convention for the compulsory exchange of populations (1923), all Muslims left Greek Macedonia and Greek refugees from Asia Minor, Pontus, Eastern Thrace and the Caucasus took their place.

The Greek-Bulgarian conflict rekindled during the Second World War, when the Bulgarians, allied to the Germans and the Italians, sought to gain the ground lost during the Balkan Wars. With the aim to transform the ethnological composition of the area –the result of the exchange of populations following the previous wars— they drove out of their zone of occupation in Eastern

Kastoria, centre of the Macedonian Stuggle. A view from the lake.

Macedonia part of the Greek population; furthermore, they managed to win over some thousands of Slavophone inhabitants of Central and, particularly, Western Macedonia by promising material gains and cultivating the impression that both Greek and Yugoslav Macedonia were to become part of Bulgaria. By 1944, those Slavophones who had commited themselves to the Bulgarian cause, along with their fellows of Yugoslav Macedonia, constituted the nucleus of a new state-formation in former Southern Serbia, which the communist leaders of new Yugoslavia endowed with the name 'Macedonia' as part of their effort to win over those Slav inhabitants who had manifested pro-Bulgarian feelings during the Bulgarian occupation.

It was a conglomerate of heterogeneous linguistic and religious elements, of Slavophone refugees from Greek Macedonia, pro-Bulgarian Slavs of Southern Serbia, Albanian-speaking Muslims, Vlach– and Greek-speaking Christians and Gypsies, who adopted the name of the ancient inhabitants of the southernmost part of the region as their common national denomination, in an attempt to curb the attraction that Bulgaria exercised

until then. However, by adopting a name which, first and foremost, refers to the Greek part of 'Ottoman' Macedonia, the leaders of this federative state of post-war Yugoslavia automatically laid claim to parts of Greece and Bulgaria. Thus, the next phase of a question that dates back to the last quarter of the previous century was inaugurated. The outcome of this phase is uncertain and, in spite of the declarations of the Skopje leaders that they are not going to give up that name, which constitutes part of the Greek cultural tradition, another ovidian metamorphosis on their part cannot be ruled out.

Greek Macedonia, the prize of long struggles and sacrifices, now constitutes a politically, economically and culturally inseparable part of the Greek national state. The various linguistic and cultural survivals in the area constitute precious, worth preserving elements of a rich heritage and evidence the age-long historical march of Hellenism, one of the most ancient cultural communities in the Balkan peninsula.

Landmarks and Principal Phases in the History of Macedonia under Ottoman Rule

Ioannis K. Hassiotis

General Observations and Periodization

The great, generally accepted, turning points in the history of modern and contemporary Macedonia are two: the first begins conventionally with the fall of Thessaloniki in 1430, the event which determined the final transition of the Macedonian world from its once glorious Byzantine past to the five long centuries of Ottoman rule. This period ended irrevocably with the Balkan Wars of 1912-13 and was succeeded by the contemporary period in the history of Macedonia, which, at the time of writing, has concluded eighty years of Greek administration.

Apart from determining these two principal periods, it should also be useful to single out the particular, minor turning points in modern and contemporary Macedonian history. The perceptible fluctuations of the historical process clearly indicate the dramatic and complex —and not always easy to explain— character of the conditions which the Macedonian world experienced, particularly during the first period. Primarily relying on the material contained in the first volume of the present work, I shall attempt to outline the most important changes during the five centuries of Turkish rule and highlight their significance to the extent at present possible. Particular emphasis will be given to the early, so-called 'dark' centuries, because they have received the least attention, mainly due to the scarcity of relevant historical sources. To be sure, references to the phases and historical phenomena of the entire period of Ottoman rule will be extremely compendious and, therefore, inevitably schematic. At any rate, the purpose of this introductory note is merely to partially reconstruct, on the basis of the specific contributions to this volume, an as coherent as possible picture of the historical development of Macedonia under Turkish rule. For this same reason, bibliographical references will also be entirely selective. Therefore, the reader, in order to approach more systematically those subjects which are of particular interest to him/her or those presented here as points at issue, is advised to refer to the respective specific articles in the present work and to the accompanying bibliography.

Ottoman rule in Macedonia certainly did not begin in 1430; the fall of Thessaloniki merely signalled the conclusion of the bloody circle of Turkish raids which had started half a century earlier. The twilight, then, of the Byzantine era witnessed not only the final eclipse of the last vestiges of the ephemeral and meteoric Serbian presence in Macedonia but also the collapse of the Greek defence —in spite of the impressive, last military stand of Manuel Palaiologos. The first bridgeheads of the Ottoman advance in Macedonia had virtually been established during the turbulent last quarter of the 14th century. At that stage, whether by force or capitulation, nearly all principal urban centres of Eastern and Western Macedonia, from Drama, Zichna and Serres to Verria, Kastoria, Monastir and Prilapos (Prilep) fell into Ottoman hands. Thessaloniki itself, before passing into the peculiar and ephemeral period of Venetian occupation (1423-1430), had already suffered a series of sieges and falls (irrespective of the disputed regime of the city during one or another temporary Ottoman occupation).[1]

During the entire period of Ottoman rule, from the early Turkish conquests to its liberation, Macedonia seemingly appears to have gone through an undisturbed winter of historical inertia. This sense is probably conveyed by the uninterrupted Ottoman domination, which, though occasionally challenged by various internal and external claimants to the Ottoman territorial 'legacy', in fact remained uninterrupted and firm for five long centuries. However, historical facts permit us to discern at least three phases in this extraordinarily lengthy period: first, the early *Tourkokratia* (Turkish domination), lasting from the 14th century to the beginning of the 18th; a second period covers the entire 18th century and the first decades of the 19th; and a third, starting with the setting up of the independent Greek state in 1830, extends itself to 1912.

The Early Period of Ottoman Domination

The early phase of Ottoman rule in Macedonia can generally be described as a period of stagnation, both

Map of Macedonia, Thessaly and Epirus (A. Kalphayan Collection - Thessaloniki)

from the point of view of demographic growth and economic and cultural development. However, the beginning of Turkish expansion in the 14th-early 15th century set off the first dramatic changes on the demographic and social map of the region. It was a process initiated by the successive Muslim colonization first of Thracian and then of Macedonian lands.[2] The settlement of these populations in Eastern and Central Macedonia, which mainly consisted of Konyar (from Konya, Asia Minor) and Yürük farmers and shepherds, caused a perceptible compression of the Christian population, particularly in the plains, and also a cultural-religious adulteration of the indigenous character of many parts of Macedonia.[3] Furthermore, the agrarian policy of the new rulers, combined with the settlement of Muslims in extensive public lands and in the former estates of Christian landowners and *pronoiarioi*, accelerated the dismantling of the traditional system of land tenure in Macedonia and the disruption of its established, agelong social structure. Towards the end of the 16th and particularly during the 17th century, the land tenure system which had been in force since the early years of the Ottoman conquest (which had also allowed some breathing space to the ordinary peasant and to at least certain categories of Christian landlords) was gradually replaced by the *chifliks* —almost exclusively in the hands of Muslims. The new system had a devastating effect on soil workers in general; the Christian rural population of Macedonia, in particular, gradually lost whatever room for semi-autonomous economic activity it had formerly enjoyed and finally lapsed into serfdom, depending upon uncontrollable large Muslim landownership. The stifling conditions so created not only undermined economic growth, but also further upset the social and demographic equilibrium. *Chiflik* ownership in Macedonia expanded during the 18th century. It was not before mid-19th century —specifically at the time of the *Tanzimat* reforms— that the *chiflik* system began to lose ground and to give way to systematically cultivated land.

The overthrow of the old order, the arbitrary rule of the conquerors and the dislocation caused by Ottoman conquest paved the way on the one hand to islamization, and, on the other, to a mass exodus of the Christian population towards the mountainous regions of Macedonia, Thessaly and Epirus or to regions still under Western control. The desperation of the people, especially of those for whom the new state of affairs meant the loss of considerable fortunes, created the ground for acts of insubordination against the Ottoman rulers, which in turn would drive part of the Christian element into a vicious circle of reprisals, spasmodic uprisings and renewed conversions.[4] As it was to be expected, these developments drained the Macedonian countryside of large sections of its productive population and also adversely affected, at least during the early centuries of the *Tourkokratia*, the urban centres of Macedonia, already devastated by siege and looting, turning them into pale shadows of their glorious Byzantine past.

These views are based, as a rule, on indicative or fragmentary sources —not on complete demographic data. This deficiency, which is primarily due to the complete lack of reliable official records and to the innate shortcomings of the Ottoman census system, is hardly made up for by the generalizing or even unreliable information provided by travellers and foreign consuls. There is also a further factor which adds to the difficulty of determining the true demographic picture of Macedonia (throughout the period of Ottoman rule): the frequent changes in the administrative division of the area conventionally called 'Greater Macedonia'. Often its boundaries came to include parts of Thessaly, Epirus, Albania or even Serbia.[5]

On the basis of available sources, however, it appears that during the early phase of Ottoman rule the Christian population of Macedonia, its central part in particular, decreased perceptibly to the advantage of the Muslim element. The latter, as already mentioned, was reinforced by resettlements and mass islamizations. Another event which, by the end of the 15th and, especially, the early 16th century, somewhat stirred the demographic and economic stalemate in Macedonia, was the arrival —to major Macedonian cities, at least— of a considerable, by contemporary standards, number of Jewish refugees. They originated either from German-speaking countries of Central-Eastern Europe (*Askenazim*) or, in the most part, from the Iberian peninsula, the Spanish dominions in southern Italy or from other parts of South-Western Europe (*Sefardim*). Yet, during the second half of the 17th century, the Jewish population of Macedonia which was eventually concentrated in Thessaloniki, Serres, Verria, Kastoria and Monastir, suffered a considerable setback too, not only as a result of the general plight of the Ottoman empire, but also due to crises exclusively concerning the Jewish communities themselves. One of the most serious crises of this sort was the split caused amongst the Jewish population of Macedonia by the movement of the pseudo-mesiah Sabetai Chvi and, primarily, his subsequent islamization followed by the conversion of his numerous adherents (*donmeh*).

It should be noted at this point that Macedonia, in spite of the dangerous drain of human resources suffered during the early *Tourkokratia* and the ethnological changes caused by the settlement of alien groups, managed to maintain its core element stable, namely its Greek-speaking, Greek-Orthodox population which lent to the region its most enduring elements of historical continuity and, consequently, the basic components of its 'ethnic' character. Eventually, the decline of the Christian population of the plains of Macedonia was arrested as a result of Greek migrations initially from neighbouring regions and then, by late 16th - early 17th century, of the reverse movement of its old inhabitants from mountainous regions to the plains and cities. That movement, which led to the slow but perceptible recovery of Central Macedonia at least, and, conversely, to a small decrease in the Christian population of Western Macedonia, should be attributed to several factors: firstly, the restoration of peace in the region which was by then far removed from the battle zone between the Ottomans and their Venetian and Habsburg enemies; and, secondly, to the encouragement of this demographic movement by the conquerors themselves, who at that point sought to increase production and open new markets. To this new climate should, perhaps, be attributed the significant reinforcement of the decimated —since the early *Tourkokratia*— Christian population of Eastern and Central Macedonia owing to the mass settlement of farmers and stock-breeders from other parts of the Greek peninsula (Epirus, Thessaly and Central Greece). Yet, in spite of these population movements, the total increase in the Christian population of Macedonia between the 16th and the 18th century was extremely low and did not exceed 0.16% annually (in contrast to the 0.5% increase in the population of Western Europe during the same period.)

These negative factors explain the generally held —though not entirely substantiated— view that economic activity in Macedonia during the early Ottoman period was minimal. This situation nearly developed into a chronic economic recession due to the perpetual crisis of administrative institutions, the state of anarchy in the countryside and the arbitrary rule of the local representatives of the sultan. At any rate, available information tends to confirm that, at least during the years between the Ottoman conquest and the beginning of the 16th century, Macedonia experienced a period of depression.

The transition into the 16th century was marked by certain encouraging signs of economic recovery. This was due to the fact that the zone of military operations had been removed far to the north or south, to the contribution of the Jewish element (which had brought from Western Europe its long experience in crafts and commerce) and to the gradual demographic recovery already mentioned. In that century, then (in the course of which similar phenomena were observed in other parts of the Greek world), there began a

marked development in textile industry (dominated by the almost monopolistic manufacturing of woolen garments (*aba*) to cater for the needs of both the Janissaries and the Jews of Thessaloniki) and all associated crafts, such as wool and cotton spinning, weaving and dyeing; leather tanning, wine production, and candle making also developed as crafts dominated by Greek artisans and producers from Central and Western Macedonia in particular. Mining also developed during the same period, particularly around the traditional mining area of Mademochoria, the villages located around Siderokausia in Chalcidice, which, by mid-16th century, thanks to the contribution of the newly arrived Jewish skilled workes, displayed an impressive activity.[6]

That auspicious trend, which, with minor ups and downs, continued almost throughout the 16th and during at least the first half of the 17th century, was abruptly reversed by the turn of the following century. This reversal, which in some sectors assumed disturbing proportions, should not be attributed solely to the inherent shortcomings of the Eastern Mediterranean mode of production (the counter-productive Ottoman administrative machinery and system of taxation, the lack of capital, the high investment risk, the permanent insecurity of the land and sea routes, et al) but also to the ruthless competition of European goods *vis-à-vis* domestic products. Western exports, especially textiles, to the markets of the Ottoman-dominated Levant benefited from the protective environment created by special commercial agreements between the European powers and the Sublime Porte, the notorious 'Capitulations'. Of course, the Capitulations had been initiated in 1535/36 but they became an established practice during the late 16th and early 17th century.[7]

In the case of, at least, the early *Tourkokratia*, sources on the organization of communities in Macedonia are entirely fragmentary. Nevertheless, on the basis of available evidence, it is possible to reconstruct an overall picture of the way Macedonian communities functioned during that 'dark' period, when, as it was the case with the rest of Greece, the Greek-Orthodox *Genos* ('Race') developed its fundamental institutions of communal organization (such as, for instance, the way of electing the usually twelve-member community councils and their jurisdiction, the role of *protogeroi* (elders) in the administration of neighbourhoods (*mahalades*) or of the entire village, the judicial authority of the Church, of the communities and, in certain cases, of the guilds, the use and validity of established sources of Byzantine law or of more recent canonical acts, et al). It appears that, during the early history of Ottoman-dominated

Macedonia, no particularly serious problems arose with regard to the respective jurisdiction of the representatives of the communities, the guilds, the Church and the Ottoman authorities. At least, this is *ex silentio* indicated by the absence of references to serious intracommunal disputes similar to those which become visible in certain Macedonian urban and semi-urban centres by the 18th and, to a greater extent, the 19th century.

The structure of ecclesiastical organization in Macedonia during the late Byzantine period was largely preserved after the transition to Ottoman rule. Naturally, frequent creation or merging of bishoprics led to several changes in the hierarchy and number of the Macedonian dioceses. These changes, a normal phenomenon throughout the Orthodox East, did not constitute any substantial departure for the ecclesiastical structure in Macedonia, which had been preserved largely immutable down the centuries. From existing evidence regarding the redistribution of dioceses, we can form a relatively complete picture of their extent of jurisdiction, a welcome contribution to the continuing debate on the geographical boundaries (especially to the north-west) of Ottoman-dominated Macedonia.

During the first two crucial centuries of Turkish rule in Macedonia the Orthodox Church had a particularly important role to play. At first, the clergy was entrusted with the protection of the Christian flock during the turbulent period of transition. Then, the Church had to intervene, as conditions permitted, so as to check the waves of mass islamization which periodically swept over certain devastated parts of, particularly Western, Macedonia. These efforts to curb the islamization process, together with the effective spiritual influence of Mount Athos over the entire area, are, perhaps, reflected in the large number of Macedonian *neomartyrs*, during both the early *Tourkokratia* and the equally trying for the Greek-Orthodox population of Macedonia conditions of the 18th century. As available evidence shows, the role of the Church and the monasteries in particular has been decisive in the founding and maintenance of institutions of elementary education in Ottoman-dominated Macedonia, especially during the 16th and 17th centuries. This special role of the Church did not diminish even when the financial burden of education passed onto the shoulders of local communities with which the Church shared, as already mentioned, the responsibilities and jurisdiction of local self-government.

Finally, several religious leaders and monks of Macedonia, literary figures in particular, often took bold initiatives which fomented the spirit of resistance on the part of the Greek-Orthodox population against domination by 'infidel' rulers, both during the early *Tourkokratia* and in later periods. Such initiatives are more frequent among those monastic and ecclesiastical circles which, on account of historical and geographical circumstances, had developed especially close ties with the rest of Christiandom, both in the western Roman Catholic and the eastern Orthodox parts of Europe. In this respect, an outstanding part was played by certain Athonite monasteries and the primates of Thessaloniki and Achris (Ochrida).[8]

Of particular importance was the contribution of Mount Athos to the historical evolution of the Greek-Orthodox world of Macedonia, mainly in matters of art, spiritual and general education. Under Ottoman domination, particularly during its early period, the Athonite community passed from the splendour of its Byzantine past[9] into a new phase characterized by insecurity and relative decline. In addition to the problems created by the imposition of Muslim rule, the Athonites had to cope with strains and stresses generated by other extraneous factors (such as the successive and destructive raids of brigands and pirates) or purely natural disasters (such as the frequent fires and earthquakes). Even the structure and rules of operation of the monastic communities themselves experienced serious internal transmutations during the early Ottoman period, which, as a rule, encouraged the centrifugal tendencies of the monks and monasteries and occasionally abetted the loosening of morals amongst the Athonite society.

Yet, the Athonites succeeded in overcoming the adverse effects of all these crises: within an impressively short period of time, by mid-16th century, they had managed not only to preserve the material property of their monasteries and the administrative autonomy of their self-styled monastic community but also to safeguard their legal and fiscal status by means of legislative acts extracted from the Ottoman autorities. At the same time, they reorganized the internal structure of their monastic communities which, after a period of readjustment (its most important characteristic probably being the decline of the traditional, strict, *coenobitic* system to the advantage of the more relaxed *idiorrhythmic* one) crystallized into the system which, to a considerable extent, prevails to this date.

Considering these facts, it is, perhaps, easier to understand the occasional retrogressions in the spiritual development of the Athonite community, but also its admirable record in the struggle of the Church to safeguard and revitalize the age-long religious, educational and artistic tradition of the Greek-Orthodox East. This record —which covers various fields, from manuscript copying, a literature

Mount Athos: its spiritual influence throughout Macedonia helped check the process of islamization.

of 'soul-benefiting' texts, and icon painting to setting-up libraries and providing teachers for the, however rudimentary, schools both inside and outside Athos[10]— should also be associated with a further fact: thanks to the prestige and respect that it had gradually acquired among the entire Orthodox world, Mount Athos occasionally attracted eminent figures such as ecumenical patriarchs and other high officials of the Orthodox Church, writers, scholars, theologians, artists, etc.. These personalities, either through their work or by their mere presence, revitalized the human potential of the holy peninsula and the self-styled but definitely compact and of quite typically post-Byzantine character, monastic community.

The prestige of the Athonite world helped attract generous donations from various Orthodox rulers — mostly of the Danubian Principalities— and even Christian monarchs of Catholic West to the monasteries.[11] Such financial support allowed the monks to engage in extensive construction projects, as attested by the numerous post-Byzantine monuments throughout the perinsula (*katholika*, monastic building complexes, *kyriaka* of *sketes* and *kellia*, et al). It should be noted that, at least during the early Ottoman period, the impressive Athonite edifices often served as models for the erection of similar religious monuments (of the 'Athonite type'), and of monastic, secular or even humble constructions for ordinary purposes in the rest of the Ottoman-dominated world. This is particularly reflected in numerous monuments surviving in many rural, urban mainly mountainous regions of Macedonia, from the eastern provinces of Drama and Serres to the westernmost villages around Kastoria, Grevena and Florina, a clear sign of the creative influence exercised by Athonite models on the gradual evolution of the traditional Byzantine architecture towards new forms, dictated by specific historical conditions and necessities.

The role of Mount Athos as an 'ark' of the Byzantine tradition is also evident in the preservation, development and dissemination throughout Macedonia and the wider Greek Levant of the 'common' artistic expression of Orthodoxy. Indicative in this respect are the views of specialists in post-Byzantine art: according to their opinion, Mount Athos, which along with Meteora exercised an irresistible attraction among the Orthodox world, had for long established itself as an 'advanced school' of religious painting for the Orthodox peoples of the Balkan peninsula (and beyond), or even into a centre, where religious art was raised to the status of an authentic and reliable model, both from the doctrinal and the aesthetic point of view.[12]

The all important role of Mount Athos notwithstanding, signs of an autonomous lively local artistic tradition are evident throughout Macedonia already in the early *Tourkokratia*. There are indications to the effect that, in spite of the extremely adverse conditions created by the Ottoman conquest, ancestral tradition was preserved (as an organic continuation of Byzantine tradition) and revitalized. There is an impressive amount of material to corroborate this view: the frescoes which have been preserved in churches of Macedonian urban centres (at Kastoria and Verria in particular) and of some small communities in mountainous regions (in Pieria and, mainly, Western Macedonia). These monuments —remarkable in both quality and numbers— are related to a further historical phenomenon: the impressive (relative to the economic conditions prevailing at the time) number of new and relatively grandiose churches built or restored and embellished already in the last decades of the 15th and the beginning of the 16th century.[13]

The best part of surviving samples of ecclesiastical art in Macedonia permits, either directly or indirectly, their approximate chronological and geographical definition. By way of contrast, the lack of definite and, more important, dated material concerning the development of folk art and of new forms of traditional culture in general, unfortunately prevents us from describing clearly the basic features of this field of human creativity in Macedonia during the early *Tourkokratia*. Naturally, the conservatism and durability which characterize the usually anonymous folk artistic creation as a whole, reflecting the slow process of change in the respective social conditions, makes it possible to approach phenomena of earlier periods by way of inference from evidence dating to the 18th, 19th or even the beginning of the present century. Yet such a deductive approach, although it leads to attractive assumptions of historical continuity, involves the danger of drawing the student into unhistorical generalizations, especially in the absence of either sufficient documentary material or even the necessary methodological equipment.

Information is equally scarce with regard to education in Macedonia during this same period. As a result, a picture of the intellectual life of the region cannot be drawn with any degree of precision. However, available historical data on the early centuries of Ottoman rule —those 'dark' years of intellectual decline and demographic and economic stagnation— confirm the absence of organized education in Macedonia. Only the initiative of a few *literati*, clergymen or monks, seemed to offer some opportunity of education to a limited number of children in certain urban and monastic centres. Conditions started to somewhat improve around the end of the 17th and, at a more encouraging pace, during the first decades of the 18th century. Only then did the educational life in Macedonia begin to gradually depart from its emaciated state and to manifest the first signs of the unquestionable 19th century bloom in this field.

The Middle *Tourkokratia*

By the end of the 17th century and, even more so, with the coming of the 18th, at least certain parts of Macedonia began to manifest the first signs of a promising demographic and economic recovery. In Western Macedonia, for instance, it has been estimated that, between 1711 and 1788, the population had grown by a relatively encouraging 50%. Once more, however, this demographic recovery was interrupted towards the end of the 18th century and the beginning of the 19th, owing to a combination of general or purely local factors. Such a combination is provided by the brigand activity of thousands of Albanians who, since the mid-18th century, had been roaming about the interior of Macedonia, raiding, looting and destroying not only isolated settlements but also villages, even towns (as it had been the case with the then flourishing city of Moschopolis, in 1768-1769). The attitude of the local Ottoman *beys* and the motley host of their minions was largely responsible for this tragic situation, along with the absence of control on the part of an already emasculated central authority.[14] At any rate, amidst conditions of arbitrariness and anarchy, a part of the Christian population of Macedonia was driven out of despair to conversion. This phenomenon, which had abated since the end of the 16th century, once more assumed disturbing proportions, at last compelling the spiritual leaders of the Orthodox *Genos* to react.

In its agonizing effort to stem the wave of islamization the Church largely rested on the mobilization of enlightened prelates and intrepid missionaries; among them, an outstanding spiritual figure of 18th century Greek world, Kosmas Aitolos (1714-1779). For more than twenty years (from the early 1760s until his death), Kosmas covered almost the entire Albanian-infested Western Macedonia and Epirus in an effort through his preachings and the opening of new schools and churches to prevent the Orthodox flock from crossing to the opposite religious side.[15] The information available on his touring and preaching is abundant but not always accurate or well documented, especially in the case of the numerous 'memoirs' and already recorded local folk tales. However, even information of this kind, combined with still surviving

Icon painters of Mount Athos: they preserved Byzantine tradition despite the adversities created by Ottoman domination.

(mostly in churches of Western Macedonia) illustrations, has a certain historical significance: it definitely highlights the extent, importance and impact of Kosmas' preachings to the Greek-Orthodox population almost throughout the north-western Greek perinsula.[16]

Part of the Christian population, in an effort to escape the misery and destitution of their native places, headed for the urban centres of Central Macedonia (Verria, Edessa, Serres and, primarily, Thessaloniki). This trend resulted in a considerable increase of the urban population and benefited the local markets, thus contributing to the commercial growth of the Macedonian cities and their eventual integration into the Balkan and international commercial system. Reversely, it aggravated the demographic drain of the countryside depriving it of its most dynamic human element. Matters deteriorated further due to a new, equally negative, factor: the expanding Albanian tyranny as a result of the increasing power of Ali Pasha. This state of affairs revived the tendency of the people of Epirus, Western and even Central

Macedonia to migrate, though to new destinations: Eastern Thrace, Constaninople and Asia Minor.

In parallel, though to a lesser extent, Macedonians tended to emigrate to the already established Greek communities of the northern Balkans, and Central and Western Europe. These movements should not be exclusively regarded as the result of the intolerable situation prevailing in the Macedonian regions but also as the consequence of new and, at last, positive economic conditions. These developments, which once again demonstrated the solid geographic and geopolitical advantages of Macedonia, were closely connected with the expansion of Western European economic activity towards the markets and ports of the Greek Levant. The establishment of free trade conditions between the Ottoman empire and the northern Balkans considerably contributed to the growth of brisk intra-Balkan trade particularly after the relaxation of the tariff clauses imposed on the Sublime Porte by the —important for the history of the entire South-Eastern Europe— Austro-Turkish treaties of Passarowitz (1718) and Belgrade (1739).

The Macedonians' response (whether they stayed in their native places, moved to Macedonian cities or emigrated to Greek communities abroad) to that historic 'challenge' was positive: they increased or diversified their agricultural production, re-activated traditional crafts or initiated new ones and, in general, developed various initiatives. Thus, already by the early 18th century, merchants from Macedonia, especially its western parts, began to cross the limits of the Greek world and to 'conquer' the principal commercial centres of the northern Balkans and Central and Eastern Europe through their trading companies.[17] Towards the middle of the century, the *speditori* of the Greek colonies in the South Slav countries took in their own hands the most important sectors of transit commerce in that area, exporting wool, cotton and tobacco from Macedonia and importing cloth, glassware and hardware from the Habsburg empire.

Initially, the main routes of Macedonian commerce crossed overland towards Central Europe, where, by 1780, half the volume of Macedonian exports was directed. However, from the late 18th and until the early 19th century, the Macedonian merchants, together with their British, Austrian and Russian counterparts, extended their activities over the sea routes linking the commercial centres of Macedonia with destinations around the central and western Mediterranean or, chiefly, with the maritime centres and ports of the Black Sea and southern Russia. Once more, the catalyst was provided by treaties favourable to Greek commercial interests, such as those signed by the Sublime Porte in the aftermath of

the successive Russo-Turkish wars in 1774, 1783, 1792 and 1798. Of cardinal importance in the development of Macedonian commerce was, naturally, the role played by the port of Thessaloniki —for a long time the only port of some account in Macedonia. In this context, it is not difficult to interpret the spectacular growth of the external trade of Thessaloniki from two to nine million gold francs in the years from the treaty of Passarowitz (1719) to the outbreak of the French Revolution (1789). By the end of the 18th century, almost one quarter of the foreign trade of the Ottoman empire as a whole passed through the capital of Macedonia.[18]

The beginning of the 19th century was marked by the decline in Mediterranean trade caused by the French Revolution, the Napoleonic wars and the British blockade of the French-occupied continental Europe. Nevertheless, merchants from Macedonia, like their colleagues from other parts of Greece, found profitable outlets for their goods in both the risky contraband trade of grain, mainly with Spain, and in the more secure transportation of various products *via* alternative routes of supply, immune from the British blockade, through the Balkan peninsula to Central Europe .

This situation lasted until the outbreak of the Greek War of Independence and its spreading to Macedonia in 1821-1822. The damage to agricultural production, the persecution of the Greek commercial class, particularly in Thessaloniki, and, most important, the flight of a considerable part of the human potential of Macedonia to southern Greece, especially after the establishment of the Greek kingdom, resulted in a lengthy period of recession. To these adverse developments were added, at the turn of the 19th century, heavy taxation (for which the needs arising from the successive crises of the Eastern Question are partly to blame), the spreading of disorder and brigandage and the endemic malpractices of local governors and state officials. Economic conditions would take a turn to the better towards the end of the third decade of the present century, which, however, marks a new phase in the history of Ottoman-dominated Macedonia.

Economic growth was also reflected in the growth of the social status of professional and merchant associations, the guilds (*esnaf* or *rufet*), of Macedonia. This fact, apart from its effects on the social stratification of the Greek-Orthodox population, also influenced the function of the communal institutions. In many cases, the guilds were represented in the leadership of the community or were under its supervision. This relation was not always easy or free from internal friction: it occasionally led to fierce internal squabbles, primarily between the rising lay members of the communities and the traditional arbiters of community affairs until the 18th century, namely the local representatives of the Church.[19]

As a means of reducing friction and opportunities for outside (mostly state) interference, Greek community and guild leaders took care to codify their jurisdiction into special community regulations which were often drawn up following general assemblies of the people. A typical case was the reorganization of the *Koinon* (Community) of Melenikon in 1813, which resulted in the elaboration of an exceptionally advanced, for its time, 'System' institutionaling with relative lucidity a new social state of affairs: the rights of laymen *vis-à-vis* those of the representatives of the Church in the administration of the community. Elsewhere, the collective bodies of communities and trade associations largely coincided, apparently as the various businessmen and property owners, wishing to safeguard their professional interests, keenly participated in the running of communal affairs as 'elders'. At Siderokausia, for instance, in Chalcidice, all villages partaking in the exploitation of the local mines —the so-called Mademochoria— constituted a cooperative 'federation'. From its establishment until, at least, the beginning of the 19th century, this 'federation', by specially decreed privilege, constituted the supreme collective authority for its constituent communities. In other cases, however, the guilds operated independently and did not accept outside interventions in relations amongst their members on the part of either community leaders or other associations of similar or different professional outlook.

The interaction between the institutional community patterns of the Ottoman-dominated Levant and the organization of Greek immigrant communities in European countries has not received systematic study as yet. Evidence of outside influence can be traced in the constitutions of guilds and communities of the native place, as, for instance, in the case of the 'System' of Melenikon, which, incidentally, was printed in Vienna by emigrants from that town. On the other hand, several of the articles of the constitutions (*statuti*) governing the communities and fraternities of Greek emigrans can be regarded as an amalgam of two traditions: the communal institutions of the Ottoman-dominated motherland and the special rules regulating the various religious, charitable, professional and commercial associations in the host country.

If the influence of the Diaspora in shaping new forms of communal and guild relations is a matter of debate, the contribution of the emigrants in the dis-

Kosmas Aitolos: an outstanding figure of the Greek 18th century.

semination of new cultural models, social mentalities and political ideologies to their native land or other regions of the Greek Levant is beyond doubt. It is significant that the first recipients of such outside influence were the small but dynamic societies set up by the old fugitives from the Macedonian plains at the principal mountain villages (especially in Western Macedonia). From the 18th century onwards, these communities began to display early and (relative to their almost inaccessible location) spectacular cultural achievements manifested in many fields of artistic creation (particularly in architecture, painting and wood-carving). The surviving examples of this creative spirit have to be seen as a blend of traditional forms (of Byzantine origin) and Western-like trends. This is also reflected in the case of folk architecture of both simple houses and mansions, the so-called *archontika* (of Central and Western Macedonia), and the impressive samples of folk, secular painting which can be seen in those or similar buildings. In these cases (such as the decorative frescoes of the *archontika* of Siatista and Verria) the meeting of the two cultures is even thematically represented (by depicting great cities of the Levant, on the one hand, and real or imaginary cities of the West, on the other). European baroque influence is manifest in the ellaborate wood-carvings on both secular (ceilings, doors, wardrobes, transom-windows, chests, etc.) and religious constructions (temples, pulpits, prie-dieu, lecterns, etc.). It is more difficult to detect Western influences in other fields of folk art (such as metal-work, ceramics, weaving, etc.), where a powerful tradition and the needs of a long standing practice apparently acted as a brake on innovations.

The creative influence of the Macedonian emigrants and of the Greeks, in general, who came into contact with the Western way of life can be observed even in the field of education during the period under discussion. Naturally, the changes were not readily accepted or immediately introduced into school practice. Yet school *curricula*, along with traditional courses and ecclesiastic chanting (the *Octoechos*), progressively began to add subjects of more immediate utility (arithmetic, physics, geography, history), particularly in schools founded in Macedonian towns by interested groups of trading residents, as it was the case with the 'Compania School' of Kozani in mid-18th century).

These changes did not necessarily mean that the role of the Church in the founding and operation of schools had diminished. Of course, financial support for the various institutions of education primarily came from generous donations of lay groups or individuals (communities, guilds, merchants, et al). Yet, the human potential manning the 'common schools' of Macedonia (as it was the case with most of the Greek world) was largely of ecclesiastical or even monastic background. Priests and monks also taught at the schools founded by emigrants both in their native towns and, to a lesser extent, in the Diaspora (as in the case of the *Ellinomouseion* of Zemun, established in 1794). However, since the social background of teachers of this period has not been the object of serious research so far, any conclusions regarding the extent of the role of the clergy in education are bound to be precarious. For the same reason, it is not possible at the moment to assess the effect of the general social debate amongst the Greek world on the Greek-Orthodox population of Macedonia, as expressed in the contest between the modernizing/secular and the traditional/religious trends in education.[20]

Irrespective of the afore-mentioned trends, the fact remains that almost throughout the 18th and early 19th centuries up to the time of the 1821 Revolution, Macedonia showed a remarkable educational activity. This activity was evident not only at the main or traditional urban centres (Thessaloniki, Serres, Verria, Kastoria and Melenikon); it also became manifest in several, up-to-then less prominent, towns of Central and Western Macedonia which gradually emerged as peripheral focuses of economic and educational activity (Naoussa, Vodena, Kozani, Kleisura, et al).

From this educational revival, the Athos peninsula could not possibly be absent. As a matter of fact, owing to the presence of scholarly clerics and monks, the age-long intellectual tradition of the peninsula had remained essentially uninterrupted. Even in late 17th century, at a time of decline for its monastic community, Mount Athos was known as the "great Academy of Orthodox monasticism".[21] Yet, the absence of a suitable institution of education to meet the needs of the monastic population in a systematic way was acutely felt. It was exactly to these needs and also to broader cultural and 'national' objectives that the founders of the Athonite Academy attempted to respond. The school, which began its operation in 1749 near the monastery of Vatopedi, soon acquired fame as an important institution of education. This was undoubtedly due to two factors: the prestige of its founders (Prince Alexandros Mavrokordatos and Ecumenical Patriarch Cyril V) and the reputation of its first teachers and deans: initially (1753-1759), the great Corfiote cleric and writer Eugenios Voulgaris and, after him (until 1761), his successor, the scholar Nikolaos Tertzoulis of Metsovo. The comparatively brief period of advance was succeeded by protracted internal disturbances —not unrelated to the negative atmosphere created by the conservative movement of the *Kollyvades*— which fatally undermined the work of the Academy, although the school continued to function in a conventional manner until 1821.[22]

The economic and social changes that took place in the Greek world during the 18th and early 19th century exacerbated the political problem of the Ottoman-dominated East. During that period, the Greek-

Orthodox population began to intensely aspire to the possibility of the 'infidel' ruler being overthrown and replaced by a more palatable Christian regime. Yet, in comparison with the anti-Turkish activity in other Greek regions, such tendencies found rather limited expression in pre-revolutionary Macedonia: intrinsic geographical and historical reasons restricted the impact of basic factors which elsewhere accelerated the process of national 'awakening'. External 'challenges', for instance, reached Macedonia distorted and with considerable delay, owing to the fact that Macedonia had for several centuries been in the heartland of the empire, far-off from the fronts of the Ottoman wars with Christian powers. What was more, the presence of a compact Muslim population in Macedonia undoubtedly tended to discourage any direct activity against the Ottoman rulers, a fact which also adversely affected the fate of the Macedonian uprising in 1821-1822.[23]

Nevertheless, it seems beyond doubt that almost the same internal causes which affected the rest of the Greek world (upheavals caused by war, extraordinary taxation, violation of traditional privileges of the Church, monastic and even communal autonomy, the debilitation of the state, arbitrary rule and daily humiliations)[24] provoked similar anti-Turkish sentiments in Macedonia. Besides, the same social groups which took the lead in rebellious movements in other Greek regions, engaged in similar activities in 18th - early 19th century Macedonia. It was that part of Macedonian Hellenism which, through emigration or frequent contact with the West, was in a position to compare the 'rule of law' prevailing in Christian countries with the plight of the Ottoman-dominated East. That was the case with Rigas Velestinlis' followers from Western Macedonia and with the first ardent Macedonian members of the *Philiki Etaireia* (the secret 'Friendly Society'). On the contrary, the motives of the swaggering band leaders of the Macedonian highlands were not clear even as late as the beginning of the 19th century: on the basis of available evidence, it seems that their activity was rather a continuation of their tradition as *armatoloi* or even brigands, largely unconnected with those initiatives which consciously sought to promote the cause of Greek liberation on a national level. However, by the second decade of the 19th century, the ideological process which led to the conscious national liberation struggle of 1821 had been decisively accelerated in Macedonia too.

The abundance of publications on the 1821 Revolution in Macedonia notwithstanding, this important chapter of the Greek War of Independence still

Archontiko *(mansion)* in Kastoria.

awaits its appropriate place in historiography. This is due to various reasons: the limited number of relevant Western and, particularly, Ottoman documents published so far, the eventual failure of the insurrection in Macedonia and the emphasis which was justifiably given by Greek scholars to the study of the positive developments of the Revolution in southern Greece. Besides, the Macedonians did not fight only on Athos, Chalcidice and Thasos (May-October 1821), in the region of Mts Olympus, Pieria, Vermion and at Naoussa (late 1821 to April 1822); they took an active part in operations on other fronts, both on land and sea (at Aspropotamos and Trikkeri of Thessaly, on Euboea and Northern Sporades, at Kompoti of Epirus, Messolongi, Kremmydi of the Peloponnese, on Psara, Crete, Chios and elsewhere).[25] Therefore the extent and significance of the Revolution in Macedonia should be viewed from the angle of the overall liberation effort of the Greeks and not as a local insurrectionary event. Indeed, such a perspective is justified by the anti-Turkish struggles in Macedonia following the establishment of the Greek state: those struggles were in essence a continuation of the national uprising of 1821.

Mansions in Siatista (left and above).

The Post-Revolutionary Period and the Preparation for the Liberation of Macedonia (1830-1912)

The outbreak of the Greek War of Independence found Macedonia at a critical stage of economic development. The end of the Napoleonic Wars and the spread of the Industrial Revolution in Europe facilitated the penetration of Ottoman markets by foreign, especially British, commercial interests, as imports of Western industrial goods (mainly textiles) in the Ottoman-dominated Levant rose sharply and, ultimately, Eastern Mediterranean economy became much more closely connected with international trade and its fluctuations. These developments, while undermining the local craft industry in the long term, helped reorientate agricultural production towards diverse, more profitable cash crops. The changing conditions created new prospects for local retailers and middlemen of all sorts, namely in those sectors which were more familiar to part, at least, of the rural or urban and semi-urban population of Macedonia.

Despite all these, the turn of events affecting the Greek population of Macedonia in the immediate aftermath of the Revolution did not favour bold economic initiatives. Ottoman reprisals, manifested in a wave of executions and mass persecution of lay notables and clergymen, deprived the Greek-Orthodox communities, especially at Verria and Thessaloniki, of their natural leadership. What was more, apart from the flight of fighting men and their families to southern Greece during the uprising, the Greek population suffered additional demographic drain due to the successive waves of emigration (out of economic motives) either to the newly established Greek kingdom or to parts of the Ottoman-dominated East.[26]

By the late 1830s, new conditions began to prevail in Macedonia and many other parts of the Ottoman empire, which had a positive impact on the economic and social development of the Christian population. The catalyst was provided by the much vaunted period of administrative reforms (*Tanzimat*) formally inaugurated by the sultanic *Hat-i Serif* of Gülhane in 1839, which coincided with another important event: the Anglo-Turkish commercial treaty of 1838 - a model for other similar bilateral agreements which provided the legal framework for economic relations between the industrialized countries of the West and the Ottoman empire.[27]

Shortly after these events, the first positive results were already evident in the economic life of Macedonia. External trade through the port of Thessaloniki soared, agricultural production expanded and local retail activities multiplied. Of course, these developments were not merely the result of commercial treaties and administrative reforms. Commercial activities in Macedonia benefited from major international events. At the time of the Crimean War (1853-1856), for instance, and the blockade of the Black Sea ports by the Western allies, the granaries of southern Russia were temporarily lost to the European markets, which were forced to look urgently for new sources of grain. To that 'challenge' the productive capacity of Macedonia responded effectively, satisfying a significant part of Western needs. This led to a threefold to fivefold rise in the prices of agricultural products stimulating economic growth in the Macedonian hinterland.[28] There followed a new period of opportunities created by ever higher demand for cotton, particularly after the shortage caused by the American Civil War. Significantly, the production of cotton in Macedonia doubled within just two years. Even more impressive —according to consular reports— was the thirtyfold increase in exports of the same product from Kavala between from 1863 to 1868, at a time that this port of Eastern Macedonia was already known as a major tobacco exporting centre. This growing dependence of the agricultural production of Macedonia on the short-term needs of the Western markets certainly involved certain perils, all the more so as it corresponded to the colonial type of integration of the international economic system. Moreover, Macedonia failed to stabilize its sectors of agricultural production, which constantly alternated depending on external demand. Yet Macedonian agriculture eventually managed to avoid several pitfalls of the system (as, for instance, the imposition of a single crop), which proved fatal elsewhere. This development should be attributed either to the changing needs of the foreign markets or to certain favourable historical circumstances.

Economic advance in Macedonia was considerably assisted by railway connection with Central Europe. This grandiose project took seventeen years to complete (1871-1888) and a few years later (1891-1896) was extended with the construction of the lines connecting Thessaloniki with Monastir to the northwest, and with Constantinople *via* Adrianople to the east. Its repercussions for the demographic and social development of Macedonia were all important. It opened new fields of activity or revitalized old ones; in addition, it was a contributing factor to the gradual expansion of urban and semi-urban centres, particularly those booming near the railway junctions under construction.[29]

Improvements in transport, the opening of banks and, more generally, the gradual expansion of the credit system along with the reactivation of traditional seasonal markets encouraged the development of the local craft industry, and, from the last decades of the 19th century onwards, the emergence of an embryonic manufacturing sector (particularly in Thessaloniki). Other factors contributing to favourable developments were the rather timid measures introduced by the Sublime Porte with the aim to protect domestic production (involving a modest increase in the import tax from the 3-5% inherited from the 18th century to 8% in 1861-62), cheap labour —owing to the influx of rural population into the cities—, increased imports of capital goods, etc. However, the perceptible growth of the secondary sector did not actually imply industrialization to any substantial degree. The reasons for this are complex: some should be sought in the permanent, by late 19th - early 20th century, political upheaval in Macedonia, other stemmed from the inherent shortcomings of the Ottoman society and economy, while external ones related to the domination of the markets of the Eastern Mediterranean by the unrivalled products of Western European craft and manufacturing industries. Yet even this limited industrial activity in a few urban centres of Macedonia resulted in the creation of a considerable work force (two-thirds of which, at least in Thessaloniki, were drawn from the poorest strata of the Jewish population) and the early (by Balkan standards) emergence of a labour movement. By the turn of the 20th century this development was felt as the first strikes (of tobacco workers, shoemakers, tannery workers, carpenters, gas workers, transport workers, et al) broke out in the main urban centres of Macedonia (Thessaloniki, Monastir, Kavala, etc.). In 1908, between August and October in particular, at a time of mounting economic crisis, labour unrest spread to engulf almost the entire working class of Macedonia. It was an event which, on the one hand, contributed to the victory of the Young Turk movement, and on the other paved the way for the formation, on Jewish initiative yet to a transethnic direction, of mass, mostly radical, labour unions and political groups.[30]

Social developments were not unrelated to the ideological and intellectual trends which began to take shape in the main cities of Macedonia. It should be pointed out, however, that, obvious cases of mutual influence and the inevitable economic interdependence notwithstanding, the various ethnic-religious groups constituted separate ideological units which functioned with relative autonomy: they had their own newspapers and publications, their own printing houses, schools, their exclusive societies and clubs, etc. In spite of some efforts towards convergence, especially within the labour movement, the particular communities maintained clearly differing ideological orientations or, at least, completely unconnected ideological points of reference. With regard to the Greek element of Macedonia, since the third decade of the 19th century the centre of gravity had moved from Constantinople to Athens, with which the Greeks (of the urban centres, in particular) increasingly communicated both on a cultural and a political level.

The Ottoman authorities, for their part, did their best to check this communication by whatever means possible: they raised obstacles to the movement of people and economic transactions between Macedonia and the Greek state; they kept postponing the connection of Macedonia to Thessaly by rail or sea; they discouraged Ottoman citizens of Greek origin from taking up Greek citizenship, etc. Despite these measures, the connection of the Greeks of Macedonia with independent Greece steadily expanded. The importance of this connection became evident already from the first years after liberation, as the Macedonian provinces were relatively quickly and smoothly incorporated into the Greek state.[31]

The Ottoman administrative reforms —particularly after their actual application which began with the solemn promulgation of the *Hat-i Humayun* in 1856— effected far-reaching changes in the traditional communal regime of all subjected Greeks. New laws and decrees issued by the Sultan obliged the Ecumenical Patriarchate —as well as the leaderships of other ethnoreligious groups— to adjust the internal organization of the Greek-Orthodox *millet* to new principles which reinforced and safeguarded the role of laymen in community organs *vis-à-vis* the representatives of the Church. These changes, which were codified in specific 'constitutional' documents, the so-called 'General Regulations' of 1860-1862, resulted in the gradual homogenization of the system of communal organization. In this way, the diversity of the traditional institutions of the Macedonian communities became a thing of the past, yet in matters of actual self-government (in the fields of executive, judicial and, occasionally, legislative authority) the hand of communal organs was strengthened. Other forms of social, professional or educational association already mentioned underwent a similar, though smaller, measure of change.

Not surprisingly, the strengthening of the position of the laymen at the expense of the clergy caused the latter to react. The ensuing rivalry between the two poles of communal authority culminated in the heated controversies which errupted in Thessaloniki during the second half of the 19th century and repeatedly led the city's prelates to abandon their see and take refuge either in Constantinople or in nearby Mount Athos.

What was more, the upgrading of the lay element *vis-à-vis* the religious one diminished the ecumenical role of the Church and fomented 'ethnic-racial' cleavages. In Macedonia, this development had serious repercussions since, in many cases, it provided the ideological grounds for centrifugal tendencies, especially those serving the secessionist effort of the Bulgarian Exarchate. On the other hand, the strengthening of the communities and the extension of their scope of authority, particularly over school matters, benefited Greek education in Macedonia which expanded and got better organized and staffed.

Indeed, within the thirty-odd years that intervened beetween the introduction of the new community regulations and the beginning of the 20th century, Macedonia experienced a genuine educational and cultural explosion. This is evidenced by the foundation and activity of hundreds of schools, educational and cultural societies and clubs, as well as by the construction of scores of impressive school buildings and cultural centres.[32] It was a magnificent financial venture jointly supported by the communities and generous sponsors —emigrants, as a rule. This event proved of decisive importance during the relentless ethnic antagonisms which broke out in the same period; during its early crucial stage, the Greek-Slav conflict shifted from the 'ethnic-racial' to the cultural field: in other words, to a field where, for historical reasons, Hellenism had maintained an undisputed supremacy over the centuries.

The economic and social transmutations which took place in 19th century Macedonia did not distract the Greek element from its firm attachment to its overriding political objective: deliverance from Ottoman domination. To this end were directed the incessant efforts of the veterans of the 1821-1822 revolutions in Macedonia and Thessaly, who had settled in the Greek kingdom as *heterochthones* (non-indigenous) and lived with a persistent vision: the

The Greek rebel Tsamis Karatasos in a 1854 engraving.

incorporation of their motherland into the free Greek state the earliest possible.[33] As it happened, most anti-Turkish movements started on the initiative of isolated band leaders and never got off the stage of preparation (as it was the case with the secret missions to Macedonia and Mount Athos of Ilarion Karatzoglou, Tsamis Karatasos and Ioannis Velentzas, in 1834 and 1840-41). Sometimes, they developed into a peculiar guerrilla warfare on land and sea (similar to the brigand and pirate raids on the islands and the shores of the Aegean in 1835-1836). There had also been cases of desperate actions by isolated groups (such as the quixotic movement of Leonidas Voulgaris in 1866). During the crises of the Eastern Question, however, liberation efforts were more systematic and ambitious. Their leaders, often in accord with the Greek government, opened small fronts, usually on the mountainous regions of Western Macedonia or at the villages of Olympus and Chalcidice with the ultimate aim to stir up matters and provoke the intervention of the European Powers. Such were the uprisings organized by Thodoros Ziakas and Karatasos in 1854 (at the time of the Crimean War) and the revolt in Litochoro, Pieria, Vermion, and Western Macedonia in 1877-1878 (at the height of the Eastern Crisis).[34]

From the late 1870s to the time of liberation, Macedonia from a field of the traditional Greek-

Turkish confrontation was transformed into the arena of rival Balkan nationalisms, the Greek and the Bulgarian in particular. Principal agents of this rivalry —which started with the ecclesiastical schism of 1870/72 and developed into a political confrontation on all levels, from propaganda to bloody armed conflict— were the numerous and overstaffed consulates of the contesting countries and interested foreign powers (particularly Austria-Hungary and Russia), the schools, the representatives of the two rival Churches (the Patriarchate which, as a rule, was aligned with Greek positions, and the Exarchate, which identified closely with Bulgarian claims), the various covertly political societies and, finally, the guerrilla bands. For the Greek cause, the extension of the borders to the fringes of Macedonia following the incorporation of Thessaly and Arta in 1881 was an all important step. The Bulgarians, too, soon tightened their grip around the Macedonian provinces from the north after annexing Eastern Rumelia in 1885. From that time and for nearly twenty years, the Bulgarians infiltrated or helped set up numerous guerrilla groups or unruly bands inside Macedonia (its northern regions and the disputed middle zone, in particular) which, under the pretext of liberating the Christian population from Ottoman oppression, prepared the ground for a forcible repetition of the 1885 *coup d'état*. At that stage, Greek reaction did not go beyond diplomatic representations or occasional spasmodic military gestures along the border.

With the coming of the last decade of the century, the Greek-Bulgarian conflict entered a new phase, characterized by the intense activity of Bulgarian revolutionary organizations. Greek reaction, led by the newly formed (in 1894) 'National Society', was stepped up and Greek guerrilla bands were sent into Macedonia in 1896. That initiative caused the Greek-Turkish relations to deteriorate further, as the activity of the Greek bands was seen in connection with the culmination of the revolutionary effort in Crete. The Greek-Turkish War that broke out in the spring of 1897 did not only end with the defeat of the Greek army; it inevitably undermined the influence of the humiliated national centre on Macedonia and brought the activities of the 'National Society' to a halt. These events gave the Bulgarians the opportunity to consolidate and expand their positions and might have proved fatal for Macedonian Hellenism if it was not for various social and patriotic groups as well as individuals from Greece and abroad, who hastened to offer their support: diplomats, teachers, clerics, doctors, professionals of all sorts and, last but not least, several armed volunteers and army officers.

Despite these initial efforts, the situation in

Bust of kapetan Kota (left) and statue of kapetan Vangelis of Strebeno (right), early protagonists of the Macedonian Struggle.

Macedonia still appeared irreversible, particularly following the death of prominent local leaders of the Greek resistance in Western Macedonia (*kapetan Vangelis* in May 1904 and Kottas in autumn 1905). These developments dictated to Athens the despatch of organized Greek units. Thus, in August 1904, the first four such units crossed the Greek-Turkish border and commenced limited operations designed to check armed Bulgarian activity. It was the beginning of a ruthless and unconventional war, the Macedonian Struggle, which eventually decided the fate of the Greek cause in Macedonia.[35] However, that early stage of the Struggle was neither spectacular nor victorious. Already during the first operations, Pavlos Melas, leader of one of these units, was killed. Yet the death of that noble figure acted as a catalyst in Athens mobilizing more, battle-hardened, volunteers who, together with the forces earlier in the field, succeeded in restoring Greek prestige and winning over the majority of the local population within a relatively short time, thus securing final victory for Hellenism in Macedonia.

The Young Turk movement in 1908 seemed to upset the calculations of all rival parties for a short while. With declarations of equality of rights and equality before the law, the Young Turks, at least in theory, seemed well placed to outflank the demands of the contesting nationalist forces. In the event, the euphoria which prevailed during the early days of the new regime soon proved excessive and premature. Manipulation of the electoral procedure by the first Young Turk government and the centralizing and nationalistic tendencies, which became manifest particularly after the abortive *coup d'état* of the Sultan in March 1909, did not augur well for the non-Muslim and non-Turkish nationalities under the new regime. The leaders of the Christian communities of the Ottoman empire and the governments of the respective Balkan countries were compelled to adopt a fresh approach. The new circumstances demanded a coordinated effort on the part of the nationalities groups involved (Greeks, Bulgarians, Armenians, Arabs, et al) in the interior of the Ottoman empire (in Parliament, by means of representations by the Patriarch, society activities, etc.). Right from the beginning, this approach coincided with similar initiatives emanating from the interested neighbouring Balkan countries. All this activity eventually produced a revolutionary result on the diplomatic level: the formation of the first ever (and, virtually, the last effective to date) Balkan alliance, which was destined to terminate Ottoman rule in Macedonia.

IOANNIS K. HASSIOTIS

LANDMARKS AND PRINCIPAL PHASE
| THE HISTORY OF MACEDONIA UNDER
OTTOMAN RULE

NOTES:

1. The best general text on the history of Macedonia under Ottoman domination still remains the work of Apostolos E. Vacalopoulos, *History of Macedonia, 1354-1833*, Thessaloniki 1973. With respect to the topics touched herein, see pp. 65-67.

2. A. Vacalopoulos, *The March of the* Genos (in Greek), Athens 1966, pp. 49-55.

3. Muslim settlements in Macedonia reappear in the course of the 19th century (as a result of the war crises in the northern Balkans or even in the Caucasus), once more threatening to upset the demographic balance that had been restored in Macedonia after particularly painful and fairly lengthy processes of integration.

4. This phenomenon is typical of other regions of the Greek world too; see I.K. Hassiotis: 'The European Powers and the Problem of Greek Independence from the Middle of the 15th to the Beginning of the 19th Century' (in Greek), in *Greece: History and Civilization*, vol. V, Thessaloniki 1981, pp. 66-68.

5. In spite of its special political significance (or, perhaps, because of it) we do not have, as yet, a systematic record of the evolution of the geographical limits of Macedonia through time, particularly with regard to the controversial period of the *Tourkokratia*. On this issue, see the remarks of I. Koliopoulos in the introductory note to the present volume; cf. A. Vacalopoulos, *Crucial Topics of Our History* (in Greek), Thessaloniki 1988, pp. 269-272. With respect to the more general problem of the definition of Greek historical-geographical places during the Ottoman period and the views of a prominent Greek geographer of the period of Modern Greek Enlightenment, Metropolitan of Athens Meletios, see the brief but comprehensive remarks of Konstantinos Kyriakopoulos in his study: *Meletios (Mitros) of Athens, the Geographer (1661-1714)* (in Greek), vol. II, Athens 1990, pp. 673ff (regarding Macedonia, see: pp. 678-679, 681, 684-685, 687, 690).

6. Information provided by 16th century travellers about the production and operation of the mines of Macedonia, in: Konst. Philopoulou-Desylla, *Travellers of the West: a Source on the Economic Life of the Ottoman Empire at the Time of Suleyman the Magnificent, 1520-1566* (in Greek), Athens 1987, pp. 171-173, 313-317.

7. For a brief account of the regime of the 'Capitulations' and its long-term negative effects on the economy of the Eastern Mediterranean, see I.K. Hassiotis, *The European Powers and the Ottoman Empire. The Problem of Sovereignty in the Eastern Mediterranean from mid-15th to the Beginning of the 19th Century* (in Greek), Thessaloniki 1976, pp. 102-122.

8. A.-P. Péchayre, 'Les archêveques d'Ochrida et leurs relations avec l'Occident à la fin du XVIe siècle et au début du XVIIe', *Échos d'Orient*, 36 (1937), 409-422.

9. The importance of Mount Athos during the Byzantine period is illustrated in: N. Svoronos, *The Importance of the Establishment of Mount Athos to the Development of the Greek Lands* (in Greek), Karyes, Athos 1987 (particularly, pp. 62ff.).

10. Regarding the wealth of the Athonite libraries, cf. the bibliographies of M.I. Manousakas, 'Greek Manuscripts and Documents of Mount Athos: a Bibliography' (in Greek), *Yearbook of the Society for Byzantine Studies*, 32 (1963), 377-419, and Ch.G. Patrinelis, *Libraries and Archives of the Monasteries of Mount Athos* (in Greek), Athens 1963. Of the numerous general works on Athos, see the recent work by Pan. Christou, *Mount Athos: Athonite Civitas, History, Art, Life* (in Greek), Athens 1987.

11. Cf. P. Nasturel: *Le Mont Anthos et les Roumains. Recherches sur*

leur relations du milieu de XIVe siècle à 1654, Rome 1986. On the relations of the Holy See and the Athonite world, see: G. Hofmann, *Rom und der Athos*, Rome 1954. Sources reporting the donations of the Catholic rulers of the West *par excellence*, the kings of Spain, to Athonite monasteries will be published by the present author. Certain indications are included in: I.K. Hassiotis, 'España y los movimientos antiturcos en Macedonia durante los siglos XVI-XVII', *Homenaje a Luis Gil Fernández*, Madrid 1992 (in print); cf. same author, 'Insurrectionary Movements in Macedonia During the Early Ottoman Domination', in *Macedonian Hellenism* (edited by A.M. Tamis), Melbourne 1990, pp. 40-41.

12. Manolis Hatzidakis, 'Post-Byzantine Art (1453-1700) and its Influence' (in Greek), *History of the Greek Nation*, vol. X, Athens 1974, p. 436.

13. It appears that this historical phenonenon has not been systematically studied. However, the commissioned reports of archaeologists on post-Byzantine monuments of 15th-16th century Macedonia, published in successive issues of the *Archaeological Bulletin* are quite indicative (see, e.g., vols. 28 (1973) onwards); cf. the summaries of certain related papers in *VIII Symposium of Byzantine and Post-Byzantine Archaelogy and Art* (in Greek), Athens 1988.

14. A. Vacalopoulos, *History of Macedonia*, pp. 322ff.

15. *Ibid.*, pp. 369ff.

16. On Kosmas' tours, see *ibid.*, pp. 371-377. For more recent bibliography see: A. Xanthopoulou-Kyriakou, *Kosmas Aitolos and the Venetians (1777-1779). The Last Years of his Activity and the Problem of the* Didaches (in Greek), Thessaloniki 1984.

17. On this topic, see the transnational assessments in the classic study by Traian Stoianovich, 'The Conquering Balkan Orthodox Merchant', *The Journal of Economic History*, 20 (1960), 234-313.

18. Regarding the growth of Macedonian commerce, of Thessaloniki in particular, see the data contained in a pioneering work of modern Greek historiography, N. Svoronos' study, *Le commerce de Salonique au XVIIe siècle*, Paris 1956. With respect to the function and orientation of the Greek economy in general during the period under consideration, see: Spiros Asdrachas, *Greek Society and Economy. 18th and 19th Centuries* (in Greek), Athens 1982, pp. 3-78, with special references to the commerce of Thessaloniki.

19. Cf. M.I. Gedeon, 'Old Communal Disputes of the Thessalonians' (in Greek), *Makedonika*, 2 (1941-1952), 1-24.

20. Cf. the significant exacerbation of similar rivalry amongst the Greek community of Smyrna analytically presented in: Philippos Iliou, *Social Struggle and Enlightenment. The Case of Smyrna (1819)* (in Greek), Athens 1981.

21. The expression belongs to a cosmopolitan Greek cleric, the bishop of Samos Iosiph Georgirinis (see reference in: Vacalopoulos, *History of Macedonia*, p. 181, note 1).

22. On the *Athonias*: A. Angelou, 'The Chronicle of the *Athonias*' (in Greek), *Nea Estia*, Christmas 1963, 84-105.

23. Hassiotis, 'Insurrectionary Movements', pp. 48-49.

24. On this subject see: I.K. Hassiotis, 'The European Powers and the Problem of Greek Independence', p. 79.

25. A. Xanthopoulou-Kuriakou, 'Macedonia and the Revolution of 1821' in the present volume; cf. S.I. Papadopoulos, *The Preparation for the War of Independence in Macedonia* (in Greek), Thessaloniki 1968.

26. Thousands of Greeks from Ottoman-dominated regions chose to relocate in the small kingdom of Greece, investing there money and expectations. This event, which did not fail to affect negatively many flourishing Greek communities of Central and Western Europe and certain important centres of the Greek *irredenta* too, is indirectly reflected in the increase in the population of the new state, which, from 850,246 inhabitants in 1840 rose to 1,035,527 in 1853 and to 1,096,810 in 1861; this development was as much due to natural increase in population as to new arrivals from the Ottoman empire and the communities abroad. This enhanced the economic and political importance of the 'national centre' and the gradual downgrading of 'peripheral Hellenism'; cf. I.K. Hassiotis: 'Continuity and Change in the Modern Greek Diaspora', *Journal of Modern Hellenism*, 6 (1989),

16. With respect to emigration to Constantinople and Asia Minor, see the data produced in K. Tsoukalas, *Dependence and Reproduction (1830-1922)* (in Greek), Athens 1985, pp. 107ff. (in which occasion, however, the reverse is the case).

27. On this treaty see: Charles Issawi, *The Economic History of Turkey, 1800-1914*, Chicago 1980, pp. 86ff. Abundant sources on the effect of these events on the economic development of Macedonia are used in several works by K. Vacalopoulos, which, however, are full of mistakes and misinterpretations. See, in particular, his book *Economic Function of Macedonia and Thrace in mid-19th Century in the Context of International Trade* (in Greek), Thessaloniki 1980.

28. Const. Svolopoulos, 'Les effects de la Guerre de Crimeée sur la condition de Salonique: L'exportation des céréales', *Actes du IIe Congrès Intern. des Études du Sud-est Européen*, vol. III, Athens 1978, pp. 459-474.

29. With regard to this interesting chapter of the modern history of Macedonia, see the DPhil thesis (to be published) of Basil Gounaris, *Social and Economic Developments in Macedonia, 1871-1912. The Role of the Railways* (Oxford 1988).

30. Regarding those novel mobilizations and the consequent rise in class consciousness in Macedonian urban centers, particularly in Thessaloniki, see the first systematic evaluations of Kostis Moskof, *Thessaloniki: a Profile of the Trading City* (in Greek), 2nd edition, Thessaloniki 1978; cf. A. Liakos, *The Socialist Labour Federation of Thessaloniki and the Socialist Youth. Their Charter* (in Greek), Thessaloniki 1985.

31. This fact is clearly illustrated in the case of Thessaloniki; see: *Thessaloniki: 2300 Years* (in Greek, a publication of the Municipality of Thessaloniki), Thessaloniki 1985, pp. 104-107, 110, 145ff.

32. Their first systematic recording in Stephanos I. Papadopoulos, *Educational and Social Activity of Macedonian Hellenism During the Last Century of Turkish Domination* (in Greek), Thessaloniki 1970.

33. Regarding this phenomenon, which concerns fighting men from other Greek regions, see: J.S. Koliopoulos, *Brigands with a Cause: Brigandage and Irredentism in Modern Greece, 1821-1912*, Oxford 1987.

34. For a concise and general overview of these movements, see: S.I. Papadopoulos, *The Revolutions of 1854 and 1878 in Macedonia* (in Greek), Thessaloniki 1970, with related bibliography. With particular regard to the diplomatic and military events during the crisis of the Eastern Question in 1875-1878, see: E. Kofos, *The Revolution in Macedonia in 1878* (in Greek), Thessaloniki 1969, and by the same author, *Greece and the Eastern Crisis, 1875-1913*, Thessaloniki 1975.

35. D. Dakin, *The Greek Struggle in Macedonia, 1897-1913*, Thessaloniki 1966.

The Ottoman Conquest

Ioannis D. Psaras

The campaigns of Stephen Dušan, king of the Serbs, against the Byzantines in Macedonia (1331-1355), which led to the establishment of the fifteen-year Serbian state of Serres (until 1371), and, particularly, the Ottoman invasion are generally considered as the origins of the modern history of Macedonia. During the late Byzantine period, Dušan bequeathed extensive areas to his successors. The Serbs still ruled over many parts of Macedonia when the Ottomans first appeared in Europe (1354). They even managed to extend, albeit temporarily (1364-1371), the rule of the state of Serres as far as Western Thrace, Chalcidice and the Athos peninsula. At that time, the first Serb clerics penetrated into Mount Athos and gained control of the holy community at the *Protaton*, inaugurating a period of the Serbian *Protoi.*

The Byzantines never gave up the struggle, occasionally managing to recover certain parts of Macedonia from the hands of the invaders. Consequently, Serbian rule should not be considered either stable or permanent. Hence the criticism of Ostrogorskij's views regarding the composition of the population and the ethnologic upheaval in Central and Eastern Macedonia as a result of Serbian conquest, in conjunction with attestations of contemporary travellers and the views of authoritative students of the history of Macedonia, which rather show that Serbian rule in the region of Strymon (Struma) did not have any serious effect on the Greek-Orthodox element, either in the cities or in the countryside, especially at its ancient cradles.[1]

At that time, social conditions in Macedonia were no different from those in other provinces of the Byzantine empire. The Serb rulers did not change the *status quo*; they themselves had already adopted the system of *pronoiai* and, like the Byzantines, distributed land to the military and to monasteries.[2] Many pertinent acts of grant from despots or private citizens have survived as a valuable source of information about the economic and social situation in the countryside, in the farms belonging to monasteries and churches, in the fields, gardens and mills of local communities, as well as about resident aliens, serfdom, forced labour and the production and transportation of goods.[3]

The way to Macedonia opened for the Turks after the capture of Philippopolis (1363) and Andrianople (1369)[4], but mainly following the decisive defeat of the Serbs at Çirmen near the Evros river in Eastern Thrace (1371). That event signalled the demise of Serbian presence in Macedonia. Groups of *ghazi* irregulars -preceding the bulk of the Turkish hordes- poured into the former Byzantine provinces spreading terror and devastation. On their heels came raiding bandits intensifying disorder and chaos.

Thus, the second half of the 14th century, one of the darkest periods of the Byzantine history, marks the beginning of a new phase in the life not only of the Greeks but of the other Balkan peoples as well.[5] The coming of the Ottomans to the Balkan peninsula was destined to influence deeply both

Byzantine tower near the Agios Vasileios lake of Thessaloniki. It was errected by Manuel II Palaiologos as part of the defensive ring of fortifications around the city of Thessaloniki.

the political system and the culture of the area, and the effects are still felt today.

The Ottoman menace failed to unite the Balkan Christians. On the contrary, it found them worn out both by internecine wars and domestic political and social upheaval. The discord among the three Balkan states –Byzantine, Bulgarian, and Serbian– and the numerous local overlords caused them to succumb to the Turks and even to participate in the expeditions of their new rulers.

Among the Christian rulers of Southeastern Europe, only Manuel II Palaiologos, son of Emperor Ioannis V and governor of Thessaloniki since 1369, stood out for his indomitable fighting spirit, ethos, prudence and education. A bright and radical mind, he has been one of the most likable figures of Macedonia of that period, the personification of the spirit of Christian resistance against the Ottoman invaders. Being the ruler of the small Byzantine Macedonian state, Manuel realized that the only way for the Balkan peoples to save themselves from Ottoman domination was to shed their differences and co-operate against the common enemy. He was surrounded by few but daring and devoted supporters. His initiative and indepedence of mind, which sometimes conflicted with the opinion of his father, already a tributary to the Sultan, certainly embarassed the Byzantine emperor.

Manuel's action began with the recapture of Serres (November 1371). After the collapse of the ephemeral Serbian state, Manuel remained the only ruler who made serious efforts to check the Turkish advance. Yet the restoration of Byzantine rule in the region of Serres was not followed by as radical changes as one might have expected. Apparently, Manuel did not concern himself with the vestiges of Serbian rule, perhaps being primarily concerned with a common Balkan anti-Turkish front. Thus, the Serb high clergy, including the bishop of Serres Theodosius, remained in their positions. The city walls were fortified so as to become the first bulwark of Macedonian Christiandom.

Manuel also paid attention to the maintenance of old castles and had new fortifications built at selected locations so as to form a defensive ring all around Thessaloniki (Chrysoupolis, Christopolis, Rentina, Gynaikokastro, Agios Vasilios, Galatista, Kassandra, Verria, Kitros, Platamon). These forts were to serve as strongholds of the local garrisons, and to provide cover for the population against the oncoming Ottomans.

Manuel even attempted social reforms, granting the military oligarchy *pronoiai* at the expense of monasteries, ignoring the complaints and protests of the bishop of Thessaloniki Isidoros Glavas.[6] In this respect, Manuel probably imitated Dušan, who, in order to maintain his army, had confiscated church estates, both in Macedonia and Epirus, and gave it to the military. However, the results of Manuel's efforts were temporary, as, in spite of their privileged treatment, a number of Greek and Serb warlords accepted Ottoman rule and even collaborated with the conquerors.[7]

After conquering Thrace, the Ottomans advanced into Macedonia, the land of Alexander the Great, the conquest of which, according to Muslim faith, would bestow to the sultans eternal glory. Within a relatively short time, the invaders succeded in capturing, one after the other, several castles which Manuel had not managed to man in time . In September 1383 the Turks besieged and then captured Serres. The city was sacked and the inhabitants, including the bishop, Matthaios Phakrasis, were taken slaves. In 1384 they captured Drama and Zichna, a year later Prilapos (Prilep) and Monastir (Bitola), which were under the Serb ruler Marco Kraljević. Both Kraljević, the Albanian Stoja brothers and Thedoros Mouzakis, rulers of Kastoria, became vassals to the Sultan. Ochrida must have fallen at about the same time. In 1386 other Turkish forces advanced southwards and captured Kitros. The city of Verria held out longer -until March 1387. After Verria, the Ottomans captured Edessa (1389), and a few years later (1393) the fortress of Servia.

Thessaloniki was first besieged and capitulated in 1387. At first, the Turks respected the inhabitants and did not sack the city; they contented themselves with only tax vassalage. This privileged treatement lasted until 1391 when it was revoked by Sultan Bayezid I (1389-1402). The city was occupied in 1394; shortly afterwards the inhuman measure of *devsirme* ('toll of boys') was imposed (whereby the Ottoman authorities could take every fifth boy from Christian families in order to raise them as fanatical Muslims and use them to supplement the ranks of the janissaries). That first occupation of the Macedonian capital lasted until 1403. Christopolis (Kavala) was also temporarily subjected to tax vassalage (1387-1391). Yet in 1391 the city was stormed and razed to the ground.[8]

According to Simeon, Bishop of Thessaloniki (1410-1420), the civil war between Ioannis V Palaiologos and Ioannis Kantakouzinos, Serbian plundering and Ottoman raids proved exceedingly destructive for late 14th century Macedonia.[9]

After 1392, the Ottoman military advance was followed by colonization; nomadic Muslim populations from Konya in Asia Minor, the so-called Yürüks or Konyars, settled in Macedonia. Thus, the end of the 14th century marked the first important ethnological changes in the region. Warlike Yürüks led by notorious chieftains settled in fertile areas, which they found either sparsely inhabited or deserted by their inhabitants who had sought refuge in mountainous and inaccessible regions. The Yürüks, fanatic Muslims (Sunnî), mostly shepherds organized in auxiliary units (ocak), settled near Drama, Kavala, Serres, Kilkis, the lake of Langada, Sochos, Ptolemais, Kozani, Sorovits, and Yenitsa[10] bringing to Macedonia the simple but savage customs of their ancestors. A certain legend about the settlement near Naoussa is connected with the conqueror of the area Ghazi Evrenos Bey.[11] At the time of the Greek-Turkish exchange of populations, the descendants of those Turkoman tribes moved to Asia Minor. However, they kept a proud memory of the fact that they were the children of the first Ottoman conquerors to the day of their departure.[12]

The destruction of the Ottoman army by Tamerlan's Mongols at the battle of Ankara (1402) gave to Manuel II, now emperor of Constantinople, the opportunity to recapture Thessaloniki (1403), Chalcidice and the coastal zone from Strymon to Tempi. Ioannis VII Palaiologos (1403-1408), Dimitrios Leontaris (1408-1415) and Manuel's son Andronikos Palaiologos (1415-1423) succeeded one another as governors of Thessaloniki and the small Byzantine part of Macedonia.

The feuds between Bayezid's sons after the defeat at Ankara caused more destruction and looting. The Ottomans came back, crossing the Macedonian plains unimpeded. Between 1410 and 1413, Suleyman's rival Musa wreaked havoc in Macedonia and reached the outskirts of Thessaloniki.[13]

Manuel II Palaiologos: the only ruler who seriously attempted to stem the Ottoman advance on Macedonia in late 14th century.

The last years of Byzantine rule under Andronikos Palaiologos were tragic for the inhabitants of the Macedonian capital, which was under siege most of the time. When Murad II (1421-1451) ascended to the throne, a new period of Turkish raids began. In June 1422, Burak Bey, Evrenos' son, laid siege to Thessaloniki and sacked Kalamaria, the region extending from the eastern walls of the city to Kassandra. It became extremely dangerous for the people to stay outside the walls and cultivate the fields. Insecurity and fear reigned over the area driving the undernourished population to despair.

Sultan Murad II, conqueror of Thessaloniki.

In September 1423, Andronikos and the patricians of Thessaloniki, unable to organize effective defence and to avert the consequences of a new Turkish assault, surrendered the city to the Venetians on condition that they should respect the communal rights of the inhabitants and their religious beliefs. However, some are of the opinion that Thessaloniki was actually sold to the Venetians by Andronikos.[14] In any case, some time earlier, probably since 1416 –when the Ottomans had once more besieged the city – Andronikos had been paying 100,000 aspers to the Turks annually as tribut. The Venetians would have to pay 150,000, which was finally raised to 300,000 aspers.[15]

During Venetian occupation (1423-1430), many Thessalonians, exasperated by the incessant Turkish attacks and sieges, left and, as a result, the defences of the city weakened while many places of worship fell into decay as the remaining inhabitants were too few to look after them. According to Zorzi Dolfin's and Venier's chronicles, and to the Zancaruola codex, Thessaloniki in 1423 had some 40,000 inhabitants. Yet the more reliable Morosini codex puts this number to only 20 to 24,000 inhabitants; one quarter of the population had already left, seeking better fortune elsewhere.[16] Therefore, during the Venetian occupation the population of Thessaloniki must have further decreased.

The Turks could no longer tolerate the Venetian wedge in the gulf of Thermaikos. Having already conquered Central Macedonia, they had no difficulty capturing the castle of Hortiatis. The Venetian senate, considering that this castle was vital to the defence of Thessaloniki, in 1424 ordered the governor, Santo Vernier, to try to reach a negotiated settlement with the Turks, spending up to 5,000 ducats, on condition that the Turks handed back the castle and all the villages that depended on it. However, these efforts were fruitless and Hortiatis remained in Turkish hands.[17]

After Manuel's II death (21 July 1425), Murad sacked the outskirts of Thessaloniki. In 1426 he agreed to abstain from further raids on condition that the new emperor, Ioannis VIII (1425-1448), surrendered the districts of Varna, Strymon and Lamia.

At the same time, Venice continued its efforts to reach an agreement with the Turks, but to no avail. The situation in the Macedonian capital continued to be desperate. A pro-Turkish faction was formed on the assumption that, sooner or later, the city would be captured and therefore, it would be better to surrender to the Ottomans peacefully, in order to avoid the consequences. Soon, the Venetians had to face the increasing hostility of the inhabitants as well. The fear of revolt made them distrustful and oppressive; they encroached upon the people's liberties openly, and even tried to prevent them from leaving the city. Frequently, dissidents were tortured or put to death, to the consternation of the inhabitants. In reaction, two missions were sent to Venice twice, in 1425 and 1429, asking the Senate to respect the terms of the 1423 agreement and, most important, to send a load of wheat to prevent famine.[18] However, promises did not prevent Thessalonians from leaving and the city from further decline. Most of the inhabitants sold their property and fled to neighbouring countries or to Constantinople, still imperial capital, or to other Venetian dominions.[19]

In the spring of 1430 Murad II decided to clear the situation. In March he marched against the Macedonian capital from Yenitsa. The Venetians sent three galleys under the command of Antonio Diedo to reinforce the city's defence. Even so, the defenders were outnumbered and ill-equiped and, most important, their morale was low. Murad demanded the surrender of the city but the Venetians refused. Then the Turks, under the command of Sinan Pasha, commander-in-chief of the Ottoman forces in Europe, stormed the walls. The defences broke first at the Trigonion tower and then elsewhere. The gates were opened and the Turkish cavalry rushed in. The conquerors sacked the city and carried seven thousand slaves to the Turkish camp. According to oriental custom, pillaging went on for three days. On the fourth day, Murad entered the city and visited the church of *Acheiropoietos*, the first to be converted into a mosque. On the eighth column of the northern collonade, counting from the *sanctum sanctorum*, the following inscription still reads: "Sultan Murad Han captured Thessaloniki in 833 (Hegira chronology)". With the fall of Thessaloniki, the seven-year Venetian occupation, which had cost the Most Serene Republic 200,000 gold ducats, ended.[20]

The fall of the Macedonian capital, prelude to the fall of Constantinople twenty-three years later, created quite a sensation among the Greek-Orthodox world. Scholars mourned and popular legends were created about that historical event. Legends resonated the story recorded by the Grand Logothete of the Ecumenical Patriarchate Ierax (c.1530-1609/1611) that Thessaloniki was betrayed by the monks of the monastery of Vlatades, who advised Murad to destroy the

The eighth column of the northern collonade of the Acheiropoietos church, upon which the inscription engraved on Murad's orders is still preserved: «Sultan Murad Han captured Thessaloniki in 833» (Hegira chronology).

The Vlatadon monastery in an early 20th century photograph.

aquaduct supplying the city from Hortiatis. Although neither the chronicler of the fall Ioannis Anagnostis nor Venetian documents mention anything pertaining to this story, it is a well-established fact that, since 1446, imperial decrees granted special privileges to the monastery and the monks paid only a nominal tax for their farms and herds.[21]

The final fall of Thessaloniki in 1430 marked the consolidation of Ottoman rule in Macedonia. One thousand Turkish families came from Yenitsa and settled down in Thessaloniki, where they were housed in churches and monasteries. Soon, many of the city's Christian monuments were either converted to Islamic temples or destroyed.[22]

As it was to be expected, military campaigns were followed by upheaval and devastation, but many such events passed unrecorded because other, more important ones, overshadowed them. The environment was also not left unaffected: plantations and fields were neglected, towns and villages were burned down, deforestation turned green hills to bald, featureless mounds, and the inhabitants either scattered or were enslaved or killed. Whatever remained of fertile land passed into the hands of the Turks. Some Christian landlords renounced their faith and became Muslim in order to keep their property. In the hinterland, some of the converted lords' vassals followed suit and islamization began to spread. In the region northwest

of Kozani and Grevena, at the foot of the Pindus range, converted peasants came to be known as *Valaades*. These ex-Christians and, later, the cast of *Sipahis* became the nuclei of the military and social structure of the Ottoman empire during the early centuries of its existence. The old serfs of the Byzantine era gradually became the familiar sharecroppers who continued to have the same obligations to the landowners. Their revocable property (*hasia* and *zametia*) passed, gradually but steadily, from the sultan's nominal ownership to the that of their usufructuaries.[23]

The consolidation of Ottoman rule was followed by the cruel *devsirme* practice, heavy taxation and, generally, the tyranic and high-handed behaviour of the conquerors. Many Christians turned against the Turks in a desperate last stand which culminated in the battle of Varna (1444) and then, it seems, wavered on in Western Macedonia for five years.[24] Those who had the means chose to flee to Venetian possessions or Italy, while many more sought refuge in mountainous regions. As a result, a number of settlements which, after the initial period of privation and hardship, acquired significance during the Ottoman period came into being: Vlasti, Galatini, Kleisoura, Vogatsiko, Kostarazi, Selitsa (Eratyra), Samarina, Kataphygio.[25]

Towards the end of the 15th century, successive waves of Jews, persecuted in their native lands of Central Europe and the Iberian peninsula, arrived to the port of Thessaloniki. An estimated 40,000 Spanish Jews found refuge in the Ottoman empire, most of them in the Macedonian capital.[26] These immigrants reinforced the nucleus of indigenous Jews, the so-called *Romanian* Jews, and helped transform the ethnological profile of the city. The Ottoman rulers proved hospitable to the new settlers because they were interested in repopulating the decaying cities. Many Jews found their way into the interior of Macedonia and settled down in other parts of the Ottoman empire. The Jews of Thessaloniki, along with their well-known commercial activities, developed textile manufacture to a degree that, like in the rest of Europe, laid the ground for early capitalism the Macedonian capital.

The movement of Christian population, fleeing Ottoman pressures, towards the mountainous parts of Macedonia led to the development of significant settlements such as Vogatsikon (above) and Neveska (Nymphaion, right).

IOANNIS D. PSARAS
THE OTTOMAN CONQUEST
NOTES

1. Apostolos Vacalopoulos, *History of Macedonia, 1354-1833* (in Greek), Thessaloniki 1969, pp. 11-34; Angeliki Laiou, 'The Serbs in the Aimos Peninsula', *History of the Greek Nation* (in Greek, henceforth *History*), vol. IX, Athens 1979, p. 178-183.

2. Georg Ostrogorskij, *Pour l'histoire de la féodalité byzantine* (translation by Henri Grégoire), Bruxelles 1954, pp. 187-221; Nikolaos Svoronos, 'Economic and Social Developments', in *History, ibid.*, pp. 70-72.

3. Vacalopoulos, *op. cit.*, p. 15.

4. A.E. Zachariadou, 'The Conquest of Adrianople by the Turks', *Studii Veneziani*, 12 (1970), 211-217.

5. Vacalopoulos, *op. cit.*, p. 25.

6. G.T. Dennis, *The Reign of Manuel II Palaeologus in Thessalonica, 1382-1387*, Rome 1960, p. 89.

7. Vacalopoulos, *op. cit*, pp. 41-46.

8. A. Vacalopoulos, 'The Published Speeches of Isidoros, Metropolitan of Thessaloniki as a Historical Source for the Early *Tourkokratia* in Thessaloniki (1387-1403)' (in Greek), *Makedonika*, 4 (1955-1960), 20-34; by the same author, 'Archbishop Gavriil and the First Turkish Occupation of Thessaloniki (1391-1403)' (in Greek), *ibid.*, 371-373; Dennis, *op. cit.*, pp. 22-25, 151-159; I. Karagiannopoulos - A. Vacalopoulos - I. Diamantouros, 'From 1204 to the Fall of Thessaloniki to the Turks', *Macedonia: 4000 Years of Greek History and Culture* (in Greek), Athens 1982, pp. 306-318.

9. Dennis, *op. cit.*, pp. 41-46, 77-102; cf. the following works by A. Vacalopoulos: "Quelques problèmes relatifs à la résistance de Manuel II Paléologue contre les Turcs Ottomans dans la Macédoine grecque (1383-1391)", *Actes du Ire Congrès International d'Études Balkaniques et Sud-Est Européenes*, vol. 3, Sofia 1969, 351-355; 'Thessaloniki: Extramural Historical Research' (in Greek), *Makedonika*, 17 (1977), 1-39; *Sources for the History of Macedonia, 1354-1833* (in Greek), Thessaloniki 1989, pp. 13-90.

10. The Turkish name *Yenice* (New Site) is rendered Yenitsa or
-according to a Greek etymological version - Giannitsa; see: Vasileios
Dimitriadis, *Central and Western Macedonia According to Evliya
Çelebi* (in Greek), Thessaloniki 1973, pp. 62-64.
11. I.K. Vasdravelis, *Historical Archives of Macedonia, A. Thessaloniki Archive 1695-1912* (in Greek), Thessaloniki 1952, 17-18, no.
13; *ibid., C. Vlatades Monastery Archive 14(4)6-1839*, Thessaloniki
1955, 7-8, nos 14-15; Georgios Ch. Hionidis, 'Hosios Theophanis the
Young' (in Greek), *Makedonika*, 8 (1968), 223-238; by the same
author, *History of Verria* (in Greek), vol. 2, Thessaloniki 1970, p. 69;
Vacalopoulos, *History of Macedonia*, pp. 53-55.
12. Vasdravelis, *Historical Archives of Macedonia, B. Verria-Naousa
Archive 1598-1886*, Thessaloniki 1954, 80-81, no. 100; Vacalopoulos, *op. cit.*, p. 53.
13. Vacalopoulos, 'Thessaloniki: Extramural Historical Research',
5-6.
14. Giannis Tsaras, 'Thessaloniki from the Byzantines to the
Venetians (1423-1430)' (in Greek), *Makedonika*, 17 (1977), 85-123,
with bibliography.
15. M. Spremić, 'Harac Soluna u XV veku', *Zbornik Radova Vizan-
toloskog Instituta*, 10 (1967), 187-194: Greek translation with an
introduction and comments by I.A. Papadrianos, *Makedonika*, 9
(1969), 33-46. It should be noted that at that time 35-40 aspers were
worth one ducat.
16. C.N. Sathas, *Mnimeia Ellinikis Istorias. Documents inéedits
relatifs à l'histoire de la Grèce au moyen âge*, r. 4, Paris 1882, p. xx;
K.D. Mertzios, *Memorials of Macedonian History* (in Greek), Thessaloniki 1947, pp. 41-44; A. Vacalopoulos, 'Contribution to the
History of Thessaloniki During Venetian Rule (1423-1430' (in
Greek), *Armenopoulos Volume, Scientific Yearbook of the University
of Thessaloniki Law School*, 6 (1952), 127-149.
17. Mertzios, *op. cit.*, p. 45; F. Thiriet, *Régestes de délibérations du*

Sénat de Venise concernant la Romania, r. 2 (1400-1430), Paris 1959,
p. 216.
18. Mertzios, *op. cit.*, pp. 46-61; Vacalopoulos, *Sources*, pp. 185-187.
19. Mertzios, *op. cit.*, pp. 53-78.
20. Ioannis Anagnostou, *Account of the Last Fall of Thessaloniki* (in
Greek), Thessaloniki 1958, pp. 30-35; Vacalopoulos, *History of
Macedonia*, pp. 85-90; Dimitriadis, *op. cit.*, pp. 17-28; Elissavet
Zachariadou, 'Ottoman Expansion in Europe to the Fall of Constantinople (1354-1453)', *History*, vol. IX, pp. 184-213.
21. Vasdravelis, *Historical Archives, A.*, 167-168, no. 129; *ibid., C.*,
xiii-ix, 18-19, no. 21, 23-24, no. 27; by the same author, 'A 1486
Unpublished *Firman* of the Vlatades Monastery' (in Greek),
Makedonika, 4 (1955-1960), 533-536; G.A. Stogioglou, *The Patriarchal Monastery of the Vlatades in Thessaloniki* (in Greek), Thessaloniki 1971, pp. 162-173.
22. A. Vacalopoulos, 'Contribution to the History of Thessaloniki
shortly after its Turkish Conquest' (in Greek), *Grigorios Palamas*, 20
(1936), 26-35, 65-73; Mertzios, *op. cit.*, pp. 77-78; Vacalopoulos,
'Thessaloniki: Extramural Historical Research', 4-5; Apostolos
Papagiannopoulos, *History of Thessaloniki* (in Greek), Thessaloniki 1982, pp. 117-131; V. Dimitriadis, *Topography of Thessaloniki during Turkish Rule, 1430-1912* (in Greek), Thessaloniki
1983, p. 16.
23. Vacalopoulos, *History of Macedonia*, pp. 317ff.
24. A. Vacalopoulos, 'A Revolt in Western Macedonia: 1444-1449',
Balkan Studies, 9 (1968), 375-380.
25. A. Vacalopoulos, "La retraite des populations grecques vers des
régions éloignées et montagneuses pendant la domination turque",
Balkan Studies, 4 (1963), 265-276.
26. I.S. Emmanuel, *Histoire de l'industrie des tissus des Israélites de
Salonique*, Lausanne 1935; by the same author, Histoire des Israélites
de Salonique, r. 1 (*140 an. J-C à 1640*), Paris 1936.

Demographic Developments in Macedonia Under Ottoman Rule

Basil K. Gounaris

The study of demographic development over such a long period is confronted with almost insuperable obstacles. For most of the period of Turkish domination, lack of data due to the limited utilization of Ottoman documents renders a complete estimate of population impossible. On the other hand, the existing statistical data are not devoid of considerable inaccuracies. In the mind of the subjects of the empire, whether Muslim, Christian or Jewish, official census was traditionally connected with conscription and taxation. Consequently, every community had a good reason to present the numbers of its members as small as possible. Furthermore, the figures given by the Ottoman censuses often mention only the male population or just the number of families. Be that as it may, data taken from Ottoman sources, whenever available, are often more reliable than the information given by European travellers and consular agents.

The data of the second category are certainly more accesible as they are fragmentary, often based on rough or arbitrary estimates and inadequate criteria. With regard especially to the 19th and early 20th century, West European and Balkan censuses far from being reliable, show at best the increase and decrease of the population. During that period, democraphic issues were directly connected with ethnological claims of neighbouring countries and the fluctuations of the Eastern Question, a fact that further adds to the problems. Finally, a serious difficulty stems from the fact that throughout the period of Turkish rule, 'Macedonia' as a geographic concept never coincided with a specific administrative area. This permitted the occasional analysts of demographic data to 'adjust' the territory of Macedonia so as to agree with the statistical conclusions they wished to draw.[1] But even post-1912 studies of the population movements are rather limited, thus making the study of demographic development an extremely difficult task.

Population changes

The first century of Ottoman rule in Macedonia is characterized by a marked decrease in the Christian population which was primarily due to Muslim-Turkic colonization. The Yürüks, a semi-nomadic Turkic tribe, represented the majority of the newcomers, having already appeared in Macedonia since the 14th century. Most of them settled in the region of Thessaloniki, in Central and Western Macedonia (Yenitsa, Kilkis, Stromnitsa, Servia, Florina) and as far north as Monastir (Bitola). At the same time, the Christian populations retreated either to the western and southern mountainous regions or to Chalcidice.[2]

Towards the end of the 15th century it was the turn of Jews to come in lagre numbers from Central and Western Europe and settle, mainly in Thessaloniki. The *Askenazim*, Jews of German and Hungarian origin, were the first to arrive, but the most numerous group was that of Spanish Jews who were expelled from Spain in 1492. Other groups came from Sicily and Southern Italy and still more from Portugal in 1497. Jews of Western origin came to be known collectively as *Sefardim* (Spanish Jews). During the 16th century the Jewish element moved towards the interior of Macedonia and by the end of the century Jewish communities had been established at Skopje (Uskub), Monastir, Kavala, Drama, Serres, Siderocausia of Chalcidice, and elsewhere.[3]

However, the Jews were not the only mobile part of the population during the 16th century. Christian populations also began to move towards the plains. One part headed for Chalcidice where metallurgy was flourishing. The most important movement of population was the resettlement of Vlachs from Agrapha and Acheloos, who began to move to Macedonia and, to a significant extent, to urbanize. The urbanization of the Vlachs as well of other local Greek and Vlach populations during the following century resulted in

Yeni Djami: the temple of the Donmeh, the islamized Jews of Thessaloniki.

the depopulation of the interior of Macedonia; this facilitated the continuous flow of peasant Slav populations southwards.[4]

These movements seem to be confirmed by a recent study on Western Macedonia, according to which the population decreased by one quarter before 1641, following the relative swell of late 16th century. After this period and until 1683 the population of the western Macedonian plateaux seems to have remained stable, but a new decrease followed during the years of the Austrian-Turkish wars (1683-1711).

During that turbulent period the islamization process, which had not ceased during the 16th century, intensified. The most characteristic example is the case of the *Valaades*, Christians turned Muslim (in the 19th century they constituted 25% of the population of the Aliakmon valley) who, however, had been hardly turkicized by the time of the Greek-Turkish exchange of populations.[5]

However, islamization in the 17th century was not the bane of Christians only. By mid-century, the Jewish communities were divided by the preachings of the pseudo-messiah Sabetai Chvi from Smyrna. After a ten-year activity, he was arrested by the Turks and eventually, in 1666, he was converted to Islam. Subsequently, many of his followers were islamized too, preserving, however, their Jewish customs. The so-called *Donmeh* (converted), although they gradually adopted the Turkish language, remained firmly aloof from genuine Muslims and Jews alike until the day of the exchange of populations.[6]

In Western Macedonia there was a considerable growth of population during the 1700s (about 50% from 1711 to 1788) followed by a decline towards the end of the century. In the *sanjaks* of Thessaloniki and Kavala it seems that the growth did not exceed 100% between the 16th and 18th centuries. Regarding the Christian population, in particular, whose ranks were decimated by islamization and emigration to Central Europe, the percentage of growth was only 50% –an annual rate of a mere 0.16%, compared to a 0.50% for the rest of Europe. For exactly the opposite reasons, which included extensive colonization, the Muslim share of the population grew. Considerable was the increase in the numbers of Jews, who, however, remained a small minority, some 40,000 in both *sanjaks*, out of an estimated total of 600,000. Of course, the value of such estimates regarding any particular district is limited. Thus, it was surmised that the Christian population of the villages in the region of Thessaloniki might have quintupled between late 15th and early 18th century.[8]

At the turn of the 19th century (1801) the traveller Edward Clarke estimated the total population of Macedonia at 700,000. The first general Ottoman

sies and 5,915 Jews). In the *vilayet* of Monastir there were 208,222 male inhabitants (120,582 Christians, 81,736 Muslims, 4,682 Gypsies, 1,136 Jews, 24 Armenians and 35 of other religious affiliations).[9]

There is a wealth of data for the years between the first general census of 1831 and the second (1881-1893) but it is impossible to draw any definite conclusions from them. Travellers' accounts and consular reports provide information regarding most regions, but their comparison across time is not feasible because of the frequent changes in administrative or even state boundaries. In any case, around mid-19th century, Nicolaidy estimated the total population of 'Macedonia' to be 1,378,000. Twenty years later, according to the British consul's estimate, the consular district of Thessaloniki (approximately the area of the *vilayet* of *Selanik*) numbered some 700,000 inhabitants (320,000 Muslims, 330,000 Christians and 50,000 Jews). During the same period, the *vilayet* of Monastir, including the *kaza* of Korytsa (Korçë), had 536,000 Christians and 386,000 Muslims (out of a total 922,000).[11]

The census that began in 1881 and was completed in 1893 provides the first all-round statistical picture of Macedonia. It recorded 'believers' and 'infidels', men and women of every age, classified as Muslim, 'Patriarchist' (Greek), 'Exarchist' (Bulgarian), Armenian, Jewish and other traditional *millêt*. Understandably, data based on religious affiliation have limited ethnological significance, at least regarding the Christian-Orthodox population. The figures for the *vilayet* of Thessaloniki, according to *sanjak*, are the following:

	Muslims		Greeks		Bulgarians		Total
	Women	Men	Women	Men	Women	Men	
Thessaloniki	108,815	116,423	89,113	103,331	44,066	51,741	552,981
Serres	69,559	74,301	33,809	36,650	58,791	64,646	339,881
Drama	38,542	40,262	6,367	7,697	1,607	1,833	96,982
Total	216,916	230,986	129,289	147,948	104,464	118,220	989,844
	447,902		277,237		222,684		

census, which was waged in 1831 and covered only the male population, proved Clarke's estimate inaccurate. According to it, the *vilayet* of Thessaloniki (*Selanik*, including probably some regions of Thessaly too) had the greatest proportion of Turkish population of all the European provinces of the Empire (41.70%). The male population amounted to 240,411 (127,200 Christians, 100,249 Muslims, 7,047 Gyp-

However, in order not to give the impression that data concerning non-Christians were free from errors, it should be noted that the number of Jews in the *vilayet* of Thessaloniki was found to be 18,463 women and 18,743 men only.[12] According to Abbot, the Jews of Thessaloniki, fearing taxation which normally followed censuses, using signals from house to house saw to it that the younger members of the family, especially boys, were removed in good time.[13] Furthermore, considerable differences emerge if the figures of the Muslim and Christian population are compared with those taken from the *salname* (annual

and Christians as well.

The census in the *vilayet* of Monastir gives the following figures for each *sanjak*:[17]

	Muslims		Greeks		Bulgarians		Total
	Women	Men	Women	Men	Women	Men	
Monastir	43,246	44,046	34,559	38,041	78,078	84,718	327,073
Korytsa	35,627	40,862	33,971	26,771	16,957	20,765	165,727
Servia	29,422	32,331	49,410	55,014	2,424	2,950	171,599
Total	108,295	117,239	107,940	119,826	97,459	108,433	664,399
	225,534		227,766		205,892		

survey) for the same *vilayet* around 1882. The increase resulting for the decade 1882-1892 amounts to 17.3% and 24% for Christians and Muslims respectively.[14] This abrupt rise seems questionable, for it had been established that, between 1875 and 1900, the mean annual increase of the population of Macedonia was approximately 0,84%, one of the lowest in the Balkans. (Greece 1.35%, Romania 1.36%, Serbia 1.71%, Bosnia and Herzegovina 1.78%).[15] Equally revealing is a comparison of these data with a British census of 1883, for the *sanjak* of Serres. The latter estimated the total population to be approximately 300,000, 11,7% less than the Ottoman census, an impressively small difference. Equally small are the differences regarding each religious-ethnic group: the Exarchist-Bulgarians were estimated at 120,000 and 123,000 by the British vice-consul and the Ottoman census respectively, the Patriarchist-Greeks at 75,000 and 70,000 (if the 3000 Vlachs, whom the British classified separetely, are added to the Greeks then the difference is still smaller), and the Jews at 1,000 and 1,112 respectively. However, in the case of the Mus-

The figures above, whether tampered with or not, confirm that the Muslim population in the *vilayet* of Monastir was only 34% of the total, which means a 5% decrease since 1831. This should probably be attributed to the administrative reform of 1861, which removed certain Albanian districts. By contrast, in the *vilayet* of Thessaloniki the percentage of the Muslim population grew from 41,7% to 45,24%.[18] Again, the reasons for this increase probably lie in the change of *vilayet* boundaries with the exclusion of parts of Thessaly as well as to the influx of a considerable number of Muslim refugees after the Eastern Crisis in 1876-1878. However, any conclusion drawn from these data with regard to Greeks or Bulgarians would be rather dubious. In any case, it is evident that everywhere, with the exception of the *sanjaks* of Monastir and Serres, the Patriarchist-Greek element was predominant.

In the mid-1890s another Turkish census gives additional information about the *vilayet* of Thessaloniki, which tends to agree with the data of the previous census:

Muslims		Greeks		Bulgarians		Jews		Total
Men	Women	Men	Women	Men	Women	Men	Women	
227,545	224,630	152,834	141,790	128,316	117,586	22,302	21,121	1,038,953

lims the picture is quite different. Even if we add to the British estimate of 94,000 the 4,000 Circassians, the 2,000 Gypsies and the 1,000 Albanians, we do not come anywhere near the 143,860 of the Ottoman census, even reduced by 11,7%.[16] From the above it becomes clear that the accuracy of such data must in no way be overestimated, not only with respect to the size of the Muslim population but also regarding Jews

It should be noted, however, that the number of the 'Bulgarians' includes Roman Catholics, Maronites, Christian Gypsies and others.[19]

After the reorganization of the Ottoman statistics Department between 1900 and 1902, another census was attempted in 1903 and was concluded by 1906.[20] In Macedonia, the census was probably completed in 1904, under the supervision of European observers.

As it was expected, the interpretation of its outcome became the cause of a long controversy between Greeks and Bulgarians in their effort to legitimize their conflicting claims over Macedonia.

A juxtaposition of statistics from three different sources of that period is revealing. Phokas Kosmetatos, relying on the 1904 census, estimated the population of the *vilayets* of Thessaloniki and Monastir as follows:

	Thessaloniki	Monastir
Muslims	425,613	220,369
Greeks	360,000	276,667
Bulgarians	200,488	148,426
Total (Thessaloniki)	1,041,819	
Total (Monastir)	609,229	

The attempt to present the Greek element as preponderant is obvious. In the above table, Muslims and Bulgarians - especially the latter - are reduced in comparison with previous statistical data, while the Greeks appear increased by 30 %.

During the same period, Brancoff defended the Bulgarian position claiming that the population of Macedonia was as follows:

	Thessaloniki	Monastir
Muslims	393,612	195,989
Greeks	147,097	42,830
Bulgarians	501,110	370,410

The Greek element, with the hellenized Vlachs arbitrarily excluded, shows a decrease of 47% in the district of Thessaloniki and 81% in Monastir, as compared to the data of the 1880s; in contrast, the Bulgarians appear to have increased by 125% and 80% respectively.[22]

The Greek-published *Statistics on Macedonia: Vilayets of Thessaloniki and Monastir* seems closer to the truth; it is based on the census of 1904, and while favourable to the Greek point of view, it is more reliable regarding method and evaluation of data. This particular study gives the exact census results, but it excludes the *sanjaks* of Divra, Elbasan and the *kaza* of Colonia of the *vilayet* of Monastir, on the grounds that they are not part of Macedonia. In short, the following numbers are given for each *vilayet* :

	Thessaloniki	Monastir
Muslims	482,414	272,100
Greeks	287,092	289,800
Bulgarians	223,537	176,500
Total: (Thessaloniki)	993,043	
Total: (Monastir)	738,400	

Copying the Ottoman census, it also mentions 43,400 Aromunes (pro-Romanian Vlachs) and 54,000 Jews in both *vilayets*. However, the points are made that the Turks had arbitrarily recorded all Vlachs as belonging to the pro-Romanian faction, and also that some 50,000 'Bulgarians' were forcibly converted Patriarchists[23].

In the last analysis, the only feasible comparison is that on the basis of the 1881-93, 1885-96, and 1904 censuses, but only regarding the *vilayet* of Thessaloniki:

	1881-93	1895-96
Muslims	447,904	452,175 (0,95%)
Greeks	277,237	294,624 (6,3%)
Bulgarians	222,684	245,902 (10,4%)

	1904
Muslims	482,414 (6,7%)
Greeks	287,092 (-2,55%
Bulgarians	223,537 (-9,1%)

The fluctuations are justified if the following factors are considered: a) the Muslim element was boosted by refugees from the north and, also, from Eastern Rumelia, after its annexation to Bulgaria (1885); b) between 1897 and 1904, part of the Patriarchist population, voluntarily or not, was converted to the Exarchate, while, after 1881, a number of Patriarchists moved to Thessaly as land-workers; c) according to Shopov, Bulgarian consul in Thessaloniki, between 1880 and 1890 some 200,000 Exarchists moved to Bulgaria where some settled permanently.[24]

During the ensuing turbulent years, the steady movement of the populations continued. Emigration to the New World certainly was the most impotant phenomenon of the period between 1905 and 1912, and, temporarily, threatened to upset the balance between Christians and Muslims. The danger of upseting the ethnological balance intensified after the Young Turks came to power and encouraged Muslim refugees from Bosnia and Herzegovina to settle in Macedonia. In 1910 alone, approximately 9,000 refuges settled in the *vilayet* of Thessaloniki. That year, the total population of the *vilayet* was estimated at 1,130,975 inhabitants (506,886 Muslims, 307,486 Greeks, 229,481 Bulgarians, 56,623 Jews and 22,288 Vlachs). According to official sources, in 1911 the population of the *vilayet* of Monastir reached 1,000,000, the *sanjaks* of Divra and Elbasan included. However, the general drain in population caused the annual rate of growth to drop to 0.66% for the decade between 1901-1910 from the 0.7% of the preceding fifteen years.[25]

The Balkan Wars of 1912-1913 marked the beginning of new population movements. During the first Balkan War there was an influx of Muslim refugees from the north into the region of Thessaloniki, while during the second Balkan War Greeks from Eastern Macedonia temporarily flocked to the same area. Tension in Greek-Turkish relations before the outbreak of the First World War kept the population movement high. During this period (spring of 1914) a gradual exodus of Muslims and Exarchists to Turkey and Bulgaria respectively was observed, coinciding with the arrival of the first wave of Greek refugees from the Caucasus, Smyrna, the Dardanelles and Eastern Thrace. Specifically, from the Balkan Wars to the end of the First World War, 65,000 refugees came to Greece from Bulgaria and Serbia (most of them to Macedonia) while 20,000 went the opposite way and 125,000 Muslims moved to Turkey. Yet, in spite of the gradual but continuous influx of refugees, the total population of Macedonia between 1913 and 1920 dropped from 1,167,617 to 1,085,531.[26]

Cities and Urbanization

Not surprisingly, the Ottoman conquest of Macedonia thinned the population of urban centres, and, particularly of Thessaloniki. According to a Turkish census, in 1478 the city had 1,119 houses, of which 584 belonged to Muslims, that is to say the total population was not more than 6-7,000 inhabitants. The census does not mention any Jewish houses, although the first Jewish immigrants must have already settled in the city. A few years later, in the 1520s, the population increased considerably: there were 4,863 houses, of which 2,645 were Jewish, 1,229 Muslim and 989 Christian. The total number of inhabitants must have been 27-30,000, of which 8,500 were Christians. In late 16th and early 17th century, while part of the Jewish population dispersed into the interior, Christian Vlachs moved to Thessaloniki;

Monastir (Bitola): the high street during the Ottoman period.

judging by their tax contributions, by 1605 Christians must have risen to 50% of the city's population.[27]

Information concerning other cities of Macedonia during the same period is limited. However, there was a clear movement towards urban centres throughout the 16th century, especially in the fifty-year period between 1525 and 1575.[28] In 1469, Monastir had 480 families (185 Christian and 295 Muslim). The same city in 1521 numbered 845 families (205 Christian and 640 Muslim). In 1477 Kastoria had 962 families (940 Christian and 22 Muslim). However, by 1518 its population had dropped to 799 families (732 Christian and 67 Muslim), to increase again later in the same century to 1,077 families (1,033 Christian, 57 Muslim and 17 Jewish). In 1465 Serres had 817 families, 1,283 in 1518 and 1,093 in the 1520s (671 Muslim, 357 Christian and 65 Jewish). Kavala was probably founded between 1520 and 1530, in the place of the ruined Byzantine city of Christopolis. Evidently, during both the 16th and 17th centuries, Muslims generally outnumbered the Christians in many important cities of Macedonia, while some of them (Yenitsa, Stromnitsa) were exlusively inhabited by Turks. On the other hand, Christians constituted the majority in the middle-sized urban centers and the small towns of Central and Western Macedonia.[29]

The urbanization of Macedonia continued through the following centuries (17th and 18th). Heavy taxation and repression, especially during the Russo-Turkish war (1768-1774), the ensuing period of anarchy, epidemics and marauding bands contributed to the thinning of the rural population. The destruction of Moschopolis by the Albanians in 1769 also played a part as Greek and Vlach populations left Northern Epirus and took refuge in Monastir, Veles, Serres and, mostly, Thessaloniki. Besides, Thessaloniki had considerably grown as a commercial centre by that time, and was able to absorb the greatest part of urban settlers at the expense of Monastir. As it was the case in most urban centers, the presence of janissaries and their families increased the population still further.

Around the middle of the 18th century the total population of Thessaloniki was approximately 40,000 with the Jewish community still the most numerous (18,000-20,000), ahead of the Turkish (10,000) and the Greek (less than 10,000). At about the same period, Verria had 3-3,500 inhabitants, Edessa (Vodena) 2,000-2,500 and Serres 12,000-15,000.[30] Yet the deterioration of living conditions in the countryside changed the picture before the end of the century. In the absence of reliable demographic data, the estimates of European travellers show a marked rise of urban population. According to Beaujour, Verria had 7-8,000 inhabitants (Cousinery mentions 18 to 20,000), mainly Greeks and Turks and very few Jews. In the surrounding area there were about 300 villages, the population of which began to decline as many were driven by Ali-Pasha's aggression to Asia Minor. Edessa numbered 2,000 houses or 5-6,000 inhabitants, Serres 25-30,000 (Muslims estimated at 50%). Thessaloniki was already a city of 60,000 inhabitants, in other words it had grown by 50% within half a century. According to Beaujour's estimate, Kastoria had 7-8,000, Naoussa 3-4,000, Yenitsa 4-5,000 (almost exclusively Turks), Skopje 5-6,000, Kavala and Elephtheroupolis (Pravi) 2-3,000 each.[31]

The continuous growth of commerce, the gradual improvement of transport, especially after the construction of railways, the climate of insecurity in the countryside, the precarious agricultural income, and, chiefly, the steady flow of rich Muslim families southwards were the determining factors that kept urbanization at a high level during the 19th century and through the first decade of the 20th. Available data on the transportation of building materials by rail after 1870 evidence a steady growth of urban and semi-urban centres in the *vilayets* of Thessaloniki, Monastir and Skopje.

In Eastern Macedonia, after 1870, despite the fact that urban and semi-urban population (i.e. towns of over 2, 500) already constituted almost one third of the total, urbanization continued at a rapid pace. Serres reached 32,000 in 1900 from 24,700 in 1870;

Kavala 14,000 from 7,000; Drama 14,000 from 8,000 inhabitants, while between 1850 and 1870 the 4,000 people of Elephtheroupolis doubled. In Central Macedonia urban centres grew considerably too. The population of Edessa from 10,000 in 1850 increased to 25,000 in 1900 – but the population of Verria during the same period grew by only 2000, from 12,000 to 14,000. Kilkis had 3,768 inhabitants in 1870 and 7,750 in 1898. Further to the north, Stromnitsa from 8,900 inhabitants in 1894 rose to over 10,000 in 1900; the population of Istip (stip), from 11,000 in 1883 grew to 15,000 in 1907. In the west, the population of Florina from 10,000 in 1888 increased to 12,000 in 1908 and that of Prilapos (Prilep) from 13,000 to 17,000. The 5,000 inhabitants of Kastoria doubled between 1850 and 1888, but during the following years the population of the city remained static. On the other hand, the population of Ochrida, dropped from 16,000 in 1888 to 12,000 in 1908 and that of Kozani from 9,000 in 1850 to 6,000 in 1908.

A similar growth in population was observed in several small towns, most of them located along the railway lines. Furthermore, during that period, several villages which were linked to Thessaloniki by rail or even railway stations soon grew into flourishing transportation centres, Gevgeli being the most characteristic example. These data evidence a progressive urbanization of the entire Macedonian hinterland, with the only exception of the western regions where armed conflict, the absence of industry and inadequate communications traditionally encouraged emigration[32].

Naturally, the greatest part of urban settlers concentrated in the capitals of the *vilayets*, Thessaloniki, Monastir, and Skopje where the economic upsurge of the period between 1870 and 1912 offered many job opportunities and the presence of the army adequate protection. Skopje, which had 20,000 inhabitants in 1870, remained an agricultural town for at least a decade after it was connected by rail to Thessaloniki. In 1886 its population was 26,000, in 1900 32,000, and in 1910 40,000. Monastir experienced a similar growth: 45,000 inhabitants in 1850, 50,000 in 1888 and 60,000 in 1912.[33]

The population of Thessaloniki, due to the Greek Revolution and Turkish reprisals, had not exceeded 60,000 until 1840. By 1870, however, it had reached 80,000 and continued to increase rapidly. Greeks from every corner of Macedonia, paticularly from Western, Turks and Circasians from Bosnia, Thessaly and East-

Florina: overview (above) and houses by the river bank (right).

ern Rumelia, Exarchist Slavophones from Central Macedonia and Jews from every corner of Europe raised the number of inhabitants to 100,000 in 1880 and probably to 120,000 before the end of the decade. In 1905 the British consul estimated the population to be around 150,000 and in 1912 approximately 180,000, which seems a rather exaggerated figure considering the fact that the census of 28 April 1913 showed a total of 157,889 inhabitants. However, one should take into account the ever increasing influx of

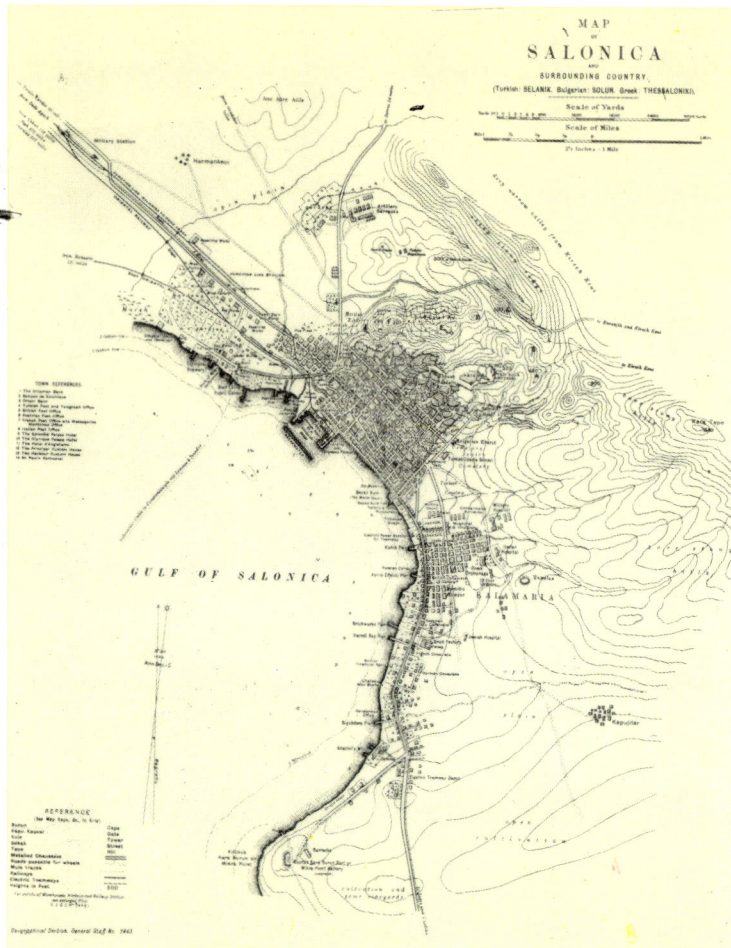

A 1909 map of Thessaloniki. At that time the city's popylation exceeded 150,000.

visitors (commercial agents, workers, Ottoman and European officials and military) who arrived to the Maçedonian capital at a rate far in excess of the ability of local inns and hotels to accomodate them, and whose numbers artificially swelled the permanent population of the city. The rapid expansion of Thessaloniki beyond both its western and eastern walls, the rise in the value of real estate and rents are indicative of the explosive growth of the city.

During the 19th century there was a change in the composition of the population according to religious affiliation. The decrease in infant mortality gave the numbers of the Jewish community a tremendous boost; between the beginning of the 19th century and 1912 it increased at least five-fold. By contrast, the share of the Muslim population, despite the arrival of refugees, declined steadily. Whereas at the turn of the 19th century Muslims compised half of the population, between the 1840 and 1890 they fluctuated between 25% and 35%, while in the 1900s their number

was definitely below 30% (in spite of the influx of Turkish refugees fleeing from the war zone, the 1913 census shows that Muslims compised 29% of the population of Thessaloniki). The Christian element, predominantly Greek, fluctuated between 20% and 30% throughout that period (1800-1912).[34]

Emigration

The origins of emigration as a social phenomenon, mainly from the western plateaux of Macedonia, are lost in the late Byzantine period, if not earlier. The political and economic conditions during Ottoman rule encouraged this trend which continued uninterruptedly until the liberation of Macedonia. Thus, for at least five centuries, the remittances of emigrants constituted a steady and much needed contribution to the low agricultural income of the population, while, at the same time, helped decongest a potentially over-crowded local labour market. The emigrant were mostly Greek- or Vlach-speaking, tradesmen and ar-

Kleisura: an important commercial centre of Ottoman Macedonia. Its inhabitants played an important role in the economic life of the empire and as members of the West Macedonian diaspora.

tisans or labourers and ploughmen who mainly sought seasonal employment both inside and outside the borders of the Ottoman empire.

From the 15th century onwards, Macedonian emigrants began to settle in Wallachia and Transylvania, where, during the 16th century, they became important economic factors in many urban centres. The wave of emigration intensified after Bohemia and Hungary were united under the crown of the Habsburgs (1699). A great number of Greek communities of, at least partly, Macedonian origins, were founded and flourished in Serbia, Austria, Hungary, Bohemia, Saxony and elsewhere. Particularly after 1760, as a result of Albanian raids against Moschopolis, followed by Ali Pasha's aggression, the settlements in South Slav lands multiplied. Western Macedonian emigrants from Blatsi, Siatista, Kozani, Kastoria, Kleisura, Monastir, Naoussa, Verria and Servia, managed over time to grow from peddlers and muleteers into merchants organized in companies, bankers and important public figures.

Despite occasional reaction from the part of the imperial authorities against their financial expansion, the immigrants were normally favourably received. Thus, the gradual concession of licenses and privileges permitted immigrant communities to build remarkable schools and churches. The most important centres of Hellenism of Macedonian diaspora were Veles, Skopje, Belgrade, Semlin (Zemun), Karlowitz, Vukovar, Mitrovica, Novi Sad, Krajina, Vienna, Budapest, and Sibiu of Transylvania. At about the end of the 18th century the Greek population of Austria was estimated at 80,000 families; in the region of Pest alone Greek communities had been established in 54 cities and small towns. One of those communities was in Tokay where Macedonian vine-growers developed the famous local variety. A large part of the considerable fortunes amassed in Central Europe returned to Macedonia not only in the form of remittances to relatives but also as investment mainly in impressive constructions or as generous donations and trusts for institutions of education.[35]

In parallel with emmigration abroad, internal seasonal migration developed too, a phenomenon which has received little scholarly attention. During the 19th century, after the end of the Napoleonic wars and with the gradual revival of commerce in the Eastern Mediterranean, it seems that the drift of population from the western mountainous plateaux of Macedonia towards every corner of the Empire gradually replaced the movement towards Central Europe. There was also migration to the south, after the establishment of the Greek state and the economic growth of Athens seemed to ensure a steady income for Western Macedonian masons and tradesmen.

By mid-19th century, seasonal migration had become an established practice, regulated by tradition. Migrants, or *gurbetsides* as they were called, used to migrate in groups early in the spring and to return in October. Longer migration was possible if financial conditions looked favourable but permanent residence in a strange land was exceptional. Normally, all migrants from the same region shared a common destination. Their trade was determined by their place of origin, in other words there was a sort of regional specialization. For instance, migrants from Prespa were carpenters and masons whereas those from Resna were gardeners and peddlers. However, the vast majority of Western Macedonian migrants were artisans, either skilled or trainees. An accurate estimate of their number on an annual basis is impossible, but it seems that in some places it was very substantial, as in the region of Resna where migrants comprised one-third of the adult male Christian population.

Boundary changes after the Congress of Berlin (1878) directed a large number of migrants towards the newly-established principalities of Bulgaria and Eastern Rumelia, where there was an acute demand for labour, both skilled and unskilled. According to Bulgarian estimates, between 1880 and 1900 approximately 200,000 persons travelled from Macedonia to Bulgaria and several settled down there permanently. This trend was not missed by the Greek government, which realized the decisive part that emigrants played in reinforcing Bulgarian irredentism in Macedonia. Similar developments occured in Greece, where Macedonian emigrants (whose numbers had increased after the departure of a great part of the Muslim population of Thessaly in 1881-1882)

were among the most ardent supporters of a dynamic policy in Macedonia.

The deterioration of the economic situation in Macedonia during the 1890s hit harder the western parts. The low prices of cereals paralyzed exports, while the Thessaloniki-Monastir railway line induced traditional customers of the local market to place their orders in the Macedonian capital. During the same period, there was a considerable influx of foreign labourers, mostly Italians, who mistakenly perceived in temporary public works an opportunity to penetrate the local labour market. Finally, uncertainty and insecurity intensified as a result of the terrorist action of Bulgarian bands, following the unfortunate outcome for Greece of the 1897 war against Turkey. Emigrants' remittances, already of crucial importance, remained static. To crown it all, came the bloody uprising of Ilinden (1903). The Turkish army and the irregulars who undertook to suppress the revolt left behind them 2,000 dead and huge material losses.

That disaster inaugurated a new wave of emigration which was destined to last longer than half a century: emigration to the New World. Formally, the door to the New World, particularly to the U.S.A., had already opened before 1880 but emigrants were few: from 1895 to 1902 only 1,678 persons emigrated from the European provinces of the Ottoman Empire to the U.S.A., one-third of them coming from the region of Florina. However, the continuing economic depression and the escalation of violence between Greek and Bulgarian bands soon led to a mass exodus of the rural population. An accurate estimate of the number of emigrants is, for the time being, impossible due to the simultaneous repatriation and departure of emigrants, the numerous ways of leaving and conflicting data. However, between 1900 and 1912, emigrants from Macedonia alone exceeded 50,000 and probably reached 75,000. Most of them were Slavophone peasants who were directed to the U.S.A., Canada and South America. For obvious reasons, Muslims constituted no more than 2% of the numbers involved.

The economic impact of this uncontrolled drain of workforce was incalculable. Traditionally, internal seasonal migrants left behind adequate working hands for farming and stockbreeding, but this balance was completely upset in the early 20th century. As a result, wages rocketed to unprecedented heights, and,

Artisans from Western Macedonia achieved high levels of artistic creativity. In the photograph, a ceiling of a mansion in Kozani (Folk Art Museum of Kozani).

naturally, carried the prices of staples along with them. Agricultural production, particularly grain, dropped sharply making necessary the import of corn and flour. The shortage of working hands left large tracts of land uncultivated and many owners, unable to pay their taxes, were obliged to sell their farms, a large part of which passed into the hands of repatriated emigrants. But the emigrants did not invest in land only; with their twenty-dollar bills, houses, stores and mills were bought, taxes were paid and, generally, the standard of living improved. It is worth noting that the annual value of the emigrants' remittances in Macedonia as a whole between 1910 and 1912 was one million pounds sterling, an adequate sum to relieve the chronic deficit of the balance of payments. Therefore, the contemporary observers justifiably expected that the repatriation of emigrants *en masse* would have incalculable economic consequences.

The political implications of emigration were equally important. The departure of a large part of the Slavophone population undermined the recruiting and financial potential of the Bulgarian bands and benefited the Greek counter-attack. Significantly, the Internal Macedonian Revolutionary Organization (IMRO) had imposed heavy levies on prospective emigrants in its effort either to check the outflow or to collect money in lump-sum contributions. This particular demand coupled with the far from negligible demands of the Turks as well as fare costs, made the usurers flourish. On the other hand, the mass exodus of Christians in connection with the growing Muslim colonization of Macedonia, momentarily threatened to upset the ethnological balance in favour of the Turks, a prospect which was averted by the outbreak of the First Balkan War.[36]

BASIL K. GOUNARIS
DEMOGRAPHIC DEVELOPMENTS IN
MACEDONIA UNDER OTTOMAN RULE
NOTES

1. Stanford Shaw, 'The Ottoman Census System and Population, 1831-1914', *International Journal of Middle East Studies*, 9 (1978), 325-338; Kemal H. Karpat, 'Ottoman Population Records and the Census of 1881/82-1893', *ibid.*, 238-249.

2. Apostolos Vacalopoulos, *History of Macedonia, 1354-1833* (in Greek), Thessaloniki 1988, 2nd ed., pp. 49-55, 99-100; Nikolai Todorov, *The Balkan City: 15th-19th Century* (Greek translation), vol. 1, Athens 1986, pp. 83-84.

3. Vacalopoulos, *op. cit.*, pp. 132, 135-137.

4. Nikos Svoronos, 'Administrative, Social and Economic Developments (1430-1821)', *Macedonia: 4000 Years of Greek History and Culture* (in Greek), Athens 1982, p. 355; Vacalopoulos, *op. cit.*, pp. 145-156.

5. Bruce MacGowan, *Economic Life in Ottoman Europe*, Cambridge 1981, p. 134; Vacalopoulos, *op. cit.*, pp. 317-327.

6. Vacalopoulos, *op. cit.*, pp. 235-237.

7. MacGowan, *op. cit.*, p. 134; Svoronos, *op. cit.*, p. 356.

8. Vasilis Dimitriadis, 'Categories of Taxation of the Villages of Thessaloniki during Turkish Rule' (in Greek), *Makedonika*, 20 (1980), 411.

9. Eduard D. Clarke, *Travels in Various Countries of Europe, Asia and Africa*, vol. 4, London 1816, p. 363; Todorov, *op. cit.*, pp. 429-430.

10. See, for example, Dimitra Giannouli, 'The *Vilayet* of Monastir, 1856-1870: Economy, Society, Administration' (in Greek), *Deltion Istorikis kai Ethnologikis Etaireias*, 30 (1987), 128-134.

11. B. Nicolaidy, *Les Turcs et la Turquie contemporaine*, vol. 2, Paris 1859, p. 339; *Parliamentary Papers: Accounts and Papers* (henceforth: *PPAP*), London 1870, vol. 66, p. 558, and vol. 67, p. 853.

12. Karpat, *op. cit.*, p. 266.

13. G.F. Abbott, *The Tale of a Tour in Macedonia*, London 1903, p. 19.

14. Todorov, *op. cit.*, vol. 2, p. 451.

15. Marvin R. Jackson, 'Comparing the Balkan Demographic Experience, 1860 to 1970', *Journal of European Economic History*, 14 (1985), 228-229.

16. *PPAP*, 1884, vol. 81, p. 242.

17. Karpat, *op. cit.*, p. 272; due to a printing error the Bulgarians in the *sanjaks* of Monastir and Korytsa appear in the 'Catholics' list.

18. Cf Todorov, *op. cit.*, vol. 2, p. 430.

19. Justin McCarthy, *The Arab World, Turkey and the Balkans (1878-1914): A Handbook of Historical Statistics*, Boston 1982, p. 60.

20. Shaw, *op. cit.*, pp. 333-335.

21. S.P. Phocas-Kosmetatos, *La Macédoine, son pasée et son présent*, Lausanne 1919, p. 37.

22. D.M. Brancoff, *La Macédoine et sa population chrétienne*, Paris 1905, pp. 17-18.

23. *Statistics of Macedonia: Vilayets of Thessaloniki and Monastir* (in

Greek), Athens 1910, pp. iii-x.

24. FO 195/2089, Biliotti to O'Connor, Salonica, 13.3.1900, ff. 85-89.

25. Georgios Mastrapas, *Statistics of the Vilayet of Thessaloniki* (in Greek), Athens 1910; *PPAP*, 1912-13, vol. 100, p. 727; Basil C. Gounaris, 'Emigration from Macedonia in the Early Twentieth Century', *Journal of Modern Greek Studies*, 7 (1989), 141-142 and note 8; Jackson, *op. cit.*, p. 228.

26. See, for example, FO 286/580, Morgan to Mallet, Salonica, 21.3, 1.5, 2.6.1914; S. Theophanidis, 'The Economic Development of Macedonia from 1912 to the Present Day', *Macedonia: 4000 Years*), p. 510; Athanasios Angelopoulos, 'Population Distribution of Greece Today According to Language, National Consciousness and Religion', *Balkan Studies*, 20 (1979), 124-125.

27. M. Kiel, 'Notes on the History of Some Turkish Monuments in Thessaloniki and their Founders', *Balkan Studies*, 11 (1970), 126-127; V. Dimitriadis, 'The *Kanunnâme* and the Christian Inhabitants of Thessaloniki Around 1525' (in Greek), *Makedonika*, 19 (1979), 339; A. Vacalopoulos, *History of Thessaloniki, 316 BC - 1983*, Thessaloniki 1983, p. 215; by the same author, *History of Macedonia*, p. 143.

28. According to data given by Ömer Lufti Barkan, the population of major cities of European Turkey during this period increased by an average 68%; see: Traian Stoianovich, 'The Conquering Balkan Orthodox Merchant', *Journal of Economic History*, 20 (1960), 243.

29. Todorov, *op. cit.*, vol. I, pp. 93-94, 103-104; Vacalopoulos, *History of Macedonia*, pp. 139-141; Kiel, 'Observations on the History of Northern Greece During the Ottoman Rule', *Balkan Studies*, 12 (1971), 433; Svoronos, *op. cit.*, pp. 357-358.

30. Vacalopoulos, *op. cit.*, pp. 251-257, 301-312; Svoronos, *op. cit.*, pp. 356, 358-359; Dimitriadis, 'Categories of Taxation...', 411; Traian Stoianovich, 'Land Tenure and Related Sectors of the Balkan Economy, 1600-1800', *Journal of Economic History*, 13 (1953), 399-400.

31. Esprit M. Cousinery, *Voyage militaire dans l'Empire Ottomane*, vol. 1, Paris 1829, pp. 195-197, 200, 207, 217, 222, 230; William M. Leake, *Travels in Northern Greece*, vol. 3, London 1835, p. 248; Vacalopoulos, *op. cit.*, pp. 466-467, 470.

32. Basil Gounaris, *Social and Economic Change in Macedonia, 1870-1912: The Role of the Railways*, unpublished PhD thesis, Oxford 1988, pp. 299-301.

33. Gounaris, *op. cit.*, pp. 301-302.

34. Gounaris, *op. cit.*, pp. 302-305; V. Dimitriadis, 'The Population of Thessaloniki and its Greek Community in 1913' (in Greek), *Makedonika*, 23 (1983), 96.

35. A. Vacalopoulos, *The West-Macedonian Emigrants during Turkish Rule* (in Greek), Thessaloniki 1958; by the same author, *History of Macedonia*, pp. 349-394; Svoronos, *op. cit.*, pp. 383-385; Stoianovich, 'Balkan Orthodox Merchant', pp. 234-313.

36. Gounaris, 'Emigration', pp. 134-149.

Economic Developments in Macedonia, 1430-1912

Basil K. Gounaris

1. Agriculture

The system of Land Tenure

Any attempt to investigate the primary sector of the Macedonian economy requires a parallel clarification of the legal conditions determining the system of land ownership. It goes without saying that in the early centuries the situation was particularly confused. Islamic Law (*Sheriat*) prescribed that all conquered land formally belonged to the sultan, who was entitled to award fiefs (*timars*), principally to Turkish dignitaries in exchange for their services. These timars were divided according to the income they yielded into *has*, *ziamets* and simple *timars*. The rights of the rural population living within the boundaries of these forms of property were limited to partial prescription. A similar situation seems to have prevailed in Macedonia, with certain exceptions to the system, such as the preferential allotment of land to Muslims and Christians as a sort of reward, or the partial retention of the Byzantine *pronoiarioi*. It would appear that the religious foundations also retained their land holdings. Most of the land, however, even as late as the middle of the 19th century, was in the hands of big Muslim landowners.

Around the middle of the 16th century an attempt was made to adjust the complex and imprecise legal terms of land tenure by means of a code which essentially prohibited full ownership. This reform, which was initially restricted to the *vilayet* of Roumeli (which included most of mainland Greece and Macedonia), provoked the violent resistance both of the big landholders and of the monks of Mt Athos. Faced with the threat of abandoned farms and the loss of substantial state revenues, Sultan Selim II (1566-1574) eventually restored the right to full ownership.[1]

In the course of the 17th century the system of land tenure entered a new phase. The petering out of the Ottoman drive for conquest, the deceleration of the rate of new territorial acquisitions and the increasing counter-attacks by the European powers towards the end of the century, all had serious social consequences. Not only was the military aristocracy no longer able to acquire new fiefs, but they were even deprived of their traditional right to the spoils of war. They were thus obliged to fall back on attempts to increase their agricultural income, which could only be done by expanding their original holdings. This was achieved by means of a variety of legal and illegal methods, such as the seizure of communal pastures or abandoned farms, the purchase of land in return either for money or for the protection of the rural population, and the acquisition of lands mortgaged for loans. The result was the gradual development of *chifliks* (heritable estates), which in the 17th and 18th centuries were still relatively limited in size (very few would have exceeded 15-30 acres) except in areas which already exported a sizeable agricultural surplus (as in the case of Serres). The development of *chifliks* in Macedonia —where land-labourer settlements were already quite widespread— was particularly marked in the 18th century and the first half of the 19th. During the final phase of this period, that is, the late 1830s and the 1840s, an attempt was made to curtail the rights of *chiflik* owners. This was continued in 1858 with the *Tanzimat* reforms: these included a new agricultural law which reinstated the various categories of land ownership (imperial, public, private, monasterial —*wakfs*— and uncultivated), facilitated the sale of land, and encouraged the acquisition of land at the expense of the chifliks.[2]

Despite sporadic initiatives on the part of the state

English map showing the roads linking Macedonia with the rest of the Balkans during the period of Ottoman domination.

in the 1860s, the ratio of large landholdings (more than 50 acres) to small throughout most of Macedonia was three to two. This proportion was probably maintained for many years thanks to a ruling in 1867 permitting land to be bequeathed even to distant relatives. The *chifliks* were cultivated by serfs, who were paid according to one of two systems: in one case the landowner provided shelter and seed, the serf a yoke of oxen, tools, and his labour, and the harvest was shared equally. In addition, the serfs were required to provide various compulsory services for their landlords, such as cutting and carrying wood, harvesting the landlord's share of the crop, etc. In the other case, the system was similar, except that a different method of sharing the harvest was agreed in advance. The labourers formed a distinct class, hired on an annual basis and paid principally in grain. At certain periods day labourers might also be hired.

Small landholdings, varying from 5 to 40 acres with an average of 10, were about equally divided between Muslims and Christians. The class of small landholders included those artisans and skilled labourers who owned land but lived in towns. The ratio of small farmers to serfs and agricultural labourers at this time (1860) was one to five. The high price of land in comparison with the humiliatingly low agricultural wages, the virtual impossibility of saving anything and the primitive agricultural methods

meant that landless farmers had virtually no hope of ever acquiring land of their own, even though vast tracts of land remained uncultivated. At the same time, accumulated debts and the outrageously high rates of interest demanded by landlord creditors had reduced a substantial number of serfs to a condition approximating slavery. Their debts were the result of transactions between creditors and in many cases were passed on from one generation to the next. The desperate situation of the rural population inspired the Internal Macedonian Revolutionary Organization (IMRO) in the period immediately preceding the Ilinden uprising (1903) to call for the dissolution of the *chifliks* and to promise redistribution of the land. It should be noted, however, that bankruptcy was not the exclusive prerogative of the landless and the small landholder. High interest charges and heavy mortgages imposed by successive poor harvests obliged many Muslim farmers to turn their land over to their Christian and Jewish creditors. This phenomenon began to take on disturbing dimensions early in the 1880s when, just fifty years after the Christians first began to acquire property of their own, the dominance of the Muslim element was already seriously threatened. The state attempted to cure this triple problem of debts, mortgages and usury through the more effective functioning of the agricultural banks which, in form at least, had been in existence since 1868. These institutions, however, do not appear to have been particularly successful, for the criteria applied for the granting of low-interest loans were not impartial. There were also accusations that these banks supported Muslim interests by the illegal sale of mortgaged Christian properties to Muslim land-owners.

Crops and Farming Conditions

Information about agricultural production in Macedonia in the early years of Ottoman rule is scanty; but it is unlikely to have been substantially different from that of the previous period, and would have consisted chiefly of cereals, vegetables, flax, fruit and olives. New crops, such as tobacco, cotton, corn (maize) and rice, appeared in the 17th century and played an important role in the subsequent development of the economy. Ottoman colonists also introduced the cultivation of the opium poppy. In general, it can be said that in Macedonia the choice of crops and the intensity of their cultivation followed the fluctuations of the world market as it responded to various political changes. During the 18th century the principal agricultural product was undoubtedly cotton. In the second half of the century its cultivation was extended from the plain of Serres to that of Thessaloniki and by the end of the century its production was nearly three quarters that of all cereals. The underlying causes of this spectacular rise can be traced in the conjunction of increased trade with Central Europe and the War of American Independence, which limited available cotton stocks. However, by the beginning of the 19th century cotton production for the whole of Macedonia had fallen to only 7,000 tons, while a few years earlier the plain of Serres alone produced 8,750 tons. At about the same time (late 18th century) tobacco production — which, it should be noted, was exclusively in the hands of the Muslim farmers — jumped from 8,000 tons in 1765 to 13,000 tons.[3] Tobacco was grown chiefly in the area between the Loudias and Axios rivers (the land to the west of the Loudias was mostly uncultivated), but also farther east, in the area around Kavala. Later, however, the heavy mobilization entailed by the Russo-Turkish wars resulted in a sharp decline in tobacco production. On the other hand, grain production increased during the Napoleonic Wars, especially that of corn -or rather the smuggling of corn, for officially

its sale was prohibited, a result of French pressure. The cultivation of cotton continued to decrease throughout the first half of the 19th century, after the re-establishment of an international equilibrium in 1815 and the opening of the Egyptian market. By 1844 it had already fallen by about 75%.[4]

The Crimean War (1853-56) gave a new spin to the wheel. This time the bulk of production was in cereals, in response to increased demand in Western Europe due to meagre harvests and the requirements of war. But this new concentration was also transitory: the American Civil War (1861-65) once again tipped the balance in favour of cotton. At the outbreak of the war annual cotton production did not exceed 1,250 tons. With American seed and British encouragement production had decupled within a few years, while the tobacco crop fell considerably. The re-opening of the American market altered the balance once more, and acres of grain and tobacco soon replaced cotton fields.[5]

The construction of the first railway line linking Thessaloniki with Skopje and Mitrovica (1871-74) ushered in a new age. Now, in theory at least, the farmers of the hinterland would be able to increase their production with a view to exports. And in fact, within a very short time the amount of land under cultivation in Central Macedonia had increased sharply, especially that devoted to cereal production, despite the temporary setbacks caused by the disastrous harvests of 1875 and 1879. Nevertheless, new and unforeseen difficulties soon appeared. A series of excellent harvests, especially between 1887 and 1897, plus the construction of the Thessaloniki-Monastir and Skopje-Vranje railway lines, led to the stockpiling of tremendous quantities of grain. But the international market was saturated with cheap American, Indian and Russian grain, and could not absorb the surplus —and considerably costlier— Ottoman produce. In 1895 grain production fell by 15%, in favour of the opium poppy, for which demand was growing. The death knell for cereal crops was struck by a combination of factors: the migration of farmers to Thessaly to take up land abandoned by Muslim farmers who had moved to Asia Minor after 1881, the war in 1897, increased emigration to the New World, plus growing urbanization. Paucity of farm labour and the consequent increase in farm wages rendered Macedonian grain production completely uncompeti-

The development of the hinterland promoted the growth of the wholesale trade in foodstuffs, which had its own quarter in Thessaloniki, known as "Ladadika" (the oil quarter).

tive, and the situation was further exacerbated by the high cost of rail transport, despite occasional adjustments, and the antiquated road network.

It was once again time to turn to new crops. The most serious contenders, and the most attractive to farmers, were cotton and tobacco, production of which had in fact been rising since the mid-1890s. From 1904 to 1912 tobacco acreage in the *sanjak* of Thessaloniki had increased by 125% and output had tripled. Similar developments were taking place in the areas around Monastir and Skopje. Cotton growing proved equally attractive, since the expansion of spinning and weaving mills permitted the absorption of ever-increasing quantities of cotton. This same period also witnessed an increase in the production of fruit and vegetables, which were carried by rail into the fast growing urban and semi-urban centres.

The failure of Macedonian agricultural products to compete with the low prices in other countries can be partially explained by the farming methods then current. As has already been mentioned, most of the land was in the hands of big Muslim landowners, who for the most part lived in the cities and left the management of their estates to overseers. Their limited knowledge of agriculture, together with their attitudes towards technological advance and modern methods of cultivation, was anything but conducive to the taking of decisions and measures which might improve the situation. Furthermore, at least until 1870, foreign capital had no interest in modernizing Macedonian *chifliks*, given the area's lack of safe and sufficient communications both with Central Europe and with the coast. The result was that farm tools remained primitive, machinery and fertilizers were completely unknown, and, instead of practising crop rotation, the traditional system of leaving fields fallow was still in vigour, which meant that every year two thirds of arable land lay uncultivated.

By the 1800s, the first unhealthy symptoms in the agricultural export market had led to the first efforts to import farm machinery in an attempt to reduce production costs. The initiative came from the wealthiest landowners but the obstacles were daunting. The system was so imperfect that appropriate benefits could not be attained. For example, the iron ploughs they began to import were unsuitable for the scrawny animals that had to draw them. The most serious problem, however, was the dogged resistance of the serfs and labourers. Although the usual reason assigned for their reaction is their attachment to tradition, it should not be overlooked that, as far as the serfs were concerned, increased production could be anything from indifferent to unfavourable, while for the farm labourers it often meant loss of employment at a time when wages were rising. Resistance must have been particularly fierce in the Kavala region, for efforts to import agricultural machinery there were totally unsuccessful. But attempts to modernize agriculture did not stop there. The founding of the Farm School in Thessaloniki in 1888 was sound in principle but did not provide an immediate solution. The systematic importing of farm machinery essentially began with the Young Turk revolt, when import duties were scrapped. It is nevertheless amazing that in 1912, after decades of encouragement, there were still only

twelve iron ploughs in the Edessa region, as compared to 1,600 wooden ones.

Although antiquated farming tools and methods were certainly to some extent responsible for the failure of the Macedonian agricultural economy to adapt to the demands of the international market, the prime obstacle appears to have been the malfunctioning of the tax system. The already heavy tax burden borne by the farmers was increased by extraordinary public levies and the outrageous demands of tax-collectors and tax-farmers. The poorly paid —and, therefore, susceptible to bribery— gendarmes were unable to protect the farmers' interests, but rather collaborated openly with those abusing their tax-collecting authority. During the final decades of Ottoman rule in particular, a prolonged budgetary crisis systematically prevented the regular payment of public employees, leaving the rural population prey to the blackmail of state officials and brigands. The escalating irredentist activity and internecine feuds between contending national factions during this period also had a negative effect on production. The reform programmes of Vienna and Mürzsteg (1902-1903) were designed to solve the problem by redefining the obligations of the farmers on a new and fairer basis: the tithe, for example, would be calculated according to the fertility of the land and the weather conditions each year. Although these schemes appeared successful on an experimental basis, on large scale they proved neither applicable nor viable. Their application required a large and well-paid police force, a luxury which the economic situation of Macedonia could not afford, even after a plentiful harvest (1903). At the same time, the large-scale emigration of farm workers resulted in a reduction in cultivated acreage, leaving the *chiflik* owners unable to meet their tax obligations.

Stock-Farming, Lumbering, Silk-Growing

Although references to these sectors are extremely scanty, it would appear that the colonizaton of Macedonia by numbers of Muslim stock-farmers reinvigorated this particular sector, in comparison with Byzantine times, at least. Further encouragement was added by the migration of Christian populations towards the mountains and the extensive deforestation, the result not only of wars but also of the necessity of providing warmth and shelter for populations on the move. Stock-farming in Macedonia followed the pattern common throughout the Balkans, that is, the herdsmen moved with their flocks up into the mountains in the spring and back down to the plains for the winter. Their movements, of course, were not limited to the confines of Macedonia, but covered the whole area of the Balkans, even after the emergence of nation states. The growth of the weaving industry as early as the 16th century guaranteed a steady market for wool, and increasing urbanization from the 19th century onwards extended the land available for grazing. To this contributed the abandonment of farms as well as from the intensive woodcutting which was fuelled by increased demand for building materials in the growing urban centres. In the 18th century the Janissaries undertook to supply the pastoral populations wintering in the plains around Thessaloniki, in exchange for the right to sell their wool. In 1815 Macedonia had more than four million head of sheep and goats and was apparently famous for the quality of its wool.[6] Thessaloniki received about a thousand tons of wool a year from its hinterland, two thirds of which were destined for export, and the remaining third for the domestic market, particularly for use in a coarse woollen cloth called *aba*. The export of raw wool decreased sharply after 1880 when new modern weaving mills were established.

Information about sericulture is more plentiful from the 18th century onwards. In the second half of that century silk production in Macedonia reached 15-20 tons a year, and was of considerably better quality than that produced in Thessaly. By the beginning of the 19th century the silk mills in Thessaloniki were producing about 1,130 Kgrs a year for local use, using cocoons from the surrounding countryside. The golden age of sericulture, however, dates from 1850 and reached its peak in the last quarter of the century. This period was marked by the export of tremendous quantities of cocoons, often exceeding 2,000 tons a year, while at the same time assuring supply for the domestic silk weavers. Silk production at this time was centred around Gevgeli. The prime factor responsible for this increase in production was indisputably the assumption of the silk tax by the Ottoman Public Debt Administration, under whose guidance the number of mulberry trees increased by 30% in 1887-88; it also initiated the importing of French silkworm eggs. It is noteworthy that state revenues from Macedonian cocoons more than doubled between 1888 and 1892.

A Jew from Thessaloniki, wearing the traditional gaberdine. The contribution of the Jews was paramount in sparking the growth of trade and the economy generally.

In 1912 the production of dried cocoons stood at 770 tons.

2. Mining and Craft Industry

The Growth of Craft Industry

One of the many economically disastrous consequences of the wars which resulted in the occupation of Macedonia by the Ottoman Turks was the loss to the cities of their Christian populations. Since the Muslim colonists were known neither for their craftsmanship nor for their tendency to consume, it is fair to suppose that this sector withered, at least until the end of the 15th century. The void left in the ranks of the artisans was promptly filled by the Jews who flocked from Spain, Portugal, Southern Italy and Northern Europe to the cities of the Ottoman Empire. Their experience, their new methods and their wide range of expertise soon established their predominance in this sector.

Cloth-making particularly attracted the interest of the new-comers from an early stage. This industry had flourished since the beginning of the 16th century, especially in the production of coarse woollen cloth (*aba*) in vast quantities for soldiers' uniforms as well as for the needs of the rural population. Towards the middle of the century the intense competition among the various workshops led the branch into a temporary crisis, from which only the creation of a guild including both manufacturers and merchants was able to extricate it. The growth of the Jewish element was paralleled by the re-emergence of Christian craftsmen, especially in the fields of wool and cotton manufacturing, dying (which had flourished in Skopje as early as the 16th century), linen and silk manufacturing, wine and candle making. These industries were for the most part centred in Western and Central Macedonia (Kozani, Kastoria, Siatista, Naousa, etc.), close to the sources of raw materials.[7]

In the 17th century the quality of the woollens produced in the city of Thessaloniki deteriorated considerably, while that of the silks and linens, in whose manufacture the Greek-Orthodox element was involved, had improved to the point where they were in great demand throughout the Empire. During the 18th century, faced with increased competition from European goods, the production of woollens decreased dramatically; but in this same period Serres, Drama and Naousa became major producers of spun and woven cottons which they exported to Central and Northern Europe.

Early in the 19th century, however, the situation changed radically. After the end of the Napoleonic Wars international trade recovered its former vigour, while the Industrial Revolution in Western Europe and particularly in Britain had permitted tremendous progress. In contrast, there was no movement towards industrialization anywhere in the Ottoman Empire. Both local and foreign capital was reluctant to cooperate with the Porte in this sector while investment in government loans, commerce and land remained so much more profitable. Thus Western industrial goods with their higher quality and lower prices had no difficulty in capturing Eastern markets. The sole exceptions to this generalized decline of Ottoman craft industry were those products of a certain irreplaceable aesthetic value, such as carpets, swords, etc. In the case of Macedonia in particular, the influx of Western products was facilitated by the industrial decline caused by the catastrophes consequent on the 1821 Greek Revolution.

The commercial treaty concluded in 1838 between Britain and the Porte gave new impetus to British trade. Tariffs on Western industrial goods remained very low (a mere 5%), while local products were subject to a host of taxes and in any case were not competitive. In 1862 tariffs were increased to 8%, and in 1864 the reorganization of industry began to be broached. Nevertheless, despite the low wages and the considerable natural resources, no progress was made in Macedonia before the early 1870s. In Thessaloniki the production of woollens was still only a cottage industry, and the only real industries left were the silk mills, which had never stopped even during the general decline of 1821-1840, one soap factory and one steam-powered flour mill.[8] A British attempt to establish cotton gins at Serres and Orphano foundered on the shoals of Ottoman bureaucracy.

The unstable conditions prevailing throughout the 1870s, together with high transport costs, served to minimize the possible benefits the construction of the first railway might have had for craft industry in the Macedonian hinterland. The sole exception was Thessaloniki, where quite noticeable progress had been made before the end of the decade. Although the silk mills lost ground to some extent, the steam-powered flour mills multiplied in order to meet the increased needs of the army and the cities. Soon two new soap factories appeared, as well as a cotton mill and a tile-works. In the years of peace which followed, the soap works, cotton mills and flour mills all expanded, while a tobacco processing plant, furniture workshops, metal works and pasta factories sprang up. Several of these new industries were soon in a

The port of Thessaloniki, in an early 20th century photograph.

position to compete with their Western counterparts. In the rest of Macedonia the situation was somewhat confused. Steam-powered flour mills had been founded between 1883 and 1886 in Monastir, Prilep, Edessa and Kilkis, and the woollen industry was enjoying an upswing; but Eastern Macedonia was in a state of stagnation.

The most important change for Macedonian industry was the construction in 1888 of the rail link between Thessaloniki and Central Europe and the consequent reduction of transport charges in 1889. On the one hand, local industries increased their production in order to offset the new wave of Central European imports, while, on the other, the cost of raw materials decreased and the market widened significantly. The tobacco industry more than doubled its production, the spinning mills were enlarged, several new steam-powered factories appeared, the Vardari area to the west of Thessaloniki was gradually transformed into an industrial zone. In the years that followed, the opening of a rail line to Western Macedonia (1894) spurred the expansion of the spinning and weaving industries in Verria, Naousa and Edessa: in Naousa, for example, production tripled between 1890 and 1906. The increase in import duties

(from 8% to 11%) in 1907 and the exemption from duty of machinery in 1908 further encouraged business, and steam-powered factories multiplied in most urban areas.

Eloquent witness to the achievements of Macedonian industry (although few enterprises were really worthy of that name) is borne by the movement of import and export traffic through the port of Thessaloniki, and the transport of goods by rail. For example, following the development of the cotton industry, exports of raw cotton from the early 1880s until the beginning of the Balkan Wars remained exceedingly low. The same was true of the wool and silk industries: exports of woollens followed those of cotton, while imports of silks decreased with the improvement in domestic production. As for rail transport, there was a tremendous increase in the volume of machinery carried (including sewing machines), as well as of chemicals and petroleum.

Mining

Of the three mining areas in Macedonia —Demir Hisar in Eastern Macedonia, Kratovo in Northern Macedonia and Mademochoria in Chalcidice— there appears to be information about the early years of the Ottoman rule only for the third. In this sector too the arrival of Jewish artisans from Northern Europe seems to have acted as a catalyst. The Byzantine Siderokausia (Siderokapsa, later Isvoro, and now Stratoniki) were lead and silver mines which were still in operation at the end of the 15th century. They were re-organized, however, in the following century, when a team of skilled Jewish workmen introduced new methods for the extraction and refining of the ore. A host of labourers from various places flocked to Chalcidice in the hope of finding steady employment. During the reign of Suleyman the Magnificent (1520-1566) the mines employed 6000 people, and state revenues from silver ranged between eighteen and thirty thousand ducats. A separate *mukata* (a tax unit let to a tax farmer) was established for the exploitation of the mines, while their management was probably sub-let to a private individual. The decline of this system towards the end of the 17th century, led, after a certain amount of experimentation and the completion of certain works of infrastructure, to the auctioning off of mine management. For about 70 years (until 1775) the mines were leased to the Çavushzade family, the highest bidders, whose heirs subsequently retained their rights for the annual payment of an adjusted rent. Meanwhile, the inhabitants of the Mademochoria were still obliged to work in the mines, even though the diminishing mineral deposits were slashing their wages. Since the middle of the 17th century, the profits of the mine tenants had come from the tax exemptions they were entitled to as managers, while the necessary ore was imported from Britain and Holland. Early in the 19th century the mine came into the hands of the Greek communities, which, although heavily taxed, maintained their rights to the mines, not for the non-existent economic benefits, but in order to retain their administrative autonomy and the consequent preferential tax rates.[9]

In the rest of Macedonia throughout the 18th and most of the 19th century the situation was discouraging. An attempt to reactivate the mines on the island of Thasos was defeated by the reaction of its inhabitants, who feared that the new enterprise would mean forced labour and additional taxes.[10] However, the principal reasons for the underdevelopment of Macedonian mining, given the existence of mineral wealth, must lie in the uneconomical methods used to extract the ore and in the lack of roads and means of transportation to carry it. Until the mid-1880s, even after the construction of the railway, no movement was recorded. The number of mining permits awarded had indeed increased, but these were essentially a sort of short term speculation, based on their resale to foreign investors.

From 1890 onwards mining both in the hinterland as well as on the littoral (Chalcidice) became more systematic. Foreign investment was by now significant and focused on the abundant deposits of chromium and antimony. New deposits were discovered in the interior of Macedonia and increased international demand guaranteed them a market. For antimony, at least, this phase did not last long. Falling prices and increased transport costs led to a cessation of production before the end of the century. In 1900 the Porte made an effort to prohibit the concession of mining rights to foreign subjects, but in the end British pressure blocked the decision. In any case, in 1901 a number of additional charges and bureaucratic requirements, in conjunction with the atmosphere of political uncertainty, sufficed to curtail mining activity. A fresh spurt occurred a few years later, particularly after the passage in 1906 of a new law fixing the duration of mine leases at 99 years. Many new permits were awarded, especially in the *vilayet* of Kosovo, and the future appeared hopeful. Unfortunately, however, in this same period cheap chromium from the vast deposits recently discovered in New Caledonia began to pour into the international markets, thus foreshadowing the end for the Macedonian mines before they had even reached their peak. By 1909 the Kosovo mines had already begun to close down, and only the coastal mines at Stratoni (manganese and iron pyrites) and Gerakini (magnesite) were still exporting at the end of this period (1912).

As this chapter has made clear, the industrial growth in the West spelt the decline of traditional Macedonian craft industry. In the final quarter of the century, however, developments occurred which favoured a regeneration and development in the secondary sector, such as improvements in the credit and loan policies, and in transportation, with the construction of railways, plus a steady increase in import duties. The most important factor, however, appears to have been growing urbanization, which provided on the one hand a class of relatively wealthy consumers, able to absorb production at a steady rate, as opposed to the rural population whose consumptive capacity depended on a good harvest, and, on the other, a source of cheap labour which was of great value in making domestic goods more competitive. Most of these labourers were Jews, who worked nine to fifteen hours a day for pitifully low wages. As a typical example, wages in the spinning mills hardly increased between 1873 and the early 1890s. Working class conditions essentially improved only after the Young Turk revolt in 1908, the waves of emigration and the labour struggles incited by the newly formed labour unions. Of course, no serious effort at industrialization could be effective outside the major urban centres —hence in the mines. Attachment to tradition and the battles which raged sporadically across the Macedonian countryside also undoubtedly played their part. Another negative factor seems to have been the failure of the rural population to acquire the mentality of the employee: this definitely led to a dearth of steady industrial labour. As for the mines, the lack of heavy industry which could have absorbed their production made them dependent exclusively on exports, with all that that entails. Generally speaking, although the development of the secondary sector in those years did provide substantial profits for certain individuals, it was unable to satisfy domestic consumers either in quantity or in style. This failure, together with purchases of machinery and raw materials abroad, explain the remarkable explosion of import trade at this time.

3. Transport and Communications

Roads

The steady refusal of the Porte to have anything to do with public works is the most telling indication that no improvement can be expected in this domain, at least in comparison with the Byzantine period. Especially after the cessation of the offensive drive of the early centuries, even maintenance of the main roads would only have caused defensive difficulties for the state. The emergence of largely autonomous provincial war lords also tended to produce a similar result, for good roads would have meant swift intervention on the part of the central authorities. Thus it was that

travellers and consular representatives complained from one century to the next of the dreadful state of the roads. For centuries the main arteries were the ancient *Via Egnatia* and those roads leading into Central Europe, either through Bosnia (Thessaloniki - Skopje - Kumanovo - Niš) or through Vidin (this latter fell into decline at the time of the clash between the Porte and Osman Pasvanoglu Pasha). The secondary network linked the major urban centres to each other (Thessaloniki, Monastir, Skopje, Jannina, Kozani, Kastoria, Serres, Kavala). Means of transportation were virtually unchanged since the discovery of the wheel: mainly horses and mules, more rarely camels, and of course the ox-carts which were notorious for their slow progress and their dreadful condition.[11]

Trade conditions in the 1860s were such that certain initiatives had to be taken; and in fact, the Porte did create a Ministry of Public Works in 1865. Despite all the efforts and regulations, the whole affair was a shattering failure. This was no means fortuitous. A partial explanation lies in the inexperience of the available engineers; but the major flaw lay in the way in which public works were carried out, namely, by forced labour, special levies on the communities affected, or a combination of the two. This system guaranteeing both free labour and the money for materials was applied during the course of this decade to the improvement of the roads from Thessaloniki to Monastir and from Thessaloniki to Serres, with the same result in both cases: the embezzlement of most of the sums collected.

In the railway age which followed, the problem shifted from the maintenance of major arteries to the construction and maintenance of the roads linking production centres with the railway stations (the problem was rendered particularly acute by the fact that most stations were situated at a considerable distance from the cities or towns they were supposed to serve). Yet, while in the beginning there was a certain amount of activity, by 1875, long before the project was completed, all work had ceased. A second attempt was made some ten years later, on the personal initiative of two exceptionally energetic pashas, in Monastir and Thessaloniki, which did accomplish a certain amount, for example improvements to the road from the Gradsko railway station to Monastir; but since their activities were focussed chiefly on roads of

Thessaloniki has been an important rail junction since the late 19th century. In the photograph, the old railway station.

military importance the benefits to trade were limited. Another effort was made following the construction of the rail line linking Skopje and Vranje, but this was largely ineffective. Moreover, the huge sums of money swallowed by the railway bonds, together with the rise in wages, left very little for public works. It was only after 1908, when road building began to be tendered to foreign companies, that some progress was made.

Railways Automobils

The construction of railways in Macedonia was nothing new for the Ottoman Empire. Railway construction in Asia Minor and the Balkans had begun as early as 1850; and the first soundings in Macedonia took place at about the same time, especially with regard to the construction of a line linking Thessaloniki and Monastir. More than ten years of negotiations were required, however, before Baron Hirsch finally signed a contract with the Porte to build no less than 2,500 kilometres of railways throughout the length and breadth of the Balkan Peninsula. One part of this project was the Thessaloniki-Skopje-Mitrovica line, construction on which began in February 1871 and was completed in December 1874. Following intense diplomatic activity and heavy pressure from the business community, construction of the promising Skopje-Vranje railway began in autumn 1886 and had been completed by May 1888, thus linking Thessaloniki with Belgrade and Vienna and thence with the entire European network.

It was not until June 1891 that, financed by the Deutsche Bank, work began on the Thessaloniki-Monastir line, which had been under consideration since 1859 at least. The terms under which it was built were excessively unfavourable to the Ottoman state, and included, besides the endless import facilities for railway material and the cession of wealth-producing operations in the surrounding area, a public guarantee to the construction company of an annual mileage profit of 14,300 francs, to be paid by the Ottoman state if not earned by the railway. It should be noted that in only three years throughout the period 1892-1911 (1908, 1910, 1911) did income from the railway suffice to cover the guarantee, and since the increased revenue was due to increased expenditure on the armed forces, in the long run it was still coming out of the state's coffers.

The Ottoman Bank building on Frangon St. Today it houses the State Conservatoire of Thessaloniki.

In September 1892 a contract was signed between the Porte and a French banker in Constantinople called René Baudouy, who represented a French group in which the Banque Impériale Ottomane was also a shareholder. Once again the terms were decidedly in favour of the foreign company. The guarantee for a line 510 kilometres long, joining Thessaloniki to Dedeagach and the Sofia-Constantinople network, was fixed at 15,500 francs, even though the prospects of increased trade were virtually nil. As was to be expected, the revenues from this mainly military line not only never covered the guarantee, not even in a year of massive military manoeuvres like 1897, but rarely reached one third of the stipulated sum. This line was built between June 1893 and March 1896.

Apart from the burden it placed on the public purse, the effect of railway construction on the development of trade in Macedonia can only be understood if the system of carriage fees is taken into consideration. For the railway companies, the lack of a decent road network meant limited traffic on the one hand and no competition on the other. This meant that the only way to increase revenue was to impose high carrying charges, very slightly below those demanded by the caravans. Charges were lowered for the first time, in order to revive traffic, after the territorial losses caused by the Russo-Turkish War in 1877-78. The problem resurfaced more sharply than ever in the late 1880s, when falling grain prices on the international market forced Macedonian growers to reduce their prices too. But the resulting 15% drop in charges even with the 1888 linking with Central Europe were not enough to provide a satisfactory solution to the problem. Representatives of railway companies in Turkey, Bulgaria, Serbia and Austria-Hungary undertook to find a solution to the problem, and the agreement which was signed in April 1889 imposed significant reductions in current rates. This agreement was particularly favourable to Austro-Hungarian trade, and soon similar facilities were conceded to Belgian and British products. Nevertheless, despite this agreement and various other arrangements made in the 1890s, the grain problem was never satisfactorily resolved. The Thessaloniki - Monastir line faced similar difficulties. Despite a 23% drop in rates in 1894, railway carriage charges remained excessively onerous for business. No further adjustments were made before the Balkan Wars.

To sum up, it appears that the company which exploited the Thessaloniki-Skopje-Vranje line was under constant pressure to reduce rates, and did finally make significant concessions, while considerably less pressure was exerted on the two companies exploiting the other lines. Several contributing factors help to explain this difference. In the first place, the Thessaloniki-Vranje line derived 70% of its revenue from freight (a large part of which was grain), and its traffic was several times that of the other two lines. Furthermore, in comparison with the other lines, the terms under which it operated were quite favourable, even permitting a certain profit for the state if traffic was heavy. In the case of the other two lines, the tithes of the regions they traversed had been assigned as security for the payment of the guaranteed sum. However, the state's economic difficulties obliged it to

proceed to an auction of these tithes. The collection of the tithe was thus in general the occasion for extensive spoliation of the rural population. If freight rates were lowered at a time when grain exports were falling irremediably and traffic was limited, then the state would have an even bigger deficit to make up to the companies. The increased expense would, of course, be offset by increasing the sum demanded for the tithes, which in the final analysis would come out of the farmers' pockets. In other words, there was no good reason for reducing the freight rates: the grain producers' fate was sealed in any case, and no one could expect any real profit.

As was to be expected, road transport in Macedonia was slow in getting started, and, before 1912 at least, it certainly posed no threat to the railways. By 1907 only two vehicles had been ordered, although permission to import had been granted the preceding year; there was some slight increase in the number of motorcycles. Although it was predicted that there was no future for motor traffic in the region because of the insufficient road network, by 1910 a rudimentary road transport system was making its debut between Monastir, Prilep and Resna.

Ports and Shipping

Inextricably linked with the development of Macedonia's foreign trade, especially with Western Europe, was the existence of good harbours at the end of natural roads. Thessaloniki maintained its predominance throughout the entire period of Ottoman rule; the port of Kavala began to develop in the 18th century, while towards the end of the 19th century the port of Orphano (Çayesi) seems to have played a small role.

With the cessation of the pirate attacks and the armed conflicts associated with the Greek War of Independence, the first regular steamship service from Thessaloniki was inaugurated in 1840. This was a weekly run between Thessaloniki and Constantinople operated by a river vessel of the Austrian Danube Steamship Company. Two years later the line was taken over by the Austrian 'Lloyd' company, which established direct steamship connections between Thessaloniki and Volos, Pireus, Syros, Corfu, Trieste and other Adriatic ports. In 1844 the Ottoman Steam Company began a weekly service between

The Customs House in the port of Thessaloniki.

Thessaloniki and Constantinople via Kavala and the Dardanelles. The 'Messageries Maritimes' began service in 1853, and were joined ten years later by another French company, 'Fraissinet'. During the 1860s Russian, Egyptian, Turkish and Greek companies all tried to acquire a share of the market, but were thwarted by the more effective organization of the companies already established and were obliged to withdraw. The 1871 attempt of the Italian company 'Trinacria' (later called 'Florio e Rubatino') to establish a line from Constantinople and Thessaloniki to Brindisi and Marseilles did however prove successful.

Simultaneously with the construction of the railways, restoration work was begun on the harbour. The demolition of the sea wall (from 1869) permitted the construction of a quay (which took ten years to build), and plans for a breakwater were prepared. Meanwhile, steamship services steadily increased. In the ten years between 1872 and 1882 Thessaloniki's maritime traffic tripled. 1886 marked the beginning of a further attempt at reorganization in view of new links with Central Europe. This period witnessed the arrival on the scene of the 'Elliniki' (Thessaloniki-Volos-Pireus), the Turkish 'Kurci' (Constantinople-Thessaloniki-Volos) and the British companies 'Bell's Asia Minor' and 'Victoria Jolly's' (Thessaloniki-Smyrna), 'Messrs. Johnstone and Co.' (Thessaloniki-Liverpool), and 'Westcott and Lawrence' (Thessaloniki-London). In 1888 the 'Messageries Maritimes' inaugurated a new and rapid fortnightly service between Thessaloniki and Alexandria. A Belgian company made its appearance and was swiftly followed by a Russian one. The next year the 'Messageries Maritimes' began service between Thessaloniki and London via Marseilles. During this same period three companies, one Austrian, one British and one Turkish, began services from Kavala to Trieste, Constantinople, Smyrna and Thessaloniki; but the port of Orphano, despite the optimistic predictions of the British in the middle of the century, did not manage to establish regular steamship services, with the exception of the Austrian 'Lloyd' for a brief period.

The breathtaking increase in maritime traffic through the port of Thessaloniki underlined the necessity for its effective renovation, a question which was of vital importance to the city's business circles. Although a study was commissioned in 1888, by 1890 nothing had been accomplished and all the problems remained unsolved: lack of a rail spur to the port, of a breakwater too, insufficient warehousing, anachronistic loading and unloading procedures. Despite the pressing nature of the problems, the radical reconstruction of the harbour was not undertaken until 1897; and progress was slow, with many technical difficulties. The bulk of the work was completed in 1903, but the rail link to the station was not finished until 1909. In the meantime, many shipping companies from a variety of countries were operating services from Thessaloniki to several ports in Western and Northern Europe. Nonetheless, the business and consular circles continued to complain, because, as they said, the French company which was building and exploiting the port had raised harbour dues, in an efforts to recover its costs, to such an extent that shipping was beginning to avoid Thessaloniki. Movement in and out of the port, however, did not bear this out. Perhaps it was a short term problem, for by 1908 total annual tonnage had again increased sharply. In contrast to the situation in Thessaloniki no work was done during this period on the harbour of Kavala, despite all its inadequacies. Nevertheless, tobacco exports kept up the level of shipping for a long time, until 1905 in fact, after which date improvements were set in hand and traffic increased.

Post and Telecommunications

Improvements in communications were largely due to increased trade in the 18th century. At that time domestic administrative correspondence was in the hands of a special body of couriers known as 'Tatars', who by the middle of the 19th century numbered about 1500 across the European provinces of the Empire. Other correspondance was carried by the 'posta', a caravan of several dozen horses. By the end of the 18th century, European postal services had begun to operate, independently of the imperial service. First in the field were the Austrians (1777), followed by the French, Russians, Egyptians, British

and Italians, who continued to offer parallel and competing services until the end of this period (1912).[12]

It appears from what information we have that at least until the final quarter of the 19th century postal services within the Empire were extremely uncertain and correspondance was certainly not inviolable. The advent of the railways, of course, improved the situation immensely. The rail link with Central Europe in particular served as a starting point for a complete reorganization of the Ottoman Post Office, with daily postal service to Belgrade. However, despite the hopes of the local population and the advocacy of the British consul in Thessaloniki, the passage of the famous 'Indian Post' remained only a dream.

From what little is known about telegraphic communications one can conclude that by about the mid-1860s Thessaloniki had direct telegraph lines to the other major urban centres in Macedonia, while communication with Western and Central Europe went via either Otranto, Scutari (Dalmatia), or Constantinople. The telegraph lines had three cables: one carried messages in Turkish for the army and the government; one used Latin characters for European correspondence; while the third was reserved exclusively for messages from India. Within about fifteen years the towns had direct telegraph links among themselves. The telephone began to appear in the first decade of the 20th century, but was reserved for use by the government, the army and the police. Telephone services began in Thessaloniki in 1907-8, and by 1912 had spread to several urban and semi-urban centres in the interior.

4. Organization of the Market.

Fairs and Caravans

Although the main centres for trade and commerce in Macedonia were indisputably the ports, especially that of Thessaloniki, there was still a need for intermediary distribution centres to serve the extensive hinterland. This service was supplied by the fairs.

Two types of fairs evolved. One was the small local weekly or monthly market fair, which supplied basic necessities (foodstuffs, clothing, etc.) to the population of the surrounding district. The other was the large annual trade fair, held on the occasion of some feast day, where suppliers and traders from a wider area met to sell or barter an assortment of products. The chief characteristic of both types of fair was the traditional display of goods. It appears that the second and more important type of fair evolved from the first sometime in the 16th century, and was held under the protection of government officials. It is known that in this period trade fairs were held at Katerini, Chroupista, Doliani (near Petrich), Zichna (known as 'the onion fair'), Kitros, Verria and Struga. There are references to fairs at Avret Hisar (Gynaikokastron) and Servia in the 17th century. In the second half of that century the Doliani fair lasted forty days. Towards the end of the century the Avret Hisar fair was relocated to Kilkis for about 15 years, but in 1706 it returned to its former site. During this period all trade fairs developed in rural areas, that is, in areas that could not support a permanent population engaged solely in trade.

By the 18th century trade fairs had begun to supply European products as well. French commercial agents regularly visited inland Macedonia, but their field of action was somewhat restricted because of the increasing activity of the brigands. The list of important trade fairs was augmented by those of Mavronoros (Western Macedonia), Serres and Nevrokopi; and most of the old names were still to be heard. It should be noted that Thessaloniki's trade was not limited to Macedonia, but extended as far as Elasson, Trikkala, Lamia and the valley of the Danube. The principal trade fairs in the 19th century Macedonia were those of Serres in February and Prilep in August. The amount of business transacted at these two fairs is the best indicator of the economic state of Macedonia at that time. For example, the business done at the 1839 trade fair in Serres accounted for almost half that city's entire annual turnover. By this time several of the older fairs had lost much of their importance and are no longer mentioned, while the length of the remainder varied from one to three weeks. With the emergence of the first nation states around the middle of the century, Thessaloniki's trading pattern was based on regional trade fairs covering most of the year and serving Macedonia, Albania and much of Bulgaria. The growth of urban centres after 1850 seems to have had an adverse affect on the remaining local trade fairs; a typical example was the competition between the town of Monastir and the fair at Prilep.[13]

Transport of goods, both local and foreign, to the markets, as well as of exports to Central Europe,

A trade fair at Monastir.

depended on the free movement of the caravans. The principal beast of burden in the Balkan caravans was the horse, which could carry a load of 130 kilos for eight hours a day. The journey from Thessaloniki to Vienna took 35 days, not counting the days of quarantine at the border. Caravans averaged 20 to 50 horses, although there are references to caravans of more than a thousand beasts.[14] They were accompanied by 20-80 men, enough to protect the caravan from attacks by brigands who lay in ambush at various places along the way, especially in the mountain passes. The sums demanded by the drivers varied according to the distance, the time of year, the political situation and the type of animal. For example, ox-carts and camels were cheaper to hire than horses because they were so much slower, even though camels could carry three times the load. At the beginning of the 18th century caravans of 100-200 beasts left Thessaloniki for the interior once a week. By 1859 the size of the weekly caravans had increased to 2-3,000 (horses and mules), rising on occasion to as many as 5,000 beasts.[15]

Banking and Credit

In order to understand the changes which occurred in the Macedonian business world in the final quarter of the 19th century, it is necessary to look at developments in the credit system. As has already been mentioned, financing of trade and agriculture was based on usury. The first bank in Thessaloniki, a branch of the Banque Impériale Ottomane, was opened in 1864 to serve the business community. At that time very few merchants had access to credit, and then only until delivery of the merchandise or at most one month afterwards. The rural population, on the other hand, was granted credit payable after the next harvest. This meant that capital was blocked in the countryside, and the lack of cash stiffled private initiative.

The amelioration of the credit system was largely due to a combination of trade growth in Thessaloniki over the following period, the profit-seeking of the European states, and the establishment of direct communication between importers and trading companies. By 1890 European trading companies were readily granting Macedonian merchants commercial credits of from three to eight months. This in turn led to improved domestic trading conditions between wholesalers and retailers, and the effects eventually trickled down to the small consumers in the villages. In the meantime, 1888 saw the founding of the Banque de Salonique, with an initial capital of two million francs and the backing of the Viennese Länderbank, the Parisian Comptoir d'Escompte, and the Thessaloniki company Allatini Bros. In 1893 the Banque de Salonique opened a branch at Monastir in an attempt to attract local businessmen, but it does not appear to have been very popular; and within a short time it had angered both Greeks and Turks by its high rates of interest. This displeasure left the field wide open for new banks, while the newly founded Thessaloniki Chamber of Commerce (1895) established trading standards and opened new horizons for commercial growth.

In 1899 the Bank of Mytilini opened a branch in Thessaloniki, with shareholder Demosthenes Angelakis as its first manager. It was followed in 1905 by the Industrial Credit Bank of Athens (which in 1907 merged with the Bank of Athens), the Bank of the East in 1906, and the Beogradska Zadruga in 1908. The first branch of the Bulgarian National Bank was not opened until 1912. Banking capital played a decisive role in the growth of trade in Macedonia in the first decade of the 20th century. During the crisis of 1906, the Banque Impériale Ottomane in Skopje guaranteed credit to local merchants, while only sizeable bank credits over the next few years enabled imports to remain at high levels. Nevertheless, it must be said that, despite consular pressures and the remarkable increase in business incomes, banking interests focussed almost exclusively on the city of Thessaloniki, with the sole exception of the Banque Impériale, which maintained branches in Monastir, Skopje, Drama and Serres.

Changes in Trading Patterns (1875-1912)

By the mid 1870s the railways were an established fact. At the same time, military upheavals and the breakup of the Ottoman Empire in the Balkans had created a new commercial situation. During the long period of peace which followed, although territorial losses meant that the geographical market was considerably reduced, new rail lines improved access to the interior considerably. The chief characteristic of this new era was the decline of the trade fairs and the caravans, the opening of shops, the transformation of business procedures, and the realignment of economic spheres of influence.

The extension of the railways from Thessaloniki to all the major urban centres in Macedonia meant that their markets could now be supplied swiftly and regularly with large quantities of goods at prices lower than before. In other words, shops could at last become viable commercial undertakings, since their stocks could follow the fluctuations of the domestic market as a whole. The situation was further improved by ameliorations to the credit system, the commercialization of agriculture, the trend to consumerism, the effect of Western European standards, and the extension of the monetary economy to the rural population. From the moment when the merchants acquired a permanent foothold in the provinces, the writing was on the wall for the trade fairs. Itinerant pedlars could not compete on an equal footing with shopkeepers, for the pedlars were burdened with travelling expenses plus the rental of their stands in the markets, while the shopkeepers now had access to the same range of goods at lower costs. The trade fairs therefore lost most of their importance, although they did not entirely disappear. The spread of shops to towns and cities, on the other hand, was as rapid as the urbanization that characterized the period.

The same fate awaited the caravans. For one thing, the rates charged by caravan drivers exceeded the highest freight rates of the railways. Then again, the border changes greatly restricted their freedom of movement. In the past, caravan drivers took their beasts wherever they felt confident there would be work for them: the system of trade fairs held regularly at specific locations made this easy. Now, however, since border duties were not imposed on goods carried but per animal, they would no longer risk a border crossing if they were not certain of finding clients to

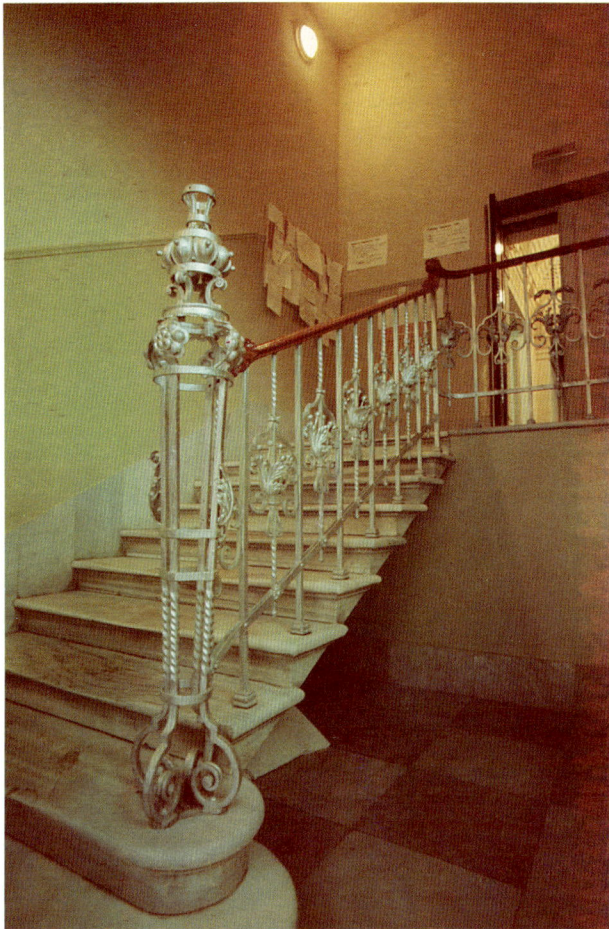

The interior staircase of the Imperial Ottoman Bank in Thessaloniki.

offset their expenses. Caravans thus became rarer, and those drivers who remained faithful to their calling mostly worked carrying goods from railway stations to outlying towns. It should be noted that at this time the stations served extensively as centres for transit trade and headquarters for commercial agents.

The spreading of new modes of transportation was accompanied by a redistribution of economic roles. Traditional trading areas found themselves cut off from the ports and fell into decline, while previously insignificant villages developed into important commercial centres. The railway from Thessaloniki to Mitrovica, for example, gave Monastir a double link to Thessaloniki: the old route via Edessa and the new railway, soon to be parallelled by a road, running through Gradsko. But although costs of transportation by the new link were 20-25% lower than by the old,

there was no corresponding benefit for local businessmen, for many of their client-villages in the region north of Gradsko were now taking advantage of the direct rail link to Thessaloniki. The construction of a direct line from Monastir to Thessaloniki had similar results: Florina, Kastoria, Kozani and Ptolemais now also had direct access to Thessaloniki. Monastir's only gain was a share of the trade with Debar and Prilep.

Developments in Northern and Central Macedonia after 1888 followed the same pattern. Niš Pirot, Vranje and especially Skopje all diverted trade from Thessaloniki. Skopje's economy became virtually autonomous: 65-70% of imports came directly from Central Europe, only those from Western Europe coming via Thessaloniki. In Veles the grain trade slumped, but Štip, Tetovo, Kumanovo, Gevgeli and Doiran all flourished. In Eastern Macedonia, Serres remained an autonomous centre until the late 1890s. The failure to build a rail link with Orphano isolated the city from its traditional seaport, while the rail line to Thessaloniki spelled the end of its autonomy. Kavala also remained outside the railway network and its trade was restricted to tobacco exports. Illustrative of the limitations of the market it served is the fact that although the total value of exports from the port of Kavala was dozens of times greater than those from Monastir (because of the demand for tobacco), imports into the two cities were about equal.

Most of these realignments proved beneficial to commercial activity in Thessaloniki, for from 1895 onwards it enjoyed an ever greater share of total trade. In this period Thessaloniki and Constantinople together accounted for about four-fifths of all trade in the European provinces of the Empire. Even Albanian trade, with the exception of a narrow coastal zone, had been sucked into Thessaloniki's sphere of influence. This predominant position inevitably led to a rapid increase in the numbers of foreign agencies and representatives in the city, as well as an influx of wealthy merchants from the provinces.

Foreign Trade

The military events that preceded the Ottoman conquest of Macedonia were fatal to trade and commerce. As is inevitable in such circumstances, trading patterns collapsed, agricultural surpluses disappeared, and capital vanished. Here too, as happened with industry, revival was sparked by the arrival of Jewish immigrants. These newcomers brought solutions to a number of problems: they were familiar with modern methods, they had contacts all over the Empire, and many had brought a certain capital with them; and they immediately began to fill the void left by the eclipse of the Byzantine business class. One significant factor behind their speedy success was their fictitious partnership with Turks, which served to assure them of exceptionally low import and export duties. During the 16th and part of the 17th century their chief trading partner was Venice, which held the reins of commerce with the East. Contacts were also established with other Italian cities and with Spain.[16]

The wars between Turkey and Venice in the 17th century had two principal consequences: one was their disastrous effect on commerce in Thessaloniki, and the other was the decline of the Jewish business class (attributable in part also to the consequences of the Sabetai Chvi movement), which facilitated the rise of the Christian segment of the population. Meanwhile, the first capitulations opened the Eastern Mediterranean to French trade. The first French merchants arrived in Thessaloniki before the end of the century, where they promptly put an end to the Venetian monopoly. The signing of the Treaties of Passarowitz (1718) and Belgrade (1739) and the lowering of tariffs in Austria-Hungary also helped stimulate trade with Central and Northern Europe, in a state of collapse since 1683. Western Macedonia's trade with Venice via Durazzo, on the other hand, began to decline. Exports towards the north consisted chiefly of wool, cotton and tobacco, while imports included cloth, glassware and iron products. A significant factor in the development of trade with this area was the existence of communities of Christians from Macedonia in the Habsburg lands, which both sustained commercial networks and multiplied trade.[17]

Concessions to other European countries were especially beneficial to the trade of Macedonia. As Thessaloniki successively welcomed British, Italian, Dutch, Scandinavian, Austrian, German and Swiss merchants during the course of the 18th century, its port became one of the most important in the Eastern Mediterranean. French pre-eminence, however, remained unchallenged, and at least until the French Revolution Macedonia's trade with Europe passed chiefly through Marseilles. The British continued to use Smyrna as a trading post, even for Macedonian products, until 1750. Despite the development of maritime trade, in 1780 approximately half Macedonia's exports still went to Central Europe. The rise of the Greek business class was perhaps the most striking development in this period. In partnership with British, Austrian and Russian traders, by the end of the century they had supplanted their French rivals in Thessaloniki and taken over two thirds of total commercial activity. Their trading colonies in southern Russia and Central Europe, their shunning of middlemen, and their use of consular sponsorship, together with the declining importance of the Muslim population in the cities, all contributed to their spectacular ascent.[18]

It should be unnecessary to stress that the principal factor in the renaissance of Macedonian trade during the 18th century was the favourable evolution of the European situation. The 1718 and 1739 treaties were followed in 1774 by the Treaty of Kuchuk Kaynardje, which opened the Black Sea to international trade thus compensating the Greeks for their losses in the previous war. Soon afterwards the American War of Independence led to an explosive increase in cotton sales (since about 1730 cotton had replaced wool as the number one export of the 18th century). Between 1719 and 1776 the value of Thessaloniki's foreign trade more than tripled, from two to seven million gold francs; and by 1789 it had reached nine million. One third of this trade was with France. By the end of the century a quarter of the Ottoman Empire's foreign trade was handled by Thessaloniki. The French Revolution and the Napoleonic Wars marked the end of French supremacy and the beginning of a long period of decline.[19]

Although the international situation in the 18th century was favourable, economic growth was severly impeded by developments at home. Brigandage and piracy, pillaging by armies on the move, poor management of the state monopolies, blackmailing by the Janissaries and armed conflicts constantly erected obstacles and imposed limitations. Nonetheless, despite curtailed profit margins the frequency and the volume of commercial transactions was such that far from negligible fortunes could still be made by the merchants of Macedonia.[20]

When the 19th century dawned, Macedonia was exporting cotton and cotton yarns, wheat, wool, silk and tobacco. The Germanic countries were taking one third of cotton exports (2,500 tons), and France only 1,250 tons at the most. Further, smaller quantities went to the Italian cities. Cotton yarns, produced in Ampelakia and Drama, went to Germany, Venice and the Russian Black Sea ports. Silk came from Zagora, but for insurance reasons and despite all the efforts of the Levant Company and the French merchants it was exported through Thessaloniki. Tobacco was shipped to Alexandria, Genoa, Trieste and Venice, which also took virtually all wool exports, some 600 tons annually. Thessaloniki handled the trade in sponges, which were gathered by divers in the Aegean and expedited to markets in Britain. Grain exports were banned, but this did not prevent Greek and Genoese merchants from smuggling considerable quantities (1,000 tons of wheat in 1809), chiefly to blockaded Spain. Imports included coffee and sugar, yarn dyes, muslins, iron, lead, tin and a variety of household goods, which then proceeded by caravan either to the rest of Macedonia or into Central Europe, desperate for new supply routes as a result of the 'Continental Blockade' imposed by Napoleon. For the record, the transport costs involved in carrying coffee and sugar to Vienna from Thessaloniki by road doubled their price.[21]

Trade in Macedonia did not recover its former volume even after 1815, when the Congress of Vienna re-established peace. Most French business activity had ceased, and all depended now on the Greeks and the British who controlled the transit trade. The Greek Revolution of 1821 dealt a fatal blow to Macedonia's foreign trade. Ravages to the countryside limited agricultural activity and exports, while the Greek business class in Thessaloniki had been so severely decimated that in 1825 the tax burden had to be redistributed among the various communities in the city. Piracy and naval battles in the Aegean were further obstacles to a full recovery of Thessaloniki's commercial activity which, despite all this, had never ceased completely. Imports during this period were limited to soap, grocer's items and citrus fruits from Syros, Samos, Crete, Trieste and Marseilles, while exports consisted of tobacco, silk, cotton and wax.[22]

Nor was there any significant improvement in the 1830s. The numerical decline of both the business and the agricultural classes caused by the Revolution, persistent banditry, heavy taxation, and decreased wool production all tended to prolong the recession. Typical of the times was the situation in the Kassandra peninsula, which saw its population falling from 700 families in 1821 to 140 eleven years later.[23] Agricultural production was not yet providing surpluses, and the results of state intervention tended to be rather negative. In 1834 the governor of Thessaloniki was banished for exploiting the wheat monopoly to his own profit, which sent consumer prices sky-rocketing. Although the resumption of river traffic on the Danube in 1835 reduced the importance of the port of Thessaloniki to the Balkans, foreign trade generally flourished over the next few years (1836-39) thanks to the revival of British commerce, only to slump again in 1840, the consequence of an outbreak of plague in 1838 followed by a fire in 1839 which emptied the city's bazaars.[24]

The benefits of the Balta-Liman trade convention between Britain and Turkey were soon felt in Macedonia. The improvement in 1841 was spectacular, and that same year also saw the arrival of the first commercial agents from Prussia. After a temporary setback in the next two years, due to poor harvests and trouble in Albania (which cut Thessaloniki off from its markets), from 1845 onwards the Macedonian economy grew steadily. Silk production was particularly satisfactory; and the grain trade flourished too, for both production and international demand rose sharply over the last half of the decade. Britain continued to be Macedonia's principal supplier of imports, chiefly cotton goods and iron. French merchants were no longer a threat to the British; but their place had been taken by the Austrians, with the result that Skopje developed into a major transit centre.[25]

Although Macedonia's trade flagged somewhat in the early 1850s, it was soon rescued by yet another favourable change in the international situation. The outbreak of the Crimean War closed the Black Sea ports just when poor harvests in Western Europe, coupled with the increased requirements of their armies, inflated the demand for grain. Similar problems faced the Ottoman Empire. The dependence of Constantinople on grain supplies from Odessa led to a tug-of-war between the Porte and the Western European merchants over Macedonian grain stocks;

but despite Turkish objections, Macedonian grain continued to flow into Europe. Prices of course jumped three to five times above pre-war levels. These higher prices more than made up for higher transport costs and, for the first time, the entire Macedonian hinterland came to life: in 1855, for example, more than 21,000 tons of wheat were shipped from Monastir to Thessaloniki. With the end of the war in 1856, grain production returned to its former levels, while exports of silk and wool began to climb again. Tobacco exports from Kavala, which had been growing steadily since the late 1840s, were also flourishing. The economic benefits of the war period also led to an increase in imports, which in 1857 amounted to 28 million French francs.[26]

Five years later a new trading opportunity appeared: the American Civil War. In the early 1860s there had been no hint of the rapid growth soon to come. Trade naturally decreased in value with the end of the Crimean War, and the most significant change in the business world was the advent of Swiss manufactures on the Macedonian market. With the outbreak of war in America, Western European industry had to seek its cotton supply elsewhere: within two years Macedonian cotton production had tripled. Exports to France flourished as they had in the previous century: by the middle of the decade (1864-66) they accounted for three quarters of the total value of exports. In 1865 Central Europe also began to import cotton. Between 1863 and 1868 cotton exports from the port of Kavala increased by a factor of thirty. As was to be expected, the tremendous amounts of cotton flooding into Western Europe could not all be absorbed, but despite significant stockpiling exports continued, and it was largely due to cotton that Thessaloniki's export totals remained high right up until 1869.[27]

By about 1870, as we have seen, the idea of building a railway network in Macedonia had matured. For the Porte this was not only to be the magic solution to a host of administrative and military problems, but, even more important, it would also increase state revenues by promoting general economic growth. The Europeans for their part had more precise goals and expectations: maritime and Central European powers alike sought cheap raw materials for their industries and markets for their products. Macedonia appeared to offer both, and the planned railway would, in theory

at least, afford equal opportunity for entry from the north and from the south.

Despite the difficult circumstances, the first benefits began to appear before the decade was over. The Franco-Prussian War curtailed trade with France, the Eastern Question crisis in 1875-78 had negative effects on domestic trade, bad weather ruined the harvest twice within ten years, and the 1879 devaluation of the Ottoman currency gave another blow to the market; but despite all this both imports and exports remained at their previous levels. The total value of imports jumped in 1872, affording substantial profits to Britain and France, who were supplying railway construction materials. Austria-Hungary seems to have lost out in the first round of this new game, while coastal trade with Ottoman ports, on the other hand, gained tremendously.

The creation of the Bulgarian state was an unforeseen and decidedly negative factor. The excessively high duties imposed by the new state on products from the Ottoman Empire severely shook the networks which traditionally supplied large sections of its territory through Macedonia. Over the next few years Britain gained substantially from the new regime: during the 1880s British exports through Thessaloniki grew by an average of almost 50%, and Britain remained Thessaloniki's principal trading partner. Imports were on the whole satisfactory, but about the middle of the decade exports, led by grain, began to fall. Farther east, nearly half of all annual trade in Kavala was with Austria-Hungary, which controlled both imports and exports.

The completion of the railway into Central Europe upset existing balance and created an entirely new situation. On the surface, the rules of the game seemed fair. Britain, France, Italy and Belgium all expected to increase their exports in the area north of Skopje, and to capture the Serbian market. Austria-Hungary, on the other hand, and to a lesser extent Germany, were set to conquer markets in Macedonia, particularly that of Thessaloniki. Baron Hirsch's railway, however, was not to betray the hopes of the Austrians, who for years had awaited the opportunity to expand southwards; and the subsidies granted to imports from Northern Europe were sufficient to upset the balance. But this preferential treatment from the railway was not the only factor in Austria's commercial success. British exports were hampered by difficulties of ad-

The substantial grain trade handled by Thessaloniki led to the construction of many flour mills.
This contemporary photograph shows the Allatini mill.

vertizing and distribution. Language problems, high prices, limited credit and a dearth of commercial agents were serious handicaps in a market where the important criteria were low prices, availability of credit, impressive appearance, packaging, and familiarity with local needs. The Austrians, the Germans, the Belgians and the Italians all seemed to grasp the situation better; and their trade increased substantially, both in the cities and in the countryside. Meanwhile, the local merchants realized in time that this stiff competition from the foreign commercial giants was threatening their businesses, and so they took the necessary steps to consolidate and expand their enterprises. Besides, the overall growth in the volume of business allowed for considerable profits.

Of course, Macedonia was still an agricultural region and its consumer potential entirely dependent on the result of the harvest. The exacerbation of the problems facing agricultural exports in 1895-96 thus led to a shrinking of the volume of imports. But 1897, despite the war between Greece and Turkey, witnessed an increase in trade, not only in Thessaloniki and Kavala but in all the other urban areas as well. The major factor in this swing was trade with the port of Volos, once more within the Ottoman domain after the Turkish occupation of Thessaly.

The final fifteen years of Ottoman rule were a period of unprecedented growth for the import trade in the port of Thessaloniki. More specifically, the annual value of imports in the years immediately after

1898 amounted to over two million pounds sterling, more than three in 1908, and more than four in 1909. This growth was completely independent of the state of the export market, which in the most favourable case barely maintained the levels of the 1880s. The trend in both Monastir and Skopje was the same. This phenomenon —spectacular import growth accompanied by shrinking exports— was the result of a combination of factors: the easy access to credit which traders enjoyed at that time, the speculation they indulged in (hoarding huge stocks in anticipation of a price rise), certain measures adopted by the Young Turks (duty-free imports of industrial machinery, abolition of the internal passport), the confidence the Young Turks inspired in the business world, agricultural imports, and the demand for raw materials and machinery to supply the needs of growing local industries. Consumer demand was fuelled by the growth of urban populations, resulting from the uncertainties of the countryside, together with increased farm and factory wages. Rural incomes especially benefitted from a spurt in invisible receipts, such as remittances from emigrants and funds channelled through various patriotic and religious organizations.

In Kavala the pattern was completely different. Imports shot up there too, of course; but their value rarely amounted to more than half that of exports, even though in the period after 1899 the value of exports from Kavala as a rule exceeded that of exports from Thessaloniki, thus making an important contribution to the commercial balance-sheet. The reason for this flood of exports was the high price Macedonian tobacco fetched on the American market. The imbalance between exports and imports was due to the fact that imports into Eastern Macedonia did not all pass through the port of Kavala, but also came in through Thessaloniki.

All this goes to show that, although Macedonia had long been part of the international market, it had never been able to concentrate on the production of one particular product. Grain, cotton, tobacco, silk and opium all rose and fell, in unison or separately, according to the weather and international developments. It was obvious that the deficiencies of the agricultural and administrative infrastructure of the country, plus the dreadful economic condition of the

The port of Kavala at the turn of the century.

Above: Thessaloniki before the great fire of 1917. From a contemporary map.

Right: The White Tower at the same date.

Ottoman Empire both diminished agricultural solvency and discouraged capital, local and foreign, from investing in this sector. The alternative of industrial growth was unattainable, for the basic prerequisites were completely lacking: there was no capital, no government protection, no technical training, no communications, no suitable labour force. The industrial revolution in Europe in the 19th century allotted Macedonia a new role, that of consumer of industrial products. The development of communications and the effects of the Western way of life helped the country perform its new role quite successfully, which meant absorbing great quantities of finished industrial products, raw materials and even agricultural produce.

ΒΑΣΙΛΗΣ ΓΟΥΝΑΡΗΣ
ΟΙΚΟΝΟΜΙΚΕΣ ΕΞΕΛΙΞΕΙΣ ΣΤΗ ΜΑΚΕΔΟΝΙΑ
ΣΗΜΕΙΩΣΕΙΣ

1. Ν. Σβορώνος, «Διοικητικές, κοινωνικές και οικονομικές εξελίξεις (1430-1821)», στον τόμο *Μακεδονία, 4.000 χρόνια ελληνικής ιστορίας και πολιτισμού,* Αθήνα 1982, σ. 359-360.

2. Bruce MacGowan, *Economic Life in Ottoman Europe,* Cambridge 1981, σ. 136-141, 171. Traian Stoianovich, «Land Tenure and Related Sectors of the Balkan Economy, 1600-1800», *Journal of Economic History,* 13 (1953), 398-403, John R. Lampe, *Balkan Economic History, 1550-1950,* Bloomington 1982, σ. 35. Κωνστ. Βακαλόπουλος, *Οικονομική λειτουργία του μακεδονικού και θρακικού χώρου στα μέσα του 19ου αιώνα στα πλαίσια του διεθνούς εμπορίου,* Θεσσαλονίκη 1980, σ. 26-27. Bistra A. Cvetkova, «Typical Features of the Ottoman Social and Economic Structure in South-Eastern Europe During the 14th Centuries», *Études historiques,* 9 (1979), σ. 129-149.

3. Σβορώνος, ό.π., σ. 371. Stoianovich, ό.π., σ. 403-404. Traian Stoianovich, «Le mais arrive dans les Balkans», *Annales,* 17 (1962), 87. Γ. Χριστοδούλου, *Η Θεσσαλονίκη κατά την τελευταίαν εκατονταετίαν,* Θεσσαλονίκη 1936, σ. 33-39.

4. Henry Holland, *Travels in the Ionian Isles, Albania, Thessaly, Macedonia etc. during the Years 1812 and 1813,* Λονδίνο 1835, τ. 3, σ. 327-329. Edward Clarke, *Travels in Various Countries of Europe, Asia and Africa,* Λονδίνο 1816, τ. 4, σ. 334, 365-366. Κ. Βακαλόπουλος, ό.π., σ. 61.

5. Constantin Svolopoulos, «Les effets de la guerre de Crimée sur la condition de Salonique: l'exportation des céréales», *Actes du IIe congrès international des études du sud-est européen,* Αθήνα 1978, τ. 3, σ. 459-474.

6. Ν. Svoronos, *Le commerce de Salonique au XVIIIe siècle,* Παρίσι 1956, σ. 240. Σβορώνος, «Διοικητικές εξελίξεις», σ. 371-372. Κωνστ. Βακαλόπουλος, «Το εμπόριο της Θεσσαλονίκης, 1796-1840», *Μακεδονικά,* 16 (1976), 78. MacGowan, ό.π., σ. 134. Απόστολος Βακαλόπουλος, *Ιστορία της Μακεδονίας 1354-1833,* Θεσσαλονίκη, 2η εκδ., 1988 σ. 133-134.

7. Σβορώνος, «Διοικητικές εξελίξεις», ό.π., σ. 374-376. Α. Βακαλόπουλος, σ. 135-136.

8. Κ. Βακαλόπουλος, «Εμπόριο», σ. 105-111.

9. Σβορώνος, «Διοικητικές εξελίξεις», σ. 372-374. Α. Βακαλόπουλος, ό.π., σ. 145-148, 506-512.

10. Α. Βακαλόπουλος, ό.π., σ. 268.

11. Holland, ό.π., σ. 324-326.

12. Ν. Πόδας, «Ταχυδρομική ιστορία της Θεσσαλονίκης ως το 1922», *Η Θεσσαλονίκη,* 1 (1985), σ. 531-542.

13. Suraiya Faroqhi, «The Early History of the Balkan Fairs», *Südost-Forschungen,* 37 (1978), 52-53, 65-67. Α. Βακαλόπουλος, ό.π., σ. 202-203, 275, Svoronos, *Commerce,* σ. 210-211. M.Ch.Ed. Guys, *La guide de la Macédoine,* Παρίσι 1857, σ. 15-16.

14. Holland, ό.π., σ. 326.

15. Svoronos, *Commerce,* σ. 207. Lewis J. Farley, *The Resources of Turkey,* Λονδίνο 1863, σ. 136.

16. Σβορώνος, «Διοικητικές εξελίξεις», σ. 376-377.

17. Σβορώνος, «Διοικητικές εξελίξεις», σ. 378. Traian Stoianovich, «The Conquering Balkan Orthodox Merchant», *Journal of Economic History,* 20 (1960), 246. Α. Βακαλόπουλος, ό.π., σ. 272-273.

18. Svoronos, *Commerce,* σ. 219. Σβορώνος, «Διοικητικές εξελίξεις», σ. 378-379. Stoianovich, «Conquering Merchant», σ. 309. McGowan, ό.π., σ. 31.

19. MacGowan, ό.π., σ. 134. Κωστής Μοσκώφ, *Θεσσαλονίκη, τομή της μεταπρατικής πόλης,* τ. 1, Αθήνα 1978, σ. 80-81· πρβλ. Svoronos, *Commerce,* σ. 300-308.

20. Σβορώνος, «Διοικητικές εξελίξεις», σ. 379. Adolphus Slade, *Records of Travels in Turkey, Greece etc.,* Λονδίνο 1832, τ. 2, σ. 449.

21. Holland, ό.π., σ. 323-324, 327-329. Clarke, ό.π., σ. 364, 366, William M. Leake, *Travels in Northern Greece,* Λονδίνο 1835, τ. 3, σ. 207.

22. Α. Βακαλόπουλος, ό.π., σ. 606. Κ. Βακαλόπουλος, «Εμπόριο», σ. 102-106. Leake, ό.π., σ. 253.

23. Urquhart, *The Spirit of the East,* Λονδίνο 1838, τ. 2, σ. 80· πρβλ. Μοσκώφ, ό.π., σ. 84. John Madox, *Excursions in the Holy Lands, Egypt, Nuvia, Syria etc.,* Λονδίνο 1834, τ. 1, σ. 81.

24. Α.Υ.Ε. 1834/36/2, Βαλλιάνος προς Υπ. Εξωτ., Θεσσαλονίκη 28 Φεβρ. 1834 (π.η). Virginia Paskaleva, «Contribution aux relations commerciales des provinces balkaniques de l'Empire Ottomane avec les états européens au cours du XVIIe et de première moitié du XIXe s.», *Etudes historiques,* 4 (1968), 283-284. FO 195/100, f. 361, FO 195/176, ff. 126-130, FO 195/293, ff. 73-84.

25. Κ. Βακαλόπουλος, *Οικονομική λειτουργία,* σ. 55-71. Α.Υ.Ε. 1844/36/2, Γερακάρης προς Υπ. Εξωτ., Θεσσαλονίκη, 25 Μαρτ. 1844, (π.η), αρ. πρωτ. 94, FO 195/495, ff. 29-38.

26. Α.Υ.Ε. 1852/36/2, Ράμφος προς Υπ. Εξωτ., Θεσσαλονίκη, 3 Μαΐου 1852, (π.η), αρ. πρωτ. 175, Svolopoulos, ό.π., σ. 459-474. Κ. Βακαλόπουλος, *Οικονομική λειτουργία,* σ. 71-75. C. T. Newton, *Travels and Discoveries in the Levant,* Λονδίνο 1865, τ. 1, σ. 121.

27. Κ. Βακαλόπουλος, *Οικονομική λειτουργία,* σ. 75-82.

Communal Organization

Haralampos K. Papastathis

Local self-government in Macedonia under Ottoman rule was closely connected with the Church. The local prelate acted as a representative of the Patriarch of Constantinople, who was accountable to the sultan for any demeanure of his Christian subjects affecting the political structure of the Ottoman Empire. The guilds were also organically related to the communities, albeit to a varying degree according to place.

The reasons which lay behind the sultan's decision to grant certain privileges to the Christians through their Church were religious, political and, primarily, fiscal.[1] Concessions had already been made on a local level with the gradual expansion of Ottoman rule and found complete expression with the fall of Constantinople. Along with the rights of inviolability, tax-exemption and invulnerability, which had been conceded to Patriarch Gennadios Scholarios, the administrative and judicial jurisdiction of the Church over the internal affairs of the *Genos* (the Orthodox Community) was expanded. The Church, then, was recognized as the 'Ethnarchy', that is, the temporal as well as spiritual leadership of the enslaved Christians. In correspondence to the Patriarch's privileges as the central organ of administrative authority, local prelates exercised extensive rights over all Orthodox Christians in their dioceses irrespective of their racial origins or ethnic self-perception. The rights of the Patriarch and the local metropolitans and bishops were reaffirmed following their election by the imperial warrant (*berat*) appointing them to office. Owing to lack of sources it is not possible to ascertain whether, during the first three centuries of Ottoman rule, specific provisions expanded the privileges originally conceded. The *berat* concerning the Metropolitan of Verria Ioakeim (1649), after a general reference to the "affairs of his jurisdiction, and that his commands may not be disobeyed", defined the prelate's authority over ecclesiastical, administrative and financial matters, marriages and control of the property of the Church.[2] Later *berats*, such as those concerning the Metropolitans Gerasimos of Thessaloniki (1788)[3], Veniamin of Servia and Kozani (1815)4, and Zacharias of Verria (1822)5, included detailed instructions regarding financial matters affecting both the Church and the State; such provisions rendered the Church a powerful economic factor. At the same time, the continuing decline of the Ottoman Empire and the ever-rising amounts of *peshkesh* (tributes) paid after each election, permitted the prelates to expand the scope of their authority, on the basis both of explicitly conceded privileges[6] and the *de facto* 'presumption of competence'.[7]

The politically leading role of the Church and, primarily, the self-government of the communities, along with the measure of participation of economic corporations in the running of local affairs, raised the Christian-Orthodox Community to the status of a political entity within the body of the empire.

Regardless of the various views on the origin of communalism in Macedonia, it seems that communal institutions had been in force and functioned before the early Ottoman invasions. The attitude of the conquerors towards communalism was positive mainly on financial grounds. During the five centuries of Ottoman domination, communalism helped preserve traditional collective and local institutions in working condition, maintain a tolerable degree of self-sufficiency for Christian-Orthodox communities, and promote their cultural, social and economic evolution. Thus, the Orthodox Community managed to survive and, from the end of the 18th century onwards, developed to a degree permitting the emergence of endogenous centrifugal tendencies during the process of ethnic differentiation in the 19th century.

In principle, the powers of the communities were

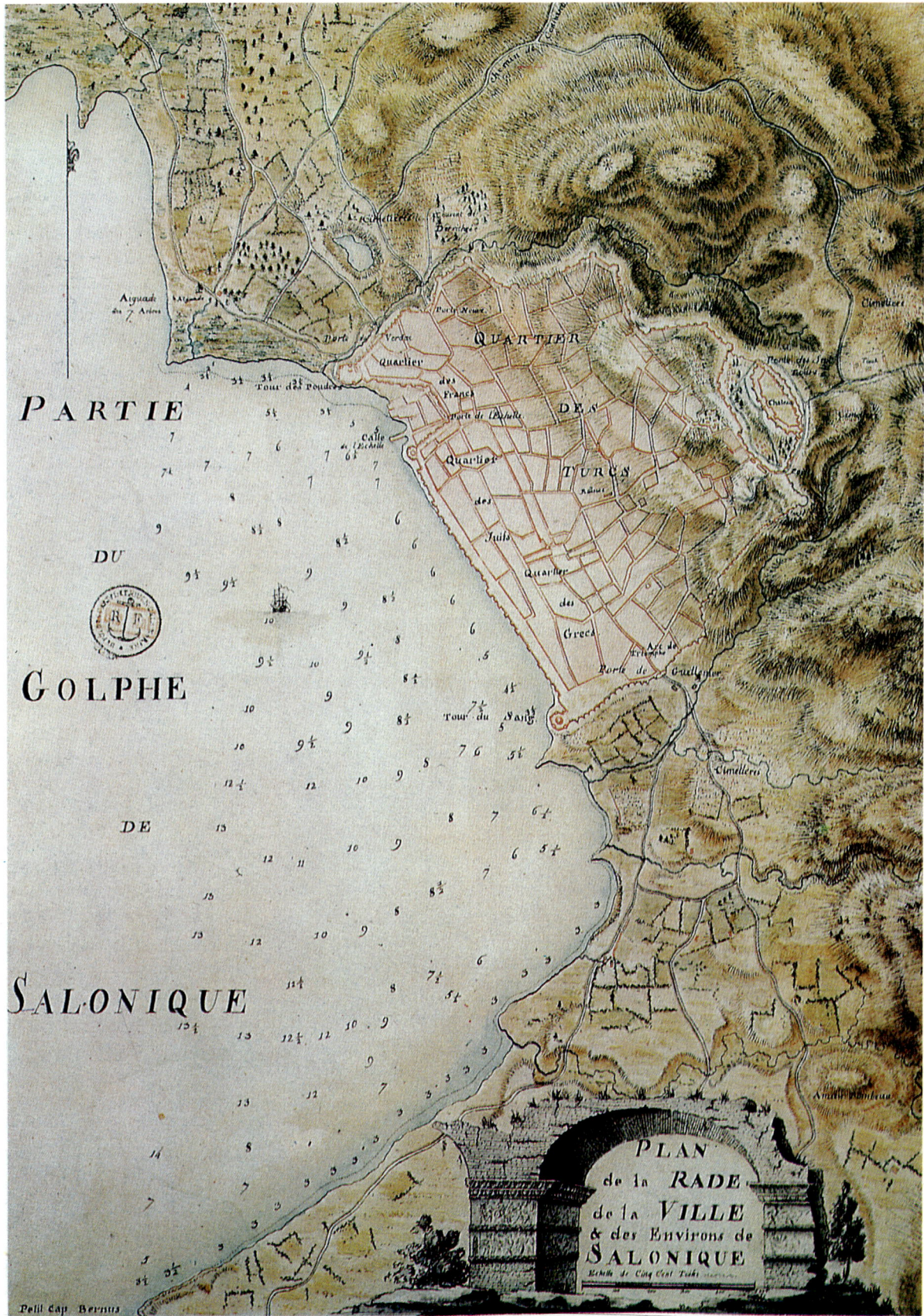

Map of Thessaloniki and its surroundings, c. 1732.

related to taxation: to assess, allocate and remit the collectively imposed tax to the State. Competence in this field facilitated the acquisition of extensive executive powers. Depending on their economic strength, they gradually acquired legislative and judicial powers, effectively disputing the exclusive rights of the ecclesiastical authorities. With regard to the structure of communal organization and the election of community organs, the system had been far from uniform in Macedonia until the time of the General (or National) Regulations of 1860-1862. In certain communities the election of the notables was within the guilds' prerogatives, elsewhere they were elected at neighbourhood (*mahalle*) level, while in other communities —as, for instance, at Moschopolis— a mixed system was in force. Of course, election to communal office was much easier for the well-to-do —the 'grandees', as they are referred to in sources on the city of Serres— than for the poorer classes. It seems, however, that there were certain property and taxability qualifications attached to the right to run for office.

Information about Macedonian communities up to the middle of the 19th century is scarce and sporadic. In the case of Serres it seems that Murad I had conceded self-government according to the established local tradition. In the same city justice was administered by a court consisting of a number of notables presided by a cleric; an Ottoman official also attended regularly as representative of state authority.[8] Metropolitan Isidoros of Thessaloniki had secured privileges for his flock (*harites* or favours) during the city's first Ottoman occupation[9], while, later, its new conqueror, Murad, exempted the inhabitants —as it is confirmed by Ahmed's I *firman* of 1605[10]— from taxation on water supply, public drainage and wall maintenance, provided that they fulfilled the rest of their fiscal obligations. In Thessaloniki there was a twelve-member community council, which in 1742, according to a report by the Venetian consul, increased its members to twenty.[11] In Serres there was also a twelve-member council (1614) which was elected by the members of the guilds voting at a special meeting of the clergy, the notables and the populace at large.[12] This meeting appears a year later to have taken measures against profiteering, threatening the offender with excommunication.[13] Each neighbourhood or parish in Serres had its own notables, the *kallistevontes* (foremost) of the *mahalle*[14], while an important office was that of the *'protogeros* ('first elder') of the castle'.[15] The

Ottoman traveller Evliya Çelebi, who vistited the area in 1670[16], described the *protogeroi* as "leaders of the infidels" of Ochrida. In Verria the term applied to the leading notables, one from each parish.[17] In Moschopolis, around 1650, the supreme council of the community was comprised of the six leading notables of the six parishes, who elected their head, the *nazir*. As the town developed, the members of the council increased to twelve with the participation of the *kodjabashis*, that is, the notables responsible for the collection of public revenues from each parish.[18]

The jurisdiction of the communities was often disputed by the Ottoman authorities, the local prelate, and even their own members in their effort, through all sorts of indirect ways, to evade their obligations. In 1747 the Venetian consul in Thessaloniki characteristically reported the following: the Greek *dragomans* (interpreters) of the consulate, who by virtue of imperial warrant were exempt from public and communal taxation, professed six rich fellow Christians to be their servants, so that they were also exempt from taxation; the latter, in turn, indicated others as 'sub-servants'; and the consul added: "it might have been tolerable had they limited themselves to avoiding the Turkish taxes only, but these people refuse to contribute to this unfortunate Greek community and, thus, alleviate its heavy tax burden".[19] Even as late as 1888, towards the end of Ottoman rule, the villagers of Blatsi denunciated to the *Kaimakam* of Kailar the interference of the local Ottoman authorities with the election of the *muhtars* (notables) of the village.[20]

Justice and the applicable law constituted the main field where the limits of authority of the Ottoman state, the Church and the communities cut across each other. Where the Christians were concerned, the Ottoman courts (*sheriat*) exercised exclusive jurisdiction over all penal offences. The *kadi* applied the Islamic holy law (*sheriat-i islâmiye*). The ecclesiastical court (which should be distinguished from that which dealt with the clerics' ecclesiastical offences) was competent, in parallel with the *sheriat*, to consider matters involving the personal and family status of the Christians and which were directly connected with the Orthodox faith, such as marriage, betrothal, divorce and inheritance. The ecclesiastical courts normally applied Byzantine law, the 'canonical provisions' —ordained by the Patriarch or the local prelate— as well as local, mostly unwritten, customary law. Community courts, consisting of laymen only, were not a common phenomenon in Macedonia and wherever they were to be found, it was by virtue of special privilege.

A typical Christian court in Macedonia was of mixed composition, including both clerics and prominent local laymen. Already in 1387, this phenomenon was noticeable in Serres in 1387; a year later the exiled Metropolitan of Serres was succeeded by the Metropolitan of Zichna in the chairmanship of the local court, which consisted of two bishops, lay notables and, once more, an Ottoman official —the latter apparently in order to monitor the situation in the newly reconquered region.[21] Clergy and laymen were also present at the local courts in Siatista[22], Ochrida[23], and Kastoria.[24] By way of contrast, the courts of first instance in economically and culturally flourishing Moschopolis were in the hands of the guilds. The appellate court was composed of the 14 guild leaders —as will be seen later; this court also tried disputes between non-guild members, with the exception of merchants who, in accordance with an age-old practice, submitted their differences to an arbitrer (*tahminci*).[25] In 1839, by decree (*buyurdu*) of the Ottoman governor (*vali*) of Rumeli, the merchants of Siatista were allowed to set up a six-member court to settle their "commercial and all other differences;" its members were to serve for a six-month term without pay.[26]

With regard to the provisions of Byzantine law applicable to each case, the Christian courts consulted manuscripts of various legal compilations. In addition to Manouil Malaxos' *Nomokanon*, which was in use throughout the Greek lands[27], the *Syntagma* (Constitution) or *Nomokanon*, compiled by Matthaios Vlastaris in Thessaloniki around 1335, was extensively used.28 After the mid-18th century the use of Konstantinos Armenopoulos' *Hexabiblos* gained ground. This compilation, which had also been produced in Thessaloniki in 1345[29], presented many advantages in comparison with those of Malaxos and Vlastaris. It offered a concise and usable codification of Byzantine civil law, which was first printed —in its demotic Greek edition by Alexios Spanos— in Venice in 1744; by 1820 it was reprinted another six times. Yet the introduction of the *Hexabiblos* into the courts of Macedonia was a slow process. When, in 1838, the eminent scholar of Byzantine Law K.E. Zachariä (von Lingenthal) visited Thessaloniki[30], he was informed that the sources of law in use at the local courts were the *Pidalion* (lit: 'Helm') compiled by monks Agapios and Nikodimos (the Athonite) and printed in 1800[31], Christophoros' *Kanonikon* ('Canonical', printed in 1800)[32] and especially—al-

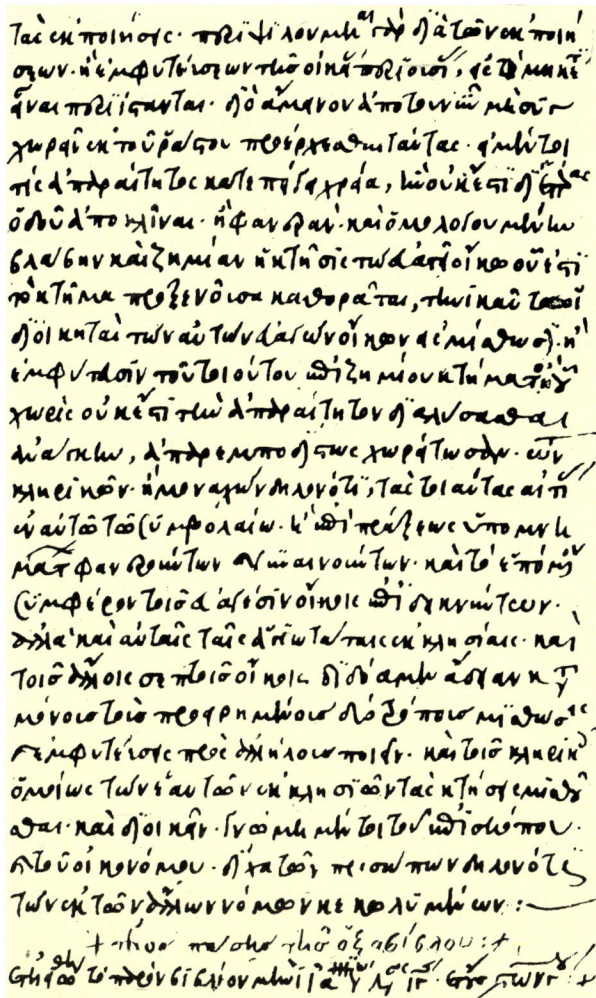

Manuscript of Konstantinos Armenopoulos' **Hexabiblos**

though in a manuscript form— the *Nomikon* of Theophilos, bishop of Kampania (Koulakia, west of Thessaloniki), drafted in 1788.[33] In fact, the then bishop of Kampania informed Zachariä that he himself exclusively used the *Nomikon*, which was held in great esteem throughout the See of Thessaloniki.[34] Apart from the indisputable merits of the *Nomikon*, its extensive use is probably attributable to Theophilos' blessed memory: in 1838 many clerics and laymen who had known him (Theophilos died around 1795) were still alive. Yet the Patriarchate had never officially sanctioned the publication of the *Nomikon*, since in some of its passages Theophilos came out with caustic remarks about the ignorance and avarice characterizing many a cleric.[35]

In addition to the afore-mentioned compilations of Byzantine law, a whole range of canonical provisions was also in force: those issued by the Ecumenical Patriarchate applied in general[36], whereas episcopal ones affected only the flock of the diocese concerned.

At that time, canonical opinions and 'certificates' —such as those issued by the Metropolitan of Kampania Theophilos[37]— were also regarded as sources of law. Normally, these documents concerned matters of family and inheritance law[38], although they often covered other cases, such as the proper attire of the faithful[39], particularly female extravagance.[40] An ordinance aimed at checking luxurious life styles was also made by the community of Kastoria in 1839.[41] Besides, the Ottoman authorities had always reprimanded any tendency on the part of the 'infidels'[42] to dress like the Muslims.

When the laws of the Orthodox Community failed to satisfy the parties concerned, family law cases of the Christians were brought before the Ottoman *kadi*. The most typical case was that of 'civil marriage' —according to the religious customs of the period— or *kepinion*[43]: it concerned marriage between a Muslim and a Christian[44], or between Christians in the

One of the last remaining coppersmiths of Kozani. The coppersmith's guild of the city had drafted its Regulations as early as 1789.

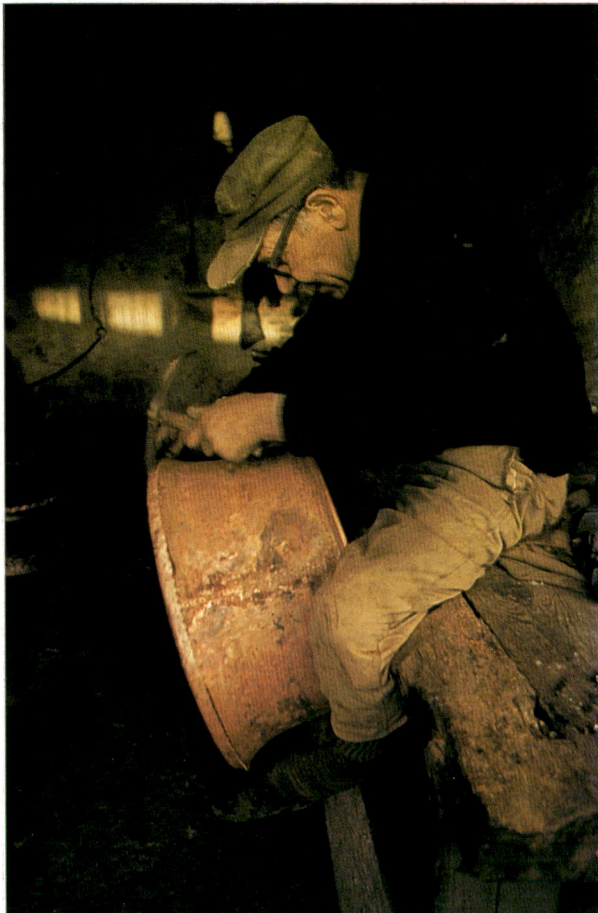

event of certain existing prohibitions, as, for instance, marriage of adulterers[45], or polygamy.[46] Ottoman sources record that almost as late as the middle of the 19th century (1838) Christians from the regions of Kitros and Kolyndros, married men and women, resorted to the *kadi* in order to contract a new marriage or to obtain divorce "against their own customs".[47] In that same year, the Ecumenical Patriarchate made representations to the Porte claiming that marriages by *kepinion* between Europeans and Greek or Armenian women[48] violated its privileged status. Excommunication was the usual response of the Church to such practices, and, with the exception of very few cases of absolution, all those people were lost to the Orthodox *Genos*.

Of particular significance was the contribution of economic associations to the organization and activities of the communities; in fact, in some parts these two entities appeared almost indistinguishable. The economic associations were known as *esnaf* or *rufet*, being guilds of craftsmen, in particular, and tradesmen. With respect to other associations of similar character, commercial partnerships (*kompanies*) were formed by Macedonian merchants in European countries[49], whereas, in the case of stock-breeders' groups (*tselingata*) in Macedonia, information is scanty.

The guilds occupied a special place in the social stratification of the Ottoman city and played an important role in the region's economic development, as the Turks were almost exclusively interested in military and administrative matters. In this way, the secondary and the existing tertiary sector of production remained in the hands of the 'infidels', Christians and Jews. For this reason, the guilds were under the supervision of the local Ottoman *kadi*. Guilds were formed by those enough well-to-do, who, in their effort to safeguard and promote their professional interests, took an active interest in the running of the affairs of the Orthodox Community.

In Macedonia there existed a unique example of a broadly-based guild, in which many communities took part. In Siderokausia of Chalcidice in early 19th century, the place of the leaseholders in the running of the silver mines was taken by the neighbouring villages, the Mademochoria, twelve large and "360 small ones", according to Urquhart.[51] This new cooperative 'federation' was granted special privileges[52]; at the same time, it constituted the supreme communal authority of the shareholding villages, insofar it administered their financial affairs. In other regions of Macedonia the guilds had a function distinct from that of the community, though organically related to its structure. The fourteen guilds of Moschopolis were under the supervision of the supreme community council. Each guild had its own council headed by the guild leader, to take care of its internal affairs. The fourteen guild leaders formed the council of the guilds, which had both administrative and judicial powers[53], and dealt with the frequently arising disputes between the guilds themselves. Among the surviving related documents there is an act of the *kadi* of Thessaloniki (1736) appointing the leader of the furriers' guild at the request of its members in order to put an end to their internal squabbles[54], as well as a *firman* of sultan Mustafa (1773)[55] prohibiting any interference from a third party in the affairs of the guilds of Western Macedonia. As a rule, outside interference had to be avoided: in 1779, the grocers of Moschopolis "having witnessed many improprieties taking place within our *rufet*, owing to the lack of order and harmony, in everything, [and] decency to each other...", agreed to draw up their guild's terms of operation. Among other provisions, it was stipulated that "if anyone is found to have entered into partnership with a Turk, ...he should be expelled from the guild".[56] Similar regulations, sometimes framed with the elders' participation and always with the approval of the local prelate, were produced by several guilds of Kozani, such as those of tanners (1786)[57], furriers (1786)[58], gunsmiths, coppersmiths (1789)[59], tinsmiths, horseshoers, et al. According to a source, joint regulations were drawn for guilds in Thessaloniki, too (1830).[60] In that same city, even the clerics came together in a *rufet*, whose regulations were drawn in 1825.[61]

In Thessaloniki some time earlier, in 1763, the community leaders and the heads of the guilds had reached eached an accord "with a common decision, opinion and will" to succour the Metropolitan, Iakovos, whenever "...an evil and perverted man might rebel... unjustly and unreasonably seeking to harm and cause damage by indescent acts...". If any of those covered by the agreement ever proved to be "defiant ...or displayed negligence and used a pretext", he would be subjected to a reprimand in church and would pay a fine to the Metropolitan, commensurate with his income.[62] Thus, the guilds *de facto* extended their presence beyond the sphere of their immediate professional interests. Indicative of the evolving social position of the guilds themselves is the case, recorded in Monastir in 1863, of guild leaders issuing a testimonial signed by them in this

Melenikon (now Melnik, in Bulgaria) was an important centre of Macedonian Hellenism. In the photograph, the old Greek school is shown.

capacity and stamped with the seal of their *rufet* for use in court before the local Ottoman *kadi*.[63]

The local guilds also took part in the setting up of the most advanced form of communal organization in Macedonia in the period before the General Regulations. At Melenikon, in 1813, "the entire Assembly of all the inhabitants in common" along and the six *esnaf* of the town drew up and endorsed the 'System or Commands', a community regulation made up of thirty articles, which was confirmed by the local Metropolitan. According to these regulations, twenty "sensible and prudent" inhabitants "of every class" met annually in order to elect three trustees and three inspectors charged with the running of the community's general administrative and financial affairs respectively. They also appointed parish wardens, and supervised all work related to public relief, schools, and even churches. Their decisions were all subject to the Metropolitan's 'confirmation'.[64] The *System* was not clear about the manner in which the twenty electors "of every class" were selected. Yet, in view of the social structure of Melenikon —there existed two classes, the *tsorbatzides* (upper crust) and the *pocheirioi* (subordinate), whose relations were marked by a great deal of discrimination visible, for instance, in questions of marriage[65]— the statute might have well introduced the election of the twenty by both classes in equal proportion. By early 19th-century standards the System of Melenikon included quite advanced provisions, particularly with regard to the rights of the laity *vis-à-vis* the administration of the Church (such as the appointment of parish wardens, the supervision of churches, etc). In this respect, it could be regarded as a precursor of the conceptions embodied in the National Regulations, the introduction of which almost half a century later marked the beneficial to the Orthodox Community conclusion of internal and external developments affecting the sultan's domain.

*
* *

The continuing decline of the Ottoman Empire had become evident particularly during the reign of Mahmud II in the early decades of the 19th century. Serious events, such as the rebellions of Ali Pasha and other provincial rulers in Albania, NW Bulgaria and Bosnia, the proclamation of Serbia to an autonomous principality, the establishment of the Modern Greek state, the secession of Mehmed Ali's Egypt, the Russo-Turkish War of 1828, taught many leading Ottomans that the only way to prevent further losses was through modernizing the state and adopting Western methods of administration.

In November 1839, Mahmud's successor, Abdul Mejid I, issued at the Palace of the Roses the *Hatt-i Sherif*, thus inaugurating the period of reforms, the so-called period of *Tanzimat*.[66] The *Hatt-i Sherif* revised all the privileges that had been granted at various times to the non-Muslim *millets*; it confirmed respect for the honour and property of all the subjects of the sultan; it introduced reforms in the administration of justice; it abolished tax farming, introduced conscription and recognized the equality of all Ottoman subjects before the law irrespective of religion.[67]

The attempt to introduce Western models into a Muslim state, the notion of equality in particular, was viewed by the Muslims as contravening the fundamental tenets of Islam. They found their 'downgrading' to the level of the 'infidels' intolerable. The Christians and the Jews for their part questioned the sincerity of the reforms and, what was more, objected to conscription. This general reaction did not lead to the annulment of the *Hatt-i Serif* but rendered it a mere declaration of intent.

In the aftermath of the Crimean War, the Porte sought the recognition of the sultan as a European leader with the right to participate in the Concert of Europe dealing with the affairs of the continent and, indeed, of the globe as a whole. Yet, in the eyes of the European Powers, such a recognition seemed to postulate the granting of equality to all the subjects of the Ottoman Empire without exception. For this reason, in February 1856, Abdul Mejid issued a new Charter, the *Hatt-i Humayun*.

The *Hatt-i Humayun* extended to all subjects of the sultan guarantees for life and property, and equal rights irrespective of religion, ethnic origin and financial status. It reaffirmed and retained in force the privileges which had been granted to non-Muslim *millets*. At the same time, each religious community was obliged to propose reforms in its internal organization, in order to meet current exigencies and the "progress of the Enlightenment and Civilization". It further confirmed the individual status of the various religious creeds, the equal participation of the laity in the running of community affairs and in the administration of justice by establishing joint administrative councils and courts (composed of religious officials and laymen). State legislation was no more to rest exclusively on the *Sheriat*. Preliminary work was initiated on the drafting of civil, penal, procedure and commercial codes, and on legislation concerning the organization of the state. The administration of the 'national' (internal) affairs of the Christian and Jewish communities became uniform throughout the Empire; it was now entrusted to a council, which, at least in principle, was elected by all adult male members of the community.

The *Hatt-i Humayun* was slowly put into effect by legislative measures, which attached a twofold content to the term 'community': in a broad sense, it referred to all Ottoman subjects belonging to the the same religion or doctrine who came under the jurisdiction of a religious authority recognized by the Porte and who lived throughout the Empire or even in large areas, considering the territorial extent of their religious authority (as, for instance, the community forming the flock of the Patriarchate of Constantinople, Alexandria, Jerusalem, etc.). In a narrow sense, it came to describe those sharing the same faith or doctrine within a particular settlement. It was often the case that within the same village or town many separate communities coexisted: Muslim, Jewish, Armenian Orthodox, Roman Catholic, Evangelical, Uniate, Christian-Orthodox, Exarchist (the followers of the autocephalous Bulgarian Church), and others; in other words, the communities were entirely constituted on the basis of religion, and not of language or national/ethnic consciousness. At the same time, in every town decentralized government was represented by a municipal authority, whose composition and function was independent of the religious beliefs of the inhabitants.

In accordance with the provisions of the *Hatt-i Humayun*, the Porte demanded from the Ecumenical Patriarchate, as well as from the Armenian and the Latin Patriarchates in Constantinople, and the Archrabbinate, the appointment of committees with the task to elaborate the fundamental regulations of each *millet*. With respect to the Ecumenical Patriarchate, the government's instructions recommended the formation of a 29-member council consisting of 7 prelates and 22 laymen, of which 10 represented the Orthodox population of Constantinople and the rest the districts of Adrianople, Bosnia, Thessaloniki, Kastamoni, Crete, Larissa, Great Tyrnovo, Pelagonia, Pisidia, Smyrna, and Philippopolis. This council was initially named 'National Assembly' —a term disliked by the Porte since it smacked too much of parliamentarianism— to be renamed 'National Provisional Council'. Its task was to formulate and approve the rules for the organization and functioning of the Orthodox communities and the Church as an administrative authority.

The National Provisional Council worked from 1858 to 1860, and over the next two years approved and put into force the "General (or National) Regulations for the Settlement of the Ecclesiastical and National Affairs of the Orthodox Christian Subjects, under the Ecumenical Throne, of H.M. the Sultan". The National Regulations contained seven parts concerning the following: 1) the election and appointment of the Patriarch; 2) the qualifications and election of prelates; 3) the constitution of the Holy Synod; 4) the 'Permanent Mixed Council'; 5) the revenue of the prelates; 6) the salaries of the employees of the Patriarchate; and 7) the monasteries. From the above it becomes clear that the community limited itself to religious matters. The self-government of the Orthodox Community as a whole included: 1) the setting up and operation of the local communities and their charitable establishments; 2) purely religious matters, such as the election of prelates and the construction of churches; and 3) the functioning of institutions of predominantly religious character (such as marriage, betrothal, divorce, inheritance), which were the object of specific courts following their own procedure.

As has seen noted, until 1860 there was no uniform system of communal organization in Macedonia. Instead, there existed a pluralism of forms and a variety of procedures. The local prelate *ex officio* represented the Orthodox community of his diocese before the Ottoman authorities and, at the same time, was accountable for its loyalty. Lay participation in the running of communal affairs was not yet an established practice, sanctioned either by the Ottoman asministrative system or by Church laws. This context was radically transformed by the *Hatt-i Humayun*, the National Regulations, and also by the regulations introduced by local communities after 1862. Such regulations are known to have existed —although not all of them have been preserved— in the following Macedonian communities: Thessaloniki (1874, 1886, 1904), Asvestochori (1906), Monastir (1896, 1905), Tyrnovo of Pelagonia (1901), diocese of Pelagonia (common regulations for a number of villages and towns, 1906 and 1911), Verria (1892, 1903, 1912), Naousa (1912), Krousovon (1907, 1912), Siatista (1902), Kavala (1899, 1907), Edessa (1885, 1891, 1911), Korytsa (1876), Kozani (1895, 1911) Serres (1877, 1892), Kastoria (1902). The National Regulations introduced a uniform system of organization. In conformity to the terms applying to the Permanent Mixed Council of the Orthodox *millet*, local officials were elected by universal male voting in parishes; the election was direct in the villages and indirect in the cities (through a number of electors). In certain Macedonian urban communities, as for instance in Monastir, the regulations did not completely exclude the guilds from community affairs; they were allowed to appoint representatives to the 'General Assembly of the Citizens' (according to the expression adopted in the 1904 regulation) who participated in a twin capacity as community members and representatives of the guilds. In other urban centres, as in Thessaloniki, following the election of the notables the body of the electors was not dissolved but it continued to function as the representative institution of the Orthodox community, that is, its legislature, while the six notables under the chairmanchip of the Metropolitan performed executive and judicial functions. More specifically, the council of the notables, always under the local prelate, represented the community before the state authorities; it determined all matters of administrative nature; it heard cases related to family and inheritance law and tried according to the procedure of the Permanent Mixed Council and the provisions of Armenopoulos' *Hexabiblos*; it elected the local notary charged with the drafting of dowry-related documents; it appointed the representatives of '*Our Genos*' to state committees; it sanctioned the election of parish committees and the

Monastir: View of the city during the Ottoman period.

decisions of parish councils; last but not least, in small towns and villages —where no special representative body existed— it appointed the inspectors of schools and other charitable establishments.

This extensive degree of self-government in its broader sense (with recognized executive, legislative and judicial authority) of the Macedonian communities was to develop further. The principle of the 'presumption of competence', which continued to be in force under the new regime, extended the jurisdiction of the community organs over fields which were not specifically covered by the *Hatt-i Humayun*. Thus, in the Orthodox communities of Macedonia the local notary performed most legal transactions between their members. The Mixed Courts situated at the prelate's seat heard private law cases in general, provided that they arose between persons of the same faith. A circular issued in 1891 by the Vizier increased the powers of school inspetors; at the same time, it provided the first official recording of the privileges of the Orthodox *Genos*, thus constituting a sort of concordat between the Ottoman State and the Orthodox Church.

The National Regulations not only infused and homogenized a form of popular sovereignty in the communal system; they also introduced lay participation in the administration of the Church itself. The *'Ephoreia ton Geronton'* (the council of elder metropolitans) was abolished and the running of the Patriarchate's affairs was entrusted to a Synod of twelve metropolitans with a two-year term, presided over by the Patriarch. Whenever the Ecumenical throne was left vacant, the prelates of the See of Constantinople dispatched ballots bearing the name of their chosen candidate for the throne. Then, a convocation was formed by the twelve members of the Synod, other hierarchs who happened to be in Constantinople, and seventy laymen. This convocation nominated three candidates on the basis of the ballots cast, from among whom the new Patriarch was elected. Friction between laymen and clerics was not uncommon. The community of Thessaloniki, which had been branded as 'ungovernable' among prelates, provides a typical example: in 1884, after spending only five years with his flock, Metropolitan Kallinikos Photiadis was forced to leave the city and take refuge in Constantinople. His successor, Grigorios Kallidis, had to abdicate twice, whereas his own successor, Sophronios, fled to Athos two years after his enthronement (1893) without showing the slightest intention to return to his 'much-coveted' diocese.

After the Bulgarian Schism and the Austrian descent on Bosnia-Herzegovina, the National Regulations in Macedonia operated almost exclusively to the benefit of the Greeks. Their democratic outlook —by the standards of the concrete place and time— favoured the spreading of education with the establishment of new schools throughout Macedonia, promoted the creation of a civil society among the Greeks, encouraged charitable initiatives, while it contributed to the gradual decline of the Ottoman Empire and the concurrent rise of the Greek element in the economic, cultural and social life of Macedonia. What is more, communal organization in Macedonia comes out very favourably in comparison with the situation prevailing in free Greece. In the Greek state local self-government languished in the strait-jacket of the strict, centralized system imposed by the Bavarian Regency, which, in the aftermath of the War of Independence, had turned the post-Byzantine communalism into a nostalgic memory. On the contrary, in Macedonia the community constituted the cell of collective activity and served as a bridge between the Hellenic origins and democratic ideals of 19th-century Europe, on the one hand, and the Byzantine tradition, on the other, a tradition which, in the political field, found expression in the Greek 'Great Idea'. In this way, the Greek-Orthodox Community managed to survive and, subsequently, to defend its position during the Macedonian Struggle and to prepare itself for political life in a free state following the Balkan Wars.   ●

The Government House (Konak), of Thesssaloniki, constructed in the late Ottoman period.

A view of Thessaloniki shortly before the end of Ottoman rule (1912).

ΧΑΡΑΛΑΜΠΟΣ Κ. ΠΑΠΑΣΤΑΘΗΣ

Η ΚΟΙΝΟΤΙΚΗ ΟΡΓΑΝΩΣΗ

ΣΗΜΕΙΩΣΕΙΣ

1. Βλ. τα γενικά έργα των: C. Papadopoulos, *Les Privilèges du Patriarcat Oecuménique (Communauté Grecque Orthodoxe) dans l' Empire Ottoman*, Paris 1921· Ν. Πανταζοπούλου, «Τα ʼπρονόμιαʼ ως πολιτιστικός παράγων εις τας σχέσεις χριστιανών-μουσουλμάνων», *Επιστ. Επετ. Σχ. ΝΟΕ ΑΠΘ*, τ. 9 («Ακροθίνια Πέτρω Γ. Βάλληνδα»), Θεσσαλονίκη 1976, σ. 813 κ.ε.· *του ιδίου, «Ο ελληνικός κοινοτισμός και η νεοελληνική κοινοτική παράδοση»*, ʼΟψεις Νεοελληνικού Βίου, Θεσσαλονίκη 1985, σ. 97-152, ό. περαιτέρω βιβλιογραφία· *του ιδίου*, Community Laws and Customs of Western Macedonia under Ottoman Rule *Balkan Studies* 2 (1961) 1-22· Μ. Καλινδέρη, *Αι συντεχνίαι και η Εκκλησία επί τουρκοκρατίας*, Αθήναι 1973.

2. Βλ. Ι. Βασδραβέλλη, *Ιστορικά Αρχεία Μακεδονίας*, τ. βʼ, Θεσσαλονίκη 1954, σ. 36-37.

3. Βλ. Μ. Καλινδέρη, *Τα λυτά έγγραφα της Δημοτικής Βιβλιοθήκης Κοζάνης, 1676-1808*, Θεσσαλονίκη 1951, σ. 78-84.

4. Βλ. Αντ. Σιγάλα, «Πατριαρχικαί πράξεις, φερμάνια και άλλα τινά έγγραφα», *Μακεδονικά* 1 (1940) 284-294.

5. Βλ. Π. Ζέπου, Ανέκδοτα τουρκικά έγγραφα εκ των Αρχείων Βεροίας και Θεσσαλονίκης, *Αρχ. Ιδιωτ. Δικ.* 11 (1944) 75-78 (αναδημ.: *Annales* [Τμ. Νομ. Σχ. ΝΟΕ ΑΠΘ] 2, 1988, 629-634), και Ι. Βασδραβέλλη, ό.π., τ.βʼ, σ. 284-289.

6. Δεν έλειψαν καταχρήσεις των εξουσιών αυτών από αρχιερείς, όπως έγινε με το μητροπολίτη Θεσσαλονίκης Μελέτιο. Υπέρ αυτού είχε εκδοθεί φιρμάνι, με το οποίο αποκτούσε το δικαίωμα να τιμωρεί «διά ραβδισμού με φάλαγγα» τα μέλη του ποιμνίου του όταν παραβίαζαν τα θρησκευτικά έθιμα. ʼΟπως, όμως, εξακριβώθηκε ο Μελέτιος εξεβίαζε με το μέτρο αυτό τους ραγιάδες της επαρχίας του, και γιʼ αυτό το Πατριαρχείο ενήργησε ώστε με νέο φιρμάνι να του αφαιρεθεί η παραχωρηθείσα εξουσία (1838), βλ. Ι. Βασδραβέλλη, ό.π., τ. αʼ, Θεσσαλονίκη 1952, σ. 526.

7. Για την αρχή αυτή βλ. Ν. Πανταζοπούλου, *Ρωμαϊκόν Δίκαιον εν διαλεκτική συναρτήσει προς το Ελληνικόν*, τχ. γʼ, Θεσσαλονίκη 1979, σ. 207, 232 επ.

8. Βλ. Απ. Βακαλοπούλου, *Ιστορία της Μακεδονίας, 1354-1833*, Θεσσαλονίκη 1969, σ. 39.

9. Βλ. Απ. Βακαλοπούλου, ό.π., σ. 69.

10. Βλ. Ι. Βασδραβέλλη, ό.π., τ. αʼ, σ. 2-5

11. Βλ. Κ. Μέρτζιου, *Μνημεία Μακεδονικής Ιστορίας*, Θεσσαλονίκη 1947, σ. 312.

12. Βλ. Π. Παπαγεωργίου, *Αι Σέρραι και τα προάστεια, τα περί τας Σέρρας και η Μονή Ιωάννου του Προδρόμου*, Θεσσαλονίκη (φωτομηχ. ανατ. από την *Byzantinische Zeitschrift* 3 [1898]) 1988, (εισαγ. Χ. Μπακιρτζή), σ. 56.

13. Βλ. Π. Παπαγεωργίου, ό.π., σ. 57.

14. Βλ. Π. Παπαγεωργίου, ό.π., σ. 58.

15. Βλ. Π. Παπαγεωργίου, ό.π., σ. 17.

16. Βλ. Β. Δημητριάδη, *Η Κεντρική και Δυτική Μακεδονία κατά τον Εβλιγιά Τσελεμπή*, Θεσσαλονίκη 1974, σ. 290.

17. Βλ. Απ. Βακαλοπούλου, ό.π., σ. 240-241.

18. Βλ. Ιωακείμ Μαρτινιανού, *Η Μοσχόπολις, 1330-1930*, Θεσσαλονίκη 1957, σ. 150-151.

19. Βλ. Κ. Μέρτζιου, ό.π., σ. 336-337.

20. Βλ. Γ. Τσάρα, «Εκλογές για μουχταροδημογεροντία στο Μπλάτσι της Κοζάνης (1888)», *Μακεδονικά*, 14 (1974) 50-54.

21. Βλ. Απ. Βακαλοπούλου, ό.π., σ. 38-39.

22. Βλ. Ν. Πανταζοπούλου - συνεργασία Δέσποινας Τσούρκα-Παπαστάθη, *Κώδιξ Μητροπόλεως Σισανίου και Σιατίστης, ιζʼ-ιθʼ αι.*, Θεσσαλονίκη 1974, passim.

23. Βλ. Ι. Snegarov, *Istorija na Ohridskata Arhiepiskopija - Patriarsija,*

(II), Sofija 1932, σ. 420-421. Για τις εγγραφές του «Κώδικα του Α-γίου Κλήμεντος», που σωζόταν στην Αχρίδα, βλ. Σ. Βαρναλίδου, *Ο Αρχιεπίσκοπος Αχρίδος Ζωσιμάς (1686-1746) και η εκκλησιαστική και πολιτική δράσις αυτού*, Θεσσαλονίκη 1974, σ. 177-181.

24. Οι περισσότεροι κώδικες της Καστοριάς απόκεινται στην Εθνική Βιβλιοθήκη. Έκδοσή τους ετοιμάζει ο καθηγητής Ν. Πανταζό-πουλος.

25. Βλ. Ιωακείμ Μαρτινιανού, *ό.π.*, σ. 151.

26. Βλ. Ν. Πανταζοπούλου - συνεργασία Δέσποινας Τσούρκα-Πα-παστάθη, *ό.π.*, σ. 141-142.

27. Ο «εις λέξιν απλήν» Νομοκάνονας του Μανουήλ Μαλαξού εκδόθηκε από τους Δ. Γκίνη-Ν. Πανταζόπουλο, *Νόμος* 1 (1982), Θεσσαλονίκη (Επιστ. Επετ. Τμ. Νομ. Σχ. ΝΟΕ ΑΠΘ) 1985. Το αρχικό σε λόγια γλώσσα κείμενο δεν έχει ακόμη εκδοθεί ολόκληρο, βλ. Αναστασίας Σιφωνιού-Καράπα - Μ. Τουρτόγλου - Σπ. Τρωιά-νου, Μανουήλ Μαλαξού Νομοκάνων, «Επετ. Κέντρου Ερεύνης Ιστ. Ελλ. Δικ. (Ακαδημίας Αθηνών)» 16-17 (1969-1970), Αθήναι 1972, σ. 1-39.

28. Βλ. την έκδοσή του από τους Γ. Ράλλη - Μ. Ποτλή, *Σύνταγμα των Θείων και Ιερών Κανόνων*, τ. στ΄, Αθήναι 1859, σ. α΄-ι΄ και 1-518.

29. Βλ. την έκδοση και εισαγωγή του Κ. Πιτσάκη, *Κωνσταντίνου Αρμενοπούλου, Πρόχειρον Νόμων ή Εξάβιβλος*, Αθήναι 1971.

30. Βλ. Κ. Ε. Zacharia's, *Reise in den Orient*, Heidelberg (φωτομηχ. ανατ. Löwenklau, Frankfurt a. M., 1985) 1840, σ. 205.

31. Βλ. Δ. Γκίνη, *Περίγραμμα Ιστορίας του Μεταβυζαντινού Δικαίου*, Αθήναι 1966, σ. 247.

32. Βλ. Δ. Γκίνη, *ό.π.*, σ. 248.

33. Βλ. την έκδοσή του από τον Δ. Γκίνη, *Νομικόν ... Θεοφίλου του εξ Ιωαννίνων* (1788), Θεσσαλονίκη (Παράρτ. Επιστ. Επετ. Σχ. ΝΟΕ ΑΠΘ) 1960.

34. Βλ. Κ. Ε. Zacharia's, *ό.π.*, σ. 205.

35. Βλ. Δ. Γκίνη, *Νομικόν, ό.π.*, σ. κβ΄-κγ΄.

36. Βλ. την έκδοση του Μ. Γεδεών, *Κανονικαί Διατάξεις*, τ. α΄-β΄, Κωνσταντινούπολις 1888-1889.

37. Βλ. την υπό εκτύπωση έκδοσή τους από τον Χ. Παπαστάθη, «Βεβαιωτήρια έγγραφα του Καμπανίας Θεοφίλου επί ιδιωτικών διαφορών», *Τιμητικός Τόμος Κ. Βαβούσκου*, τ. γ΄, Θεσσαλονίκη *(ΕΜΣ - Δικ. Σύλλ. Θεσσ.)* 1991.

38. Όπως ήταν η εγκύκλιος περί τοπικών θεσμών σε γάμους, αρραβώνες κ.ά. του μητροπολίτη Σερβίων και Κοζάνης Θεοφίλου (1796), βλ. Μ. Καλινδέρη, *Τα λυτά έγγραφα, ό.π.*, σ. 93-97, και ο *Κανονισμός των αρραβώνων στη Σιάτιστα* (1867), βλ. Κ. Οικονόμου, «Γαμήλια έθιμα εν Σιατίστη», *Μακεδονικά* 1 (1940) 274. Γενικότερα για πατριαρχικές διατάξεις σε θέματα σύναψης γάμου βλ. Ελένης Κύρτση-Νάκου, «Αι περί προικοδοσιών «νομοθετικαί» ρυθμίσεις των Κανονικών Διατάξεων του Οικουμενικού Πατριαρχείου, (1701-1844)», *Αρμενόπουλος. Επιστ. Επετ. Δικ. Συλλ. Θεσσ.* 1 (1980) 55-78.

39. Ο Βενετός πρόξενος Θεσσαλονίκης αναφέρει ότι τον Αύγουστο 1753 αναγνώσθηκε σε όλους τους ναούς διαταγή του μητροπολίτη, με την οποία απαγόρευε στους Έλληνες και τις οικογένειές τους να ντύνονται με γούνες, μεταξωτά υφάσματα, κεντητές ζώνες και άλλα είδη στολισμού. Τους παραβάτες των εντολών του τους επαπειλούσε με αποκλεισμό από τη λειτουργία, τον ασπασμό του Ευαγγελίου, τη λήψη αντιδώρου και την εξομολόγηση· έφτανε μέχρι αυτή την επιβολή αφορισμού, βλ. Κ. Μέρτζιου, *ό.π.*, σ. 362-364.

40. Βλ. εγκυκλίους του μητροπολίτη Σερβίων και Κοζάνης Θεοφίλου (1789, 29.8.1803 και 24.10.1803) κατά του στολισμού των γυναικών, στον Μ. Καλινδέρη, *Τα λυτά έγγραφα, ό.π.*, σ. 90-93, 97-98 και 99-102 αντίστοιχα.

41. Εκδόθηκε από τον Δ. Γκίνη, *Περίγραμμα, ό.π.*, σ. 358-360.

42. Το 1636 ο Βενετός πρόξενος Θεσσαλονίκης αναφέρει ότι ο σουλτάνος απαγόρευσε σε όλες τις χριστιανές («φράγκισσες, Ελληνίδες, Αρμένισσες») και τις Εβραίες να φορούν σκούφιες, βλ. Κ. Μέρτζιου, *ό.π.*, σ. 184. Στα 1703, δημοσιεύθηκε διάταγμα που απαγόρευε στους Έλληνες, Αρμενίους και Ισραηλίτες να φορούν χρωματιστά ενδύματα, κίτρινα παπούτσια και γούνες, βλ. Κ. Μέρτζιου, *ό.π.*, σ. 188.

43. Βλ. Ν. Πανταζοπούλου, *Κεπήνιο, Αφιέρωμα στον Αλέξανδρο Γ. Λιτζερόπουλο*, Αθήνα 1985, σ. 205-235.

44. Βλ. Ι. Βασδραβέλλη, *ό.π.*, τ. β΄, σ. 2-3.

45. Βλ. Ν. Πανταζοπούλου, *Κεπήνιο, ό.π.*, σ. 219-220, με σχετικά στοιχεία των αρχών του 16ου αι. από τους κώδικες Καστοριάς.

46. Βλ. Ν. Πανταζοπούλου, *Κεπήνιον, ό.π.*, σ. 222, με πληροφορίες των μέσων του 16ου αι. από τους ίδιους κώδικες.

47. Βλ. Ι. Βασδραβέλλη, *ό.π.*, τ. β΄, σ. 336.

48. Βλ. *Turski Dokumenti za Makedonskata Istorija, 1827-1839*, Skopje 1958, αριθμ. 101/64.

49. Οι ελληνικές κομπανίες της Κ. Ευρώπης απαρτίζονταν κυρίως από Μακεδόνες εμπόρους, βλ. Olga Cicanci, *Companiile Grecesti din Transilvania si comeptul european in anii 1636-1746*, Bucuresti 1981, και το υπό δημοσίευση βιβλίο της Δέσποινας Τσούρκα-Παπαστάθη, *Η Ελληνική εμπορική κομπανία του Σιμπίου Τρανσυλβανίας*.

50. Βλ. Ι. Βασδραβέλλη, *ό.π.*, τ. α΄, σ. 214.

51. Βλ. Απ. Βακαλοπούλου, *ό.π.*, σ. 505-513.

52. Βλ. τα σχετικά φιρμάνια των ετών 1705, 1762 και 1820 στον Ι. Βασδραβέλλη, *ό.π., τ.α.΄*, σ. 51-52, 202-203 και 428-430 αντίστοιχα.

53. Βλ. Ιωακείμ Μαρτινιανού, *ό.π.*, σ. 151.

54. Βλ. Ι. Βασδραβέλλη, *ό.π.*, τ.α., σ. 214.

55. Βλ. Σ. Σαλαμάγκα, «Τα ισνάφια και τα επαγγέλματα επί της τουρκοκρατίας», *Ηπειρωτική Εστία* 8 (1959) 565-566.

56. Βλ. V. Papacostea, «Despre corporatiile moscopolene», *Revista Istorica Romana* 9 (1939) 13.

57. Βλ. Κ. Γουναροπούλου, «Κοζανικά», *Πανδώρα* 22 (1872) 492.

58. Βλ. Μ. Καλινδέρη, *Αι συντεχνίαι της Κοζάνης*, Θεσσαλονίκη 1958, σ. 27-30.

59. Βλ. Μ. Καλινδέρη, *Αι συντεχνίαι, ό.π.*, σ. 35-37.

60. Κατά την άποψη της Ελένης Βουραζέλη-Μαρινάκου, *Αι εν Θράκη συντεχνίαι των Ελλήνων*, Θεσσαλονίκη 1950, σ. 93.

61. Βλ. Χρ. Γουγούση, «Ιστορία του συντάγματος (ισνάφι, συντεχνία, σωματείον) των ιερέων Θεσσαλονίκης», *Γρηγόριος ο Παλαμάς* 10 (1926) 278-293.

62. Βλ. Μ. Καλινδέρη, *Τα λυτά έγγραφα, ό.π.*, σ. 49-51.

63. Βλ. Δέσποινα Τσούρκα-Παπαστάθη, «Μια δικαστική διαφορά στο Μοναστήρι (Βιτώλια) και οι ελληνικές συντεχνίες», *Ελιμειακά* 6-7 (1983) 287-294.

64. Βλ. Π. Πέννα, *Το Κοινόν Μελενίκου και το σύστημα διοικήσεώς του*, Αθήναι 1946, σ. 23-46 αναδημοσιεύεται η δυσεύρετη έκδοση του *Συστήματος ή Διαταγών*, Βιέννη 1813.

65. Βλ. Π. Πέννα, *ό.π.*, σ. 19.

66. Για την περίοδο αυτή βλ. ενδεικτικά τα έργα των: E. Engelhardt, *La Turquie et le Tanzimat ou Histoire des Réformes dans l' empire Ottoman depuis 1826 jusqu'à nos jours*, vol. I-II, Paris 1882-1884· B. Lewis, *The Emergence of Modern Turkey*, Oxford (University Press) ²1969, σ. 74 κ. έ.· A. Schopof, *Les Réformes et la Protection des Chrétiens en Turquie, 1673-1904*, Paris 1904· G. Young, *Corps de Droit Ottoman*, vol. I-VII, Oxford 1905-1906· Δ. Νικολαΐδου, *Οθωμανικοί κώδικες*, τ. α΄-δ΄, Κωνσταντινούπολις ²1889-1891· C. Papadopoulos, *ό.π.*, passim.

67. Βλ. Δ. Νικολαΐδου, *ό.π.*, τ. γ΄, σ. 2849-2854.

The Greek Orthodox Church in Macedonia Under Ottoman Rule

Andreas Nanakis

Organization of the Orthodox Church in Macedonia

The administrative organization of the Greek Orthodox Church in Macedonia did not change considerably with the transition from the Byzantine period to that of Ottoman rule. Its administrative division into dioceses, archbishoprics and bishoprics, as well as the function of Patriarchal monasteries –the direct jurisdiction of the Ecumenical Patriarchate– were substantially preserved throughout Ottoman rule, with the exception of rather inevitable changes, such as the merging of bishoprics, or the change in the status of monasteries.

Thessaloniki remained, of course, the most important religious centre of Macedonia. By the end of the Byzantine period, its prelate had risen from eleventh to eigth place in the list of order of the Ecumenical Throne. According to the metropolitan system of administration, he had six to eight bishoprics within his jurisdiction.[1] Their number varied: a late 15th century *taktikon* (ordinal) mentions the following ten: Kitros (first in order), Kassandreia, Servia, Kampania or Kastron, Petra, Herkoulia or Ardamerion, Ierissos and Mount Athos, Liti and Rentina, Polyani and Vardariotes, and Platamon and Lykostomion.[2] However, a 15th century codex lists twelve of them: Kitros or Pydna, Verria, Koudrovitia, Kassandreia or Potidaia, Kampania or Kastron, Petra, Herkoulia or Ardamerion, Ierissos or Mount Athos, Liti, Vardariotes or of the Turks, Lykostomion or Thessalian Tempi, and Platamon.[3] Another 16th century ordinal mentions the same bishoprics with the addition of that of Servia.[4]

However, neither the number nor the order of these bishoprics remained unchanged. Thus, the bishoprics of Verria and Kassandreia were promoted to dioceses under a Metropolitan and became independent of the See of Thessaloniki. The bishoprics of Liti and Dragouvition merged into the bishoprics of Verria, Kampania and Polyani. The bishopric of Vardariotes merged with Polyani in the 'Diocese of Polyani and Vardariotes' with Doirani as its seat.[5]

From 1880 onwards, due to boundary changes between Greece and Turkey, the bishopric of Platamon was split and abolished, with the part still in Turkish territory going to the bishopric of Petra, the remainder merging into the bishopric of Larissa.[6] In 1896 the bishopric of Petra followed suit and merged into the diocese of Elasson and the bishopric of Kitros.[7]

At an earlier stage, there had been other important modifications. Between 1584 and 1588, the bishopric of Servia was temporarily attached to the archbishopric of Achris. Due to the extensive islamization of the local population, on Bishop Meletios' initiative the seat of the same bishopric was transferred in 1745 to Kozani, where it still remains.[8] On 10 June 1882, one month after the Patriarchal edict which ceded the provinces of Thessaly to the Church of Greece, the bishopric of Servia and Kozani was separated from Thessaloniki and was raised to the rank of diocese, with Eugenios as its first Metropolitan (1882-1889).[9] Therefore, at the turn of the 20th century, only five bishoprics remained under the metropolitan of Thessaloniki: Kitros, Polyani, Kampania, Ardamerion, and Ierissos and Mount Athos.[10]

The metropolitan of Thessaloniki and the bishops under him constituted the diocesan or episcopal Synod of Thessaloniki, chaired by the bishop of Kitros. This synod held two regular sessions a year, during the third week of Lent and in October right after St Demetrius' Day.[11]

The Cathedral of Ochrida, St Sophia, built in the 11th century

The Archbishopric of Achris

Achris (Ohrid), the most important city of Northwestern Macedonia in Byzantine times, had been the seat of an archbishopric. It seems probable that, after the dissolution of the Serbian state and the Ottoman conquest of Bosnia in 1463, its ambitious archbishops annexed it to the archbishopric of Ipek (Peć). By late 15th - early 16th century, the archbishopric included thirty-two bishoprics, of which twelve were in Macedonia, namely the bishoprics of Grevena, Kastoria, Sisanion and Siatista, Stromnitsa, Moglena, Monastir (Bitola), Kičevo, Dibra (Debar), Polozka, Skopia (Skopje), Kratovo, Kyustendil, and Prespes. In 1538, the archbishop of Achris temporarily annexed the bishopric of Verria.[12]

The archbishoprics of Achris and Ipek remained active until 1767, when they were suppressed by Ecumenical Patriarch Samuel I. Until then, the archbishopric of Achris was autonomous, although, from 1676 onwards, the Patriarchate repeatedly intervened in its internal affairs. After its abolition, its bishoprics were gradually promoted to dioceses.[13]

Towards the end of the 18th century and early 19th, there were the following dioceses in Macedonia: the archbishoprics of Kassandreia and Achridae, the dioceses of Thessaloniki, Kastoria, Pelagonia and Prilapos (Prilep), Vitolia (Monastir), Edessa (Vodena), Karisia (Korytsa) and Selasphoron, Tiveriopolis and Stromnitsa, Velegrades and Konitsa (Kanina), Grevena, Serres, Philippi and Drama, and Melenikon; and the bishoprics of Kitros, Kampania and Panion, Platamon-Lykostomion, Servia and Kozani, Polyani and Vardariotes, Petra, Adramerion, Ierissos and Mount Athos, Sisanion and Siatista, Moglena, Molossaioi, Prespes, Dibra, Zava, Chora (probably Gora) and Makris (Mokras).[14]

The **Katholikon** *of the Vlatades Monastery.*

Monasteries

During the gradual conquest of Macedonia by the Ottomans, the monasteries, particularly those that resisted the conquerors (as, for instance, the monastery of St John the Baptist near Serres) suffered much pillaging and destruction. Thus, of the many monasteries known in the late Byzantine period, only few survived. Most of those which flourished later, were built during the first years of Ottoman domination.

Among the monasteries of Ottoman-ruled Macedonia the following are worth-mentioning:

a) The Vlatades Monastery, founded in the 14th century, was exceptionally well treated by the Ottoman conquerors. In 1446 Mehmed II himself issued the first in a series of imperial decrees (*firman*) which sanctioned the privileges of the monastery. The legend of the contribution of its monks to the fall of Thessaloniki as an explanation to its privileged status has been referred to elsewhere. The early centuries of Turkish rule were a period of great prosperity for the monastery, primarily due to its extensive property (*metochia*) in the region of Thessaloniki. From 1527 onwards the monastery became known as Çaus-monastery. In 1633, a decree of Patriarch Cyril Loukaris temporarily annexed it to the Iviron Monastery of Mount Athos, a sign of relative decline. At that time, the churches of St Nicholas Orphanos and St Athanasius are mentioned as dependencies of the Vlatades in the city of Thessaloniki. These temples were donated to the monastery by the metropolitan of Verria Theophanis Mallakis. The convent of Zoodochos Pigi of Thessaloniki, known as Lagoudiatos, was also within its jurisdiction.[15]

b) The monastery of St Anastasia at Galatista, Chalcidice, had been erected by Empress Theophano in the 10th century and was rebuilt by St Theonas, metropolitan of Thessaloniki, in 1522. In 1789 the monastery was destroyed by fire. In 1821 it suffered extensive damage as a result of Turkish reprisals for its contribution to the insurgency in Chalcidice. However, thanks to its wealth, the monastery played an

The Church of St Nicholas Orphanos.

important role throughout the Ottoman period.[16]

c) The monastery of Eikosiphoinissa which lies at the foot of mount Pagaion. Its grandeur during the Ottoman period was based on extensive property and large numbers of monks, estimated at 150 in 1632. Its eminence is evidenced by the title of *Protosyngelos* held by its abbot. To this monastery Ecumenical Patriarch Dionysius I retreated after his abdication in 1439; there, on account of his generosity, he was proclaimed second founder of the monastery.[17] In 1632, the Cypriot abbot Theoliptos toured Western Europe, where, in addition to his fund-raising mission, he sounded Christian rulers, the duke of Savoy in particular, regarding an initiative against the Ottomans in Cyprus.[18]

d) The monastery of *Hosios* Dionysios of Olympus, founded in the name of Agia Trias (Holy Trinity) in the 15th century, was reconstituted by Dionysios, a monk of the Philotheou Monastery of Mount Athos a century later. Dionysios turned the monastery into a spiritual centre of the area. According to a folk tale,

he was denounced by local villagers to the Ottoman authorities for allegedly having built the monastery without permit, which then might turn into a hide-out for local brigands (*klephts*). According to Apostolos Vacalopoulos, as the monastery is located in such a wild and remote area, the story may contain an element of truth.[19]

e) The monastery of Zavorda in the region of Grevena, built by the Thessalonian *Hosios* Nikanor. It was dedicated to the Transfiguration of Our Saviour and was renowned thanks to the personality of its founder as well as a centre of letters. Until 1767 it depended on the archbishopric of Achris.[20]

g) The monastery of St John the Baptist of Verria also became an important centre of monastic life. Several important figures of the monastic order lived there, including *Hosios* Dionysios, *Hosios* Nikanor, *Hosios* Antonios, founder of the hermitage named after him, and the Docheiarian monk Theophanis of Ioannina, founder of the Asomaton monastery near Naoussa.[21]

The monasteries of Macedonia belonged either to the jurisdiction of the local bishop or to that of the Ecoumenical Patriarchate, as it was the case of St Anastasia in Chalcidice and *Hosios* Dionysios in Olympus. But their status was not immutable. Depending on the circumstances, a patriarchal decree could convert a monastery to episcopal and *vice versa*.

Major Ecclesiastic Figures of Ottoman-dominated Macedonia In spite of the decline of education and the generally adverse conditions of the Ottoman period, a number of eminent personalities created a considerable tradition in the religious and literary life of Christian Orthodox Macedonia; among them, *Hosios* Nikanor, Dionysios, Antonios, the Thessalonian Niphon, Patriarch of Constantinople, the scholarly Theonas, metropolitan of Thessaloniki, Damaskinos Stouditis, Bishop of Liti and Rentina, the Cretan Athanasios Pattelaros, metropolitan of Thessaloniki and later Ecoumenical Patriarch, and Josiph, metropolitan of Thessaloniki, from Drama.

Hosios Dionysios of Olympus was born in Thessaly. He spent some time in Meteora before moving to Mount Athos. While serving as abbot of the Philotheou Monastery, he was expelled by Bulgarian monks and took refuge to Verria and then to Jerusalem. He declined an appointment to the vacant bishopric of Verria, prefering monastic life on Mt Olympus, where he founded the monastery of the Holy Trinity. He also founded the monastery of Sourvia at Makrynitsa. He died in the monastery that bears his name, at Olympus.[22]

Hosios Antonios the Young, was born in Verria. As a monk, he lived first at the prosperous monastery of Peraia and then he went into retreat in a cave where he spent fifty years in self-denial and pray. He died alone and his holy relic was brought to Verria where a church was built in his memory. Later, in the cave where he died the *skete* of the Baptist was built.[23]

St Niphon of Thessaloniki, who rose to the Ecumenical Throne three times (1486-1489, 1497-1498, 1502), together with monk Zacharias of Mount Athos, first settled at the monastery of Theotokos in Achris. After Zacharias was elected archbishop of Achris, Niphon went to the Dionysiou Monastery on Mount Athos. While he was still there, he was elected archbishop of Thessaloniki and, later, Ecumenical Patriarch. He died at Dionysiou and was canonized for his holiness, piety and spiritual activity.[24]

St Theonas, archbishop of Thessaloniki, was born in mid-15th century. As a novice he had been near neomartyr Iakovos Iviroskitiotis. He spent his years of ascetism at the Iviron *skete* on Mount Athos and later at the Simonow Petras Monastery, where he stayed for two years. Then he went to Galatista of Chalcidice, where he rebuilt the ruined monastery of St Anastasia and became its abbot. Later he was ordained bishop of Paronaxia, he was appointed Patriarchal Exarch, and, finally, he was elected archbishop of Thessaloniki. Theonas, whose virtues as a righteous and scholarly figure had been widely praised, was canonized *post mortem*.[25]

Damaskinos Studitis, bishop of Liti and Rentina, was born in early 16th century in Thessaloniki. He studied at his native city and later went to Constantinople where he was a student of the eminent scholar Theophanis Eleavoulkos. He was tonsured as Damaskinos and he preached in various churches as subdeacon. His literary work *Thesaurus* was the product of his preachings and patrological studies. In 1558 he was ordained priest and a little later he became bishop of Liti and Rentina, where he stayed until 1574. In 1565 he appeares as a member of the Synod which deposed Patriarch Ioasaph. He served as chairman of Polyani and also of Dominikon and Elasson. He was sent by Patriarch Mitrophanis III as Exarch to Russia, and was appointed deputy archbishop of Constantinople by Jeremiah II Tranos (1572-1579), who had been his pupil, at the time of the latter's tour of the Peloponnese (October 1573- July 1574). An erudite man, versed in both ancient and demotic Greek, a prolific writer of both religious books and treatises, he is regarded as one of the foremost intellectual men of his time. He died in 1577.[26]

Athanasios Pattellaros, Ecumenical Patriarch, was born in Rethymnon, Crete. He first took the monastic vows on Mt Sinai and later stayed for a while on Mount Athos. Athanasios was a man of broad education, both Classic and Christian, fluent in Latin, Italian and Arabic, with a deep knowledge of the Holy Scriptures. In 1631 he was elected archbishop of Thessaloniki and three years later he succeeded Cyril Loukaris to the Ecumenical Throne. He was suspended and reappointed in 1652. Athanasios died in Russia, in April 1654.[27]

Josiph Daliviris, metropolitan of Thessaloniki, was born in Dimitsana. M. Gedeon described him as

The St Anastasia Monastery at Galatista, Chalcidice. It was rebuilt by St Theonas, Metropolitan of Thessaloniki, in the 16th century.

"a worthy, educated and art-loving cleric". He displayed much ecclesiastical and spiritual activity. In 1821 he fell victim to Turkish reprisals following the outbreak of the Greek Revolution: he martyred at Neochori of Constantinople.[28]

These religious personalities excelled as prelates, abbots or simply monks. They turned their places of activity into centres of letters and spiritual influence, nurseries of intellectual revival during the difficult years of Ottoman rule. Their preachings, their general activity and example bolstered Christian Orthodox faith and helped check the tide of islamization which threatened the Christian population of Macedonia, particularly during the 17th and the first half of the 18th century. In addition to the afore-mentioned personalities, other eminent men of the Church had been active in Macedonia: Theophanis Eleavoulkos and Athanasios Parios, later Patriarch of Alexandria,

Gerasimos Palladas the Cretan in Kastoria, and Kosmas Aitolos, who travelled through Central and Western Macedonia founding schools and bolstering morally and spiritually the enslaved population.

Islamization in Macedonia

Islamization was not only the result of official policy but also - and foremost - the product of the desperation of the oppressed Christian population. Mass islamization was pursued during the reign of sultans Selim I (1512 -1520), Selim II (1566-1574) and Murad III (1574-1595). The phenomenon intensified from late 16th to late 18th century due to maladministration, the ruthless exploitation of the enslaved Christians by uncontrollable local beys and pashas, the virtual state of anarchy, heavy taxation and economic hardship. Conversely, prospects for personal advance held out to would-be renegades induced many Christians to renounce their faith in order to avoid the evils of servitude.

Conditions in Macedonia deteriorated during the Russo-Turkish War of 1768-1774 and the ensuing period of Albanian raids. Islamization particularly spread in Northwestern Macedonia and Southern Albania, although converts often preserved some elements of their ancestral faith as 'Cryptochristians'. One of the most interesting examples of religious syncretism was the case of the *Valaades* of the region of Anaselitsa in Western Macedonia. Despite their islamization in late 17th century, this group retained many elements of Christian faith, such as their belief in the miraculous qualities of Saints and the worship of the Holy Virgin, as well as cordial relations with their Christian fellow-countrymen.[29]

Another striking example of islamization in Northern Greece was the case of the Vlach-speaking community of Notia, in Central Macedonia. Founded in early 18th century, the village survived as a Christian enclave until it was finally converted in 1779. The reasons were similar, albeit more acute, to those that had compelled parts of the Christian population elsewhere in Macedonia. In the case of Notia conversion was encouraged by the local prelate himself. Yet, until the day of the Greek-Turkish exchange of populations, the community preserved a gospel in which their anscestors had recorded their apostasy. According to a legend, the apostate metropolitan of Moglena, Ioannis, changed his name to Ali and served as kadi at Larissa. One day, however, he went to the crowded mosque of Turahan, by the Pinios bridge, stood on the pulpit, made the sign of the cross and started reading a passage from the gospel provoking the fury of the crowd and, ultimately, his own violent death.[30]

The afore-mentioned episodes and other, such as that of Lialovo in Eastern Macedonia, are characteristic cases of mass-islamization. Yet individual conversions were a more frequent phenomenon throughout the Ottoman period. The Orthodox Church strived with every means available to curb the apostasies, which occasionally threatened to reduce its flock dramatically. Enlightened clerics and scholars undertook to stimulate the religious sentiments of the, largely uneducated, population through preaching and teaching. Kosmas Aitolos' tireless

touring of Western Macedonia is a typical example of this missionary campaign.[31]

Neomartyrs in Macedonia

Neomartyrs were the symbols of the spirit of resistance against islamization and Ottoman oppression. Martyrdom represents the struggle of many Greek Orthodox who stubbornly stood by their ancestral faith. Their self-sacrifice was a sort of a passive resistance to the conqueror, which, however, often had an immense impact on people's morale. As Nikodimos of Mount Athos put it, "these novel martyrs reinforce, invigorate and revive the waning, withering faith of the Christians of today." Their number in Macedonia is especially high, perhaps owing to the proximity of the holy community of Mount Athos.[32] The following list gives, in alphabetical order, the names of some martyrs who either were martyred in or came from Macedonia:

Avvakoum (1628). According to Codex 89 of Lavra, "on the 6th of August 1628, the neomartyr *Hosios* Avvakoum was martyred at the capital, Thessaloniki, to the glory and pride of Orthodox Christians".[33]

Akakios, *Hosiomartyr* (1816). Born Athanasios at Neochori, near Thessaloniki, he moved to Serres with his family and from there to Mount Athos where he was tonsured. He was beheaded on the 1st of May in Constantinople.[34]

Athanasios Koulakiotis (1774). Born at Koulakia of Verria, he attended the Greek school of Thessaloniki near Athanasios Parios, and then the Athonite Academy before moving to Constantinople. He came back to his native land and died a martyr's death outside Thessaloniki.[35]

Aquilina (1764). Born at Zagliveri, the daughter of a renegade. When her father attempted to convert her too, she refused, and so, according to the legend, she was put to death by the Turks.[36]

Alexander (1794). Born in Thessaloniki, at the parish of Panagia Laodigitria. He went to Smyrna where he was converted and joined the dervishes order. Eighteen years later he recanted and was subsequently martyred (26 May 1794).[37]

Anastasios (1794). Born at Radovitsi, near Stromnitsa, he came to Thessaloniki where he trained as a gunsmith. Pressed to renegade he refused and was tortured to death on 8 August.[38]

Argyros (1806). A taylor from Epanomi. At the age of 18 he was hanged at the *kapani* market on 11 March, because he refused to be circumcized.[39]

Ioannis, the dwarf (1802). Born in Thessaloniki, he moved to Smyrna with his father where they worked as shoemakers. He was beheaded at the Soan Bazaar of that city on 24 May.[40]

Ioannis the tailor (1652). Originally from Thasos, he worked in Constantinople. He was slayed for his refusal to become an apostate.[41]

Kyranna (1751). Born at Vissoka (Ossa) near Thessaloniki. A janissary tax-farmer attempted to islamize and then marry her, but she refused and was put to death.[42]

Hosiomartyr Kyrillos. Born in Thessaloniki in 1544, he dwelled at the quarter of Acropolis. At the age of 14 he went to the monastery of Hilandari, on Mount Athos, where he was tonsured. He came back to Thessaloniki where, after refusing islamization, he was put to death in front of the church of Sts Constantine and Helen on 6 July 1566.[43]

Hosiomartyr Makarios (1527). A student to Patriarch Niphon, he spent his monastic life at the monastery of Vatopedi on Mount Athos. He was beheaded in Thessaloniki and his memory is honoured on 14 September.[44]

Michael (1544). Born in Agrapha of Eurytania, he came to Thessaloniki after his marriage and worked in a bakery. He was a regular attendant at the preachings of Archbishop Mitrophanis, who recounted his life and martyrdom. He refused to be islamized and the Turks burned him alive in front of Church of the Purification.[45]

Christodoulos (1777). Born at Valta of Kassandra, he came to Thessaloniki to work as a taylor. He was hanged in front of the Church of St Minas on 28 July. The Christians bought his body and buried it with honours.[46]

Chrysi (1795). Born at Slatena of Moglena, she was tortured to death.[47]

Worship and Centres of Worship

Christian Orthodox practice, including the observance of feast and rites, was nominally free under the Ottomans. However, in practice, apart from the fact that many churches had been either destroyed or

Acheropoietus: the first church of Thessaloniki to be converted into a mosque by the Ottoman conquerors.

turned into mosques, various obstacles and restrictions curtailed the religious rights of the Empire's Christian subjects.

According to Ioannis Anagnostis, after the fall of Thessaloniki, Sultan Murad appropriated all Christian temples, and only after long and persistent efforts Metropolitan Grigorios managed to persuade him to release four churches: "He left us only these four churches, the ones called catholic, after our Shepherd's strenuous endeavours. All the rest of the houses and temples he gave away".[48] Murad distributed the best monasteries to his officers who turned them into residences. Ottoman domination in Thessaloniki began with further damage of Christian sanctuaries: the sultan had their marbles removed and sent to Andrianople as material for paving the floor of the city's baths.

Unable to maintain the remaining temples the Church entrusted this task to private citizens. Already in July 1432, Archbishop Grigorios conceded the Church of St Paraskevi to a certain Odigitrinos and his two sons, Dimitrios and Ioannis. The Archbishop's description of the condition of the Church contained in the relevant document is revealing: "The holy and great temple of St Paraskevi has long been neglected and has now reached such pitiful condition, gradually descending into decay, with no holy hymns sang in it except on the Saint's Day alone, ... is entrusted to three persons ... who have to take charge of it from this very day, and to saw to it first that psalms are sang, candles are lit ... as well as to restore the building and to look after it and its holy water cistern too".[49]

During the second half of the 17th century, Thessaloniki had thirty churches, although the Basilica of St Demetrius, the 'Myhr-exuding' saint, had been turned into a mosque. Around 1733 their number was reduced to about twelve or thirteen. Another church of St Demetrius, which was located in the place of present-day Church of St Gregorius Palamas, probably served as cathedral. Other important churches of that period were St Athanasios, St Nicholas and St Minas.[50]

The memory of St Demetrius was still celebrated

Our Lady 'Koumbelidiki', a typical example of church architecture in Kastoria.

in Thessaloniki and all over Macedonia with due ceremony. All bishops within the jurisdiction of the Archbishop of Thessaloniki took part in the great

The church of St Athanasias, built in the early Ottoman period.

The church of St Demetrius. During the Ottoman period it was turned into a mosque along with many other Christian places of worship.

liturgy, and, the Prelate, who was actually the head of the community, delivered the traditional encomium to the Saint.[51]

Conditions in the other urban centres of Macedonia were similar to those in Thessaloniki. Servia, where the Ottomans respected all seven churches of the town, and Kastoria, where in the 17th century there existed seventy churches, were rather exceptional cases. Generally, there were restrictions on the building of new churches and the restoration of old ones, although they were not so strictly imposed as in the case of Crete, for instance. In fact, during periods of peaceful coexistence between Christians and Muslims, many churches were built and frescoed. That was the case particularly of prosperous centres such as Kastoria and Kozani, where the expansion of guilds and commercial advance allowed the communities to build numerous and magnificent churches.

Privileges and Obligations of the Ecclesiastical Hierarchy

Orthodox metropolitans were elected and ordained by the Ecumenical Patriarchate, while bishops were appointed by local episcopal synods, wherever, as in the See of Thessaloniki, they functioned. The procedure was concluded by imperial decree (*berat* or *firman*), which, validated the election and confirmed the prelate's prerogatives. A 1882 decree regarding the metropolitan of Verria outlines the status of Orthodox prelates. According to this document, bishops, priests, monks and nuns ought to submit to the local metropolitan's authority, who was entitled to punish, as well as to ordain or dethrone bishops. Excommunication was among his indisputable prerogatives. He was the single authority to settle matters of marriage or divorce affecting the Christian subjects of the Empire, according to canonic law, and to impose penalties in cases of invalid wedding. The metropolitan was free to exercise his authority in both religious and financial matters affecting the Church without undue pressure from the Ottoman authorities. Accusations brought against him by Muslim political or religious authority would be unacceptable until verified. The prelate also had the right to tour his diocese under official protection.[53]

A much older decree (1696), whereby Methodios, metropolitan of Thessaloniki was deposed and replaced by Ignatios, defined the rights of the new prelate as follows:

"I commanded that the afore-mentioned Ignatios takes charge of the Metropolis of Thessaloniki and the attached bishoprics in the place of Methodios, and all infidels within his diocese, living or deceased, shall recognize him as their metropolitan and resort to him for any matter related to the diocese and obey the words of God. When the afore-said metropolitan, according to their custom, discharges or appoints priests, monks and bishops, no one should interfere.

When any of the bishops, priests, monks or nuns dies and the metropolitan appropriates the estate of the deceased on behalf of the Patriarch, it should be unlawful for any treasury or property records official to interfere... No one should interfere in case the metropolitan punished priests or monks. Parish priests should not sanction weddings of infidels without the knowledge and approval of the afore-said prelate. Within the jurisdiction of the afore-said diocese, if a tithe payer, whether a woman or a man, divorces her or his spouse, no one but the metropolitan has the right to interfere. The afore-said cleric, according to the (infidels') customs, shall reap the benefits from all property, farms, vineyards, gardens, estates (*metohia*), pastures, fields, holy fountains, mills, and whatever objects and livestock are dedicated to the Church and shall manage them in the same way as his predecesors.

The former Metropolitan Methodios, or anyone else, should not annoy or disturb him. Thus, My holy symbol should be recognized and respected by all.

It was written on the 16th of Ramazan 1107 (20 April 1696) at the camp of Daout Pasha"[54]

Each prelate to have the decree of his appointment issued was obliged to pay to the Ottoman administration a fee. Moreover, he owed annuities both the Sublime Porte and the Patriarchate. In case of a delay or failure to meet these obligations, the Patriarch could have a *firman* issued and claim his tribute effectively. The following is a typical example of a *firman* issued in 1695 at the request of Patriarch Kallinikos, concerning metropolitans Methodios of Thessaloniki, Makarios of Verria, and the bishop of Petra whose annuities were overdue:

"When the present firman reaches you, let it be known that cleric Kallinikos, current patriarch of the infidels living in Constantinople and the *kazas* of the Empire, has submitted to the Porte of My Beatitude stating that the metropolitan of Thessaloniki Methodios, the metropolitan of Verria

Makarios and the bishop of Petra ... have not as yet appeared to renew their appointment, have not met their public dues, have delayed payment of many public taxes, and he begged me to notify them through My servant, Osman Haseki, and through the *kadis*, that they will not be permitted to hold their office while they fail to renew the *berats* and settle their accounts. A *firman* has been already issued to that effect. I have commanded that, upon the arrival of afore-mentioned Haseki bearing the present high *firman*, you should act accordingly, and for as long as the afore-mentioned metropolitans and bishops still owe public taxes, have not had their verats renewed, and refuse to pay public fees, they shall not be pemitted to hold their office.

Thus, you should recognize and respect My holy symbol.

It was written on the 4th of Jemazi ul Evel 1107 (11 December 1695) in Istanbul"[55]

The Contribution of the Orthodox Church in Education

As a result of Ottoman conquest, conditions in Macedonia were far from conducive to the development of education. Instruction of the most rudimentary character was available to boys only either near the churches or inside them. The teacher, usually the priest himself, taught writing and reading using ecclesiastical books, such as the *Horologion*, the *Octoechos* and the *Psalter*, as textbooks.[56]

In mid-16th century Thessaloniki, the deacon of the Ecumenical Church Dimitrios, the Athenian Georgios and the Cretan Mathaios are mentioned as teachers. The circular of Patriarch Jeremiah II Tranos in 1593 marks an important period in the history of education during the Ottoman period. Thereby, prelates were urged to found schools "so as the divine and holy letters may be taught, and to help those willing to teach and those wishing to learn". The close relationship between Church and education of the Byzantine period became even closer under Ottoman rule, with the Church setting up various teaching institutions. Father Synodinos from Serres recounts in his chronicles that in 1603 his father took him to Kaladendra, a village where father Dimos taught him his first letters; in 1619 he received further education from Father Parthenios at the local metropolis, includ-

The St John the Baptist Monastery, overlooking the Aliacmon river.

ing passages from Cato, Pythagoras, Aristophanes as well as the Canon of Christmas and Epiphany.[57]

One century later, in 1735, a better organized school was founded at Serres by the scholarly metropolitan Gabriel (1735-1745). Among the teachers who served there, Nektarios, later bishop of Litza and Agrapha, and Minas Minoidis, who taught philosophy and grammar from 1815 to 1819.[58]

Of paramount importance was the contribution of monasteries. The monastery of Zavorda, in the region of Grevena, was one of these centres of learning. It contained a voluminous library and contributed a great deal to the developement of education in Western Macedonia. Monasteries also supported financially young people who wished to study.

In fact, education progressed in regions where local prelates proved able, educated men of initiative, in addition to favourable economic conditions. Such had been the case of Achris, where its adroit and learned primates, most of them Phanariots, promoted a considerable cultural and theological movement, sisble in the amount of theological works, copies and original, produced at the local monastic communities.[59]

The Orthodox Church in the Macedonian Struggle

The turn of the 20th century found the Orthodox Church in Macedonia facing the grave consequences of nationalistic rivalries. Since the previous century,

Balkan peoples had entered the phase of growing ethnic awareness and irredentism. By the turn of the century, however, nationalistic antagonisms had become extremely acute leading to violent ethnic strife. Regarding Macedonia, the crisis broke out after the founding of the Bulgarian Exarchate (1870). By that means, Bulgarian nationalists purported to define as well as to expand their religious and national limits, at the expense, of course, of the Ecumenical Patriarchate.

The situation was more critical wherever the local population had not yet acquired a clearly-defined national consciousness, particularly in the predominantly slavophone regions. In those areas the collective identity of *Romiosini* had largely survived under Ottoman domination as it had developed during the Byzantine period. The simple peasants, who constituted the large majority of the population, by remaining in the jurisdiction of the Ecumenical Patriarchate distanced themselves from the Exarchate, which openly represented Bulgarian nationalism, and were regarded part of modern Hellenism, the natural heir to *Romiosini*. Conversely, the Exarchate's main target was to win over the Slav-speaking element, either peacefully or forcibly, and to press the Greek population into accepting its ecclesiastical domination.

Under the great Patriarch Joachim III (1901-1912) the Ecumenical Patriarchate, to which Macedonia belonged ecclesiastically, embarked upon a formidable struggle to contain Exarchist expansion. The struggle, waged in religious-ecclesiastical terms, aquired a crucial national dimension too, as the term 'Exarchist' soon became identical to 'Bulgarian' as 'Patriarchist' came to mean 'Greek'. Joachim took advantage of the deténte between Turkey and Greece

The St John the Baptist Monastery: the interior.

The Sts Anargyroi Monastery of Kastoria, a centre of the Macedonian Struggle.

following the latter's defeat in the 1897 war, and staffed the dioceses of Macedonia with young prelates whose Greek nationalist fervour matched their religious prowess.

Among these men, certain figures stand out, such as Ioakeim Phoropoulos, metropolitan of Melenikon (1901-1903) and Pelagonia (1903-1909),[62] Chrysostomos Kalaphatis of Drama (1902-1908),[63] Theodoritos of Nevrokopi (1903-1907),[64] Aimilianos of Grevena (1908-1911),[65] Germanos Karavangelis of Kastoria (1900-1907),[66] Grigorios Zervoudakis of Serres (1892-1909),[67] Grigorios of Stromnitsa (1902-1908),[68] and Alexander of Thessaloniki (1903-1910).[69] During the Macedonian Struggle, these prelates carried on the difficult task of preserving their flock's loyalty to the Patriarchate and encouraging the Greek national sentiment in the hearts of the simple Macedonian peasants. They had to face, particularly from 1906 onwards, the reaction of the Turkish authorities, which in the end demanded their recall, as they did with their principal associates, the Greek consuls. As a result, they were temporarily suspended, until some of them transferred their activity to Asia Minor, where the Greek element was in grave peril in face of the rising Turkish nationalism. Germanos Karavangelis worked to hearten his Greek flock in Pontus at the peak of the Young Turk fanaticism. The activity and tragic end of two other prelates, who had contributed to the national cause in Macedonia, Chrysostomos of Drama and, then, Smyrna, and Grigorios of Stromnitsa and, then, Kydonies, are well known.

ANDREAS NANAKIS
THE GREEK ORTHODOX CHURCH IN
MACEDONIA UNDER OTTOMAN RULE

NOTES

1. *Religious and Ethic Encyclopedia* (in Greek), henceforth *REE*), vol. 6, Athens 1965, p. 454.

2. Ap. Glavinas, 'The Bishopric of Liti and Retina' (in Greek), *Yearbook of the Faculty of Theology of the Univ. of Thessaloniki* (henceforth *Yearbook*, vol. 24 (1979), 338.

3. Glavinas, *op. cit.*, 337.

4. *Ibid.*, 343.

5. Ath. Angelopoulos, *The Church of Thessaloniki* (in Greek), Thessaloniki 1984, p. 77.

6. Angelopoulos, *op. cit.*, pp. 77-80.

7. *Ibid.*, p. 80.

8. Ap. Vacalopoulos, *History of Macedonia, 1354-1833* (in Greek), Thessaloniki 1969, p. 327.

9. Angelopoulos, *op. cit.*, p. 80.

10. *Ibid.*, p. 83.

11. A. Angelopoulos, *The Episcopal Synod of the Diocese of Thessaloniki* (in Greek), Athens 1977.

12. Vacalopoulos, *op. cit.*, p. 137.

13. *Ibid.*, p. 207.

14. *Ibid.*, p. 435.

15. G. Stoyoglou, *The Patriarchal Monastery of Vlatades in Thessaloniki* (in Greek), Thessaloniki 1971.

16. Glavinas, 'The Monastery of St Anastasia Pharmacolytria' (in Greek), *Yearbook*, vol. 26 (1983), appendix 33.

17. Glavinas, 'Notes on the Eikosiphoinissa Monastery', in *In Memoriam to Iakovos, Metropolitan of Konya* (in Greek), Athens 1984, pp. 97-115; by the same author, 'Unpublished Documents on the Eikosiphinissa' (in Greek), *Yearbook*, vol. 29 (1988); by the same author, 'A Circular of the Diocese of Thessaloniki in Recourse of the Eikosiphoinissa' (in Greek), *Makedonika*, vol. 21, Thessaloniki 1981, 351-372.

18. George Hill, *The History of Cyprus*, vol. 4, Cambridge 1952, pp. 56-57.

19. Glavinas, 'St Dionysios on Mount Olympus' (in Greek), *Yearbook*, vol. 26 (1981), appendix 30; by the same author, 'St Dionysios on Mount Olympus. An outline of his Life, Activity and Personality' (in Greek), *Yearbook*, vol. 27 (1982), 128-143. 'The Patriarchial Monastery of St Dionysios during the Second Half of the 18th Century' (in Greek), *Yearbook*, vol. 26 (1981), 173-201, *et. al.*.

20. *REE*, vol. 9, Athens 1966, l. 460.

21. Vacalopoulos, *op. cit.*, pp. 120-121.

22. Sophronios Eustratiadis, former metropolitan of Leontopolis, *Hagiology of the Orthodox Church*, Athens, undated, p. 116.

23. Eustratiadis, *op. cit.*, pp. 48-49

24. *Ibid.*, p. 350.

25. *REE*, vol. 6, Athens 1965, l. 502-503.

26. Glavinas, 'The Bishopric of Liti...', *op. cit.*, 341-342.

27. Glavinas, 'Metropolitans of Thessaloniki during the 17th century' (in Greek), *Yearbook*, vol. 22 (1977), 111-117.

28. T. Gritsopoulos, 'The National Martyr Joseph, Bishop of Thessaloniki' (in Greek), *Makedonika*, 4 (1955-1960), 470-494.

29. Vacalopoulos, *op. cit.*, pp. 317-329, whith further bibliography.

30. *Ibid.*, pp. 327-328.

31. *Ibid.*, pp. 34 Off.

32. *To the Neomartyrs, ad Honorem et in Memoriam* (in Greek), *Minutes of Theological Conference* (17-19 November 1986), under the aegis of Rev. Panteleimon, Metropolitan of Thessaloniki, Thessaloniki 1988.

33. Eustratiadis, *op. cit.*, p. 2.

34. Eustradiadis, *op. cit.*, p.21. Chrysostomos Papadopoulos, Archbishop, *The Neomartyrs* (in Greek), Athens 2 1934, pp. 70-71.

35. Eustratiadis, *op. cit.*, p. 15. Rev. Makarios of Corinth, Nikodimos of Mount Athos, Nikiphoros of Chios, and Athanasios Parios, *Compilation of the Lifes of Neomartyrs* (in Greek), Thessaloniki 1984, p. 60.

36. Eustratiadis, *op. cit.*, p. 23.

37. Papadopoulos, *op. cit.*, Athens 3 1970, pp. 83-84.

38. Eustratiadis, *op. cit.*, p. 37.

39. *Ibid.*, p. 53.

40. *Ibid.*, p. 240.

41. *Ibid.*, p. 238.

42. *St Neomartyr Kyranna of Ossa, Life and Service Hymns* (in Greek), Thessaloniki 1989, Preface by St. Papathemelis, Introduction by A. Glavinas.

43. *Service and Life of the Glorious St Neomartyr Kyrillos of Thessaloniki* (in Greek), Thessaloniki 1980. The Service is by Father Gerasimos Mikroyiannanitis and the Life by Stephanos Papoutsakis from the manuscript 347 of the Dionysiou Monastery.

44. Eustratiadis, *op. cit.*, pp. 283-284.

45. Glavinas, 'Neomartyr Michael of Granitsa, Agrapha, 20-21 March 1544', in *Report in Memoriam to Maximos, Metropolitan of Sardeis, 1914-1986* (in Greek), Metropolis of Switzerland, Geneva 1989, pp. 53-60

46. Eustratiadis, *op. cit.*, p 475.

47. Eustratiadis, *op. cit.*, p.481.

48. Glavinas, 'The First Metropolitans of Thessaloniki during Turkish Rule' (in Greek), *Yearbook* (in Greek), vol. 23 (1978), 335.

49. *Ibid.*, 341.

50. Vacalopoulos, *op. cit.*, pp. 288-289.

51. *Ibid.*, p. 290.

52. *Ibid.*, pp. 244-247.

53. *Ibid.*, pp. 435-436.

54. Glavinas, 'Metropolitans of Thessaloniki during the 17th century', *op. cit.*, 153.

55. *Ibid.*, 149.

56. Vacalopoulos, *op. cit.*, p. 200.

57. *Ibid.*, p. 201.

58. *Ibid.*, pp. 396-397.

59. *Ibid.*, p. 138.

60. On the definition of and relationship between Romiosini and Hellenism, see G. Metallinos, *Tourkokratia* (in Greek), Athens 1988, pp. 68-72; and I. Romanidis, *Romiosini* (in Greek), Thessaloniki 1975.

61. E. Kofos, 'The Greek-Bulgarian Question', *History of the Greek Nation* (in Greek), vol. 13, Athens 1977, pp. 238-305.

62. A. Geromichalos, *The National Activity of Ioakeim Phoropoulos, Metropolitan of Pelagonia, and his Reports* (in Greek), Thessaloniki 1968.

63. On Chrysostomos of Smyrna, see the works (in Greek) of S. Loverdos (Athens 1934), K. Politis (Athens 1934), Chr. Solomonides (Athens 1971, vols. 1-2), and Deacon Andreas Nanakis, 'The Impact of the Macedonian Struggle during Chrysostomos' Tenure at the City of Drama and his Election to the See of Smyrna', in the *Records of the XIth Panhellenic Historical Conference* (in Greek), Thessaloniki 1991, 135-156.

64. A. Karathanassis, *The Metropolis of Nevrokopi during the Macedonian Struggle* (in Greek), Thessaloniki 1987.

65. E. Kostaridis, *The Contemporary Greek Church* (in Greek), Athens 1921, pp. 169-171.

66. Germanos Karavangelis, Metropolitan, *Memoirs* (in Greek), Thesssaloniki 1959.

67. V. Stavridis, *The Ecumenical Patriarchs, 1860 to the Present* (in Greek), Thessaloniki 1977, pp. 481-489.

68. Kostaridis, *op. cit.*, pp. 193-195.

69. Panteleimon Chrysophakis, Metr. of Thessaloniki, *Hagiological and Patrological (Essays)*, Thessaloniki 1990, pp. 149-150.

The Monastic Community of Mount Athos

Christos G. Patrinelis

The Place and its History

Of the three peninsulas of Chalcidice, the one lying farthest to the east, Mount Athos[1], is the most mountainous and least accessible from land. The Great Vigla, which blocks the entrance to the peninsula, is succeeded by a range of densely wooded mountains culminating in the steep, conical mass of Athos (2033 m.). Coasts are coveless and rocky, whereas in the hinterland the ground is riven by precipitous gorges forming violent winter torrents and abundant streams in the summer. Vegetation is dense and extremely diverse: gardens and orchards, small vineyards and olive groves in sheltered places, forests of pines, oaks and horse-chestnuts higher up, beech and firs on the edge and slopes of Mount Athos. The climate, although generally temperate, also varies in places. The east coast, in particular, is buffeted by violent northerly and northeasterly winds (*Vorrias* and *Thrakias*, i.e. from Thrace), stirring the sea "most brutally", according to Herodotus.

In ancient times, Mount Athos and the peninsula bearing its name had been connected with both myths, legends as well as historical fact, such as the destruction of the Persian fleet of Mardonius at Acrathos in 493 BC and the attempt of Xerxes to cut a canal through the neck of the peninsula ten years later. Archeological finds and literary sources confirm that the region had been settled continuously until the first centuries AD, when it was deserted, probably as a result of barbaric invasions.

Only in late 8th - early 9th century the first Athonite monks appear. The earliest related reference dates from 843, when Mount Athos is mentioned as a monastic centre equivalent to the then famous monastic settlements on Bithynian Olympus and Paphlagonian Kyminas. During that early period, when monastic life on Mount Athos was not yet organized in monasteries, there were numerous ascetics living either hermitically in caves or tents, or in *lavres*, groups of huts with an embryonic coenobitic or-

ganization. Such *lavres* were mainly formed near Ierissos and by the neck of the peninsula, in the place where the ancient 'seat of the Elders' was located and where the monks convened to elect the *Protos*, their administrative and spiritual head. That period was marked by certain ascetic figures, such as Petros the Athonite and Euthymios. A novice of the latter, Ioannis Kolovos, founded the monastery of Siderokausia, with which the Athonite ascetics clashed bitterly. That dispute compelled them on the one hand towards tighter organization, and, on the other, to move the seat of their community to *Megali Mesi*, the place where Karyes is located today.

A new era in the history of Mount Athos was inaugurated by Athanasios the Athonite who settled there in 958. Athanasios, born in Trebizond, had already spent a few years at the monastic community of Kyminas, where he was associated to the general and, later, emperor, Nikiphoros Phokas. Later, when on Mount Athos, Athanasios received generous contributions and lavish offerings from Nikiphoros, mostly coming from the spoils of the emperor's triumphal campaign against the Saracens in Crete (961). Athanasios used that wealth to build the monastery of *Megisti* (Greatest) *Lavra* (963), the first monastery to be organized as a coenobium on Mount Athos. Later still, Nikiphoros Phokas, always intending to retreat on Mount Athos one day, aided the newly-founded monastery. His example was followed by his successor Ioannis Tzimiskis, who, in 972, issued the first *typikon*, the monastic community's charter. Athanasios, the father of coenobitic monasticism on Mount Athos, died in 1004, bequeathing to the ever increasing Athonite ecommunity his own Charter and his *Diatyposis* (Will), which constitute the basis of the internal organization of the Athonite monasteries to date.

Meanwhile, new monasteries were founded on Mount Athos, on the model of Megisti Lavra. Around

The Iviron Monastery: the cistern.

980, monks of Lavra, who had come from Iberia (present-day Georgia), built the Ibiron (of the Ibires) monastery. In 985 three brothers from Adrianople founded the monastery of Vatopedi. At about the same period the monasteries of St Paul and Xeropotamou were founded, both associated with *hosios* Paul of Xeropotamou, a man renowned for his severely ascetic life, who had opposed the reforms of Athanasios the Athonite. In the 11th century, the monasteries of Xenophontos, Docheiariou and Zographou were founded. It is the time when the first Russian monks appear on Mount Athos, settling first at the monastery of Xylourgos and later at Panteleimonos. In late 11th century or early 12th another monastery, Koutloumousiou was built. The Serbian monastery of Hilandari was founded around the end of the 12th century by Prince Sava, son of the Serbian ruler Stephen Nemanja. Finally, the monasteries of Pantokratoros, Dionysiou, Simonos Petra and Grigoriou were established in the 14th century, while

Our Lady, the 'Portaitissa'.

the monastery of Stavronikita, which had existed as a *skete* since the 11th century, acquired individual status as late as 1536.

The twenty monasteries just mentioned are the ones still existing to date. However, between the 10th and the 15th centuries, a number of other important monasteries were founded, which, for various reasons, were dissolved or annexed to others. In the *typikon* of Emperor Tzimiskis (972), for example, 58 Athonite monasteries are mentioned, whereas in that of Constantine the Gladiator their number stands at 180.

The proliferation of monasteries and the swelling monastic population, particularly during the 11th and 12th centuries, gave rise to multiple problems, administrative, financial and moral. Monastic life especially suffered from endless disputes over property rights. The task of settling these controversies belonged to the local monastic authorities, the *Protos* and the Assembly of the Elders, although issues of some significance often caused the Ecumenical Patriarch or even the Emperor to intervene.

During the 13th and 14th centuries the Athonite community went through periods of serious crises as a result of the Crusaders' domination of the Near East, the raids of pirates who had infested the Aegean, and the incursions of the mercenaries of the so-called Catalan Society in the early 1300s. The Athonite world took an active part in the religious disputes that shook the empire during the late Byzantine period, such as the Hesychastic movement and the question of the unity of the Churches. To compensate for these mishaps, the Byzantine emperors, especially the Palaiologoi, by successive *chrysoboulla* (golden-bulls) granted the Athonite monasteries various privileges and endowed them with lucrative estates, particularly in the Strymon valley, in Thrace and on the Aegean Islands. The Serbian rulers proved equally generous, primarily Stephen Dušan, who, however, extracted from the Athonites his recognition as suzerain in return.[2] However, the Serbian domination, which Dušan attempted to consolidate, collapsed ingloriously in 1371. The power vacuum that ensued was exploited by the 'king' of Thessaloniki - and, later, emperor of Byzantium - Manuel Palaiologos, who did not hesitate to expropriate monastic lands in order to reinforce local defences. Yet the Ottoman pressure proved impossible to sustain, until, in 1387,

The Panteleimonos Monastery, on the west coast of the Athos peninsula.

Thessaloniki and most of Macedonia fell to Turkish hands. A large part of Athonite property in Chalcidice and the Strymon valley was confiscated and the community was obliged to pay tribute to the sultan. Among the first acts of Emperor Manuel II Palaiologos after the partial restoration of Byzantine rule (1403) was to reinstate the monasteries in their previous ownership on condition that they transferred to the imperial treasury one third of the tribute imposed by the Ottomans. The following twenty years were dreadful. In 1423, the last governor of Thessaloniki, Andronikos Palaiologos, having surrendered the city to the Venetians, withdrew to Mount Athos. Foreseeing a bleak future, he advised the monks to accommodate with the inevitable in good time. A 'memorandum' in a codex of Vatopedi informs us that "in the year ϛπλβ´ (1423-24) the Holy Mountain paid homage to sultan Murad at the city of Adrianople following the advice of the late despot, lord Andronikos Palaiologos"[3]. A new chapter in the history of Mount Athos began.

The Legal and Fiscial Status of Mount Athos

The attitude of the Athonite monks towards secular authority and the powerful of the day was dictated by their constant and fundamental concern to protect their estates and to safeguard their autonomy. The kind of settlement the Athonites reached on these vital issues with Murad II at their meeting in Adrianople is not known. However, certain conclusions can be drawn from the attitude of the Ottoman authorities during the ensuing years, as well as from fragmentary information in later documents: first, the new rulers respected the autonomy of Mount Athos and, second, not only they abstained from encroaching upon the property of the monasteries but they also conceded very favourable terms of taxation, as it had been the case with other communities voluntarily subjecting themselves to the sultan. However, ten years later, after a general inquiry into the ownership of all lands in Macedonia (1432/33), Murad changed tactics and ordered that "all monasteries and churches be taken and their revenues and property be seized", according

The **Katholikon** *of the skete of St Andrew.*

to the contemporary historiographer Ioannis Anag-nostis. Although it is not clear what followed, it seems that the Athonite monks recovered their land, which they now possessed only as usufructuaries (*tasarruf*), while the sultan retained the ownership; whatever property, however, the monks subsequently acquired (purchases, donations, etc.), it fully belonged to them (mülk). They also secured some tax exemptions and favourable terms of payment.[4] Moreover, the Ottoman authorities were persuaded to recognize the monastic communities as legal entities, capable of any transaction. Thus, they became entitled to inherit members of the community incontestably, especially when the deceased were registered as owners of monastic estates, of which they were in fact only stewards.

These legal and economic arrangements were sanctioned by Murad's successors without significant changes. In 1568, however, Sultan Selim II decided to repeat Murad's *coup de main*. He seized the assets, both land and chattels, of churches and monasteries throughout the empire with the intention to cede their use for a price (*Maktu*), either to their former owners or to the highest bidder. According to an Athonite document of that period, "the royal *el-emin* (supervisor of public property) of sultan Selim came bearing his order, to include all the belongings of the monks and the monasteries, movable and real, estates, mills, gardens, vineyards, farms and everything else, not only of Mount Athos but of everyone within his realm. So, they mercilessly sold them to laymen as if they were the owners...".[5] In order to redeem their property some of the Athonite monasteries resorted to Turkish or Jewish pawnbrokers of Thessaloniki pledging whatever of value was left to them, while others appealed to generous and pious lords for help. For instance, the debts of the monasteries Dionysiou, Karakalou and Docheiariou, amounting to over 200,000 aspers, were paid off by the prince of Moldavia Bodgan Lapusneanu and his mother Roxane.

The immediate and practical purpose of Selim's 'robbery', as it was described, was to raise money to cover the expenses of his impending expedition against Cyprus. There was, however, legal covering. Specifically, during the reign of the previous sultan, Suleyman, the distinguished *Seyhülislâm* (grand master of Islamic law) of Constantinople, Ebü'l Su'ud (1545-1574), had inspired the gradual harmonization

*The **Katholikon** of the Xeropotamou Monastery.*

of the current customary law with the Islamic holy law (*Seri'a*). According to the latter, monasteries, being institutions dedicated to the worship of God, could be classified - along with their property - as *vakf*, a privileged status which, at least in theory, rendered them inalienable. For this reason, along with the hasty redemption of their property or, rather, in connection with it, the monasteries of Mount Athos, collectively in 1569 and separately too, a little latter, hurried to obtain the relevant documents, the so-called *vakfname*.[6]

Regarding the fiscal terms of the final arrangement, a *firman* of Sultan Selim (1569) indicates that the Athonite monks paid for the redemptiom of their property within Mount Athos 14,000 florins (840,000 aspers) and for the rest, outside the peninsula, 130,000 aspers (at a time when the Ecumenical Patriarchate paid tribute 246,000 aspers a year, while the annual salary of a Janissary stood at approximately 2,700 aspers)[7]. It should be noted that by the same *firman* the status of the monasteries as legal entities, first recognized by Murad II, was finally confirmed.

At about the same time, further developments in the fiscal status of monastic estates included the fact that a considerable part of them, apparently on the Athonites' initiative, was declared *Mukata'a*, i.e. subject to taxation on a predetermined basis (*maktu*), which was infrequently adjusted to keep up with inflation, irrespective of the fluctuating annual crop. Thus, the monks avoided the risk of their produce being arbitrarily assessed, as well as the danger of encroachment upon their land.

From then on and until the beginning of the 19th century, a considerable number of sultanic *firmans* confirmed and protected the fiscal position of Mount Athos, threatening penalties against any public servant who violated the 'privileges' of the Athonite monks as well as against any layman who deared trespass monastic property.

Administrative Dependence

Although very little is known about the administrative organization in Macedonia during the early Ottoman period, it seems that from the outset Mount Athos became part of the *kaza* of Siderokausia of the *vilayet* of Thessaloniki. Already in mid-15th century, both the *aga* of Siderocausia and the pasha of Thessaloniki frequently intervened - apparently at the monks' request - in property disputes between Ottoman landowners and monasteries or between the monasteries themselves. The practice of the Athonite monks to appeal to the Ottoman judicial authorities of Thessaloniki was castigated by Patriarch Jeremiah II

in his 1574 *sigillion* (bull) which constituted the fifth *typikon* of the holy community.

At the time of Suleyman I the Magnificent (1520-1566), Mount Athos was given as a fief to the commanding officer of the élite palace guard, the so-called *bostanciler*. The Athonites had to contribute annually a rather mediocre sum in exchange for powerful protection from inside the imperial palace. Their feudal lord was represented locally by an *aga* who served for two years, first situated at Thessaloniki, and, from 1575 onwards, at Karyes. The so-called *zabit* of Mount Athos kept a Turkish scribe and a guard of ten to twenty men, the *seymen*. The holy community was obliged to pay his salary and to provide him food and board. The presence alone of the *aga* and his guard were supposed to protect Mount Athos from armed incursions of Turks from nearby Siderokausia and pirates. The *aga* often participated in the meetings of the *Iera Synaxis* (Holy Assembly), where he time and again exercized his authority arbitrarily. The Athonites responded either by appealing

"Reclining Christ": a detail from the frescses of the **Protaton** *at Karyes.*

to the *bostancrbashi* in Constantinople, or, more often, by extending additional *baksheesh* to the *aga*.

In order to expedite their secular affairs in Constantinople and Thessaloniki, the Athonites had, since mid-18th century, maintained permanent 'trustees', usually local notables (Phanariotes, big merchants, bankers, etc), such as Goutas Kautantzoglou in Thessaloniki, who offered their services free of charge. One or two Athonite monks also served in both cities as liaison between the trustees and Mount Athos.

Apart from their rather loose dependence on secular authority, the monasteries of Mount Athos were under the spiritual supervision of the Ecumenical Patriarchate, having almost since their founding been proclaimed *Stauropigiakes* (Patriarchal). After the fall of Constantinople, the ties between Mount Athos and the Patriarchate were strengthened, as a result not only of the broadening of patriarchal jurisdiction but also of the fact that many deposed or retired patriarchs usually retreated to Mount Athos, where they took an active interest in communal affairs and dedicated their small or large property to the monasteries. Besides, the Athonites frequently brought their internal disputes before the Patriarchate as a court of appeal. However, the limits of the Patriarch's jurisdiction over Mount Athos were quite unclear, as patriarchal *sigillia* often dealt with rather trivial matters, which could well have been settled by the Holy Assembly at Karyes. Yet, over important spiritual and institutional questions, the Patriarchate fully retained its jurisdiction. Thus, the Fifth (1574) and Sixth (1783) Charters of Mount Athos were drafted on the initiative of Patriarchs Jeremiah II and Gabriel IV respectively. The Patriarchate also intervened drastically in the case of the *kolyves* dispute in the second half of the 18th century.

More direct and frequent was the intervention in Athonite affairs of the bishop of Ierissos and Mount Athos. Especially after the eclipse of the office of the *Protos* ('the First') in late 16th century, the bishop not only participated in but also presided over the Holy Assembly. During the 17th century in particular, he spent more time at Karyes than at his seat. Apparently, certain excesses on his part provoked a *sigillion* of Patriarch Cyril Loukaris (1622), whereby the bishop was reminded that he should not consider Mount Athos "as his own diocese" since the monasteries were *stauropigiakes* and, therefore, belonged to the Patriar-

A view of the Iviron Monastry.

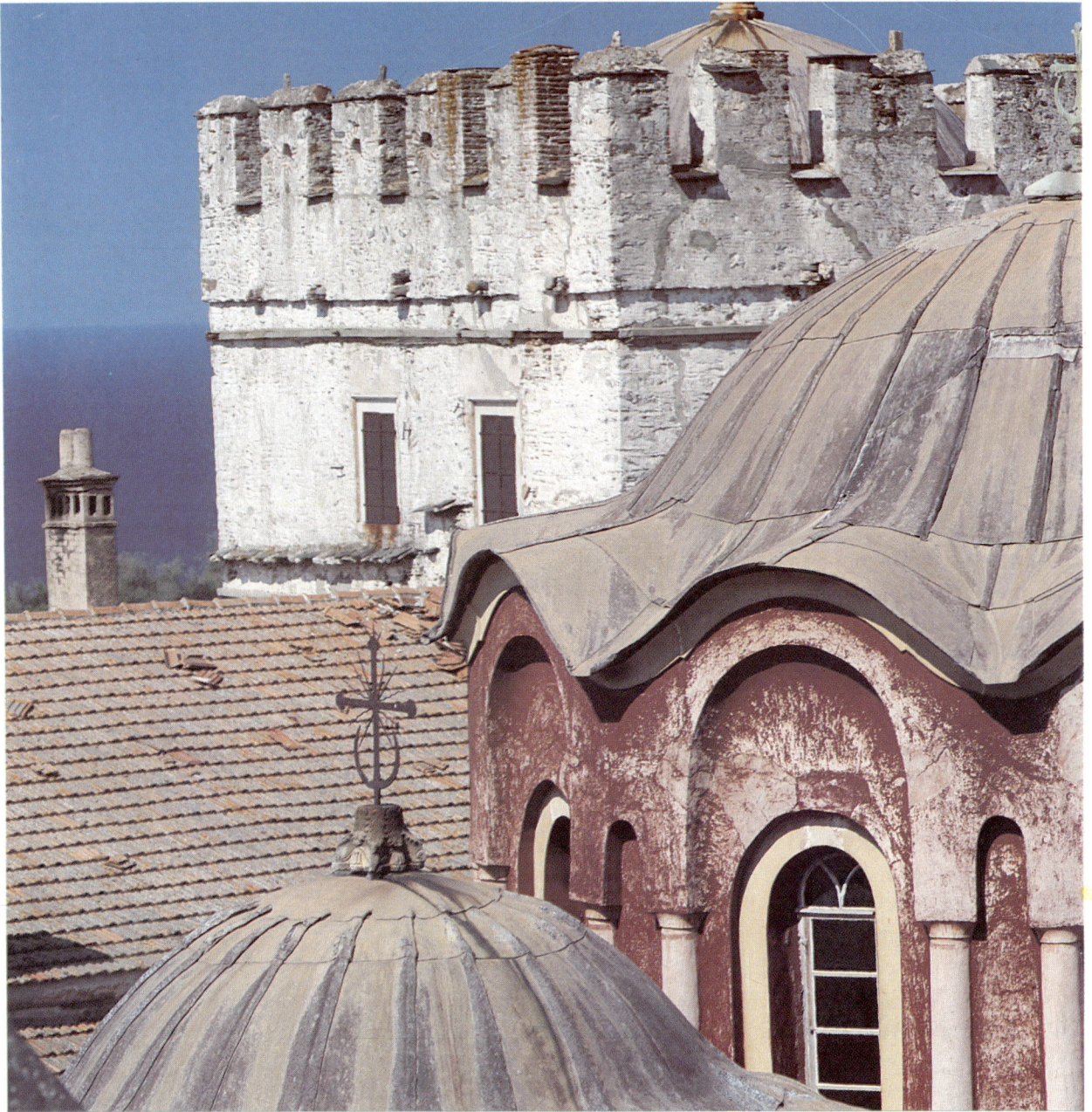

A view of the Vatopedi Monastery.

chate. However, the interventionist practices of the bishop of Ierissos continued well into the 18th century.

Internal Organization

At the core of Athonite monasticism was, naturally, the monastery. It constituted an officially recognized legal entity, self-governed and capable of any transaction. Until the end of the 14th century Athonite monasteries were organized as *coenobia* (communes)

on the model of Megisti Lavra, regulated by the successive *typika*. More specifically, administration and spiritual guidance in each *coenobium* were in the hands of the hegumen who was elected by its members for life. The monks owed reverence and absolute obedience to him, and also undertook to offer their services gratuitously (ministrations), and to give up any right on private ownership. However, from the end of the 14th century onwards, a different form of organization and self-administration, the so-called *Idiorrhythmia*, began to gain ground and to generate other, secondary administrative and spiritual effects. *Idiorrhythmia* was not a novel phenomenon in the history of Eastern monasticism; yet the reasons for its immergence and spreading in Mount Athos have not been adequately explained. It is worth noting, however, that long before *idiorrhythmic* monasticism was almost universally accepted in Mount Athos, at the turn of the 17th century, the coenobitic system had undergone serious transformation: the hegumen's term of office became annual or, at least, temporary, with part of his authority going to a whole range of *offikialioi* (functionaries, such as the sacristan, the ecclesiarch, the administrator), whose narrow circle also appointed the hegumen. Finally, the title of the hegumen itself almost eclipsed, or, wherever it was still in use, was deprived of its original meaning. The *idiorrhythmic* monasteries were run by a two- or three-member comittee of *proïstamenoi* (superintendents), who were usually elected from among the *offikialioi* or from a circle of spiritually and finacially influential, monks. The *Idiorrhythmia* had a more serious impact upon the Athonite way of life and morals: private ownership was permitted, the monks could regulate their diet and choose their occupation themselves, they received payment for their services to the monastery or they could hire less well-off monks as servants.[8] Furthermore, the annual elections for the various offices soon gave rise to intense electioneering. On the other hand, the introduction of *idiorrhythmic* monasticism freed the monks from the potential despotism of the hegumen, and permitted a measure of private life and the development of one's own inclinations. Indeed, *Idiorrhythmia* could be described as a transition from a 'monarchic' to an oligarchic or partially democratic system, with all the advantages and distortions the latter entails.

The flaws of *Idiorrhythmia*, above all the loosening of discipline and moral austerity induced many scholarly clerics and patriarchs to exercise their influence in favour of the restoration of the coenobitic system. The efforts of Patriarch Jeremiah II in late 16th century brought only ephemeral results. Then some monasteries, including the two most important, Lavra and Vatopedi, returned to the coenobitic system, only to revert to *Idiorrhythmia* a little later. It was not until after two centuries that a tendency towards

St Peter: fresco in the Lictor's cell at Karyes.

the coenobitic system led, between 1784 and 1813, the monasteries of Xenophontos, Esphigmenou, Kastamonitou (Konstamonitou), Simonos Petra, Panteleimonos, Dionysiou and Karakalou back to the coenobitic system.

Apart from the turn to *Idiorrhythmia*, other centrifugal tendencies emerged among Athonite monks during Ottoman rule. Alternative forms of monastic life and organization developed, such as *sketes*, *kellia* (cells), hermitages, *kathismata* (seats), all revivals of early monastic forms which spread considerably after the 16th century. Yet all these secondary monastic institutions were subordinate to the main monasteries, not only as a result of a degree of administrative dependence, but also because they were established on the latter's property.

The *sketes* - a revival, in a way, of the ancient *lavra*- consisted of several *kalyves* (lit. 'huts') –often quite large edifices– around a central church, the *kyriakon*, and was usually organized on the basis of *Idiorrhythmia* under an elected Father Superior, the so-called *dikaios* (prior). Each hut served as domicile of a 'senior' and his 'retinue' of two or three monks. Among the Athonite *sketes*, that of St Anna (belonging to Lavra) is the oldest, having been founded in 1605. At the turn of the 18th century, the famous *skete* of Kausokalyvia (also of Lavra) was established, almost simultaneously with the –still existing– sketes of Prophet Elias (of Pantokratoros), St Demetrius (of Vatopedi), Nea Skiti (of St Paul), St Demetrius of Lakkos (of St Paul too), Evangelismos (Xenophontos), Prodromos (Iviron) and St Panteleimon (of Koutloumousiou).

Regarding the other alternative monastic settlements, *kellia* (cells), together with the chapels and gardens attached to them, were ceded by the dominant monastery to a 'senior' for a fee; the latter usually employed two servants who lived with him. Seats were located near the monastery, which apart from shelter provided food as well to their single occupant, usually an old monk who desired isolation.

In early 19th century, there existed eleven *sketes* on Mount Athos with some 500 monks, and 290 cells with approximately 750 ascetics.[9]

The most austere monastic category is that of hermits or anchorites. Hermits live completely isolated in inaccessible places, usually caves converted into crude dwellings or simple huts (*kalyves*). Such hermitages are scattered all over the barren, rocky southwestern slopes of Mount Athos, at Katounakia, Karoulia, Kerasia, and elsewhere.

Some sort of central administration existed in Mount Athos already in the 9th century, although each monastery retained its autonomous status. An assembly of representatives of the monasteries, called the Holy Assembly of the Elders or 'Great *Mesi*', constituted the supreme administrative organ of the Athonite community. It was considered a legal person and functioned as a *skete* or *lavra*, with property of its own, mainly cells near Karyes. The Holy Assembly elected the *Protos* of Mount Athos for a life term. The *Protos* was the chief executive with the right to convene the Holy Assembly whenever there were serious matters to be considered.[10] He was seated at the *Protaton*, the historical temple of Karyes. This structure was preserved into the early Ottoman period. Gradually, however, the power of the *Protos* diminished, his term of office was recuced to one year, and, after 1593, the office was abolished altogether.[11] It seems that the fiscal changes of 1569 and the arrival of a Turkish *aga* to Karyes in 1575 were not unconnected with the eclipse of that institution. In contrast, the prestige and authority of the Holy Assembly increased, albeit temporarily: in 1661 it was practically dissolved as its members decided to sell its property to the monasteries in order to meet the "enormous and unbearable" debts of the Athonite community. Furthermore, the status of *vakf* accorded to Mount Athos, with only twenty officially recognized monastic institutions, did not allow much legal ground for the autonomous existence of that peculiar *skete* or '*lavra* of Karyes'. In effect, the Holy Assembly was transformed into a *Koinon* (Common) or Holy Community of Mount Athos, which again consisted of *proestotes* (representatives) of the twenty monasteries. Soon, however, the dignitaries from the big three monasteries - Lavra, Vatopedi and Iviron - virtually assumed full power. Only in 1744 a *typikon* approved by the Community and sanctioned by Patriarch Paisios II, somewhat helped redress the balance between the major and the lesser monasteries. Its provisions were consolidated –with small modifications– by the *typikon* of 1783, formulated by Patriarch Gabriel IV and the Patriarchal Synod with the assistance of the Athonites. Specifically, that latter document provided for the division of the twenty monasteries into four groups of five and the appointment by the Holy Community of four *epistates* (superintendents) annually, one from each group. Significantly, one of them should come from one of the five major monasteries (Lavra, Vatopedi, Iviron, Hilandari and Dionysiou). Each of them held one fourth of the official seal of Mount Athos; therefore, no act of the *Epistasia* could be authorized unless it was unanimously taken by all four. An important novelty of the 1783 *typikon* was that, unlike the previous one, it recognized no precedence to any of the four *epistates*. By a 1810 resolution, a permanent consultative body of twenty representatives –one from each monastery– was appointed by the *Iera Epistasia* (Holy Superintendency).

The main tasks of both the *Epistasia* and the Com-

A view of the Vatopedi Monastery overlooking the Aegean.

munity, as it had been the case with the *Protos* and the Assembly, were to settle the disputes arising between monasteries, and, primarily, to allocate the various taxes, in proportion to the human and material resources of of each monastery.

Finances

As legal entities and populous institutions with extensive landed property, the monasteries, their religious character notwithstanding, were important economic units: they produced goods and services, maintained economic relations with one another as well as with third parties, and were, of course, subject to regular taxation and extraordinary leves. If one attempts to concentrate the various economic activities under the general 'assets - liabilities' categories, the following sources of income and cause of of expenditure may be defined:

A. Main sources of income, cash or in kind:

a) Cultivation or exploitation of monastic farms within or without Mount Athos. In addition to stretches of timber, agriculture had developed considerably on Mount Athos. In 1764, for instance, there existed 172.7 hectars of vineyards, 21.5 hectars of gardens, 35,837 olive trees, 1,005 hazels, and 1,990 beehives.[13] Monastic estates, the so-called Athonite *metohia*, were much more extensive outside the peninsula. Most of them were in Chalcidice[14], mainly in the peninsulas of Kassandra and Sithonia (Longou) and in the region of Kalamaria. In 1722 there were 32 Athonite *metohia* in Chalcidice, 58 in 1766 and 55 in 1806.[15] Other were to be found on the islands of Thasos, Lemnos, Imvros, Skyros, Proikonisos, Samos, in Moudania, even in Crete and Zakynthos. But the most lucrative estates were those in Wallachia and Moldavia, donations of the various rulers, local or Phanariot, of those countries. Monastic lands outside Mount Athos were cultivated by share-croppers or farm labourers under the supervision of two or three monks.

b) Livestock. Both inside and outside Mount Athos the monasteries grazed substantial flocks in extensive pastures. In 1801 the monastery of Vatopedi alone owned 8,000 sheep and goats, while in 1815 the flocks belonging to all Athonite monasteries numbered some 25-35,000 heads.[16]

c) Leasing of land and premises, houses and shops, in Thessaloniki, Constantinople, Adrianople, Bucharest, Iasi and elsewhere –mostly the donations "in eternal commermoration" of devout people.

d) Donations in cash or in kind, and annual allowances, mostly from rulers and high officials of the Danubian principalities[17] and the czars 'of all Russias'. The following top the list of donors and sponsors: Mistress Maro, daughter of the last Serbian king George Branković and step-mother of Sultan Mehmed II the Conqueror, the rulers of Wallachia Radu the Great (1495-1508), Neagoe Basaraba (1512-1521), Gabriel Mogilas (1618-1620), Constantine Brâncoveanu (1688-1714), Nikolaos Mavrokordatos (1715-1730), Mathaios, Alexandros and Grigorios Gikas (mid-18th century), the rulers of Moldavia Stephen the Great (1457-1504), Petre Rares (1527-1538), Vasil Lupu (1652-1661), Ioannis and Skarlatos Kallimachis (1758-1761 and 1807-1819), Czars Ivan III (1462-1505), husband to Zoe Palaiologos, his son Basil IV (1505-1533), and Ivan IV the Terrible (1533-1584). Thanks to their contributions, monasteries and churches, which had been destroyed by fire, were rebuilt, church interiors were adorned, debts were paid, and confiscated property was redeemed. The above as well as many other rulers devoted to Athonite monasteries the proceeds of many rich monasteries and churches, and scores of shops and houses in the Danubian principalities.

e) Alms-raising (ziteies: mendicancies), which the monasteries launched almost continuously from the end of the 15th century onwards, especially in Constantinople, the Danubian principalities, Russia, even in Venice. The famous scholarly monk Kaisarios Dapontes, for example, during his eight-year tour of the Danubian countries managed to collect 50,000 kurus on behalf of the Xeropotamou monastery - at a time, when a teacher expected to make between 250 and 500 kurus a year.

B. Main causes of expenditure and consumption of capital and goods.

a) Food, which absorbed the best part of Athonite agricultural production. Cereals, in particular –which did not grow inside Mount Athos– as well as wine, were mainly consumed by the monks and their guests. In 1801, for instance, the monastery of Vatopedi –containing approximately 300 monks– needed some 1,600 pounds of bread and more than 130 gallons of wine a day.[18]

b) Repairs and decoration of churches and monasteries, especially after the frequent disasters, earthquakes and fires, that afflicted Mount Athos. The donations of Danubian princes and philo-Athonite prelates and laymen were mostly used for these purposes.

c) Payment of debts and redemption of property pawned or confiscated by the Ottoman authorities. In these cases too, the Orthodox rulers and other "noblemen of our Genos" rendered generous assistance.

d) Legal expenses and related 'gratuities' which at times amounted to exorbitant sums. For instance, at the turn of the 18th century, a litigation between the monasteries of Vatopedi and Zographou, which was eventually settled by the Grand Vizier in Constantinople, cost the winning part - Vatopedi - 100,000 kurus, a sum equal to the annual tax paid by the monastery to the Turkish authorities.

e) Purchase of new property. Although monastic lands mainly came from donations and bequests, during the rather intermittent periods of prosperity the monasteries invested in real estate. In 1620, for instance, the Dionysiou monastery bought from the inhabitants of Gomato in Chalcidice a pasture for 101,000 aspers; in 1636, another pasture in the region of Kitros for 100,000 aspers - at a time when 200,000 aspers represented the value of 400 oxen or 2,500 sheep.[20]

g) Payment of fines (cereme) imposed by the Turkish authorities for various reasons. In 1743, for instance, when the authorities found out that the known Russophile metropolitan of Sofia Anastasios took refuge on Mount Athos, "royal wrath came unto us and the Porte... sent a vizier's delegate... and he exacted forty purses (20,000 kurus) from us".[21] Later still, the turbulent period of Russo-Turkish wars afforded so many occasions for the imposition of fines that the Athonites were driven to despair, as, according to a 1785 record of the Holy Community "no strength was left to the poor monasteries to meet the all so frequent".[22]

h) Gifts (peskes) and gratuities (baksheesh). Although in theory optional, these forms of bribery had become established and inviolable practice. A gift, either in cash or in kind, was offered to every new governor (vali) of Thessaloniki, to the agas of Mademochoria and of Mount Athos and to their associates. Since these officials changed every one or two years, the *peskes* turned into a regular contribution. *Baksheesh* was paid to anyone who could expedite the Athonite affairs or to anyone who might harm the monasteries if he were not pleased. The records of the Holy Community include numerous accounts of such cases, as the following examples show: In 1773, "we gave the Maten *aga* (of Mademochoria) two watches as *peskes*... 102 kurus". In 1777, "I paid to the new pasha from Morea 1,300 kurus". In 1810, "some gift to be bought and offered to the *vali* of Thessaloniki who declined the donation in cash, and in order to satisfy the mullah, who demands a large sum because of the events with which you are familiar". In 1819, "what was offered as yet to the said *vali* of Thessaloniki...: 2,625 (kurus) for a snuffbox to his excellency, 600 for a watch to his blood-brother, 250 to his steward, 250 to his treasurer, and 120 in gradulities to guards, sergeants and coffee-caterers" of the *vali*.[23]

i) Regular taxes. They were levied on persons, property and production. The list included poll-tax, the taxes paid to the *bostanci* guard and to the treasury of the sultan, the tithe, the salary and board fees of the local *aga*. Normally, taxes were apportioned and then collected from each monastery by the Holy Assembly, and, later, by the Holy Community.

Poll-tax (*cizye* or simply *haraç*) had been imposed since at least the middle of the 15th century. Every year the Athonites had to pay for 3,000 persons, irrepective of their actual number. From the 18th century onwards the conventional 3,000 taxable monks of Mount Athos formed three distinct categories: wealthy (approximately 10% of the total), medial, and poor (another 10 %), paying 12, 6 and 3 kurus per capita respectively.[24] *Haraç* represented 25% of all regular taxes levied on Mount Athos.

The tax paid to the *bostanci* guard appoximated 8% of the total, while that paid to the imperial treasury another 25%. The tithe on the goods produced within Mount Athos approached 15% and the expenses of the *aga* (*agalik*) almost 12%. Minor taxes covered the rest. However, extraordinary taxes were frequently imposed, particularly in wartime.

Information regarding the total amount of regular taxes imposed on Mount Athos during the first centuries of Ottoman rule are sporadic and, not infrequently, vague and contradicting. According to the Russian monk Isaias of Hilandari (1489), Mount

Students of the Athonias School.

Athos paid to the sultan 14,000 aspers annually[25], not a particularly heavy burden, if one considers the fact that in 1469 an estate of the monastery of Esphigmenou near Ierissos was sold for 30,000 aspers. According to two Ottoman fiscal registers, in 1530 annual taxation stood at 27,760 aspers, and a little later at 25,000.[26] A firman of Selim II mentions that in 1569 the Athonites agreed to pay 70,000 aspers as *haraç* annually.[27] However, by 1601-1602, the total of fiscal obligations of the Mount Athos monasteries had reached the sum of 700,000 aspers, an exorbitant amount, even considering the devaluation of the Ottoman currency after 1586 (the amount was equivalent to the price of 1,500 plough oxen or 2,000 cattle or 10,000 sheep). In 1678 the total amount of taxes was 17,000 kurus, while in 1724 and 1744 it rose to 35,000 and 102,000 respectively (at a time when a farmhouse cost some 120 kurus, and the annual salary of a teacher was 250-500 kurus). Between 1789 and

1806 –a period of rocketing inflation– taxes ranged from 37,000 to 75,000 kurus[28] (in 1794 the daily wage of a labourer stood at 1 or 1,5 kurus) .

From the beginning of the 16th century until 1568, thanks to donations of Orthodox rulers mainly, Mount Athos knew a period of exceptional prosperity, which permitted many monasteries to launch costly construction projects and to ornate their churches (*katholika*) with magnificent frescoes. Since, however, their estates were seized and they were obliged to take on loans to recover them, the monasteries went through severe financial distress which threatened even the major ones with collapse. In a 'memoir' of 1583, for example, a monk laments the decline of Megisti Lavra, which "was reduced to utter poverty, so that most of the cells collapsed and there is no one to open his eyes and see the disaster... but everybody lost his mind watching the debts rising and the contest for primacy; alas, then, alas!".[29] Around 1630, the monastery of Panteleimons "fell into great losses and debts; the vestments of the clergy were pawned... and its property mortgaged, with the debts rising, however, the monks themselves were thrown to jail where they suffer...". In 1661, as mentioned previously, the enormous debts of Mount Athos obliged the Holy Community to sell more than seventy cells at Karyes. In 1784 the Dionysiou monastery "suffered great distress due to its very large debts... as the *Konyars* (Turks) would not leave the Fathers in peace, every so often coming after their aspers like wild wolves". In 1789 the monks of Lavra were thrown to jail after having failed to pay their amount of tax (7,200 kurus), while ten years later, for the same reason, they were obliged to strip some precious gospel off "its golden, beautiful decoration".[30]

However, it should be noted that the term 'debt' implies not only taxes owed to the Ottoman authorities but also loans that the monasteries had occasionally taken, and, chiefly, the usually delayed amortization. Thus, the total debt of Mount Athos at the turn of the 19th century was almost three times as high as its taxes due, reaching 215,000 kurus in 1801, and then dropping to 102,000 in 1809, and to 77,500 in 1820.[31]

The monastic population

The movement of monastic population on Mount Athos was related to the general political, social and cultural conditions prevailing in the wider area as well to the specific situation within Mount Athos. Although there is a good deal of information about the population of Mount Athos in general and of each monastery individually, only a fraction of it can be considered reliable. The numbers given by travellers (6,000-12,000 monks) are obviously conventional and exaggerated. On the contrary, evidence from Ottoman and Athonite archival sources is sparse but accurate. Inevitably, one should rely on the latter. The earliest data come from an Ottoman tax register of 1525/1530 and provides the exact number of Athonite monks: 1,440 persons.[32] Another, slightly later, register concurs: 1,442. Yet there are no reliable data for the next two centuries. Indirect evidence, however, suggests a thinning down of the Athonite population during the first half of the 17th century.

In 1764 a detailed census conducted by Ottoman officials showed a population of 2,908 monks and 58 laymen, a total of 2,966.[33] In 1808, a similar census produced a number of 2,390 monks and 315 laymen, 2,705 in all.[34] It must be noted, though, that at least the last two censuses did not take into account monks who were outside Mount Athos at the time. Therefore, the numbers of monks should be increased by about 30%, since it has been adequately established that approximately one third of the Athonite monasteries' personnel was normally out to the monastic estates or on fund-raising tours.[35]

A thorny and controversial issue, which in the 19th century assumed international proportions, referred to the ethnological composition of the monastic population at the period under discussion. Foreign monks had always been present on Mount Athos - from the Caucasus, Russia, Bulgaria, Serbia and elsewher - but their numbers were limited until the second half of the 15th century. Subsequently, their presence was increasingly felt, a phenomenon which has not been adequately explained yet. More specifically, at about the end of the 15th century, the following monasteries were reportedly staffed with foreign monks: Panteleimons with Russians (it had already become known as the monastery of the Russians or 'Russian'), those of Hilandari, Grigoriou and St Paul with Serbs, Zographou, Simonos Petra, Koutloumousiou and Philotheou with Bulgarians, Iviron with Georgians. Their presence is evident, particularly during the fifty-year period between 1480 and 1530, in Athonite documents signed by representatives of the monasteries or other monks as witnesses: in many cases 25% to 50% of the signatures are Slavonic (including Rumanians who still used the Cyrillic alphabet).[37] Subsequently, foreign presence diminished. Shortly after the mid-17th century the monasteries of Panteleimonos, Hilandari, Zographou, St Paul and Xenophontos are mentioned as Slav.[38] A century later the monastery of Panteleimonos was almost abandoned, while the *sketes* of Prophet Elias and St Demetrius (of Lakkos) were restored by Russian and Moldavian monks. At the turn of the 19th century Slav monks still manned the following monasteries: Hilandari, Zographou, St Paul and Xenophontos.[39]

Regarding the presence of foreign monks on Mount Athos, two points should be made clear: a) Before 1830 there was no ethnic antagonism on Mount Athos. Greek and foreign monks coexisted harmoniously, even within the same monastery. The tendency of monks of common origin to concentrate to the same monastery or *skete* reflects a localistic –not nationalistic– spirit. b) The presence of many or few foreign monks never created an image of Mount Athos as a neutral, multi-national community; foreigners always constituted a minority. The region itself belonged to the ecclesiastical, cultural and geographical space of the *"Genos ton Romaion"* (the Greek-Orthodox Race). Greek monks were regarded natives, while the Slav and Rumanian foreigners. In a 1501 *sigillion* Patriarch Joachim I refers to the Bulgarians of the monastery of Koutloumousiou as "monks from a foreign land". In 1541, Patriarch Jeremiah I informs us that the Bulgarians of the latter monastery "were succeeded by monks of our *Genos*".[40]

With regard to the geographic and social origin of the monks, as well as the reasons that compelled them to take refuge on Mount Athos, the British Colonel W. M. Leake, a most discerning traveller who visited Mount Mount Athos in 1806, observed: "The inhabitants of Mount Athos come of course from every corner of Turkey and they are mostly aging men, who retire there, either moved by piety or, more often, in order to secure the rest of their life from the hazzards of Turkish despotism. Anyone who brings money with him is welcome. If he is an old man, he is not accepted without money, but a young and hard-work-

The Assumption of Virgin Mary, fresco in the **Protaton** *church at Karyes.*

ing man could be accepted even without, and, after serving for a few years as a layman, he becomes a monk. Since these persons only seek to make a living, they generally come from the lower classes. Some, of all ages, are fugitives for some crime or are hiding from the just or unjust revenge of a Turk. I met several who had once been converted to Islam and afterwards recanted and sought refuge here, the only place where they can return to the Church and avoid the punishment awaiting Muslim renegades".[41]

Factors of Decline

Apart from the almost permanently adverse economic and political conditions, other factors contributed to the hardships of Athonite life, afflicting people and installations, even causing monastic communities to disintegrate: frequent fires, earthquakes, epidemics, raids of brigands or pirates upon Mount Athos.

Every so often, fire completely or partly destroyed

*"The expulsion of the tradesmen from the Temple", in the **Katholikon** of Hilandari.*

the monasteries of Grigoriou (1500, 1761), Dionysiou (1534, 1539), Esphigmenou (1491), Iviron (1740), Koutloumousiou (1487, 1767), Kastamonitou (1717), Xenophontos (1817), Xeropotamou (1517, 1609), Pantokratoros (1733), Simonos Petra (1580, 1622), Stavronikita (1607, 1741), and Hilandari (1722).

Frequent earthquakes, a predicament common to all monasteries, have been recorded as follows: in 1456 ("a most horrible tremor of the earth"), 1511, 1526, 1564, 1572 ("an earthquake so great that the premises were torn apart and rocked from the foundations"), 1585 ("such a great earthquake, that towers collapsed and the church walls cracked... and even the sea retreated..."), 1684, 1719, 1765 ("more than forty terrible shocks" and, after eight months, "an earthquake with a most terrible convulsion that the walls of churches and houses cracked again"), 1779, 1790 ("the Mount was shaking like a reed"), 1800, 1811.

There is little information regarding epidemics. It is known, however, that in 1734, 1760, 1771, 1783 and 1810, "plague afflicted Mount Athos".

The monastic communities equally suffered from the devastating raids of brigands and pirates who had been infesting Mount Athos since the earliest recorded times; for this reason monasteries were built on the model of castles. Since the 15th century and throughout the Ottoman period, the maintainance and reinforcement of their fortifications had been among the monks' main concerns. In early 19th century, the defences of Lavra included cannons as well. Some of the most important incidents are given here as recorded in various 'memoirs' and archival sources:

In 1527, "along with the other evils inflicted by the sea-pirates on Mount Athos, they burned down the (erstwhile) monastery of Mylopotamos".[42]

In 1534 "the (monastery of) Esphigmenou was conquered by the godless *Agarinoi* (Mohammedans)... who having plundered all its belongings and having destroyed the church, and burned the holy icons after tearing them apart... took seven monks as prisoners and left the same way they came; that is how the monastery was devastated".[43]

In 1650 - during the Cretan War - Occidental (*Frankoi*) pirates "upon arriving to our ports capture the priests and monks; first they deprive them of even their vests, as if they were not humans, something that not even the Turks do, and then they beat them mercilessly...". In case they captured any of the Turkish guards of Mount Athos, "that (is) the greatest of evils; not only it is a matter of great necessity to set the (the captive) free for ransom, whatever those holding him decide, and they usually demand, quite inhumanly, many thousands of reals... but also to pay the freed as much as he wishes... Then, the said Christians (pirates) seize whatever we need to live on... and when they leave, still worse evils await us as the rulers (the Turks) claim that we have invited them...".[44]

In 1692, with the "turmoil of the Turco-Venetian wars, suddenly, clamour and disorder filled Mount Athos, so that this place of retreat of souls came close to becoming refuge of bandits", such as "that villain bandit Tzepelis", who, in 1693, "came with many others to capture the *aga* and, by divine Providence, for Mount Athos not to be destroyed, he failed in (his) task".[45]

In 1755 the monks themselves organized a squad and "chased out of Mount Athos all the thieves... who came at night and killed monks of *kellia*".[46]

During the Russo-Turkish wars (1770-1774 and 1787-1792), contrabandists, particularly from Hydra, smuggling Macedonian wheat, flooded Mount Athos, thus provoking the damaging incursions of Turkish detachments. The Athonites preferred to bribe the Turks in order to rid themselves of their 'protection': "I paid *cereme* (fine) to the *müsellim* and the mullah for the twelve soldiers of the pasha who came to Mount Athos because of the Hydriots and the thieves... 123 *aslans*", the treasurer of the Holy Community notes. Further down he adds: "67 soldiers were on their way to Mount Athos... to search for thieves and other calumnies... but we fixed them... and gave (them) 2,260 *aslans*".[47]

In 1773, "on the break of dawn of All Saints' Day, the Christian thieves, who had been going round Mount Athos in two caiques, went to the *skete* of Prophet Elias and took father Paisios the calligrapher and heresiarch of the *kolyves*... together with his senior, and brought them to their caiques at the *skete* of St Paul, they sailed out and threw them into the sea and drowned them, declaring that they drowned them as free masons and the like".[48] Some religious sensitivity for pirates!

Education and Intellectual Activity

One of the earliest visitors to Mount Athos, the French naturalist P. Belon (1549), among other valuable pieces of information, notes that the Athonite monks showed no interest in classic education and that it was doubtful whether there were two or three in each monastery who could read and write. Similar remarks are to be found in the accounts of later travellers but also in texts of 18th - 19th century Greek scholars. That criticism —sometimes exaggerated— was not unfounded but it lacked a sense of historical perspective: these critics used as yardstick the impressive record of the Western monastic orders in letters, science and education. For Eastern monasticism, however, education, although admitted as valuable, was never raised to primary improtance or consindered a *sine qua non* quality of a good monk.

Anyhow, the long monastic tradition of the Orient recognized at least one craft as neccessary to the functioning of a monastery: the 'ministration' or

St George: mosaic in the Xenophontos Monastery (detail).

'handicraft' of the calligrapher, which is mentioned already in the will of Athanasios the Athonite. The Athonite tradition of calligraphy - the artistic copying of primarily liturgical books - survived and flourished during the period of Ottoman rule - although, in the second half of the 15th century, only one calligrapher is mentioned on Mount Athos, "the meanest of monks" Nikiphoros, who, between 1478 and 1493, copied manuscripts in Vatopedi. He is the last known Athonite scribe who copied texts of ancient Greek authors.

During the 16th and the 17th centuries, copying workshops (*scriptoria*) operated in at least two monasteries (Dionysiou and Xeropotamou), producing works of excellent quality and impressive quantity. From that period, some forty Athonite scribes are known and more than five hundred of their manuscripts survive; hundreds of others have been

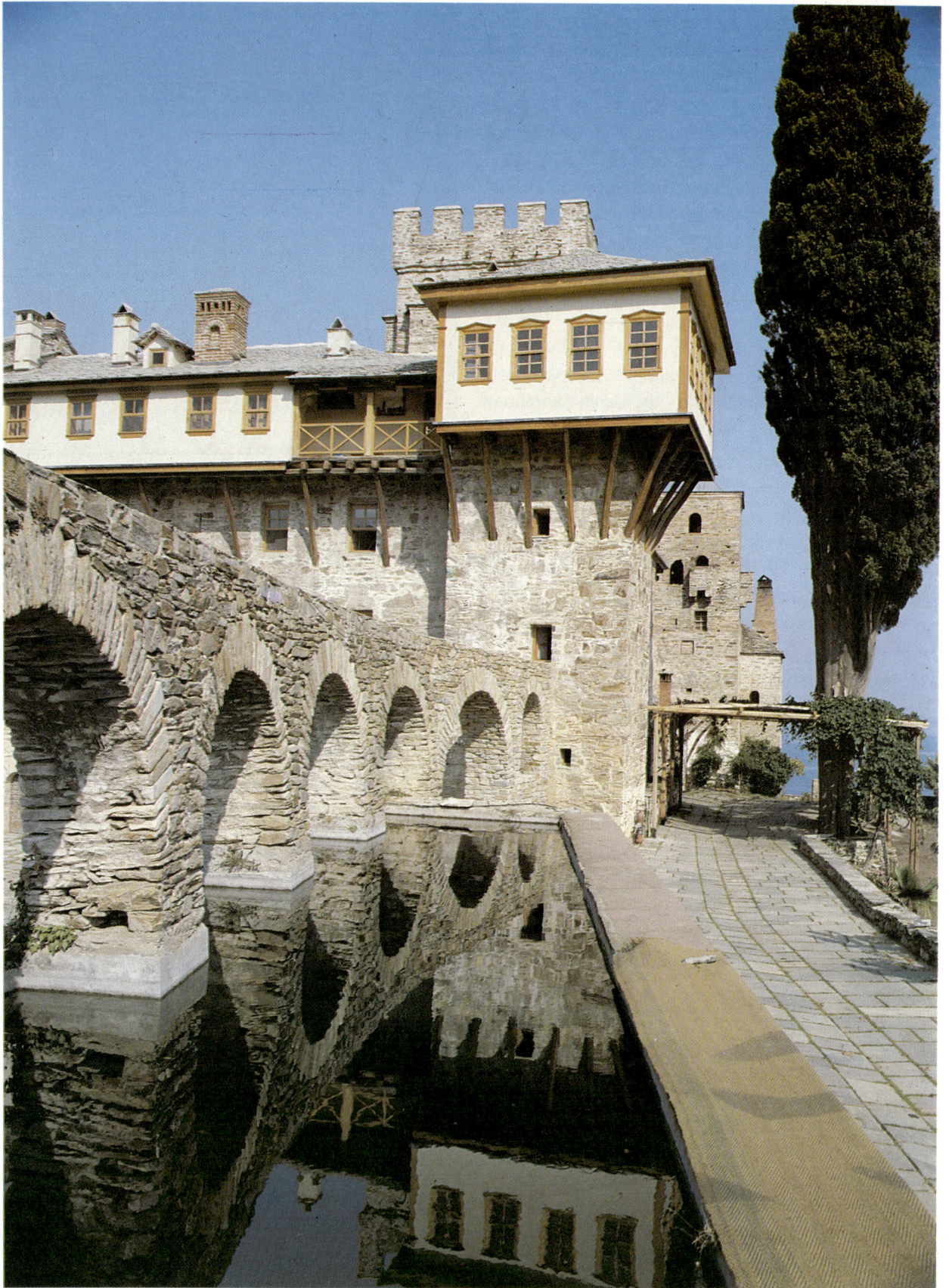

The Stavronikita Monastery: a view of the interior.

destroyed by various causes. The Georgian scribe Theophilos, for example, noted in a manuscript which he copied in 1523 that, until then, he had copied twenty-nine codices, giving their titles too. However, only one of the thirty-one known manuscripts of Theophilos is older than 1523, indicating a tremendous loss of approximately 93%!

Next to this wide circle of scribes, one should consider the various Athonite bibliophiles who bought or commissioned the copying of a specific manuscript for their own use.[49] Therefore, the generalizations regarding widespread lack of education among the Athonites seem rather exaggerated. Admittedly, however, in comparison with the early centuries of Athonite history, Ottoman domination signalled a period of decline, at least with regard to the number of Athonites who distinguished themselves in scholarly pursuits, as well as to the size and quality of their work.

The earliest Athonite writer of some calibre was Dionysios (+1606), the so-called 'Orator' or *Studitis*, who mainly paraphrased patrologic texts into demotic Greek. His contemporary, *proïstamenos* of the Stauronikita monastery, Ierotheos Koukouzelis from Cyprus (+1626), was a distinguished scribe and author of the travelling account *Of a Certain Itinerary to Jerusalem and Palestine* and of a *Story and Wonderful Vision... on Paradise and Hell*.[50]

The mid-17th century marks the activity of the archimandrite of the Iviron monastery, Dionysios (1672), who repeatedly travelled to Russia and died as metropolitan of Hungary-Wallachia. In Moscow he was involved in the movement for the revision and new edition of the liturgical texts of the Russian Church, becoming himself the proof reader. Dionysios also completed the Russian translation of the so-called Chronicle of Dorotheos of Monemvasia and wrote an unpublished *History, or Account of the Origin of the Russians*.[51]

The foremost 17th century Athonite writer was Agapios Landos (+1657). A man of mediocre education but an extremely talented writer, Landos wrote in popular style stories "for the benefit of the soul", and compiled lives of the Saints from Byzantine works translated "into the common dialect". His twelve books, first printed in Venice between 1641 and 1664, were reprinted more than 150 times until 1820 and over forty since. One of his works, the *Salvation of*

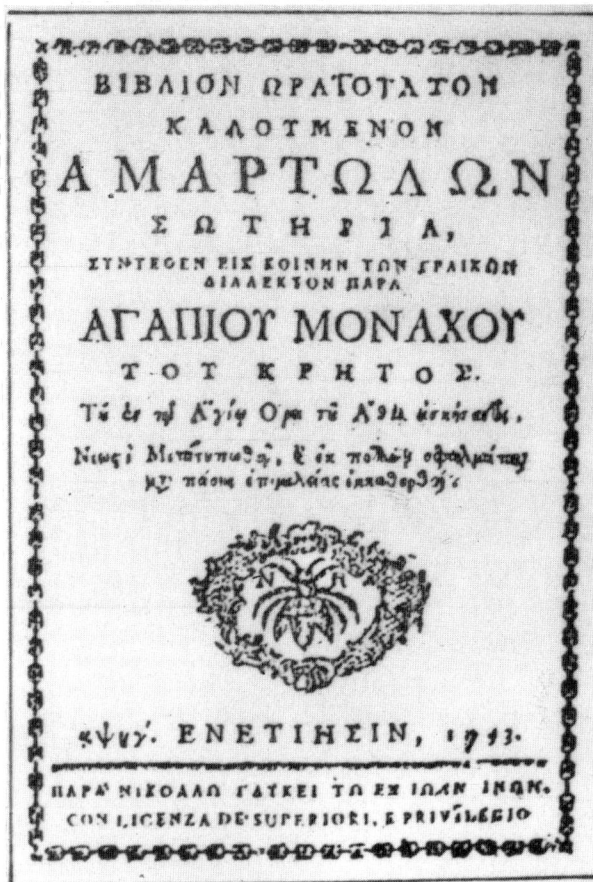

Agapios Landos' Salvation of Sinners (over), the most widely read book of the Ottoman period.

Sinners (1st ed., 1641), was the most popular book of the Ottoman period, reprinted 27 times until 1820 and ten times afterwards.[52]

During the first half of the 18th century, two 'lesser' scholars are found on Mount Athos, Dionysios from Fourna (+1745), a hagiographer and author of the famous *Interpretation of the Art of Painting*,[53] and the hieromonk (i.e. monk ordained as priest) Ierotheos Iviritis (+1745), who worked as a teacher on Skopelos (1723-1736) and published the book *Speeches and Counsels... of Ephraim the Syrian in Simple Expression* (1721).[54]

One of Ierotheos' pupils on Skopelos was Kaisarios Dapontes (+1784), possibly the most prolific 18th century Greek writer. After studying in Constantinople, serving as secretary to Constantine Mavrokordatos in Wallachia and Moldavia, a spell in jail in Constantinople, and an unfortunate marriage, he became a monk at Xeropotamou. An astonishingly gifted versifier, a genuinely talented popular narrator with the wisdom of an experienced and sorely tried man, he wrote dozens of works in both verse and prose. In his work, the conventional Phanariot language and easy rhyme is compensated for by his spontaneous humour, his candid sense of life and a love for the goods 'of this world', a surprising proclivity for a monk. His most important works in verse include the *Mirror of Women* (1766), in which he depicts the most famous women of history, the *Garden of Graces*, a chronicle of his tour of the Danubian principalities, and the unpublished *Historical Geography* and the *Bible of Regna*, a synopsis of Byzantine history in some 30,000 verses. Of his prose, worth-noting are the *Dacian Journals*, a diary of events of the Austro-Russo-Turkish War (1736-39), the so-called *Chronographer*, referring to the history of the Ottoman empire between 1656 and 1704, and the *Historical Catalogue... of Roman Officials*, a biography of some 130 eminent Greek scholars, clerics, Phanariots and merchants of the period 1660-1784.[55]

Analogous to Dapontes' work –but lacking his verve– is that of Kyrillos of Lavra (+1809), verse writer, chronographer and traveller. He entered Lavra in 1760 after studying at Patmos and Smyrna. In 1766-1767 he taught at the Greek Gymnasium of Bucharest and in 1768 and 1770 he toured Russia collecting alms for his monastery. His impressions

from that journey are contained in his long verse *Description of Russia*. On his return to Lavra he was elected hegumen. In 1779-1780 he was in Venice editing the publication of a *Proskynitarion* (Book of Worship) for the monastery of Lavra. His most important work is the unpublished *True Political and Ecclesiastical History*, where, in some ten thousand fifteen-syllable verses, he gives a synopsis of the history of the Greek East from the 11th century to 1809. Moreover, Kyrillos organized the extensive archives of Lavra, copied the most important documents in special codices, occasionally adding his own critical comments. For this work, he is now regarded as the introducer of Byzantine diplomatics.[56]

A wide circle of Athonite monks and other scholars of late 18th - early 19th century is associated with the so-called movement of the *Kolyvades*.[57] It was the most important spiritual movement on Mount Athos during the Ottoman period, not only for the unprecedented controversy it generated but also for its persistence and far-reaching effects.

The immediate cause triggering the dispute was a quite insignificant one: In 1754 the monks of the *skete* of St Anna claimed that it was highly irregular to hold memorial services on Sundays, and not only on Saturdays as tradition demanded. The controversy soon divided the Athonites into two contending factions. Lavra, to which the *skete* belonged, hastened to con-

The Docheiariou Monastery.

demn the *Kolyvades*, as the adherents to tradition were named; the latter, however, secured the support of the former teacher of the Athonite Academy Neophytos of Kausokalyvia, a "quarrelsome critic". Finally, the escalation of the dispute and, perhaps, his own exclusion from the Athonite school forced Neophytos to leave Mount Athos in 1759 and to continue as a teacher in Chios (1759-63), Adrianople (1763-67), Brasov of Trasylvania (1770-73) and Bucharest (1767-70, 1773-84), where he died. It should be noted that Neophytos also had some connection with the Athonite pres, which was set up at Lavra at the expense of Archimandrite Kosmas of Epidavros (Monemvasiotis). The printer was Dukas Sotiris from Thasos, better known for his rather unsuccessful attempt to set up a publishing business in Iasi of Moldavia. The only product of the Athonite press appeared in 1759, a *Selection from the Book of Psalms*, paraphrazed into purist prose by Neophytos of Kausokalyvia.[58]

The *Kolyvades* dispute intensified anew after 1770. The one who "rekindled the furnace of scandals in Mount Athos" was the then scholarch at Thessaloniki, father Athanasios Parios, a scholarly and fighting spirit.[59] In a series of treatises, memoranda and letters, Athanasios defended and articulated theologically the tenets of the movement. The approach of its subsequent leaders, Makarios Notaras (+1805)[60], former metropolitan of Corinth, and Nikodimos the Athonite (+1809)[61], had a clear mystical dimension. With their joint works –*Philokalia of the Holy Niptics* (an anthology of some thirty asceticmystical Fathers), *Evergetinos* (Benefactorial), and *The Complete Works of Symeon, the New Theologian*, appearing between 1782 and 1790– they attempted to associate the movement with the Byzantine mystics and Hesychasts of the 14th century. On the other hand, theological treatises such as the *On Continuous Holy Communion* (by Neophytos Kausokalivitis, Makarios Notaras and Nikodimos the Athonite), seemed to connect the *Kolyvades* with the ascetic-liturgical theories of the Western Church. The Jesuit practice, in fact, of daily communion had drawn the severe criticism of the so-called Jansenist theologians of the 17th century. What were the links and circumstances that associated the *Kolyvades* movement with Western mysticism has not been established as yet. However, it should be noted that Nikodimos, before coming to

Manuscripts in the Vatopedy Library.

Mount Athos, while he was still serving as notary to the diocese of Naxos (1770-1775), had contacts with local Jesuits, who, it seems, also taught him Italian. Moreover, it has been established that Nikodimos' two most popular works, *Invisible War* (1796) and *Spiritual Exercises* (1800), are simply adaptations of two products of Western ascetic literature, bearing similar titles, Lorenzo Scupoli's *Combattimento spirituale* (1589) and Ignazio Loyola's, founder of the Jesuits, *Esercisi spirituali*. Even Athanasios Parios translated for the use of his students in Chios the work of abbot Antonio Genovesi, *Elements of Metaphysics* (1802). Therefore, it is difficult to regard the tenets of the *Kolyvades* as a whole "the essence of Orthodox spirituality", as it is often claimed.

A leading opponent of the *Kolyvades* movement was Theodoritos Lavriotis from Jannina (+1823), a self-taught but erudite scholar who travelled to Germany and Wallachia and later became hegumen of the monastery of Esphigmenou. His best known work is an interpretation of the Apocalypse (1800), a venture into the allegorical method of interpretation, the outcome of which was condemned by the Patriarchate as precarious. His history of Mount Athos, based on Athonite primary sources, has been lost. Some of his works dealing with the *Kolyvades* question have been preserved in manuscripts of the *skete* of St Anna, with controversial passages bolted out by the hand of a *Kolyvas*.[63]

The *Kolyvades* dispute reached its peak during the

Nikodimos the Athonite.

sojourn of Athanasios Parios on Mount Athos (1771-72). At that time the Patriarchate intervened and with various synodic resolutions first attempted to reconcile the rival factions but, a little later, it condemned Athanasios and the leaders of the movement (1776). Nikodimos, a newcomer to Mount Athos and "a sweet-tempered and graceful man", evaded condemnation. However, the most active adherents were obliged to leave Mount Athos and to settle on various Aegean islands (Chios, Ikaria, Paros, Hydra and elsewhere). The monastery of Annunciation, founded by father Niphon on Skiathos, developed into the most important centre of the movement –frequently referred to in the short stories of Papadiamantis and Moraitidis.[64] On the whole, the dispersion of the *Kolyvades* contributed to the spreading of their ideas and liturgical practices among a significant part of the Greek people. Certain elements of their teachings survived in later religious movements, such as that of Apostolos Makrakis, as well as in contemporary religious organizations. Yet the most profoundly Eastern element of their beliefs failed to survive: their interest in the ancient ascetic literature and the tradition of the so-called *niptic* Fathers. In contrast, this particular tendency survived in Russia, at least since

the time of Nil Sorsky (+1508), whose spiritual tradition was revived by Paisy Velichkovsky (+1794) in the 18th century. Both had strong ties with Mount Athos.

Very little is known about Sorsky's sojourn on Mount Athos. However, it seems that knowledge of Greek permitted him to study the Byzantine mystics and then carry to Russia many elements of hesychast doctrines. The theoretically self-evident but extremely subversive, for its time, view of Father Nil that monastic life and extensive private ownership are imcompatible was ardently supported by Maximos the Greek (+1556), who paid for his beliefs with thirty years imprisonment. Maximos, whose secular name was Michael Trivolis, started as a promising young scholar in Italy before becoming a monk at Vatopedi (1505-1516). Then he moved to Russia, where, through his writings and ecclesiastic activity in general, he came to be considered not only a leading intellectual of his time but also the main contributor to the re-establishment of Greek-Russian spiritual and ecclesiastical relations.[65]

Paisy Velichkovsky arrived to Mount Athos in 1746, determined to uncover there the true origins of Orthodox asceticism. While still young, he had already been dissillusioned by both secular education and formalized, conventional monasticism. During his stay on Mount Athos (1746-1764), he began to collect and translate into Slavonic numerous texts of ascetic literature, of Byzantine mystics and Hesychast theologians. He continued his work –which had developed into a pious obsession– after moving to Moldavia. There, he learned of Makarios Notaras' and Nikodimos' the Athonite similar pursuits, whom he was able to communicate only indirectly by writing and through common friends and students. Their spiritual kinship was confirmed by Paisy himself, who translated into Slavonic and published (1792) Makarios' and Nikodimos' *Philokalia*. Paisy left more than 300 codices containing translations of passages from the Greek ascetic and hesychastic literature, which later on –in manuscript or printed form– attracted not only the unwordly *stare* but also those "Slavophile" Russian intellectuals who countered the ideals of "Holy Russia" to Western European culture.[66]

Equally far-reaching were the implications and effect of the work of Paisy, the Bulgarian monk of

Hilandari. His *Slav-Bulgarian History of the Peoples, the Kings and the Saints of Bulgaria, Compiled by Paisios, a Monk of Mount Athos for the Benefit of the Bulgarian People*, completed in 1762 –and widely circulated in manuscript until 1844– was the first serious effort to check the Bulgarians' linguistic and cultural Hellenization and to inspire them with pride for their all but forgotten medieval past. For this work –of however little historical account– Paisy was declared by posterity the father of Bulgarian nationalism.[67]

At the time of the *Kolyvades* dispute and Paisy Velickovsky's ascetic-literary pursuits on Mount Athos, an initiative of altogether different character materealized: the foundation of the Athonite Athonite Academy. It has already been noted how distant from Eastern monastic practice and principles was the study of science and letters, let alone secular education. Indeed, even at its time of prosperity, apart from the expected interest in theological studies and the copying of related manuscripts, no schools or systematic study of wordly disciplines are to be found among the Athonite community. Sporadic evidence to the contrary merely confirms the rule. Later on, however, echoes from Renaissance humanism, the practice of Counter-Reformation and, particularly, the spirit of Enlightenment reached Mount Athos, where they were not unanimously or completely opposed, as it might have been expected. Thus in 1636, quite surpisingly, the Greek Jesuits Kanakis and Nikolaos Rossis –delegates of *Propaganda Fide*– founded a school at Karyes which was attended by a score of student-monks until 1641, when it was closed –not as a result of Athonite reaction– by the Turkish authorities.[68] A century later, Neophytos Mavromatis, the scholar and former metropolitan of Naupaktos (Lepanto) and Arta (+1746), then in retreat on Mount Athos, unsuccessfully attempted to found a school at Karyes, despite the generous support of Nikolaos Karagiannis, a patriotic merchant in Venice.[69] The failure of this particular effort was, probably, partly due to the conviction of the Patriarch of Jerusalem, Chrysanthos Notaras, that a school could not possibly operate on Mount Athos.

Yet, in 1748, the monastery of Vatopedi, on the advice of deputy hegumen Meletios, established a "preparatory school of Greek studies, comprehensive education and teaching of Logic, Philosophy and Theology". For this purpose impresive premises were built with class rooms, a library and a hundred and seventy rooms for boarding students. The project was aided by Cyril V, the progressive and energetic Patriarch, who undertook to secure the Athonite Academy's permanent funding. Initially, the monks of Vatopedi seemed inclined to appoint a German professor from Halle,

Eugenios Voulgaris: his five-and-a-half years at the Athonias were, perhaps, the most fruitful of his life.

Saxony, as director, something quite unprecedented for Athonite standards. Finally, Neophytos of Kausokalyvia was chosen (1749), who, however, fell short of expectations. In 1753, at the suggestion of Neophytos himself and with Patriarch Cyril's wholehearted approval, Eugenios Voulgaris was recalled from Jannina as the new director. His term of five and a half years at the Athonite Academy constitute a most productive period in Voulgaris' life, a turning point in the comparatively short period of the reorientation of Modern Greeks towards 'enlightened Europe'. Of the two hundred students of the Athonite Academy of that period, many distinguished themselves later as teachers and scholars, such as the ardent apostles of Enlightenment Iosipos Moisiodax and Christodoulos Pamplekis, as well as the "unenlightened' Athanasios Parios, Sergios Makraios, Kosmas Aitolos and others. But the period of achievement and developement was short-lived. After 1758, Patriarch Cyril, the patron of the Athonite Academy and then in retreat on Mount Athos after being deposed, intervened rather obtrusively into the affairs of the

Athonite Academy. Moreover, reaction to Voulgaris seems to have come from Meletios Vatopedinos and assistant teacher Panagiotis Palamas. The students were also divided into contentious factions rendering the director's work quite impossible. In the event, Voulgaris was forced to leave Mount Athos (1759), without even being able to collect his personal belongings.

Decline was rapid. Voulgaris' successors, Nikolaos Tzerzoulis, Kyrillos Agraphiotis, Kyprianos Kritikos did not manage to attract but a few students. In early 19th century the Patriarchate widely appealed for the Athonite Academy's revival, contacting even Korais, but to no avail. The scholarly Metropolitan of Philadelphia Dorotheos Proios would express his bitter dissapointment: "A Museum (school) on Mount Athos shall never be established, and if established it will be demolished shortly".[70]

Dorotheos Proios' distrust of the Athonite monks was not an isolated phenomenon. Since the end of the 18th century, the magnificence surrounding Mount Athos in popular imagination had began to fade. The secular ideals of Enlightenment and the widespread anticlericalism of that period began to influence an ever-increasing number of scholars and, through them, to infiltrate wider social strata. Even clerics, who otherwise would not challenge the Church, rejected monasticism as socially useless, and the Athonites, in particular, as being "drones plundering the produce of the bees", according to Neophytos Doukas.[71] Archimandrite Anthimos Gazis was more emphatic: "Our good monks, secure like herds in their monasteries, emasculated in their idleness, fatten on the poor laymen's labour, whom they delude with their superstitions".[72] Deacon Iosipos Moisiodax did not reject monasticism outright, but he gave priority to the needs of education: "While the mountains of Mount Athos are filled with luxurious palaces, the unfortunate schools of ours lack even the essential books".[73]   Finally, the enthusiastic 'Anonymous' of the *Hellenic Nomarchy* believed that Mount Athos epitomized all human evils and that monasteries in general posed a grave national danger: "so many hundreds of monasteries... as many sores on the body of the motherland, because they feed on its products without doing any good at all"![74]

These views, although considerably mitigated later, as the initial fervour of Modern Greek Enlightenment abated, augured far-reaching cultural changes, which were decisively initiated by the 1821 Revolution and the establishment of the Greek state.

From the Revolution of 1821 to Liberation

Due to its geographical isolation and its religious character, Mount Athos for a long time remained practically untouched by the armed conflict and the political developments affecting the Balkans. However, since the time of the Russo-Turkish wars (from 1770 onwards), as it has been noted, the impact of military events was increasingly felt on Mount Athos. At the turn of the 19th century, for instance, when the *Klephts* of Olympus intensified their activity, several bands, such as that of the notorious Nikotsaras and, later, of Vergos, Harisis and others, often took refuge in the peninsula or used it as a base for their raids upon the Turks.

With the outbreak of the Greek Revolution in 1821, first in the Danubian principalities and within a month in the Peloponnese, Roumeli, Mt Pelion and the Aegean islands, Mount Athos could not possibly remain outside the vortex of history. A leading hero and tragic victim of the dramatic events of November 1821 was Emmanuel Pappas, a rich merchant from Serres and member of the *Philiki Etairia*.[75] Pappas was sent by Alexander Ypsilantis, leader of the Revolution in the Danubian Principalities, to Mount Athos in the spring of 1821 escorting a ship full of ammunition. A small group of monks sided with him from the start, but the elders of the holy community hesitated; however, Pappas' prestige and the rumour that Ypsilantis had crossed the Danube and was moving southwards, persuaded them to embark upon the big adventure. The Turkish *aga* of Mount Athos was arrested, and, following a *Te Deum* at the *Protaton*, Pappas was proclaimed 'Leader and Defender of Macedonia'. Thus, by the end of May 1821, the revolution has spread to Mount Athos. Polygyros had already revolted while other districts of Chalcidice followed suit. The impromptu revolutionary units, consisting of a few hundreds of monks and villagers, throbbed with patriotic enthusiasm but lacked battle experience, discipline and suitable weapons. After some spectacular initial success, they were forced by inflowing Turkish reserves to retreat to the peninsulas of Kassandra and Mount Athos; there, disillusionment, squabbles and lack of money, food and ammunition created a hopeless situation. Living conditions had become particularly dramatic on Mount Athos where the influx of more than 5.000 women and children from all over Chalcidice –in violation of the traditional *avaton* (the ban on the female sex)– exhausted supplies and created acute sanitation problems.

The impending Turkish invasion paralyzed the holy community; the spirit of resistance died out amidst a state of panic which neither Pappas' delegate Nikiphoros Iviritis nor the pleas of Dimitrios Ypsilantis could dispell: "All holy monasteries, their glory, your peace, your life depend on the salvation of our *Genos* as everything is endangered along with the *Genos*, if we display ill-considered negligence. Shew that the clerics of our

The Megisti Lavra Monastery: a view from the inner yard.

Church are not indifferent to the freedom of our faith and our *Genos*".[76] Yet, when Emmanuel Pappas returned to Mount Athos in November 1821, he was received with coldness bordering on enmity. He decided to give up the effort and boarded his ship, intending to go to southern Greece, where the Revolution was in full swing; his bitter frustration, however, was such that he died of apoplexy still on board at the age of forty-nine.

A few days later, an Athonite delegation was sent to Kassandra to "pay homage" to the pasha, while renouncing the "gang of criminals" which had incited the rebellion. The monks begged for amnesty and for the return of their property in Chalcidice, offering 1,500,000 kurus as well as double their regular taxes to appease the sultan. The pasha, however, failed to keep his part of the arrangement: not only did he arrest dozens of prominent Athonites –many of whom died of ill-treatment– but he also stationed military garrisons at all monasteries, which were withdrawn only in 1830, after causing incalculable damage to buildings, works of art and libraries.

Meanwhile, already in the first month of the revolution, a gradual outflow of monks soon took the form of mass exodus. Thus, from the 2,980 monks of Mount Athos in August 1821, only 1,062 and 590 were to be found in 1824 and 1826 respectively. Almost all foreigners left. Of the Greek monks some fled to the Aegean islands and others to the Peloponnese, taking with them whatever valuable they could salvage.[77]

The monks began to return to Mount Athos after the military occupation was lifted. Governor Kapodistrias offered a ship of honour to carry Athonite treasures back to their place. He also mediated to the Russian government for the latter to release the revenues from Athonite estates in Bessarabia and thus alleviate the financial plight of the monasteries. At the same time, the Athonite community managed to recover part of its property in Chalcidice which had been hurriedly sold or mortgaged in order to meet the demands of the Ottoman military occupation.

Athonite relations with the Ottoman administration were modified in 1826 when the *bostanci* Guard was disbanded and Mount Athos was brought under the ministry of Finance. The governor of Mount Athos became a palace official with the title of *voyvoda*. After the 1869 reforms and until 1912, Mount Athos was governed by a *kaymakam* with both tax-collecting and policing functions.

A new crisis in relations with the Turkish authorities was threatened in 1854, at the time of the Crimean War. Tsamis Karatasos, the Macedonian chieftain, arrived at Mount Athos and tried to induce the monks into another rebellion. Yet very few responded to his invitation. The holy community, led by recent bitter experience, asked

him "to leave the *rayalik* (subservient regime) of the holy place undisturbed" and offered him a sum of money to withdraw. Karatasos withdrew to the neck of the peninsula after sending a sharp rebuke to the Athonite leaders: "I notice that you persist on your subservience and remain wholly devoted to the Ottoman government".[78] In the event, Turkish reprisals following Karatassos' defeat were rather mild.

In 1860-1861, the Turkish governor of Macedonia, Hüsnü Pasha, attempted to curb the administrative autonomy of Mount Athos, but he was foiled as the Athonites successfully appealed to the sultan.

Athonite finances received a heavy blow when the newly established Romanian state first (1852) attached and, finally (1863), expropriated all monastic and Church endowment in the former Principalities. A significant portion belonged to Athonite monasteries: 35 monastic establishements, 3 churches, 211 metohia, 77 buildings, and hundreds of vineyards and farms. The indemnity offered by the first ruler of the Romanian state, Alexander Couza, was considered –and actually was– so small that it was rejected by the Athonites. Legal proceedings against the goverment in Bucharest came to nought. Another financial blow was the decision of the Russian government in 1873 that only two-fifths of the rents of Athonite *metohia* in Bessarabia and the Caucasus could be remitted.

Relations between Mount Athos and the Ecumenical Patriarchate suffered periodic crises and remained more or less tense throughout the 19th century. The tendency of the Patriarchate to intervene into the administrative and spiritual affairs of Mount Athos rallied the Athonites in a common effort to safeguard and, if possible, to increase their autonomy. At first, friction started over economic matters. Since the time of Patriarch Gregory VI (1835-40), the Athonites were increasingly called upon to contribute to various charitable purposes (building a lazaretto in Constantinople, aid for the fire-stricken, erecting the School of Chalki, etc), a fact which was much grumbled at and led to protests even before the Ottoman government. The tension almost developed into a break with the Patriarchate when Joachim II (1860-1878), in his attempt to codify the mostly unwritten administrative principles of the Athonite community, elaborated a charter (1877) which, although sanctioned as a state law, was rejected by the Athonites on the –not unreasonable– grounds that they had not been consulted. The long period of coldness that ensued was terminated on the initiative of Patriarch Joachim III, who had spent a long time on Mount Athos: the new *General Regulations of Mount Athos* appeared and were duly approved by both the Athonites (1911) and the patriarchal synod (1912), but were not sanctioned by the Ottoman authorities owing to the outbreak of the First Balkan War.

However, the issue that turned Mount Athos into a battlef of nationalistic antagonisms and diplomatic bargaining was the attempt of the Russians to alter its ethnological character and use it as a springboard of Panslavist designs.[79] That effort was part of a more general tendency to exploit Orthodoxy politically, which became manifest in the case of other religious centres of the Levant, such as the Ecumenical Patriarchate and the Holy Lands, which the Russians also tried to bring under their control.

The Russian penetration of Mount Athos was rapid and followed two complementary ways: mass settlement of Russian monks at thinly populated and heavily indebted monasteries or *sketes* and an ever increasing interest in Athonite affairs, manifested by frequent visits of Russian officials and lavish funding of building programmes. The first targets —and, later, centres of Russian propaganda— were the old 'Russian' monastery of Panteleimonos, the *skete* of St Andrew of Vatopedi,

also known as *Serai* –near Karyes– and the *skete* of Prophet Elias of Pantokratoros. Although in 1830-1834 there had been no Russian monk in these monastic establishments, during the following seventy years the number of Russian monks and 'pilgrims' exceeded 2,500 and in the entire peninsula 3,500. Among them, there were several former officers of the Russian army and scholars, such as Andrei Muraviev and the historian Peter Sevastianov.

Meanwhile, during the second half of the 19th century, the Russians constructed churches and multi-storeyed buildings of unprecedented size and luxury to provide for the hundreds of monks and pilgrims who kept coming every year. In addition to unlimited financial backing, visits of high officials were employed by the Russians in their effort to foster their hold on the monastic community of Mount Athos. Grand Dukes Constantine Nicolajevic in 1845 and Alexios Alexandrovic in 1867, Prince Ignatiev, the Russian ambassador in Constantinople, escorting his American and

Megisti Lavra: the dining-hall.

Xenophontos: cupola.

German colleagues in 1874, Grand Duke Constantine Constantinovic in 1881, and Admiral Alexei Virilev in 1900, all visited and paid their respects to the Russian monastic establishments of Mount Athos.[80]

The Russians tried to secure and augment their gains in the monastic field by means of diplomacy too. They added to the –abortive– San Stefano Treaty (1878) a specific clause granting the Russian presence on Mount Athos (the monastery of Panteleimonos and the *sketes* of St Andreas and Prophet Elias) autonomous status; Russian *kellia* throughout Mount Athos (until then belonging to various Greek monasteries) were also recognized as annexes to the main three Russian establishments with the right to own land. Thus, the Russians laid the ground for further expansion over the entire peninsula. Naturally, the Greek, Ottoman and other interested governments reacted. The Congress of Berlin, a few months later, decisively curbed Russian ambitions; the particular provision on Mount Athos was annulled and the ancient status was restored.

Monastic life on Mount Athos was less affected by the rising Balkan nationalisms. Romanian monks mainly concentrated at the *skete* of St Demetrius and their number never exceeded 300. The Serbs, who began to return to Mount Athos after 1830, limited themselves to the monastery of Hilandari and never exceeded 50. They resisted Russian influence and contended themselves with the financial aid they received from Serbia. Until the middle of the 19th century, the Bulgarians of the monastery of Zographou (230-300 monks) coexisted with Greek monks. After the Bulgarian Schism, they took care to remain loyal to the Ecumenical Patriarchate, but their relations with their Greek colleagues deteriorated during the Macedonian Struggle and the Balkan Wars.

Athonite affairs entered a new phase on 2 November 1912. On that day, a squadron of the Greek fleet led by the flagship *Averof* anchored off the port of Daphni and a detachment landed at the neck of the peninsula. Within a few hours the Turkish authorities surrendered. After five centuries, the Ottoman domination of Mount Athos had ended.

From Liberation to the Present

The radical changes brought about by the Balkan Wars kept the question of the international status of Mount Athos open. During the Ambassadors' Conference in London, Russia –through her representative but indirectly too, through an inspired 'petition' of the Russian monks of Athonite cells– submitted afternative proposals for the status of the Athonite community: internationalization, neutrality, joint protection or joint suzerainty by the three Balkan countries and Russia. The Ecumenical Patriarchate and the Greek government, seriously engaged in other fronts, put up a rather mild resistance. The Athonites, however, declared in a special resolution their determination to resist with all means available any solution revoking the autonomy of Mount Athos and the "Greek sovereignty over it".[81]

With the outbreak of the First World War that particular fermentation was suspended, while the success of the Bolshevik Revolution put an end to Russian interest in Athonite affairs. The treaties of Neuilly (1919), Sèvres (1920) and Lausanne (1923) expressedly or implicitly recognized the –de facto, until then– Greek sovereignty over Mount Athos.[82] Yet relations between the Greek state and Mount Athos as well as the internal regime of the Athonite community remained legally unspecified until 1926, when the Greek parliament ratified the *Constitutional Charter of Mount Athos*, largely based on the *General Regulations* of 1911-1912. Moreover, specific articles were added to the Greek Constitution of 1927 –with passed into all subsequent constitutions– stipulating, among other things, that Mount Athos constitutes "a self-governed part of the Hellenic State, whose sovereignty thereon remains intact". According to these texts, the Greek state is represented by the Governor of Mount Athos, seated at Karyes and answerable to the Ministry for Foreign Affairs. The governor sees to it that constitutional order is observed, participates in the meetings of the Holy Community in advisory capacity, and is in charge of the local public authorities (police, customs, etc). Mount Athos remains under the spiritual supervision of the Ecumenical Patriarchate, but relations between the two were, and still are, lukewarm, if not cold. The reasons are the introduction in 1923 of the Gregorian calendar which the Athonites –with the exception of Vatopedi– rejected, and the tentative steps of Patriarch Athenagoras (+1972) and his succesors towards a rapprochement between the Roman Catholic and the other Christian Churches.

The Second World War, enemy occupation and the events that followed did not leave Mount Athos unaffected.[83] A few days after the entry of German troops into Thessaloniki, the Athonites sent a letter to Hitler asking him "to assume this holy place under his high personal protection". Indeed, throughout the occupation, there was only a small German guard stationed at Karyes. In December 1944 representatives of EAM (National Liberation Front) convened a 'Panathonite Meeting' at Karyes, which proceeded to draw up a new Charter. The draft was sympathetically received by the *kelliotes*, because it satisfied their agelong demand for emancipation from the dominant monasteries, but it was never applied: in April 1945 the EAM authorities were withdrawn from Mount Athos.

The manifestations of 1963 marking the millenium of Mount Athos constituted an important event of the post-war period. They were attended by government officials, Patriarch Athenagoras, representatives of Orthodox and other Churches, the universities of Athens and Thessaloniki, scientific societies and leading Byzantinists.

Perhaps, the most positive intervention of the state in Mount Athos during the last decades has been the work of the Archaeological Service, which undertook the restoration and conservation of many historical buildings and frescoes. In 1965 the entire peninsula of Mount Athos was declared a cultural and natural preserve and a special archaelogical service was established whose branch is the Centre for the Preservation of Mount Athos Heritage. However, cooperation between these two public agencies with the Athonites has not always been smooth with the latter frequently complaining of state intervention in their internal affairs. Discontent intensified in 1969, when the military regime of the Colonels, in pursuit of its programme for 'Church reform', issued a decree which provided for fiscal control of the

Virgin Mary and the Child, in the **Protaton.**

monasteries, measures for the protection of their treasures as well as other forms of state intervention in their function.

The Athonite community for its part has only a limited scope for reaction, since it financially depends on the state to a great extent. In 1924, 20,000 hectares of monastic land were permanently leased to the state for the settlement of Asia Minor refugees. In return, the state undertook to pay the Athonites a 6% annual interest on the presumed value of that land in the form of public bonds, which, however, were annulled in 1944. Since then, the state has been paying an annual allowance which is allocated among the twenty principal monasteries in proportion to the land leased by each of them. It should be noted that the 'dependent' monks have no share in state funding: the *kelliotes* earn their living by cultivating their fields, *skete*-dwellers and anchorites by selling their handicrafts. Other sources of income for the Athonite monasteries comprise the remaining *metohia* in Chalcidice, rental from several buildings in Athens and Thessaloniki and lumbering. Further, there is a 3% duty on the value of goods transported through Mount Athos for the benefit of the Holy Community and the Athonite Academy.

In the field of education, the most noteworthy event of the last hundred and fifty years has been the re-establishment of the Athonite Academy in 1874, which –with short intervals– still functions as an ecclesiastical school. Among the many, but generally 'lesser', Athonite scholars, the following stand out: Vartholomaios of Koutloumousiou (+1851), a student of Nikodimos the Athonite, who taught on Imvros, at the Flaghinian School of Venice, the Ionian Academy, the theological school of Chalki and the Athonite school. He wrote a history of his native island, Imvros, a history of the Virgin Mary Monastery of Chalki, and published the first critical editions of the *Minaia* and other litugical books.[84]

Gerasimos Smyrnakis and Kosmas Vlachos simultaneously published, in 1903, two still useful general histories of Mount Athos. Other scholars distinguished themselves in historical research, codicology, and edition of texts and documents: Alexandros (Eumorphopoulos) of Lavra (+1905), Spyridon Kampanaos of Lavra too, physician, Gabriel of Stauronikita, Ioakeim Iviritis, Panteleimon (Davos) of Lavra, Alexandros (Lazaridis) of Lavra and the erudite but not equally methodical, Christophoros Ktenas (+1940) and Eulogios Kourilas (+1961). Certain elements of the spiritual tradition of the Kolyvades revived in the persona and writings of the former hegumen of Dionysiou, Gabriel Kazasis (+1984).

Over the last centuries, the libraries and archives of the Athonite monasteries have attracted the interest of many students and researchers as depositories of the intellectual tradition and history not only of Mount Athos but of the Byzantine world in general.[85] The monastic collections of manuscript codices, the origins of which can be traced to the time when the monasteries were founded, should have been much richer in the early 18th century than they are at present not only in number but in material, too. In addition to the host of Athonite scribes, who kept working even during the period of Ottoman domination, monastic libraries were occasionally enriched with collections of manuscripts bequeathed by philo-Athonite scholars and prelates, such as Theophanis Eleavulkos (+c.1555), Maximos Margounios (+1602), Patriarch Dionysius IV (+1694), Neophytos Mavromatis (+1746) and others. Already since the Renaissance, there had been talk in humanist circles about the *celebratissimas bibliothecas... quae in Atho monte sunt*. This fame aroused the collecting zeal of various bibliophile rulers as well as the interest of relevant state services: from the end of the 15th century onwards, special missions to Mount Athos were organized with the task to locate and obtain by any means available the valued manuscripts. Thus, in 1491, Ianos Lascaris, a leading philologist of his time, visited Mount Athos and, on behalf of Lorenzo di Medici, got hold of a rich manuscript collection, today at the Laurentian Library of Florence. In 1543 Nikolaos Sophianos, a scholar from Corfu, procured some 300 codices from Mount Athos and the monasteries of Thessaly for the Spanish diplomat Diego Hurtado de Mendoza (today at the Library of Escorial in Spain). In mid-17th century the Cypriot Athanasios the Orator, a delegate of Cardinal Mazarin, carried to France numerous Greek manuscripts, among them 109 from Mount Athos (today at the Bibliothèque Nationale in Paris). In 1654 the Russian monk Arseny Sukhanov left Mount Athos with 498 old patrological and liturgical manuscripts in his baggage (today at the Historical Museum of Moscow). The drain of manuscripts from Mount Athos continued at least until the middle of the 19th century. In 1837, for instance, Robert Curzon, a British noble, took dozens of codices to England; many more were taken away by Minas Minoidis (+1860) to France and Porphyry Uspensky (+1877) to Russia.

However, although expatriated, these manuscripts were not lost to science. Certainly many more have been irretrievably damaged as a result of the all too frequent fires, the turmoil of war years, particularly between 1821 and 1830, moisture and the generally bad conditions of storage, plus their use for the basest practical needs. Already in early 19th century, Korais had suggested to the Patriarchate certain measures to stem further loss, but eighty years lapsed before Professor Spyridon Lampros laid the ground for the restoration, classification and cataloguing of the Athonite manuscripts. His work was later completed by others so that at present there have been published descriptions of content of nearly 12,000 Athonite manuscripts. Most of them have been photographed by the Patriarchic Institute of Patrological Studies of Thessaloniki.

Today, the Athonite archives constitute a 'treasury' of Byzantine documents, the richest in the world, a valuable source for the study not only of Athonite history but also of the legal and fiscal institutions of Byzantium. Monastic records have been preserved with much greater care than manuscripts since they are mostly titles of ownership and proofs of various financial trancations. In any case, until the mid-19th century, foreign researchers were not interested in Athonite records, which, therefore, escaped the fate of manuscripts. Porphyrio Uspensky was the first to take transcripts and to publish an extensive catalogue of Athonite Byzantine documents (pilfering several of them too, and smuggling them into Russia). Later, the most important documents of seven Athonite monasteries were published on the basis of Uspensky's transcripts. Between 1918 and 1920 Gabriel Millet, a French student of Byzantine Art, and in 1941 the leading German Byzantinst Franz Dölger photographed many official documents which were then published in remarkable editions. Since 1962 the Byzantine Research Centre (of the Athens-based National Research Foundation) has undertaken several missions to Mount Athos to photograph latent Byzantine and, particularfly, post-byzantine documents. Finally, the Modern Greek Research Center (a branch of the same Foundation), has inaugurated a cataloguing programme for old printed books of the Athonite libraries (among them several hundreds of 'archetypes' and 'paleotypes', i.e. books printed before 1600).

Following liberation, the monastic population of Mount Athos sharply declined. In 1913 there were 6,345 monks (3,707 Greeks, 1,914 Russians, 379 Romanians, 243 Bulgarians, 89 Serbs, 14 Georgians). Thirty years later, in 1943, their numbers had decreased by 55% to 2,878 monks (1,800 Greeks, 700 Russians, 220 Romanians, 120 Bulgarians, 35 Serbs, 3 Georgians). Over the next thirty years there was a further 60% decline down to 1,146 monks (1972). Since then, however, the Athonite population has been steadily on the increase: 1,200 monks in 1974, 1,445 in 1981. Along with this considerable rate of growth (20% in a decade) two significant developments can be observed: the average age of the monks has decreased and their level of education has risen. Specifically, while in 1960-1964 the percentages of secondary and higher education graduates were only 12,3% and 2,8% respectively, ten years later the corresponding percentages stood at 28,2% and 17%.[86]

This apparent recovery in numbers as well as the qualitative change in the composition of the monastic population is due to both external causes and recent spiritual trends within the Greek society. More specifically, over the last few decades, the sweeping tide of tourism did not leave monastic places unaffected, thus orientating a number of monks and novices towards the, comparatively, less accessible Mount Athos. On the other hand, the perceptible turn of the Greek and Orthodox theology in general, during the 1960s –under the influence of Russian theologians of the diaspora– away from German Academism and towards the so-called patricist and mystic tradition of Orthodoxy contributed to a positive re-evaluation of Eastern –and particularly

Interior aspect of the Xeropotamou Monastery.

Athonite– monasticism. This fact –in connection with the more general reaction to the model of consumer society– led several young people to Mount Athos, students of theology or not; many of the latter came from among the once thriving 'Christian movement' which, at exactly that time (1959-1960), after an internal crisis, split and almost collapsed. Finally, indicative of the new trends is the quite extraordinary presence on Mount Athos of some fifty proselytes to Orthodoxy from various countries of Western Europe and the USA.

C.G. PATRINELIS
THE MONASTIC COMMUNITY
OF MOUNT ATHOS
NOTES

1. For general and specific bibliographies of Mount Athos see: I. Doens, 'Bibliographie de la Sainte Montagne de l'Athos' in *Le millenaire du Mont Athos 963-1963*, vol. 2, Venice-Chevetogne 1964, pp. 337-495; I. Doens - H.K. Papastathis, 'Legal Bibliography of Mount Athos, 1912-1969' (in Greek), *Makedonika*, 10 (1970), 191-240; K. Delopoulos, *Contribution to the Bibliography of Mount Athos, Books, 1701-1971* (in Greek) Athens 1971. Among the older general histories of Mount Athos the following are still useful: M. Gedeon, *Mount Athos, Memories, Documents, Notes* (in Greek), Constantinople 1885; Kosmas Vlachos, *The Peninsula of the Holy Mountain, Athos* (in Greek), Volos 1903; Gerasimos Smyrnakis, *Mount Athos* (in Greek), Athens 1903. More recent general histories include: I. Mamalakis, *The Holy Mountain (Mount Athos) through the Centuries* (in Greek), Thessaloniki 1971; Monk Dorotheos, *Mount Athos. Initiation into its History and Life* (in Greek), vols. 1-2, Katerini 1986; P. Christou, *Mount Athos, the Athonite State, History, Art, Life* (in Greek), Athens 1987. For a comprehensive study of the early history of Mount Athos, see the introductory chapters in Denise Papachrysanthou, *Actes du Protaton*, Paris 1975.

2. G. Soulis, 'Stephan Dušan and Mount Athos', in *Yearbook of the Society for Byzantine Studies* (in Greek), 22 (1953), 82-96.

3. N. Oikonomidis, 'Monastères et moines lors de la conquête ottomane', *Südost-Forschungen*, 36 (1976), 1-10. The author considers plausible the tradition that the Athonites had already submitted to the sultan before 1372.

4. Elissavet A. Zachariadou, 'Ottoman Documents from the Archives of Dionysiou (Mount Athos), 1495-1520', *Südost-Forschungen*, 30 (1971), 1-35 (partic. 21-27).

5. Christophoros Ktenas, 'Sigillate and Other Patriarchal Documents of the Athonite Holy Monastery of Docheiarios', in *Yearbook of the Society of Byzantine Studies* (in Greek), 5 (1928), 109-110. Also see, I.K. Hassiotis, *The Greeks on the Eve of the Naval Battle of Lepanto* (in Greek), Thessaloniki 1970, pp. 21-22; A. Vacalopoulos, *History of Modern Hellenism* (in Greek), vol. 2, Thessaloniki 1976, pp. 195-196; I. Mamalakis, *op. cit.*, pp. 252-254.

6. John C. Alexander, 'The Monasteries of the Meteora during the First Two Centuries of Ottoman Rule', *Jahrbuch der Österreichischen Byzantinistik*, 32/2 (1982), 99-100, 102-103.

7. P. Lemerle - P. Wittek, 'Recherches sur l'histoire et le statut des monastères athonites sous la domination turque', *Archives d'Histoire du Droit Oriental*, 3 (1984), 411-474 (partic. 442 ff)

8. Maximos the Greek gives an interesting account of the internal organization of the monasteries and monastic life in early 16th century; see, G. Papamichail, *Maximos the Greek, the First Enlightener of the Russians* (in Greek), Athens 1950, pp. 363, 414. Negative consequences of *Idiorrhythmia* –in mid-late 16th century– are described and castigated by the scholarly monks Pachomios Rousanos (see, I. Karmiris 'Unpublished Speech of Pachomios Rousanos' (in Greek), *Theologia*, 14 (1936), 38-40, and Ph. Meyer *Die Haupturkunden für die Geschichte der Mount Athosklöster*, Leipzig 1984 p. 213-214) and Dionysios the Orator (see, Meyer, *op. cit.*, p. 218-223).

9. Nikodimos the Athonite, *Pidalio*, Athens 1841, p. 479.

10. Ch., 'The Protos of Mount Athos and the Megali Mesi or Assembly' (in Greek), *Yearbook of the Society for Byzantine Studies*, 6 (1929), 241-281.

11. A list of the known *Protoi* of Mount Athos in Papachrysanthou, *op. cit.*, pp. 129-150.

12. An edition of *Typika* of Mount Athos, in Meyer, *op. cit.*, 13. Alexandros Lavriotis, 'Mount Athos after the Ottoman Conquest' (in Greek), *Yearbook of the Society for Byzantine Studies*, 32 (1963), 113-261.

14. J. Koder, 'Die Metochia der Mount Athos-Klöster auf Sithonia und Kassandra', *Jahrbuch der Österreichischen Byzantinistik*, 16 (1967), 211-224, and *ibid.*, 17 (1968), 117-125.

15. Mamalakis, *op. cit.*, p. 284; W.M. Leake, *Travels in Northern Greece*, London 1835, p. 135.

16. Alexandros Lavriotis, *op. cit.*, 81.

17. G. Cioran, *Relations between the Romanian Countries and Mount Athos* (in Greek), Athens 1938; P. Nasturel, *Le Mont Athos et les Roumains, Recherches sur leurs relations du milieu du XIV siècle à 1654*, Rome 1986.

18. K. Simopoulos, *Foreign Travellers in Greece*, vol. 3, 1st ed., Athens 1975, p. 106.

19. Leake, *op. cit.*, p. 132.

20. P. Nikolopoulos - N. Oikonomidis, 'The Holy Cloister of Dionysiou; Archive Catalogue' (in Greek), *Symmeikta*, I (1966), 301.

21. Alexandros Lavriotis, *op. cit.*, 48, 112.

22. *Ibid.*, 51.

23. *Ibid.*, 17, 27, 31, 35.

24. *Ibid.*, 18; Leake, *Travels*, p. 251.

25. B. de Khitrowo, *Itinéraires russes en Orient*, Geneva 1889, p. 259.

26. H.W. Lowry, see note 32.

27. N. Oikonomidis, 'The Holy Monastery of Stauronikita; Catalogue of Codices' (in Greek), *Symmeikta*, 2 (1970), 449.

28. Alexandros Lavriotis, *op. cit.*, 112; Mamalakis, *op. cit.*, pp. 284-86.

29. Sryridon Lavriotis - Sophr. Eustratiadis, *Catalogue of the Megisti Lavra Codices* (in Greek), Paris 1925, pp. 335-336.

30. Dorotheos, *Holy Mountain* (in Greek), pp. 230, 300, 419.

31. Alexandros Lavriotis, *op. cit.*, 125; Leake, *Travels*, p. 136.

32. H.W. Lowry, 'A Note on the Population and Status of the Athonite Monasteries under Ottoman Rule (ca. 1520)', *Wiener Zeitschrift für Künde des Morgenlandes*, 72 (1981), 115-135; also see, *Byzantion*, 52 (1982), 496-499, and 55 (1985), 493-414.

33. Spyridon Lavriotis, 'Transcripts of Documents of Megisti Lavra' (in Greek), *Byzantinisch-neugriechische Jahrbücher*, 7 (1927-29), 408.

34. Alexander Lavriotis, *Athonite Documents of the Great Greek Revolution 1821-1832*, Athens 1966, pp. 25-28.

35. Leake, *Travels*, p. 125; Simopoulos, *op. cit.*, p. 106 (testimony of Carlyle and Hunt 1801)

36. Isaias Hilandarinos; see de Khitrowo, *op. cit.*, p. 25-29.

37. Christou, *op. cit.*, pp. 219-20; N. Oikonomidis, *op. cit.*, p. 9.

38. Ioseph Georgeirinis, *A Description of the Present State of Samos, Nicaria, Patmos and Mount Athos*, London 1678, pp. 92-96.

39. Leake, *Travels*, pp. 120, 121, 141.

40. P. Lemerle, *Aktes de Kutlumus*, Paris 1945, pp. 163, 173, 174.

41. Leake, *Travels*, p. 137.

42. Alexandros Lavriotis, *The Holy Mountain after the Ottoman Conquest* (in Greek), p. 45.

43. S. Lampros, *A Catalogue of the Greek Codices at the Libraries of Mount Athos* (in Greek), vol. 1, Cambridge 1895, pp. 170, 172.

44. Spyridon Lavriotis, *'Athonite", Grigorios Palamas, 5 (1921), 362-363.*

45. Alexandros Lavriotis, *op. cit.*, p. 46-47.

46. Spyridon Lavriotis, 'Transcripts of Documents...', *op. cit.*, 427.

47. Alexandros Lavriotis, *op. cit.*, pp. 49-50.

48. S. Kadas, 'A Manuscript with Kaisarios Dapontes' Autographed Notes' (in Greek), *In Honore E. Kriaras*, Thessaloniki 1988, p. 200.

49. Linos Politis, 'Athonite Bibliographers of the 16th Century' (in Greek), *Ellinika*, 15 (1957), 355-384; by the same author, 'Athonite Analecta' (in Greek), *ibid.*, 16 (1958-59), 126-36; by the same author, 'Persistances byzantines dans l'écriture liturgique du XVIIe ciècle', in *La paleographie grecque et byzantine*, Paris 1977, pp. 371-373.

50. Ch.G. Patrinelis, 'History of the Stauronikita Monastery', in *The Stauronikita Monastery* (in Greek), Athens 1974, 36.

51. Ch.G. Patrinelis, 'Dionysios Iviritis, Archbishop of Hungary-Wallachia, Translator of Dorotheos' Chronography into Russian' (in Greek), in *Yearbook of the Society for Byzantine Studies*, 32 (1963), 314-317.

52. Despoina Kostoula, *Agapios Landos the Cretan*, Ioannina 1983.

53. K.Th. Dimaras, 'A Life of Dionysios from Fourna by Theophanis from Agrapha' (in Greek), *Ellinika*, 10 (1937-38), 213-279.

54. T. Gritsopoulos, 'Ierotheos Iviritis the Peloponnesian' (in Greek), in *Yearbook of the Society for Byzantine Studies*, 32 (1963), 94-112.

55. D. Paschalis, 'Kaisarios Dapontes (1714-1784)' (in Greek), *Theologia*, 13 (1935), 224-250.

56. Eulogios Kourilas, *Kyrillos, Prehegumen of Lavra* (in Greek), Athens 1935.

57. Ch.Z. Tzogas, *The Controversy Concerning Memorial Services in Mount Athos during the 18th Century* (in Greek), Thessaloniki 1969; K. Papoulidis, *The Movement of the 'Kollyvades'* (in Greek), Athens 1971.

58. N.E. Skiadas, 'The Press of Mount Athos, the Athonite Academy and Eugenios Bulgaris' (in Greek), *Nea Estia*, 90 (1971), 1194-98.

59. D. Oikonomidis, 'Athanasios Parios' (in Greek), *Yearbook of the Society for Cycladic Studies*, 1 (1961), 347-422; L.I. Vranousis, 'Unknown Patriotic Pamphlets and Unpublished Texts of the Time of Rhigas and Korais' (in Greek), *Yearbook of the Medieval Archives of the Athens Academy*, 15/16 (1965-66), 252-329.

60. K. Papoulidis, *Makarios Notaras (1731-1805), Archbishop of former Corinthia*, Athens 1974.

61. K. Papoulidis, 'Nicodème l'Hagiorite (1749-1809)', *Theologia*, 37 (1966), 294-313, 390-415, 576-590; 38 (1967), 95-118, 301-313.

62. K. Papoulidis, 'The Relationship of Nikodimos' the Athonite *Invisible War* to *Combattimento Spirituale* of Lorenzo Scupoli' (in Greek), *Makedonika*, 10 (1970), 23-33; see also, *ibid.*, 11 (1971), 167-113.

63. Eulogios Kourilas, 'Prehegumen Theodoritos Lavriotis, Scribe' (in Greek), *Byzantinische Zeitschrift*, 44 (1951), 343-346.

64. G. Veritis, 'The Reforming Movement of the *Kollyvades* and the two Alexanders of Skiathos' (in Greek), *Actines*, 6 (1943), 99-110.

65. Papamichail, *op. cit.*; J.V. Haney, *From Italy to Muscovy. The Life and Works of Maxim the Greek*, Munich 1973.

66. A.-A. Tachiaos, *The National Revival of the Bulgarians and the Emergence of a Bulgarian National Movement in Macedonia*, Thessaloniki 1974.

68. G. Hofmann, *Rom und Athos*, Rome 1954. Two or three of Rossis' Athonite students continued their studies at the Papal college of St Athanasius in Rome; see, Z.N. Tsirpanlis, *The Macedonian Students of the Greek College of Rome and their Activities in Greece and Italy (16th century-1650)* (in Greek), Thessaloniki 1971, pp. 109-112.

69. Sophronios Eustratiadis, 'Neophytos Mavromatis, Metropolitan of Naupactos and Arta' (in Greek), *Romanos Melodos*, I (1933), 161-249.

70. Alkis Angelou, 'The Chronicle of the *Athonias*. A Treatise on the History of the Athonite Academy Based on Unpublished Texts' (in Greek), *Nea Estia*, Christmas 1963, 84-105.

71. Soph. Lolis, *The Religious Views of Neophytos Doukas* (in Greek), New York 1949, p. 176.

72. Anthimos Gazis, *Vivliothiki Elliniki* (in Greek), Vienna 1807, preface.

73. Iosipos Moisiodax, *Apologia* (Alkis Angelou ed., in Greek), Athens 1976, p. 39.

74. Anonymous the Greek, *Elliniki Nomarchia* (G. Valetas ed., in Greek), Athens 1957, p. 173.

75. I. Mamalakis, *The Revolution in Chalcidice in 1821. The Participation of the Athonites and the Role of Emmanuel Pappas* (in Greek), Thessaloniki 1962; Alexandros Lavriotis, *Athonite Documents of the Great Greek Revolution....*

76. I. Mamalakis, 'New Evidence Regarding the 1821 Revolution in Chalcidice' (in Greek), *Bulletin of the Historical-Ethnological Society*, 14 (1960), 455.

77. P.M. Kontogiannis, 'The Treasures of Mount Athos at the Time of the Revolution' (in Greek), *Theologia*, 4 (1926), 144-52.

78. Alexandros Lavriotis, *Mount Athos. Struggles and Sacrifices, 1850-1855* (in Greek), Athens 1962, pp. 146-148.

79. St. Papadatos, *Slavic Penetrations into Mount Athos* (in Greek), Ioannina 1961.

80. I. Smolitsch, 'Le mont Athos et la Russie', *Millénaire du mont Athos, 963-1963*, Venice-Chevetogne 1963, 279-318.

81. Meletios Metaxakis, *Mount Athos and Russian Policy in the Orient* (in Greek), Athens 1913.

82. N. Antonopoulos, 'La condition internationale du Mont Athos', in *Millenaire...*, 381-405.

83. Gabriel, Hegumen of the Dionysiou Monastery, 'Fifty-Five Years of Athonite History' (in Greek), *Yearbook of the Athonite Academy*, Athens 1966, 56-57; D. Tsamis, *Mount Athos. An Approach to its Contemporary History* (in Greek), Thessaloniki (1985).

84. K. Dyovouniotis, *Bartholomeos of Koutloumousiou* (in Greek), Athens 1938.

85. M.I. Manousakas, 'Greek Manuscripts and Documents of Mount Athos: a Bibliography' (in Greek), *Yearbook of the Society for Byzantine Studies*, 32 (1963) 377-419; Ch.G. Patrinelis, *Libraries and Archives of the Monasteries of Mount Athos* (in Greek), Athens 1963.

86. G. Mantzaridis, 'Recent Statistical Data Concerning the Monks of Mount Athos' (in Greek), *Yearbook of the School of Theology of the University of Thessaloniki*, 19 (1974), 335-345.

Greek Schools in Macedonia under Ottoman Rule

Athanasios Karathanasis

The year 1430 was one of the most dramatic moments in the history of Thessaloniki, the year when the co-capital of the Byzantine Empire fell to the Turks, to remain under Ottoman dominion for nearly five hundred years. This baneful event had grievous effects on the formerly glorious cultural life of the city, for the scholars fled and the intellectual side of the city's life withered away. Today it is extremely difficult to trace its constituent elements and recombine them into a clear picture of the period, for there is virtually no original material available: it has all been lost over the centuries, whether from indifference or as victim of the general perniciousness of the times. There remains only indirect evidence to help us form an image, however imperfect, of the intellectual face of the city in the centuries prior to the Greek Revolution. What is clear, however, is that organized education as we understood it before 1430 no longer existed in Macedonia, and that what education there was, was assumed by monasteries and churches, using ecclesiastical books, a situation which has passed into history in the form of the 'hidden schools' legend.

The *Vilayet* of Thessaloniki

It is likely that a certain Ioannis Moschos taught in Thessaloniki early in the Ottoman period (1490). It also appears that by 1520 the monastery of Agia Anastasia, under Theonas, who later became Metropolitan of Thessaloniki, had established itself as an important centre.[1] Krousios tells us that in 1585 Georgios Athinaios had ten pupils in Thessaloniki; other teachers at that time were Matthaios of Crete, tutor to Patriarch Jeremiah II, Maximos, and probably Halikopoulos.[2] In the 18th century there was a Greek school in Thessaloniki, taught by the celebrated scholar Giannakos, who had studied in Italy.[3]

In the first decades of the 18th century what was known as the 'Hellenic School' flourished under Ioannis of Thessaloniki, who appears to have been a notable Greek and Latin scholar.[4] A few years later, in about the middle of the century, these two schools numbered among their teachers Akakios, the Thessalonian Ioannis Ioannou, and (until 1758) Kosmas Balanos from Jannina; he was succeeded by Athanasios Parios, who taught until 1762 and again from 1778 to 1786. Parios was succeeded by Ioannis Kontos from the Sparmou monastery on Olympus.[5] A leading role in educational matters during this period was played by certain notables of the Greek community in Thessaloniki, including two outstanding figures, the metropolitan *Logothete* Andronikos Paikos, and Ioannis Gouta Kautantzoglou.[6] As we have seen, Athanasios Parios was invited a second time to teach, from 1778-1786. This period coincided with the restoration of peace after the disturbances connected with the succession to the Metropolitan's throne of Thessaloniki.[7] During this period Athanasios Parios enjoyed the support of the entire Greek community in Thessaloniki. It was also at this time that he translated and illustrated the life of Agios Grigorios Palamas, with the assistance of the Metropolitan of Thessaloniki, Iakovos. His purpose in preparing this translation was two-fold, to expound the spirit of Orthodoxy to the people of Thessaloniki, and to teach them about their saint. In 1785 Parios published the *Antipope*, thus making Markos of Ephesos more widely known. It is interesting to note, in this context, that before having the book printed Parios sought the opinions of Theophilos, bishop of Kampania, of Ignatios, bishop of Servia, and of "the blessed Oikonomou, of Kozani".[8] It appears most probable that Parios also composed *The Grammar of the Neophyte*, which he revised for his students and published in Venice in 1787 "for use in that semi-

Teachers and pupils of the vilayet of Thessaloniki at the turn of the 20th century.

nary", meaning of course his school in Thessaloniki.[9]

In the period 1787-1807, immediately after Parios, that is, Ioannis Sparmiotis taught in Thessaloniki, with the assistance of Anastasios Kampitis and Doukas Apostolidis. As was to be expected, the School of Thessaloniki suspended operations with the outbreak of the Revolution, but it soon re-opened under the direction of Naouseans Nikolaos Angelakis (beheaded in 1822 for his part in the Revolution), and Emmanouil Photiadis.[10] After the dramatic events of 1821 and the deaths of Metropolitan Iosiph and many lay leaders, Matthaios of Ainos attempted to revive the Greek-Orthodox spirit; but in despair he two years later requested, and was granted, a transfer to the Metropolis of Kyzikos, leaving the School of Thessaloniki to get on as best it could, despite the fact that the revenues of the church of Agios Antonios near the Hippodrome had been assigned for its use.[11] His successor, Makarios of Lemnos, proved equally unable to revive the former glory either of the School or of the general life of the community, which was still suffering the effects of Turkish savagery; he retired in discouragement to the Iviron Monastery.[12] His successor was Meletios Pangalos (1831-1841), who was succeeded in his turn by Ieronymos of Lemnos, who worked enthusiastically during the twelve years of his pastorate to reorganize the city's schools. He was helped significantly by a committee of twenty distin-

guished citizens of Thessaloniki, who undertook to collect money, draw up regulations and select suitable staff for the two schools serving the community, the Greek school in the suburb of Agios Athanasios and a monitorial school. A very significant contribution to the organization of schools in Thessaloniki was made by community leaders such as the Harisis family (especially Theagenis), and the Abbott, Prasakakis, Angelakis, Pharangas and Rongotis families, among others. The first Greek school for girls in Thessaloniki was founded in 1845, thanks to the efforts of M. Karanikola and Elisavet Kastritsiou.[13]

The second half of the 19th century saw the beginnings of educational antagonism among the Balkan states, each of which had its eye on Macedonia and was striving to establish a presence in and a claim on that area by founding schools there. This policy, in fact, was the result of the well-published opinion of many foreign diplomats that Macedonia should be recognized as belonging to whichever state had the most schools there.[14]

As far as Greece is concerned, we know that the Church, the Ecumenical Patriarchate and its local metropolitans, was responsible for the education of the enslaved Greek people. The *Hatt-i Humayun* (February 1856) and its sequel, the General Regulations of the Patriarchate (1860), gave a new impetus to the intellectual life of Macedonia. From this period the Church's interest in education was supplemented by that of leading social groups in the Greek community. One of the vehicles these groups used for the broader dissemination of Greek education throughout Macedonia was the various educational and cultural societies.[15] These societies were based on the pioneering Athenian Society for the Dissemination of Greek Letters (1869) and the even older Hellenic Philological Society of Constantinople (1861). Each town and city in Macedonia soon had its own society, thus ensuring that teachers were sent to every corner of the land. These teachers worked passionately to maintain the people's attachment to Hellenism and Orthodoxy, thus supplying an essential element of moral support for the oppressed Greek population which, thanks to this peaceful revolution, was later able to take an active and successful part in the Macedonian Struggle. One hardly needs to emphasize here the longer-term benefits of these measures and the fact that within a very few years Macedonia was flooded with capable teachers, of whom we shall mention only a few in this chapter, for it would be impossible to cite them all.

We shall also look, as succinctly as possible, at the remarkable flowering of educational and intellectual life in Thessaloniki during the last decades of Ottoman rule, under the guidance of famous teachers such as Nikolaos Nikolaou (1855-1888), Margaritis Dimitsas (1865-1869), Antonios Oikonomou (1880-1886), Dimitrios Dimitriadis, and Pantelis Kontogiannis, who was the first professor of Modern Greek History at the University of Thessaloniki. In 1870 the Greek School was re-designated a Gymnasium, and housed in a building bequeathed by Pulcheria Prasakaki. The policy of the Greek state towards education in Macedonia was three-pronged: first, to subsidize all Greek communities, via the nearest consulate, for educational purposes; second, to provide teachers, books, etc; and third, to ensure that capable teachers were formed from among the people of Macedonia themselves.[16] In the meanwhile, the Vardari *Astiki* school was built in 1866, and included a gymnasium, a central primary school and a school for girls. To these schools flocked boys and girls from all over Macedonia who, after graduation, went on to found schools in villages and *chifliks* throughout the area, and thus to make their contribution to the work of national revival. In 1875 the first

teacher training college was founded by the Thessaloniki Educational Society[17], and largely funded by the Society for the Dissemination of Greek Letters; its first director was K. Oikonomou, and shortly afterwards the well-known educationist Harisios Papamarkou from Velvendos. The college building was located opposite the church of Agios Alexios, but was destroyed by fire in 1890. Ch. Hatzidimitriou founded his school for girls at the Vardari quarter in 1878.

By the final decades of the century Thessaloniki had ten schools: a three-year teachers' college, a six-grade gymnasium, a high school for girls, a four-grade primary school for girls, a central nursery school, a six-grade central school in Agios Athanasios, a primary school in Vardari, and three nursery schools (Ippodromiou, Agios Athanasios and Moni Vlatadon), for a total of 44 teachers and 2,200 students.[18]

Their expenses were met from a variety of sources: bequests, donations of money and buildings, special subscriptions, private loans, contributions from church funds, collections for schools, revenues from the chandlery, an annual community lottery, receipts from the sale of handwork, concerts, etc.[19] Early in the 20th century the teachers college was closed; two tower colleges were founded, however, one for boys and one for girls, and a new local primary school. This period also saw the founding of the first private schools, such as Stephanos Noukas' Hellenic Commercial High School (later re-named the Marasleion Hellenic School), the Girls Standard High School, which functioned until very recently under the name Aglaia Schina School[20], the Agios Pavlos Crafts School, and of course the famous Papapheion Orphanage.[21] The early years of the 20th century saw the building of the Ioannideios School[22], and the Educational Society's Night School. It should also be noted that in the first decade of the century Thessaloniki also had 64 schools for other nationalities: 26 Turkish, 2 German, 6 Italian, 1 English girls' school, 1 American farm school, 7 French schools, 8 Hebrew, 6 Bulgarian, 4 Serbian, 2 Romanian and 1 Armenian.[23]

The complete intellectual picture of the city also included the printing houses[24], which have been discussed in the appropriate chapter, as well as the activities of the various societies and associations.[25]

The nearby village of Asvestochori (Kirech-Köy)

Inmates of the Papapheion Orphanage in an early 20th century photograph.

had a primary school as early as 1860; in 1870 it was re-located and a nursery school and a girls' school added[26]; by 1906 it had become a municipal school with a good library.[27] By that same year the neighbouring village of Aivati had a six-grade municipal school and a nursery school, Saoud Bali had a small school, Neochorouda a school and a nursery school, Gradebori a four-grade school and a nursery school, etc.[28] A school was functioning at Baltza before 1840, but it was 1870 before it had its own building; in 1897 the Baltza Municipal School was re-named the Hellenic Primary School, while 1906 saw the founding of the Friends of the Arts Society.[30] Laïna had a school and a nursery school, Hortiatis a mixed six-grade municipal school, Pylaia a four-grade mixed primary school and a nursery, Epanomi a nursery and a six-grade school with G. Philidis as headmaster, as well as the 'Agapi' Educational Fraternity.[31] Vasilika had a monitorial school, founded by Metropolitan Neophytos of Kassandreia, and later a municipal school and a primary school.[32]

In the diocese of Kampania in 1891 there existed a municipal school, a nursery school, and four primary schools; a primary school at Koryphi which served five other villages, and elementary schools at Tsianophoron, Kleidi, Kaïlesi and Koryphi, for a total of 14 schools and 850 pupils, according to the local bishop. There was also a primary school in the Anargyron Monastery. By 1909 the number of schools in the district had increased to 25, despite the constant friction between the bishop and the school committees.[33]

In 1906, according to a contemporary report, there were 4243 students in Greek schools in the *kaza* of Thessaloniki, out of a total rural population of 31,827 (13%), a number that, by contemporary standarts, appears satisfactory, as does the teacher-pupil ratio of 1:54.[34]

The *vilayet* of Thessaloniki also included the *sanjak* of Drama. The *kaza* of Drama had a Greek school by 1870, and by 1876 a monitorial school, a school for boys and a school for girls. The city and the surrounding area flourished particularly around the turn of the century, during the prelacy of Metropolitan

Chrysostomos Kalaphatis (later martyred at Smyrna), when a nine-grade boys' school, an eight-grade girls' school, a nursery school (with 100 youngsters) and a primary school were all founded in the city. The intellectual life of the city was supplemented by the activities of the Progressive Fraternity of Drama (1874), which founded a library and reading room, and took an active interest in the collection of antiquities.[35] Intellectual life in the area was anything but slight: there were three schools at Tsataltza (Choristi), supported by the merchant Stergios Michai-lidis, then living in Smyrna, and two societies; by 1913 Doxato had a six-grade boys' school, a five-grade girls' school and a nursery school (founded in 1874), as well as an archaeological society ('Philippi'); Prosotsani had a Greek school, and the 'Eos' Educational Fraternity (1873).[36] In Eleftheroupolis (Pravi), in the *kaza* of Pravi, there were two municipal schools; Mesoropi had an Educational Fraternity (1906), and Podochorion had schools for boys and girls by the turn of the century.[37] In the neighbouring *kaza* of Kavala the Greek community had organized a boys' and a girls' school; by 1876 there was a Greek school, a monitorial school and a girls' school.

The rapid development of the city of Kavala also had repercussions on education, so that by the end of the century there were an eight-grade girls' school, two boys' schools, a six-grade girls' school with a gym sponsored by the Kavala Educational Fraternity, the Friends of the Muses Fraternity of Macedonia and the 'Aristotle' Educational Society, which latter had also built a municipal boarding school for students from other cities and the surrounding countryside.[38] In 1850 a Greek school was established in the village of Theologos, on the island of Thasos: an invitation to teach there was extended to the archimandrite Kallinikos Stamatiadis (originally from Thasos), who had fought in the 1821 Revolution and was the vicar of the Greek community in Munich. He refused, pleading his age; but he nevertheless took the opportunity to remind his compatriots of the benefits of education which, as he wrote, is "better than apiaries, better than vineyards, better than olive orchards, for while all these are useful, without education they are nothing". Theologos' efforts were imitated in Panagia and Kazaviti, but in 1864 a French observer, Perrot, could still reproach the citizens of Thasos with not having assured their smooth operation. Dr Melirrytos wrote in 1871 that there were schools all over Thasos,

but a traveller named Loher disagreed: he found only four, in Theologos, Kazaviti, Kalirahi and Panagia. An attempt by the people of the island in cooperation with the Chedive Ismael of Egypt to establish a gymnasium or college was unsuccessful.[39]

In the *sanjak* of Serres the Greek population had always faced great problems in the development of their intellectual life. In Upper Djumaja, for example, the tiny Greek community maintained a school with only one master and one mistress. In the *kaza* of Nevrokopi the situation was not too bad, especially in contrast to the tremendous problems facing the Greek population in the rest of the region. Thanks to the efforts of Metropolitan Germanos of Drama, Nevrokopi had a school as early as August 1835, located at the Varosi quarter; and we know that its teachers in 1858-1860 were Petridis and Athanasiadis, and that in 1863-1864 there was a teacher who was paid by the church of Our Lady (*Hyperagia Theotokos*). In 1862 the Greek population founded a communal school. The interest of the Patriarchate did not lapse, however, nor that of the Greek consul in Serres, the Greek merchants in Nevrokopi, or the Macedonian Educational Association of Serres. By 1885 Nevrokopi had a five-grade primary school, a five-grade girls' school and a nursery school. In the rest of the area belonging to the bishopric of Nevropkopi, including Kato Nevrokopi (Zirnovo), Perithori (Startista), Kato Vrontou, and Terlitsi, there were primary and municipal schools. By 1896 the *kaza* of Nevrokopi had a primary girls' school, a nursery school, three elementary schools and a municipal school in Nevrokopi itself (1899). In 1904 the energetic Metropolitan of Nevrokopi, Theodoritos Vasmatzis (1903-1907), proposed to the Ecumenical Patriarchate the addition of two more classes to the primary school and the nursery/girls' school.[40]

The city of Melenikon, in the eponymous *kaza*, was a well-organized town with its own constitution and a host of Byzantine churches; by the end of the 18th century it also had a Greek school. Among the first notable teachers there, early in the 19th century, were Adam Tsapekos and Christophoros Philitas, followed by Dimitrios Kalampakidis (1830-1840 and 1847-1850)[41], who after studying in Vienna had set up a printing press in Melenikon which published certain of his works.[42] Other schools followed: a nine-grade girls' school, a five-grade girls' school (1853), a four-grade municipal school at the parish district of Potamos and a nursery school (1865), all of which were largely funded by Dr Anastasios Pallatidis.[43] A significant contribution to the intellectual and patriotic life of the city was made by the Melenikon Cadet Association, which continued its activity at Sidirokastron after 1913.

In the neighbouring *kaza* of Petrich and in the villages Startsovo and Bogorovista there were a total of four schools. The first Greek school in the *kaza* of Demir Hisar (Sidirokastron) was founded in 1832; until 1861 this school taught from a liturgical song book, the *Oktoechos* and the Book of Psalms. A Greek school was founded in 1844; some of its graduates taught the younger pupils, with the help of a number of graduates of the famous Zosimaios Academy in Jannina, who were arriving in waves from Epirus. In 1861 the monitorial system was introduced by a local resident who had studied in Serres. In 1844 there was a teacher from Melenikon in the Greek school and several from Zagora. The expenses of the school were covered by the revenue from the sale of candles in the churches, and the interest on a capital fund.[44] By 1909 education in the city was fairly well advanced: the catalogue of schools was completed by a municipal school, a girls' school, and a girls' school with a nursery; all these were principally financed by their patrons Simetsos and Alexidis, as well as by the Progressive Fraternity and the Friends of Progress Fraternity. Considerable progress had also been made in the rural areas of the district: there were 14 Greek schools with 16 teachers and 400 pupils.[45] In the *kaza* of Zichna there was an outstanding school, the Alistrati Central Hellenic School, founded in 1841; its first teacher was D. Kalampakidis from Melenikon. By 1870 there were also a six-grade girls' school and

The Central Nursery School in Monastir.

two nursery schools. The Central School taught religion, language and literature, philosophy, mathematics and German; its graduates could open their own schools, "not merely tutor in private homes, but establish a public School".[46] The Amphipolis Conservative Fraternity was founded in 1874, and revived in 1903.[47] By 1876 there were three Greek schools running smoothly in Rodolivos; the cultural life of the town was supplemented in 1905 by the founding of the 'Anagennisis' ('Renaissance') fraternity. The educational contribution of the Monastery of Eikosiphoinissa was in all respects remarkable. Brothers from the monastery studied at the Alistrati School, and in 1844 opened, in the monastery, a Hellenic School which functioned until 1916.[48] In Dovista (Emm. Pappas) there were a boys' school, a girls' school, a nursery school, two fraternities (1883) and a music society (1910).[49] In general, then, it could be said that the educational situation in Zichna was reasonably satisfactory, despite the problems associated with the Turkish-speaking Greeks; these problems were gradually overcome by the establishment of nursery schools and girls' schools, which educated the mothers of the future.[50]

As for the *kaza* of Serres, the city itself had a particularly good educational system, the result of a well-established and flourishing intellectual life. The *Chronicles* of a priest called Synadinos are an excellent source of information on the organization of the school: fathers Parthenios, I. Politis and Kyriazis taught grammar, Cato, Pythagoras, Aristophanes and hymnography.[51] Our information about education in the city is somewhat more complete for the period 1696-1730; there were several well-known teachers at that time, including Anastasios Papavasilopoulos (1696-1702), Anastasios Popas (1719-1742), Spiridon Ioannou, and Nikolaos Scholarios (1742-1748).[52] Shortly before 1730, the school in Serres faced a number of problems, the solution of which was made possible by the extremely generous donation of 250 piastres by the ruler of Moldavia, Nikolaos Mavrokordatos.[53] An organized school was founded in 1735 on the initiative of Metropolitan Gabriel (1735-1745), but it closed in 1780. It seems to have been re-opened in 1787 by Metropolitan Matthaios, with one Theodoros as master, who suggested that Catholic members should be appointed to the school board. Early in the 19th century (about 1811), merchants from Serres then living in Vienna and Brasov

(Kronstadt) contributed to the establishment of a Greek School, to be taught by "Konstantinos Oikonomou of the Oikonomou family". The expenses of this school were to be met from a surcharge on each shipment of cotton.[54] During this same period (1834), Metropolitan Grigorios Phourtouniadis founded a monitorial school, with the assistance of teacher Paparrizou and the financial support of a wealthy gentleman, K. Spandonis. The first monitor in this school was Neophytos of Koutloumousiou. By 1852 the Greek school had acquired a new building;[55] it was being taught by N. Argyriadis with Brother Ignatios as his assistant. The first girls' school in the city was founded in 1853, with the assistance of K. Doumpas (from Vienna), N. Stergiou and V. Krikotzios.[56] The 'Grigorias' Girls' High School, named for its patron, Grigorios K. Rakitzis, was founded in about 1880.[57]

In 1858 the Serres Greek School, which we have already mentioned, became a semi-gymnasium under the headmastership of a well-known figure in education, Ioannis Pantazidis; he was succeeded by N. Halkiopoulos, Chr. Samartzidis, Dim. Maroulis and I. Kalostypis.[58] The years 1870-1880 marked a period of decline for the Serres School, however, because of jealousies in the community. In 1884 the School became a full gymnasium, with the German-educated Ioannis Dellios as its first headmaster.[59]

In 1872 the Macedonian Educational Society of Serres established a teacher training college for men, with one preparatory and three regular classes. Its first director was D. Maroulis, who was financed by the Protestant community of Barmen, on the Rhine; his irascibility, however, and probably his pro-Protestant sentiments, too, led to conflict with the Society, and he was replaced by Vranos Vozanis. Maroulis then opened his own teachers' college, but it closed in 1874; the first one, that founded by the Society and run by Vozanis, closed in 1881.[60] Of all the associations in Serres, the Macedonian Educational Society deserves special mention, for it contributed in many ways to promoting education, countering Bulgarian propaganda, and endowing scholarships. The Society was dissolved shortly after the death of I. Theodoridis, one of its most distinguished members. Other organizations included the 'Ourania' Friends of the Muses Society (1879), the 'Orpheus' Society for music and gymnastics, and the 'Prussia' Society.[61]

In Iraklia (Varakli or Djumaja), there were a nine-grade municipal school, a six-grade girls' school, two nursery schools, and a gym built by the community. It should be noted that many of the boys from the school went on to complete their education at the secondary school in Serres, and then returned to teach in various rural schools in the kazas of Serres, Drama and Melenikon.[62] Iraklia also had a National Association, with D. Rotskas as president.[63] In Nigrita (and in Sourpa or Syrpi, two separate villages which together constituted Nigrita) there were the Nigrita Greek School and the Sourpa four-grade primary school, while by the end of the 19th century there was also a municipal school.[64] The St John the Baptist (Prodromou) Monastery ran a small elementary school, which became an ecclesiastical school in 1878-1879.[65] The remainder of the kaza of Serres (wherever Greek communities were predominant) had 73 Greek schools, with 104 teachers and 4,461 pupils.[66]

The sanjak of Thessaloniki also included the kaza of Stromnitsa, where there had been a Greek school since the middle of the 19th century, taught in 1866-1869 by Harisios Papamarkou. Four years later there were also a primary school, a girls' school and a nursery school. After 1878 the area developed rapidly, and school enrolment reached a total of 378. A committee was formed in 1880 to reform and strengthen the schools in Stromnitsa, and by 1883 there were a semi-gymnasium, a High School, and 13 urban and rural primary schools, supported after 1893 by the Tsouphlis endowment. There were also a National Political Association, a Ladies' Friends of the Muses Society, a Hunting and Sports Society, and a Philharmonic society belonging to the National Political Association.[67] A similar situation prevailed in the remaining rural areas of the district (Eleousa, Vasilovo, Gabrovo, Kolesino, Neochori).[68]

Moving on to the kaza of Doirani, in the capital, Doirani (the seat of the bishop of Polyani) and in the villages Pyravos, Valantovo, Phourka and Potaros, there were 8 schools with 12 teachers and 330 pupils, funded by the Tsouphlis endowment.[69] Another source, from around 1890-1891, mentions 17 Greek schools. In 1904 Bishop Parthenios of Polyani noted the existence of a number of Bulgarian and Uniate schools in his diocese, and recommended the immediate construction of a new building for the gymnasium in Doirani.[70]

In the *kaza* of Gevgeli the educational situation improved tremendously after the completion of the rail link with Thessaloniki (1872): the Greek school was supplemented by a seven-grade boys' school, a nursery school, a four-grade girls' school and a school for handwork, all housed in a two-storey building belonging to the Tsouphleion Educational Foundation.[71] In 1908-1909 there were, apart from those in Gevgeli itself, 26 Greek schools with 44 teachers and 1,054 pupils.

In the *kaza* of Yenitsa the education of the Greek population had to contend with great difficulties, especially in the city, because of the overwhelmingly Muslim population and, since the middle of the 19th century, intensifying Bulgarian propaganda. Nonetheless, there was a Greek school as early as the 17th century. In 1810 the headmasters were Konstantinos of Naousa and Konstantinos of Thessaloniki, and in 1822 D. Barlaoutos. Besides the Greek school, founded in the mid-19th century with the help of a bequest from Baron Sinas, by the end of the century there were also a three-grade secondary school, a co-educational primary school, a girls' school and a nursery school. By the beginning of the 20th century there were a six-grade boys' school, a four-grade girls'school and three nursery schools, supported by the 'Pella' society and the Friends of the Poor Fraternity.[72] In Kilkis, capital of the *kaza* of Avret Hisar, and in the surrounding countryside, there were three Greek schools, under the supervision of the episcopal warden of the bishop of Polyani.[73] Langadas had a Greek school before 1860, which grew into a four-grade municipal school, later supported by the Progressive Fraternity; the neighbouring villages of Sochos, Giouvezna (Assiros), Visoka (Ossa) and Ligovani (Xylopolis) all had smoothly running Greek schools. It should be noted that this area had been the target of heavy Romanian (Apostolos Margaritis) and Bulgarian (Papapetrou) propaganda. The Progressive Fraternity, founded in 1892, was also very active [74]

The *kaza* of Vodena, with its capital of Edessa (or Vodena), had a number of educational institutions. We now know that in the middle of the 18th century the Greek school was taught by Amphilochios Paraskevas from Jannina, well-known for his educational zeal elsewhere; in 1764 a certain Konstantinos, a former pupil of Eugenios Voulgaris, was also a teacher there. Nevertheless, the first systematically organized school in the city was founded in 1773.[75]

The codex of the Greek school in Edessa[76], which is one of the chief sources of information for the period, tells us that in 1785 there was a properly constituted school, and that in about 1797 its teacher was Dimitrios Logothetis of Vodena.[77] The school closed for the duration of the Revolution, and re-opened sometime after 1840. In 1861 a monitorial school was opened. In 1857 there were seven elementary schools (of which three were private and one communal) with a large number of teachers, most notably Ioannis Tsikopoulos from Kataphygi (1870). By 1863 the city also had a girls' school. One of the greatest contributors to the development of the schools was Hatziparisis. By the early years of the 20th century Edessa had a three-grade semi-gymnasium, a six-grade municipal school, a six-grade girls' school and two nursery schools.

We can also follow the educational and cultural flowering of the city of Edessa through the reports of the Vodena Educational Society, which took an active interest in founding schools in the countryside for the purpose of reinforcing the national sentiments of the population.[78] Teacher D. Plataridis, who was also the secretary of the society, gives us a vivid picture of the educational campaign in the rural areas of the district.[79]

Verria, capital of a *kaza* (Karaferia), had a Greek school in the years 1650-1665, taught by Kallinikos Manios from Verria.[80] Much later, in 1849, Verria had two schools, a secondary school and a monitorial school, thanks to the efforts of the Ecumenical Patriarch Chrysanthos, and Manolakis Antoniou and Ioannis Theocharis. In 1864 the Greek school was at last housed in its own building, followed by the monitorial school in 1865. A girls' school was founded in 1870, taught by Polyxeni and supported by Meletios.[81] The progress of the schools was accelerated by Metropolitan Prokopios, thanks to whose efforts there were in 1876-1877 a three-grade secondary school, a monitorial school, and a girls' school with a nursery department, and in 1898 a three year semi-gymnasium, a six-grade municipal school, a six-grade girls' school and a two-year girls' school. These schools were financed by D. Raktivan, Brother Meletios Konstamonitis and Emmanouil Zampakias, among others. The Verria Educational Society was founded in 1874, but was soon dissolved. The 'Athena' society, with a wide range of activities, succeeded it in 1880: it is largely to this society that we owe the organization of the girls' school, the library, the reading room, and support for poor students; this society was dissolved in 1898 and replaced by 'Melissa'. The city also boasted a music society, 'Orpheus', and a sports club, 'Theseus'.[82]

Naousa had a school as early as the 18th century. Its teacher in 1750 was Theophanis D. Anasiotis (1762-1773), while for ten years its headmaster was Brother Amphilochios Paraskevas;[83] he was succeeded by Kampitis, N. Angelakis and E. Photiadis. The city was destroyed in 1821, but with its resuscitation the schools re-opened, so that by the end of the century there were an eight-grade boys' school, a five-grade girls' school and two nursery schools. In the meantime, the 'Pieria' educational society had been founded in 1875 and later the Friends of the Poor Fraternity, the 'Improvement' society, and the People's League.[84] The *kaza* had a total of 43 Greek schools, with 55 teachers and 2,475 pupils.[85]

Katerini had a Greek school in the 19th century, housed in a small building belonging to the Ascension Church. The active interest of the Greek Consul in Thessaloniki and Bishop Parthenios, together with the efforts of "certain citizens of Katerini" under the ledership of Lanaridis, led to the establishment of a school which in 1906 had 442 pupils. One source indicates that in 1906 there was also a six-grade mixed municipal school and a nursery school. Greek education felt the effects of Romanian propaganda, but this did slacken after 1904.[86] Kolindros had a school as early as 1753, taught by Father Paisios from the St John the Baptist (*Prodromos*) Monastery.[87]

In Vratsi, Bishop Agapios founded the first school in 1850, but it was destroyed in the uprising of 1878.[88] Both a boys' and a girls' school were founded in 1871-1872, and there is a reference in 1906 to a mixed five-grade municipal school and a nursery school.[89] Libanovo had a four-grade primary school with a junior teacher, G. Samartzidis; and there were elementary schools in Katacha under Papakonstantinos Matakos, in Kitros under an Epirote teacher named Igoumenidis, and Agios Ioannis under Tsikopoulos.[90] Finally, we know that Litochoro had a two-storey school building in 1870, which housed both a monitorial and a secondary school; it also had a Fraternity for Progress and Education.[91]

The first Greek school in the *kaza* of Kassandreia was founded at the capital, Polygyros, by Metro-

politan Iakovos; between 1864 and 1912 there were three schools: a nursery, a primary and a secondary school. This first school also housed the library of G. Chrysidis (1873), but it soon closed. The schools were supported by the Pavlidis and Phrantzis endowments.[92] There was a small school in Liarogovi (Arnaia) in 1871. In 1877 Bishop Amvrosios founded a Greek school; by the beginning of the 20th century there were a nursery, a primary and a municipal school.[93] The same was true of Ierissos, which in 1891 had a school which followed the Thessaloniki school system.[94] Theodoritos Vasmatzidis (later Metropolitan of Nevrokopi[95]) taught in Liarogovi and Ierissos from 1886 to 1888. According to the bishop of Ierissos and Mt Athos, there were well-organized municipal schools in all the villages in his diocese, as well as a girls' school in Liarigovi and nursery schools in Ierissos and Isvoros (Stratoniki); these were supported by the receipts from the sale of candles in the churches and donations from those notables who took an interest in education. Ardameri had a municipal school before 1891; and there were schools in Zagliveri, Livadi, Doumpia and the village of Adam, which all operated satisfactorily and followed the programme of the municipal school in Ardameri; the remaining twelve villages in the diocese of Ardameri had elementary schools supported by revenues from church receipts and land leases, and by subscriptions from Greeks living in Zagliveri.[96]

The *Vilayet* of Monastir

The *vilayet* of Monastir was subdivided into three *sanjaks*, those of Monastir, Korytsa and Servia. The eponymous *kaza* was the first (1830) to have an eight-grade school, which provided teachers for the schools being established throughout the area.[97] From 1851-1865 there was a private school in Monastir, run by Margaritis Dimitsas; but it closed with the proliferation of communal schools in the city and the surrounding countryside: by 1883 there were 11 schools.[98] The secondary school taught Ancient Greek, Latin, French, the Old and New Testaments, mathematics (arithmetic and geometry), Greek and Roman History, and geography. The Gymnasium taught Ancient Greek, Latin, French, Turkish, the Old and New Testaments, mathematics, experimental physics, botany, zoology, world history, philosophy and gymnastics. The nursery schools were patterned on those in France. The city's three girls' schools had, in 1883, 469 pupils and 4 teachers. The Bulgarian community in Monastir had five schools, and the Romanian one. This extraordinary educational activity on the part of the Greek community was even favourably commented upon by foreign diplomats.

Also significant was the contribution of the medical school in Monastir, established on the initiative of the Greek consul in Monastir, G. Dokos, and the Society for the Dissemination of Greek Letters, and which in 1883 had 37 students and 8 teachers. This school was obviously of prime importance in the fight against Exarchist propaganda in the sensitive Monastir area.[99] By the end of the period of Ottoman rule the *kaza* had 17 schools, the most important being the Central Girls' School, the Central Municipal School and the Seminary. These schools could not have functioned without the generous support of Greeks living abroad, such as Baron Doumpa, Dim. Mousikos, I. and Th. Dimitriou, and many others.

The first Greek society in Macedonia was founded in Monastir in 1850. This was the '*Dimotikon Katastima*', or '*Kazinon*', which quickly developed considerable national activity '*Karteria*' ('Perseverance') and the 'Hellenic Club' were two other societies, whose sole purpose was social service.[100]

Krousovon (Krushevo), an important local centre, had a school as early as 1835; in 1847 a bequest from N. Michail enabled the community to erect a new building for it, complete with a library. A secondary school was founded in 1875, and housed in a new building in 1901. Graduates continued their studies first in Ochrida and then in Athens –like I.Pantazidis, for example.[101] By the turn of the century there were nine schools, with 567 pupils and 150 teachers, despite the intensive Romanian propaganda. It is worth noting that many graduates of these schools went on to become distinguished scholars, university professors, and the like. The patriotic and intellectual life of the town was further supplemented by two societies, the 'Aristotle' (1874) and the Greek Political Club.[102]

Megarovo had a Greek school, taught by Oikonomos Papadimitriou, and later Ioannis Morokis; the secondary school was founded in 1845, and a girls' school in 1860, which four years later acquired a building of its own. Education in Megarovo owed a great deal to its generous patron, Stergios Stylidis. By

The boy's school at Krousovon.

the turn of the century the town had a six-grade primary school, one year of gymnasium, a six-grade girls' school, and a nursery school. Megarovo also had various societies and fraternities: 'Elpis' (Hope), the Friends of the Poor (1890), and a Political Club.[103]

There were two Greek schools in Nizopolis, three in Milovista and Gopesh, while Resna had a six-grade municipal boys' school and a four-grade girls' school (1869) run by the 'Anagennisis' (Renaissance) Society. Ochrida, in spite of all the Exarchist propaganda, supported nine Greek schools, with 10 teachers and 515 pupils.[104] The *kaza* of Prilep had a total of seven Greek schools in the first decade of the twentieth century.[105]

A school was established in the *kaza* of Florina shortly after 1850; a girls' school was built on a site purchased by the pro-Greek pasha Izet in 1906-7. By the first decade of this century, however, the educational situation in the city was reasonably satisfactory: there were an eight-grade girls' school, a four-grade girls'school and three nursery schools with facilities for boarders, as well as a music society (the 'Orpheus'), the Hellenic Club, and the Ladies' Fraternity.[106] It is interesting to note that books were brought from Monastir and Thessaloniki by a comrade of Pavlos Melas, Lakis Pyrzas; and many graduates of Florina's schools fought in the Macedonian Struggle.[107] In 1867 a girls' school was founded in Neveska (Nymphaion) by Zoe M. Tsirli, the wife of a wealthy gentleman, as well as a municipal boys' school which was run from 1878-1897 by Antonios Kyrizidis from Epirus, and later by V. Papageorgiou. The Nikeios School, built by I. Nikos, still stands today as a monument to the interest of the people of Neveska in education. The Agios Spyridon Educational Fraternity also contributed greatly to education in the area.[108] Pisoderi had an impressive boys' school founded by a patron of the town, the cleric Modestos, and a girls' school. There were a boys' school and a primary school in Negovani (Phlampouron); Sorovits (Amyntaion) had a primary and a boys' school together, and a Ladies Philanthropic Society. The whole *kaza* had a total of 47 Greek schools, with 65 teachers and 2,650 pupils.[109]

In the *kaza* of Kastoria, the capital, Kastoria, was exceptional for its intellectual activity. It is said that Gerasimos Palladas, later Patriarch of Alexandria (1688-1710), taught in a school in Kastoria until 1682. According to Anastasios Michail from Naousa, the affluence of the city permitted many of its young people to study in Venice, when not in Siatista. The first organized school in Kastoria was that founded by a leading member of the local gentry, G. Kastriotis, who had made his fortune in Wallachia at an early age and, at the suggestion of the Patriarch of Jerusalem Dositheos Notaras and his nephew Chrysanthos, and with funds deposited in the Zecca bank in Venice, founded this school. Its first teacher was a monk, Brother Amvrosios. There was probably a 'common school' operating at the same time, financed by G. Kyritzis, with the help of his confessor Christophoros Borokomitis; this school was initially taught by Christophoros, later succeeded by Methodios Anthrakitis. In 1711 the people of Kastoria erected a new building for it, with funds provided by their patron Kyritzis. When the headmaster of the Kastriotis School, Amvrosios, died in 1713 (shortly after the death of his brother and assistant master Ioannis), the people of Kastoria asked Chrysanthos Notaras and his compatriots in Adrianople to send someone to replace him. The tragic events of that year, with the death of Bassaraba, ruler of Wallachia and a friend and patron of Kastriotis, meant that their request went unheard. Meanwhile, Kastriotis had named as titular beneficiary of his bank deposits the Church of the Holy Sepulchre; and the reigning confusion disrupted the transmission of funds for the School for a number of years. This difficult situation was made worse by

the death in 1716 of Christophoros, who was succeeded as headmaster of the Kastriotis School by the archdeacon to Dionysios, Metropolitan of Kastoria. The Kyritzis School, in the mean-time, continued to operate more or less satisfactorily under Anthrakitis, despite the opposition of his rival, the philosopher Ierotheos Iviritis, who accused him of unorthodox teaching, more specifically, of having adopted the views of the heretic Molinos. After his condemnation, Anthrakitis was succeded by Sevastos Leontiadis. By this time the financial problems of the Kastriotis School had been solved, and the Kastoria schools entered on a period of ascendancy that lasted until the middle of the 18th century.[110] Our information about the teachers in the Kastoria schools is much fuller after that date. In 1876 the Greek school had, besides the three secondary school classes, three high school classes under the headmastership of Ph. Sakellariou. By 1890 there was also a semi-gymnasium; there had been a monitorial school under G. Manidakis since 1844; in 1858 a girls' school was founded, which in 1890 became a municipal girls' school under V. Maltou as the first headmistress. The girls' school also included two nursery schools. Another institution of importance was the Sunday School, open on Sundays to teach illiterate youths.[111]

In about 1775 the famous scholar Ioannis Pezaros was teaching in neighbouring Kleisoura. We have more complete information on education in this town for the period after 1830, thanks to the surviving published regulations of the schools. Thus, we know that in 1830 there were a primary and a secondary school, in 1866 a girls' school and a nursery school, and in 1889 a municipal boys' school. A great part of the success of the schools in Kleisoura is due to the interest of emigrants such as Archimandrite Sophronios Bartzoulas (Bucharest), Giannakis Simotas, Simos Simotas, and the Darvaris brothers, among others.[112]

Argos Orestikon (Chroupista) had both boys' and girls' schools before 1870; by the turn of the century these had developed into a five-grade boys' school and a four-grade girls' school, despite the solid organization of Bulgarian and Romanian propaganda.[113]

Tradition has it that the first school in Vogatsikon was founded early in the 19th century. By about 1860 there were a four-grade primary school and a three-grade municipal school under a teacher from Thes-

The Nikeios School at Nymphaion.

saloniki, G. Rousis. In 1875 Menelaos Mikas financed the founding of a girls' school.[114] There were organized schools in Nestorion, Mourboutsiko (Eptachori), Losnitsa (Germas) and Zelovo (Antartiko). To sum up, the *kaza* of Kastoria had a total of 83 schools, with 118 teachers and 5,202 pupils.[115]

In Blatsi, in the *kaza* of Kailar, the village priests were teaching school as early as 1761; from 1819-1843 the teacher there was D. Popovik. The school was re-organized in 1847, on the initiative of the Doumpas brothers, Dr G. Serganos, and Neophytos, the metropolitan of Moglena. A girls' school was founded in 1856. Bequests from K. Thomaidis, K. Dosios, Th. Doumpas and D. Mousikos (who founded the Mousikeion Hellenic Girls School) led to further growth in the period 1860-1881. By 1911 there were a seven-grade boys' school, a four-grade girls' school and a nursery school. The *kaza* had a total of 15 Greek schools, with 24 teachers and 1,020 pupils.[116]

The *kaza* of Anaselitsa was dominated by Siatista, where the school was taught by Methodios Anthrakitis (1710). Information is somewhat richer for the period after 1871, by which date there were two secondary and two monitorial schools. In 1899 the secondary school had become a full six-grade gymnasium; its first headmaster was G. Mousaios, who was succeeded by I. Papias (1891-1907) and Th. Natsinas (1907-1909). At a later date the Trampantzeio Gymnasium (1888) served as a secondary school: this school housed the Manouseios and the Rodopouleios Libraries, with 5,000 and 2,000 volumes respectively, as well as a more than respectable natural history collection. There were also several societies and associations which contributed to the intellectual development of the city.[117]

In Selitsa (Eratyra) D. Manakidis was teaching a school before 1800; in 1861 the teacher was D. Veniamin. This school was financed by revenues from the Synaskios grazing lands and from an endowment provided by Theophanis, then bishop of Mantineia and Kynouria. In 1870 a secondary school was established with funds provided by Loukas K. Kotoulas. There was also a girls' school. The school was obliged to close in 1880, when Loukas Kotoulas' brother, Thomas, suspended the funding of its operation; but with the help of D. Georgiadis, a merchant in Kraiova, it was able to re-open.[118] By the turn of the century there were also a six-grade municipal school, a two-year high school, a four-grade girls' school and a nursery school.[119]

Zoupani (Pentalophos) had a school by the middle of the 18th century, which seems to have existed until the early years of this century; in the meantime, emigrant natives such as Evangelos Kokkinos[120] had helped to build a girls' school and a nursery school.

One very significant school in the history of Western Macedonia was the gymnasium at Tsotyli, which was founded in 1871 with 80 students, of whom 30 were Ottoman. It was supported by the 1,045 members of the Macedonian Educational Fraternity, and, to an even greater degree, by on West Macedonians living in Constantinople, including such figures as Thomaidis, Papavasileiou and Antoniou, who were responsible, among other things, for the construction of the school building (1874). The smooth running of the school was assured by the

appointment of trustees at in various places (Siatista, Dolos, Lipsista). The school was closed from 1877 to 1881, but it re-opened, and by 1890 was a full-fledged gymnasium under headmaster Ph. Sakellarios; in 1894 accommodation for boarders was added. By 1893 its graduates were being admitted to the University of Athens without preliminary examination; and both staff and students contributed much to the Macedonian Struggle.[121] In total, the *kaza* of Anaselitsa had 49 Greek schools.[122]

As for the *kaza* of Servia, the eponumous town very probably had a school as early as the middle of the 17th century; and it seems that one of its students was the famous 17th century scholar Grigorios Kontaris, bishop of Servia and later metropolitan of Athens. The school was taught for many years (1678-1694) by his classmate, Brother Neophytos. It slowly fell into decline, but donations early in the 19th century from Manouil Serviotis and Bishop Veniamin of Servia and Kozani enabled the school to recover. By the end of the 19th century Servia had a six-grade municipal school, a girls' school and a nursery school.[123] The first substantiated reference to a school in Velvendos dates from 1773, when the priests and leading citizens of the town requested that one be founded; this request was approved by Ecumenical Patriarch Samuel Hantzeris in July 1774. The school was closed in 1821, but re-opened in 1845 as a municipal school under G. Goletidis. By 1870 it was flourishing, as was the girls' school which had been established in the meantime, and which had 5,624 pupils and 1,090 infants.[124]

By the end of the 19th century there were a mixed six-grade Greek school and a two-grade infant school, as well as a girls' school. Kataphygi had a school by the beginning of the 19th century, taught by D. Birdas from Velvendos. It soon became a municipal school, and its graduates were appointed to teach in the elementary schools in neighbouring hamlets. The school owed much to its well-known (and local) teacher I. Tsikopoulos, and its more or less permanent (after 1875) trustee, Asterios Varvarezos.[125]

The *kaza* of Grevena had schools in Grevena, Samarina, Krania, Perivoli, Smixi and about sixty other smaller villages. There must have been a school in Grevena before 1821, which closed at that time and re-opened in 1845 under Christos Igoumenidis. By 1882, in any case, the city had a secondary, a primary

The Modesteios 'Hellenic Boys' School' at Pisoderi.

and a nursery school, and two societies.[126] Samarina presents the same picture: a school functioning before 1821 which closed during the Revolution and re-opened later; its teacher in about 1867 was Zisis G. Hotopoulos. By 1882 there were a secondary, a primary and a nursery school, and an educational society; soon there were two others as well.[127]

There is evidence that Kozani had a school in the first half of the 17th century, which even had a school library. This school was later (1688) taught by Grigorios Kontaris. After the departure of Christakis of Livadi (1738) the school was closed for two years; but ex-patriot citizens of Kozani in Hungary built a new school at Stoa and appointed Evgenios Voulgaris to teach it. For six years he taught a whole new range of subjects: logic, physics, metaphysics, algebra and mathematics. This brought him into conflict with the conservative teacher Amphilochios Paraskevas, who taught only the traditional subjects: grammar, rhetoric and logic. When Voulgaris resigned to become the Director of the Athonite Academy, he was succeeded

by N. Varkouris, who taught there for eight years.

Education in Kozani was largely supported by the city's tradesmen. The Company School was founded in the second half of the 18th century; it owes its name to the association of local merchants in Hungary who in 1745 decided to support the existing school and, subsequently, agreed in 1765 to build this new school. It closed in 1772 when the Company was dissolved. A new school was founded in Kozani in 1798, on the initiative of ex-patriot Pagounis in Leipzig. Kozani merchants in Vienna and Budapest sponsored the establishment of the 'School' in 1809. The first monitorial school was organized by G. Manidakis in 1832; thirty years later a girls' school was founded. There were a number of outstanding teachers in Kozani at this time (1875 and after), including D. Argyriadis from Siatista, Th. Sarhatlis, S. Michailidis, I. Tsikopoulos, and I. Kalostypis, and subsequently Ph. Sakellarios, Anastasios Pichion, I. Pavlidis, D. Karapatsidis, G. Michailidis, A. Pouliadis and N. Valagiannis. Another important figure was P. N.

Liouphis, the headmaster of the gymnasium from 1894 to 1910 and 1911 to 1916, who was the co-author of a history of the city. By the end of the 19th century Kozani had a four-grade semi-gymnasium, a six-grade municipal boys' school, a six-grade girls' school and a nursery school, while by 1908 it had a gymnasium, two municipal boys' schools and a nursery school, run under the supervision of the Community's Council and with the support of a number of distinguished citizens. The city's various societies ('Phoenix', the 'Pandora' Cultural Fraternity, and the Ladies Philanthropic Fraternity) also made a significant contribution to the development of national and educational life in Kozani.

The way was paved, then, for an extraordinary renaissance of Greek letters in Kozani, and for the consequent appearance of a number of remarkable scholars, including D. Sakellarios, G. Karagiannis, D. Karakasis, G. Sakellarios, Euphronios Raphael Popovic and G. Lassanis.[128] This effusion of intellectual activity has left a living monument in the shape of the celebrated Kozani Municipal Library, which grew out of the initial donations to the community by Bishops Theophilos of Servia (1768-1811) and Veniamin of Kozani (1815-1849), assembled in what was then called the 'House of Improvement. According to a document from 1819, "the students would from time to time gather there for study, reading and discussion". In 1919 the library was administered by the Kozani Reading Society, under the presidency of Photios, then bishop of Irinoupolis and susequently Ecumenical Patriarch. In 1923 the Library was taken over by the Municipality of Kozani.[129]

We shall add just a few more details about education in the area. In Aiani, the first mention of a school occurs in 1781; its original teacher was Ioannis Gerasimos Manakos from Samarina, and it was supported by the Kozani 'Phoenix' Society.[130] Daphni (of Voion), birthplace of Stephanos Noukas, had a school in 1825, which was also attended by pupils from neighbouring villages (Zoni, Polykastro, Avgerino) and which was mainly taught by the village priests.[131] The same was true of Dragasia[132] and Liknades[133], whose schools dated from 1860 and 1840 respectively.

Having assembled this wealth of information, we can now advance certain general conclusions. The schools provided the Greek population of Macedonia not only with a basic education, but with other even more important services, namely, the promulgation of national issues and the cultivation of a national consciousness, which was in fact their fundamental purpose. Many of their graduates went on to become teachers in schools of every type all over Macedonia. These teachers, together with the clergy, formed the basic nucleus in which was rooted the struggle of the Greek population of Macedonia: first came the schools and then armed insurgence. For our conclusions we shall necessarily limit ourselves to the period covering the end of the 19th and the beginning of the 20th century; complete information is available only for that era.

In the two *vilayets* which constituted Macedonia, then, those of Thessaloniki and Monastir, there were, prior to 1912, 1,041 educational institutions with 1,704 teachers and 68,000 students. Put another way, the students in the Greek schools represented 10.33% of the total population. The ratio of teachers to pupils was 1:40, reasonably satisfactory even by today's standards. Thessaloniki was the principal educational centre, with 32 schools, 127 teachers and 3,898 pupils. Next came Monastir, with 19 schools, 55 teachers and 2,500 pupils, followed by Serres with 16 schools, 50 teachers and 2,000 pupils. Kozani, Kastoria, Kavala, Verria and Siatista had, on average, 5 to 9 schools, 30 teachers and 1,000 to 1,300 pupils. Some 1,500,000 francs were spent on running these schools, of which 1,000,000 came from local revenues, 250,000 from personal subscription and gifts, and the rest from funds supplied by the Society for the Dissemination of Greek Letters, the Hellenic Philological Society of Constantinople, and local educational societies.[134]

As we have seen, the educational and philanthropic associations and societies in Macedonia played a special role in the educational and patriotic affairs of the Greek population. There was one society for every 3,727 inhabitants, for a total, at first count, of 48 educational societies, 39 philanthropic societies and fraternities, 11 gymnastic clubs, 18 musical, theatrical or cultural societies, 12 libraries, and one publishing house. These societies were for the most part founded in the 1870s, and based on two principal models, the Hellenic Philological Society of Constantinople and the Society for the Dissemination of Greek Letters.[135]

ATHANASIOS KARATHANASIS
GREEK SCHOOLS IN MACEDONIA
UNDER OTTOMAN RULE
NOTES[*]

1. T. Evangelidis, *Education during the* Tourkokratia *(Ottoman domination)*, vol. 1, Athens 1936, pp. 101, 112; regarding Moschos, see: Andreas Moustoxydis, 'Ioannis, Georgios and Dimitrios Moschos', *Ellinomninon*, 7 (1845), 386; on Theonas, see: A. Glavinas, 'Life, Service and Paracletic Canon to St Theonas, Metropolitan of Thessaloniki', *Yearbook of the Faculty of Theology of the Aristotle University of Thessaloniki*, 25 (1980), 289-290.

2. Evangelidis, *op. cit.*, pp. 111-118.

3. M. Gedeon, 'Old Communal Disputes of the Thessalonians, *Makedonika*, 2 (1941-1952), 18.

4. N. Tsoulkanakis, 'Ioannis, Son of Ioannis, Teacher at the Thessaloniki School', *Klironomia*, 7 (1975), 353-386.

5. Evangelidis, *op. cit.*, p. 114-116.

6. G. Stogioglou, 'Unpublished Sources on the Panagouda Church in Thessaloniki (1757-1905)', *Yearbook of the Faculty of Theology*, 19 (1974), 377.

7. D.B. Oikonomidis, 'Athanasios Parios (1721-1813)', *Yearbook of the Society for Cycladic Studies*, 1 (1961), 351-352.

8. Athanasios Parios, Monk, *St Gregory Palamas and the Anti-Pope*, Thessaloniki 1981 (reprint), p. 255.

9. As the heading of the afore-mentioned publication reveals, Parios was schoolmaster of the Thessaloniki 'seminary'.

10. H. Papastathis, 'The Cultivation of Letters in Thessaloniki under Ottoman Rule', *Nea Estia*, Christmas 1985, 224, which provides useful additional information on our subject.

11. *Loc. cit.*

12. A more detailed analysis in G. Stogioglou, *The Greek Schools in Thessaloniki under Ottoman Rule. Notes from University Lectures*, Thessaloniki 1988, pp. 15-16.

13. *Ibid.*, passim.

14. Stephanos I. Papadopoulos, *Educational and Social Activity of the Macedonian Hellenism during the Last Century of Ottoman Rule*, Thessaloniki 1970, pp. 7-14; this is a classic study on education in 19th-century Macedonia, which the interested reader may consult for more information on the schools of Thessaloniki (pp. 97ff.)

15. *Ibid.*, passim.

16. Eleni D. Belia, 'The Educational Policy of the Greek State towards Macedonia and the Macedonian Struggle', in *The Macedonian Struggle*, Thessaloniki 1987, pp. 29-40.

17. *Curriculum of the Model Elementary School of Thessaloniki*, Athens: Society for the Dissemination of Greek Letters, 1879, p. 60.

18. Papadopoulos, *op. cit.*, pp. 98-102; cf. V. Dimitriadis, *Topography of Thessaloniki during the Period of Ottoman Rule 1430-1912*, Thessaloniki 1983, p. 392.

19. Sidiroula Ziogou-Karastergiou, *Makedonika*, 16 (1976), 92-96.

20. *Makedonikon Imerologion*, 4 (1928), 177-180, and 8 (1932), 92-96.

21. For detailed information on these schools, see the related titles in K. Hatzopoulos (ed.) *Bibliography of Thessaloniki*, Thessaloniki 1987, pp. 43-57.

22. S. Mitsopoulou-Liparidou, 'The Ioannideios School of Thessaloniki', *Makedoniki Zoi*, 133 (1977), 24-25.

[*]   All sources in this chapter are in Greek.

23. Papadopoulos, *op. cit.*, p. 108.

24. H. Papastathis, 'The First Printing Presses of Thessaloniki', *Makedonika*, 8 (1968), 239ff.; N. Christianopoulos, 'Greek Publications in Thessaloniki under Ottoman Rule (1850-1912). First Recording', *Diagonios*, 6/1980, 235-309; and by the same author, 'Literary Books and Periodicals Printed in Thessaloniki (1850-1950)', *Diagonios*, 4/1980, 56-79.

25. Papadopoulos, *op. cit.*, p. 122ff.

26. Harilaos Tsekos, *History of Asvestochori*, Thessaloniki 1957, pp. 154-155.

27. S.I. Papadopoulos, 'The Condition of Education in the *kaza* of Thessaloniki in 1906 (an Unpublished Report by Dimitrios Sarros)', *Makedonika*, 15 (1975), 117-119.

28. *Loc. cit.*

29. For additional information, see: D.I. Kampasakalis, *History of Baltza*, Thessaloniki 1974, pp. 133ff.

30. Papadopoulos, 'Sarros Report', passim, and *Educational and Social Activity*, pp. 129ff.

31. Papadopoulos, 'Sarros Report', 126-138.

32. Papadopoulos, *Educational and Social Activity*, p. 19.

33. *Codex of Episcopal Synod*, Thessaloniki, Archives of the Department of Pastoral Studies, Aristotle University of Thessaloniki, ff. 143-144.

34. Papadopoulos, 'Sarros Report', 144-145.

35. Papadopoulos, *Educational and Social Activity*, passim.

36. N.G. Philippidis, 'Tours of the Macedonian Provinces of Drama, Zichna and Eleutheroupolis', *Parnassos*, 1 (1877), 126-134.

37. *Ibid.*, 17ff.

38. Papadopoulos, *op. cit.*, pp. 25-27.

39. Apostolos E. Vacalopoulos, *History of Thasos, 1453-1912*, Thessaloniki 1984, pp. 132-136.

40. A.E. Karathanasis, *The Metropolis of Nevrokopi during the Macedonian Struggle*, Thessaloniki 1988 (Yearbook of the Faculty of Theology, Annex).

41. A. Vacalopoulos, *History of Macedonia*, Thessaloniki 1969, pp. 398-399.

42. *Loc. cit.*; Christianopoulos, 'Greek Publications', 26-28.

43. P. Pennas, 'Contribution to the History of Melenikon. Anastasios Pallatidis and His Manuscripts', *Serraika Chronika*, 2 (1957), 67-125.

44. Anonymous, 'Certain Annotations on Demir Hisar', *Parnassos*, 2 (1878), 543.

45. G. Stivaros, 'Demir Hisar', *M.I.P.S.* (1910), 213; cf. Papadopoulos, *Educational and Social Activity*, p. 37.

46. A. Giompliakis, 'The Central School of Alistrati', *Makedonika*, 4 (1955-1960), 383-390.

47. Papadopoulos, *op. cit.*, p. 41.

48. *Ibid.*, p. 44.

49. D.K. Samsaris, *Contribution to the History of the Community of Emmanouil Papa. The Church of St Athanasios and Its Unpublished Codex*, Serres 1970, pp. 59, 70.

50. *Ibid.*, p. 46; cf. Philippidis, 'Tour', 126-134 (particularly on Ziliachovo, Rakovo, Skritovo, Stravolakkos, Silinos, Angista, Krommista, Rodoleivos, where schools operated on monitoral basis).

51. Vacalopoulos, *History of Macedonia*, pp. 396ff.; cf.

Papadopoulos, *op. cit.*, pp. 48ff.; Pennas, *op. cit.*, p. 408; Elli Angelou-Vlachou, *Education in Serres under Ottoman Rule*, Athens 1935.

52. E. Stratis, 'History of the Schools of Serres', *M.I.P.S.* (1909), 144-149.

53. Vacalopoulos, *loc. cit.*

54. *Ibid.*; Stratis, *op. cit.*, pp. 145, 147.

55. Pennas, *op. cit.*, p. 472; Stratis, *op. cit.*, p. 147.

56. Pennas, *loc. cit.*

57. *Ibid.*, pp. 407-408; Stratis, *op. cit.*, p. 150.

58. Pennas, *op. cit.*, pp. 416-420; Stratis, *op. cit.*, p. 150-151; Vlachou, *op. cit.*, pp. 28-29.

59. Pennas, *op. cit.*, pp. 420-425; Stratis, *op. cit.*, p. 152-154; Vlachou, *op. cit.*, pp. 38-40.

60. Pennas, *op. cit.*, pp. 402-407; Stratis, *op. cit.*, p. 33-38; Vlachou, *op. cit.*, pp. 33-38.

61. Papadopoulos, *op. cit.*, pp. 54-58.

62. 'Defender of Macedonia. The Plain of Serres and the Town of Varakli-Djumaja', *M.I.P.S.* (1908), 260; Papadopoulos, *op. cit.*, pp. 58.

63. *M.I.P.S.* (1909), 316.

64. D.G. Dapani, 'Nigrita-Sypa', *M.I.P.S.* (1911), 122.

65. Papadopoulos, *op. cit.*, p. 61.

66. *Loc. cit.*

67. *M.I.P.S.* (1909), 316.

68. A. Angelopoulos, *Northern Hellenism. The Hellenism of Stromnitsa. Topography, History, Church, Education, National and Communal Life. Memoirs of K. Bonis*, Thessaloniki 1980, pp. 61-64.

69. Papadopoulos, *op. cit.*, p. 69.

70. *Codex of Episcopal Synod*, ff. 142-143.

71. Ioannis G. Xanthos, *History of Gevgeli and National Activity of the Inhabitants of the Town and the Surrounding Villages*, Thessaloniki 1954, pp. 17-18; Papadopoulos, *op. cit.*, pp. 69-73.

72. Georgios P. Oikonomou, *Macedonian Diary, the Gordian Knot*, Thessaloniki 1915, pp. 173-174.

73. *Codex of Episcopal Synod*, ff. 142-143.

74. N.B. Kosmas, *Langadas. History-Folklore*, Thessaloniki 1968, p. 18; Papadopoulos, *op. cit.*, pp. 77-80.

75. *Edessaika Chronika*, Sept.-Dec. 1972, 13-15.

76. K.G. Stalidis, *Codex of the Hellenic School in the city of Vodena in 1785*, Edessa 1979, pp. 15-17; *Ekklisiastiki Alitheia*, 3 (1882), 119-122, 158-159.

77. K.G. Stalidis, 'Dimitrios, *Logothetis* of Vodena. A Teacher of the Hellenic School of Edessa in 1792', *Edessaika Chronika*, 3 (1972), 35-36.

78. This is the subject of a study being prepared by the author in collaboration with A. Satrazanis, titled 'The Records of the Educational Association of Edessa. Contribution to the Cultural Activity in Macedonia during the Last Decades of Turkish Domination'.

79. D[imitrios] P[lataridis], *Report on the Intellectual Development* (sic) *in the Province of Vodena*, Constantinople 1874.

80. Z.N. Tsirpanlis, *The Macedonian Students of the Greek College of Rome and Their Activity in Greece and Italy (16th c.-1650)*, Thessaloniki 1971, p. 200.

81. For more on this subject, see G. Hionidis' detailed studies: 'Three

Regulations of the Greek Community of Verria towards the End of Ottoman Rule', *Makedonika*, 10 (1970), 106, 111, 134; 'The Schools of Verria between 1849-1912 according to Unpublished Documents', *Makedonika*, 11 (1971), 1-27.
82. Papadopoulos, *op. cit.*, pp. 85-88.
83. Vacalopoulos, *History of Macedonia*, p. 332.
84. E. Stougiannaki, 'Naousa', *M.I.P.S.* (1911), 125, 153, 156-157; Papadopoulos, *op. cit.*, pp. 86-90.
85. *Ibid.*, 90.
86. Papadopoulos, 'Dimitrios Sarros'.
87. Kleopatra Polyzou-Mameli, *History of Kolindros*, Thessaloniki 1972, p. 61.
88. *Loc. cit.*
89. Papadopoulos, *loc. cit.*
90. Polyzou-Mameli, *op. cit.*, p. 265.
91. Papadopoulos, *Educational and Social Activity*, pp. 92-93.
92. S.A. Kotsianos, *Polygyros, Unknown Pages of Its History*, Thessaloniki 1961, p. 17.
93. Papadopoulos, *op. cit.*, p. 95.
94. *Codex of Episcopal Synod*, f. 22.
95. Karathanasis, *The Metropolis of Nevrokopi during the Macedonian Struggle*, (Annex to the Yearbook of the Faculty of Theology), Thessaloniki 1988, p. 55.
96. Report of bishop of Ierissos and Mt Athos, and of bishop of Ardameri, in *Codex of Episcopal Synod*, f. 22.
97. Sophia Vouri, *Education and Nationalism in the Balkans. The Case of Northwestern Macedonia, 1870-1904*, Athens 1992.
98. Papadopoulos, *op. cit.*, pp. 133-137.
99. K.A. Vakalopoulos, *Northern Hellenism during the Early Phase of the Macedonian Struggle (1878-1894). Memoirs of Anastasios Picheon*, Thessaloniki 1983, pp. 178-189.
100. Papadopoulos, *op. cit.*, pp. 136-140.
101. N. Ballas, *History of Krousovon*, Thessaloniki 1982, p. 29-32.
102. K.A. Vavouskos, *The Contribution of the Hellenism of Pelagonia to the History of Modern Greece*, Thessaloniki 1959, pp. 9, 12, 22, 26; and Papadopoulos, *op. cit.*, pp. 140-143.
103. G. Kazas, 'Megarovo', *M.I.P.S.* (1910), pp. 239-250; Papadopoulos, *op. cit.*, pp. 145-148.
104. Vavouskos, *loc. cit.*; Papadopoulos, *op. cit.*, pp. 148-151.
105. Papadopoulos, *op. cit.*, pp. 152-154.
106. *Loc. cit.*
107. D.N. Pepis, 'Intellectual Activity in the District of Florina before and after Liberation', *O Aristotelis*, 59-60 (1966), pp. 56-62.
108. Papadopoulos, *op. cit.*, pp. 154-155.
109. *Ibid.*, pp. 155-157.
110. G.P. Kornoutos, 'Schools in Kastoria under Ottoman Rule', in *Prize of Antonios Keramopoulos*, Athens 1953, pp. 426-468; Stathis Pelagidis, 'A Bibliographic Outline on the City and Region of Kastoria', *Makedonika*, 24 (1984), 289-291.
111. Papadopoulos, *op. cit.*, pp. 154-155; P. Tsamisis, *Kastoria and Its Monuments*, Athens 1949, pp. 83-87.
112. A. Sigalas, 'Codex of the Schools of Kleisoura', *Makedonika*, 1 (1940), 500-506; Evangelidis, *op. cit.*, vol. 1, pp. 122-123; cf. Papadopoulos, *op. cit.*, pp. 170-172.
113. Papadopoulos, *op. cit.*, p. 173; D.K. Rouphas, 'Chroupista', *M.I.P.S.* (1910), pp. 130-134.
114. K. Bentas, *History of Vogatsikon*, Kastoria 1952, p. 6; Papadopoulos, *op. cit.*, pp. 173-174.
115. *Ibid.*, pp. 175-177.
116. M.A. Kalinderis, *The Community of Blatsi during the Period of Ottoman Rule*, Thessaloniki 1982, pp. 92ff.; Papadopoulos, *op. cit.*, pp. 178-181.
117. I. Apostolou, *History of Siatista*, Athens 1929, pp. 49ff.; Papadopoulos, *op. cit.*, pp. 182-186.
118. I.N. Photopoulos, *History of Selitsa (Eratyra)*, Athens 1934, pp. 101-109.
119. Papadopoulos, *op. cit.*, pp. 186-187.
120. G.P.S. Panagiotidis, 'Zoupanion', *M.I.P.S.* (1913), pp. 187-189.
121. I.K. Hassiotis-N. Delialis, 'Stephanos Noukas (1836-1931), the "Macedonian Educational Fraternity" and the Founding of the Tsotyli School (1871)', *Makedoniki Zoi*, 37.6 (June 1969), 18-26; cf. Papadopoulos, *op. cit.*, pp. 189-193.
122. *Ibid.*, p. 196.
123. Minas E. Maloutas, *Servia*, Thessaloniki 1956 and supplement 1965, pp. 49-59; cf. A. Sigalas, *Archives and Libraries of Western Macedonia*, Thessaloniki 1932, pp. 73, 115; Papadopoulos, *op. cit.*, pp. 196-198.
124. N.P. Delialis, 'Founding Documents of the Greek School of Velvendos', *Makedonika*, 6 (1965), 266-274; Papadopoulos, *op. cit.*, pp. 196-198.
125. *Ibid.*, pp. 200-201; Kleanthis Nastos, *Kataphygio of Pieria-Kozani*, Thessaloniki 1971, p. 48.
126. Evangelidis, *op. cit.*, vol. 1, p. 110; Papadopoulos, *op. cit.*, pp. 201-202.
127. A. Vacalopoulos, 'Historical Research in Samarina, Western Macedonia', *Grigorios o Palamas*, 21 (1937), 429-430; Papadopoulos, *op. cit.*, pp. 202-204.
128. P.N. Liouphis, *History of Kozani*, Athens 1924; cf. Papadopoulos, *op. cit.*, pp. 204-211.
129. Regarding the library, see: Sigalas, *Archives of Western Macedonia*, p. 73.
130. K.E. Siampanopoulos, *Aiani, History-Topography-Archaeology*, Thessaloniki 1974, pp. 421-435.
131. Alekos A. Adamidis, *History of Daphni of Voion*, Thessaloniki 1980, pp. 48-50.
132. A.A. Adamidis, *History of Dragasia of Voion*, Thessaloniki 1977, p. 34.
133. A.A. Adamidis, *History of Liknades of Voion*, Thessaloniki 1979, p. 82.
134. Papadopoulos, *op. cit.*, pp. 242-246; by the same author, 'Education in Macedonia and Its Contribution to Setting the Conditions for the Success of the Macedonian Struggle', in *The Macedonian Struggle*, Thessaloniki 1987, pp. 225-227; regarding the increase in the number of schools to 1,041, suffice to note that in 1878 there existed 574 schools with 26,939 pupils and in 1885 610 with some 40,000 pupils: G. Hassiotis, *L'instruction publique chez les Grecs*, Paris 1881, pp. 499-501, 509, 512-513, 515-517.
135. Papadopoulos, *loc. cit.*

Post-Byzantine Painting in Macedonia

Nikos Nikonanos

Post-Byzantine art is the period of Greek art conventionally taken as beginning with the fall of Constantinople and ending with the formation of the modern Greek state in 1830. This is the stage in Greek artistic production in which Byzantine art continued, though under foreign (Ottoman or Venetian) domination. For that reason –though still conventionally– the latter date given above has to be shifted forward in the case of Macedonia to 1912, when the area was liberated. The post-Byzantine stage then handed on the baton –at an earlier time in some forms of art and a later one in others– to modern Greek vernacular art, which had been taking shape during that period together with the other outward appearances of modern Greek life. In religious painting, however, which is the subject of brief treatment in the text which follows, post-Byzantine characteristics were retained in the overwhelming majority of the works until the late 19th and early 20th century. As a result, the borderline of 1912 is not merely conventional in the case of religious art, but corresponds more or less exactly to the true situation.

Religious painting was one of the most important achievements of the period of Ottoman rule. Although conditions were unfavourable for the production of art after the fall of Thessaloniki in 1430 and of Constantinople in 1453, painting was able to overcome the difficulties of the time, to survive and to evolve in the new circumstances, continuing the Byzantine traditions and at the same time constituting the principal artistic language throughout south-eastern Europe down to the end of the 18th century. This phenomenon, whose duration is unique in the history of European art, was the result[1] of two main factors: a) the fact that the Orthodox Church, under the leadership of the Ecumenical Patriarchate, played a decisive part in the spiritual, intellectual and artistic development of the Orthodox peoples of the Balkans, and b) the significance of Mt Athos as a centre of Greek and Orthodox learning and in particular as a place from which the art of painting could be spread through the Balkan peoples.

Mt Athos and, to a lesser extent, Meteora and the other important monasteries exerted an inexorable pull over artists and served as spiritual and intellectual models. They were places of advanced learning and of artistic creation of unquestioned prestige: as Manolis Hadzidakis aptly put it, "they were the decisive factor in the dissemination of the Greek art of the day through the Orthodox Balkans and the Near East, and even as far as Russia. They art acquired the significance of a model which was authentic and valid from the doctrinal and aesthetic points of view".[2]

The rest of Macedonia, too, continued its artistic and intellectual production without interruption under Ottoman rule. In the particular case of religious painting, the following comments of a relatively general nature can be made. In urban centres such as Verria and Kastoria (we mention those two towns in particular since it happened that they have preserved a significant number of monuments down to the present day, thus allowing us to watch their art develop) the production of paintings continued after 1453 with scarcely a gap. During this period, there was a parallel increase in the number of painters who were not from urban centres, and there were even cases in which the residents of small mountain communities specialsied in the production of paintings and other kinds of art. This, however, is bound up with the growth in the population of such districts as the residents of urban centres took refuge in inaccessible –and thus safer– areas in order to escape oppression.[3] We should also note the frequent presence of priest and monk icon-painters in areas other than Mt Athos.

In Thessaloniki, which had been an important artistic centre in the Byzantine period, we find no painting studios –by way of contrast to the smaller towns– particularly during the first and particularly difficult years of adjustment to the new conditions. This was only natural, for the Greek Orthodox population of the city had shrunk considerably. In the 17th century, however, the painters returned, and by the 18th century the Greek nucleus of the population swelled to the point where Orthodox Greeks gave the city its national character.[4] At this time, Thessaloniki was a centre for artistic activity (apart from the murals of around 1730 recently discovered in the Nea Panayia church,[5] a large number of portable icons have also been identified[6], and it also seems to have developed into a centre for trade in Athonite icons.

In the second half of the 15th century and the opening

Panaghia Eleousa (Our Lady of Mercy), early 15th century. In the Panaghia Eleousa hermitage on Lake Megali Prespa.

decade of the 16th, there were no mural painters who could stand as worthy continuers of the Palaeologean painting of the 14th century. The surviving murals, of which there are quite a number, are simplified works displaying misunderstandings of earlier figures, statements which often lay outside the classic tradition, and, as a rule, a more or less vernacular, regional and provincial character. In general there was a manifest drop in quality.

It should be noted at this point that recent research has shown that despite the Ottoman rule imposed over almost all Macedonia in the late 14th century, new churches were built and decorated throughout the 15th century, and in particular in its first and last quarters. Other churches had their wall-paintings renovated.[7] However, the new churches were all simple chapels which did not afford the wall space for compositions on a large scale. As a result, the need to apply even a rudimentary iconographic programme to the paintings meant that the scenes were depicted on a small scale. This usually confined the iconography to the figures which were absolutely essential, and had consequences for the designing of the forms and for the structure of the composition in general.

The Virgin Mary, in the depiction of the Annunciation (late 15th century). In the church of Aghios Georgios on the island of Aghios Achilleios in Lake Mikri Prespa.

Among the wall-paintings which could be mentioned in this connection are those of the churches of St George[8] and Our Lady 'Porphyra'[9] at Mikri Prespa, of Our Lady 'Kountouriotissa'[10] and of the Monastery of St George at Ritina[11] in Pieria, of St Menas[12] at Velvendo, of the Sts Theodore[13] and Sts Cosmas and Damian[14] in Servia, of St Demetrius[15] Aiani, and of St Nicholas[16] at Vevi. In Kastoria, the decoration of the churches of St Nicholas of the nun Eupraxia (1485/86)[17], of St Nicholas of the Lady Theologina (c. 1490-1500)[18], of St Spyridon (c. 1490-1500)[19], of St Nicholas 'Magaleiou' (1505)[20], and on the west outer wall of Our Lady 'Koumbelidiki' (1485)[21], among others, together with earlier examples from the first half of the 15th century (including St Andrew 'Rousoulis', the Three Saints and the Taxiarchis Mitropoleos), show that the town was the most important centre for painting in Western Macedonia.[22] The surviving works in Verria –Our Lady 'Haviara', Our Lady 'Kyriotissa', Panagouda, Gorgoepikoos, Our Lady 'Palaioforitissa', St Nicholas 'Gournas', St Patapius and others– testify to similar activity in this Central Macedonian town.[23] On Mt Athos, the murals in the refectory of Xenophontos Monastery (1496/97) and in the chapel of John the Baptist in the Protaton at Karyes (1526) make it clear that the conditions were not such as to prohibit the decoration of holy establishments.

Although we cannot speak of a 'school' painting, some of the works from this period with which we are familiar share certain features. They were all produced by the same studio –undoubtedly the most important of its age– which decorated small churches in the closing decades of the 15th century and the first years of the 16th. The names of the artists have not survived. Yet the fact that the decoration in at least six churches in Kastoria (those of St Nicholas of the nun Eupraxia, the greater part of the murals of St Nicholas 'Magaleiou', sections of the decoration of St Nicholas of the Lady Theologina, the surviving wall-paintings from the demolished church of St Spyridon, some of the wall-paintings in St Demetrius, in the Eleousa quarter, and the depiction of St Nicholas in the esonarthex of Our Lady 'Koumbelidiki') have been attributed to this studio, and the relationship between these works and earlier wall-paintings from Kastoria leave no room for doubt that there were painters from the Western Macedonian town itself or from its environs. For that reason, the studio is known as the 'Kastoria studio'.[24]

Perhaps the most interesting feature about this studio is the marked degree to which it moved around, as can be seen from the fact that works attributed to it are to be found in Servia (the Sts Theodore, Sts Cosmas and Damian), Prespa (St George), Verria (the murals in the sanctuary and the narthex of Our Lady 'Haviara'), Thessaly (the old main church of the Monastery of the Transfiguration in the Meteora) and also in Serbia, Bulgaria and Romania.[25]

The painters in this team employed a standardised variety of art, as a result of which their works lack the power of their original models. They tried to imitate the Palaeologian painting of Macedonia, but their imitations are often vernacular in nature and are frequently lacking in skill. Among the characteristics of their work are the broad, soft surfaces of the faces, with a little light shadowing, the expressive features, the relatively accomplished –though not always entirely successful – drawing and the figures, which are sometimes elongated and affected in posture and sometimes short, stout and inelegant. The old main church of the Monastery of the Transfiguration at Meteora (1483), which is the earliest example of the studio's work yet known to us, and the church of St Nicholas of the nun Eupraxia in Kastoria are today seen as particularly important since each is an almost complete iconographic unit and because of their outstanding quality. One last point to be made in reference to this Kastoria studio is that the date of its appearance, the fact that the art of its painters was accepted and known far beyond Kastoria itself and Western Macedonia and, in general, the quality of its painting and the survival of elements from it in later works make it one of the most significant artistic phenomena of the late 15th and early 16th centuries. The observation has been made that the work of the studio could be described as urban, while the decoration not attributed to it is of a rural and monastic nature.[26] This decorative work is in a variety of artistic styles, but certainly lacks any particular claims to distinction and is little diversified in terms of its morphological diversity. Of interest in relation to the level of artistic production during the chronological period in question are the wall-paintings in the chapel of St John the Baptist in the Protaton at Karyes (1526): they demonstrate the gradual falling away in quality and at the same time explain why painters from Crete had to be invited to work in the great centres of monasticism.

This seems to be the place for a brief introduction to Cretan painting.[27] In the 15th century, Crete developed into an artistic centre of the greatest importance, and it flourished in the arts and letters almost to the end of the 17th century. In painting, in particular, its achievements were most impressive. It is indicative of the progress made in this sphere that between 1453 and 1526, over a period of seventy years, we know the names of 120 painters from Herakleio alone.[28]

By way of contrast to Ottoman rule, the power of Venice in Crete displayed religious and professional toleration towards painters, who could also derive material and intellectual benefit from the fact that they were allowed to travel to Venice and work there. Even in the first half of the 15th century painters from Constantinople had settled in Crete, revitalising the provincial painting of the island, and after the fall of Constantinople in 1453 still more artists took refuge there. Thus the Cretan school, one of the finest examples of post-Byzantine Greek painting, took shape and acquired its principal features in terms of technique, style and iconography during the 15th century, in an advanced intellectual and artistic atmosphere, and against an urban background which had transcended its medieval setting.

The Cretan school was at the height of its development during the second and third quarters of the 16th century, and it survived down to about 1700. The period of its finest flowering, from the early 16th century until about 1570, is dominated by the figure of Theophanes Strelitzas[29], whose works served as models for those who came after. The iconography of the Cretan school is spare and austere; buildings act as a discreet accompaniment to the human figures which are predominant in the compositions, and the Western elements –few in number and secondary in importance– are organically integrated into the scenes depicted. The human figures are elegant but unaffected, with nobility in their poses and gestures. The faces are grave –often gloomy– and the bare limbs are modelled with highlights on the brown blocking. The lines are firm, the folds of the garments are stylised, the colours used are normally the primaries and the execution is faultless.

After the beginning of the second quarter of the 16th century Cretan painters made their appearance in mainland Greece, where they were invited to the major monastic centres. In 1527, a year after the simplistic example of the paintings in the St John the Baptist chapel of the Protaton, we find Theophanes at the Meteora, where he was invited to paint the little church of the Monastery of St Nicholas 'Anapafsas'. Theophanes, who must by now have had the reputation of a great painter, then went to Mt Athos, where the paintings of his maturity are to be found.

This major monastic centre had been able to choose from among the most outstanding painters during the Byzantine period, as we can see in the case of Panselinos and the other great artists whose names have not come down to us. Now that the Cretans had begun to acquire a name for themselves outside their native island, Mt Athos commissioned portable icons from them and invited them to decorate churches, chapels and refectories with wall-paintings. In 1535 Theophanes was at Megiste Lavra Monastery, where he painted the main church - the building erected in 1004 by St Athanasius of Athos, the founder of the Monastery. In the little church of St Nicholas 'Anapafsas' at Meteora, with its single area and narthex, most of the scenes were of necessity small and sustained Theophanes' relations with the portable icon. By way of contrast, the church of Megiste Lavra was a large building of the Athonite type, and Theophanes' artistic talents had to adapt to the monumental dimensions of the mural, in which his technical and stylistic characteristics crystallised. Across these large surfaces he spread an exemplary and varied iconographic programme, organising on a black ground compositions which are superb in line and colour, which are structurally tight and simultaneously vivid, and which are permeated by calm and melodic rhythm. The human figures are grave, of impeccable ethos, and their presence dominates the entire church. As Manolis Hadzidakis, an expert on Theophanes' work, points out, the wall-paintings which adorn Megiste Lavra "are a great achievement for their period, with the rational distribution and completeness of the iconographic cycles, the thematic wealth of the iconography, and with their outstanding artistic quality". For that reason, "these paintings will attain and retain the status of a model for the decoration of monastery churches in the Orthodox countries".[30]

Theophanes and his two sons Symeon and Neophytos (who also became painters) stayed on at Megiste Lavra. Theophanes was closely linked to the Monastery, becoming a member of the brotherhood in 1536 and, according to recent research, painting a second work on an equally large scale: he must have been the artist responsible for decorating the interior and the facade of the refectory.[31] This building had been damaged by earthquake in 1526, and with the assistance of Gennadios, Metropolitan of Serres, its roof was renovated and the entire building painted with murals. The painting must have been done around 1541: that was the year in which Gennadios died, and he is depicted on the facade with St Athanasius, the founder of the Monastery, and the Emperors Nicephorus Phocas and Ioannis Tzimiskis, under whose patronage it was built. Gennadius is shown holding the refectory and is surrounded by a halo, an indication that he was no longer alive when the mural was painted. In addition, it has been observed in relation to the attribution of the decoration to Theophanes and his studio that it would be unlikely for such an important project to be entrusted to any other

The Acension (detail), 1546. In the church of the Stavronikita Monastery on Mt Athos.

artist when the painter and his sons were living in the Monastery. A third major composition is the painting, in the years 1545-1546, of the main church of Stavronikita Monastery, which was founded at this time. According to a note in a Monastery codex, "the church was painted by Theophanes the monk and Symeon, his son".[32] Research has also led to the attribution to Theophanes and his associates of the decoration of the refectory of this Monastery and its little chapel of St John the Baptist.

However, Theophanes' artistic activities were not confined to these compositions. To judge by the technique, the iconography and the distinctive style, a number of other works should also be attributed to the great Cretan painter, including the icons on the stands in Megiste Lavra Monastery, the Protaton and Stavronikita Monastery. Yet regardless of the exact number of wall-paintings and portable icons which can be attributed to him with greater or lesser degrees of certainty, there is no doubt that the painters of the 16th and 17th centuries took Theophanes' art as their model.

During the 16th century many other churches, refectories and chapels on Mt Athos were painted, a striking number of them by painters of the Cretan school who were more or less closely associated with Theophanes and his studio. In 1536 the 'Molyvokklisia' in the vicinity of Karyes was painted, followed in 1540 by the main church of Koutloumousiou and the refectory of Philotheou, and in 1547 by the main church and part of the refectory of Dionysiou. Here the artist who painted the murals was Tzortzis[33], who work closely resembles that of Theophanes.

Also of the first half of the 16th century is part of a wall-painting showing the prophet Ezekiel in Pantokrator Monastery, a work which confirms that Cretan painters worked in this monastery, too.[34] Later in the century, in 1568, the main church of Docheiariou Monastery was painted: these extensive wall-paintings have survived in perfect condition. The main church of Iviron Monastery was painted late in the 16th century. One should also note at this point that apart from the wall-paintings, a large number of portable icons of the Cretan school have survived. These works, by Theophanes[35], Euphrosynos[36], Damascenos[37] and a number of nameless artists, show the extent to which the Cretan school predominated on Mt Athos during the 16th century.

The Last Supper (detail). In the church of the Stavronikita Monastery on Mt Athos.

We should conclude this brief reference to the work of the Cretan painters on Mt Athos by citing the conclusion drawn by Hadzidakis in relation to Theophanes' presence in the major monastic centres of Turkish-occupied Greece: that the contact between the educational, cultural and artistic traditions of Crete and mainland Greece "came at the right moment and proved decisive for the future of ecclesiastical painting. It raised the level of local artistic production and set up a firm point of reference for the painting of the Greek world and also for the remainder of Orthodoxy".[38]

However, there were also on Mt Athos at this time monastic circles which preferred the painting of mainland Greece, with the anti-Classical tendencies familiar from the Palaeologue era and recycled constantly throughout the 15th century and in the early 16th century. In the case of the old main church of Xenophontos Monastery, for example, which was renovated in the 16th century, part of the wall-paintings were executed by the painter Antonios[39] in 1544, and these murals can be used as evidence for attributing to him two compositions in smaller churches: the wall-painting of the Prokopiou keli of Vatopedi Monastery (1537) and that

of the chapel of St George in Ayiou Pavlou Monastery (1552). Antonios was familiar with the Cretan paintings of the Athonite monasteries (Megiste Lavra, Stavronikita, etc.), which had undoubtedly influenced his technique and iconography, but his works continued to be anti-Classical in nature. They lack the smooth flow and restrained but noble style typical of the Cretan works, and the iconographic programme differs from that of the Cretan compositions. However, it is indicative of Antonios' quality and technique that until recently he was thought of as a pupil of the Cretans: this demonstrates that contact with Cretan painting had allowed him and the other mainland Greek painters to enhance their artistic language by comparison with the earlier works of the 15th and 16th centuries, as a result of which they were invited to decorate not only chapels but also the main churches of monasteries, as was the case with Xenophontos. Another Theophanes[40] –the shared name is merely a coincidence– also worked at the Xenophontos Monastery, and in 1563 he painted the murals in the narthex of the old main church.

In parallel with the Cretan school and the provincial art of Antonios and the Theophanes who decorated the

The Tree of Jesse (detail), 1568. In the church of the Docheiariou Monastery, Mt Athos.

narthex of Xenophontos, there was also another school of painting at work in north-west Greece in the 16th century, a school which crystallised its modes of expression at this time. This is known as the 'north-west Greek school', or the 'local school in mainland Greece', or the 'Thiva school' since three of its representatives were from Thiva (ancient Thebes).[41] This school focused on the Ioannina district and relied on the Palaeologue artistic tradition of Macedonia and its neighbouring areas as well as on the Kastoria studio enriched with elements from earlier and contemporaneous Cretan painting to form an independent system which accorded with the cultural traditions of north- west Greece. In connection with the Cretan school, it should be noted that local artists came into contact with Cretan painting, soon succeeded in modernising their own work and, "advancing in parallel with the Cretan icon-painters of the major monastic centres [created] mural groups which display a different sensibility and which enriched the art of the 16th century with original forms"[42], as M. Acheimastou-Potamianou notes in her study of the paintings in the Filanthropinon Monastery.

Among the features of the art of the north-west Greek school are its narrative complexity (in which the scenes are enriched with secondary incidents), its wealth of figures in motion, its preference for sharp contrasts of colour (especially in the garments), its ability to convey the emotions being experienced by the figures, and the numerous buildings which fill almost all the ground as if a stage set were being designed. By way of contrast with the calm and restrained air of the Cretans, the north-west Greek school expresses a baroque tendency and its art is realistic and rather rough. However, it resembles the Cretan school in incorporating some features of Western (specifically, Italian) art.

The painters of this school constituted the most important artistic movement in mainland Greece. They worked on the island in the lake of Ioannina (at the Philanthropinon and Diliou Monasteries), in Epirus more generally (the churches at Veltista and Krapsi), in Aetolia (the Myrtia Monastery), in the Meteora (at the Varlaam Monastery, whose founders were from Ioannina) and in Macedonia (the Zavorda Monastery, Kastoria and Mt Athos). Works by them can also be found further south, and some features of their artistic language survived even after the 16th century.[43]

The school made its appearance on Mt Athos with Frangos Katelanos[44], who is better known for the reputation he enjoyed after his death and for the number of paintings attributed to him. In 1560, Katelanos decorated the chapel of St Nicholas in the Megiste Lavra Monastery. This chapel was attached to the main church of the Monastery, which, as we have seen, had been painted by Theophanes twenty five years earlier, in 1535. The monks' choice after the death of Theophanes (in 1559) to commission the decoration of the chapel within the same church from Katelanos shows that he must have had a reputation as an outstanding painter. These wall-paintings are indeed mature works. By way of contrast to previous compositions, the figures are less restless and, in general, the quality is higher. There is another reason, too, for which the wall-paintings of the St Nicholas chapel are important: they are the only work to bear Katelanos' signature. In the inscription of ownership his name is given as the painter of all the murals, and it is on the basis of the decoration at Megiste Lavra

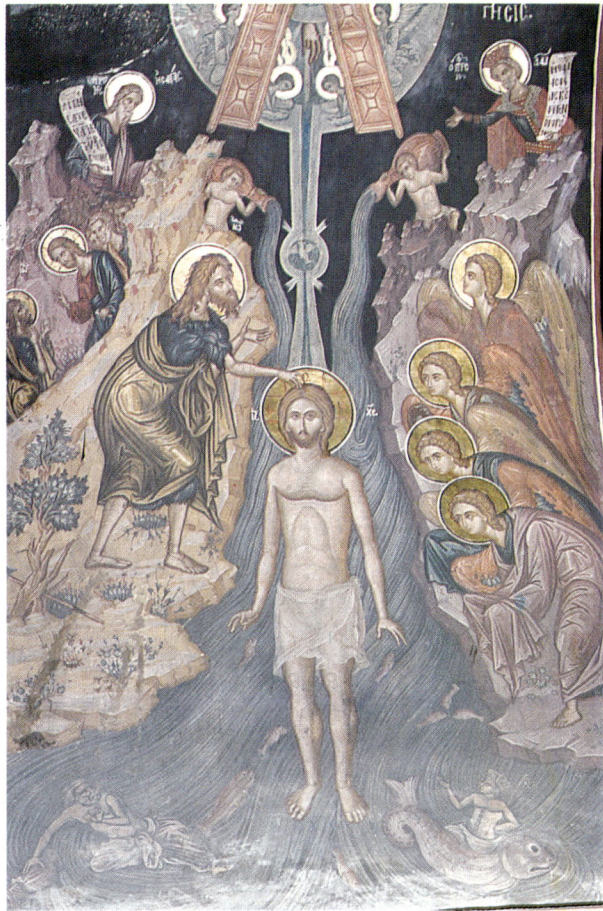

The Baptism of Christ, 1560. In the chapel of Aghios Nikolaos in the church of the Megisti Lavra Monastery, on Mt Athos. below : Saints Peter and Paul, 1552. In the chapel of Aghios Georgios in the church of the Aghios Pavlos Monastery, on Mt Athos.

that scholarship has attributed to him the wall-paintings of the Myrtia Monastery (1539), of the narthex and part of the main church of the Philanthropinon Monastery (1542), of the main church of the Varlaam Monastery at Meteora (1548), at Our Lady 'Rasiotissa' in Kastoria (1553) and in the main church of the Zavorda Monastery, Grevena. However, although these works are similar to each other they also differ, which makes it impossible to attribute them all with certainty to the artistic activities of Katelanos.[45] Of the works in Macedonia, only Our Lady 'Rasiotissa'[46] (a small and simple wooden-roofed church) has been published in full, while St Nicholas at Megiste Lavra[47] and the main church of the Zavorda Monastery[48] lack the special studies which would enable us to form a complete picture of the work of Frangos Katelanos and his associates in Macedonia.

Off Mt Athos and elsewhere in Macedonia, ecclesiastical painting flourished in the 16th century, especially in Western Macedonia and around Verria. Almost all these works display a preference for the anti- Classical tendencies familiar from Palaeologue painting, which survived and prevailed in the area in the 15th century. However, subsequent tendencies and the later achievements of painting were not entirely unfamiliar, and such painters as did not remain completely committed to their local idioms were able to benefit from their contacts with the iconography and techniques of the Cretan school and the north-west Greek school. Depending on their talent, they were then able with greater or lesser degrees of success to revitalise their means of expression and improve the quality of their art more generally.

Among the painters whose names have come down to us is Onoufrios. Inscriptions on the monuments which he decorated –especially in the Berati and Kastoria areas– tell us that he was born in Berati, that he served as archpriest in the metropolitan bishopric of Neokastro (Elbasan), and that he was a noted scholar of Greek. Apart from wall-paintings, he also produced portable icons, but the work in Macedonia for which he is best-known today is the decoration of the relatively spacious church of the Holy Apostles in Kastoria[49]. A second set of works in the same town –the wall-paintings of Sts Cosmas and Damian 'by the School'– was lost for ever when the church was renovated in 1867.[50] Onoufrios, a man of learning and an urban background, was familiar with the Cretan school and the north-west Greek school of his times, with the earlier Palaeologue tradition and with the characteristics of Italian art; however, he cannot be classed as belonging to one school or the other. His art –careful, with noble and often elongated figures

neatly organised into compositions– expresses his own personal artistic idiom.

Another painter whose name has come down to us is the priest Efstathios Iakovou, protonotary of Arta; of his work, we know of sections of the decoration in the main church of the Monastery of the Dormition of the Virgin at Molyvdoskepasti in Epirus (1537) and the set of wall-paintings in the chapel of St John the Divine in Our Lady 'Mavriotissa' at Kastoria (1552).[51] Iakovou was a painter of moderate talent whose main characteristics are bright colour, mobile compositions, garment folds which are often stiff, stylisation of natural settings and frequently of faces, and the inclusion of much architectural detail. Efstathios knew of the Cretan manner, but he did not succeed in assimilating it creatively: he uses it in parallel with elements of the earlier Palaeologue tradition of the Macedonian monuments.

Kastoria preserves a number of other examples of 16th century painting, such as the wall-paintings in the narthex of St George 'of the Mountain' and of St Nicholas 'of the Cathedral' (1593). These are of more or less the same type as the St John the Divine chapel of Our Lady 'Mavriotissa' - that is, they belong to local northern Greek studios which were loosely connected to the Cretan school and the north-west Greek school. One could make the same comment on the paintings in the chapel of St Sotera (1591) in the Prefecture of Florina. By way of contrast, one of the painters who decorated the church of St Zacharias[52] in the village of the same name in the Prefecture of Kastoria –specifically, the artist who painted the murals on the west outside wall– was connected with the north-west Greek school. Indeed, from one point of view these paintings could be included within the circle of activities of Frangos Katelanos.[53]

According to their inscriptions of ownership, the churches of the Archangel Michael (1549)[54] and St Nicholas (1552)[55] at Aiani, Kozani, were built and painted in the mid-16th century. In the case of St Nicholas, we even have the name of the painter: "Zacharias, monk-deacon". The decoration in the ruined church of St Nestor[56] in the same town must date from the same period, if we are to judge by the few fragments of wall-paintings which have survived. The painter Zacharias, to whom all three works are attributed, worked in a non-urban and simplified style, with anti-Classical tendencies which reflected misunderstood earlier models in an often mechanical manner.

In Verria and its surroundings, a large number of wall-paintings from the second half of the 16th century have survived as evidence of the frequency with which

St John the Theologian (1552). In the chapel of Aghios Ioannis Theologou in the Mavriotissa Church in Kastoria.

churches were erected, repaired and decorated at this time. They also suggest that there was the scope, and the inclination, for similar activities elsewhere in Macedonia. We have already seen support for this view in the example of Aiani, where two —or more likely, three— churches were built and decorated in the course of a very few years. In Verria and the surrounding area the wall-paintings in ten churches can be dated to this period by their inscriptions, and this number will undoubtedly increase with other examples not documented by inscription when a detailed study of all the town's churches is conducted. By way of indication, we could mention the murals in the churches of St Nicholas of the monk Anthimos (1565), St Nicholas of the nobleman Kalokratas (1570), the Monastery of Our Lady in the village of Asomota (1570), St Nicholas 'Makariotissa' (1571/2), Sts Ceryx and Julitsa (1589), and Our Lady 'Haviara' (1598).[57] The wall-paintings in the churches of St Nicholas (1588) and St Dimitrios 'Gratsianis' at Velvendo[58] are from close to the end of the century; like the wall-paintings of Verria and its surrounding area, these are simplified and anti-Classical works. Taken together, all these murals are the work of local studios in northern Greece which were not especially familiar with the advances made at the time by the Cretan school and the north-west Greek school. Wherever relationships with either of those major artistic trends can be discerned, they are loose and largely superficial. The artists tended to remain loyal to the local traditions, often

misunderstood their Palaeologue models and, as far as we can tell, the variations in the quality of their work was the result more of their differing personal talent and less of an established artistic vocabulary in each local studio.

The last third of the 16th century saw the appearance of painters from the mountain village of Linopoti, near Kastoria.[59] Over the centuries to come, the involvement in painting of the inhabitants of certain villages in mainland Greece —most of them in mountain areas— was to become quite a common phenomenon. These teams of painters were organised on a family basis, leaving their homes to work in the spring and returning in the autumn. The churches decorated by the painters of Linopoti, who are the earliest known team, were mostly in Macedonia and Epirus, though they did work even further away. Their work can be found at the Fotmou Monastery in Aetolia (1589), in the church of St Athanasius in Riljevo, Prilep (1627), in the Monastery of the Prophet Elias at Tyrnavo (1632-1642) and in the Monastery of St Athanasius at Zagora, Pelio (1645-1646). The evidence we have today shows them working over a period of eighty six years, from 1570 to 1656. Their art incorporates element of the earlier artistic tradition of Macedonia and the areas bordering on it, of the north-west Greek school, of the Kastoria studio and of the Cretan school. As a result, their works are varied in form and stand out for their eclectic combinations of earlier and more recent artistic tendencies; yet the painters of

The Presentation in the temple (detail), 1552. In the church of Aghios Nikolaos, Aiani, Kozani.

Linopoti, with their rural origins, managing to translate these tendencies into a simple and vernacular language which often misinterpreted its models but would always be comprehensible to those to whom it was addressed. Three of the most interesting sets of wall-paintings of the Linotopi studio are in Macedonia: those of St Demetrius at Palatitsia, Verria (1570), St Nicholas of the nobleman Thomanos in Kastoria (1639), and the Monastery of the Transfiguration at Dryovouno, Kozani (1652). In the paintings of St Demetrius at Palatitsia[60], a three-aisled basilica with a narthex, Nikolaos, the earliest of the Linotopi painters of whom we know (and one of the most gifted), drew primarily on the Palaeologue tradition and that of the Kastoria studio, succeeding in giving his composition ease of organisation and a monumental air. However, the work as a whole is uneven, as a result of the varying talent of Nikolaos' associates. In addition, the scene of the Second Coming which covers the entire east wall of the narthex, with its elongated figures and meticulous modelling of the faces, must be the work of another painter. In St Nicholas, Kastoria –which before the modern repairs was a simple colonnaded church with a wooden roof[61]– the artist, also called Nikolaos, skilfully selected elements from the local tradition and the Cretan school and incorporated them into his painting. However, by comparison with St Demetrius at Palatitsia, his statements are of a clearly anti-Classical nature. In the main church of the Monastery of the Transfiguration at Dryovouno, a cruciform church with two lines of columns, a narthex and a later exo-narthex), the painter –a third Nikolaos– took elements from the Cretan school, the north-west Greek school, the Macedonian tradition in painting and also Western models, all of which he blended with skill. The composition he produced is an attractive work whose main features are smoothly-proportioned scenes, carefully rendered faces, ornamentality and a quest for grandeur. The eclectic trend we have seen in St Nicholas, Kastoria, and more generally in the painting of the 17th century was expressed with particular grace at Dryovouno, thanks to the talent of the painter.[62]

In the 17th century, conditions became more favourable for the economic activities of the enslaved Greeks, and this new situation in turn encouraged the founding of new monasteries and churches. In Pieria, the frequency with which churches were erected and painted is striking,[63] particulary by comparison with the previous century, from which no monuments have survived. At the Monastery of St George of Ritina, the wall-paintings in the main church, the painted sanctuary door (1619) and the portable icons on the screen give us an interesting picture of the painting of the early years of the century. Two churches were founded at Skotina in the first decades of the 17th century: the church of Christ (the sanctuary was painted in 1618 and the nave in 1627) and that of St Athanasius (dating from the third decade of the century). The wall-paintings of St Nicholas of Vounene at Litochoro and those recently discovered in the sanctuary and the north aisle of St Athanasius at Aiginio also date from the first half of the 17th century.

The situation in Chalcidice has been observed to be similar to that of Pieria at this time. More specifically, almost all the wall-paintings in the church of Our Lady at Kalandra (1619)[64] have survived, as have parts of the murals in the churches of Our Lady Faneromeni at Nea Skioni,[65] Our Lady the Life-Containing Fount in the Maroutsa district, St Athanasius at Fourka, the Holy Trinity at Kassandrinos, and the Dormition of Our Lady at Nikiti, Sithonia. With the exception of the wall-paintings in Nikiti, all these works are in the Kassandra promontory, which must be connected not only with the independence of the Bishopric of Kassandreias from the

Metropolitan Bishopric of Thessaloniki but also with the prosperity which the area gained from its international trade in wheat.[66]

In the 17th century, as in the 16th, a significant number of churches were painted in Verria: St Nicholas in the Vlach quarter, St Nicholas 'Gournas', St Procopius, St Paraskeve, St Andrew, Our Lady of the Annunciation, etc.[67] The same was true of Kastoria, where we have already dealt with the wall-paintings in the church of St Nicholas of the nobleman Thomanos (1639) by Nikolaos of Linotopi. The murals in the churches of Our Lady of the nobleman Apostolakis (1606) and St Nicholas of the noblewoman Theologina (1663) also belong to this period, as does a section of the decoration of the church of St Nicholas 'Kyritsis' (1654), inter alia. Series of wall–paintings have survived in a number of other towns and villages, especially those in mountainous areas: the Monastery of Our Lady at Spilaio, Grevena, the Monastery of the Transfiguration at Dryovouno, Kozani, the church of St George at Kato Grammatiko, Pella, in Siatista, and elsewhere. The chapel of the Company of the Archangels in the

Aghios Dimitrios, 1570. In the church of Aghios Dimitrios in Palatitsia. below: The Holy Trinity (1619). In the Panaghia Church in Kalandra, Chalcidice.

Monastery of St John the Baptist in Serres was painted at this time (1634)[68], as was the corridor in the south colonnade of the main church (1630), and the murals in the church of Our Lady at Theologos on Thasos also dates from the 17th century.

In the 17th century, the number of painters of rural origins –especially those from Western Macedonia– increased. Painting became a speciality among the inhabitants of Mt Grammos (Grammotsa) and other mountainous areas, quite apart from the village of Linopoti of which we have already spoken. Icon-painting became vernacular and simplified as a rule, continuing the anti-Classical tradition of Palaeologue painting. Artists were frequently incapable of escaping from purely linear compositions, and smooth flow was often unattainable or not even attempted; indeed, the drama of the scene depicted was emphasised. The trend towards eclecticism which we have seen in the 16th century became more general and can be seen in very many works, although it did not always prove possible to blend the various elements with great success. However, in those cases in which the artists had unusual ability and talent their work is most attractive even today, regardless of the tendencies which are predominant in their work. These artists had learned the lessons of technique to be taken from the great painters of the Cretan school and the north-west Greek school and applied them satisfactorily; but when they tried to emulate their distinguished colleagues in other respects, their art found it difficult to escape from the generally vernacular atmosphere of the age – quite apart from its descent into stylisation (usually without any breath of inspiration) and misinterpretation.

Much decorative painting of the 17th century has survived on Mt Athos, although only in refectories in three instances: the remainder is all in chapels.

In the early decades of the century, a considerable number of works –most of them of the greatest value– followed in the tradition of the Cretan painters of the 16th century. As a rule, though, wall-painting was notable for its stylisation, often in combination with a vernacular atmosphere. On Mt Athos, too, the painters were usually from rural areas –whether they were monks or members of the laity– and urban artists whose cultural level would undoubtedly have been higher are rarely encountered.

The best-known sets of wall-paintings[69] are those in

The Last Supper, 1605. In the Dionysiou Monastery on Mt Athos.

a large part of the refectory of Dionysiou Monastery (1603), the refectory of Chilandariou Monastery (1621), the refectory of Docheiariou Monastery (late 17th century), the dome of the phiale in Megiste Lavra (1636), chapels in Dionysiou, Vatopedi, Iviron, Chilandariou and Megiste Lavra Monasteries, and the keli of St George at Provata. Although the names of these artists have not usually survived, some have come down to us: Mercurios, Daniil, Ioannis, Germanos, Anastasios, Atzalis and the Serb Mitrofanevic.

A series of portable icons with distinctive features –broad faces, highly ornamental garments and furniture, decorated haloes– from Mt Athos and Thessaloniki[70] bear witness to the fact that Mt Athos had moulded a stylistic and technical tradition of its own, and that the painting of Thessaloniki had, by the 17th century at least, made a fresh start characterised primarily by its relations with the Athonite studios.

In the 18th century a great deal of decorative work was produced on Mt Athos and elsewhere, and there is a marked increase in the number of painters whose names we know. The conditions in which the Christian subjects of the Ottoman Empire lived had by now improved considerably, leading to the building of numerous churches, monastery churches and chapels. Epirus and Western Macedonia emerged as important artistic centres, and icon-painters from these areas did much work elsewhere.[71] Even on Mt Athos, painters from Epirus and Western Macedonia were usually summoned when it was necessary to use artists from 'the outside world', and thus undoubtedly had a positive effect on the reception and dissemination of their work. Most of these icon-painters came from mountain towns and villages –such as Ioannina and Kastoria– and they kept up their local traditions. They were prepared to incorporate features which they came across in their work farther afield, but their style and manner of expression became steadily more vernacular. The narrative became more verbose, the iconography was enhanced with contemporary features (notably in the garments of the figures depicted) and with baroque and rococo characteristics, depictions of the Apocalypse became more widespread and scenes of the Second Coming, with the punishment of sinners, were rendered with the immediacy of the vernacular language. These features certainly enhanced and revitalised icon-painting, but since they were accompanied by a decline in technique, ecclesiastical painting was progressively transformed into a vernacular art form. It grew to resemble high-quality handicraft work, thus justifying the description of the painters as 'journeymen', at least for the 19th

Aghios Theodoros, 1743. In the church of Aghios Germanos, in the village of Aghios Germanos (district of Florina).

century. The same artists as painted icons also worked on the decoration of urban houses,[72] and features of secular painting –such as vases of flowers and other floral motifs– became easy to interpolate into religious art. This phenomenon was largely the result of eclecticism on the part of the icon-painters and of the acceptance of such trends in ecclesiastical circles.

On Mt Athos, however, instances of the imitation of earlier works –which had first appeared in the 17th century– became more frequent and, in the first half of the 18th century, took the form of a local artistic trend, a purely Athonite style and technique was aim was to return to the Palaeologue models of the monastic community. Indeed, this movement had its theoretical exponent, the priest-monk Dionysios from the village of Fourna in Evrytania.[73] Taking into consideration earlier texts and the vast number of wall-paintings to be found on Mt Athos, Dionysios produced his Interpretion of the Art of Painting between 1728 and 17833 (with the

Aghios Dimitrios, 1783. In the church of the Xeropotamou Monastery on Mt Athos.

assistance of his pupil Kyrillos). This is a true manual of icon-painting, with technical and iconographic instructions and advice to young painters to model themselves on

Panselinos, the great artist of Thessaloniki, in whom the Athonite monks identified all the Palaeologue painting which had developed around that northern Greek city.

The Flower decoration in the church of St Aschangels in New Potidea, Chalkidiki (1872), is a typical and extreme case of a secular subject used in religious painting, as flowerpots constituted the only painted decoration on the walls of the church (Photo by N. Nikonanos, 1968, before the church was whitewashed).

St Luke the Evangelist, 1711. In the chapel of the Baptist in the cell of Dionysius of Phourna, in Karyes, Mt Athos.
Below: "The Dance of the Apostles" (1721). In the chapel of Aghios Dimitrios in the church of the Vatopedio Monastery on Mt Athos.

Dionysios went to Mt Athos at the age of only sixteen, became a monk and taught himself icon-painting "by studying from boyhood and, as far as possible, imitating" Panselinos, as he tells us in his Interpretation. Wall-paintings and portable icons by Dionysios are to be found on Mt Athos and elsewhere, but his reputation –though moderate– rests chiefly on the wall-paintings in the chapel of St John the Baptist in his keli –the keli of Meletios– at Karyes (1711). In the numerous figures, most of them isolated, which make up a considerable part of the decoration of the chapel, Dionysios tried to imitate the similar scenes depicted by Paneslinos in the nearby church of the Protaton. He was not entirely successful in escaping misinterpretation, but in terms of technique, and especially in the use of bright tones and the modelling of the faces (which are broad, with delicate shading) his efforts were rewarded. Dionysios also incorporated into his art elements from the iconography of his own day, both vernacular and Western. This can be seen in the scenes from the life of St John the Baptist, for which there was no model in the Protaton, and when he copies specific figures, as in the case of Christ Recumbent, the picturesque landscape behind Christ, and the baroque surround with its floral decoration.

Apart from the keli of Dionysios, there are numerous other works of this period on Mt Athos which show this tendency to return to Palaeologue painting, some of which stand out for their outstanding quality. These works include the decoration of the chapel of St Demetrius in the church of Vatopedi Monastery (1721)[74] and the narthex in the 'Koukouzelisa' chapel of Megiste Lavra (1715)[75]. In both cases, the painters were artists of talent who took Palaeologue models –though not necessarily those of Panselinos– as their starting-point for interesting scenes and isolated figures. The 'Koukouzelisa' painter is known to us: he was David of Avlona. Two works outside Mt Athos, the wall-paintings in the church of St Nicholas at Moschopoli (1726) and of the church of St John the Baptist at Apozari, Kastoria (1727), are also attributed to him. In the same style are the wall-paintings recently discovered in the 'New' church of Our Lady in Thessaloniki (c. 1730).[76] However, these three examples do not substantiate any theory of the wider dissemination of the Athonite movement, since when David was called from Mt Athos to paint the churches of St Nicholas at Moschopoli and St John the Baptist in Kastoria he would have applied there the art with which he was familiar. The wall-paintings in the 'New' church of Our Lady are simply confirmation of the relationship between Thessaloniki and Mt

Athos which had begun in the previous century. As has been aptly observed, "this mural decoration, with its deliberate revival of Palaeologue models, its eclecticism and its delicacy of colour quality is an artistic entity and an achievement in painting of a purely Athonite nature".[77] Although the movement was not destined to have continuity, it made a major impression on Athonite painting in the second half of the 18th century, and echoes of it are also to be found in the 19th century. Thus was created an Athonite tradition which can be traced back to the movement to return to the Palaeologue models in the first half of the 18th century. The bright colours and broadly modelled faces, with their delicate shading, enriched an iconography which also embraced elements from the engravings of the West. This school of painting was not only assimilated by the painters who came to Mt Athos from elsewhere and worked there: it also spread to wider areas. As a result, works along the lines of the Athonite models, often maintaining more faithfully the earlier anti-Classical tendencies, were produced throughout Macedonia.

It should be noted that the wealth of wall-paintings and portable icons of the 18th century –such as, for example, the vast number of icons in Thessaloniki– have never been published. As a result, although it is possible to trace the general lines of the art of this period and the decisive role played by Mt Athos in formulating it, the nuances of 18th century ecclesiastical art are more or less unknown.

Our knowledge is also inadequate where the 19th century is concerned. We know a little more about the Athonite studios[78] and the painters from Galatitsa in Chalcidice[79] and Kolakia[80] near Thessaloniki. However, after the second half of the 18th century, ecclesiastical art –by now a purely vernacular handicraft– took on an almost entirely uniform character, a development in which Mt Athos was instrumental. The number of new foundations set up on Mt Athos, the monastic community's insistence on tradition, and the generally accepted view that the works produced there were exemplary in terms of doctrine and aesthetics, were the factors most important in binding this tendency together and at the same time were decisive in sustaining the Byzantine forms of art into the 20th century.

To sum up, we can state unreservedly that the post-Byzantine ecclesiastical painting of Macedonia –and of Greece as a whole– is an organic continuation of Byzantine art, though one which constantly revised earlier types in accordance with the circumstances of Orthodoxy and the Greek people at any time.

●

181: Saints Nikitas, Georgios the Younger of Ioannina, Tryphon, et al. In the church of Saints Kirikos and Ioulitta in the Monastery of Aghia Anastasia, Chalcidice.

NIKOS NIKONANAOS
POST-BYZANTINE PAINTING
IN MACEDONIA
NOTES

1. M. Chatzidakis, "Post-Byzantine Art (1453-1700) and its diffusion", in "History of the Greek Nation", (Ekdotiki Athinon), vol. 10, Athens 1974, p. 436.
2. *Ibid.*, p. 411.
3. A. Vakalopoulos, "History of Modern Hellenism", vol. 2, Thessaloniki 1964, pp. 80ff.
4. I. Hasiotis, "The Turkish occupation. Demographic, economic and social evolution", Thessaloniki 2300 Years, Thessaloniki 1985, pp. 91ff.

5. S. Kissas, 'Thessalonian Painters in the Eighteenth Century. A Preliminary Study', BS 24 (1983), 478. S. Kissas, "The Nea Panaghia Church", Thessaloniki and its monuments, Thessaloniki 1985, p. 148. Cf. Arch. Bulletin 33, 1978 (1985), Chronicles B2, p. 244, Arch. Bulletin 34, 1979 (1987), Chronicles B2, pp. 286-287.
6. Kissas, *op. cit.*, p. 478.
7. E. Tsigaridas, 'Monumental Paintings in Greek Macedonia during the 15th Century', Exhibition Catalogue, Holy Image, Holy Space. Icons and Frescoes from Greece, Athens 1988, p. 54. Cf. E. Tsigaridas, "Monumental painting in Macedonia in the 15th century", Eighth Symposium on Byzantine and post-Byzantine art and archaeology", Athens 1988, abstracts of papers, p. 16.
8. S. Pelekanidis, "Prespa's Byzantine and post-Byzantine monuments", Thessaloniki 1960, pp. 85-94. N. Moutsopoulos, "Churches in the Prefecture of Florina", Thessaloniki 1964, p. 4. N. Moutsopoulos, 'Byzantinische und nachbyzantinische Baudenkmler aus Klein Prespa und aus Hl. German', BNJ, 20 (1970), pp. 1ff.
9. Pelekanidis, *op. cit.*, pp. 94-108. Moutsopoulos, *op. cit.*, p. 56. Moutsopoulos, *op. cit.*, pp. 4ff.
10. E. Tsigaridis, Arch. Bulletin, 28 (1973), Chronicles B2, pp. 489-492. P. Lazaridis, Arch. Bulletin, 29 (1973-1974), Chronicles B3, pp. 759-764. Cf. E. Tsigaridas, K. Loverdou-Tsigarida, "Archaeological Research in Velvendo, Kozani", Macedonica, 22 (1982), p. 312. T. Papazotos, "Post-Byzantine painting in Pieria", Archaelogists on Pieria Thessaloniki 1985, pp. 64-65.
11. Papazotos, *op. cit.*, p. 64.
12. Tsigaridas, Loverdou-Tsigarida, *op. cit.*, pp. 311-312.
13. A. Xyngopoulos, "The monuments of Servia", Athens 1957, p. 75ff. Tsigaridas, *op. cit.*, p. 58.
14. Xyngopoulos, *op. cit.*, pp. 102ff. By the same author, "Sketch of the history of religious painting after the fall of Constantinople", Athens 1957, p. 67ff. Chatzidakis, *op. cit.*, p. 419. Tsigaridas, *op. cit.*, p. 57.
15. S. Pelekanidis, "Researches in Upper Macedonia", Macedonica, 5 (1962), pp. 380ff. T. Pazaras, Arch. Bulletin, 33 (1978), Chronicles B2, pp. 271-273.
16. Moutsopoulos, *op. cit.*, pp. 46-50. G. Subotic, L'Ecole de peinture d'Ochrid au XVe sicle, Beograd 1980, pp. 86-93 and 201-202 (in Serbo- Croat with French summary). Tsigaridas, *op. cit.*, p. 57.
17. A.K. Orlandos, "The Byzantine monuments in Kastoria" ABME 4 (1938), p. 167. S. Pelekanidis, "Kastoria I, Thessaloniki 1953, p. 18, plates 179-188. Chatzidakis, *op. cit.*, p. 419. Tsigaridas, *op. cit.*, p. 56.
18. Orlandos, *op. cit.*, pp. 158-159. Pelekanidis, "Kastoria" *op. cit.*, pp. 248-262. By the same author, "Prespa's Byzantine and post-Byzantine monuments", *op. cit.*, p. 91. Chatzidakis, *op. cit.*, p. 419. Tsigaridas, *op. cit.*, p. 56.
19. Orlandos, *op. cit.*, p. 182. Chatzidakis, *op. cit.*, p. 419. Tsigaridas, *op. cit.* pp. 56-57.
20. Orlandos, *op. cit.*, pp. 165-166. Pelekanidis, "Kastoria", *op. cit.*, p. 18, plates 168-177. Chatzidakis, *op. cit.*, p. 419. Tsigaridas, *op. cit.*, p. 56.
21. Orlandos, *op. cit.* pp. 134-136. Pelekanidis, *op. cit.*, plate 117b. Xyngopoulos, "Sketch", *op. cit.*, p. 73. C. Mavropoulou-Tsioumi, "13th century murals in the Koumbelidiki in Kastoria", Thessaloniki 1973, pp. 41-43, plates 55-58.
22. Tsigaridas, *op. cit.*, pp. 56-57 and 60. Cf. E. Tsigaridas, "Research in the churches in Kastoria", Macedonica, 25 (1485-86), 379-389.
23. Tsigaridas, *op. cit.*, pp. 57-60.
24. For the Kastoria studio, cf. principally Xyngopoulos, "Sketch", *op. cit.*, pp. 63-69. Pelekanidis, "Prespa's Byzantine and post-Byzantine monuments", pp. 91ff. S. Radojcic, 'Une ecole de peinture de la deuxime moiti du XVe sicle', Zbornik za Likovne Umetnosti, 1 (1965), 68-105. Chatzidakis, "The chronology of an icon from Kastoria", Bulletin of the Christian Archaeological Society, period D 5 (1966-1969), 305- 306. Chatzidakis, *op. cit.*, p. 419. G. Gounaris, "The wall paintings in the churches of Aghii Apostoli and Panaghia Rasiotissa in Kastoria", Thessaloniki 1980, pp. 158-159. M. Chatzidakis, "Post-Byzantine art 1430-1830", Macedonia, 4000 years of Greek history and culture" (Ekdotiki Athinon), Athens 1982, pp. 414-415. M. Chatzidakis, "Greek painters after the fall of Constantinople

(1450-1839)", (Centre for Modern Greek Studies E.I.E) Athens 1987, pp. 77-79. Tsigaridas, *op. cit.*, pp. 56-57. E. Yeorgitsoyannis, "Anonymous artists' workshop in the second half of the 15th century in the Balkans and its influence on post-Byzantine art", Epirotica Chronica 29 (1988/89), pp. 145-172, which provides all the relevant bibliography. For the incorporation of the depiction of St Nicholas into the 'Koumbelidiki' in the studio, see Mavropoulou-Tsioumi, *op. cit.*, pp. 36-37.

25. See note 24.

26. Chatzidakis, "Post-Byzantine art 1450-1830", *op. cit.*, p. 415. By the same author, "Greek Painters", *op. cit.*, p. 78.

27. Of the voluminous bibliography on the Cretan School and the Cretan painters, see in particular Xyngopoulos, "Sketch", *op. cit.*, pp. 1ff and especially pp. 80ff and Chatzidakis, "Post-Byzantine art (1453-1700)", *op. cit.*, pp. 420ff. Chatzidakis' recent work "Greek painters after the fall of Constantinople (1450-1830), pp. 21-63, gives a wealth of bibliography both on Cretan painters and painting and on the other artists and post-Byzantine painting in general.

28. Chatzidakis, "Post-Byzantine painting (1453-1700)", *op. cit.*, p. 420.

29. See, in particular, Xyngopoulos, "Sketch", *op. cit.*, pp. 94-112. K. Kalokyris, "On the frescoes of the Cretan artist Theophanes at Meteora and Mt Athos", in "Athos, archaeology and art", Athens 1963, pp. 54-98. M. Chatzidakis, "The painter Theophanes Streblitzas toupiklin Bathas (biographical check)", Nea Estia 74 (1963, special issue on Mt Athos), pp. 215-226. By the same author, 'Recherches sur le peintre Thophanes le Cretois;, DOP 23-24 (1969-1970), pp. 309-352. By the same author, "Post-Byzantine art (1453-1700)", *op. cit.*, pp. 422- 424. A. Karakatsanis, "The icons of the Stavronikita Monastery", The Stavronikita Monastery, History-Icons-gold embroidery", National Bank of Greece, Athens 1974, pp. 41-60. M. Chatzidakis, "The Cretan painter Theophanes. The final phase of his work on the frescoes of the Stavronikita Monastery" (published by the Stavronikita Monastery Press), Mt Athos 1986.

30. Chatzidakis, "Post-Byzantine art (1453-1700)", *op. cit.*, pp. 422-423.

31. Chatzidakis, "The Cretan painter Theophanes", *op. cit.*, p. 37.

32. *Ibid.*, pp. 34-34 and appendix, fig. 31.

33. *Ibid.*, pp. 40-41. Chatzidakis, "Greek painters", *op. cit.*, p. 297.

34. E. Tsigaridas, "Frescoes and icons in the Pantocratoros Monastery on Mt Athos", Macedonica 18 (1978), pp. 191-192.

35. See note 29.

36. M. Chatzidakis, "The painter Euphrosynos", Kritica Chrinica 10 (1956), pp. 273-291. By the same author, "Greek painters", *op. cit.*, p. 289.

37. Chatzidakis, "Greek painters", *op. cit.*, pp. 241-253, with the relevant bibliography.

38. Chatzidakis, "The Cretan painter Theophanes", *op. cit.*, p. 119.

39. Chatzidakis, 'Note sur le peintre Antoine de l'Athos', Studies in Memory of David Talbot-Rice, Edinburgh 1975, pp. 83-93. By the same author, "Post-Byzantine art (1453-1700)", p. 424. By the same author, "Greek painters", pp. 171-172.

40. Chatzidakis, "Greek painters", *op. cit.*, p. 312.

41. See primarily M. Acheimastou-Potamianou, "The Philanthropinon Monastery and the first period of post-Byzantine painting", Athens 1983, pp. 197ff, with all the relevant bibliography.

42. *Ibid.*, pp. 214-215.

43. *Ibid.*, p. 185.

44. Xyngopoulos, "Sketch", *op. cit.*, pp. 113ff. Chatzidakis, "Post-Byzantine art (1453-1700)", *op. cit.*, pp. 424-425. Gounaris, "Frescoes in the Aghii Apostoli and Panaghia Rasiotissa churches", *op. cit.*, pp. 162ff. Acheimastou- Potamianou, *op. cit.*, pp. 197ff.

45. Acheimastou-Potamianou, *op. cit.*, pp. 197ff.

46. Gounaris, *op. cit.*, pp. 105-182.

47. Xyngopoulos, "Sketch", *op. cit.*, pp. 113ff. Hadzidakis, "Post-Byzantine art (1453-1700)", *op. cit.*, p. 418. Acheimastou-Potamianou, *op. cit.*, p. 178.

48. Michailidis, "New elements in the painted decoration of two monuments in Thessaloniki", AAA IV (1971), pp. 346-352.

49. Gounaris, *op. cit.*, pp. 21-104 and 179-182. Cf. Chatzidakis,

"Post-Byzantine art (1430-1830)", *op. cit.*, pp. 418-419.

50. Gounaris, *op. cit.*, p. 80.

51. Gounaris, "The frescoes of Aghios Ioannis Theologos in the church of the Mavriotissa in Kastoria", Macedonica 21 (1981), pp. 1-78. Cf. Chatzidakis, "Greek painters", *op. cit.*, p. 286.

52. Michailidis, "The church of Aghios Zacharios, in Kastoria", Arch. Bulletin, 22 (1967), 1st Studies, pp. 77-86.

53. Chatzidakis, "Post-Byzantine art (1430-1830)", *op. cit.*, p. 418.

54. Pelekanidis, "Researches in Upper Macedonia", pp. 400-405.

55. *Ibid.*, pp. 405-414.

56. *Ibid.*, pp. 396-400.

57. T. Papazotos, The frescoes in the church of the Panaghia Monastery on the Aliakmon", Macedonica 21 (1981), pp. 99ff.

58. Tsigarida, Loverdou-Tsigarida, *op. cit.*, pp. 315ff.

59. A. Tourtas, "The churches of Aghios Nikolaos in Vitsa and Aghios Minas in Monodendri. An approach to the work of the painters from Linotopi", Thessaloniki 1986, with all the relevant bibliography.

60. *Ibid.*, especially pp. 1-5, 267-280, 321-325.

61. *Ibid.*, especially pp. 22-23, 291-294, 328.

62. *Ibid.*, especially pp. 26-28, 301-308, 329-330.

63. For painting in Pieria in the 17th century, see Papazotos, "Post-Byzantine painting in Pieria", pp. 65-68.

64. I. Papaggelos, "The church of the Presentation of the Virgin, in Kalandra, Chalcidice", from "Churches in Greece after the fall of Constantinople", Athens 1979, pp. 47-53.

65. L. Toska-Zacharof, "The frescoes in the Panaghia Phaneromeni church in Nea Skioni, Chalcidice", in the Proceedings of the First Panhellenic Symposium on the History and Architecture of Chalcidice (7-9 Dec. 1984)" Thessaloniki 1987, pp. 211-255, with references to the wall-paintings in the other churches.

66. Papaggelos, *op. cit.*, p. 52.

67. See in this respect Papazotos, "The work of an anonymous painter in Veria", Macedonica 19 (1979), pp. 168-192.

68. A. Stratis, "The fresco decoration of the chapel of the Archangels in the Timio Prodromo Monastery, Serres", Third Symosium on Byzantine and post-Byzantine art and archaeology", Athens 1983, abstracts of papers on pp. 75-76.

69. See Chatzidakis, "Post-Byzantine art (1430-1830)", p. 420.

70. *Ibid.*, pp. 420-421.

71. Chatzidakis, "Intellectual life and culture 1669-1821" History of the Greek Nation (Ekdotiki Athinon), vol. 11, Athens 1975, pp. 250-255.

72. Makris, "The Hionadites, 65 folk artists from Hionades, Epirus", Melissa Press, Athens 1981, p. 34. Garidis, "New copper-plate types for secular decorative painting in the 18th and 19th centuries", Macedonica 22 (1982),p. 11.

73. Xyngopoulos, , pp. 292ff. By the same author, "Dionysius of Phourna", Nea Estia 74 (1963, special issue on Mt Athos), pp. 227-230. Chatzidakis, "Intellectual life" pp. 248-250. Chatzidakis, , p. 276.

74. Xyngopoulos, "Sketch", pp. 306ff. Chatzidakis, "Intellectual life" p. 249.

75. Chatzidakis, "Intellectual life", p. 250. By the same author, "Greek painters", pp. 235-237.

76. See note 5.

77. Chatzidakis, "Intellectual life", p. 250.

78. G. Smyrnakis, Mount Athos, Athens 1903, p. 365. Kalokyris, "Contemporary icon painting on Mt Athos", Athos, Art and Archaeology Topics, Athens 1963, pp. 253ff.

79. D. Pallas, "Painting in Constantinople after its fall", Arch. Bulletin 26 (1971), p. 258. M. Chatzidakis, "A few words on the Constantinople school", Arch. Bulletin 27 (1972). p. 133. By the same author, "Intellectual life", p. 250. Papaggelos, "Artists workshops in Chalcidice in the 19th century", First Symposium on Byzantine and post-Byzantine art and archaeology, Athens 1981, abstracts of papers on pp. 68-70. L. Boura, F. Tsigakou, "Sketches of the work of post-Byzantine painters from Galatista, Chalcidice", Zygos November-December 1983, pp. 22-30. Chatzidakis, "Greek painters", pp. 187-188, 295.

80. Evyenidou, "A 19th century painters' guild in Kolakia", Macedonica 22 (1982), pp. 180-204.

Monastic Architecture

Ploutarchos Theocharidis

The group of monastery buildings, as the expression in architectural form of a particular kind of monastic life, is designed to serve a series of complex functions across the areas of the religious worship and everyday life of the monastic community and the production and storage of its commodities. The introversion for which the overall design is notable (and which stems from the anchorite ideology of renouncing the world) finds its extreme architectural expression in the walls which surround the building, isolating the community from the world while at the same time protecting it and its goods against all threats from outside.

In terms of their general character, monastic buildings –with the exception of churches, which are exclusively associated with worship– are closely related to buildings of similar kinds in secular architecture (houses, farming and handicraft buildings, fortifications, etc.). However, they also differ from such buildings, sometimes deviating from them in certain basic functions (as is the case with houses) and sometimes displaying particular traditions which developed in monastic architecture. In the case of these buildings, intended for everyday use, it was thus natural that the conservatism we can see today in icon-painting and church building, especially in the monastic works dating from after the fall of Constantinople –a conservative which is charged directly by the religious ideological framework[1]– should have been much less rigid. There are two main factors which determine how close or loose was the relationship between monastic buildings and the secular architecture of their time:

a) The particular nature of their function and, consequently, the degree to which they were charged by the ideological framework of monasticism; among typical examples are buildings such as the refectories at one extreme, or towers, mills and labourers' houses at the other.

b) The intention of the particular owner and user (or, rather, of his age) to lay a greater or lesser emphasis on the monastic –that is, non-secular– nature of the building, or to operate within the framework of a particular architectural framework, as was the case from time to time on Mt Athos.

In studying the architecture of the Macedonian monasteries of recent centuries, it should be borne in mind that the overwhelming majority of the monuments which have been published date from the 18th century and after. The material at our disposal on earlier periods is much more limited in quantity and is mostly preserved on Mt Athos, whose large monastic foundations were for centuries a model for the spiritual lives and artistic activities of the Orthodox monasteries.

In the first centuries of Ottoman rule there must, of course, have been a certain continuity in, and development of, the earlier Byzantine modes in building (for example, in the construction of churches), since the Orthodox church and monasticism continued to exist as official institutions even after the Ottoman conquest. However, although it is relatively easy to watch the manner in which Byzantine and post-Byzantine architecture evolved in the field of church-building (where we have an almost uninterrupted serie of monuments which have long attracted the interest of researchers), our knowledge of the course taken by monastic architecture down to the 18th century is limited because of the relative rareness of such monuments and because of the retricted amount of research which has taken place in this area. In the particular case of the more humble functional buildings (which then, as now, tended to give the specific monastery complex its overall architectural character), our knowledge is scanty and fragmentary in relation to the Byzantine period; in the case of the early Ottoman period, it is only recently that we have begun to recognise the material which has been preserved in the 'arks' of the Athonite monasteries. On the other hand, we are equally ignorant of the corresponding humble secular architecture of these two periods –that is, of housing and production in urban and rural areas –in northern Greece in general.

In the brief outline which follows it will not, of course, be possible to cover separately each of the different types of monastery building. Readers will find an excellent overall picture of them in the comprehensive study of the subject by A. Orlandos[2], which continues to be a unique work. What we shall try to do is present in summary form the evolution of the general features of the groups of buildings, with particular emphasis on Mt Athos and the architecture of the early Ottoman period which has survived there.

In the 15th century (a period of transition, which saw the Ottoman Turks complete their conquest of the Byzantine lands and consolidate their empire), many monasteries declined and were dissolved, yet many of the larger and wealthier foundations were able to carry on normally. The monastic community of Mt Athos is the most characteristic example of this continuity. But soon, with the recovery which began in the closing decades of the 15th century and lasted for about a hundred years –the Golden Age of the Ottoman Empire– many of the dissolved monasteries were refounded and new foundations were set up throughout Greece. The initiative for this lay largely with the Ecumenical Patriarchate and with individuals associated with it and Mt Athos. In very many cases, the necessary work was performed thanks to generous donations from the princes of the Danube states, and this elevated patronage is reflected in the scale and high quality of monastery architecture.

The same wind of reconstruction continued to blow on Mt Athos in the late 15th and early 16th centuries, when almost complete rebuilding of many monasteries took place (even involving extension of the precincts[3]), and many of the main churches and refectories were repaired, remodelled and reconstructed from the foundations up. Quite apart from the various historical sources which testify to this frenzy of reconstruction, a reading of the buildings themselves will allow us even today to sense this particular feature of the period. The uncommon economic power, special legal status and consequent continuity of life which are features of the Athonite monasteries led to the preservation, in most groups of buildings, of an almost continuous stratification of building activity dating from the 16th century at the latest. According to our research, the percentage of structures dating from the early Ottoman period is strikingly high. These older structures (or remnants of them) are very often encapsulated within buildings dating from later periods, making it possible to recognise them only when we intervene to support or restore them. It is worth recording that apart from the numerous fortificatory walls, towers, refectories and monumental buildings of other kinds, this centuries-long stratification of structures also preserves a whole host of important traces of humbler buildings (wings of cells, store-rooms, etc.) –that is, a type of architecture of which, as we have seen, we know nothing in northern Greece at this early date. In fact, more specialised studies have revealed quite a

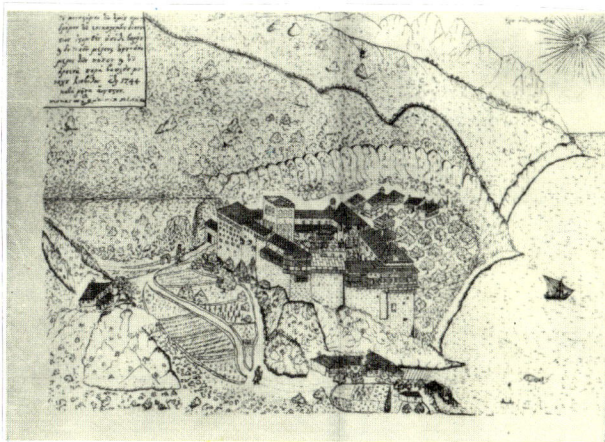

Phot.1. The Dionysiou Monastery, in a drawing by Barski (1744).

Phot.2. The Docheiariou Monastery, in a drawing by Barski (1744).

number of such buildings from this period which have survived down to the present day in a more or less complete form.[4] A systematic study of this material, which will be of importance for the history of Athonite architecture and will also cast light on many issues of the secular architecture of the Late Middle Ages in the Balkans, is still in its initial stages. Specialised and detailed research into the buildings themselves is necessary to bring these features out and assess them, and great sensitivity should be displayed when repairing and restoring buildings. If this is not done, such buildings are in danger of being spoiled or even lost for ever, since the majority of them are wooden or of lath-and-plaster construction and, when repairs take place today, they are usually seriously damaged or are removed and replaced.[5]

In the 16th century, the architecture of the rural monasteries (those which lay outside the walls of large towns) was still strongly fortificatory in nature. In the case of all the Athonite monasteries which were renovated at this time –and of Stavronikita Monastery

Phot.3. The Docheiariou Monastery, seen from the west, with the boatsheds in the foreground.

which was built then, on the site of an earlier, much smaller and ruined foundation– high, strong walls continued to be seen as essential, and were reinforced with tower-like projections. Most of the earlier towers of any size, which were free-standing fortresses, forming part of the monastery precinct or outside it, connected to a smaller monastic foundation, a kelli or an arsanas, were repaired or largely rebuilt, and new structures of a similar nature were erected from the foundations up.[6] Most of the fortified buildings on Mt Athos, and in particular those by the coast, were constructed with special cannon-ports at this time (fig. 1), demonstrating their strength and their degree of modernisation. We are also told by historical sources of the use of cannon, and small and early examples of such weapons (or of their parts and accessories) are to be seen in some monasteries even today.[7] The monastery's landing place on the coast (the arsanas) would also be protected by such a tower, standing above it and equipped with machicolations, embrasures and often cannon (photograph 5). The danger from the sea was very great in the early period of Ottoman rule, when the pirate fleets were enormous and heavily armed. There is historical and oral testimony to frequent raids and even to the plundering of monasteries, such as the disaster which befell Esphigmenou in 1533.[8]

With the exception of what the few fortified small monasteries to have survived[9] can tell us, we know very little about the appearance of the minor monastic foundations on Mt Athos in the early Ottoman period: the numerous kellia which stood at some distance from the monasteries[10]. However, our research has revealed that some of the surviving kellia preserve the remnants of structures of this period –or even their entire nuclei– and these have been incorporated into the more recent buildings in just the same way as happened in the case of the monasteries. Many of the more important kellia seem to have had fortified towers for their protection, and it is far from impossible that the numerous towers with which the promontory is studded may have formed a network for keeping a watch on the coast and passing on information. In this respect, it is especially interesting that the Holy Council of Mt Athos continued in the early 16th century to maintain its fortified tower in the otherwise ruined small monastery on the site later occupied by Stavronikita.[11]

As a result of the strictly fortificatory function of the monastery complexes, the building masses seem to have been generally heavy, with few architectural features on the facades - although this was not always the case, as can be seen, for example, in the older east wing of Dionysiou Monastery, built in around 1500[12], where the external facade is articulated around high arched windows in successive rows (figs. 2, 3).

In most cases, walls consisted of simple filled rubble masonry. The use of bricks was confined to some of the domes and arches, and occasionally to joints. Little decorative brickwork was used on the facades. It would also seem –naturally enough– that the use of lath-and-plaster balconies on the outer sides of the complexes of buildings was less common than it is today, when we are struck by the number of successive open (aplotaria) and closed (sachnisia) balconies. This earlier appearance of the buildings –heavy and austere– was largely retained until the early 18th century, as we can see in the extremely accurate drawings produced on the spot in 1744 by the Russian monk and traveller Vasily Grigorovich Barskij.[13] If we bear in mind that very little building was done on Mt Athos between c. 1603 and c. 1750, then it is reasonable to suppose that the architectural picture of the monasteries given by Barskij closely reflects the activities of the 16th century, and this is often confirmed in our work on the buildings themselves. As for the frequency of wooden external balconies on successive storeys during the early Ottoman period, the only sure evidence today comes from a multi-storey building added outside the south side of Dionysiou in the mid-16th century: here the holes into which the beams of the balconies which the building had on its four uppermost floors fitted have survived.[14] However, Dionysiou Monastery stands in a particularly strong position, on the top of a steep coastal cliff (photograph 1), as do Gregoriou, Simonopetra and Ayiou Pavlou Monasteries, in whose drawings by Barskij we can also see successive balconies on the upper floors.[15]

In the few residential wings to have survived on Mt Athos from the 16th and early 17th centuries, the outer facades corresponding to the successive corridors by which the rooms were reached usually consist of stone pillars or wooden columns bearing wooden beams on which the floors rest. Lines of arches are only occasionally used on these facades, and even then are always confined to the ground level of the buildings[16] (photographs 6, 7). The material we have at our disposal today suggests that the proportion of wooden or lath-and-plaster structures in the humbler buildings which served the functions of everyday life must have been very great. The example of the refectory of Stavronikita (first phase built shortly before 1546) demonstrates that the lath-and-plaster system could even be adapted to buildings which in other respects were approached with a monumental cast of mind.

It is difficult to talk today of the monastery architecture of the rest of Macedonia in the early Ottoman period, since such groups of buildings as have survived have not yet been studied. To judge by the general impression given by certain large monastic foundations in the general area of northern Greece, it would seem that the overall nature of such complexes did not differ much from that of Mt Athos (e.g., the Monastery of St John

Phot.4. The sea front fortress of the Karakallou Monastery; the monastery itself is visible in the right rear corner (photo 1978).

the Baptist near Serres[17], the Monastery of St Anastasia near to Vasilika[18], the Monastery of St Dionysus on Mt Olympus[19], the Dousikou Monastery near Trikala, the Flamouriou Monastery on Pelion[20]). Of course, the monasteries located in towns are always an exception, since they did not have the overpowering need for fortification of those situated in rural areas.

However, some of the surviving smaller foundations are of outstanding interest. These include the two metochia of St Anastasia Monastery –both ruined today– one of which is at Kritziana near Epanomi and the other (of the Holy Trinity) is approximately 2 km to the south-west of the Monastery. The former is built in the form of a little fortress, with a peripheral wall strengthened by three small towers on the south side of the precinct and a strong tower-house in the middle of the north side, which may have been another tower in an earlier phase (photograph 8). The remaining buildings in the group (now demolished) were arranged inside the precinct along its sides, as was the small, simple church,

Phot. 5. The tower of the Iviron Monastery.

which stood at the eastern extremity of the north side. The initial phase in the building of the tower-house has been dated to 1530[21] and the precinct must have been laid out at the same time, as can be seen from the architectural features of its two surviving small towers. The second of the two metochia, which is in a much worse state of repair, seems to have been protected only by a surrounding wall. It was rectangular in layout with low single-storey buildings on all four sides around a courtyard. Its humble wooden-roofed church, whose apses preserve 16th century wall-paintings[22], is incorporated into the buildings on the north side of the precinct. Small groups of buildings of this kind, fortified to a greater or lesser extent and intended either as residences or to protect the produce of large estates, could perhaps tell us something about the form in which the large feudal residences must have been laid out in the early Ottoman period. In this respect, a comparison between the more recent metochi complexes of Chalcidice and the premises of the large privately-owned estates dating from the same period[23] is of particular interest.

As early as the reign of Selim II (1566-1574), Mt Athos had begun to sink into a long period of recession which soon assumed the dimensions of decline and lasted until the first half of the 18th century. Similar difficulties faced the monasteries of the rest of Macedonia at the same period.

The 17th century seems to have been a period of transition in monastic architecture, as we can see in the surviving buildings on Mt Athos. During that century the last of the large and purely fortificatory towers were built[24], while in the residential wings we can see a shift towards a preference for a type of monumental facade looking on to the courtyard of the monastery, with successive open lines of arches corresponding to the number of floors and particularly lavish decorative brickwork[25]. This type of facade was to prevail throughout the 19th century and would become one of the distinctive features of the Athonite monasteries (photographs 9, 10). At this time, too –if not even a century earlier– the basic simple type of small unprotected group of buildings of Athonite kellia outside the monasteries as we know it today had already become predominant. It consisted of a small church with a house abutting on it on the west, although such rudimentary arrangement of functions could easily have been widely applied at an earlier time. Today, we are familiar with this type of small kelli from the numerous 18th and, especially, 19th century examples (photograph 11). The

Phot.6. Megistis Lavras Monastery: the north side of the wing known as "Aghios Athanasios".

Phot.7. Megistis Lavras Monastery: the west side of the wing known as "Aghios Athanasios".

Phot.8. The Aghia Athanasia Monastery estate at Kritziana, near Epanomi (photo by Th. Pazaras, in about 1963).

churches which as a rule belong to them are of a special and characteristic type –condensed cruciform with a drumless dome– whose ealiest dated examples in the kellia of Mt Athos can also be traced back to the start of the 17th century.[26]

Early in the 18th century Mt Athos embarked upon a long period of great prosperity and intensive economic activity which lasted down to the War of Independence

Phot.9. The Helandariou Monastery, seen from the courtyard of the south wing. The arcades on the two lower levels date from the 17th century, and the rest of the building from 1784. (Photo 1980)

Phot.10. The Xeropotamou Monastery, seen from the courtyard of the north section of the east wing (1780).

of 1821. It seems that many monasteries reconstructed all their buildings at this time, beginning with the main church itself and the refectory. This practice continued (and was in some cases completed[27]) in the period after the War of Independence and into the early 20th century. Many of the smaller monasteries built extensions which sometimes more than doubled the area of the precinct.[28] There was prosperity and activity off Mt Athos, too, especially after the 1770s, when the Russo-Turkish wars were over. The funds for these building projects were provided by various senior clergy, monks and rich laymen and also stemmed from the alms which the monasteries themselves collected from the Orthodox population.

Although the design of monastery complexes continued to obey the general rules of safety and fortification, they progressively lost the outward appearance of castles after the 18th century. Rather than large and purely fortificatory towers we begin to see smaller tower-shaped masses, while the windows which give on to the outer side of the monastery increase in size and balconies (covered or open) start to become more frequent, especially on Mt Athos. The arsanades of the monasteries built at this time do not have towers. Contemporary sources tell us that by the first half of the 18th century the monasteries on the promontory no longer used their cannon other than for firing salutes to distinguished visitors. The Athonite landscape became

studded with small and unfortified kellia and idiorhythmic sketes, in the form of miniature settlements consisting of units of buildings similar to those of the kellia, became more numerous.

Towards the end of Ottoman rule, the monasteries off Mt Athos acquired an architectural character identical to that of the vernacular architecture of the time[29], although, of course, they are often on a larger scale[30] (photographs 12, 13). The same was true to a large extent of church-building off Mt Athos, in which the modes of vernacular architecture were widely applied at this time.

Phot.11. The Marda (Maroudadio) cell near Karyes. The house dates from 1797 (photo 1977).

Phot.12. The "Timio Prodromo" Monastery in Serres: projecting enclosed balconies on the west wing (photo 1978).

Phot.13. The "Timio Prodromo" Monastery in Serres: view from the courtyard on the north wing (photo 1979).

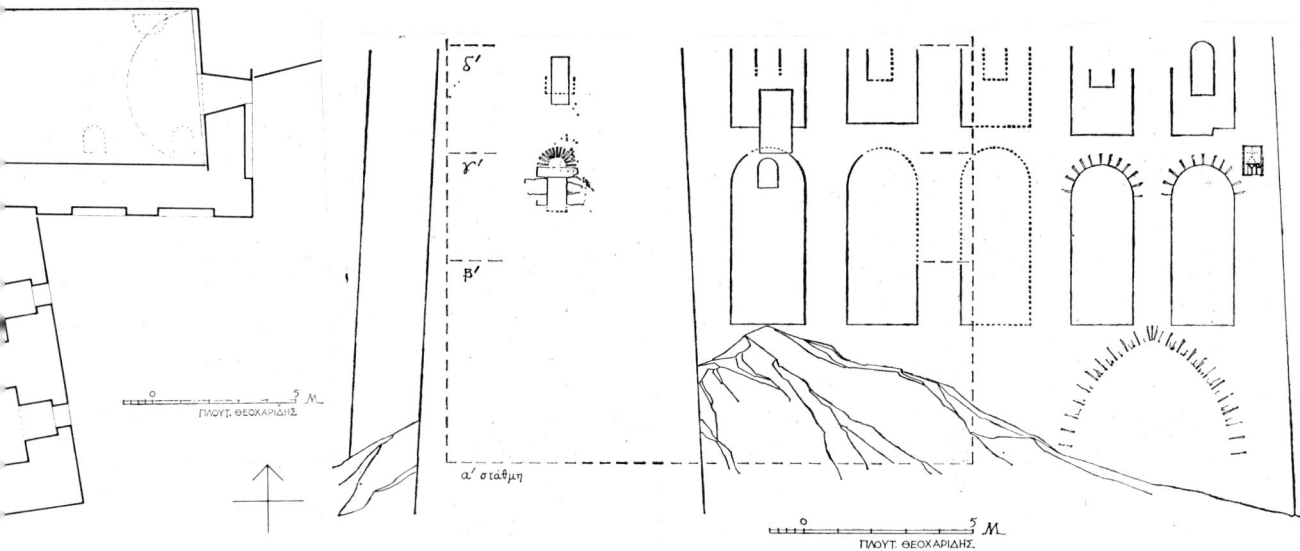

*ng in the southwest corner of
mid 16th c.*

Fig.3. The Dionysiou Monastery, sketch of the outside of the old south wing (built circa 1500).

op. cit.

11. C. Patrinelis, A. Karakatsani, M. Theochari, "The Stavronikita Monastery, History - Icons - Gold Embroidery", National Bank of Greece, Athens 1974, p. 21.

12. See note 3, above.

13. On Barskij's journeys and drawings, see K. Chrysochoidis in the series "Places and Images", vol. 2, Athens 1979, pp. 7-30 and figs. 1-119.

14. See Theocharidis, "Observations", *op. cit.* pp. 448ff and note 2.

15. On the balconies of Simonopetra, see Theocharidis, Simonopetra, *op. cit.*, p. 82. It has been ascertained that the rows of balconies shown on the drawing of Ayiou Pavlou belong largely to buildings of the late 17th century: see P. Theocharidis, "Observations on the structural history of the Aghios Pavlos Monastery on Mt Athos", Eighth Symposium on Byzantine and post-Byzantine art and archaeology (abstracts), Society of Christian Archaeology, Athens 1988, pp. 41-42.

16. P. Theocharidis, "The residential wings of the Athonite monasteries (1500-1900)", Greek Traditional Architecture, vol. 8, Melissa, Athens 1991, p. 256.

17. See photographs 12. 13. They have survived on the two lower levels of a building dating from 1544/5. P. Theocharidis, *op. cit.*, p. 260, note 21.

18. P. Theocharidis, "An initial approach to the structural history of the Aghia Anastasia Monastery complex", The Archaeological Oeuvre of Macedonia and Thrace, Thessaloniki, 12-15 February 1992.

19. C. Siaxabani-Stefanou, "The church of the Dionysius Monastery on Mt Olympus", Churches in Greece after the fall of Constantinople, vol. 3, National Technical University, Athens 1989, pp. 111-124.

20. G. Kizis, "The Phlamourion Monastery on Mt Pelion", Churches in Greece after the fall of Constantinople, vol. 2, Athens 1982, pp. 151-166.

21. According to an inscription which has survived: see V. Pazaras, "The inscription on the Aghia Anastasia monasterial domain at Kritziana, Epanomi", Macedonica 10 (1970), pp. 143-151.

22. Recorded by the 10th Inspectorate of Byzantine Antiquities.

23. See, indicatively, the examples given by N. Moutsopoulos, "Settlements, manors, monasterial domains", Thessaloniki 1977, and G. Kizis, "Official and Traditional architecture: the influence of the

centre on the provinces in the Ottoman Empire", Greek Traditional Architecture (Thessaly-Epirus), vol. 6, Athens 1988, pp. 269-290, figs. 17, 19.

24. See, for example, the arsanas with tower at the Iviron Monastery (1625/6) and the tower of the Protaton at Karyes. See P. Theocharidis, "Examples of houses", *op. cit.*, pp. 275-276.

25. For example, the north wing of Vatopedi Monastery, sections of the west wing of Chelandari Monastery and the buildings in the south-east corner of the precinct of the same monastery. On the latter, see S. Nenadovic, 'Les bÄtiments (Konaks) du complexe sud de Chilandari', Hilandarski Zbornik, 5 (1983, in Serbo-Croat), pp. 215-256. See also, more generally, P. Theocharidis, "Residential wings", *op. cit.*

26. See the text by M. Polyviou in this volume.

27. For example, the Xiropotamou, Kastamonitou and Zographou Monasteries.

28. For example, the Xenophontos and Ayiou Pavlou Monasteries. On the former, see P. Theocharidis, "Preliminary review of the Byzantine aspects of the enclosure of the Xenophontos Monastery on Mt Athos", XVI Internationalen Byzantinistenkongress, Akten II/4, Jahrbuch der âsterreichischen Byzantinisk, 32/4 (Vienna 1982), pp. 443-455. On the latter, see note 15, above.

29. See, for example, S. Voyiatzis, "The Monastery of the Dormition at Torniki, Grevena", Bulletin of the Christian Archaeological Society, period D, vol. 15 (1989-1990), pp. 241-256.

30. E.g. the Monastery of Our Lady at Kleisoura, Florina, and the Monastery of the Holy Trinity at Vytho, Kozani. On the latter, see P. Leonidopoulou-Stylianou, "The church of the Aghia Triada Monastery at Zoupani", Churches in Greece after the fall of Constantinople, vol. 1, Athens 1979, pp. 67-82. See also the short text on the Macedonian monasteries by N. Moutsopoulos in "Macedonia, 4000 years of Greek history and culture", Athens 1982, pp. 427-429.

31. See N. Moutsopoulos, "Kudarei, Macedonian and Epirote Master Builders", The First Greek Professional Technicians in the Period of the Liberation, Technical Chamber of Greece, Athens 1976, pp. 353-370, and N. Moutsopoulos, "Macedonian Architecture", Thessaloniki 1971. See also P. Theocharidis, "Residential wings", p. 265.

32. See, for example, S. Stefanou, "Small non-monasterial architecture and complexes on Mt Athos", Greek Traditional Architecture, vo.. 8, Athens 1991, p. 295.

Ecclesiastical Architecture of Mt. Athos

Miltiadis D. Polyviou

It is a matter of common knowledge that Mt Athos is a unique example of a monastic state. As a consequence, it is not at all surprising that the building of churches in this unusual place should constitute a special case for Macedonia and, indeed, for Greece in general. The general co-ordinates of church-building do not, of course, differ from those of the rest of Macedonia: the doctrinal framework was undoubtedly the same and the general historical background was shared, while the teams of builders were not completely alien to each other. The causes of the differences are equally clear and understandable. In terms of ideological co-ordinates, an open society of citizens is one thing, and a closed society of monks is quite another. In terms of its liturgical function, the church does not cover a parish, but a monastery, a skete or a kelli. In terms of the church's significance for the social formation to which it refers and of the expenses which that formation can make available, the different between monastery and village is equally clear.

The building (or rebuilding) of churches on Mt Athos during the five centuries of Ottoman rule did not, of course, always occur at the same pace, since the more general conditions on which it depended were not always identical. Those conditions included relations with the Ottoman authorities, the state of security in the area, the finances of the monasteries, and the cash support emanating from the Danubian principalities. As a result, the tide of church-building ebbed and flowed. Along general lines, it could be said that the first century of Ottoman rule was –quite understandably– a period of great recession. This was followed by eighty years of increased activity, and then by a similar period of decline.[1] The next period, from the mid-17th to the mid-18th century, was one of consolidation[2] which paved the way for the next upsurge in church-building; this began immediately and lasted until the time of the War of Independence of 1821.[3] In the two decades which followed, almost no churches were built because of the catastrophic consequences of the Athonite community's participation in the unsuccessful revolt in Macedonia.[4] However, a fresh wave of church-building now began, as a result –among other factors– of the large

sums of Russian money being channeled on to Mt Athos.[5]

The Athonite churches can be classified, first of all, in terms of their function and role. The most important category contains the katholika (main churches) of the monasteries, which, naturally enough, are the most outstanding examples of Athonite church-building in terms both of size and the quality of their architecture. The kyriaka (churches for common Sunday worship) of the anchorites make up another significant category, and these buildings often approach the katholika in size and importance. (We should, perhaps, include in our examination of the kyriaka a number of other churches of a similar size.) By way of contrast to the categories of katholika and kyriaka, which are familiar and limited in number, the third category of Athonite churches consists of the countless smaller church buildings which might be described as chapels or kelli churches. Some of these are attached to katholika, and are katholikon chapels; others are free-standing, inside or outside the monastic precinct, as in the case of wayside chapels or cemetery churches; a third group form part of the wings of monasteries or sketes, and the fourth and final group –also the largest– contains the churches specific to each kelli or kalyva.

Each of these categories, of course, has its own features and its own history. In general, it could be said that the shared characteristic most typical of Athonite church-building is its conservatism. Conservatism is not, of course, a general feature of every church or of monasticism itself, of which it is the most extreme version. But on Mt Athos the conservative trend is much more distinct, precisely because it is a purely monastic community which acts as the ideological centre of Orthodoxy and the guardian of its values. It should not be forgotten that architecture is much more dependent than the other arts on the conditions of place and time, and so the role of 'conservatism' has by definition a significance quite different from that which is has in, for example, painting. It should also be noted that the power of this conservatism has fluctuated wildly from area to area and from age to age. Thus it could be said –in general– that conservatism is stronger in terms of the overall type than in morphology or decoration (typologi-

Churches on Mt Athos in the late Turkish period: top left, Xeropotamou (1761-4), top right, Zographou (1801), and bottom right, Esphigmenou (1808).

cal changes are more difficult than the introduction of a new morphological element), while in terms of the category of church it is much weaker in the kelli churches and the kyriaka than it is in the katholika, which have shouldered the responsibility of continuing the Byzantine ecclesiastical tradition. However, it should be noted that –with very few exceptions– all the categories of church have the common feature of a dome. Even the few wooden-roofed churches (which appeared in the late 19th century, usually attached to Russian kellia) have a dome or false dome of some sort. The only domeless churches are the chapels on the lower levels of the monastery wings, which of necessity use as their ceiling the floor of the storey above.

Post-Byzantine Katholika

Most of the katholika of Mt Athos –all, indeed, except six– are buildings of the post-Byzantine period.[6] The katholika of Koutloumousiou, Dionysiou, Stavronikita, Karakallou, Docheiariou and Simonopetra Monasteries all belong to the first period of revival (16th century).[7] The katholika of Philotheou, Xiropotamou, Grigoriou, Zographou, Esphigmenou and Ayiou Panteleimonos Monasteries date from the period of the great upsurge in building activity between the mid-18th century and the outbreak of the War of Independence in 1821, as does the new katholikon of Xenophontos Monastery, which was completed after the War of Independence. Lastly, the period of revival in building in the mid and late 19th century produced the katholika of the Ayiou Pavlou and Kastamonitou Monasteries.

The post-Byzantine katholika of the Holy Mountain are all of the so-called Athonite type: that is, they are complex four-pillared cross-in-square churches with an esonarthex and lateral apses. These churches are faithful

applications of the type of Byzantine katholikon which was formulated on Mt Athos in the period between the late 10th and early 14th centuries.[8] It should be noted at this point that the archaeological research necessary to determine whether, and how far, this perseverance with the Byzantine katholikon in the Athonite type was influenced by the typological commitments involved in rebuilding the churches on top of the remains of earlier katholika has not yet been conducted. However, the case of the katholikon of Philotheou Monastery –built in 1746– reveals a clear typological choice, since the new building was in the form not of a basilica, asthe previous katholikon on that site9 had been, but in the Athonite type. Another example of a deliberate decision to implement the Athonite type can be seen in the rebuilding of the katholikon of Xiropotamou Monastery, in 1763: we can be certain that this church did not follow whatever remains there may have been of its predecessor, since that church had a different orientation.10 However the case may be, it is a fact that in the extant post-Byzantine katholika the deviations from the typology of the Byzan-

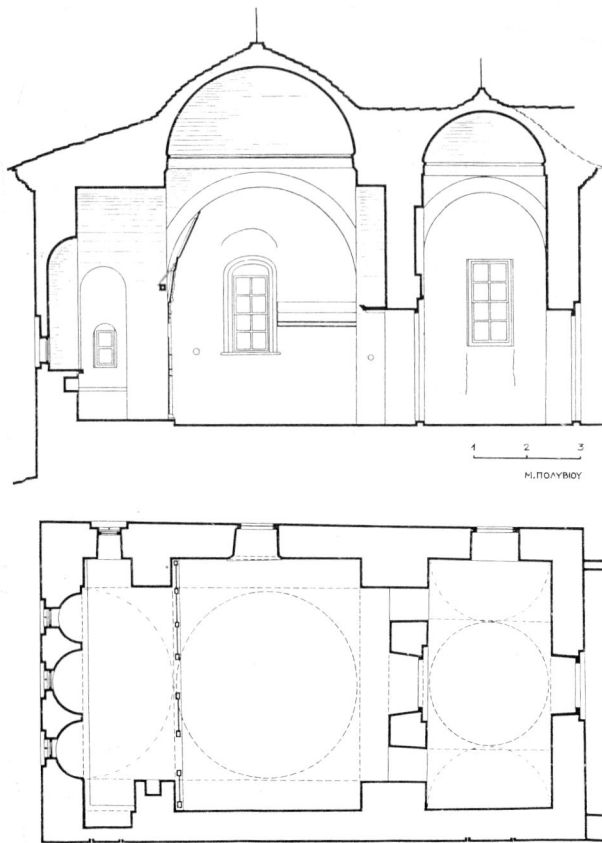

Cemetery church of the Xeropotamou Monastery.
Vertical section and ground plan.

tine Athonite church are negligible and concern not the basic type itself but only certain of its individual details. The most significant of these deviations can be seen in the katholikon of Stavronikita Monastery, which lacks the choir apses that are the most distinctive feature of the Athonite type. This deviation should, however, probably be attributed to the confined space of the precinct rather than to any desire for originality.

In the Athonite type, the main church consists of the area marked out by the four arms of the cross, with the spaces contained in the angles of the arms and the large dome in the centre, and of the choir apses which protrude on each side. The dome is borne, as usual, on four pillars and is hemispherical with windows in the drum. The arms of the cross are roofed with semicylindrical vaults, while the spaces in their angles are covered with hemispherical vaults, cross vaults or semicylindrical vaults. The choir apses are semicircular on their inner side and have three or more outer sides; they are roofed with quarter-spheres. The central section of the sanctuary is formed by an extension of the east vault of the cross (borne on an additional pair of pillars or columns) and

the central apse, which is semicircular on the inside and triangular on the outside, with a quarter-sphere roof. The lateral parts of the sanctuary are topped with small domes and their apses are semicircular inside and triangular outside, with quarter-spherical roofs. In some cases, domed peripheral rooms –called typikaria– protrude from the two corners of the east wall and are roofed with domes. The spacious esonarthex has a roof divided into a number of parts in various forms (domes, vaults, cross-vaults, etc.) borne on between two and eight pillars. To the side of the esonarthex are chapels (one or two in number), which as a rule are in the compressed cross-in-square chapel type; these communicate with the esonarthex but may also be entered from their western sides. Further to the west is the narthex itself (or in some cases the exonarthex), whose facade consists of open or blind arches and which is roofed with small drumless domes or cross-vaults.

Apart from these general features, which are to be found in more or less all the post-Byzantine katholika of Mt Athos, each church has its own special characteristics. For example, in the case of three katholika of the late Ottoman period (Xiropotamou, Zographou, Ayiou Pavlou), there is a small dome above the roof of the centre of the sanctuary vault. This feature does not derive from the Byzantine tradition, but may reflect the influence of Moldavian models.[11] Another original feature about the katholikon of Xiropotamou is the absence of dividing walls between the chapels and the esonarthex. In the katholika of Esphigmenou and Ayiou Pavlou Monasteries –which, like that of Xiropotamou, date from late Ottoman times– there are no dividing walls between the main church and the esonarthex. These phenomena demonstrate a tendency to redesign the type– a tendency which, although not abandoning the shell of traditional typology, now begins to see it as a uniform and integrated whole which does not always need to make plain its accretive origins. In the typology of the katholikon of Docheiariou Monastery, the choir apses do not have the usual floor plan in which the external side is triangular or polygonal: here it is rectangular. In the Grigoriou and Ayiou Pavlou Monasteries, the lateral apses of the sanctuary do not protrude but are inscribed in the masonry of the walls, while the katholikon of Ayiou Pavlou Monastery has two apses which protrude from the north and south walls of the sanctuary. This original feature of apses on the north and south walls of the sanctuary is also to be found in the new katholikon of Xenophontos Monastery, and in an even bolder form, since these apses are similar both in size and in the arrangement of their surfaces to the choir apses.

The church of the cloister of Kausokalyvia (built in stages between the 17th and the early 19th century).

The special features to be found in each case are not, of course, confined to the examples cited above. What is of importance is that they do not constitute part of a clear evolutionary trend in the type, which could be said to have remained generally undeveloped down the centuries which have elapsed since its inception. This phenomenon could be seen as one more manifestation of the extreme conservatism typical of all aspects of Athonite life.

This conservatism could be said to be less marked in the case of morphology, and the effect of evolution is more easily distinguished than it is in the typology. Of course, in the katholika of the first post-Byzantine period (16th century), adherence to tradition is more or less absolute and there are very few new features. Walls are usually of rubble-filled masonry, involving the irregular addition of brick and the familiar articulation along lines of arches, while vaults and domes were built purely of brick. Cornices are sometimes toothed and sometimes in concave section, and on the domes they consist of arches rather than running straight. The katholikon of Docheiariou Monastery stands out among the churches of this period: its exaggerated ratio of height to width and the square pillars in its rectangular choir apses give it a rather more Western appearance.[12]

In the katholika of the eighty years prior to the War of Independence, the basic constitution of the building continued to be faithful to tradition, but the details which betray evolution are more distinct. The wall surfaces now consist of hewn masonry framed in brick and with intervening bands of brick, while continuing to be articulated in lines of blind arches. The use of the traditional toothed cornices also continued, although concave or undulating forms because more common. The cornices of domes were not always in the traditional form of arched sections, now often being laid out in continuous straight lines. The pointed arches reminiscent of Muslim models and typical of the period made their appearance on Athos, too (see the windows in the katholikon of Philotheou Monastery), as did door openings with the familiar undulating column capitals (katholika of the Xiropotamou, Esphigmenou and Zographou Monasteries). The new katholikon of Xenophontos Monastery –the most innovative of all the katholika of this period, perhaps because it was completed after the War of Independence– has glass lenses in the shape and section of advance 'Turkish baroque'.

In the katholika of the period since the War of Independence, the individual features which go beyond the Byzantine tradition continue to evolve and now reflect the trends of the later 19th century without abandoning the conservatism of insistence on the traditional juxtaposition of masses. A characteristic expression of the nature of this period is to be seen in the katholikon of Ayiou Pavlou Monastery, built in the mid-19th century, where the walls are entirely faced with dressed masonry (as is also the case with the slightly later katholikon of Kastamonitou), while on the facades elements of advanced 'Turkish baroque' (e.g. lenses with complex curved shapes) co-exist with purely neo-Classical features such as the pediments which crown the windows.

The Kyriaka of the Sketes

Apart from the buildings which date from the Byzantine period, we shall also have to exclude from our

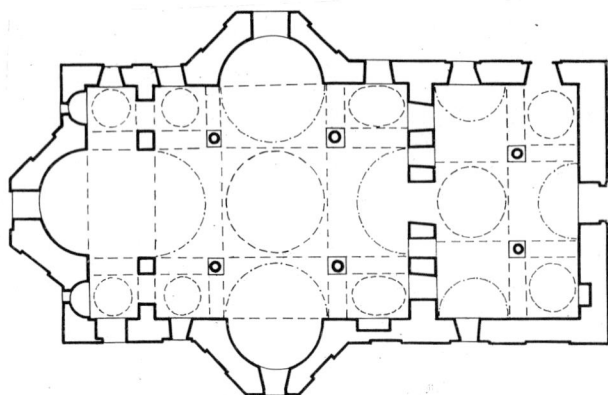

Floor plan of the church of the Iviritiki cloister.

examination of the kyriaka of the twelve sketes the structures of the last fifty years of Ottoman rule, since they lie outside the traditional framework and are much closer to the Eastern European neo-Renaissance style. Thus we shall be dealing with only seven examples in this category of church-building which, if we also consider the additions made to the majority of them, cover almost the entire period of Turkish rule.[13] The earliest of these buildings is the kyriakon of the skete of St Ann, whose initial nucleus pre-dates the 17th century. The kyriakon of the Kavsokalyvia skete is also quite old: the first stage in its construction must date from the 17th century.[14] The other five kyriaka were all built in the 80 years before the War of Independence –a period which, as we have seen, was one of much church-building.

The typology of the kyriaka is as conservative as that of the monastery churches. Of course, the radical changes and additions to many of them mean that the original form of the buildings is not always clear. Most of the changes involved the narthex and were intended to make the esonarthex more spacious: this can be seen, for instance, in the kyriakon of St Ann, whose lateral apses are subsequent additions.[15] However, in general it could be said that the kyriaka which fall within the scope of this study are of the Athonite type – in their final form, at least. In other words, they are of the cross-in-square type with lateral apses and a lite, just like the katholika. The typological differences between the kyriaka and the katholika are effectively non-existent in some cases; in others, they are quite distinct, depending on how far the type applied in each case is fully in line with the Byzantine models or contains simplifications such as the absence of columns in the esonarthex or a reduction in the number of supporting pillars in the church itself. The kyriakon of the skete of Iviron Monastery, for instance, cannot be distinguished typologically from the katholika

(apart, perhaps, from the fact that it has only one apse rather than three on its eastern wall). The kyriakon of the Kafsokalyvia skete, on the other hand, differs from the katholika in having an apse only on its eastern wall, in the fact that the body of the church has two columns (as opposed to the complex four-column layout), and in its single-space esonarthex.

These general observations on the typology of the kyriaka also apply more or less equally to their morphology. However, it is immediately clear that in this respect they are less conservative than the katholika. Needless to say, the basic principles in the form taken by the shapes and in the general articulation of the planes do not change and the arrangement of the facades relies on the same traditional features; yet there is a degree of development and a departure from the attempt to faithfully imitate earlier models. The apses and domes are proportionally larger than in the katholika; the articulation of the planes is less subtle and careful; the pointed 'Islamic' arches typical of the period are more frequently employed; cornices normally have a simple concave section, and the walls are of rubble or semi-dressed stone with occasional admixtures of brick, especially in the domes and arches.

Chapels and Kellia Churches

In general, it could be said of these churches that they are far less conservative than the katholika or even than the kyriaka. This is easy to explain: such small churches did not serve as symbols after the manner of the katholika, nor were they intended to express the survival of the Byzantine ecclesiastical tradition. In any case, the kelli churches extant today are more recent and consequently more highly developed buildings: none of the surviving examples dates back beyond the mid 17th century.[16]

In terms of typology, the great majority of these churches are in the compressed cross-in-square type and its variations. This is the type of church produced when the ordinary cross-in-square type is compressed so that the distance between the walls and the supports of the central dome is cancelled out; those supports thus become columns, the corner areas disappear and the width of each of the arms of the cross (apart from the east arm) is equal to the distance between the columns. The basic type consists of the body of the church and the sanctuary. The body of the church is the square area between the columns, roofed with a hemispherical (or slightly flattened) drumless dome carried on three semicircular arches and a semicylindrical vault on the east side. The

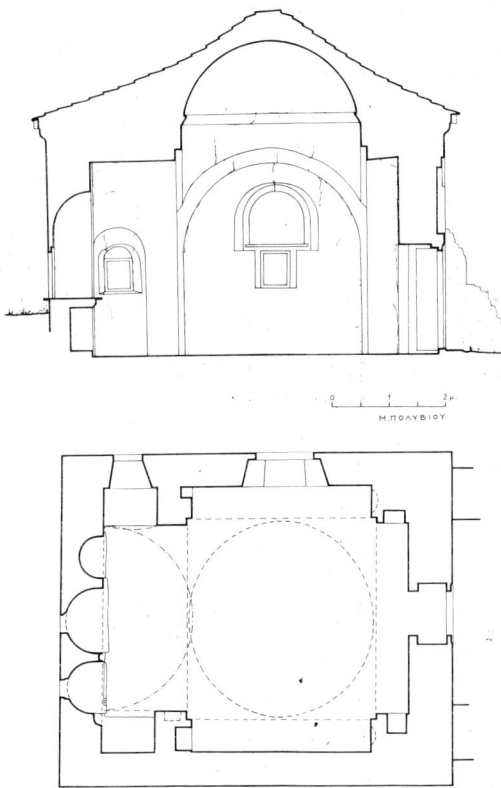

Above, church of the "Aghios Georgios" cell in the Provata district. Vertical section and ground plan. Right, two typical chapels on Mt Athos: above, the Panaghia chapel of the Zographou Monastery (2nd half of the 18th century) and below, the cemetery church of the Xenophontos Monastery (1817).

vaulted area is the sanctuary, usually without apses on the outer side: its three small apses are recessed into the masonry of the wall. In most cases, the basic type has an additional open-sided and wooden-roofed exonarthex on the west. Certain typological variations are produced when the dome has a drum or when the central apse of the sanctuary protrudes on the outer side.

The compressed cross-in-square type was known in the Byzantine period,[17] but it was under Ottoman rule that its use became most widespread. In terms of the floor plan, it remained almost unchanged. The only real difference from the Byzantine type was that there the dome always had[a] drum, while these later buildings –under the influence of Islamic architecture18– use the familiar drumless dome. The compressed cross-in-square type of

church with a blind drumless dome seems to have appeared early in the 17th century (the chapel of the St George keli at Provata, built in 1631, must be the earliest known example) and to have been most widely used in the late 19th century. Apart from the basic type, there were also a number of variations, most of them involving the addition on the west of a narthex roofed with a vault, a cross-vault (more rarely) or a dome supported on lateral arches. In some cases, this variation on the type has the further supplement of choir apses on each side of the body of the church. Between the narthex and the main church is the trivilo, with a wide opening in the centre and smaller doors on either side –one of the most characteristic features in the architecture of the Athonite chapels of the late Ottoman period.

The little churches of Aghios Georgios and Aghios Theodosios at the Xeropotamou Monastery (1837) are a lovely example of adjacent chapels within the monasterial complex.

Vaulted churches consisting of a single space are rare, as is the variation in which there is a drumless dome in the centre of the vault.[19] Equally uncommon are dome-roofed single-space churches with two lateral apses incorporated into the thickness of the masonry. However, the greatest typological interest is to be found in another rare example: the tripartite church with a rectangular floor plan (for example, the chapel of St Andrew in the skete of the same name at Karyes). The main church is roofed with a low drum and a dome with eight supports using pendentives. It has two shallow lateral apses sunk into the masonry of the wall. The altar is roofed with a quarter-sphere, and the wings of the sanctuary have drumless hemispherical domes. The esonarthex is roofed with a navicular dome in the centre and two drumless hemispherical domes at the sides. There are also some variations on this type, differing chiefly in the manner in which the esonarthex is roofed.

A certain number of wooden-roofed churches were built during the mid 19th century, primarily as churches for the Russian kellia. These were simple structures with false or wooden domes and, in some cases, a narthex;[20] until that time, the only wooden-roofed churches on Athos had been the lower chapels of the pairs of superimposed chapels in the wings of monasteries. The superimposition of one chapel on top of another was a fairly common practice on Mt Athos in Ottoman times: it probably stemmed from the need to provide the bearing structure of the upper chapel with firm foundations, thus creating beneath it an area with an identical floor plan which was suitable for arrangement as a chapel with the floor of the upper chapel as its ceiling.

In general, it could be said of the typology of the kelli churches and the chapels that their conservatism is less marked than it is in the case of the katholika and the kyriaka. Once more, of course, only one basic type of church is used –and one with Byzantine origins, at that– yet there was clearly much more scope for variation and tradition did not function as quite such an oppressive burden.

Naturally enough, the churches in this category offer fewer opportunities for morphological investigation than do those of the other categories. Not only are they inferior in terms of typology, size and elaborateness of construction: they are also frequently not free-standing, and are enclosed within the monastery or kelli buildings of which they form part. Nonetheless, such churches are often of considerable interest, not only because they reflect the character of their age but also because some of them are true architectural achievements. In most cases, their external appearance is humble, with simple flat rubble-masonry walls and no apses or other features, and with slate roofs broken by a half-concealed drumless dome and edged with a continuous horizontal cornice. The only features which betray some sense of variation

Floor plan of the cell church of Aghios Andreas (Serai) in Karyes.

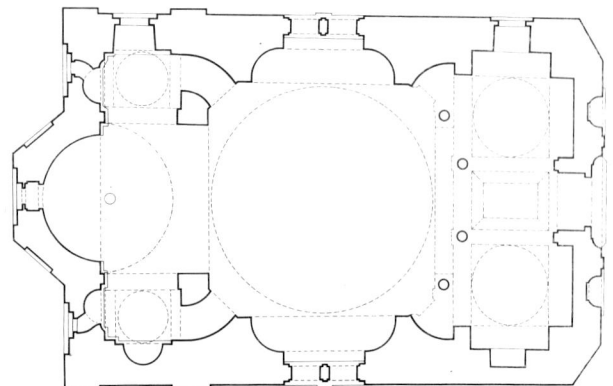

are the brick-arched windows, the simple decorative brickwork on the facades, the serrated or undulating brick cornices and, in a few cases, blind arches on the facades. These churches are, of course, more striking in appearance when they have domes on the roof or apse; the polygonal drum of the dome can be articulated around pillars and elongated windows with simple or complex frames and may be crowned with a cornice which is simple and horizontal or discontinuous and arched, while the apse will be articulated around blind arches. There are some chapels dating from the late 18th to the mid 19th centuries which manage to escape from this rather impoverished framework –one example would be St George in the east wing of Xiropotamou Monastery– and in which the familiar 'vernacular baroque' style of the age reaches its climax. In the most recent of such buildings, the first influences of neo-Classicism can be detected: great care has been taken with the facades, which are in dressed masonry set in brick; the pillars and window frames are entirely of dressed stone, and the cornices are undulating and skilfully worked. In other chapels, by way of contrast, the exterior is relatively simple and out interest is directed to the interior (as with the church of St Andrew at the skete of

The tiny church of the cloister of Kausokalyvia.

the same name in Karyes, also known as the Serai). Here the elaborateness of the typology (tripartite, pseudo three-apsed, octagonal support for the dome) makes it possible for the interior to impress us with its highly baroque treatment of the surfaces and its decoration.

●

MILTIADIS K. POLYVIOU
ECCLESIASTICAL ARCHITECTURE
OF MT. ATHOS
NOTES

1. See Panayiotis K. Christou, "Mount Athos", Athens 1987, p. 216.
2. *Ibid.*, pp. 216-217.
3. *Ibid.*, p. 267.
4. *Ibid.*, pp. 271-274.
5. *Ibid.*, p. 381.
6. For a brief presentation of the most important stages in the building of all the katholika on Mt Athos, see the article by Miltiadis D. Polyviou and Ploutarchos L. Theocharidis, "The churches in the monasteries on Mt Athos", Special Edition 1986 , off-printed from, Centre for the Preservation of the Athonite Heritage, Thessaloniki 1986.
7. The dating of the katholikon of Simonopetra is not yet certain. According to M. Gedeon ("Patriarchal journals", Athens n.d., p. 93) and an inscription in the Monastery library, the church was renovated in 1623, when Timotheos was abbot, and this date seems to correspond to all the other facts.
8. *Ibid.*
9. The type of the old katholikon of Philotheou Monastery can be seen very clearly in the drawing by Barskij (1744). For an enlargement of this drawing, see Paul M. Mylonas, Athos though old engravings and other works of art, Athens 1963, p. 131.
10. See the Barskij drawing, *Ibid.*, pp. 106-107.
11. The argument for the Moldavian origins of this feature is presented by Pavlos Mylonas in his article "The Dolianon, or Kranias, Monastery on Mt Pindos", in Churches in Greece after the fall of

Constantinople, in Athens 1979, p. 107. On Mt Athos - apart from the katholika already mentioned - there is also a dome above the altar in the kyriakon of the Romanian skete of St John the Baptist (1864), which is further indirect evidence of the Moldavian connection.
12. See also Pavlos Mylonas, "The architecture of Mt Athos", Nea Estia no. 876, Christmas 1963, p. 202.
13. See Pavlos Mylonas, "Kyriaka and other similar churches on Mt Athos", in Christian Archaeological Society: Third Symposium on Byzantine and post-Byzantine art and archaeology - Programme and summaries of texts., Athens 1983, pp. 61-62, which gives a very brief description of the typology of the kyriaka and the fundamental stages in which they took shape.
14. *Ibid.*
15. *Ibid.*
16. It would seem that the earliest kelli chapel is that of St George at Provata (1631). See M. Polyviou, "Observations on the architecture of the Aghios Georgios chapel in the Provata area of Mt Athos", in Christian Archaeological Society: Third Symposium on Byzantine and post-Byzantione art and archaeology - Programme and summaries of texts., Athens 1982, pp. 81-82.
17. See C. Bouras, "Aghios Stephanos, Rivion, Acarnania", Scientific Annual of the Polytechnic School of the Aristotelian University of Thessaloniki , and A. Portelanos, "Aghios Nikolaos Horefto, Mt Pelion", Churches in Greece after the fall of Constantinople vol. 2, Athens 1982, p. 172.
18. See Anastasios K. Orlandos, "Ecclesiastical architecture in Greece during the Turkish occupation", Athens 1953, off-print from the periodical L'Hellenisme Contemporain, p. 214.
19. See Pavlos M. Mylonas, "Kelli churches on Mt Athos", in Christian Archaeological Society: Second Symposium on Byzantine and post-Byzantine art and archaeology, Athens 1982, pp. 70-73, which gives a brief but full typological classification of the kelli churches of Mt Athos.
20. *Ibid.*

Macedonian Ecclesiastical Architecture (Excluding Mt Athos)

Kalliopi Theocharidou

The two first centuries (15th-17th)

During the first two centuries after the Ottoman conquest–the darkest and most difficult years for the Greeks– it was only natural that very few churches should have been built in towns, rural areas or monasteries. The difficulties facing the inhabitants of low-lying areas and of towns strongly occupied by the Turks were clearly much greater: here direct and strict control could be exercised over compliance with the measures to restrict church-building.[1] By way of contrast, there was more building activity in the upland areas, where control was less easy, and under the auspices of monasticism and the relative degree of autonomy which the Ecumenical Patriarchate had managed to safeguard. This difference in the general conditions of life–which continued into the subsequent period– is apparent in the number of churches to have survived in the areas in question and in their size and quality of architecture.

Monastery church-building

During this period, many Byzantine monasteries were dissolved as a result of destruction by warfare, of depopulation and of general impoverishment. However, work began after the mid 16th century on the construction of a number of important monasteries throughout Macedonia (Monastery of the Holy Trinity on Olympus 1542/3, Zavorda Monastery 1534, St Anastasia Monastery in Chalcidice approx. 1525, Monastery of Our Lady at Spileo near Grevena 1633)[2], while a number of earlier Byzantine monasteries were renovated and flourished once more. The Monastery of St John the Baptist at Verria became a coenobium and was renovated in around 1540 by the Blessed Dionysius the Younger. The Monastery of Our Lady belonging to 'kyr-Joel' was renovated by the Blessed Theonas in approximately 1540. The 'Eikosiphinissa' Monastery near Drama, which had been devastated in 1507, was refounded in the 17th and seems to have flourished, since we know that it had 150 monks in 1632. The Byzantine Monastery of St John the Baptist, on the other hand– which had had privileges and prestige under Gennadius

Scholarius ([3] 1468)– declined during the 16th century.[4]

Of the two categories into which monasteries can be divided in terms of their affiliation, the stauropegic foundations, which were loosely dependent on the Patriarchate, were wealthier than the 'parish' or 'provincial' monasteries, which were under the jurisdiction of the closest bishop and, as we can see in the source materials, often ran into difficulties. There are, however, three important religious personalities who seem to have played an important part in the prosperity of the Macedonian monasteries after the mid 16th century. These were men who made their appearance in the area early in the century and founded large monasteries after first acquiring renown and numerous disciples: St Dionysius the Younger, who renovated the Monastery of St John the Baptist at Verria and founded the Monasteries of the Holy Trinity on Olympus and Sourvia on Pelio, the Blessed Nikanor (1491-1549), a lay preacher who was active in Western Macedonia and founded the Zavorda Monastery in the mountains near Grevena, and the Blessed Theonas, who founded the famous Monastery of St Anastasia in Chalcidice and, as Metropolitan Bishop of Thessaloniki, renovated the 'kyr-Joel' Monastery in the city.[5]

The fact that many important monasteries were founded by monks who had spent part of their lives on Mt Athos indicates one of the most direct paths by which the influence of the Holy Mountain spread throughout Macedonia. Apart from the Blessed Dionysius the Younger and the Blessed Theonas, both of them Athonites, to whom we have already referred, we also know that the Monastery of the Heavenly Host at Naousa was built in the late 16th– early 17th century by Theophanes, monk of Docheiariou.[6] The state of our knowledge today does not give us a full picture of all the channels through which the Athonite models spread through Macedonia, or of the processes by which this occurred, but the spiritual leadership of Mt Athos is manifest in every aspect of monasticism, including monastic architecture.

From the point of view of church typology, the

Phot.1. Aghios Georgios Monastery at Asprovalta. The church seen from the northwest.

Athonite type–the cross-in-square with lateral apses– was used in all the monasteries in mountain areas, in the larger and more important foundations (such as the stauropegic monasteries of Zaverda, the Holy Trinity on Olympus and Our Lady at Spileo) and also in smaller monasteries such as those of St George at Asprovalta (second half of the 16th century, diagram 1) and St George at Eptachori on Mt Grammos (Bourboutsiko[7], 1625).

This is clearly connected with the influence of Mt Athos, but it is also related to the impact of the Meteroa monasteries on the architecture of these areas. The difference lies in the fact that in the examples cited above the spacious esonarthex of the Athonite church gives way to a narrow narthex divided into three parts, while with the sole exception of the Holy Trinity on Olympus the tripartite sanctuary is simple and lacks typikaria. Both the simple and the complex four-column arrangements of the central part of the church were used, and even more complicated variations with addition pair of pillars on the west were not unknown: such an arrangement can be seen in the Spileo Monastery (diagram 2).

As a rule, the central part of the church was topped with the usual high-drummed Byzantine dome, although the St George Monastery at Asprovalta is a rare example of the use of a large cross-vault for this purpose.

In general, the construction of these churches continued the best of the Byzantine tradition, with bands of dressed blocks (usually limestone) alternating with two or more rows of bricks, a structural technique used in vaults as well as in the drums of domes and the side apses. In vertical walls, this type of masonry was often used in conjunction with the skilful rubble masonry of the building traditions of Epirus and Pindus (fig. 1).

Phot.2. The Spilaiou Monastery at Grevena. View of the church from the southeast.

Externally, the facades were enlivened with blind arches on the lateral apses, the sanctuary apses and the domes which protrude above the one-piece slate roof (fig. 2).

By way of contrast to these impressive churches in mountain areas, the monastery katholika of the plains and urban centres are as modest as the parish or family churches of the same districts.

Almost all the few katholika of this period with which we are familiar –such as St George at Ritina, Pieria (1494)[8], Our Lady 'Porphyra' at Prespa (1522)[9], the Monastery of the Prophet Elijah near the village of Asomati, Verria (before 1570)[10]– are simple wooden-roofed buildings of very modest proportions. Examples of single-arched vaulted churches are relatively rare: one could city the cemetery church of the Monastery of St George at Eptachori (mid 17th century) or the upper floor of Our Lady at Tourniki (1400)[11], both of which fall within the architectural style of the mountainous regions.

Our knowledge of the urban monasteries of this period is even more incomplete, as a result of the damage and confusion caused by the constant changes in the urban environment. In the former Byzantine centres, of course, there were certainly monasteries at this time: they include St Nicholas of the monk Anthimos in Verria (1565)[12], St Nicholas 'Gornas' (wall-paintings of the 15th-18th centuries), also in Verria, which is thought to have been a monastery katholikon[13], and St George 'of the Mountain' at Kastoria (late 14th century, 16th century additions), which is mentioned as a monastery in 1749.[14]

Church-building in the towns and villages

The very modest churches to have survived from this period in the larger or smaller towns of Macedonia reflect vividly the general impoverishment of the countryside and the tremendous difficulties facing the Christian populations of the Ottoman-occupied urban centres. It is indicative of the atmosphere that Thessaloniki, the region's largest city, has no churches dating from the early Ottoman period, nor are there any in the environs of the city. In Chalcidice, some of the few early churches to have survived were monastery metochia, as is the case with the chapel of Our Lady 'Phaneromeni' at Nea Skioni (late 16th century), which is a metochi of Flamouri Monastery, or the church of the Presentation of the Virgin at Kalandra (before 1619), which was most probably a metochi of Chilandari Monastery.[15]

The type of building predominant in both small family churches and parish churches had a wooden roof, a single room (with or without a narthex), a characteristic elongated layout (e.g. the church of Our Lady at Trigoniko, Kozani, 1593, diagram 3, or St Athanasius at Ayios Yermanos, Florina, 1604[16]) and very often no windows at all: there are simply skylights in the roof. The inferior quality of these buildings–unplastered rubble masonry as a rule, with wooden ties– and the modest proportions imposed by Ottoman law meant that the churches very often resembled houses rather than places of worship. The floor of the church often lay considerably below the outside ground level, so as to give it the necessary height inside.

Even in urban centres such as Kastoria, which had a valuable Byzantine tradition in church-building, the use of this type of church–modest, wooden-roofed and simple, though richly-painted inside– became general. In some cases, of course, the best Byzantine structural tradition survived: these include St Nicholas 'Magaleiou' (1505), with its incomplete brick surrounding for each masonry block and its use of blind arches in the

apse. But by now the rule was rubble masonry with wooden ties; this was usually unplastered on the outside, although churches with external wall-paintings are not unknown (e.g. St Nicholas of the nun Eupraxia, 1486)[17].

At Aiani near Kozani, another former Byzantine centre, there are three simple wooden-roofed churches dating from the 16th century.[18] Here, too, great care has been taken with the masonry, which is isodomic and uses dressed stone and limestone blocks alternating with rows of bricks. The walls and the sanctuary apse have blind arches, there is decorative brickwork and serrated bands are used (church of the Archangel Michael, 1549, fig. 4).

It is only in Verria and its vicinity that we find–in addition to the usual simple churches– a number of spacious three-aisled wooden-roofed buildings serving as parish churches (Our Lady 'Haviara' 1498, St Nicholas in the Ayios Antonios quarter 1575, etc.).[19] This interesting local phenomenon -of the early appearance of a church type which had of course been known in Byzantine times but was not to be generally used in Macedonia until the subsequent period–is not easy to explain satisfactorily today, since the available material has not been systematically studied. The building history of the churches of Verria is very often complex, as can be seen in those examples which have been investigated in rather more detail, and this prevents us from saying with any certainty that the three-aisled churches we see today were always in that form (e.g. St Nicholas 'Amoleftos', which dates from before the second half of the 16th century, and the Transfiguration of the Saviour in the Ayios Patapios district, whose early phase pre-dates 1602).[20] As for the origins of the type, the three-aisled Byzantine churches which already stood in the town –perhaps on the same sites as those we see today– must certainly have served as models. It is indicative that the foundations of an earlier three-aisled basilica have been found beneath St George 'Grammatikos', today a three-aisled basilica with a wooden roof.[21]

Mid 17th century– early 19th century

In the crucial period of the 16th and 17th centuries, considerable demographic upheavals took place as large Christian populations left the low-lying areas to escape Turkish oppression and built new villages in the mountains. As a result, Kozani, mentioned as a village in 1534, soon grew into a town,[22] while Siatista must have been a place of some importance as early as the second half of the 17th century: at least five large churches were built there between the mid 17th century and the opening years of the 18th.[23]

The insecurity and destitution from which the countryside had suffered during the previous period must have begun to recede after the signing of the Treaty

Phot. 3 The Spilaiou Monastery, Grevena:
interior view.

Phot. 4. The church of the Archangel
Michael at Aiani in the district of Kozani.
View from the south.

of Karlowitz (1699), and a perceptible economic recovery took place after the Treaty of Passarowitz (1718). Of course, insecurity returned in the second half of the 18th century, with the Russo-Turkish wars, which triggered waves of migration towards Central Europe. In 1769, the Vlach-speaking villages of Mt Grammos were looted by 'Turk-Albanians', who laid waste the prosperous town of Moschopoli.[24]

The economic well-being of the upland parts of Macedonia, which relied on trade and manufacturing, is to be seen very clearly in that area of architecture which involves the building of churches, and it can be distinguished in terms both of quality and of quantity. The number of churches increased everywhere throughout the 18th century and the three-aisled basilica type predominated as it did in the rest of Greece. The flourishing Christian communities found the small simple churches of the past inconvenient now, and their clear preference for large and richly-decorated buildings was directed into projects of renovation from the foundations up. We can see testimony to this in the numerous inscriptions which refer to the earlier "unsightly and very small" church and contrast it with the "new, beautiful and admirable" building.

The need which dictated the adoption of the three-aisled basilica type was undoubtedly that of providing space for a larger congregation. In addition, such a church would allow the members of the community to gather in a clear and organised member, by generations and in accordance with the social hierarchy.

Many of the models used for this purpose were still standing in the vicinityu (e.g. the cathedral churches of Edessa, Ochrid and Serres and the churches of Kastoria), since the type was in use down to the late Byzantine period. In Verria, as we have seen, three-aisled basilicas were built during early Ottoman times. Much influence may also have been exerted by contemporary models which possessed particular prestige, such as the new Patriarchal church in Constantinople (1720), and by the tendency to return to Orthodox sources of much earlier times which can be observed at this time in various aspects of religious life.[25]

This was a suitable atmosphere for the emergence of personalities such as the Patriarch Kallinikos, who during his exile in the Monastery of St Catherine on Sinai (1757-1762) studied Justinian's basilica there. On his return, he designed a standard church based on it, with all the necessary instructions, and this was used for all the churches commissioned by him.[26]

The characteristic phenomenon of the differing architectural traditions of the mountainous and low-lying areas which we saw in the early period of Ottoman rule continued to exist in the centuries under examination.

In monastic church-building, the Athonite type was still widely applied (katholikon of the Monastery of the Holy Trinity at Vytho, 1800, Our Lady 'Bounasia', 1816)[27], but here, too, the three-aisled basilica with all its variations was introduced. Some churches were in the familiar wooden-roofed form (Our Lady 'Kleisoura', Florina, 1813), others had unusual variations on the wooden roof (such as the katholikon of the St Athanasius Monastery at Selitsa, 1797[28], where lateral apses have been added to the classic three-aisled basilica), and a third group had a vaulted roof with or without a dome (Petra Monastery, Olympus, 1754–repaired 1815– and St Paraskeve Monastery outside Samarina, 1713).

However, the prosperity and ingenuity of the age can be best seen in the large parish churches of the towns and villages. Most of these churches continued to be in the classic wooden-roofed basilica type, with two lines of columns or, more rarely, piers (e.g. the Prophet Elijah, Siatista, 1701). The taller central aisle is often roofed with a false arch, while the side aisles have lower, flat roofs. On the outside, wooden-roofed open-sided balconies along one or more sides provided even more weatherproof accommodation for the faithful (fig. 5).

In the mountain areas of Western Macedonia, the vaulted basilica type is also common: here there is usually a cylindrical vault over the central aisle and a series of flattened arches over the side aisles (e.g. St Achilles, Pentalofo, 1742, fig. 6, St Athanasius, Pentalofo, 1816). Sometimes we encounter a variation in which the vaulted basilica is combined with the cruciform church (e.g. St Paraskeve, Siatista, 1677)[29], where a rudimentary cruciform nucleus, visible only in the arrangement of the vaults and with a blind dome beneath the one-piece roof, can be seen in the centre of the church (diagrams 4a, 4b).

Inside, the women's gallery is also found in a variety of forms, with a straight eastern wall or with a Greek [30]-shaped recess in the centre, and on the same level as the floor of the main church or a few steps above in (in which case it is shut off with slatted doors, e.g., the Prophet Elijah, St Paraskeve, Siatista, St Nicholas, Eratyra, 1737, or by a wall pierced with simple or decorated apertures, e.g.,St Achilles, Pentalofo, Our Lady, Samarina, 1816). Where the building is sufficiently tall, the women's gallery becomes a separate floor, with a simple straight eastern side or with lateral projections in the shape of a Greek [31] (St Athanasius at Pentaplatanos in the Prefecture of Pieria, the Monastery of Our Lady at Kleisoura, St Athanasius at Griva, Kilkis,

*Phot.5. Aghios Achilleios, at Pentalophos,
seen from the southwest.*

Phot.6. Interior view of Ag. Achilleios, Pentalophos.

Phot.7. Aghios Athanasios, Pentalophos. Eastern aspect.

1801). The centre of the gallery is often enlivened with protrusions of a composite curved nature revealing a baroque approach.

Although the three-aisled basilica type was spreading, other types familiar from the post-Byzantine tradition of other areas were still used, especially for smaller churches. These included the domed basilica with aisles and a cupola (e.g. the Holy Trinity at Pisoderi, 18th century) or the simple square type with a dome (e.g. the Holy Trinity at Kleisoura, 1813)[32]. Simple rubble masonry was the rule in constructing the outer walls of these churches, with the exception of the apse, which was usually polygonal and over whose dressed masonry and blind shallow decortive arches great care was lavished. The lines of columns inside the church might be of masonry (this was usual in mountain areas) or consist of wooden poles in the centre faced with plastered wooden slats. The arches, whether semicircular or low and undulating in the Turkish style, are usually false arches formed out of plastered slats.

Towards the end of this period, and during that which followed it, much stone-carving was done, especially on the doors of the main entrances to the churches or on the peaks of the arches on the apse (figs. 7-8).

The interiors of these churches were particularly splendid: the walls were covered with murals, the ceilings were lozenged and covered with richly-painted panels, and the wooden screens were abundantly carved and gilded to match the bishop's thrones and icon-stands. The impressive atmosphere of prosperity and nobility in these churches–an atmosphere akin to that of the mansion-houses even in terms of the decorative features– makes one feel that here the enslaved Greeks strove to live in a world of imagined liberty and grandeur, to feel proud and superior to their conquerors, with

Phot.8. Aghios Athanasios, Pentalophos. Details of the apse.

the striking figures of their priests and bishops as their real overlords.

Mid 19th century– early 20th century

After the War of Independence of 1821 and the Treaty of Adrianople (1829) which marked the beginning of the end of Ottoman sovereignty in the southern Balkans, the strict constraints on the Christian populations seem to have slackened somewhat. The reforms of 1839 were an important stage in this process, but those of 1856, under which freedom of religion and protection for non-Muslim Ottoman subjects were promised, are of even more importance for the topic of ecclesiastical architecture which concerns us here. The restrictions on the dimensions and height of churches were lifted, it was permitted–for the first time– for churches to be built on sites not already occupied by churches (and even in Muslim villages), and bell-towers could also be erected.[33]

Yanitsa, a sacred city to the Muslims of Macedonia,

is a case in point: the Christians of the town did not obtain their first church until 1867.[34] Of course, in more isolated areas where Turkish control was looser, the Christians seem to gave plucked up their courage at a much earlier date, and some churches built in the early years of the 19th century were large in dimensions and height (e.g. the parish church of St Athanasius at Spileo, Grevena, 1804, the parish church of St Athanasius, Pentalofo, 1816).

From the point of view of typology, the three-aisled basilica continued to predominate as it had during the previous period (as a vaulted basilica with dome, e.g., St

Phot. 9. Monastery of Aghia Anastasia Pharmakolytria. View of the church from the southwest.

Phot. 10. The Theotokos Church in Naousa, seen from the southwest.

Phot.11. Aghios Dimitrios in Athytos, Chalcidice, from the northwest

Demetrius at Ayios Dimitrios, Pieria, 1874, St Antony, Verria, 1860, or St Demetrius at Athytos, Chalcidice, 1895, or as a combination of basilica and cruciform arrangement with domes, as in the new katholikon of the St Anastastia 'Pharmacolytria' Monastery, 1834).

The most characteristic feature of the churches built during this period is their high, cubic, bulky appearance; this is usually simple and unembellished, but could be broken up with porches or lower roofed galleries along one side only or continuing as a Greek [35] around as many as three. The roof is one-piece and double-pitched, truncated at the east and west pediments, and above it one (or occasionally more, as in the katholikon of St Anastasia 'Pharmacolytria', fig. 9) protrude in a rather ungainly manner.

This increase in the bulk of the main church also caused a change in the outside gallery, which came to be a weighty structure in which piers or short columns supported either a straight wooden architrave (Our Lady 'Mikri', Samarina, 1865, St Athanasius, Skotina, south gallery addition, before 1876)[36] or a full-scale colonnade (Dormition of the Virgin, Skotina, St Constantine, Filippai, Grevena).

Since the considerable height of the church allowed the women's gallery to be built as a proper second storey, there was room beneath it for an open arcade, usually only on the west facade (St Athanasius, Thessaloniki, 1818, Our Lady, Naousa, 1833, Dormition of the Virgin, Vavdos, 1811, fig. 10) or on three sides in the case of monumental churches (St Menas, Thessaloniki, 1852[37], Dormition of the Virgin, Yanitsa, 1867).

The spacious and–above all– lofty interior of the church was now lit by large windows. Those on the east and west walls, in particular, made use of highly decorative shapes: circular, oval, quatrefoil, lozenged or, most

Phot.12. Aghios Georgios, in Mesi Milia, Pieria. The bell-tower on the southern facade.

characteristic of all, foliate.

One completely new element during this period is the belfry, which takes the shape of a tower on a square or octagonal ground plan and revives the entire architectural composition by adding the contrast of a vertical element next to the serene but heavy mass of the church. The belfry was built either as a free-standing structure at some distance from the church, in which case it was a straightforward tower with a solid base and walls pierced with large apertures on the upper floors (Our Lady 'Megali', Samarina, St Paraskeve, Siatista, 1862, St George, Naousa, 1869, Dormotion of the Virgin, Vavdos, 1871), could be attached to one edge of the western facade or might be placed diagonally to one side of the main entrance, operating as a monumental porch (eg. St Paraskeve, Ano Milia, Pieria, 1854, St Demetrius, Kleisoura, 1856, where it is on the south side, fig. 12). Nor was it unknown for a light and perforated belfry to be erected on the roof above the west facade of the church (e.g. St Demetrius at Athyto, Chalcidice, 1859, fig. 11).

Fig.1. The Monastery of Aghios Georgios at Asprovalta: a) floor plan of the church, b) vertical section of the church.

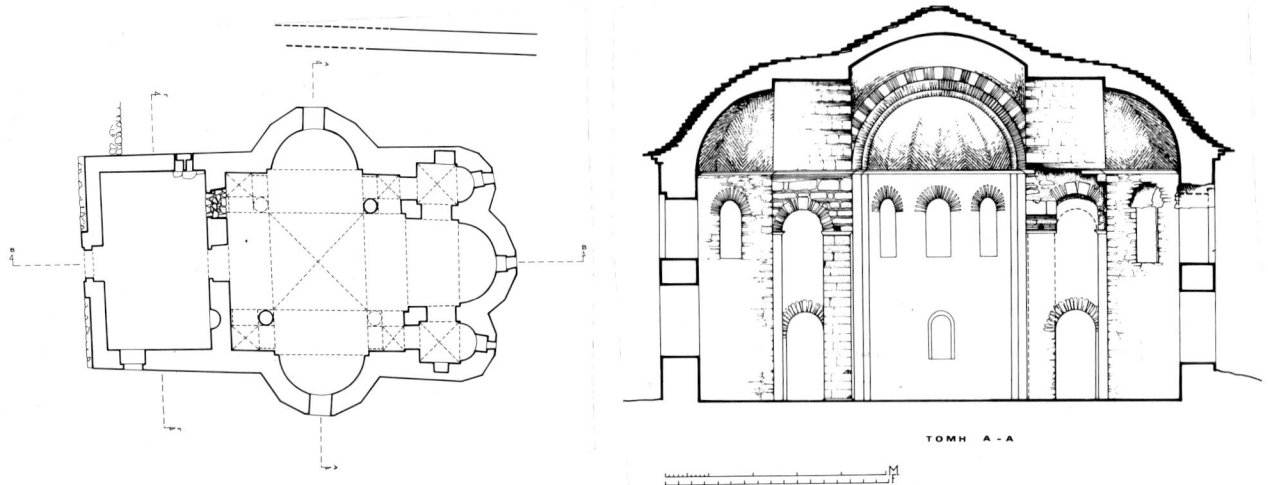

TOMH   A - A

KALLIOPI THEOCHARIDOU

MACEDONIAN ECCLESIASTICAL

ARCHITECTURE

NOTES

1. G. Velenis, "Historical sections of post-Byzantine architecture in Thessaloniki", Thessaloniki 2300 years, (published by Friends of the Folk and Ethnological Museum of Thessaloniki) Thessaloniki 1985, pp. 20-21.

2. See, respectively, A. Glavina, "Aghios Dionysius, Olympus", 26 (1981), pp. 8ff; N. Deliali, "The testament of Aghios Nikolaos of Thessaloniki", Macedonica 4 (1955-60), pp. 193-199; N. Kotzia, "Spilio, Spylio, Spelaion, Pylaion, and its Monastery", Archaeological Society 1950-51, pp. 14-30.

3. "History of the Greek Nation", vol. 10, pp. 140-141.

4. See note 2, above.

5. ' "Service" of our Blessed and "Theophoros" father Theophanes the Younger, of Ioannina, anchorite and miracle-worker, who lived as a hermit in the mountains of the proud city of Naousa', Venice 1976, p. 33.

6. K. Theocharidou, A. Tourta, "The Monastery of Aghios Georgios outside Asprovalta", Churches in Greece after the fall of Constantinople, vol. 3, Athens 1982, pp. 45-64.

7. M. Polyviou, "The Monastery of Aghios Georgios at Eptachori (Bourboutsiko), Voio-Grammou", Churches in Greece after the fall of Constantinople, vol. 2, Athens 1982, pp. 35-45.

8. T. Papazotos, "Mediaeval frescoes in the Prefecture of Pieria", Historicogeographica 1 (1986), p. 32.

9. N. Moutsopoulos, "Churches in the Prefecture of Florina", Thessaloniki 1964, pp. 14-15, fig. 11.

10. T. Papazotos, "The frescoes in the church of the Panaghia Monastery at Aliakmon", Macedonica 21 (1981), pp. 93-107.

11. S. Pelekanidis, "Mediaeval Macedonia", Arch. Bulletin 16 (195),p. 228, and S. Voyiatzis, "The Monastery of the Dormition in Torniki, Grevena" Bulletin of the Christian Archaeological Society 15 (1989-90), pp. 241-256.

12. C. Chionidis, "History of Veria", vol. 2, Thessaloniki 1970, p. 191.

13. *Ibid.*, pp. 180-181.

14. A. Orlandos, "The Byzantine monuments of Kastoria", ABME 4 (1938), and E. Tsigaridas, "Research into the churches of Kastoria", Macedonica 25 (1985-96), pp. 379-389.

15. I. Papaggelos, "The church of the Presentation of the Virgin in Kalandra, Chalcidice", Churches in Greece after the fall of Constantinople, vol. 1, Athens 1979, pp. 47-53.

16. Moutsopoulos, *op. cit.*, plate 33 (55-56), fig. 58.

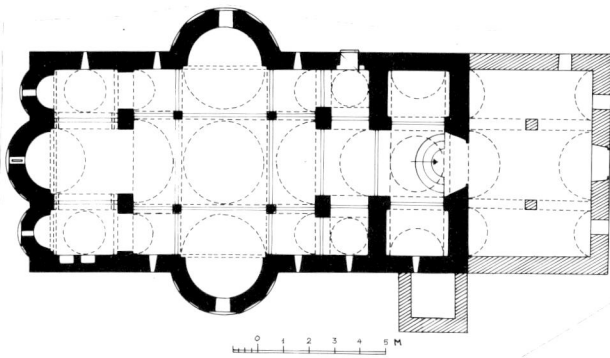

Fig.2. Church of the Theotokou Monastery at Spilaion, Grevena: a) ground plan (by N. Kotzia), b) vertical section.

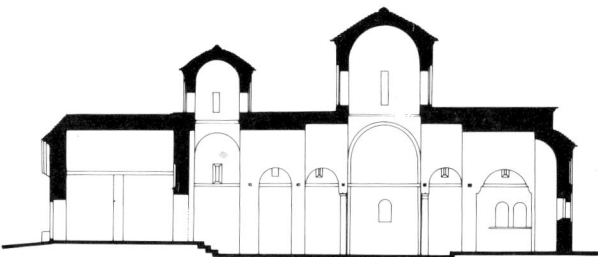

**Fig.3.
Theotokos Church at Trigoniko, in the district of Kozani: ground plan and facade.**

17. Orlandos, *op. cit.*, pp. 165-166 and 167.
18. S. Pelekanidis, "Researches in Upper Macedonia", Macedonica 5 (1961-63), pp. 396-414.
19. Chionidis, *op. cit.*, and 18 (1963), p. 250 and Arch. Bulletin, Chronicles 26 (1971), pp. 444-445.
20. See, respectively, Arch. Bulletin, chronicles, 29 (1974), pp. 729-758, and T. Papazotos "Supplement on Veria", *op. cit.*. p. 493.
21. Arch. Bulletin, chronicles 33 (1978), B2, pp. 270-271, diagram 1.
22. M. Kalinderis, "The guilds in Kozani during the Turkish occupation", Thessaloniki 1958, p. 7.
23. K. Theocharidou, "The Prophet Elijah, in Siatista", Churches in Greece after the fall of Constantinople, vol. 1, Athens 1979, p. 63.
24. "Macedonia. 4000 years of Greek history and culture", Ekdotike Athinon, Athens 1982, pp. 426-429.
25. "History of the Greek Nation", vol. 11, pp. 266-269.
26. C. Bouras, "The architectural type of the basilica during the Turkish occupation, and Patriarch Kallinikos", Churches in Greece after the fall of Constantinople, vol. 1, Athens 1979, pp. 159-168.
27. See, respectively, R. Stylianou, "The church of Aghia Triada, Zoupani", Churches in Greece after the fall of Constantinople vol. 1., pp. 67-82, and V. Nikita-Skartadou, "The Bounasia Monastery and its stonework reliefs", Macedonica 17 (1977), pp. 212-233.
28. A. Stefanidou-Fotiadou, "The church of the Aghios Athanasios Monastery, Eratyra (Selitsa)", Churches in Greece after the fall of Constantinople , vol. 2 (1982), pp. 21-34.
29. A. Portselanos, "Aghia Paraskevi, Siatista", Reconstruction, Preservation, Protection of Monuments and Complexes, Athens 1984, pp. 77-100.
30. Moutsopoulos, *op. cit.*, plates 53-55, fig. 97 on the Holy Trinity at Pisoderi, and plate 135, diagram 236 on the Holy Trinity at Kleisoura.
31. D. Nikolaidis, "Ottoman Codices", Constantinople 1869, p. 33.
32. V. Dimitriadis, "A decree for the erection of the first church in Genitsa", Macedonica 9 (1969), pp. 324-335.
33. C. Siaxabani-Stefanou, "Aghios Athanasios, in Skotina, Pieria", Archaeologists on Pieria Thessaloniki 1986, pp. 65-71.
34. M. Kambouri, "The church of Aghios Minas, in Thessaloniki. A new type of ecclesiastical architecture", Churches in Greece after the fall of Thessaloniki, vol. 3, pp. 13-32.

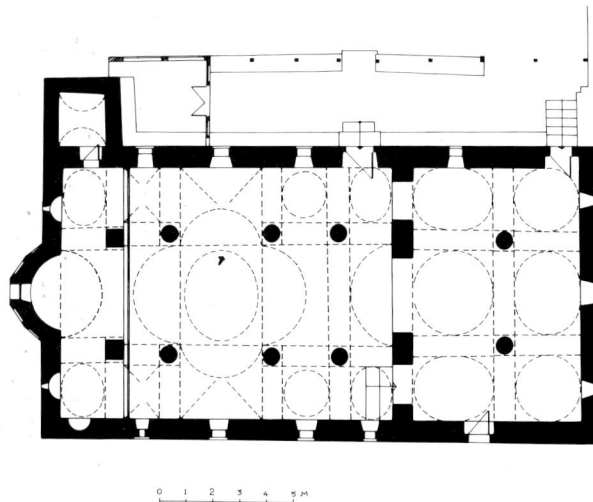

Fig.4. Aghia Paraskevi, Siatista: a) floor plan (by A. Portelanos), b) vertical section (A. Portelanos).

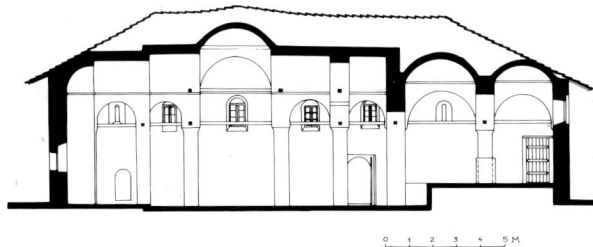

The houses of the Macedonian communities: 15th - 19th century

N.C. Moutsopoulos

Theoretically, the popular residence of a place must be studied as the continuation of the ancient residence as it developed in the same geographical and cultural area. However, the indisputable relationships of the independent agrarian unit or the «line of the row houses» in urban areas are very difficult to be ascertained; but they must be studied very carefully and must be faced critically.

Paralleling the various forms and types of the Byzantine residence that developed in the Macedonian countryside, about which our information is scanty, there had always been and had survived, much more conservative forms and types of residence which had preserved various vestiges of older models. This type continued to exist during the years after the turkish conquest.

Initially, these were residences (konacs) of the «two-home» nomad-stockbreeders (Saracatsans and Vlachs).

Near the strunga (pen) we see two types of dwelling; circular and orthogonal. Between them, there is a number of transitional types leading from the circle to the square and rectangular plan of the dwelling. A researcher can perceive, in this rich typology of primitive dwelling, all the desperate effort man has made, since the dawn of the time, to create a home for him, his family and his livestock[1].

The dwelling of the paraboloid of revolution form («the hut with a cowl») is remarkable both for its perfection and longevity -although it is constructed of cheap material- and, also for its survival. It is a type that orginates in the far past, in as much as we believe that the ancient tombs (the Mycenean treasures) imitated some model of a «holy residence»[2].

Furthermore, the existence of such a type of paraboloid of revolution on the mountain that towers above the Diacofto canyon, in Aegialea, in a location between the ancient towns of Voura and Eliki, constitutes a strong link in the chain of evolution of the circular buildings[3].

The rectangular type of hut, with a two-pitched roof - and, very rarely, with a four-pitched roof - when

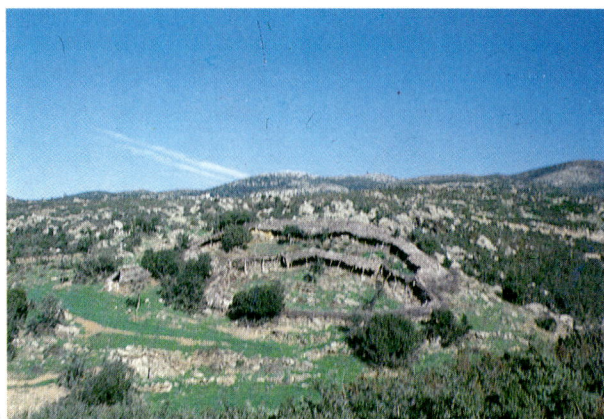

Konak «Fold» of Sarakatsans on Mt. Chortiatis, near Thessaloniki, in the region of Peristera.

Pericentral konaks of Vlach shepherds in Pano Machalas of Vitsa, Epirus.

Circular Sarakatsan huts with a «cowl».

Circular (pericentral) Sarakatsan huts of a konak.

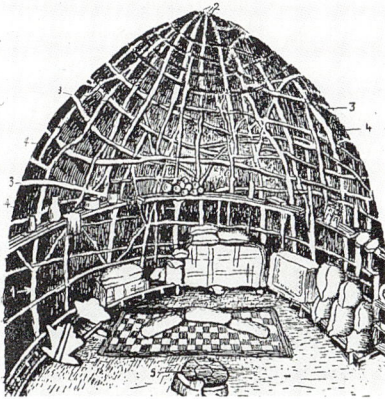

Schematic section of a pericentral Sarakatsan hut.

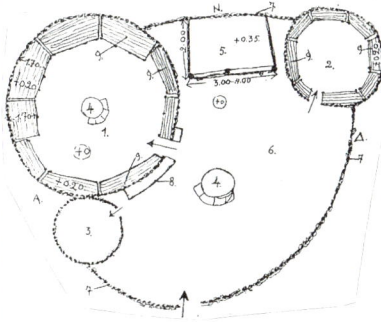

Sarakatsan settlement with a central circular hut and corresponding smaller circular ones.

Pericentral Sarakatsan hut in the stage of construction (Museum of Sarakatsan folklore of Serres).

Orthogonal Sarakatsan hut.

Orthogonal Sarakatsan hut with «ovoros».

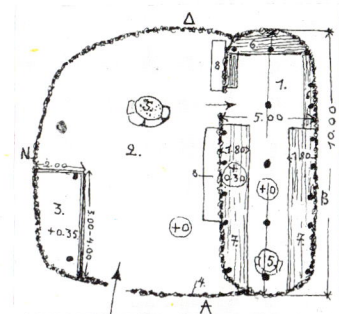

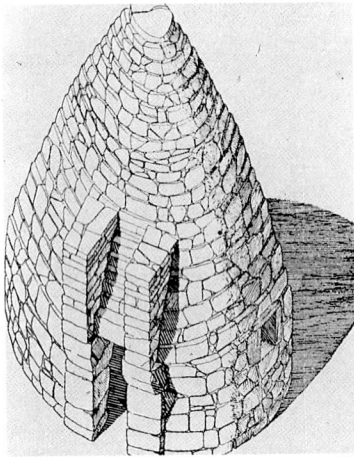

The dome of Gaios on Mt. Aghia Triada in Aigialeia (according to N. Moutsopoulos).

Transverse section of a Mycenean tomb according to Dôrpfeld.

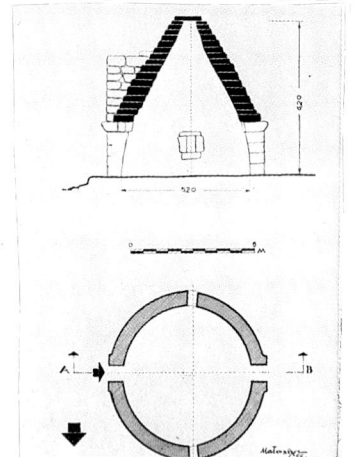

The dome of Gaios on Mt. Aghia Triada (N. Moutsopoulos).

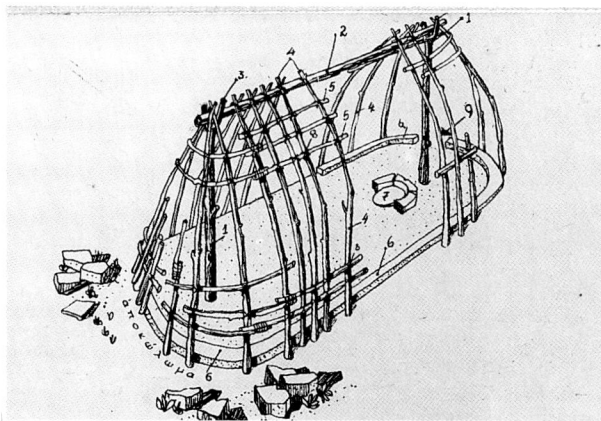

Sketch of the construction of a rectangular sarakatsan hut with curved narrow sides.

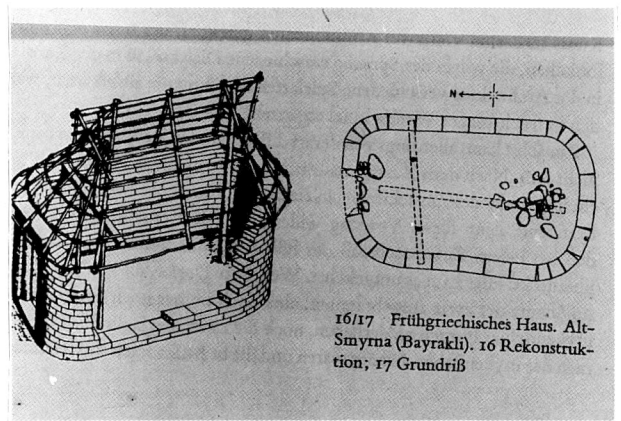

16/17 Frühgriechisches Haus. Alt-Smyrna (Bayrakli). 16 Rekonstruktion; 17 Grundriß

On the right, plan, and on the left perspective of a dwelling of the early Greek period in Old Smyrna (Bayrakli).

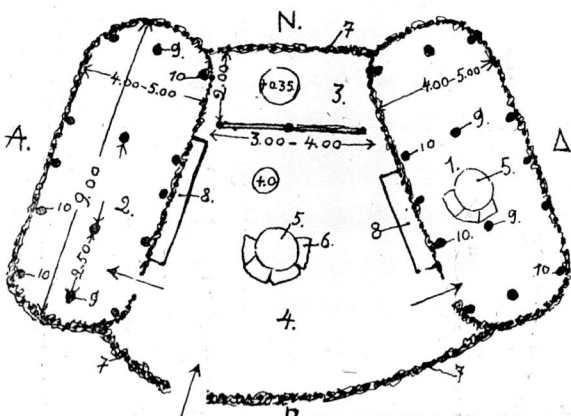

Sarakatsan settlement with two opposite rectangular huts and interior «oboros».

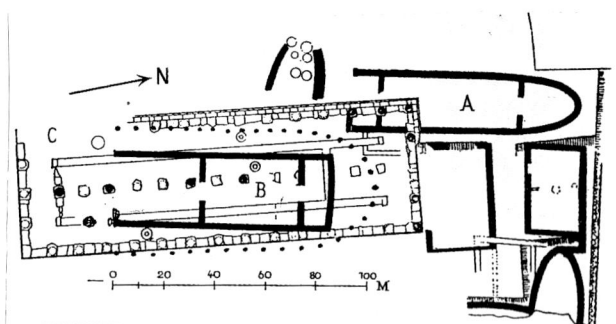

The temple of Apollo at Thermos (Building A).

it does not belong to the «wide-front» type, in other words, when it does not have the entrance on the wider side, then, with a multitude of variations (with a semicylindrical narrow side covered with a half cone, or arched and a portico on the side of the entrance) shows us the line of evolution of buildings of an

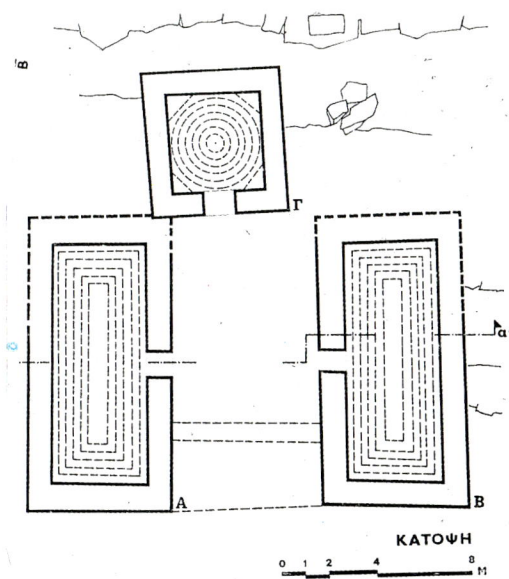

Plan of the «Draconhouse» of Palli-Laka (Drago) in the region of Styra (N. Moutsopoulos).

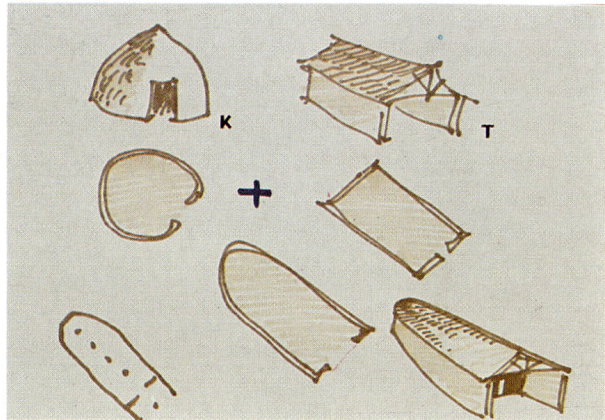

Sketched of the theoretical transition from the circular (pericentral) form to the rectangular.

The Psarades settlements on the shore of the lake Megali Prespa (photographed in 1959).

Aerial photograph of Castoria (1991).

ellipsoidal plan, from the time of Troy and ancient Smyrna to the earliest phases of the great temple of Apollo, at Thermo.

*

This type of construction survived in the Macedonian area too, from the far past to our time, that is, as long as nomadic life survived.

Also, the form of the initial cell of stone architecture, which, since the ancient times was continued through the Byzantine era and survived during the turkish rule, orginated in this antique type of abode.

Exactly, this single-room type of dwelling, which, in earlier times, was erected crosswise on the contour lines, constituted almost the exclusive type of dwelling in the Macedonian agrarian, and stock-breeding areas, and, also, in mixed settlements and has preserved the appelation, depending on the case, cottage, farmhouse, and when it had a basement or, later, one more floor, family house.

In certain cases, a clearly-defined area around it, was fenced and formed the court-yard or «ovoros» (probably from the slavic dvor).

Inside the yard, a lean-to was used as a kitchen, with the oven next to it and in another part of the yard the barn and the stable were erected.

The dwellings of the serfs and sharecroppers, which worked in the fiefs of the turkish aghas and beys (*patospita, spitotopoi*) belong to the same type[4].

View of Veria (photo: in 1958).

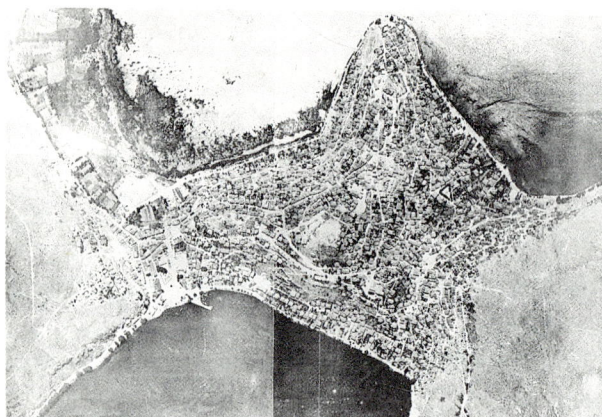

Pre-war aerial photohraph of Castoria.

These were one-storey, (*strota* or *hamila*), duplex houses[5], rarely two storey-buildings («high houses»), with their secondary annexes (storeroom, ovens). Sometimes there was a threshing floor inside the court-yard.

Certain pieces of information recorded by old-timers, are valuable because they help us to understand the construction and function of this primary cell of dwelling during the period of the turkish rule.

In our research, the information given by the priest of Calloni, Euthymios Gregoriou, which was published in the newspaper of Kozani, «North Greece» (March 13, 1932, p. 2) is valuable:

«Their first abodes (that is, the abodes of the nearest ancestors) were wooden huts roofed with thatch, canes, or slate, or small, stone houses, without embellishements, so that they could leave them behind whenever they wanted to relocate. Later, when the settlements began to be permanent, they built their houses according to a better design, adding one more floor... They got logs for their houses from near-by places. I have seen such big logs that I used to wonder how they carried them from the forest. And the old men said that they did not have to carry them because the place where the village now stood had been a forest full of wild animals, bears and others. The flooring consisted of rough, split logs on a layer of mud; one might see an occasional sideboard made of rough planks smoothed with an adze, and, very rarely, cut with a saw. The windows were very small, with shutters made of planks, without panes, open all day long. Only when it snowed did they hang a heavy blanket across them[6].

In the continuation of his account, the priest of Calloni attributes the improvement of these primitive huts «to the emigration, which showed them that there were better living conditions elsewhere». Antonios Keramopoulos, commenting on this says: «There was, also, the influence of the bigger towns or cities of the West Macedonia from where traders went to central Europe and brought back the modern civilization, and founded schools before south Greece had awakened»[7].

We are familiar with the problem of the demographic rearrangement during the period of the turkish invasion, and the coming of the turkish tribes of the *ghazis* and, later, the *yuruks* to the regions that concern us, during the reign of Sultan Murat.

The Turks settled in thinly-populated areas, in the rich farms of the Byzantine nobility, which, after 1430, at least in the vilayet of Thessaloniki, were divided into several *ziamets*, yuruk villages, various *timars* and the big fief of Ghazi Evrenos-Bey.

The turkish *spahis* were also given pieces of land. The Turks defined the property of the monasteries as «vakuf» and they protected it.

The inhabitants of these regions who were forced to stay, became serfs of the ottoman landholders, Turks first, and, later, some Albanians, and many of them were islamized, like the «Valaads» of the villages of Voion and the province of Anasselitsa.

The inhabitants of places where the settlements of the turkish nomadic populations, especially Yuruks and Koniars, were dense, as, for instance, in the plains from Kozani to the Lake of Ostrovo, fled to the mountains[8]. This compulsory exodus must have been either a mass relocation, or a gradual movement of small groups, or tribes.

In the new places, usually in pre-established mountain settlements, the newcomers picked or were shown, locations at some distance from the initial nucleus. If the newcomers came from the same

Old photograph of Castoria (1920?).

Old photograph of Castoria (1920?).

original nucleus - which was rare - they were easily assimilated. If they came from other places and they arrived much later than the first settlers - whose memories were filled with the pain and labor and toil and losses of lives which they suffered in hewing a home out of the wilderness – then settled in separate places giving different names to their settlements.

The different place of origin of the new groups or even individuals, is remembered and recognized by the designation of the newcomers (strangers) either by the general term «stranger» or by the derivative of their place of origin: «Maniatis - Maniatica», «Moraitis - Moraitica», «Cretan - Cretica», «Rumeliot - Rumeliotica», «Cravarites - Cravaritica», «Chasiotis - Chasiotica», «Thracian - Thraciotica»; also by their racial designations: «Vlach - Vlachica», «Pharserot - Pharserotica»[9], «Copatsaros - Copatsarica», «Gypsy - Gyptica»; and by their trade or occupation: sayakas (a maker of a special woolen garment called «sayaki» - sayak, in turkish), terzis (the turkish word for tailor), taliadouros (the carver), boyadzis (the turkish word for painter), hadzis (from the turkish word «haci», the pilgrim), etc.

And from their trades or professions, the names of the villages: Hionades (from the collection and selling of quantities of snow), Chalkiades (coppersmiths), Chouliarades (culturely makers), Carbounades (coal sellers), Melissourgi (apiarists), etc.

At first the settlements had no name. The name which appeared later was given either by the inhabitants themselves or by their neighbors. When the name was picked by the settlers themselves, it often explained the cause of the formation of the settlement, e.g. «Cataphygion» (Refuge)· Or, they gave the village the name of the patron saint of their guild or the patron saint of their old home town. Theyqsometimes,

gave it the name of the family of the founder or the name of their old home town. Sometimes the name of the village derived from the main occupation of the inhabitants Psarades (Fishermen), Asvestochori (Limestone village) or from their production Capnochori (Tobacco village), Vamvakia (Cotton Village) or from a certain important landmark of the district «Melia (Apple tree), Achladia (Pear tree), Itia (Willow), Mylos (Mill) or from the morphology of the area Livadi (Fields), Limna (Lake), Cherso (Barren).

The largest part of the population, after the invasion, fled to the wooded bulks of Mt. Pindos and all its branches, which cover most of West Greece, or to Mt. Gramos, Mt. Vermio, Mt. Pieria, Mt. Olympus and Mt. Chasia. The untrodden mountains gave protection to the christian population. Many villages still have the name «Cataphygi» (Refuge), like the well-known village on Pieria[10]. According to the stories, its inhabitants once lived in the rich village of Podari, on the bank of the river Aliacmon, but due to the turkish oppression, they left their village - it is not known when - and took refuge on the plateau, above the steep slopes of Flaburo, where they had their folds. «They built their village with logs which they cut from the forest on the plateau; their village was literally covered with snow in the winter, but it was beyond any turkish authority and the most independent village of the district»[11]. Scattered pices of information bring to light the sites of some villages that were deserted by their inhabitants during the first decades of the first turkish rule. However, these ruins probably were the second homes-refuges of inhabitants of other regions, and, in turn, they were deserted after more recent raids.

Eustathios Stougiannakis has preserved the following information: «The deserted villages on the

Siatista: Poulkos' mansion.

Siatista: Nerantzopoulos' mansion.

slopes of Mavri Petra are: Stari, Poti, Touvaritsi, Alkeri, Bella Voda (Asproneri), Fetitsa and Fourca. Those on the slopes of Dourlia are: Koutsoufliani, Drasilovo, Perisiori, Upper Giannaco, Golema Reca, Dedovo, Ramnista, and Gymnovo. The destroyed villages on Seli are: Palioseli, or Main Seli, Marousia, Scotina, Volada and Dichalochori»[12].

According to information and to the scanty available data, (church inscriptions, place-names and ruins) many villages of West Macedonia and N.E. Epirus were formed in this way, as, for instance these mountain towns of Pindos: Samarina, Perivoli, Avdella, Sinatsico (Askio), Siatista, Eratyra (Selitsa) Vlasti (Blatsi), Galatini (Kontsico), Cleisura, Pentalophos, Vogatsico, Costarazi and others[13].

«The poor soil», Apostolos Vacalopoulos writes, «forced them to live with frugality bordering on undernourishement, so they turned to stock breeding which became their main and important source of income, giving them both food and clothes[14]. Under these particularly tough living conditions, the moun-

The mansion of Emmanuel brothers in Castoria, covered with snow (1962).

The «sahnisi» of Poulkides' mansion, in Siatista, surrounded with a high wall.

View of the exterior of Nerantzopoulos' mansion in Siatista.

Kyra Sanoucos' mansion in Siatista (photo: 1960).

tain populations developed their full power of survival; the continuous fight against nature needed alertness; the clearing of forests needed vigilance, for if you stop, the forest comes back to claim the lost ground. And as John Philemon says, «if the Greek was forced to live on the toughest mountains and the rockiest of islands, he benefited from this experience; his loss was not irreparable. Now stronger and wiser, he made progress only by honest means»[15].

On Mt. Pindos, we find a numerous Vlach-speaking population. Vacalopoulos writes that the density of their population in a small area made them scatter to other places, even in the region of Olympus. Thus, the Vlachs of the villages of Neochori, Fteri, Melia, Vlacholivado and Kokkinoplos preserved the tradition that they came from the mountains (probably Mt. Pindos) several hundred years before founding the village of Livadi[16]. This is supported by the similarities of names, dialects, accent and customs, between the Vlachs of Olympus and Pindos (Samarina and others)[17].

So, most of the mountain villages of Macedonia were formed by the union of various scattered but contiguous settlements («catounes») of Vlach herdsmen mainly, and those villages of mixed population consisting of Vlachs, latin-speaking mountaineers, bilinguals and other Greeks, flourished and prospered during the next centuries[18].

The village of Ambelakia, in Thessaly, was also founded during the beginnings of the 16th century, as it was evidenced by a liturgy book dating back to 1580, which Nicolaos Gameos bought and donated to the church of St. Paraskevi[19].

A statistical table compiled by Heleni Antoniadou - Bibicou gives the number of the villages which were destroyed or deserted after the Turkish conquest (15th c. - 19th c.)[20].

Twin menhirs at Pelecan (Pelca) of Western Macedonia
(photo: 1989).

15th c. 1st half :	65
2nd half :	58
16th c. 1st half :	16
2nd half :	25
17th c. 1st half :	27
2nd half :	103
18th c. 1st half :	30
2nd half :	50
19th c. 1st half :	662
Total :	1036 villages.

It is particularly interesting that the legend reffer-ring to the «inauguration» of the village and, at the same time, its protection against all evils (death, the plague, etc.)survived in Macedonia. The legend dates back to the far antiquity and its origin is, probably,

pre-Hellenic; it means that two first-born twins must mark the boundaries all around the village («belting» the village), driving two twin calves. In Pelca (the Pelecanos of today) the inhabitants show visitors two erect stone slabs (menhirs) marking the grave of the slain calves[21].

There is a legend about the founding of Naussa by general Ghazi Evrenos. Old inhabitants of Naussa say that the general asked the Sultan to grant him that region and the Sultan answered that he could build his city on an area «not larger than the area covered by one stretched ox-hide. The clever general, a descen-dant of the islamized byzantine Vranas family, cut the hide into thin, fine filaments, tied them end-to-end, formed a very long thread and managed to enclose a large area within the perimeter[22].

Another way to define the boundaries of a village so as to give «protection» is the planting of four trees at some distance from the village, approximately defining the four points of the horizon. The priest of the village planted the trees and placed also a piece of the «prosphora» inside them. These trees were taboo and noone could touch them[23].

The same category of protection against evil in-cludes the preventive religious processions. In Dar-nacochori - Neo Souli of Serres (Subaskioi) a great procession takes place on St. George's day. The procession starts at the chapel of the cemetery. First come the sacred vessels and crosses made of flowers inscribed in circles, at the top of high poles[24]. The young men carrying these crosses certainly do not know the meaning of the heliacal symbols incised on the rocks of the slopes of Mt Paggaion, probably the work of the ancient Sintoi[25].

A protective measure (protection against epidemics or long drought) corresponding to the aforementioned customs, is the Cypriote custom of enclosing the village with a rope[26]

The destiny of the European territories of the Byzantine Empire was decided after the fall of Cal-lipoli. In 1359, Turkish armies appeared in front of the walls of Constantinople. After they established the «Rumeli hisar», the Turks reinforced their positions in Thrace. During the reign of Murat I (1362-1389) the Turkish spread in the Balkan peninsula[27].

Murat's general, Lala Sahin entered Philip-poupolis in 1363 and acquired the title of the «Beylerbey of Rumeli». The sultan transferred his seat to Didymoteicho (Demotica) and, after 1365, to Andrianoupolis. In less than twenty years the Turks captured Serres (1383), Sofia (1385) and Thessaloniki (1383/1387). After the notorious defeat of the Serbian forces at Kossyfopedio (Kossovo) (June 15, 1389) the destiny of the Balkans was decided irrevocably. Now, Bayazit I was on the throne.

The Byzantines tried to salvage whatever could be salvaged. The times were difficult and the western peoples faced the situation with malicious indifference. The long centuries of enslavement for the Balkan peoples began.

The Turks were already familiar with the coastal Balkans. The Byzantine themselves had invited them as allies in the endless conflicts between legal and illegal heirs to the Byzantine throne. They had realized that the natural inner power of resistance of the people had weakened by the long conflict and civil wars and the defenses of the fortified cities were in a deplorable condition.

The Byzantine historiography, deriving its facts from contemporary sources, paints a black picture of the first years of the turkish conquest and how the conquerors dealt with those who offered the slightest resistance to them[28].

The Turkish invasion could not have been accidental, or impulsive or, simply, expansionistic. The Turkish professor O.L. Barkan, who has studied the subject, maintains that the Turkish conquests in the Balkans were based on a well-organized plan. Internal socioeconomical concurrences obliged the ottoman administration, to find land for the Turkomanic tribes elsewhere; and after organizing these tribes in military units, to undertake an expedition against the Balkans where, as they knew quite well, the fertile plains were thinly populated due to the long civil wars and the Bulgarian raids[29].

The aim of the invasion was not a sort of colonial control of the territories but a place to relocate the surplus of population of the regions of central Asia Minor.

According to a well-studied plan, agrarian populations were transported to arable plains, and stockbreeding nomads were transported to regions suitable for them. Of course, the Turks aimed, at the same time, to displace the christians, break up the solid, christian

Miniature of Constantinople (1422) from Cristof Buondelmonde's book «Liber Insularum».

communities and so, to change the demographic picture of the territories.

A more effective means to accomplish this was the system of relocating whole groups of homogeneous populations to regions with inadequate work force. Those groups sometimes included christians from conquered territories. Therefore, we can explain the appearance of groups of Slavs in regions of East and West Macedonia whose inhabitants had deserted their land during the invasion. O.L. Barkan himself claims that it was natural for a State, with its own ideas of right, to force its subjects to relocate when it was necessary[30].

Specifically, sources dating from 1385 report that during the years of Murat I and Bayazit, nomadic populations were brought to Magnesia, to the plains of Serres and to the Axios valley from Saruhan. For some of these groups, that relocation was some sort of exile because they had broken the law of the monopoly of the salt imposed by the Sultan Yildirim Bayazit. The Sultan himself ordered his son Ertugrul to supervise the relocation of the nomads of Saruhan

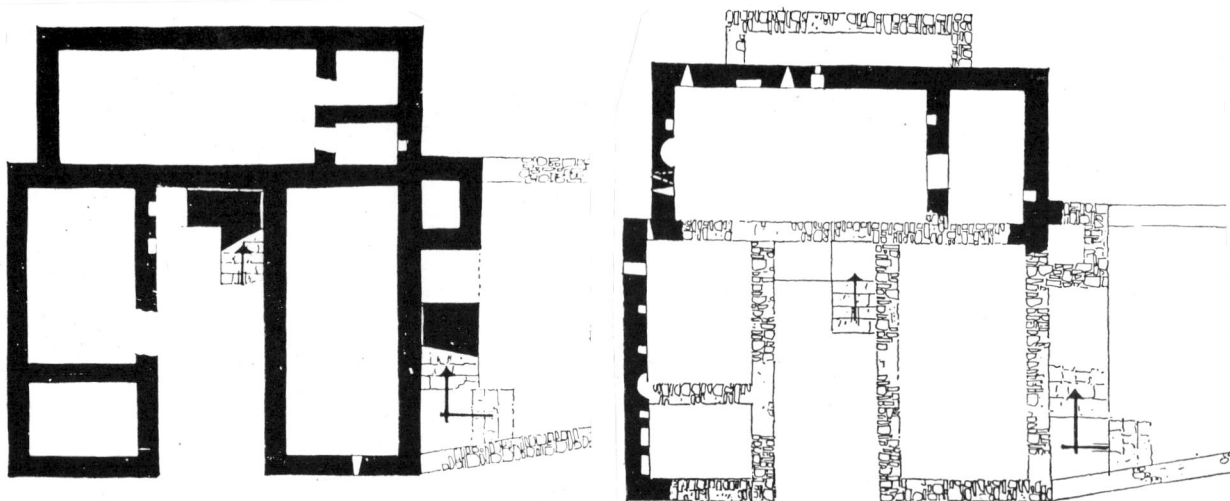

Plans of houses of Gardiki, Northern Epirus (Emin Riza, Monumentet, 17, 1979, plate III).

from Menemeni, where they had their winter pens to the plains of Philippoupolis (Filibe)[31]. It was at that time that the first nomadic Yuruks, militarily organized, came and settled in regions of Macedonia[32].

To solidify its conquered territories, the ottoman administration, apart from the compulsory and expedient relocations, imposed a control over the relocation of individuals from the country to the cities[33].

To pave the way for the conquest of the entire country, the Turks had a system of precursory, peaceful invasion by disciplined and fanatical members of the order of the dervishes. The dervishes, the vanguard of the turkish armies, came to the Balkans and established monasteries (the «tekkes») near the feet of the mountains, grew families and founded villages round the monasteries[34].

To understand the formation, organization and the type of abode of the earliest settlements which were founded immediately after the turkish conquest, we must go back to the mountain settlements on the almost inaccessible mountains of Macedonia and Epirus. Because many of these settlements flourished during the 17th century and their original nucleous changed, we have to look for authentic forms in older samples which were, later, deserted by their inhabitants. Such vestiges of old settlements have been preserved in the northern and northwestern extensions of Macedonia, in places in N. Epirus.

Near the Dervitsani of today (Dervican), in the district of Argyrocastro (Djirokaster) there was a ruined settlement named Coucoula and was within the region of Dropolis (Dropul)[35]. It was built on the plain and its ruins still exist.

In old Turkish records of the census of 1431-32[36], Dervitsani is mentioned as a settlement with 70 houses. The census of 1582-1583 mentions that it numbered 194 houses.

During that period probably, the inhabitants of the settlement relocated to regions of arable land. One can still see in the ruins of the settlement vestiges of very small, one-room houses built of field-stone[37].

The ruins of Kamenitsa, the old Saranda (Sarande), date back to the 14th or 15th century. The records of 1431 show that the village numbered 208 houses with a higher revenue than that of Argyrocastro. The data of the census of 1582-1583 show that Kamenitsa numbered 222 houses, 550 including the suburbs. The village was deserted at the turn of the 17th century. The condition of the ruins proves that it was a mass exodus of the population. The village had many churches. The houses are of the one-room, rectangular type with a mezzanine. The construction of these houses has many similarities to the castle-houses of Mani[38]. The tall buildings have a cistern in the ground floor.

The typology of the buildings has many similarities to the typology of the residences in Mystra and Mouchli, in Arcadia[39].The ruins of 7 churches, of which two probably date from the 13th-14th and the 14th-15th c.[40], have been preserved.

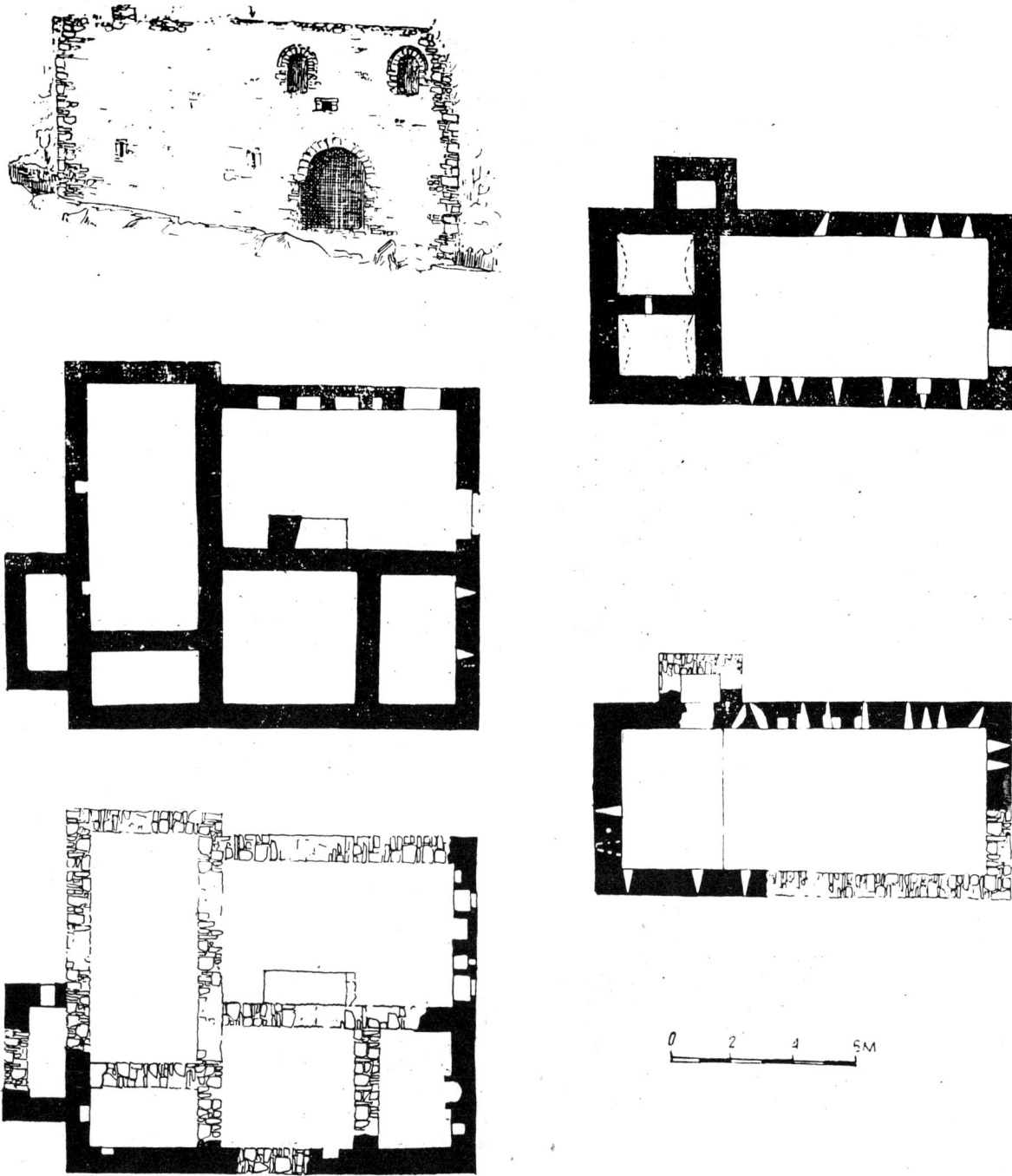

Plans of houses of Gardiki, Northerm Epirus (Emin Riza, Monumentet, 17, 1979, plate IV).

The construction is of stone exclusively and parts of the walls are built with mortar of an excellent quality and show good workmanship. Some vestiges of wooden ties («hatil»,«belts») are preserved and also, over some openings, gutters such as those used by the Byzantines. The openings are small and the wooden roof was covered with slate.

Another important old village in the region north-west of Argyrocastro is Gardiki (Kardhiq). The castle of Gardiki was either built or repaired in the 13th or

14th century[41]. According to a record of 1431-32, it numbered 30 houses. The well-known Turkish traveller Evlia Celebi says that in the middle of the 17th century the village numbered 150 houses. It was a prosperous village in the 18th century. In 1811, Ali Pasha, wishing to expand the pashalic of Ioannina and settle his old accounts with some beys, captured Gardiki and slaughtered most of its inhabitants[42]. Many typological and morphological features of the village buildings are similar to those of the urban residences of Mystras[43].

Of the original settlement, no buildings have been preserved. By studying the ruins which belong to constructions dating from the 17th century, one can conclude that, typologically, the abode of that period belonged to the Γ or Π type. Most of the houses were two or three-storey buildings. The house of the type had the staircase inside the legs of the[44]. Each house was independent with its own defensive system, which was, perhaps, due to the custom of vendetta.

The fate of the ancient town of Nicolitsa (the Nicopolis of Epirus) was similar to the fate of its neighboring settlements. The Vlach inhabitants were displaced by the Albanians who envied their prosperity. Nicolitsa was an important village and had a very good school which had become famous. Some of the inhabitants fled to Monastiri (Bitolia) and others to Kroussovo[45].

East of Premeti (Permet) on the eastern coast of Voosa one can see the ruins of two old settlements, Darda (Dardhes) and Stoyan (Stojan). The census of Korytsa (Korce) and Premeti of 1431-32 shows that Dardica (Darditsa) had 6 houses and Stoyan was a deserted village; but other sources report that it was an inhabited settlement. The census of 1520 records that Darda numbered 15 houses and Stoyan 17. Later, around 1582-1583, the number of houses of Darda increased to 23 whereas the houses of Stoyan decreased to 4. It seems that after these villages were abandonned, they were built again later[46].

The engineer Emin Riza, head of the Restoration Service of Tirana studied the typology and the technique of construction twice and came to the conclusion that the buildings are older.

However, it seems that the end of the 16th century was also the end of Stoyan although some constructional details of the ruins seem contemporary with those of Darda[47].

The foundations of the houses of Darda lie across the contour lines of the ground, like the Byzantine houses of Mystra, Mouchli[48], Carytaina[49] and Geraki[50].

The two-pitched roofs were, then, covered with slate. The area of the ground floor was small[51] but, many times, it was a split-level construction. Several small alcoves (small built-in sideboards) can still be seen in the walls of the ruins.

East of Premeti on the right shore of Sopoto, there are the ruins of a settlement which the Albanian researchers Emin Riza and Pirro Thomo believe to be the ruins of the old Byzantine Cochni (Kokni); the census of 1431-1432 records that Cochni then numbered 14 houses. The houses of the settlement are built of rubble, and only one (of those whose condition permits study) is built of mortar. The houses had the familiar mezzanine. In the walls of the raised part of the ground floor there are alcoves[52].

The writers are not sure about the reasons for the desertion of such settlements as Camenitsa. Borsh (St. Saranta), Lekdush (Tepeleni), Darda, Stoyan and Gardiki and attribute it to various reasons. These settlements are mentioned in the ottoman censuses of 1431-1432, which shows that they had been founded before then and continued to exist through the period of the turkish rule[53].

In these settlements, it is very difficult for one to discern any kind of «center» (commercial, social, etc.) Frequently, at some central point one can discern vestiges of a «genetic» nucleus near some point of reference such as a tree of immense height. The church is usually built outside the village, perhaps because the cemetery is near it[54]. The rocky ground usually makes access to the scatered houses difficult, and the houses are built across the contour lines of the ground. The excellent construction of the houses leads us to the conclusion that, even then, house construction was in the hands of experienced masons.

Moschopolis was one of the most important centers of N.Epirus. Ioakim Martinianos, who has studied the problem of the demographic rearrangements after the ottoman conquest of N. Epirus, has preserved valuable information. He writes that from the middle of the 14th century to the beginnings of the 17th, Moschopolis was a group of huts[55]. We also have the information that, in 1600, Moschopolis was a small town[56].

Many people believe that this Greco-Vlachic capital of N. Epirus derived its name from the word «Voscos» (shepherd) so that from Voscopolis became Moschopolis.

However, Ioakim Martinianos protests about this etymological (mis)interpretation; he writes: «This is the most ridiculous misconception that has ever been expressed. Who knows what ignorant daydreamer created this myth, since it is a proven fact that the nomad shepherds never found a city nor do they know the meaning of the word; and the near-by, or even the remote populations, all around, do not speak Greek but albanian, vlachic and, occasionally, slavic so they would not have been able to give the settlement a name derived from a language which thay do not know». And he adds that the name of the town probably came from the name of the original settlement which had the albanian name *Votscop*, therefore the Albanians correctly pronounce the name Votscopolia[57]. Furthermore, the second component of the compound word Votscopolia, whether «pole» or «polie», is of slavic origin, the first meaning «plateau» and the second «valley»[58].

Socrates Liacos also contradicts the prevailing interpretation of the word - that is, that Moschopolis or Voscopolis was founded by shepherds - exlaining that the root of the word in Vlachic means «wooded valley», and he believes that the town was founded by Vlachs «who were the most progressive people of Romania and, following their bishop, they left their ancient city, the Davlia of the Macedonians and Deavoli of the Byzantines (near the Maliki of today, west of Korytsa) and, as one of their Patriarchs wrote, thay abandoned the land of their fathers and came to find refuge here[59].

Moschopolis reached a peak of prosperity and became a big and rich town in the period between 1600 and 1767[60]. Then the town began to decline (1767-1770). It revived and flourished again for about a century and a half (1770-1916) until its population was massacred on the 16th of October of 1916[61].

During the period of its prosperity, a lot of people, mostly Vlachs, flowed into the city. Spyros Lambros writes that «many estimated the population of the city to be 200.000; this is probably an exaggeration, but

the city numbered at least 85.000 inhabitants»[62]. Athanasios Aravantinos in his «Chronicles of Epirus» (Athens, 1856) writes that the city had 12.000 families[63]. Lambros suggests that this number should be multiplied at least by 7 because, at that time, in Macedonia and Epirus, married children and their own children lived with the parents in the same house, forming one family[64].

The general belief is that Moschopolis, had 6.000 houses. When W.M. Leake (1805) visited the city, the decline had begun. On a wall of the church of the near - by monastery of St. John, an inscription bore the date «1632». Other visitors saw inscriptions on walls of other churches bearing the dates 1700 and 1760. These inscriptions lead us to the conclusion that Moschopolis flourished between 1650 and 1750. They say that the first raid against the city was made in 1769[65] and the second in 1788. The final and decisive blow was dealt - as always - by Ali Pasha[66].

Apart from Moschopolis, many other important big villages of Pindos were destroyed, too: Gramutsa, Linotopi, Nicolitsa - which, from a mere farm grew into an important town - Nitsa, and Vithkuki[67]. Their inhabitants fled to the region of Monastir[68], where they founded important Vlachic communities, such as Molovista (Melovitsa)[69]. Gopes[70], Megarovo[71], Tarnovo[72], which is separated from Megarovo by the Ydragora river, and which in 1932, numbered 500 families, Nizopoli with 500 families of herdsmen[73], and Krusovo with 10.000 inhabitants[74]. Villages with pure Vlachic populations - with a few Albanian Vlachs - were the following: Vlachokleisura, Nevesca (Nymphaeon), Belcameni, Pisoderi, Abdela, Samarina and Pervoli.

Vlachokleisura, with 3.000 inhabitants, had been the most important Vlachic village of West Macedonia. All these were important villages of West Macedonia during the 18th century. Matsuki was, then, a town, while later, in the 19th century numbered only 25 houses[25]. Syrraco and Calarytes had 500 houses each - about 5.000-6.000 inhabitants each of them - while, during the previous century each of these villages had only five houses[76]. The two villages flourished because their inhabitants developed an important manifacture, especially goldsmithing and silversmithing.

Calarytes (Calar), Syrraco and Matsuki are located

in the upper basin of the eastern branch of the river Aracthos, one of the most secluded regions of our peninsula. In 1822 these villages were destroyed by the Turks and never revived again[77].

According to old sources, Metsovo was founded by Flocas' Vlachic tribe. The inhabitants specialized in wool processing; according to a french commercial traveller wool cape manufacture reached a peak at the turn of the 18th century[78]. The settlement became richer and richer due to the commerce that developed through Ioannina.

The inhabitants of Calarytes transported their goods by sea and thanks to their connections with the sultana Valide, they were not oppressed by the Turkish authorities, and they were exempt from taxation. However, in 1800, Ali Pasha revoked all privileges and imposed a taxation on all the villages of the district[79]. The annual tax that the inhabitants of Calarytes paid, from 14.000 piasters soon rose to 45.000 piasters and the permit for a church bell cost another 15.000 piasters[80].

With the liberation, the border separated the villages; Calarytes was included in the free Greek State, whereas Syrraco, the native town of the poet Zalocostas, remained under the Turkish rule. The inhabitants of Calarytes scattered all over the Greek State and the place was deserted. And the inhabitants of many other important villages of West Macedonia and Pindos, which had been destroyed in the 17th and 18th century by the Albanian raiding bands, also scattered and their villages were deserted.

Socrates Liacos reports that the Vlachs of the destroyed villages of Voscopoulea (Moschopolis), Sypsca, Bithkoukia, Frassiari, Zavaliani, Valiani, Linotopi, Gramusta, Nicolitsa[81], Arza and other villages which had begun to decline when W.M. Leake visited them (beginning of the 19th century), scattered to all corners of the ottoman empire and Europe carrying along the Greek culture and contributing a lot to the developement of commerce in Austria-Hungary, where they transplanted their highly developed trade unionism[82].

The distance between Bithkouki and Moschopolis is 18 kilometers. Inscriptions on churches mention them as «cities with a large population»; and the prosperity of these cities had reached a peak when the near-by cities of Castoria and Korytsa had only 300-

400 houses each[83].

The 18th century was the period of their greater economic and cultural development; the two towns were subdivided into many districts and their inhabitants had formed many guilds, according to their trade. There were extensive pastures around the cities so the inhabitants could grow large herds and benefit from the products (skins, milk, butter, etc.).

The most important organization was the guild of metal-workers, especially the guild of copperworkers which had a special place in the social hierarchy; and also in Bithkouki, where one of the districts was called «Kovacas» (from the slav. word konac = smith).

There was a special «market day» that attracted many merchants so that the fame of the local tradesmen reached faraway Venice, where they came to be known as «mercanti Arbanesi». Paralleling this commercial growth, was the cultural progress. It was at that time that a college, the «New Academy» was founded in Moschopolis[84] and most of the churches were built; more than 20 in Moschopolis and around 12 in Bithkouki. The monastery of St. John the Baptist of Moschopolis and the monastery of St. Peter of Bithkouki competed with each other in wealth and fame.

After the repeated destructions of the 18th century (1769, 1789) Moschopolis was deserted; also, Bithkouki was deserted after 1823. Their inhabitants scattered to other neighboring towns or emigrated to other countries of the Balkans and Europe[85].

An interesting extract from D.A. Sachinis' «History of Siatista gives an account of how thiw town was built by fugisitives from regions where settlements had been destroyed by albanian raiding bands:

«Siatista is a more recent town. During the reign of sultan Murat I, who had conquered the entire West Macedonia (1395) hordes of Ottomans from the region of Konia (the coniars) came to the plains of Thessaly and Macedonia where they setlled in the fertile valley of Karayannia, and the Christian inhabitants fled to the high, rocky plateaus of Siatista, a naturally fortified place, secure and almost inaccessible to the Turks, so that they could preserve their faith, national consciousness and freedom. Also the inhabitants of the near-by villages of Tsiroutsino, Trapezittsa, Pelka, Palaeocastron, Exarchon,

Sarakina, Giancovi, Tservena, Petrovo and some others, not tolerating the oppression, plundering and forcible islamization, gradually abandoned their homes and went to the hideaways on the plateau of Siatista»[86]. In another extract, the author writes: «Later, refugees from other regions came to Siatista. Especially from Thessaly and Epirus where opression, plundering and persecution had reached a peak after the Albanian revolt (1612). Many came from the Peloponnese as it is evidenced by some family names - «Moraites», etc. - (probably after the Orlof revolt), from Moschopolis (the families of Pericles, Canatsulis, Zoupan, Liacos, and others), from Darda, from Lagga, even from the heroic villages of Suli, as it is evidenced by the family names Papasuliotes, Natsinas, Karaliolos, Samaras, and others[87].

The codex of the monastery of St. Nicanor at Zaborda (1692) contains a list of 124 christian villages in the then province of Grevena, now nomos of Grevena.

This list mentions the villages: Pontini (Torista), Kolokythaki, Lagadikia (Gotsizino), Agalaeoi (Agaloe), Kentron (Vendzi), Nesi (Nesinico), Agapi (Ratsi), Pegaditsa, Kyrakali, Myrsini (Trano Koplari), Elaphi (Piniari), Vatolaccos (Topratovo) and Kivotos (Kryfidzi) as purely christian villages, whereas during the last years of the turkish rule their inhabitants were exclusively muslim; this proves that islamization of these villages took place much later, probably during the 18th century[88].

This information is valuable not only because it has preserved the old names of 124 villages of West Macedonia, especially of the region of Grevena, but also because it proves indisputably their age, since they must have been founded before the end of the 17th century.

Regarding the islamization of the inhabitants, several data dating from the middle of the 18th century exist.

In 1760, the inhuman treatement, the persecutions and the heavy taxation forced 36 villages of christian Skipetars of Karamouratia, in the region of Pogoniani and Konitsa to be islamized. In spite of the long and bloody battles, - the result of the despair to which they were driven and which lasted for a half a century - they were finally subdued by the Turks of Premeti. Even bishops and priests succumbed and made the

Cells with architectural projections in the monastery of St. John Prodromos, in Serres (Photo: 1961).

horrible decision to be islamized so as to prevent the physical annihilation of the inhabitants[89]. The same things happened in the region of Moglena (Karad-

A Street of Smyrna. Sketch by Thomas Allom, lithograph by T. Higham.

A picture of Portaria (Simone Pomardi, 1806).

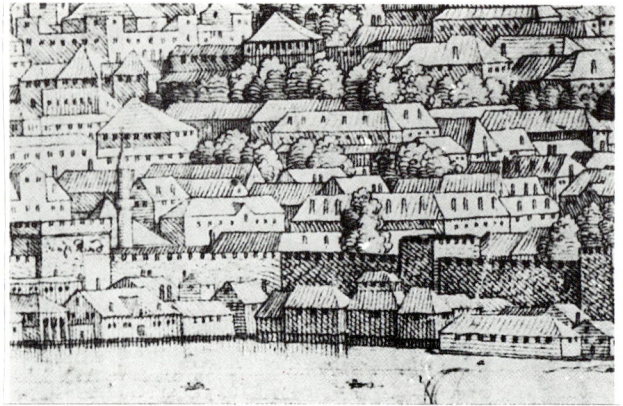

View of the districts of Constantinople, according to Lorich (Middle of the 16th century).

zova) and elsewhere (Rodopi, etc.).

This brief introduction was necessary in order that the reader may understand and differentiate the various regions where the christians took refuge after they had lost their homes, especially those of the villages of the fertile plains, and the formation of new, mixed populations which, after the conquest, gravitated to such depopulated cities as Constantinople and Thessaloniki. The old historical urban centers continued their life, but now with a mixed population.

After the conquest, the Turks kept, in a way, the old, Byzantine administrative division. But new important centers began to develope either on the ruins of the old or in new locations, depending on the new demographic rearrangements. Thus, apart from Thessaloniki, other centers, such as Serres (Siroz), Veria (Karaferia), Drama (Dirama), Monastiri (Bitola, Tolimonastir), Yanina, Lamia (Zeitoun), Kavala, Zichna, Vera (Feredjik), Edessa (Voden), Kastoria, Florina, Achrida, Stromnitsa, and others, began to grow. On the contrary, other populous towns such as Servia, Gynaecocastro (Avret Hisar), Maximianoupolis, Anastasioupolis (Burukale), Chrysoupolis, Redina, and a large number of mountain fortified villages and villages in the fertile plains were deserted.

After the conquest, the Turks founded some new settlements in strategic places, especially in the middle of fertile areas where they brought immigrants from Asia Minor, mainly Yuruks, and settled them on the farmlands, for instance in Yanitsa (Yenise Var-

dar), in Chrysoupolis (Sari Saban) by the Nestos river in Gioumouldzina, the old Byzantine castle of the Kamoutsines[90], in Lagada (Lagaza), in Naussa, in Kozani, in Alexandroupolis (Dede Agac) in Larissa (Nefsehir) and in some other towns.

Apart from a few exceptions, the Turks were not interested in building new forts and castles (they built the Kara-baba fort in a region contiguous to the Venetian dominion). But they did repair and maintained the road network and they built bridges; they also built caravanserais for the comfort of travellers. In the fortified historical urban centers, such as Thessaloniki, Kamoutsina (Gümüldzina), Serres, Drama, Veria, Castoria, Larissa, Yannina and others, they founded new shopping centers, shopping malls, public baths (hamam), mosques and monasteries for the orders of the dervishes who played an important part in the period of the invasion.

As the time passed, order and safety began to be restored especially in the hinterland where the inhabitants had suffered from the long war and the continuous raids from land and sea during the last years of the Byzantine Empire. People began to return to their daily occupations and the traders opened again their shops and stores. Now, there began a marked change in the demand for the goods they produced; the products began to be orientalized somewhat, in order that they might compete with those offered in the big markets of the East, especially in Constantinople. The Turks protected the guilds (isnaf) in order to control the production for military reasons.

The enslaved Greek populations, the Rums, the

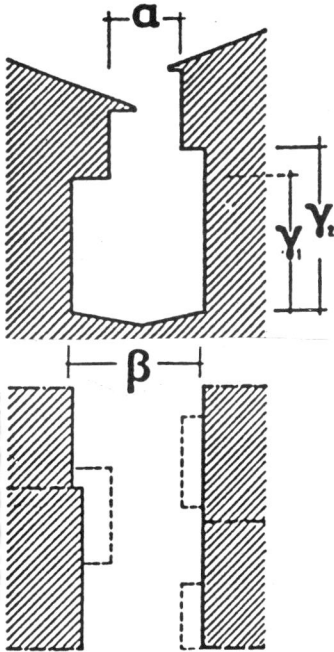

Schematic representation of a byzantine street in plan and transverse section (4,5).

SOURCES	a*	β*	γ*
1. Corpus Juris Civilis, *"Decree of Onorios and Theodosios, AD 243.*	10*		
2. Corpus Juris Civilis, *"Decree of Zenon, AD 531.*	10*	12*	
3. *Justinianian Codex (*Cod. Just. *VII, 10 12c)*			15*
4. Preliminary Act, *Basil I, AD 872.*	10*	12*	
5. Recalt *(Jus Graecoromanum, AD. 879-886)*		12*	
6. Vasilika, *AD 900*	10*	12*	
7. Eparchic book of Leon the Wise, *10th c.*	10*		15*
8. Novel 113 of Leon the Wise *PG 107, p. 652-653 10th c.*	10*		
9. "Hexabiblos" of Armenopoulos, *AD 1345*	10*	10*	15*
10. "Nomicon" of Theophilos of Ioannina, *AD 1788.*	$3^1/_3$**	20**	

* The dimensions are given in Byzantine feet (1 b.f.=0.3088m)
** The dimensions are given in Byzantine "pechys" (cubitus)
(1 b. pechys=0.4632m)

rayas[91] of the ottoman empire, gathered round their natural, spiritual leadership, the clergy, the bishop and the elders of each place who were responsible for the administration of justice and the collection of taxes, to the ottoman authorities.

In the urban centers and the large villages of the period, the only social center of the neighborhood was the church where, in addition to the divine liturgy, other social activities took place - weddings, baptisms, funerals. The square in front of the church was used for the dances and other activities. On the church gallery (hayat), the older women advised the girls, and, especially, newly-wed young women how to become good housewives, and, among themselves they arranged matches and brought about future marriages; and the elders apportioned tax obligations, picked the most gifted of the young men to support financially, they decided what help to give to the needy, the orphans and the widows and, there, on the church gallery the committees chose the teacher and made the decisions about building a new school. The social work of the elders was both valuable and difficult. Their work helped the nation to survive; thanks to the elders some excellent men had been able to progress and, in turn, to help others, the multitudes[92].

Another basic institution of the period of the turkish rule was the guilds which helped the in-

Schematic representation of the articulation of the parts of a byzantine residence based on the byzantine laws. Open-air solaria (N. Moutsopoulos).

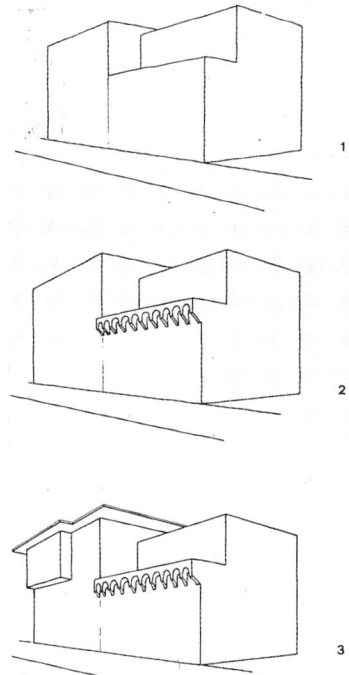

habitants of the settlements not only financially but also socially by organizing public relief committees in which the members of the guild and their families participated.

The building construction continued, developing from the building construction of the Byzantine period. The laws which, since the Byzantine time,

Front view of a «sahnisi» of a mansion in Siatista.

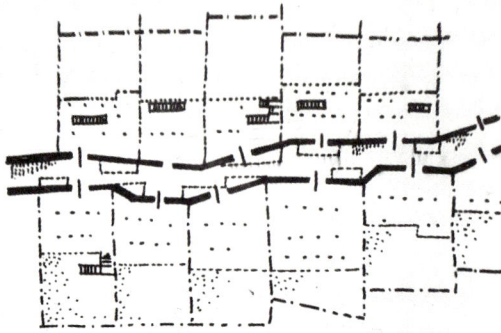

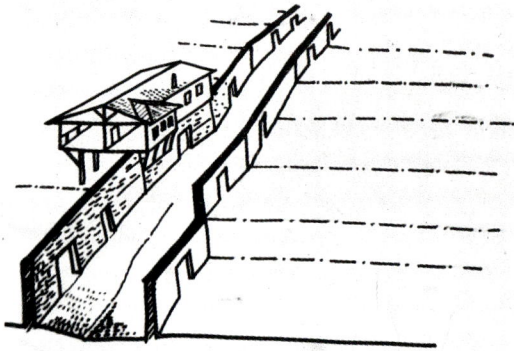

*Schematic representation of the manner
of arrangement of plots of land and «row-houses»
in Veria (N. Moutsopoulos).*

*View of the facade and the «sahnisi» of Jonos' mansion in
Siatista.*

P. Tzindos' townhouse in Veria.

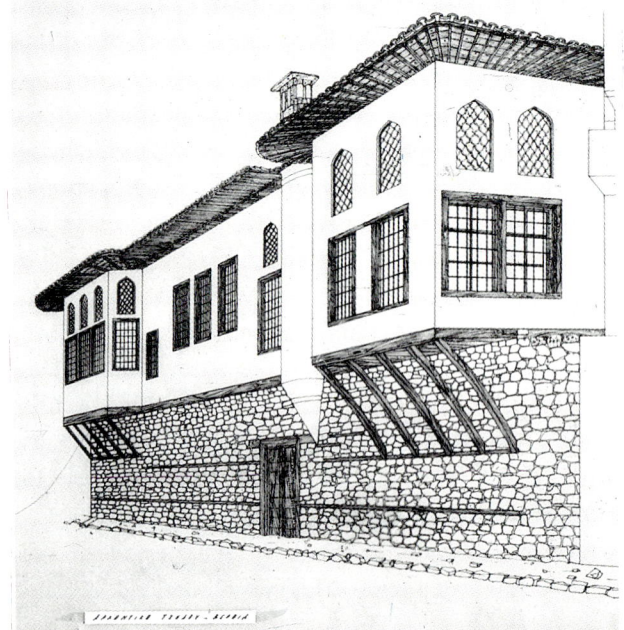

defined the proportions of the height of the buildings
to the width of the streets, and defined a minimum
width of thoroughfare, so that the street could be
sunned and aired, and at the same time, give some
protection against fires, continued to be in force. A
consequence of this continuation, especially in the
lines of row-houses of the cities, was also the continuation of the same architectural types and the logical development of the forms in proportion to the
progress of the building construction.

Morphologically, through the years, certain building types began to take a more oriental form. The
relieving arches over window lintels, from semicircular - as we see them in older monuments of Brusa -
changed to pointed and, finally, to four-centered arches of a pure islamic morphology. In building construction, at first the form of the Byzantine wall construction of bricks was continued. Later, the isodomic
system, according to the seljuk models, began to
appear.

Old houses on Dialetti str., Thessaloniki,
with triangular solaria.

Old houses with solaria on the small street leading
from «Camara» (Galerius' Arch of Triumph)
to the St. George Rotonda.

A house with a deep «hayat» (front porch)
in Chalcidiki.

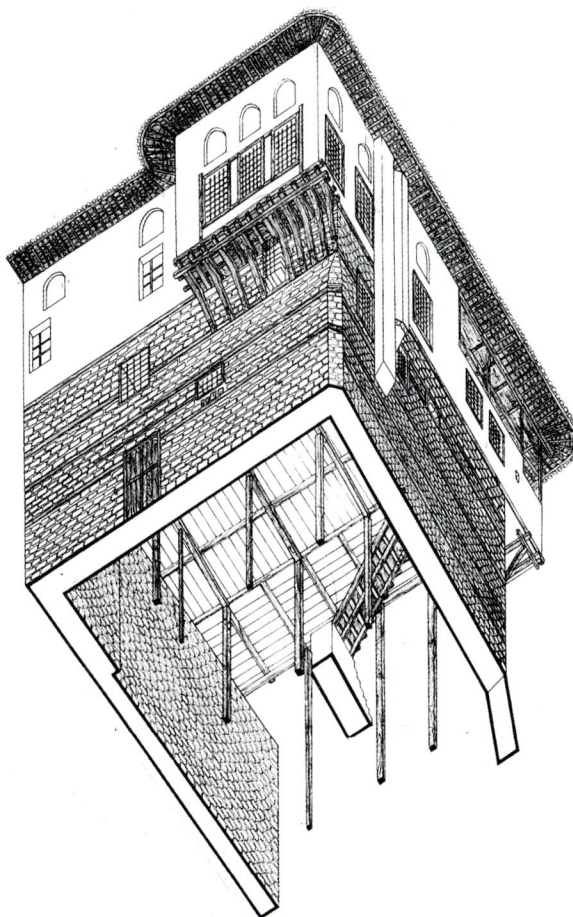

Isometric representation of Sapountzoglou's mansion
in Veria (N. Moutsopoulos).

In the 17th century, the Ottomans had already completed their morphology which was, essentially, a combination of Byzantine and oriental (iranian and seljuk) types and forms.

In settlements where the continuous system of construction was applied, the wall defining the building line was the only element of the building made of stone.

This wall varied according to the district. Sometimes it was fairly low, and sometimes fairly high, as in examples of architecture in Veria. The width of the building lot depended on many factors. The party walls were sometimes built of stone and sometimes of brick or other, cheaper material such as rubble and extended to the depth of the building. From that point on, the distance to the symmetric building across the yard varied according to the depth of the block. Usual-ly the ground floor was not used unless the occupation of the inhabitants required auxiliary space. One can

Twin wide-front dwellings.

see the timber pillars (direk) which supported the upper floor; they are either simple or they have, at the top, knee braces that give them the appearance of trees that have shed their leaves. The bedrooms and sitting-room were on the first floor, facing the street and, sometimes, some of them jut out over the sidewalk.

The interior gallery usually has the width of the closed spaces; but, sometimes, it is wider. Sometimes part of the gallery is superelevated, forming a sort of split level floor, sometimes with protrusions, which evinces a sensitivity of choice of suitable optical effects for the benefit of those who sit on the wide benches enjoying both the view and the hospitality of the host and hostess.

In cases of rustic construction, the nucleus consists of a wide-front building, similar to the nucleus of the continuous construction, but independent.

We have scant information about the urban centers of Macedonia during the 16th century. There was no safety in the country. The packtrains which carried the products of the various regions to Europe, were often waylaid by armed bandits. The small garrisons stationed at the cols and crossroads, and the armed guards that accompanied the packtrains offered only nominal protection.

The monasteries also felt the general depression. In the first quarter of the 17th century, the monastery of Megisti Lavra in Athos could barely provide food for six monks; only after 1630 did it begin to prosper. The monasteries of Vatopedi and Iviron were also suffering a decline. The economic crisis forced the monasteries to restore the «peculiar» system which continued through the next centuries. The monastery

of Prodromos of Serres faced the same difficulties; in 1650 it was almost dissolved and most of its monks took refuge in Athos. The older monks, who stayed in the monastery could barely live and sold all their possessions to buy food.

It seems that the lack of safety, apart from creating a stream of emigrants to the European countries, it also created a smaller stream of local migrants to the larger urban centers and important, large villages. The well-known Turkish traveller Evliya Tselebi, who visited these districts in 1662, wrote that Veria and Naussa (Niagusta) had approximately 4.000 houses each. Castoria had 2.500, Vodena 1.060, and Florina and Yenitse Vardar 1.500 each[93]. On a map of 1560, Samariana has the name Santa Maria de Praetoria.

Around the end of the century the war between Turkey and Austria ended in an Austrian victory which was validated by the Karlovic treaty (1699), and gave hopes of a recovery. After the new Passarovic treaty (1718) whose terms were favorable to the development of commerce, there was an upward economic development which lasted to the middle of the 18th century[94].

The Greeks took advantage of the existing possibilities and got rich. Manufacture, cotton thread dyeing, and fur processing began to grow. Exports to Venice, Serbia, and Austria and Hungary multiplied. Trading in the Macedonian hinterland was done in the town fairs, such as the fair of Avret Hisar, the fair of Doliani, near Petritsi[95], the fair of Serres and, of course, the oldest of them, the fair of Demétria, at the western exit of Thessaloniki. In West Macedonia, the most important fair was the fair of Mavronoros and,

A wide-front dwelling.

Wide-front dwelling.

Wide-front house in the St. Achillios' settlement on the homonymous island of Mikri Prespa (1991).

later, the fair of St. Mamas in Chalkidiki.

This economic growth is reflected best in the construction of new churches and their decoration with elaborated temples of carved wood and new frescoes.

Siatista is a characteristic example of the economic growth; the town must have been founded before the 17th century since, in 1612, it resisted a violent attack of Albanian irregulars. Immediately afterwards, we see waves of refugees coming to the town from Moschopolis, Epirus, Thessaly, Suli, even from the Peloponnese. Between 1610 and 1647, seven churches were built in Siatista, evidencing that the settlement had grown into a large central village[96]. Between 1700 and 1792 another seven churches were built in Siatista.

The 18th century really brought many changes throughout the ottoman empire. The sultan decided to open the gates wide to the West. In 1721, the ottoman government sent the first ambassador Yirmisekiz Mehmed Efendi to Paris, accompanied by a large retinue. From that time onwards, the traditional etiquette of the palace began to be influenced by the French manners which were soon transmitted to the people outside the palace walls. At the same time the sultans attempted to westernize training in the military schools. The traditional reserve towards western systems and western technology began to disappear. During this period the new artistic milieu began to be established in the capital of the ottoman empire[97].

During the period of the Russo-Turkish war (1736-1738) the unsafety in the country reached a new peak and local insurgencies hindered the smooth transportation of goods. People from West Macedonia again

began to emigrate to Europe in order to avoid the heavy taxation imposed and covered by the pretext of the war. A firman of 1742 admits the anarchy that reigned in the cazas of Thessaloniki. The new Russo-Turkish war broke out in 1768 (1768-1777). In 1769, Turkoalbanian bands sacked and destroyed the Vlachic villages of Grammos: Nitsa, Nicolitsa, Linotopi, Virtianic. Their inhabitants were forced to flee to safer regions. Most of the inhabitants of Nitsa and Nicolitsa formed a new settlement: Crousovo. The inhabitants of Linotopi and some Albanian-speaking inhabitants of Bithkouki fled to Megarovo.

Moschopolis was sacked and destroyed in the same year. The inhabitants scattered to Korytsa, Yanena, Delvinaki, Ambelakia, Thessaloniki, Serres, Bitolia (Monastiri), Crousovo, Velesa, Belgrade, Budapest and Vienna and, through their hard work and abilities, they invigorated the economy of their adopted countries. We know that 100 families settled in Chrupista and many others in Vlachokleisura.

The destruction of Moschopolis was a heavy blow to the christians. That town had been the center of arts and manufacture, of the wool trade, of goldsmithery. It had been the center of letters and education and the books that were published there, invigorated the spirit of the enslaved christians. The inhabitants of Moschopolis who went to Monastiri (Bitolia) founded their own market place, the Vlahtsarsi[98]. After the end of the Russo-Turkish war a new period of anarchy began in Macedonia; the various local beys began to fight and kill one another. The period of terror affected the safety and threatened the life of the enslaved christians.

House with «hayat» (front porch) in the settlement
of Psarades, Megali Prespa (1991). Along the front
of the hayat, fish from the lake are hanging to dry.

A ruined house in the settlement of Psarades,
Prespa (photo: 1991).

In spite of the unsafety and anarchy, a revival could be perceived everywhere. The morale of the enslaved population had risen[99]. The Greek emigrants had come in contact with the European ideals of the enlightenment and had become more confident and sure of themselves. The Greek merchants were more educated now and came in contact with the emigrant scholars of their time. The new ideas travelled fast and reached the large, rich villages and are reflected in the work of art and architecture of the period. The biggest and most beautiful mansions of Macedonia were built in the 18th century.

In spite of the persecution, many mountain villages managed not only to survive, but also to flourish and grow due to the abilities and energy of their inhabitants which impressed the foreign visitors who came in the 18th and 19th c. to study the system of their self-government and, particularly, their guilds[100].

N. Pantazopoulos writes on the subject: «certain mountain settlements and main villages that happened to acquire some special privileges, for instance, the villages of Pelion, or villages with a flourishing commerce and manufacture, as, for instance the mountain villages of West Macedonia, or villages with powerful guilds, like the village of Ambelakia and the villages of Pelion, grew rapidly and bloomed»[101].

Around 1700, the Greek population in the Ottoman empire was estimated to be 1.500.000; the continuous wars of the 16th and 17th c., the massacres, slavery, islamization and mass emigration had caused a deplorable shrinkage in the number of the Greek subjects of the empire. N. Svoronos writes: «in spite of the adversities the Greeks tried to organize, taking advantage of the small margin of freedom left to them by the Turkish authorities. This is the period of adaptation»[102]. Their main protection against poverty was the development of manufacture and, generally, the development of the primary production through the system of cooperative associations. As N. Pantazopoulos writes, «The Greeks, organized in cooperatives, religious (clergy), political (communities, societies), military (captaincies, guerrillas, corsairs) and economic (guilds, and companies) managed to preserve their religion, their language and their laws and by making the bond between those four forms of associated groups tighter, to succeed in freeing themselves»[103].

An important form of association was the economic which was represented by every guild. At the same time, entire districts organized in guilds and even managed to obtain privileges from the Ottoman government, which granted them a monopoly of production, and paid a special tax, either pecuniary or in kind, to the representative of the sultan who was the nominal supervisor of the «trust» of guilds, which, as N. Pantazopoulos writes, often superseded the community organization[104]. In many areas of the country, the two forms of organization, that is the guilds and the community, established a system of coordinating the independent activities of each organization, as, for instance, Thessaloniki, Serres, Melenico, Veria,

Naussa, Kozani, Siatista, Castoria, Moschopolis, Korytsa, Monastiri, Crousovo and others[105].

Summarizing what we mentioned in the previous chapters, we could suggest a simplifying form of the demographic rearrangements which followed the turkish conquest and the consecutive settlements of the Yuruks, the Ghazis and other Ottomans during the 14th, 15th and 16th centuries.

Nicolaos Svoronos writes that «the legal status of the subject christian populations was defined according to the principles of the islamic law which recognised the right of life and property and gave religious liberty to anyone who had submitted to the Ottoman rule without resistance; but they were obliged to pay a tax per capita, the old arabic *djizya*, which the christians called «haratsi», which defined the property tax mainly. The first sultans applied the principle of the islamic law. Anyway according to the same law, all the conquered lands belonged to the sultan who could apportion it to his soldiers, the ghazis, and to various officials, for services rendered»[106].

It is a fact that the population of the plains, whether urban or rural, abandoned their homes. Those who stayed, continued cultivating their land, but under a different legal status of land tenure. It is impossible to estimate the number of the inhabitants who left their homes, fleeing either to regions that were still free, or to dominions of the Serinissime or even to regions and centers which had already been conquered by the ottomans. A considerable number of inhabitants fled to mountain areas, a movement which had taken place again, in the past, during barbarian raids. It is not easy to determine how long it took the refugees to adapt to the new conditions in their new settlements; the living conditions, however, must have been extremely tough, which makes us wonder whether there were any city dwellers among these refugees.

Certain nuclei of mountain settlements of Macedonia and Pindos had been formed during previous demographic rearrangements which are beyond the scope of the present study. However, in the new mountain homes of the 15th and 16th century, the enslaved Greek populations organized their new pattern of life and managed to survive and preserve their traditions and faith. The development of the manufacture of processing dairy products and, especially, wool and skins grew into the most important source of wealth.

From the accounts of the Turkish traneller Evliya Tselebi we learn that in the 17th century (c.1670) there was a flourishing silk manufacture and silversmithing[107] in Yanina, and «in Moschopolis, the carpet and textile manufacture contributed a lot to the prosperity of the population»[108]. The wool was processed and turned into thread or wooven cloths before it was offered for sale. The technique of red dyeing of the thread was particularly developed in Ambelakia and Rapsani of Thessaly. The artisans of Castoria, using a special, traditional technique, processed imported parts of fur (cords), which were smaller cutouts masterfully sewn together and exported them as furs, and it was not easy to distinguish them from one-piece furs.

The transit commerce had been systematically organized and was tolerated, even supported by the Ottomans, who took care of the permits which would allow the packtrains to pass through the check points at the cols and provided a military detachement to see that they crossed the borders safely. The muleteers, the so-called «kyradzis» were, usually, Vlachs. The packtrain system contributed much to the economy and ensured the transportation of goods to the farthest corners of the Ottoman empire, and even to the northern countries of Europe and, at the same time, helped the communication between distant places[109].

Telemachus Katsuyannis writes that «the packmasters, from primitive muleteers developed into entrepreneurs and were, indisputably, the pioneers who opened new ways and new horizons of commercial activities to the still developing urban middle class. The surplus population - the unemployed - turned to manifacture and urban trades where they found work. This fact, in its wider sense, was the beginning of the formation of a lower middle class». And he concludes with the remark: «this transition had already begun before the turkish conquest»[110].

We know that the Vlachs of Pindos used packtrains to transport their goods to Yanena, Bucharest, Thessaloniki, Serres and Constantinople[111]. And anyway, the first traders and peddlers had been, mostly, Vlachs. The organization of the community of Ambelakia is a striking example. And according to W.M. Leake and others, «The Vlachs were important manufacturers and traders in many other cities of the European provinces of Turkey, except in Thrace where the Greek refugees from Asia Minor and the Armenians competed with them successfully»[112].

There was a vigorous commercial activity in Ambelakia of Thessaly, during the last quarter of the 18th century and the beginning of the 19th. The town boasted several hotels and the active, polyglot merchants were always ready to get in contact with the European merchants and frequently visited the commercial fairs or France and Germany[113]. «During that period, that mountain town looked like an oasis in the middle of the desolation and poverty of the area of Thessaly[114]. And the society of the little town resembled the societies of the European towns and many Germans sojourned there to transact their business». I. Leonardos writes: «And one could see here young men in European attire, and most of them were German commercial travellers»[115].

The inhabitants of Moschopolis had founded a populous community in Korytsa. Also, Sipischa flourished during the 17th and 18th c. The merchants of the two towns had established branches in Venice, Vienna, Budapest and Leipzig. The flourishing greek communities of Vienna consisted mostly of Vlachs from Moschopolis and as W.M. Leake (1805) writes, most of the inhabitants of Siatista and Selitsa spoke German because of their commercial connections with Vienna[116]. The inhabitants of Zagori, as several foreign tourists say, had developed vigorous commercial activity. The rich merchants of Kapesovo and Veitsa had established branches in Vienna, Moscow, Breslau, Leipzig and Amsterdam, and most of them had accounts in german banks. Those who had settled permanently in Russia and the Dunabian countries were mostly fur traders[117].

As we have already mentioned, emigrants from Kozani, Siatista and Castoria had established well-organized nuclei in the big cities of Hungary and some of them were Vlachs. The communities of the immigrants were centered around their churches which were always beautifully adorned with carved woodwork whose style tended towards the post-Byzantine, Greco-oriental baroque[118]. In one of these churches, the work of a certain Theodoros Gruntonicos of Moschopolis is still preserved[119].

A heavy blow to the emigrant Greeks was the decision of Ali Pasha of Yanina to turn the 40 villages of Zagori over to his youngest son, Salibey. No Greek

had the right to own land, and, suddenly, in March of 1815, 5.350 families became serfs. Kyriakos Simopoulos writes that «the consequences were disastrous. The merchants were at the mercy of the satrap because their families were hostages of the Pasha. Those with families in the villages were obliged to return. The others settled permanently abroad[120].

The Swedish traveller Jacob Jonas Björnstähl (*Briefe auf seinen ausländischen Reisen*, Leipzig 1780)[121], who visited Ambelakia in 1779 as a guest of the bishop Dionysios, got acquainted with most of the scholars and merchants of the town and was astonished by the high intellectual level of the persons with whom he came in contact. He was particularly impressed by the erudition of the teachers of the Greek School of Ambelakia and the polyglotism of the merchants who had travelled to the farthest corners of Europe. He mentions professor George Triantafyllides who had studied under the guidance of the famous scholar Eugenios Voulgaris, and taught Aristophanes and Homer and Latin, and he had a long discussion with him on the subject of the «beginnings of decline of the Greek language». They also talked about botany and the Swede suggested that the Greek scholar systematically collect the various herbs and record them with their contemporary names along with the names that Theophrastus and Thucidides had given them. He also advised him to study other Greek botanists, to read Lenaeos' «botany» and complete with comments and addenda Meletios' *Geography* (which was done by Anthimos Gazis in 1807), and to record the ancient inscriptions on some buildings of the town[122]. Björnstähl also found that bishop Dionysios, his brother Nicolaos Michael, who had lived in Leipzig for 15 years, doctor Nicolaos Perinis and several other merchants spoke German[123].

The Greek children of the town and its district, attended the «Greek Museum» of Ambelakia whose curriculum, apart from the usual subjects, included ancient writers, natural sciences, philosophy and advanced mathematics. We have information from many sources and, mainly, from wills and donations and the constitution of the famed Ambelakia Company (article 14), that many young men were sent abroad to study and learn at least one foreign language to be able to make a career in commerce. The tourist Bartholdy who visited Ambelakia in 1803 says that he met young men who had attended colleges in Jena and Leipzig[124].

Many of the best-known scholars of the period taught school in Ambelakia; the famous sage Eugenios Voulgaris, the scholar archdeacon Gregorios Constantinos - he and Daniel Philippides coauthored the «*Modern Geography*», printed in 1791 in Vienna -, the mathematician Ionas Sparmiotes, the historian Constantas Coumas, the scholar Daniel Magnes or Magnetas, the scholar priest Polyzoes and others[125]. Koukkides writes that «all these scholars held conferences with other erudite inhabitants of the town, such as the hellenist and iatrophilosopher Assanis, the Drosos brothers, the physician and translator Sakellaris, a graduate of the university of Vienna, and talked about ways to revive the Greek nation». And one of the leaders of the «Friendly Society», Anthimos Gazes, and the scholar Gregorios Constantas suggested that an «Academy» be founded in Ambelakia[126].

We know that through the 19th century «the education of the children of the enslaved Greeks was the job of the local communities, the church and, sometimes, of the guilds or even some individuals»[127].

Certain political events and treaties, such as the treaty after the 16-year long war between Turkey and Venice, Austria and Poland which is known as the Karlovic treaty (January 26, 1699)[128] contributed a lot to the growth of the economy of the mountain villages of Macedonia and the surrounding areas. The period of peace favored the development of the transit commerce. The prosperity of the Greek communities of the diaspora was reflected in the home towns. Many manufacturer guilds were formed during this period and became powerful, especially in the towns and villages in the region of Olympus and Kissavos (Rapsani, Tirnavos, Ambelakia, and others). Especially after the Passarovitz treaty (1718) new horizons opened to the Greek merchants and their prosperity was reflected in the growth of letters, arts and architecture[129] in spite of the disasters and devastations of the years 1715, 1721, 1738 and 1744 and the perceptible fall in commercial transactions[130]. However, the privileges that the sultan granted to the patriarch after the conquest and other privileges that some villages obtained, contributed a lot to the survival and the growth of Hellenism[131].

*

Helen Papatsa's house in Athytos, Chalcidiki. 1: Ground floor plan 2: 1ˢᵗ floor plan.

Isometric representaion of the typology of a wide-front house.

Interpretation of a castle-like, wide-front house of Macedonia.

Reception of the bishop of Salona on the «hayat» of a house in Chryso.

Coming back to the subject of residences, we see that the oldest type which is prevalent both in the alluvial valleys and the semi-mountainous regions of Macedonia and Thrace is the wide-front type of abode with a front porch. This type, through various transfigurations of the basic cell, led to the variety of types we find elsewhere[132], for instance in Albania[133], Bulgaria[134], and Turkey[135]. The upper floor covered balcony (*hayat*), was called *cardak*[136] in slavic, but the Byzantine name was «doxatos»[137], a name which was preserved through the centuries both in the Greek regions and in the slavic[138] and was given to all covered open spaces[139].

This space was protected from the sun and the wind and combined the advantages of a closed and open space together. The villagers spent most of their time on this «cardak», working, or cooking their meals in open hearths and rested after the toil of the day. But the most important advantage of these half-closed spaces was the protection they gave against the weather. In the winter, they were well protected from the wind; in the summer they were protected from the heat. The origin of these half-closed spaces dates back to the dawn of time when the entire abode was half-open.

A color copperplate by Edward Dodwell picturing a dinner on a «cardak» gives an ideas of its uses. It is a dinner given by the bishop of Amphissa, at Chryso[140]. The bishop is sitting cross-legged, according to the oriental custom, on a low mattress, blessing a christian who bows before him. Several elders and «nobles» of the region are sitting round a very low table and another who had just come into the «hayat» is washing his hands in a basin while a servant is pouring water from a copper pitcher. A woman is serving the dinner. The scene is characteristic of the life in the beginnings of the 19th century and shows the attire and customs of the period which little differed from the turkish customs. Even a small child, in the background, in baggy trousers, vest and turban does not differ from the son of an ottoman agha of a neighboring village.

Wide-front house.

A house with a «doxatos» in Siderocastro (photo: 1960).

Houses in Sidi-Bou-Said, Tunisia (photo: 1976).

However, the function of a «hayat» of a village dwelling was different from the function of the «doxatos» of the mansions of the rich merchants and affluent traders, but it did not differ from those of the turkish population. But the «hayats» were very useful to the agrarian population[141]. One might also say that a specific kind of agrarian occupation, for instance, the processing of the tobacco leaves, made the construction of a «hayat» necessary to a village dwelling.

We tried to gather information about the time that the cultivation of tobacco first spread, but, unfortunately, there are no related historical studies. A friend, professor Haluk Sezgin informed me that a spanish ship first brought the tobacco to the ottoman empire in 1483, in other words, during the period that the Sefaradin Jews started coming. But when tobacco began to be systematically cultivated, and, especially, where, is not known. Doubtless, it is an important event which affected the agrarian economy of the empire. Apostolos Vacalopoulos, the historian of modern Hellenism, gives an important piece of information in his study «Macedonia in 1715». It is an extract from the diary of commander Constantine, a Greek nobleman of the court of the ruler of Wallachia Constantine Bracoveanu (1688-1714) who helped the grand Vizier Ali in his expedition against the Venetian dominions in Peloponnese at the head of an army of Vlachs[142].

The commander describes the fortified city of Xanthe and says that «the famous tobacco produced in the district was called «pirsitsan»[143]. It is, probably, a corruption of the turkish words «bir secen» which

mean «tobacco of first quality». As far as I know this is the oldest reliable piece of information about the cultivation of tobacco and it is doubtlessly correct because, today, the district of Xanthe produces tobacco of excellent quality. Also, W.M. Leak mentions tobacco exportation in 1835[144], but a more systematic cultivation must have begun in the decade from 1890 to 1900. We have more specific information about the extensive tobacco cultivation which was systematized by the hard working refugees from Asia Minor, later; records mention the production of tobacco: in 1922 , 25.000 tons; in 1924, 80.000 tons[145]. Furthermore, Jacques Ancel says that a systematic cultivation of tobacco began «at the turn of the century»[146].

However, we cannot depend on this information to ascertain that the construction of a «hayat» in village dwellings of tobacco producing districts had any connection with the product because we know that

Houses in Sinassos, Cappadocia (photo: 1982).

Houses with projections in the 1ˢᵗ floor at Orta Hissar of Cappadocia.

«hayats» were built before the introduction of the tobacco cultivation, and in districts where tobacco was never cultivated. Anyway, we have noticed such constructions in the capital of the empire dating back to the 16th century[147].

Therefore, the covered balcony, no matter what name it was given (doxatos, hayat etc.) constitutes an essential typological and morphological element of the traditional residence of the Hellenic areas and also of the Balkans and Asia Minor and originates in much older constructions. It had existed as part of the functional spaces of the residences in the Byzantine empire and also in the countries of Near East and the north African coast.

Certain researchers regard the perfectly symmetrical type of residence which is prevalent in the towns of West Macedonia, and in Asia Minor, where the rooms are placed in the four corners of the upper floor (and sometimes some of them protrude outwards) and the sofa running crosswise in the space between them, as oriental[148]. This view would be correct if it is proved beyond any doubt that, later repairs have not altered the type of the famed Cinili Kiosk, in Constantinople, which we know it was constructed between 1472 and 1473[149].

After a correct analysis, Godfrey Goodwin marked clear similarities to, if not influences of, the famous Fatihpur Sikri of India, where the form of the plan is justified by the centrobaric position of the throne of Akbar[150].

In any case, the Cinili Kiosk (turk. kösk) brings to Constantinople the completed, perfectly symmetrical architectural type[151]. The ottoman konak also originates in the Cinili Kiosk[152].

*

However, we must mention here artisans and masons, the «coudareoi» who built those houses.

The regions that produced most of the multitude of «coudareoi» during the Turkish occupation, are: in North Epirus, the villages of Korytsa : Chotsta, Biglitsa, Plikati, Elovo, Radimisi, Zoupani, Chouliarochoria, Chouliarades, Vastavetsi (the Petrovouni of today), Michalitsi, the Tzumerka villages, Pramata, Agnanta, Sclupo, Koutsovitsa, Raftanaeoi, Koukoulitsa, Gratista. The villages of Konitsa: Pyrsogianni, Vourbiani, Stratsani, Castaniani, Cerasovo, Koutsico, Zerma, Leskatsi, Chionades - which also produced famous painters and, particularly, icon painters -, Tournavo, - well-known for its wood car-

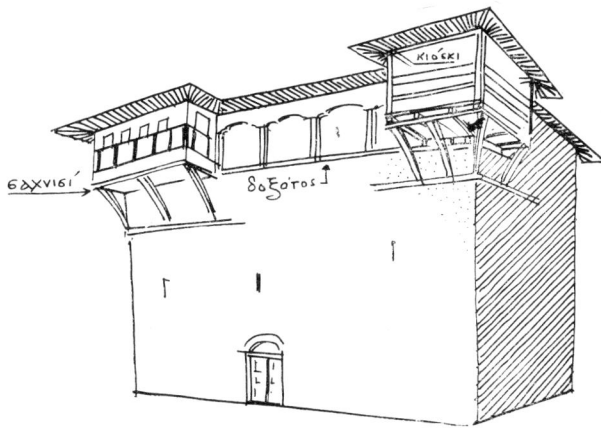

Sketch of a house with architectural projections.

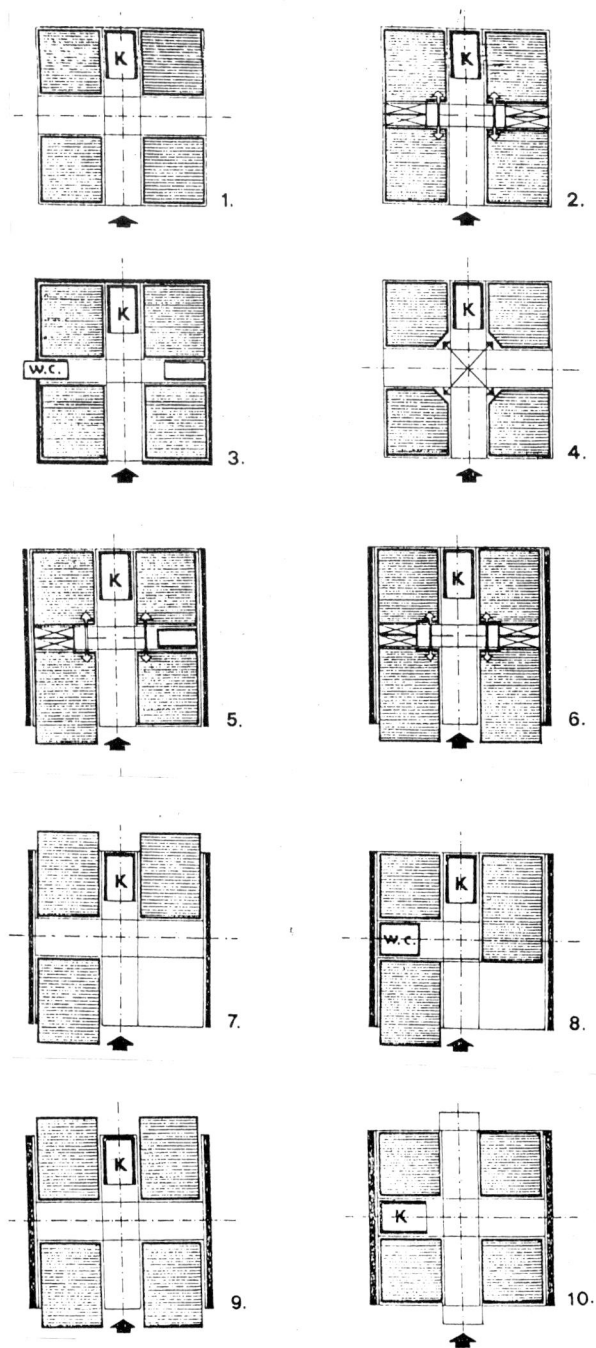

Theoretical typological analysis of the symmetrical type of residence.

vers -, Isvoro, Leskoviki, Plavali, Blethiki, Cantzaco, Molista and the villages of Arta and Paramythia. The villages of West Macedonia and, particularly, the mountain villages of Florina: Negovani (Flabouro), Belcameni (Drosopege), Pentalofo, Eptachori, the mountain villages of Anaselitsa, Microcastro and the villages of Kozani[153].

In the Balkans and, also, in Asia Minor, houses with certain common morphological features were built, but they were clearly different and each settlement acquired an individual, local physiognomy. Also, the houses of the mountain settlements differed from the houses of the plains. These differentiations were due to the ways of construction and the materials which ought to be easily available and suitable for the construction. The masons themselves, of the villages of West Macedonia and Pindos, state clearly that wherever they went, they built the houses according to the local custom.

A guild of builders had artisans of every specialty; miners, quarry workers, carters to carry the stones from the quarry to the site of construction, carpenters, wood-carvers, stone-dressers and painters-decorators. These artisans had acquired experience from their work in the public works of the ottoman government, road construction, bridges, hydraulic works, caravansarai construction, mosques and also from their work in church and monastery construction[154].

The work of these artisans in the public works department must not be underestimated. During the first period, immediately after the deterioration of the Byzantine empire, and even before the fall of Constantinople, Byzantine influence was evident in the morphology of the governmental buildings of Prussa. Later, through the years, naturally, an ottoman style began to form and it was also natural that the builders who were always from the same mountain regions,

«Navel» in the ceiling of the NE room (oda) of the 1st floor of the mansion of Kyra Sanouko in Siatista.

Ceiling panel in Poulkides' mansion in Siatista.

were influenced by their experiences in the Ottoman public works and carried elements of their morphology - particularly decoration - back to their places.

These are the elements we mentioned previously; the wooden ceilings of the rooms of the mansions in Siatista and Castoria, whose arabesques sometimes

Bevelled corner of a house with isodomic wall construction in Veria (photo: 1960).

Bevelled corner of a house with pseudo-isodomic wall construction in Koukouli of Zagori, Epirus (photo: 1960).

Timber bearing framework of a traditional residence in Philippoupolis (photo: 1965).

Details of «hayat» in the monastery of Rozinou (near Melenico).

show a distint oriental technique. The houses of the mountain settlements differ from the houses of the plains. The differences are due to the different ways of construction, and the different materials which must serve different needs.

In wooded regions where structural timber was abundant, sometimes the whole building was of wood, as in Aimos (Balkan). In regions where stone is the only existing building material, the houses were built of stone (in many villages of Epirus, Gortynia, Cynuria, and Mani). An important intermediate type is the mixed; the ground floor and the frame of the building are of stone and the upper floor is constructed of wood (West and Central Macedonia, Rodope, Pelion and elsewhere)[155].

Regarding the technique, the walls are constructed of stone and mud and, at intervals, are braced with cross timbers (hatil). The walls of the upper floor are constructed of lighter material; a wooden latticework braced with slats and coated with mortar.

Bearing structural members are extended through the upper floor and support the roof which is covered with tiles of the Byzantine type, or slate, depending on the location and habits.

In mountain villages the entire house is built of stone. The tower-like form of the houses is evident everywhere. The sitting room of the upper floor is in the center. The small windows let some light into the rooms. The interior staircase goes from the ground floor to the sitting room.

We are going to look more closely at the types of construction of a small Macedonian district, Chalki-

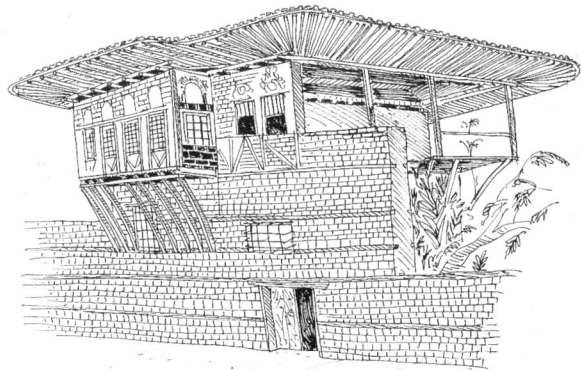

Sior Manolakis' mansion in Veria (N. Moutsopoulos).

Old house of Veria (composite construction: stone, brick, slatting) (1960).

diki. The materials of construction, as is the case in traditional architecture, were those provided by nature; local stone carried from near-by quarries - which

Timber houses in Djeravna, Bulgaria (1975).

*«Hayat» of a house in Djeravna (Aimos), Bulgar
ia (1975).*

are abandoned today -, timber from the forests, especially the famous chestnut of Athos and finally, clay for the hand-made bricks, which were mixed with straw and constituted the main building material for walls; the walls, braced at vertical intervals with twin wooden «belts», especially under the sills and lintels of openings, gave a perfect earthquake-proof construction. Special clay was used for the construction of ornamental bricks and tiles, when the roof was not covered with local slate.

The walls were sometimes built of stone reinforced at vertical intervals with wooden braces (belts), the «straps» of the byzantine builders[156], and sometimes of both stone and timber, or they consisted of a wooden frame filled with a lighter material, the so-called «çatma».

The inside partitions were built of even lighter materials; wooden stats of a trapezoidal cross-section, with their short dimension nailed to the wooden framework. The two surfaces were covered with red clay reinforced with fine straw, or plaster reinforced with goat hair anf flattened with the trowel. These walls were known as slat walls. The same materials were used, later, to cover the beams of the roof and form the ceilings of the rooms, replacing the old traditional elaborately constructed wood panel ceiling.

The construction of the Macedonian mansions was composite; stone and wood. Depending on the region, sometimes more stone was used, sometimes more timber. In certain cases the construction was entirely of stone or of timber. In a final analysis, in the

Timber house in triavna, Bulgaria.

Macedonian architecture, timber was the main building material; the bearing structural members were timber posts; the wall frame consisted of vertical timbers and horizontal and diagonal cross-braces and struts. The spaces were filled with hand-made bricks, small tiles and clay. The interior partitions were even lighter; they were constructed of wooden slats[157].

In elaborate constructions, the ground floor and the mezzanine were built of stone with timber cross-braces at intervals. Some parts of the walls rose through the first floor for constructional reasons. This difference in the thickness of the walls is very pleasing to the eyes of an observant visitor. It is the same with certain parts of the partition walls, where they constructed built-in wardrobes or closets, almost like those of today. This tendency of the builders to «clear» the spaces and leave the surfaces free, creates an interior architectural quality, which, much later,

The interior «hayats» of Sior Manolakis' mansion in Veria (photo: 1962).

Houses with timber architectural projections in Molyvos, Lesvos (photo: 1960).

Garden wall constructions with rubble, in Monodendri, Epirus.

Garden wall construction with rubble, in Vitsa, Epirus.

the western architecture, also influenced by the spirit of the Japanese architecture, understood and pursued.

In Castoria, the construction of the foundations

was easy because the entire Castle is built on rock. The same rock gave the materials for the walls. Many times the builders brought stone from the near-by mountains. For the quoins they always brought hard and durable stone from Tsiuca. The outside walls were bonded with clay and their thickness sometimes exceeded 1 meter. These walls were reinforced at vertical intervals of 1.50 m. with timber braces, oak on the outside and chestnut on the inside. The two zones of bracing were interconnected by means of bonding ties so that the entire construction became a continuous bearing frame transmitting the stresses smoothly to the rock. The rough stones were cut by the scabblers and the walls were built by the master mason himself. The partitions and outside walls of the last floor were built of small bricks and clay, covered with plaster mixed with straw. Plaster was also used to cover the interior surfaces of the walls and to fill the joints of the outside walls. Sometimes, lack of sand forced the masons to use local yellow clay[158].

The timber was carted from the forests of Gramos,[159] and, as Yannis Aivazis, a local old-timer remembers, «it was ironwood, very durable, oak, poplar, pine; they carried them to the Aliacmon river and from there, by boat, to the lake. I saw some large holes in the beams of the floors; they were not those holes that remain when you take out the knots, they were punched by the workers to pass the ropes with which they pulled those big logs and carried them from the places where they cut them, far beyond the lake, where there was the great forest called «Petra». These beams were 0.15 x 0.15 m in cross section and were spaced at intervals of 1.50 m and their ends

Ph. Koutsogolis' family house in Syrraco.

Krystallis' house in Syrraco (photo: 1978).

*Cobblestone street in Kato Mahalas of Vitsa, Epirus
(photo: 1965).*

rested on the stone wall. On them other cross-beams were placed at wider intervals, and they had a cross-section of 0.12 x 0.15 m. On these, additional beams were placed cross-wise, or parallel to the main beams, and the planks of the flooring, whose dimensions were 2.00 x 0.02 x 0.27 m, and were of soft, white timber, were nailed on them. In certain spaces and very rarely, they put a layer of a special coloring material over the flooring.

To construct the roof they first laid the wall plates, thick timbers up to 8.00 m long, and on them they nailed the pole plates and the purlins. The purlins were of pine with the suitable grain. In certain cases, instead

Front view of a mansion in Arnea (Liarigova) (N. Moutsopoulos).

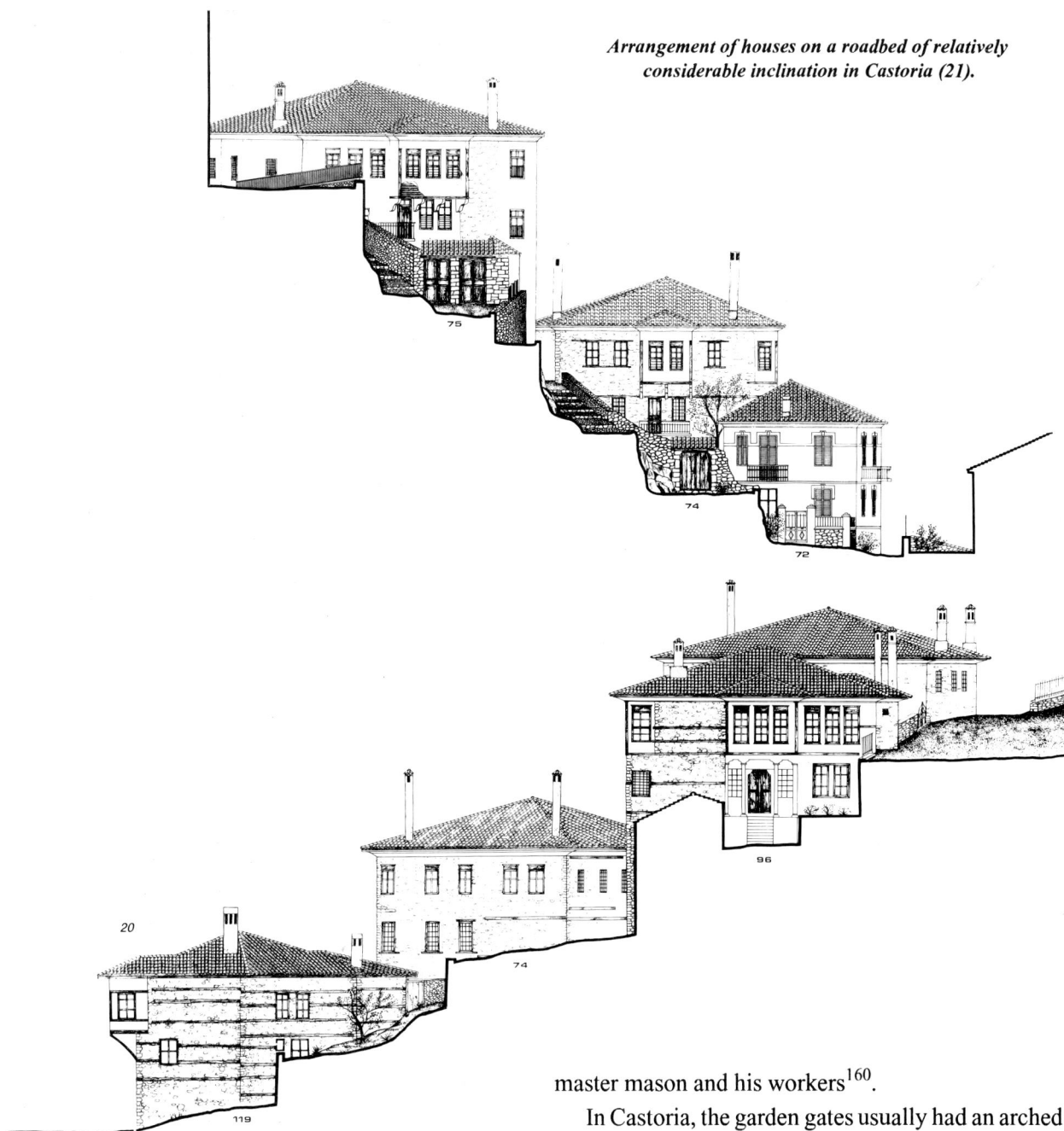

Arrangement of houses on a roadbed of relatively considerable inclination in Castoria (21).

of purlins they used thick cane. The roof rested on the outer walls and the posts, which were tied together with braces. The principal rafters were nailed to the king post and supported the roof. The rafters completed the frame of the roof and created the characteristic protrusions all around the building. According to the custom, before the tiles were placed, the landlord and his neighbors brought some gifts to the master mason and his workers[160].

In Castoria, the garden gates usually had an arched lintel, and they were made of hard and durable wood studded with big, flat-headed rivets and they were secured with bots, latches and bars. The big, iron ring of the door is called «tsucalidi» in Castoria[161]. On either side of the gate, there were low parapets where, in those times, the old women of the neighborhood sat and exchanged the news of the neighborhood and talked the evening away until the oil lamps were lit and it was time to go inside.

As soon as we crossed the gate, we were in the large courtyard which was paved with flags and surrounded by a high stone wall. Always, at least a part

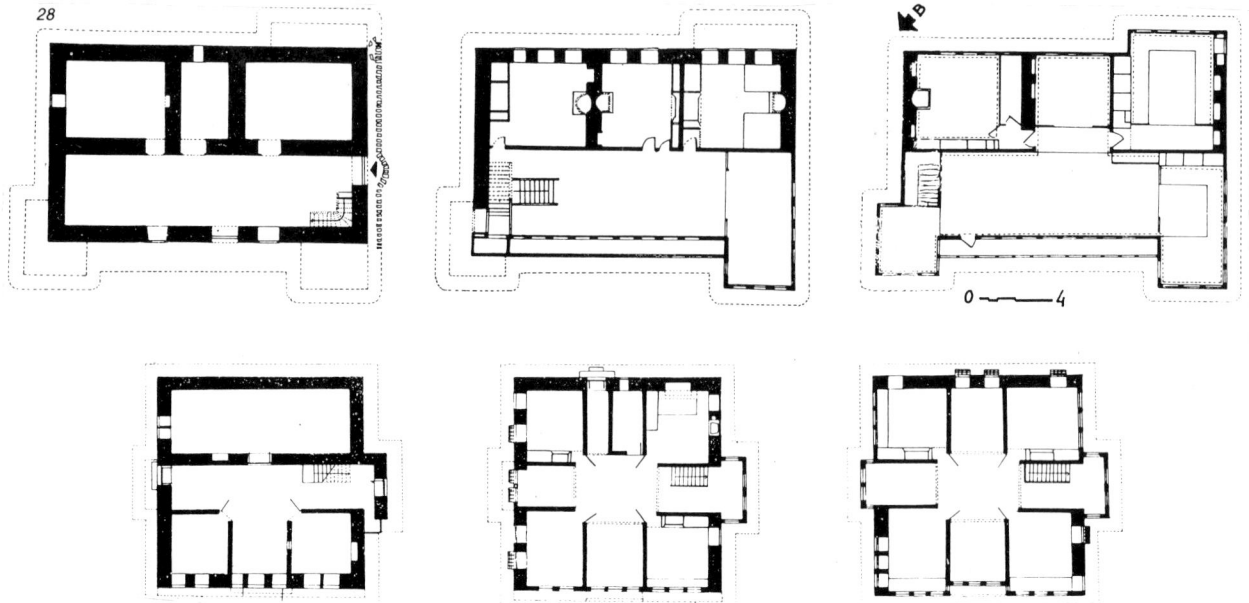

Schematic typology of the Castorian house. From left to right: Ground floor, 1ˢᵗ floor and upper floor plans.
Top: Tsiatsapas' mansion. Bottom: Metousis' mansion (21).

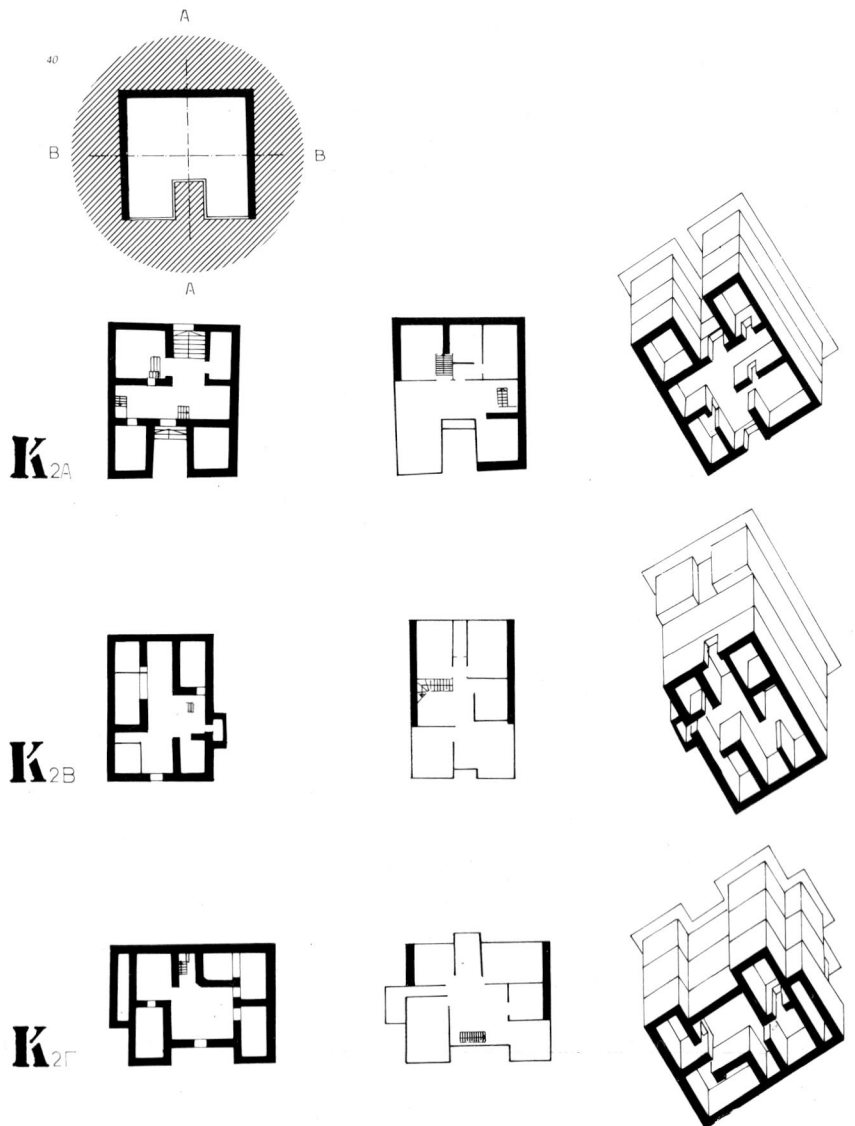

K₂ₐ

K₂ᵦ

Typology of the Castorian house
(Type K2) (21).

K₂ᵧ

of the yard was paved with flags with white-washed joints. Across the yard was the porch and, on each side, the auxiliary places, the kitchen, the cellars, the toilet and the place where they kneaded the dough. When the house faced the lake, the courtyard reached as far as the shore. Sometimes, in a corner of the courtyard, they placed a rectangular block of stone (about 0.20 x 0.20 x 0.45 m) with a hemispherical depression in the middle. This was the place where they ground coffee beans. In Castoria, certain natural cracks in the ground were used to form sewers, and the toilet was sometimes constructed over such a crack to facilitate drainage. The ground floor kitchen had a fireplace that could take two big kettles; its hearth was constructed at a height of about 1.20 m from the floor for convenience. The upstairs kitchen whose fireplace had a big trivet for the kettle, sometimes protruded over part of the yard and formed an inner portico with stone or timber columns (the Nandjis mansion is an example). The basements of the mansions were hewn out of the living rock and were covered with a thick layer of red clay. The ground floors did not have windows; thay had narrow ventilation slits (e.g. the Tsiatapas mansion).

As we have mentioned previously, the rectangular horizontal section of the building was divided into two by a wall parallel to the long dimension. One of the spaces was subdivided into smaller, auxiliary rooms. In one of them there was a big, wooden container which could take about 10 to 15 thousand okas, where they put the grapes. The other, smaller rooms were storerooms. The other big space was not subdivided. The front door opened into an inner court, paved with flags, where a staircase led to the upper floor and another to the basement. Very often there was a mezzanine between the ground floor and the upper floor, where there were additional auxiliary rooms and the workshop, if the owner was a fur-dresser. In older times the opening at the top of the flight of stairs, over the landing of the mezzanine, was closed with a trapdoor which was secured by means of a bar.

The landing of the staircase at the upper floor was a continuation of the sitting room and on either side were located the winter rooms of the family. The second floor often protruded so that the rooms could be square or orthogonal and become more spacious, forming the various oriels and balconies which were supported by elaborately carved wooden corbels. This

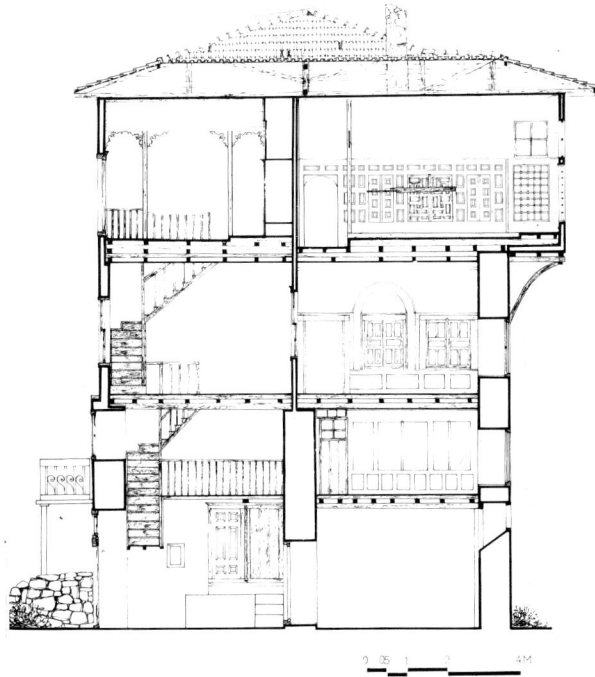

Vertical cross-section of Tsiatsapas' mansion, in Castoria.

floor was the «summer residence» and, also, the place where the family received their guests and gave parties in the large salon. But if the owner were a fur-dresser, the large room was used as a place of work. The large salon was called «doxatos» (toxarion = arch)[162], and took the name from the interior wooden arcade along the side parallel to the street. Sometimes there was a «doxatos» on the lower floor[163] and, according to Orlandos, «it corresponds to the ancient Greek peristyle or to the Roman atrium; the colonnade itself can be regarded as a descedant of the peristyle». The columns of the «doxatos» usually had a square cross-section and a horizontal capital with concavoconvex brackets of the type we see in most of the post-byzantine basilicas with wooden roof. Sometimes at either end of the «doxatos» there were daises constructed at a height of 0.15 - 0.20 m above the floor with small wooden pillars with curved capitals and low, wooden latticework forming their faces, which were called «kioskia» or «krevates»[164].

However, apart from the rich mansions of Macedonia, which evidence the craftsmanship and personal taste of the old builders, there is a large

Development of the decoration of the vertical surfaces of the third floor of Tsiatsiapas' mansion.

number of popular, middle-class houses with a very clear and greater typification. These houses show, more clearly, the uniform morphological features that prevailed in the entire Balkan peninsula and Asia Minor, so that it is often difficult to distinguish a house of Eski Sehir from a house in Edessa, or a house in Kiutachia from a house in Florina. In this architectural type we must look for the older, medieval origins. The intercomparison of the basic nuclei of this architecture, the room, the sitting rooms and the balconies, gives us a variety of typology whose boundaries start in the Balkans and are lost in the Middle East and North Africa.

The oriental influence is due to the work these masons did in the capital of the ottoman empire, Istanbul, the former Constantinople. Furthermore, Turkey, in addition to her own architectural tradition, accepted any kind of local influences and did not prevent other ethnic groups from developing their own architectural tendencies. But Turkey accepted influences from the West, too. The influence of the Western baroque was so widespread in the 18th century that the style became the dominant motif, the basic warp. The numerous other local styles developed from this nucleous and achieved remarkable results which, however, create many problems for anyone who may want to discover the percentage and origin of the local architectural constituents[165].

The mansions of Phanari have preserved another feature which constitutes a transition from the rooms we have studied to the byzantine triclinia; an example is the mansion at 302 Phanari str., whose door bears an inscription, published, in French, by general L. De Beylie[166]: «May Christ protect the inhabitants of this house. In the month of August, 1676 A.D.» C. Joja[167] writes that: There is no other structure similar to the

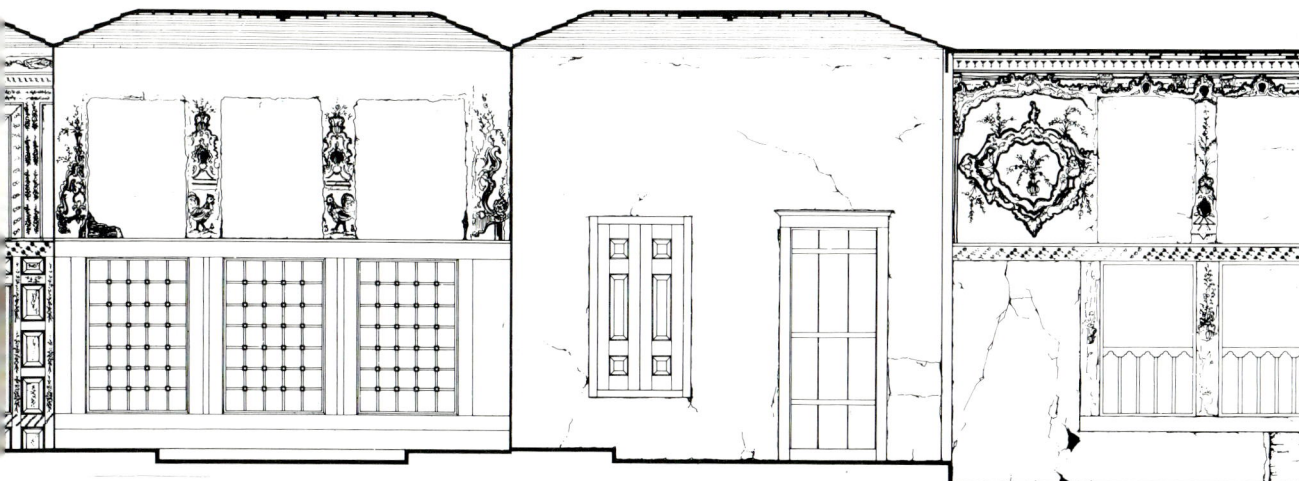

The same in the bottom drawing.

Two-storied house in the sinaitic «metochi» in Phanari, Constantinople (photo: Prof. Haluk Sezgin, 1980).

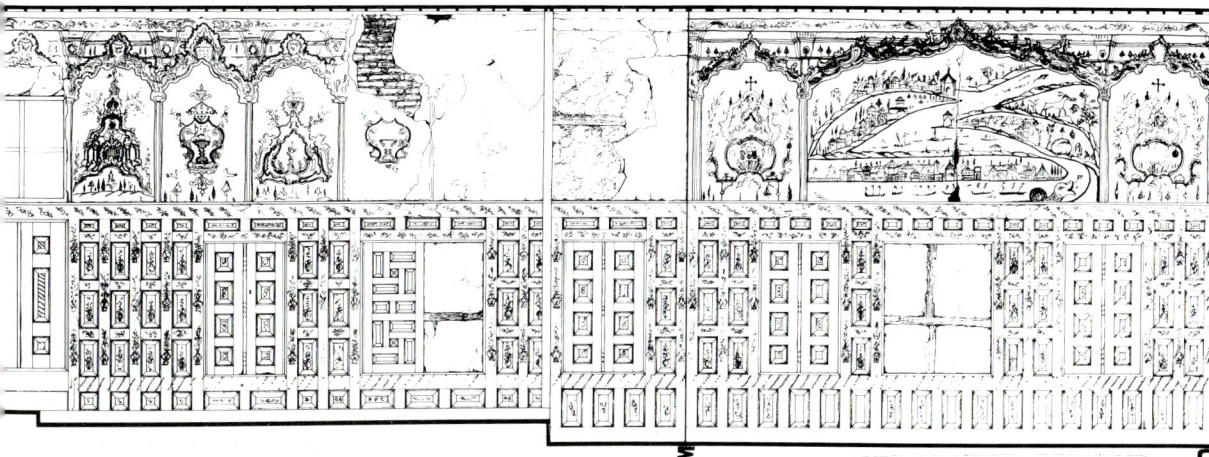

stone buildings of Constantinople, either in Asia Minor or in the Balkans, or even in the old ottoman capital, Brussa: The houses of Phanari have no ottoman architectural feature. However, their morphology is not western, because nowhere in the West has such an example been preserved. The Byzantines called the rooms «heliacos» - sundecks - exactly as they call the flat roofs and verandahs in Thrace, Mesenia and Skyros, today[168]. They also called «heliacos» the «doxatos» and any room that protruded outwards. Leon, in his 113th Novel gives the exact definition of the term «heliacos»[169]. These are, so to speak, open air porches used as places for seeing, which have been invented for the sole purpose to afford the enjoyment of fresh air; they took their name from the sun, that is why they are called «heliacos». Phaedon Coucoules writes that «the Byzantine heliacos had neither a specific shape nor a specific

Details of the windows of a mansion in the sinaitic «metochi» in Phanari, Constantinople (photo: Prof. Haluk Sezgin, 1980).

location». The «heliacos» could be constructed on the ground floor level (ground floor «heliacos») or on the upper floor (upper floor «heliacos»)[170]. The plan of the «heliacos» was oblong like the plan of the «doxatos» of Castoria. The «heliacos» could be located on one side of the building or on two or three. Bessarion, in his «Laudation of Trapezus»[171], writes: «There were balconies all around the buildings, turning every which way, open to the winds». Eustathios[172], in his «Folklore», writes: «The house of Priamos was described as beautiful, with its halls of hewn stone, certainly, with its stone arcades open to the hot sun, as the name of the hall means, which in the vernacular, was corrupted to "heliacos"».

In Constantinople, certain buildings are called «heliaca», as, for instance, the «round, heliacos of Magnavra» which was built in the time of Mauricius,[173] «the heliacos of Pharos»[174] «the heliacos of Boucoleon»[175] and the «heliacos of Nea»[176].

The phrase of Neophytos Egleistos[177] «the butler's pantry and the five-arch space over it» definitely means a covered balcony with five arched openings, more elaborately built than the ground floor where the butler's pantry was located, or built of lighter materials, even of wood with timber arches. However, apart from the Byzantine «room-heliacos»[178] and the open air «heliacos» or «doxatos», there were the «closed heliaca», the «closed verandahs»[179], in other words the «hayats». Phaedon Coucoules[180] writes: «The Byzantines called heliacos what the ancient Greeks called balcony, that is, a closed orthogonal part protruding at right angles to the main wall facing the street and usually built of timber, and was called «tavlato[181] or tavloma or sanidoton (structure made of planks)». This type of heliacos was also called solarium, or verandah or balcony. Niketas Choniatis writes that during the reign of Manuel Comnenos (Bonn 205): .....«these balustrades, then, on either side of the street through which the triumph was to pass, attached to two-storey or three-storey buildings, caused the admiration of anyone who saw them, and their effect on those who watched was not small...». Furthermore, those «sahnisins» remind us of a detail that has been recorded by Constantine Porphyrogenitus (*De ceremoniis* v. I, Bonne II, 18 p. 600): «and the fenestrato hanging in the middle of the hall where the kings sit on their throne ....» (see *Anthol. Graeca* XVI 380).

There are certain interesting miniatures in the well-known manuscript of the Chronicles of Skylitsis, of Madrid, dating back to the end of the 13th century[182]. Some of them picture «heliaca» of the palace. André Grabar managed to discern and isolate the various artists who decorated the manuscript and, even, locate the local schools. Another manuscript of the 14th century which, as we know, was illustrated in Mystras, is interesting because of the strong, gothic morphological features of the miniatures fol 19r and fol 29v picturing balustrades[183]. Manuel Tzycandyles copied this manuscript of Iob and the copy dates back to 1362[184].

Therefore, the «sahnisi», this peculiar morphological and functional element has been located in Byzantine constructions. Therefore, this morphological feature that prevailed in the Balkan post-byzantine architecture, in other words the architecture of the period of the Turkish rule, cannot be regarded as a feature of ottoman influence. On the contrary, it must be understood that the muslim populations of Asia Minor inherited it from the Byzantine tradition. But about the Byzantine house our information is scanty[185].

As we said, the architectural protrusions, «heliaca» and «sahnisins» (oriels) constitute an important morphological element of architecture. The word «sahnisin» is Persian and means «the throne of the king»; the name is given to any part of the building that protrude outwards, and became the prevalent architectural element of the ottoman architecture after the 16th century, although it was known during the Byzantine period[186].

The forms and construction of the «sahnisins» must have originated in a very old wooden model which, later, took the form of the «sahnisin» of the houses of Phanari. These constructions were regarded, earlier, as pure byzantine and many researchers believed that they dated from the 10th century. However, they must have been constructed much later, probably after the middle of the 15th century, in other words, after the fall of Constantinople because most of the mansions touch the coastal walls in places that they render the defensive system useless. These reasons and their structural features evidence that they date from the 17th or 18th century when Phanari had turned into a well-known commercial center[187]. The protrusion of a closed space beyond the building line was introduced as a necessity. The lack of light and sunshine in the strongly fortified cities of the middle ages, influenced the morphology of their residences and led to the solutions we mentioned previously. And, anyway, to these elements, light and sun, owe their names the various morphological features we have studied so far (heliaca, solaria). The forms of the architectural protrusions are also associated with the small, sometimes very small area of the plots in cities surrounded by walls. These architectural protrusions increased the living space especially of the upper floors which constituted the main residence (in the form of the various triclinia).

However, these protrusions served a social function too. They were the «eyes» of the people; in periods when the circulation in the streets was not easy, the women, half-hidden behind the balustrades, could watch what happened outside, in the street. The «sahnisins» were also useful because the inhabitants of the house could rest there and they were, probably, a place of honor, as their name implies (sahnisin = the throne of the sah)[188].

This architectural solution was applied widely to the Byzantine residence. In the «Vasilica», there is an illuminating paragraph about solaria: «From now on, the solaria will be of the Romaic (Greek) type; the distance between one another should be ten feet; if these conditions are not observed, a solarium should not be constructed; and their height from the ground should be at least fifteen feet, and they should not be supported by either pillars, whether stone or timber, or walls so as not to obstruct the airing of the street and uglify the public thoroughfare; and staircases leading up to the solaria should not be constructed under them, in the street». The byzantine legislature prescribes a minimum distance of 10 feet (approx. 3 meters)[189] between any two architectural projections. However, it is also known that, in spite of all the laws and penalties[190]q the mansions of many nobles had such long protrusions» that they formed a tunnel over the street»[191].

The byzantine legislature defined the manner of construction in the building blocks of the byzantine cities and where architectural projections were not permitted, mainly for both social and airing reasons. The Justinianian codex[192] prescribed a height of at least fifteen feet from the ground for any architectural

A residence in the district of «Psamathia» (Kum-Kapu),
Constantinople (17th c.) (g. De Beylier).

projection which should be constructed without supports which would make the street narrower[193]. Staircases under the projections were forbidden because they would block the traffic, but also to avoid the danger of fire[194]. If the buildings across the street were public offices, then the distance from the architectural projection to the nearest point of the opposite building should be at least fifteen feet. If the street was very narrow, that is, if its width was less than ten feet, then the balconies should alternate[195] or they should not be built[196]. In the following sketches we tried to express architecturally the spirit of the byzantine legislator. The result is important because it revealed a similarity to the corresponding solutions of such architectural problems of the years of the Turkish rule, because it is known that the byzantine regulations governing house construction were still in force during these years (16th - 19th c.) (Armenopoulos, and «Law» by Theophilos of Ioannina). Thanks to this legislature (and its prohibitions) the byzantine and post-byzantine architecture reached the peak that is still admired both in the Balkans and Asia Minor. The following sketches give a clearer picture of the limitations and prohibitions of the legislature which is, essentially, a «building code»[197]. In the sketches always a>10 (byz. feet) b> 10-12 (byz. feet) and γ>15 (see memorandum)[198].

We know that the traditional residence of the nobles and despots of the byzantine period was a tower-like building with, later, protrusions in the top floor. This type has been preserved in isolated structures which were the headquarters of the garrisons that protected remote villages (such as the tower of Galatista) and those that protected the share-croppers of the Athonite monasteries. Other towers protected cols, hills (observatories) or mooring docks of monasteries. The residences of the Byzantine landowners and, later, of the Turkish feudal lords, had the same austere, tower-like form with the main entrance located at the level of the upper floor (for instance, the tower of Vasilica, near Thessaloniki). L. Heuzey's wonderful sketch which has been preserved, gives us an example; it pictures the three towers of the village of Damasi, near Tournavo, with his own explanation that this form, without any protrusions, is the oldest[199].

This form of the tower-like residence, in which the cellars were located in the ground floor space and the entrance at the level of the first floor, influenced the byzantine dwellings both in the cities and in the country, as we see in the preserved mansions of Mystras which, at one stage of their development, have a turret in one corner of the residence, which rises to a height of two additional storeys[200]. The facade of this type of residence had the shape of an L and structures like this were built till the end of the 18th century in many regions of the country, from Mani and Mesenia[201] to Thrace and the Aegean islands. In many regions where there was unsafety, they added this fortified turret for protection, as, for instance, in Albania, where it was known as the «kula» or «kulia»[202], and in Mani.

The form of the isolated, fortified tower, comprised the nucleus of the later development of the urban mansions, when there was more order and safety, and they became parts of larger settlements, and their castle-like appearance began to change; the top floor was, now, of lighter construction and architectural protrusions began to appear. This transition is well-known because of information given by

several tourists and especially the table published by Ed. Dodwell in 1819, in Portaria of Pelion[203]. about such residences of Greece, but also of Yugoslavia, Bulgaria, Albania and Rumania[204]. About Ambelakia of Thessaly, Leonardos says that «the city is adorned with lofty residences, towers and stately buildings».

The old bishopric of Ambelakia, according to reliable information and, especially, according to an inscription dating back to 1767, is the oldest of the buildings of this type in Ambelakia. This building has been the residence of the bishop of Platamona and Lycostomio since 1767, but its form has undergone many changes. The ground floor and the mezzanine have preserved most of the old morphological features and, particullarly, the main entrance and the right-hand window with the semicircular arches which are similar to their contemporaries (for instance the Alexios mansion, which has an inscription dating 1760) in Siatista[205]. Later, a «sahnisin» was added to the upper floor, whose brackets were covered with planks and mortar. According to an inscription «the repairs were completed during the time of bishop Ambrosios, 1799». The characteristic feature of the tower-like buildings of this period is that, instead of the very small windows and the defensive narrow openings, the builders started to arrange the rooms of the upper floors along the faces of the residence, with windows looking out on the street.

From the middle of the 18th century onwards, the new mansions that were built (but also those which were repaired, as, for instance, the bishopric mansion) began to have large balconies and «sahnisins» in the top floor. However, the ground floor and the mezzanine still preserved their castle-like appearance. The Swedish traveller J.J. Björnstähl, who had been a guest of the bishop in 1779, gives some information about the buildings[206].

According to the aforementioned descriptions, «the new, Greek type» of Leonardos is this new architectural tendency to replace the tower-like construction with the very small windows - for instance, such a residence which has been preserved in Tempi, even has the medieval scalding water spouts - with the new type, which we will now study, with the tower-like ground floor and the mezzanine, and the «sahnisins» and large openings in the top floor.

However, when Leonardos said that the mansions which he admired were built «according to the beautiful, new Greek and European models» he meant that either the whole construction was a mixture of Greek and European architecture, or in certain points the architecture was Greek and in others European.

Leonardos, an erudite, widely-travelled man, could distinguish the european neoclassic and baroque architectural morphology from the purely Greek morphology, in the mansions of Ambelakia. Furthermore, A. Anacatomenos says that «most of the buildings have three floors whose walls still preserve their red color and the embellishments that won the admiration of the neighboring Turks»[207]. This information leads to the conclusion that the mansions of Ambelakia were built according to the byzantine model, replacing the semicircular arches with other decorations, as, for instance, in the G. Schwarz mansion. And Leonardos' phrase «European models» refers rather to the interior decoration - which, as we will see, had been influenced by European models - than to the overall morphology of the mansions. In our opinion, the aforementioned remarks and information are important because they shed light on the controversial question of the «european influences» on the Greek architecture of the 18th and 19th c. and, especially, on interior decoration.

The apothegmatic view of Yannis Cordatos («*Ambelakia*» p. 117), a usually careful writer, that «the mansions of Ambelakia were big and built according to plans of models brought from Germany, modified to suit local needs» is not based on careful analysis. And his remark, in a footnote on the same page, in which he refutes professor G. Megas who correctly maintains that «the architectural style has not been imported from Europe, but it constitutes the splendid peak of the Thessalian popular architecture»[208], is even more erroneous. Cordatos refutes Megas' opinion, but he never justifies his view, that «these mansions were residences of rich merchants who had travelled abroad, and brought back the plans and the masons built their houses according to their instructions».

That many of the mansions of Ambelakia and, also, of other towns in Thessaly, Macedonia and Epirus, were residences of rich merchants who had lived abroad is an indisputable fact; furthermore, Leonardos (p.153) writes: «Because many of the nobles and rich merchants had lived in Germany for a long time, they felt pangs of nostalgia for their

adopted country and her customs and building style, so they did not hesitate to spend a lot of money on the betterment of the town generally and on building houses with some of the beautiful architectural features of Europe»[209].

However, Cordatos claims that the merchants of Ambelakia «brought the plans from Europe». This is impossible, because no European architect would undertake to make the plans for a house without knowing either the morphology of the ground with the steep slopes or the locally available materials of construction and the capabilities of the local masons. Even if an architect prepared the plans similar to those they made in Europe, the buildings would have been constructed of stone and their morphology would have been either baroque or neoclassic, which was never applied in Ambelakia. Finally, even if the merchants of Ambelakia had brought with them a complete design and plans for their houses (complete because there would have been no supervision of the work) no mason of that time would have been able to read and understand the plans and apply the architectural drawings to practice.

The mansions of Ambelakia, both typologically and morphologically, belong to the architecture of Siatista; and this is another proof that the plans for the buildings were not brought from Europe. Contrary to Cordatos' opinion, El.- P. Georgiou (*History and guilds of Ambelakia*, p. 58) writes: «those nobles, lovers of the beautiful, gave those simple artisans the opportunity and the means to practice their craftsmanship and express their innate tastefulness»[210].

It is evident that the mansions of Ambelakia, as well as their contemporaries elsewhere in Greece, constitute a development of the local popular architectural tradition with many foreign influences on the morphology, especially on the interior decoration. But the foreign influences have no relationship to the architectural plan and the basic form of the building. The personal preferences and taste of the rich owners may have affected the interior decoration and some small details, and, certainly, they, themselves, or the groups of masons had patterns of decorative motifs, copperplates or pictures of European mansions, or patterns of skylights, transoms, etc. However, these models did not affect the architectural morphology; on the contrary, these elements were copied, as wholes, inside decorative frames, on the friezes and the walls of the rooms of the buildings (as in the examples of mansions we mention). These patterns were used almost without any change, because they did not have either the knowledge or the ability to reduce the picture of a facade, or a perspective of a European mansion to practice. Even today, this can be done only by an architect.

*

It must be noted that this architecture has local variations according to the area, especially on the Greek islands. The architecture of continental Greece is more uniform and has interesting similarities to the architecture of areas farther north (north Epirus, Achrida, Monastiri, Velessa, Crousovo, Stromnitsa, Argyrocastro) and to the architecture of North Rodopi (Melenico, Smolian, Philippoupolis), of Aimos (Djeravna) and to the architecture of the coastal East Romelia (Mesimvria, Sozopolis), and, of course, to the architecture of East Thrace and Asia Minor (Kiutachia, Prussa, Sinassos), the most representative examples being in Kula, Amaseia and Pontus[211]. Now, we are going to examine the morphology of the residence, as it developed from the end of the 18th c. through the 19th in the areas that interest us.

Spyridon Lambros writes: «Moschopolis was adorned with many beautiful mansions built according to the European style, because the inhabitants of Moschopolis frequently travelled to Hungary and Austria and managed to expand their activity as far as the heart of Northern Europe»[212]. Ioakim Martianos writes on the subject of architecture: «The buildings are of the veneto-macedonian style rather than turkish; stately, archaic and imposing, have succumbed to the fate and to the relentless time and do not exist any more; they collapsed, one after the other, and were ruined. And the ruins were cleared to make room for cultivation and the entire region became fields and pastures dotted by the ruins of the former stately residences, and even the streets have disapeared...»[213].

Daniel Philippides and Gregorios Constantas in their «Modern Geography» write that «Ambelakia had about 550 houses, and some of them are very beautiful, because they were built in the European way»[214]. Felix Beaujour says that Ambelakia look rather like a town of Holland than a turkish village[215].

Also, I. Leonardos gives an interesting description: «The town is small, numbering about 500 houses; but this small town, famous all over Europe, is the second capital of the region of Kissavos, adorned with lofty, tower-like residences and splendid public buildings which climb up the slope of the mountain as if they are built one on top of the other. Most of them are of the Greco-European style and many have three floors. And among them, a few stand out and look like palaces. Their style and appearance draw the attention of the foreign visitors and add to the overall beauty of the town. Therefore the opinion of certain travellers that Ambelakia look rather like a Dutch town than a turkish village is justified»[216].

The «Demetrians» (Daniel Philippides and Gregorios Constantas) whose account refers this picture of the town to an earlier period than the year 1791 when their «Modern Geography» was published, say that «some of the 550 houses are beautiful» because the most beautiful mansions were built later.

An example of older architectural style is the bishopric mansion which was built during the time of bishop Dionysios, in 1767 and was modified later during the time of bishop Ambrosios. The two writers justify their admiration by adding, «because they were built in the European way». Leonardos makes the same remark: «of the Greco-European style». Since all these writers make the same remark, it is obvious that these mansions were not similar to the usual turkish or Greek mansions of the period because, then, they would have written only that «they are big, beautiful, rich». In the first case, we see that the writers considered these mansions beautiful because they were built «the European way», although this phrase could mean that they were built either according to European methods of construction or according to the European morphology. However, as we will see, the construction faithfully follows the traditional post-byzantine technique, with the castle-like ground floor and, sometimes, of the mezzanine, whose walls are reinforced with timber cross-ties at vertical intervals and timber structural bearing members in the upper floors whose outside walls are built with a wooden frame and small bricks and tiles. The partitions in the upper floors are made either of light slats nailed to the bearing members, with narrow spaces between them to provide a better bond for the plaster, or of wooden panelling. This was the general type of construction at least from the beginning of the 18th century onwards in all the regions of Turkey (the Balkans, Asia Minor, Syria, Egypt, Mesopotamia, North Africa)[217]. Consequently, the characterization refers to the architectural morphology and not to the construction. We will now see whether they mean the exterior formation of the construction and the architectural forms ("heliaca", "sahnisins", cornices, etc.) or the interior decoration[218].

Leonardos attributes the beauty of the mansions of the town to the fact that they were built «according to the Neo-Greek and European style». By «Neo-Greek», he obviously means a type of construction different from the old, traditional types and, naturally, from the turkish architectural morphology of the mosques and seraglios, or he would not have said «neo-Greek», but what he says, when he describes the ruins of the rooms of the seraglio of Veli Pasha (Ali Pasha's son): «beautifully adorned in the best asiatic style.»

Leonardos also mentions the «european style», so he probably knew from personal experience or pictures the rich houses of Europe and, of course, he could distinguish neo-classic or baroque architecture which had influenced the architecture of free Greece, from the traditional style of the Greek popular residence of which many examples were preserved.

However, we can easily define the form of the old Greek residence with which he makes the comparison, by studying the available examples in Ambelakia and other neighboring districts of Thessaly and Macedonia. It is evident, that the comparison will be between middle-class residences and upper-class mansions and not between humble, agrarian dwellings which had no particular style, but they only served a practical need, and were built according to the form of the wide-front dwelling of Olynthos, with some changes because of the addition of various, new auxiliary rooms. Nor shall we make a comparison with the humble agrarian dwellings of Thessaly[219] which were built of simple brick and which, as B. Zafranas says, were called «izbas».

The square, multi-story isolated towers, at first, had no architectural protrusions in the upper floors and the entrance was located at a certain height from the ground and it was accessible by means of a movable timber staircase, and later, by means of a stone permanent staircase.

Gradually, as living conditions improved and other towers were built near-by to form a settlement, and the danger of robber raids and the feuds marked by violent conflicts disappeared, the residence began to change; it gradually lost the characteristics of an isolated tower and began to take the form of a mansion of a society that started to be urbanized.

Another point that must be stressed is the continental character of this architecture, at least as it was formed between the end of the 17th century and the beginning of the 18th. We have been accustomed to calling this type of construction with the strong, solid walls and the balconies and «sahnisins» in the upper floors, «macedonian architecture» because, for several years, the most representative and beautiful examples have been those preserved in Macedonia. But we must not forget that similar mansions with the same basic architectural features exist or existed in Thessaly, Epirus, Thrace, Middle Greece and on many islands (Skopelos, Thassos, Lesvos, Samos) and that before the Revolution constituted the uniform type of the Hellenic post-byzantine architecture[220].

The exterior morphology and the basic principles of the functions of the interior constitute the common elements between the mansions of the various regions of Macedonia. However, a more careful examination discloses basic typological differences, which are limited to the spatial organization of the ground floor where are the auxiliary rooms - storerooms and cellars - and the arrangement of the main room («doxatos») and the solaria of the upper floor. A common feature is the castle-like construction of the basic building which includes the ground floor rooms and the mezzanine. Special care was taken for the security of the entrance; sometimes (as in Siatista and Ambelakia) the plan of the building looks like an L whose short arm rises like a tower with loopholes to protect the entrance which is between the legs of the L[221].

We will not describe the spaces of the mezzanine because their overall arrangement is the same with the upper floor which is the summer residence and also includes the hall for entertaining guests. The nucleus of the upper floor is a central hall which was called «doxatos» or «crevata» or «crevati» or «mesia». The staircase ended at this hall and, all around it, doors gave access to the bedrooms. The hall had various shapes. It could be rectanglular with the long dimension perpendicular to the side facing the street, with

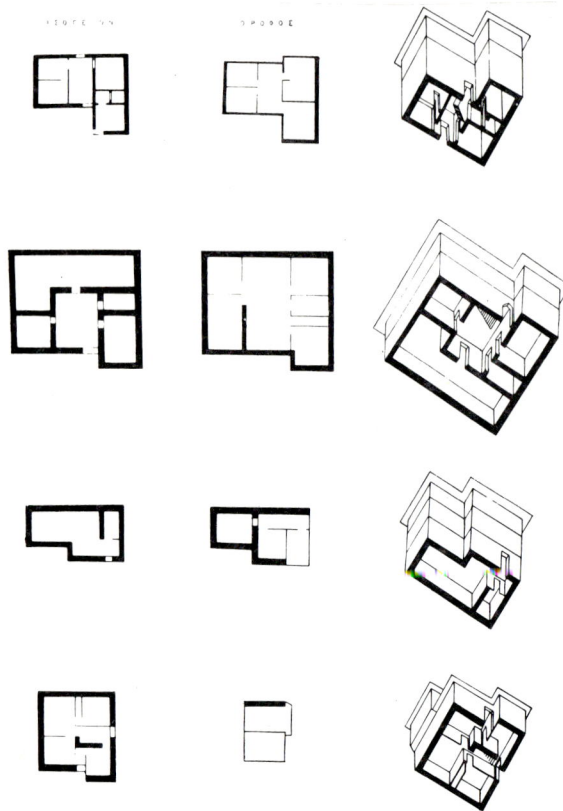

The Σ 1 architectural type of residence in Siatista.

The Σ 2 architectural type of residence.

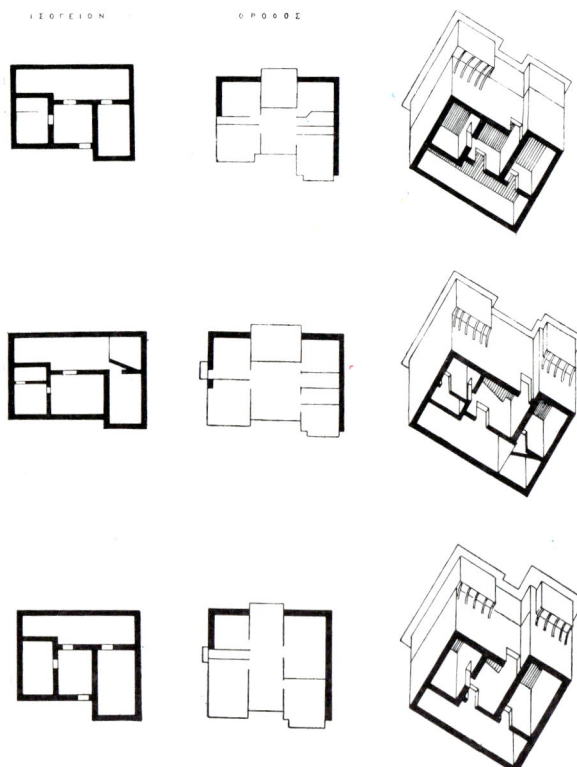

windows on both sides. Sometimes its long dimension was parallel to the face of the building. And sometimes it formed a cross whose arms were turned into «sofas», resting places with low divans which sometimesqprotruded outside forming oriels[222]. The overall arrangement of the rooms of this hall has many variations which reveal unknown sides of the ability and sensitiveness of the craftsmen of the period who could create such pleasant and variagated motifs and utilize the small openings so as to light the beautifully adorned rooms.

Another remarkable feature was the creation of different levels of the floor of the hall, not because they were functional, but just because they offered a pleasing sight. These elevated parts of the floor were sometimes constructed in other rooms, too, and were of two kinds: The sofas of the «doxatos» could be elevated by two steps, one at the exterior side - something like an anteroom to the main sofa - and a second step, that gave access from that «theoretical anteroom» to the sofa, at the point where the lattice was located[223]. The «sofas» sometimes had couches all around the walls. They did not differ much from the other rooms except that one of their sides was open, so that one who entered the «sofa» walked along the axis of the «doxatos» and not diagonally as was the case with most of the other rooms also, there were no fireplaces or «mousandres» (built-in wardrobes) in the sofas. The overall shape of the «doxatos» and the sofas varied. The sofas were, usually, rectangular, square, or they ressembled polygonal kiosks and then they were called «kioskou». Sometimes they protruded outside, forming «sahnisins» whose projection was either orthogonal or curved (mostly in the regions of Thrace and Bulgaria). If there were couches, they were constructed either against the wall of the sofa that faced the street, or they formed a Π. The proper lighting, the decoration of the walls and the ceiling and the flooring completed the atmosphere of comfort the craftsmen wanted to create[224]. These were the basic rooms of a typical upper floor of the macedonian architecture, and, as we saw, they were designed to be both functional and pleasant and comfortable[225].

The basic principle governing the layout of the plan of the building was the independence of each room and, at the same time, an harmonious overall composition, with the sofas giving the impression of isolated kiosks. However, the decoration of all avail-able spaces and the arabesques of the ceiling, and the artistic panelling evince oriental influences.

Evliya Tselebi's account, dating from 1660, about the multi-story mansions («seraglios») of Castoria, especially those built on the waterfront, which im-pressed him most, is unique[226]. It would be safe to assume that the first Greek mansions of Castoria which were built in the 17th century belonged to people who became rich thanks to the flourishing trade with Venice and other cities on the coast of the Adriatic sea, about which there is a lot of information in the public records of Venice[226a].

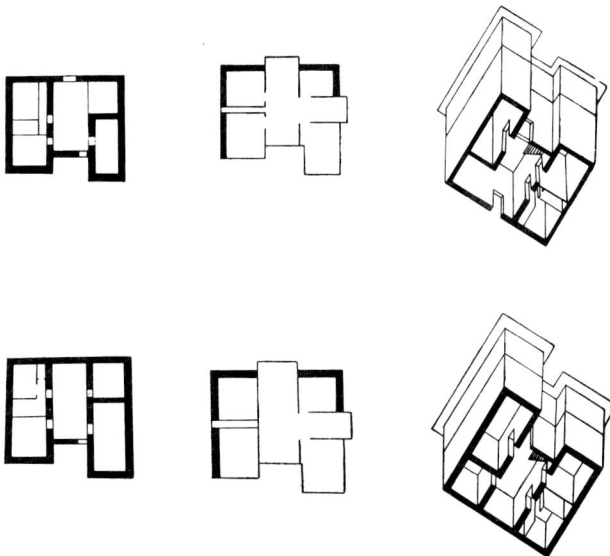

Arabesques on the ceiling of an upper floor room of Manousis' mansion in Siatista (16).

The Σ 3 architectural type of residence in Siatista.

Siatista. In 1753 the mansion of Nanos Nislis, and in 1750 the mansion of Giannakis (Nantzis) in Castoria; in 1754 the mansion of the noble Moralis (Tsipas) in the district of Apozari in Castoria.

The mansion of the ethnomartyrs Emmanuel brothers, Regas' comrades, and many other mansions which have been destroyed, belong to the same period. In 1754, the mansion of Hadjiyiannides (Nerandzopoulos) was built in Siatista, and in 1756 the mansions of Jonos and Gerechtes in Geraneia. In 1759 the mansions of Alexiou and Argyriades

In chronological order, and according to local sources, in Geraneia (Siatista), Mustapha's mansion was built around the end of the 17th century and in 1710, the new owner, Naum Nerandzis, repaired it. In Castoria, Chrysos Athanasiou's mansion was built in 1721. In Siatista, Tsouras' mansion was built in 1725. In Castoria, Constantine Rallis (Vasdecas)' mansion was built in 1728. In Siatista, Sanoucos' mansion was built in 1742 and in Castoria, Theocharis Malcos' in 1745. In 1746, the mansions of Nicolaos Chad-jimichael and Athanasios Canatsoulis, and in 1752 the mansions of G. Manousis and Poulkides (Pulkos) in

The ceiling of the sitting-room of Jonos' mansion (16).

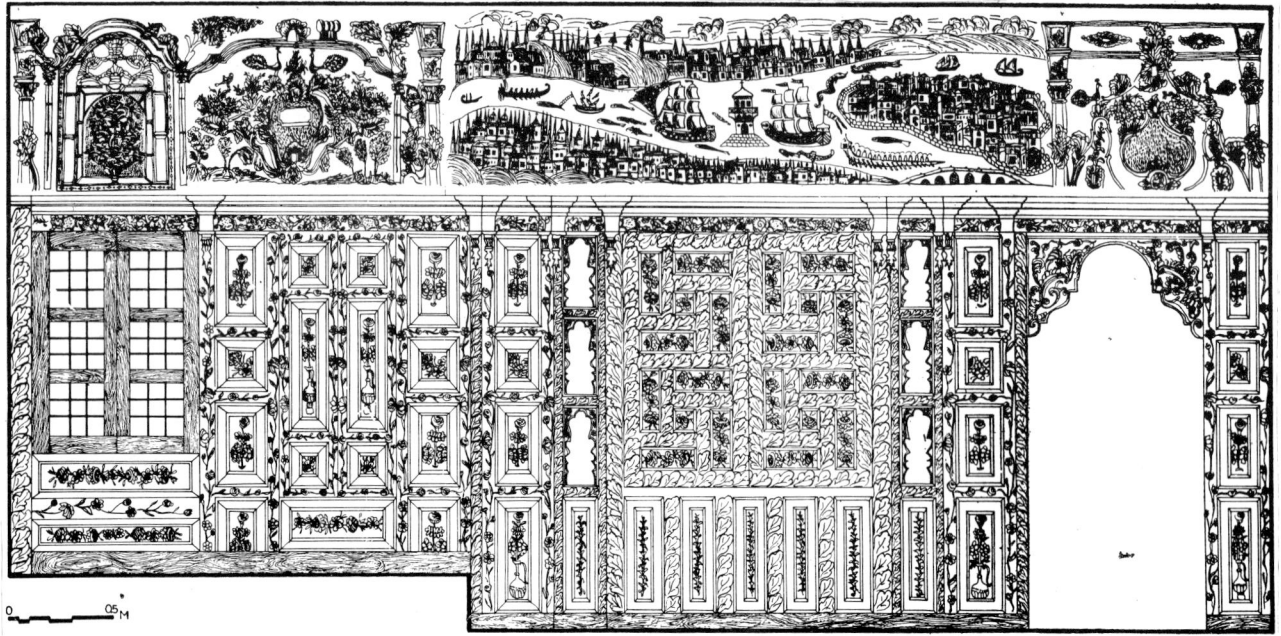

Panelled closets and frescoes on the frieze in the sitting room of Jonos' mansion in Siatista (21).

(Maliogas) and in 1760 the house of Ioannis Cottulas in Geraneia[226b]; around 1770 the mansion of Sior Manolakis in Veria, and a little earlier, the mansion of Rachtivanouda. As an inscription on a fresco in the «doxatos» of G. Schwarz in Ambelakia says, the mansion was built in 1797.

This constructional activity in the 18th century was definitely due to the emigrant Macedonians who had developed vigorous business activity abroad; and one of the deeply implanted ambitions of the emigrant

Longitudinal section of Poulkides' mansion.

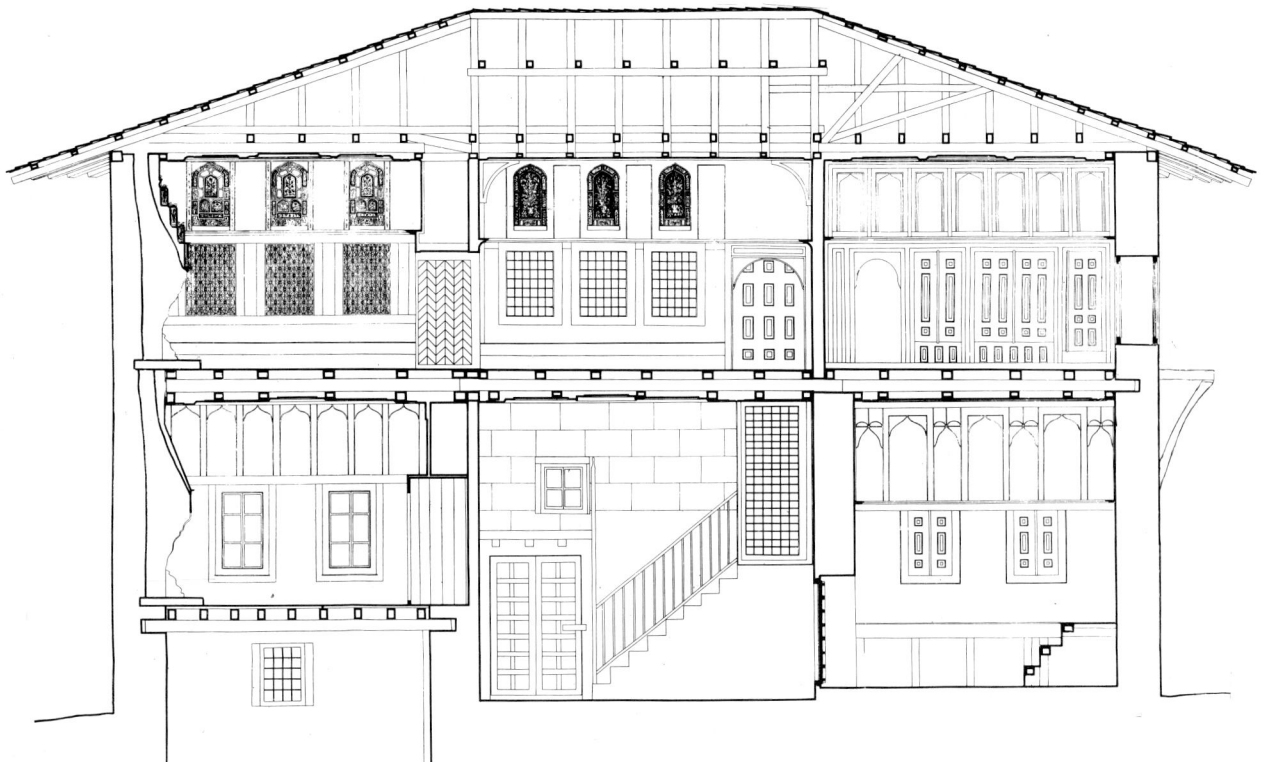

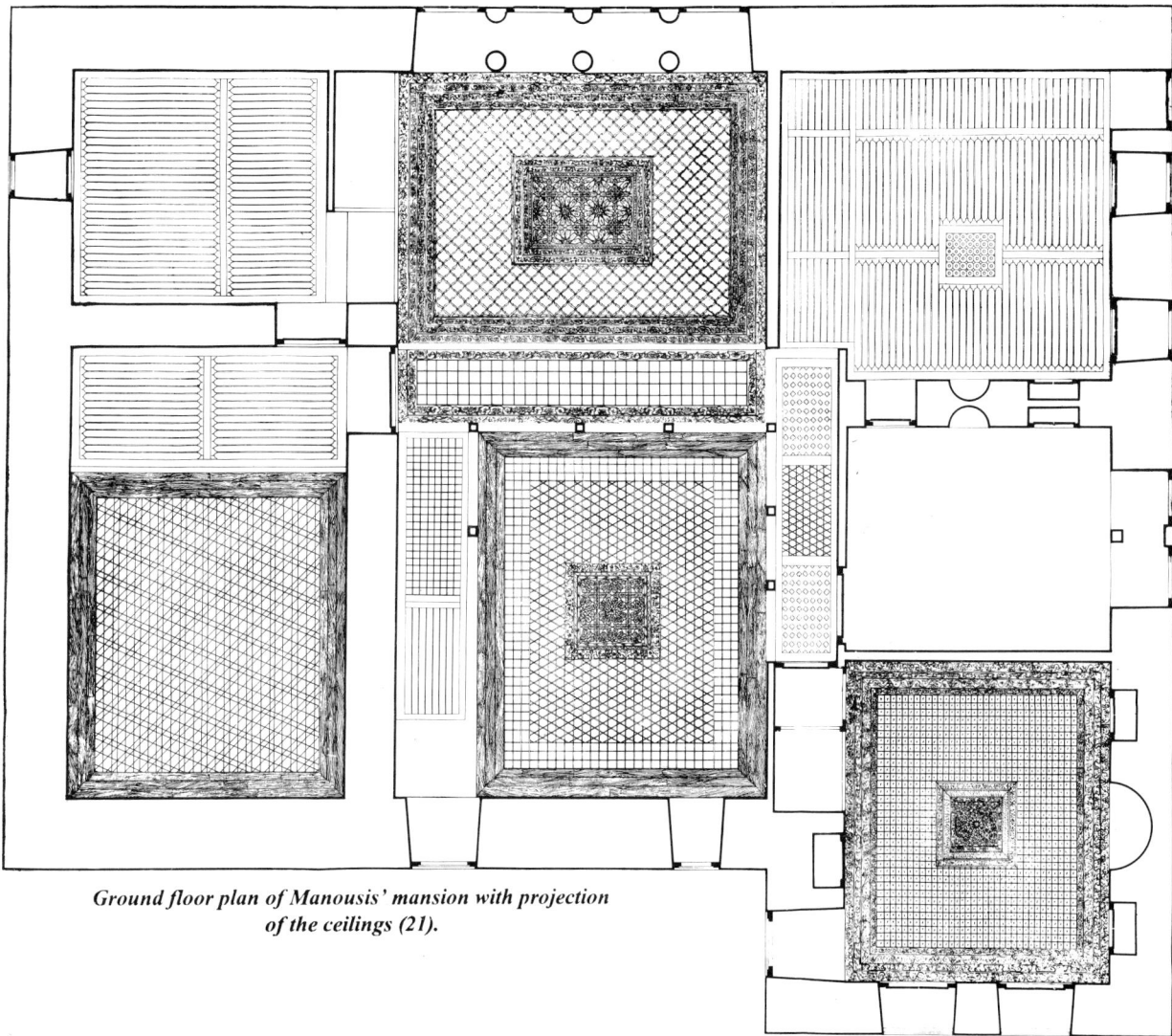

*Ground floor plan of Manousis' mansion with projection
of the ceilings (21).*

Greek, even during the turkish occupation, was to
built an imposing and beautiful house in his home
town, which would, also, evidence the success of its
owner. The bigger and more beautiful the house, the
bigger the admiration of his fellow citizens. But the
emigrants of Siatista did not come back home richer
only, but, also, more educated.

W.M. Leake, who visited Siatista in 1805, says
that, at least one member of each family lived abroad,
in Italy, Hungary, Austria and in several cities of
Germany. Very few of the older inhabitants had not
spent at least a dozen, or more, years abroad. All the
people of the town spoke German and Italian[227].
Pouqueville, who visited Siatista one year later, says
that their long stay in foreign countries and their
contact with people who, at that time, were more
cultured, influenced their whole life[228]. Those people
wanted to improve their living conditions, and hired

*Fresco in the «doxatos» (drawing room) of the upper floor
of the mansion, picturing G. Schwarz mansion (1798)
(N. Moutsopoulos).*

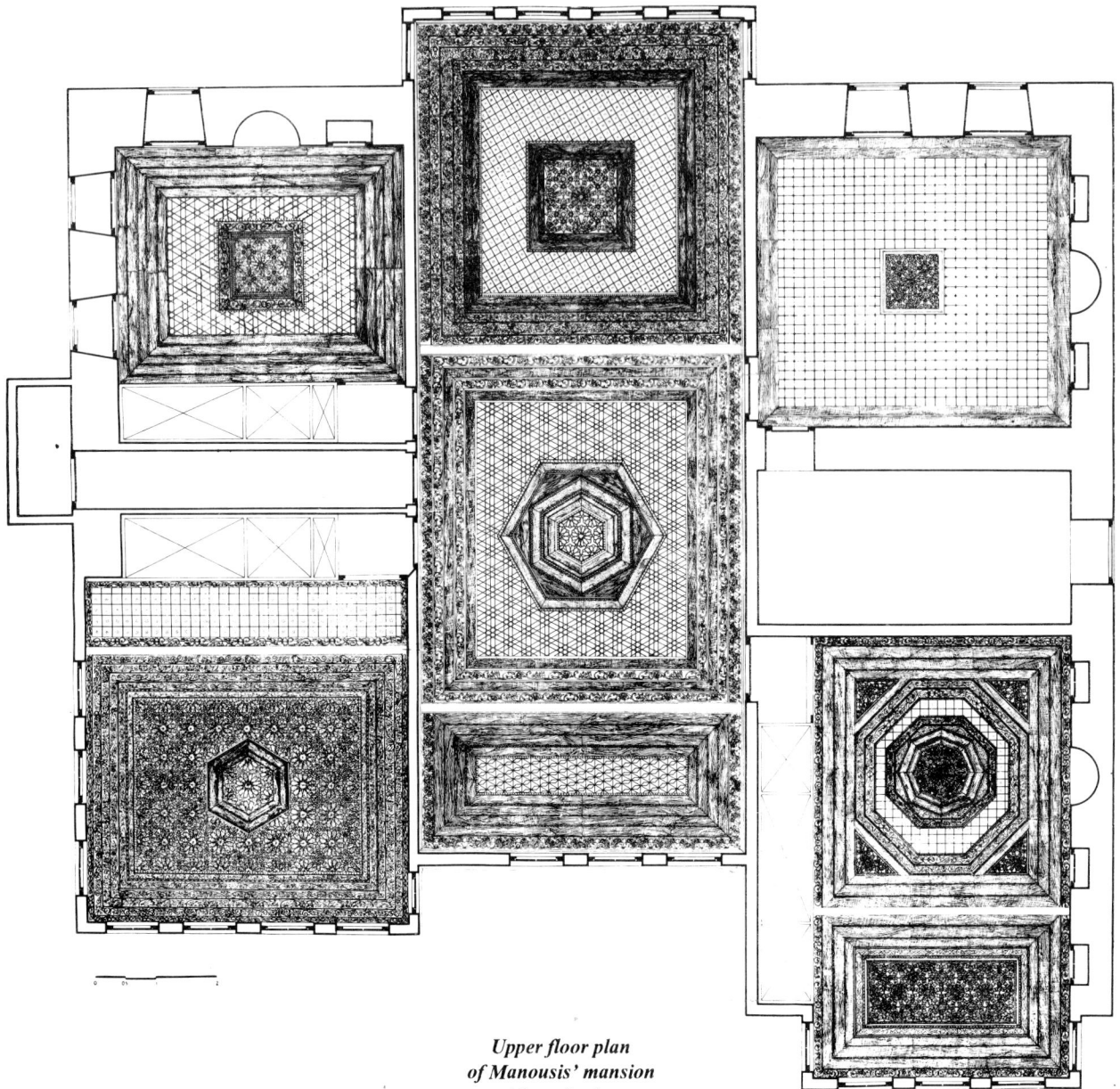

*Upper floor plan
of Manousis' mansion
with projections
of the ceilings (21).*

the groups of builders of West Macedonia and Epirus to build their houses bigger and better than the old ones. And since most of the members of the family - especially the female members - spent long hours indoors, they wanted them to live in beautiful surroundings. From the aspect of typology and building methods, they stuck to the ageless local traditions. But the decoration shows the deep changes it underwent after the 18th century.

There was no furniture or other movable objects in the macedonian houses. There were no beds; the mattresses, in the morning, disappeared inside built - in closets. Every built - in wardrobe had its special use and every object had its special place inside the built-in wardrobes or sideboards[229].

Now, we will get back to the morphology of the room. One of its partition walls had a built-in wooden wardrobe, the so-called «mousandra», a typified construction, with frescoes on its cornice and, usually, a picture of an important city such as Constantinople and Vosporos, in the center. In front of the «mousandra» there was a narrow space where the door

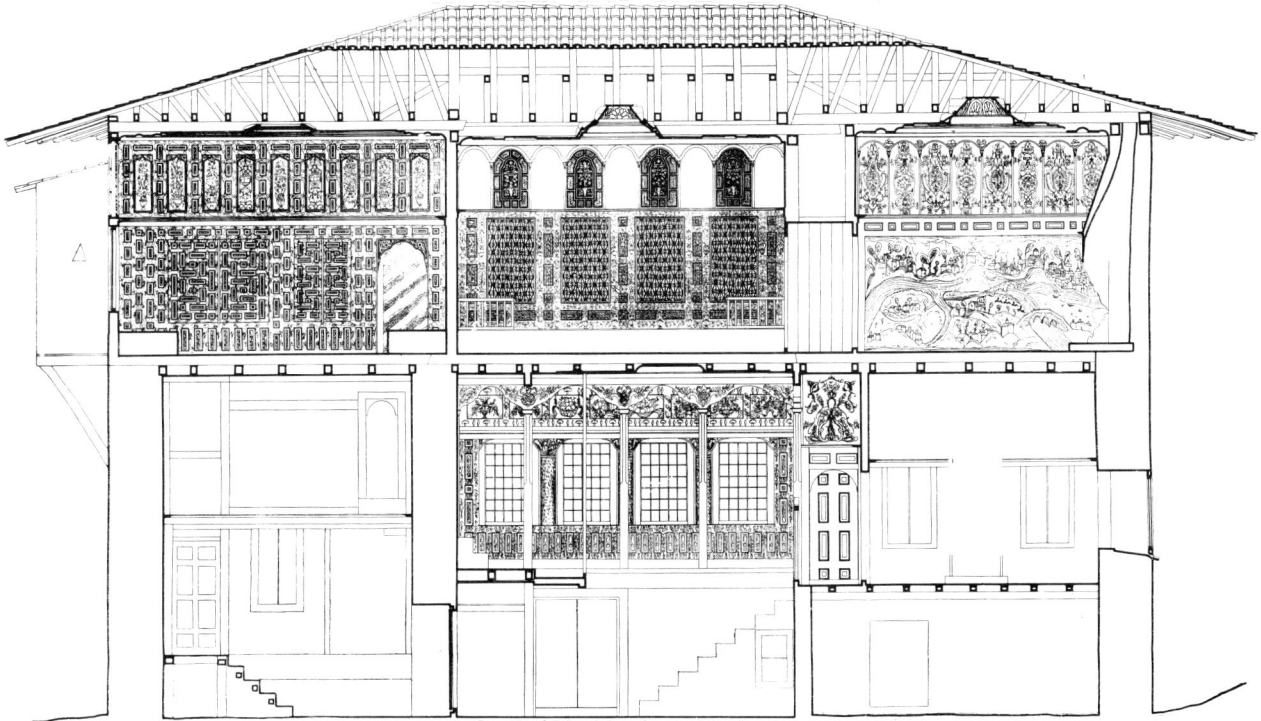

Longitudinal section of Manousis' mansion (21).

of the room opened. The main «oda» was, usually, higher by one step than the hall, it was square, and was separated from the space of the «mousandra»-entrance by a «tribelon», two very slender columns with elaborate capitals, painted in the same color with the room[230]. Around the three walls there were low couches which had various names (tiklizia, mideria[231] etc). When the room protruded outward, then a «sahnisin» was formed[232]. The fireplace was sometimes built in the wall facing the street. The rooms were called «oda», a turkish word meaning room, and so is the word «coubé», for the beautiful arabesques of the ceiling. In more recent examples, the strong islamic features of the ceiling have been superseded by a mixture of local and oriental style, the so-called turkobaroque. The same style was also prevalent in constructions in Asia Minor. The ottoman style of the details was prevalent everywhere, especially where colors are concerned[233]; this was natural because the type of the architecture that developed during the ottoman period was an expression of the style which was prevalent in every part of the empire, but always with local variations. Although the partial elements of a building were the same - even the terminology, a mixture of turkish, arabic and iranian was the same[234]

- the morphology and typology often are different in various places; thus the architecture of S.E. Bulgaria (Romelia), of Aimos (Balkan), of Korytsa, Ar-

Axonometric section of Kanatsoulis' mansion (21).

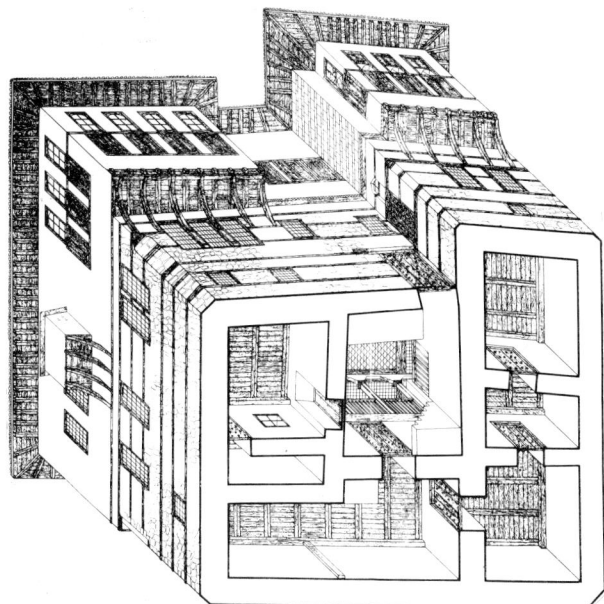

*Painted «mousandras» (built-in closets) in the eastern wall
of the SW room of Poulkides' mansion in Siatista.*

gyrocastro, Achrida, Thessaly (Pelio, Rapsani, etc) or
Thrace is not the same[235].

It is an indisputable fact that the artisans and
masons who built those houses were Greeks; and they
also built the houses of Turks. According to reliable

*The ceiling panel with the arabesques in the winter sitting room
of Manousis' mansion in Siatista.*

information, they also built public works (bridges,
market places, caravansarais and also the paved
roads). All this work helped them to apply, in the 18th
century, their experience to practice and create such
works of art. Especially these works of art[236] evidence
their long experience acquired by working in ottoman
religious buildings (the artistic arabesques of the ceilings of the mansions of Siatista constitute an additional proof)[237].

According to the descriptions of travellers and the
pictures which have been preserved, the konaks of the
Turkish and Turkoalbanian (muslim Albanians) beys
and aghas were different from the mansions we have
described. They were lower and the spatial organization of the «odas» was linear; the interior elevation
differences were greater and the «odas» were connected by means of deep sofas while the front staircases were heavier and more elaborate.

In the Greek mansions, sometimes they constructed a rectangular dais against the wall of the long
side of the «doxatos», as, for instance, in the
Sapoundji's mansion[238]. The long couches were
covered with straw mattresses and on them they
spread multi-colored blankets[239], and pillows. The
staircase, whose landing was part of the «doxatos»,
was either open or separated from the hall by a
wooden latticework. Over the landing there was,
sometimes, a platform for the band - the «instruments», as they were called.

It would be interesting to picture a social gathering
on a cold winter night, in an old mansion of Castoria.
A big fire is blazing in the fireplace; on the threshold
of the hall the guests have left their dirty boots, and in
slippers, they have reclined on the divans; the
grandfather sits at one end of the sofa and the
grandmother at the other. Many guests sit, cross-
legged on the floor. The housewife has already put the
best white pillow cases and the low table is covered
with local food.

In certain rare cases, the ceilings of the mansions
of Castoria were covered with plaster intaglios; but
more often, the ceilings were made of wood rhomboidal panels colored in red or green, with a central
pseudodome. The decorations of the walls were at a
certain height from the floor, above the cornice which
was in a line with the lintels of the doors and the
windows. All the openings, the wood panelling and
the built-in wardrobes and closets were located below

the cornice. The section of the wall above the cornice, which was something like a frieze, included the transom windows (the byzantine «skylights») and it was adorned with painted decorations inside arch-like frames which enclose a multitude of baroque anthemia whose basic colors are pink, red with a little blue or violet. To the aforementioned decoration we should add the usual representations of imaginary landscapes with imaginary animals, cities and harbors and, chiefly, pictures of Constantinople viewed from the Ceratius[240].

There were several types of windows that were used, depending on their place and function. We have already mentioned the narrow slits in the ground floor walls that ventilated the auxiliary rooms. These narrow openings were wider on the inside and tapered to a slit on the outside. The winter rooms of the first floor or the mezzanine had narrow windows with bars which protruded outwards so that one could see who was at the door. These windows were called «richta». The «doxatos» and the summer rooms of the second floor had larger windows. When there was no «sahnisin», the windows were opened in the thickness of the stone wall and, if the owner wanted more light, several windows, close to one another, were constructed along the exterior course of the stones. But the construction presented difficulties in the formation of the wooden lintel which had to be supported by a series of wooden pillars corresponding with the mullions[241]. The «parakyptika» windows of the «doxatos» always had a wooden lattice and had no panes; they had wooden shutters which, earlier, were called «kepéghia». But the most beautiful ornament of the mansions of Castoria was the transom window; the transom windows were in the shape of pointed or broken arches with multi-colored small panes forming various geometrical or floral patterns[242].

The oriental influences are due to the influence that the western baroque had on the architecture of the entire ottoman empire during the 18th century, and, particularly on the architecture of Constantinople. And all the various local artistic expressions were, in turn, influenced by this, and gave such remarkable examples of art.

From the beginning of the 18th century onwards, the baroque style rapidly gained ground and it appeared, sometimes more evident (as, for instance, in Constantinople) and sometimes less (in the provincial

Painted «mousandras» in the eastern wall of the SW room of Poulkides' mansion in Siatista.

towns of the empire). Apart from the partial «grammar» of the baroque, in the details of decoration, the whole style had been assimilated and the common models were interpreted faithfully enough but leaving

Decoration of the corner «deliacos» (solarium?) of Manousis' mansion in Siatista.

«Mousandras» in the SW wall of Poulkides' mansion in Siatista (eastern wall).

a margin for the existing local artistic tradition to express itself, the tradition whose carriers were the popular and anonymous artisans of the various guilds[243]. The tricliniums of certain local traditions are undoubtedly similar to the representative type of «oda» of the ottoman residence.

The professor of the School of Fine Arts of Constantinople Onder Kücükerman[244] in his *Anadolu'daki Geleneksel Türk evinde* makes an important analysis of the turkish «oda», its location in the building, its relationship to the semi-closed spaces, the sitting arrangement, the fireplace, the built-in wardrobes and closets, the doors, the openings generally, the ceilings, the panelling, the furniture and its function.

In my opinion, pure byzantine elements in the typology of the «triclinium» are the perimetric couches in the form of a Π, the three openings leading to the «oda» which is higher by one step than the lobby, and the built-in closets of the lobby which, we know, were constructed, later, in the Greek mansions of Phanar. On the contrary, the type of decoration, the color scale and the interior atmosphere evince more or less ottoman influences. However, the panels and central «navels» of the ceilings, especially of some mansions of Castoria and Siatista, belong to the pure ottoman morphology.

Some Turkish architects claim that each room (oda) of a turkish house constitutes an independent unit. Most probably each room belonged to a separate family and functioned independently exactly as, in order times, the cell of the turkish family lived under one, nomadic tent[245]. I personally believe that the «oda» is a direct descendant of the Byzantine *triclinium*, the essential and dominant element of the byzantine residence (*domus*).

As we have already mentioned there were no pieces of furniture or movable objects in the Macedonian bedrooms. Each of the «mousandra» had a special purpose; each object had a pre-arranged place in the «mousandra». Even the smallest objects, such as glasseware, had their specific place, sometimes visible («pulitses») and sometimes closed.

In the rooms of the houses, which we tried to describe, the members of the Greek families were born and grew-up; and in those rooms they lived and acquired their first experiences, and that is where the tradition was transmitted from generation to generation, and the ageless customs survived. Old and young, women and children constituted a disciplined group which actively participated in the events of everyday life.

The social life of a Greek family within the closed space of the residence and outside must be studied as an integrated whole; in the rooms and in other places, especially in the church which, apart from its religious function, participated in the social life of the people - marriages, births, baptism, deaths and even after death. Towns of Macedonia, such as Castoria, Siatista and Veria constitute a garden full of the fruits of the popular tradition whose shell is the residence, covering one half of the human activity.

The mansions of Macedonia, especially of W. Macedonia, of Thessaly (Rapsani, Ambelakia, Pelion) and of Epirus have their own interior morpohology which belongs to the larger category of popular architecture, the one we call macedonian architecture and, if the morphology has some influence on the function of the rooms, the influence is of oriental origin. This sentence means that in the construction of these mansions, the largest part of the whole building was used for the creation of «odas» (good odas, «bas-odas», «coffee-odas») and sofas and kiosks, «heliacos», «doxatos», in other words places for comfortable living according to the oriental style, with «minderia» (or «miderlikia») , «tiklizia», and other low divans around the fireplaces where the inhabitants or their guests could recline or sit cross-legged and relax («rahat» or «houzur», in turkish).

There is no mansion in north Greece which does not have similar interior spatial organization strikingly contrasting with the European style. The furniture, which, in its various forms and styles, was the basic equipment of a european residence was absent. There were no beds and the mattresses were hidden inside special «mousandres», the built-in closets (in turkish «musandira»): There was no dining room, or table or chairs[246].

The «mousandres» were also the strongboxes, the safes of the owners, especially of the merchants. There is an interesting description about the strongboxes of the period in a will of 1889[247]. «Now I shall reveal to you where my money is hidden in the house. On the fireplace, in the bedroom, in two holes, I have hidden two pails full of money with all the invoices; in the same room, above the aforementioned holes, I have a kettle full of florins with the invoice. In the same room I have merchandise and the ledgers; in the upper floor there is a locked «mousandra» full of merchandise. I have merchandise in the workshop, and in the cellar, in the corner, under the coal, there is a pail full of money with the invoice».

The paintings on the doors of the built-in cupboards were of the same style with the decorations of the ceilings and the wooden partition walls, especially in the «good rooms» and together with the colored transomsq created a pleasant and impressive atmosphere.

The walls were vertically divided by means of horizontal cornices, the so-called «poltses» («gilvia») which in the «sahnisins» projected outwards and, at the same time, formed the lintels of the windows and the base of the transoms. The surfaces between these cornices were covered with wooden panelling with anthemia or, in some places, they formed the doors of the built-in cupboards. If a partition wall was con-structed of thin slats, then it was also decorated with anthemia or pseudo-windows. The spaces between the transom windows were also decorated with pictures of flowers and so were the wall spaces above the «mousandres», and the thin, partition walls were decorated with whatever the mind of the Macedonian popular painter conceived. Nothing, not even the smal-

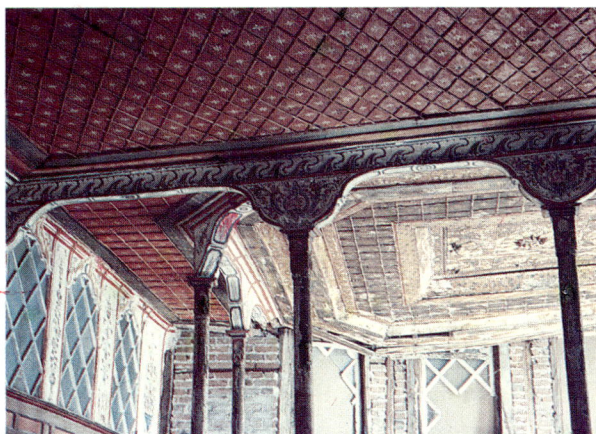

Detail of the ceiling of the «doxatos» of G. Schwarz's mansion im ambelakia (photo: 1960)

Detail of decoration of a ceiling in Siatista.

Detail of the ceiling of the «deliakos» (solarium) of Nerandjopoulos' mansion in Siatista.

lest corner or the smallest pillar was left without some decoration. There are pictures even on the «frieze» formed over the cornice which is level with the transoms. The entire interior of the Macedonian mansions was adorned with frescoes and pictures and this feature makes the deepest impression on the visitors.

Detail of the ceiling of G. Schwarz's mansion in Ambelakia.

Detail of the painted dome in the drawing room of G. Scharz's mansion in Ambelakia (photo: 1960).

The transom windows, high in the wall, over the windows of the upper floors of the mansions, had no panes; they had only wooden shutters «kepeghia» or «canatia»). Over every window there was a transom on the top of the lintel, which, in the Macedonian style of construction, projected outwards and inwards and formed a cornice. A wooden lattice protected the windows. In the evening, when the shutters were closed, the only light that came into the room was through the multi-colored panes of the transom windows. However, transom windows were not constructed only over the windows of the outside walls; they were also constructed in the partition walls, between the rooms. Anyway, one thing is certain: the multi-colored panes of the transom windows, if not the plans of the transoms, too, came from Europe.

«Navel» on the ceiling of Tsatsapas' mansion in Castoria.

«Navel» on the ceiling of Tsatsapas' mansion in Castoria.

Decoration in the Tsatsapas' mansion in Castoria.

*Fresco on the wall of the «deliacos» (Solarium) of Manousis'
mansion in Siatista.*

Athanasios Economou in a letter he sent from Vienna to G. Schwarz in 1798, writes: «... she cost to Belegrad, of four boxes full of panes for Mr. George D. Schwarz sent according to his order through Gabriel Banvenesis, florins 180...»[248].The frame of

the transom windows was made of plaster of Paris and for its additional protection against weather, there was another transom window, simpler and stronger, on the outside, so that the rhomboidal cross-pieces of the two windows coincided. The multi-colored panes were

*Decoration of the SW wall of the upper floor NE sitting room
of Sanoukos' mansion in Siatista.*

*Decoration of the frieze in the SW sitting room of Poulkides'
mansion in Siatista (W. wall).*

Decorative braids on the NW wall of the SE sitting room of Manousis' mansion in Siatista.

Painted frieze of the NE room of Sanoukos' mansion in Siatista (S.W wall).

Detail of decorative painting in a partition of the frieze in Sanoukos' mansion in Siatista.

fitted inside the rhomboidal spaces between the cross-pieces of the window. Sometimes, the panes were all carved or bore inscriptions and other designs. In the thorough study of the transom windows of the man-

Decoration of the frieze in the upper floor winter sitting room of Poulkides mansion on Siatista

Painted panel of the SW wall of the upper floor winter room of Manousis' mansion in Siatista.

sions of Siatista we said that the construction of such complicated patterns with so slender cross-pieces made of plaster of Paris must be regarded as an achievement of the Macedonian craftsmen of the period[249]. The perfection of the composition can be seen from the inside. The small panes were fitted from the exterior side of the transom window and were glued with plaster, that is why the horizontal cross-section of a cross-bracing was triangular with the vertex towards the inside, and the base flush with the outside surface; in this way, the panes were stuck more firmly. Along the base of this triangle, the artisans constructed narrow grooves where they fitted the panes and then they filled the groove with plaster. It was up to the artisan to surmount the difficulties that this work presented. When

the transom window was constructed in this manner, and all the small panes were firmly glued in place, the

*Detail of a fresco in the «deliacos» of Manousis' mansion in
Siatista (NW wall).*

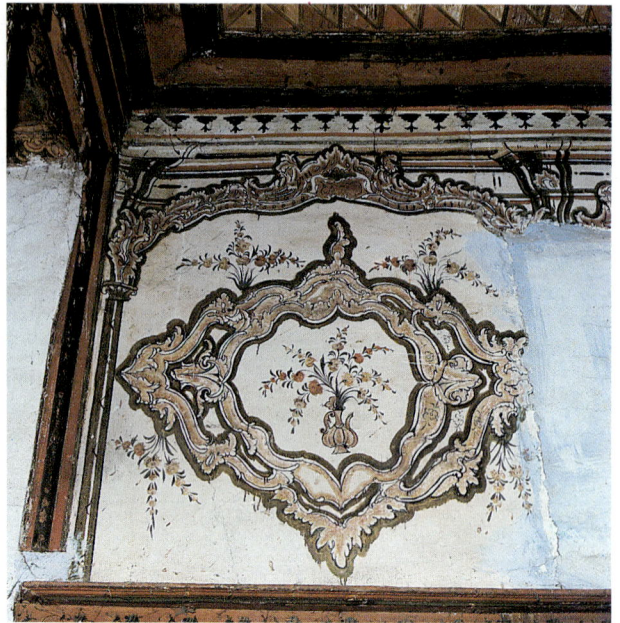

Decorative motif in Tsiatsapas' mansion in Castoria.

*Decoration of the ceiling in Kyra Sanouco's mansion
in Siatista.*

whole window was like a perforated rigid frame. The
shapes of the transom windows varied greately, but it
is obvious that they were constructed on the same
model which was, probably, brought from Europe.
Similar patterns could be seen not only in the
glasswork of Europe, but also in the elaborate plaster
or wooden frames of the mirrors of the period which,
in the 18th century, were known as «Chippendale».

Today, we cannot estimate or imagine how deeply

*Theoretical sketch of the form of a byzantine domus in the
district of Phanari, Constantinople (N. Moutsopoulos).*

*Column capital of carved wood in the upper floor of
Nerantzopoulos' mansion in Siatista (photo: 1960).*

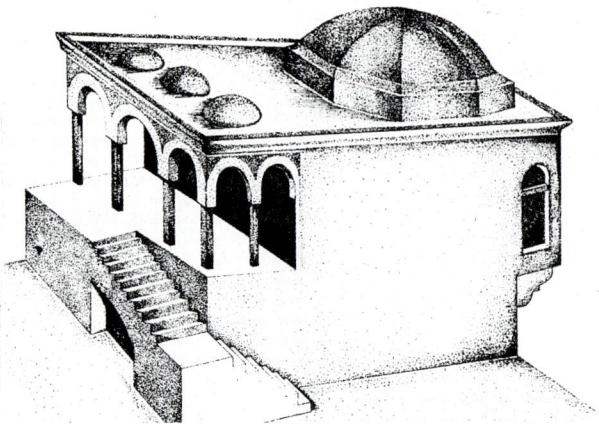

The interior of an ottoman war tent; among the spoils taken by the polish expeditionary force during the siege of Vienna (Museum of Warsaw) (photo: N. Moutsopoulos)

this foreign style influenced the local craftsmen; however, their work evinces long familiarity with the baroque and the rococo as applied to painting and constructions made of plaster of Paris. However the coexistence of various forms in different materials shows long experince[250].

The appearance of secular painting in the interior of the rooms, kept step with the tendencies towards Europeanization which started to develop in the higher strata of the ottoman society during the reign of Achmet III[251]. In the big ottoman center, Constantinople, started these tendencies which shaped the secular painting of the familiar turko-baroque, the popular baroque and the rococo and, from there, they spread throughout the provinces of the empire[252]. In that city, the Greek artists got acquainted with those models and were taught the style and the way to create that particular effect in the rooms, naturally, adding their personal taste and ethnic traditions, and con-

Fresco in the «Pantheon» of Kanatsoulis' mansion in Siatista.

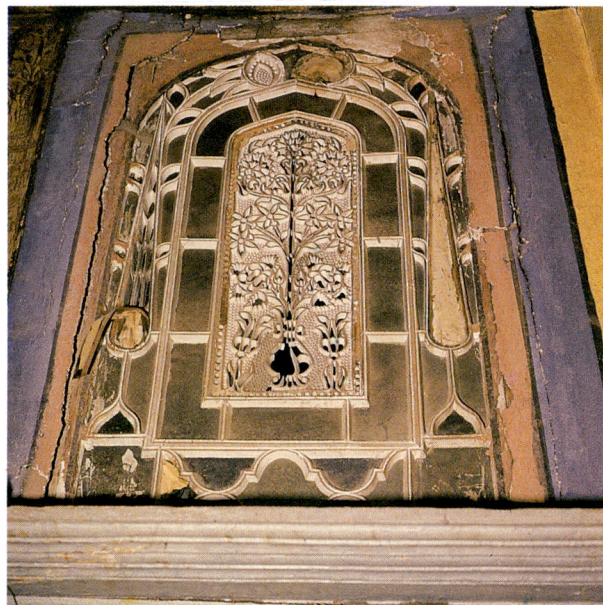

structed these works of art of which many examples have been preserved in several variations.

Sometimes, rarely though, the outside faces of the walls of the upper floors were decorated, too. In Macedonia, some examples have been preserved and we are going to mention only the most important: for instance, the outside of the sahnisi of the «good room» of George Schwarz's mansion in Ambelakia[253], and D. Schwarz-Avramopoulos' mansion[254] in the same town, which we included in the study because architecture transcends geographical boundaries. In certain mansions of Siatista there are frescoes on the outside walls of the «sahnisins»; one of the oldest and most orientalized is the fresco on the wall of Pulkides' mansion, which has rosettes between the transom windows and the picure of a ship[255]. In an important center of Hellenism, Philippoupolis (Plovdiv), frescoes on the outside walls of the mansions were very usual. The most important examples are the houses of Argyres Kuyumtzoglou (1847)[256], of B. Stambolian[257], of Veren Stambolian (middle of the 18th c.)[258] and the gable over the door of the house of Stephan Hindilian (1835-1840), a work of Mocas and Mauvroudes, with an architectural pattern similar to that of the house of D. Schwarz in Ambelakia[259]. The

Fresco on the S. wall of the NW sitting room of Keradzis' mansion in Siatista.

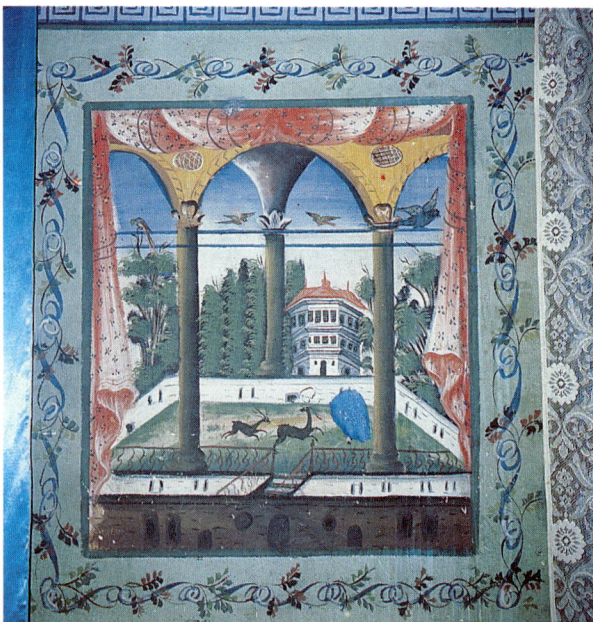

beautiful architectural projection in the konak of Agoushev in Mogilista of Smolyan (Rodope) has also pictorial representations[260].

In Siatista, there are the oldest examples of these decorations. Chadjiyannides, a rich emigrant from Siatista who had settled in Budapest, in 1754 built a luxurious mansion in Siatista and, later, gave it to his daughter as her dowry. Today the mansion is known by the name of its last owner, Nerantzopoulos. The wonderful transom windows of this mansion are elaborately adorned with plaster shapes which support the colored panes. The transom windows were constructed on site, as an inscription written in sgraffito on the panes says in ancient Greek verse:

«Now God in excelsis generously cared for this house, a source of joy and splendor, like Pandora's box out of which do not come gifts of guile, but graces. In Siatista, the 15th of September of 1755 A.D. Michael Papageorgiou»[261].

On the frieze of the mansion, some admirable pictures of imaginary cities, interspersed with anthemia, baskets of flowers, garlands and rosettes, have been preserved and can still be seen.

The interior of the mansion of Chadjimichael (Canatsoulis), which was built in 1757, was decorated in two stages. The older was completed in 1767, and includes the ceilings with the artistic arabesques of geometrical braids with evident oriental influence. Particularly, the fresco on the wall of the «women's room», which represents a bridge and, in the background, an island with a castled city, is a variation of the well-known fresco in Topkapi[262]. Doubtless, there must have been a certain old model with which, the painter who included the theme in his repertory when he painted the more recent frescoes in Topkapi (1779)[263] was familiar.

The Poulkides' mansion, which definitely dates from 1752, is one of the most important mansions of Siatista, and its preserved frescoes are the most important of those which date from the middle of the 18th century (1759). On the ceilings one can still discern the vestiges of very small, polygonal panels.

The transition started with the decoration of the vertical surfaces where the baroque supersedes all the other styles. However, among the anthemia and flower bunches, one can discern some islamized models, braids and other familiar, popular ottoman motifs. In the friezes, over the wall panelling, one can discern, inside the rectangular spaces created by the slender outlines of the baroque pillars, elaborately painted vases with flowers and panniers on top of the miniature pieces of furniture of western style. Many parts of the decoration are similar to that of Tsatsiapa's mansion, in Castoria.

However, the most interesting representation in Poulkides' mansion is a representation of Constantinople. But here, it has a strange, symbolic character. The picture shows western-style churches, steeples, lofty towers, similar to contemporary copperplates picturing monasteries of Athos; and among the houses, one can discern a priest with a cross in his raised hand. Bosporus is full of ships and fish as big as the ships. The fishes have a monstrous shape and look like the dragons of hell, as they used to paint them in pictures of the Last Judgement. The monster-fishes probably expressed the innate fear of the sea of the simple, mountain painters of the Macedonian mansions. High in the sky, winged dragons fly around a blue-gray ikon of a cherub. Although it is high noon, the sky is full of red and yellow stars. However, the most important feature of the picture is the way the artist painted the clouds which reflect and disperse the light of the sun, and the effect accentuates the blend of reality and symbolic myth.

Another important point is that the construction reminds us of certain miniatures such as the ones in the well-known «Pilgrimage to the Holly Land», of the library of the monastery of Gregorios of Athos, which has the inscription «By the hand of Daniel the physician:1680»[264], and those in the codices of the monasteries of Iviron (no. 874) and Docheiariou (no.129).

However, in the frescoes of the Macedonian mansions, the symbolic representations we mentioned are charged with the ethno-ideological content[265], as, for instance, the frescoes in Siatista and Castoria. Doubtless, that picture of Constantinople, which was, as all the Greeks knew, the seat of the patriarchs and the former capital of the Byzantine empire, symbolized their lost fatherland; and it was charged with the hopes and expectations for deliverance from slavery and restoration of the symbols of Hellenism: Constantinople and St. Sophia. Probably, grandmothers used those pictures to teach their grandchildren the history of the capital and the future resurrection of the race.

Fresco on the W wall of the NW sitting room of Keradzis' mansion in Siatista.

The various mythical gigantic birds that tear snakes apart also hide some symbolism; we saw many such pictures on the walls of mansions in Siatista and, in

Fresco on the S wall of the NW sitting room of Keradzis' mansion in Siatista.

Fresco on the E. wall of the NW sitting room of Poulkides' mansion in Siatista.

the form of bas-reliefs, on the parapets of the fountains in monasteries, or, as woodcarvings, on the doorjambs of churches, and the walls of the low-ceiligned basilicas of the period.

However, the attention of the visitor may be drawn to certain themes whose symbolism puzzles even those who have read the prophecies ascribed to the emperor Leo VI the Wise (886-912)[266] and only the initiates can understand them: The gigantic bird takes the snake apart, sometimes in a clearing of a dense forest; sometimes the gigantic bird flies over the globe; and sometimes, as on a wall of the Manousis' mansion - the inscription, which is not clear, says: «*10 April 1787. The bird ...*»-[267] the gigantic bird perches on the top branches of an immense tree, while deer graze in the near-by field[268]. By the way, on a wall of Maliogas' mansion, there is a picture of an Austrian hussar surrounded by deer[269].

It is not easy to determine the origin of these symbols because some of them have been repeated through the centuries. The artists of various denominations used these imposing but innocent-looking symbols in various locations. The most popular themes had always been the dragon and the bird with the serpent[270], or the serpent, either alone or next to a chained lion. We have seen those representations even on the faces fo some Armenian Christian churches, on walls of seljuk ruins and even on the face of an oven in upper Thessaloniki and on the wall of a house in Mesoropi of Cavala[271].

The multi-colored decorative braids on the frieze of the Pulkides' mansion reminded us of the initial letters and the decoration of a series of Athonite manuscripts of the 16th century[272], a familiar techni-

que of the period which survived in later representations with well-defined outlines and uniform
colors but showing strong oriental influences, on
embroidery (without gold).

The mansion of C. Alexiou (Gerechtes), in Siatista
was built during the period from 1755 to 1760. The
Jono's mansion, which was built in Gerania in 1756,
was probably decorated later, perhaps in 1786, according to the inscription on a transom. A remarkable
painting is a fresco picturing Constantinople and the
familiar «Tower of Leander», of the well-known
legend,- which is known today as «The tower of the
maiden» - on the island that was named after it[273].

As we have said, the picture of Constantinople
seems to have been a necessary decoration, usually of
the space over the «mousandra». Doubtless the oldest

Detail of a fresco in the SW corridor of the upper floor of Manousis' mansion in Siatista.

Fresco in Poulkides' mansion in Siatista.

Fresco in Manousis' mansion in Siatista.

ti). These representations followed two different ways, according to the ideology and artistic education of their creators: on the one hand, through the visitor-artists of the West and on the other, through the orientalized expressions of Turkish, Arab or Iranian miniature painters, as, for example, Matraki Nasuh (1536-1537). Adding to these the copperplatings that West Macedonian merchants brought from abroad, we can form an idea about the models those traditional local artists used in their creations. A proof of this is the fresco picturing Frankfurt in the mansion of Argyriades (Maliogas), in Siatista (1844) with the inscription «*Frankfurt am Main*[274], or the picture of Anadolu Hisar (1671)[275] or the landscape of Divan-i Ilhani in Topkapi Saray (Museum Library) (H. 912 f. 36). Furthermore, the unforgettable Kitsos Makris managed to locate the model that the popular artist

examples were the cartographic representations of the capital of the ottoman empire which had been widely known since the fall of Constantinople (Buondelmon-

Fresco representing Adrianople, over the fireplace in Maliogas' house in Siatista.

«The palace in the river —which can also be seen in Maliogas' mansion— where they locked up the princess to protect her from being killed by the dragon, as it was ordained by fate...».

used. It was a large copperplate by Johann Balthassar Probst who died at 75 in 1748. Probst copied, with some changes, a copperplate made by Mautthäus Merian (1593-1650) dating from 1619. The Greek artist has not made a faithful copy of the model,

The fresco picturing Constantinople in the sitting room of Jonos' mansion in Siatista.

although he has put the ribbon with the name of the city in his picture[276]. There is another fresco picturing Madrid on the cornice over a window of one of the rooms[277]. M. Garides writes that «in this case, the popular painter had the work of another Probst, George Probst, who worked in Augsburg in the 18th century, as his model»[278].

However, in addition to those western models, the Greek popular artists of secular painting of the 18th and 19th century had another source of inspiration: Greek and Balkan copperplates and wood engravings, usually picturing saints or monasteries often surrounded by passages from the story of the life of the patron saint of the monastery. Many times these artists take «poetic license» and transform certain elements or replace familiar figures with others, more or less similar, but their work always has the freshness and grace of popular creation.

«Frankfurt am Main». Fresco on the frieze of a room of Maliogas' house in Siatista.

Exterior murals picturing animals in Mesoropi, Kavala.

On a partition wall of the Manousis' residence (1762) a fresco pictures the monastery of Vatopedi; and in some other frescoes depicting Constantinople, the Athonite monastery of Vatopedi is in the place of St. Sophia[279]. All these themes - including Constantinople with St. Sophia and the Tower of Leander, the most favorite themes of the artists - are sometimes confused with each other, or transformed or some elements are interchanged, according to the importance that the popular artist wanted to give them. And apart from the gigantic fishes and ships, there are many other symbolic themes: sometimes Constantinople is protected by the Ikon of a Cherub and sometimes by the two-headed eagles[280].

Eratyra, Kozani: A fresco with the two-headed eagle.

There are representations of Constantinople in the mansions of Natzis and Tsiaparas (1798) in Castoria, in the mansions of Maliogas (1787,1844), of Jonos (1756,1786), of Lioutaris (Caryophilis) (1850) in Siatista, in the mansion of G. Schwarz (1798) in Ambelakia of Thessaly, in Chamorigas' mansion in Drakia of Pelion and in many others.

The pictures of Constantinople do not express only the Greeks' yearning for freedom but also their admiration for the city of their dreams, the former

A perpesentation of the monastery of Simon Petra «by the hand of Ioannis» March 27, 1870.

«reigning city» and capital of the empire where the ecumenical patriarch has his seat, and, now, the sultan, too. There are similar frescoes, in the same places of rooms of mansions throughout the vast empire, as, for instance in Tsakiraga's mansion in Coula[281] and in several mansions in Saframpolis[282]. There are the same rococo decorations, and the same anthemia on the walls of the rooms throughout Asia Minor, Syria,

Epirus, Albania, Middle Greece[283], the north Aegean islands[284], Euboea[285] and Crete. The stylized and orientalized representations of cities which were very popular at least from the 16th century onward, were transferred to the walls of the rooms of the mansions in Asia Minor.[286] The oldest models are probably the miniatures of the Turk Nakkas Matrakci, as, for instance, his Constantinople (1534)[287] and his «city of Erzerum»[288]. The local peculiarities in various regions of Asia Minor are due to interior proportions of the spaces[289].

The depiction of architectural landscapes was popular, particularly during the reign of Selim III. A typical example is the picture of the palace of Versailles on the wall of the staircase leading to the rooms of Valide Sultana[290]. There is a similar picture in the upper floor sofa of the mansion of D. Schwarz (Avramopoulos) in Ambelakia, with some alterations; the central pool has been replaced by a lawn and a clock tower has been added in the center of the picture[291]. There are similar depictions of architectural landscapes in Oslekov's house in Koprivtitsa[292] and in an alcove called «alafranga» in Stephan Hindlian's house in Philippoupolis[293]. Many times, these pictures of imaginary architectural landscapes were painted only on the interior friezes of the rooms, as, for instance, in various rooms of Topkapi Saray (Aynalι oda of Abdülhamit)[294], in the wing of the harem (Valide Sultan Oturna Odasi)[295], in the Harem Dairesi (Valide Sultan Yatak Odasi)[296].

An important, dated decoration has been preserved in the mansion of Manousis, in Siatista. This was also completed in two stages. The older stage dates back to 1763. But the richest frescoes were painted later, in 1787. In the eastern, winter rooms there are pictures on the built-in wardrobes and on the friezes, which depict, among other themes, greek mountains (Sniatsico, Kissavos, Olympus, Othrys, Burino, Agrapha). Obviously, many artists comprised the group that worked here because there are apparent differences between the manner of painting the panels of the friezes and the capitals of the timber pillars and the large panels of the walls.

The frescoes on the walls show a different theme; they depict pastoral scenes, shepherds and flocks of goats something strange because the stockbreeders of the region, the so-called Saracatsanos, hated goats so much that they left their care to the women. However,

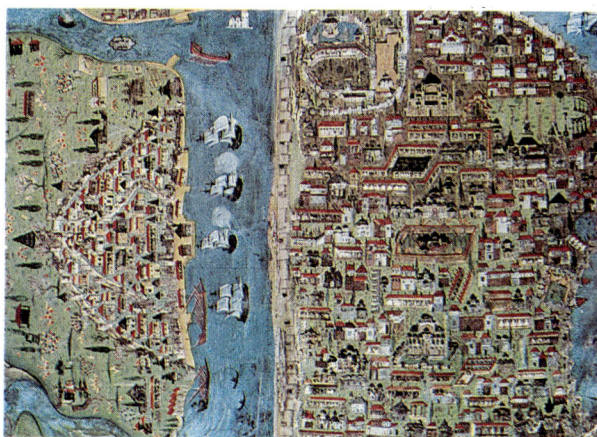

Constantinople and the Golden Horn-Miniature from the «Description of the landmarks of Suleiman's expedition against the two Iraqs» by Al Matraki, 1537.

the painter knew mountain landscapes very well; he had probably lived on a mountain or was born in a mountain village of Pindos. His pictures of cities located near rivers are only developments of the front elevations. But his interest is centered around the trees and the big birds that perch on them, loooking as if they are about to fly and join the flight of birds seen in the distance. The river is full of beautiful, full-rigged ships and fish, and its banks swarn with water birds.

The interior of the mansion of Giannakis (Natzis) in Castoria, which was built in 1750, by masons from Debreli, was decorated in 1796. Here, the rococo has

Miniature from the «Description of the landmarks of Suleiman's expedition against the two Iraqs»q op. cit.

Veria: Fresco in the house of Sior Manolaki.

reached its peak. The friezes of the rooms are adorned with fine compositions interlaced with flowers and garlands. A picture of Constantinople reminds us of the picture in the mansion of Maliogas (Tsirliganis), in Siatista.

A mansion in Selitsa (Eratyra), near Kozani, was

Fresco with the two-headed eagle over a door in Avramopoulos mansion.

decorated in 1798. The decoration of the rooms of the mansion, which the noble Moralis built at the turn of the century, was completed during the same year. Later, in 1754, the new owner, Demetrios Tsiatsapas repaired and remodelled it[297]. The fresco of Constantinople in the «good room» is a special work of popular art of the 18th century. It is a completely stylized imaginary drawing of a perfectly schematized city divided into coastal sections by long, narrow strips of water running into the land. Doubtless, it is Constantinople; however, no mosques or minarets can be seen anywhere. There is a long line of sailships in the foreground accompanied by the favorite theme, the big sea dragons, which, in some cases, are bigger than the ships. The overall decoration, with the baroque anthemia, resembles the decoration of the mansion of Poulkides, in Siatista (1759). The details are also similar. The clock tower in the fresco of Poulkide's residence, which is also the belfry of a church, can also be seen in a fresco of Tsiatsapas' mansion. In both houses, the way of drawing the outlines of the architectural developmnets reminds us of the miniatures of manuscripts of the period and, particularly, the «Pilgrimage to the Holy Land» of the 17th and 18th centuries we mentioned before.

The rich frescoes with the strong rococo decoration in the mansions of Sior Manolakis, in Veria, which, unfortunately, does not exist today were probably painted during the same period[298]. It was painted by artists from Chionades. The frescoes, inside frames, pictured western cities interspersed with a lot of baroque decorative details. All the decoration of this house, but especially the pictures of the cities are similar to some landscapes painted in the konak of Tsaciraga at Birgi, where a fresco showing a panoramic view of Smyrna has been preserved (1830)[299].

The mansion of Nerantzis Aivazis, near Doltsos, in the district of Serviotis of Castoria is more recent than the others but its decoration has followed the tradition faithfully[300]. Here, too, one can discern the desire of the owner to decorate even the smallest space of the interior with the wealth of themes we have described and which are still admired by visitors. On every vertical surface of this house, too, wherever there were no pseudo-windows, they painted frescoes of anthemia, mythical monsters or wild animals of the jungle, hunting scenes, baroque and rococo frames,

Detail of the hood of the decorative fireplace in the room of the «eagle» of G. Schwarz's mansion in Ambelakia.

garlands and baskets full of either fruit or flowers, pictures of french-style furniture, even the picture of a Hussar - as in the mansion of Maliogas - with the inscription «*Le Houssare d'Autriche*»[301], pictures similar to those of the mansions of G. Schwartz in Ambelakia[302] and the two-headed eagles of the mansions of Malioga, Keradzis and Nerandzopoulos with the inscription «the month of May, 20, 1755»[303].

Hunting scenes became a favorite theme too. The painter pays special attention to detail. The falconers with the trained falcons perched on their arms, can be seen very clearly; the hunting dogs, and everything else, even details which are clearly the product of the artist's imagination are pictured with remarkable vividness. Sometimes the pictures of the owners of the houses, in period costumes, are included in the picture - as, for instance, in the house of D. Keradjis, in Siatista[304].

At the turn of the 19th century, something like a fresh breeze blew away the established traditional scenery of the interior of the houses. The multi-colored baroque decoration disappeared. The «color» ceases to play an essential part in completing the symbolic representation; it was superseded by «history», the historiated painting. It was like a revival of older times, already familiar to the rich Macedonian merchants who had travelled to the big European centers, especially to the big cities of Austria and Hungary; also, some messages had come through the pamphlets which were printed in Venice, Vienna, Paris or even in Moschopolis. However, it was a familiar but welcome change; it was especially welcome to the Macedonians because it brought Greek themes and the enslaved Greeks were proud of it. And this current became prevalent a little later when South Greece was freed and Athens became the capital of the Greek Nation.

From that time onwards, the influence of neo-classicism began to be evident even in the horizontal cross-sections of the mansions which now became

Detail of fresco in Argyriades' house in Siatista.

Gradually, the typical themes of the frescoes, Constantinople, plants and flowers, rococo and colors were replaced by mythological representations. The arabesques of the ceilings were replaced by the neo-classic rhythmology, friezes, classical cymatia, spiraliform meanders and anthemia. All these figures of mythology or ancient history, the scantily-dressed godesses and nude nymphs probably shocked the overdressed old women of that period, but they «swallowed» them because on the one hand they were «Greek» and on the other they were fashionable in «civilized Europe». They were remote from ordinary experience, but so were the distant cities from which the new fashions and ideas came and with which they were familiar only through the stories that the men of the family - those who had travelled abroad - told

more symmetrical, especially in the Vlachic villages of Macedonia. A few gables began to make their timid appearance over the facades of the mansions. The architectural projections, the «sahnisins», began to be supported by ternary columns: with a base, a shaft and a capital. The openings began to be constructed with frames. There were regions where neo-classicism came to mean hellenism. The schools which were built during this period had a distinct neo-classic morpohology.

Inscription in an upper floor room of Maliogas' mansion. It informs us that «Repair work began on March, 6, 1844, and ended on April, 15. Siatista, D.A.».

Detail of a fresco in the drawing room of Maliogas' house in Siatista.

about them.

Thus, in 1811 the «good room» of the old mansion of Nicolaos Chadjimichalis, built in 1757, - which is known today as the Canatsoulis mansion, from the name of a more recent owner - was redecorated with themes of the Greek mythology, and because of this, it was called Pantheon[305].

In the old mansion of Djouras (1725), in Siatista, new frescoes were painted in 1827 in certain rooms. In the frescoes, on a white background, inside big rectangular frames, one can see fine, linear paintings of lions, anthemia and even human figures; somewhere, among them, there is even the picture of a

«The four seasons». Detail of a fresco in Kariophilis'
mansion in Siatista.

pendulum.

The old mansion of Argyriades (Maliogas) in Siatista, which, as we saw, was built in 1759, has an inscription that says: «*On the 6th of March, 1844 the remodelling began; it was completed on the 15th of April*». During this stage, the new themes, in frames, were painted, for example the equestrian portrait of the Austrian Hussar, probaly copied from a popular pamphlet of the period, the deer, a picture of the globe with two symmetrical lions on each side and a chapleted eagle over it, pictures of ostriches and two symmetrical human figures in the center, one having

«The four seasons held by the Day and the Night,
between them, the Earth» Fresco in Kariophilis' mansion,
in Siatista.

A picture of the owner on the W wall of the NW room of
Keradzis' mansion in Siatista.

the features of Rigas Pheraios and the other, probably, those of Lord Byron.

In the mansion of Liutaris (Kariofilis), in Siatista, there is a fresco picturing the four seasons inside large circles, and, symmetrically, two women in ancient Greek attire, symbolizing the Day and the Night. These frescoes were painted when the house was remodelled in 1850[306]. An important fresco of an old theme but adopted to neo-classic style, is a repre-

Fresco picturing animals in the drawing room of Maliogas'
mansion in Siatista.

Interior decoration in
Michaelides-Tsirlis
house.

sentation of Constantinople, full of mosques and minarets and other public buildings, including the Incili kiosk, drawn with such accuracy that, in spite of the alterations and replacements that the painter

made, evince the existence of a model. The sea is full of steamships with paddle-wheels while the scenes on the shore with the gentlemen on horseback and the

Fresco with Constantinople as its theme, in Kariophilis' house
in Siatista.

Detail of fresco in Kariophilis' house
in Siatista.

*Fresco in the upper floor
of a mansion, Nympheon,
Florina.*

*Classical landscapes (top and bottom) of free Athens in
Keradzis' mansion Siatista.*

ladies in western apparel walking by the seaside, all those folkloric details, evidence that the painter had a personal experience of the life in Constantinople in the middle of the 19th century. This fresco reminds us of the technique they used, during the same time, in pictures of Constantinople in Asia Minor, in Amasya and Merzifunda and in the period of Beyazid II in the region of Küulliyesi Sandirvani[307].

In the mansion of Michael N.Tsirlis, in the mountain town of Neveska (Nymphaion), which was built in 1887, neo-classicism is evident in the interior decoration. Especially, in pseudo-alcoves, the painter tries to give the illusion of sculpture to his picture of deities of the Greek pantheon (Artemis, Aphrodite, Aris) by using chiaroscuro in very soft tones. This Artemis particularly has been identified with the well-known marble copy of the phidian Amazon of the Mattei collection[308]. I. Touratsoglou, who has studied the fresco - which, in 1975 was separated from the wall[309] - believes that the painter was Italian or he had studied in Italy. Another fresco, picturing a philosopher, was discovered in the mansion of Th. Tsirlis. I. Touratsoglou who, published it, writes: «the philosopher pictured in the fresco of the upper floor

of Th. Tsirlis will enrich the meager collection of neo-classic copies of ancient works of sculpture which are still preserved in houses dating back to the second half of the 19th century.» The picture was identified with the seated figure in the Galleria of Palazzo Spada of Rome which, according to some specialists, depicts Aristotle and according to others

Fresco in Karakitsios' mansion. Eratyra, Kozani.

Detail of a ceiling of the Cathedral of Siderocastro.

Detail of a ceiling of Annicas' house in Kleisoura, Castoria.

Aristippus. Touratsoglou believes that the painter had a picture contained in E.D. Visconti's «*Iconographia Greca*» (Milano 1823 fig. XXa)[310], as his model. There are other important frescoes of the period in the mansions of Theodoros Litsis, Gitsas, Lustas, K. Missios and C. Boutaris[311] of the same town.

From now on, it is not easy to follow the neo-classic development because it spread and became a general current throughout the ottoman empire[312].

In the mansion of D. Keradjis, in Siatista, we see now classical landscapes of free Athens: Hadrian's

Arch, with a cart right in front of it and two symmetrical trees, the Olympieion[313], and Constantinople inside an oval of laurels. Among all these, there is a human figure, standing near a chair - a favorite pose of that period - which is interesting because it discloses some information on the usual attire of the era[314].

Meander is the basic motif now in the form of either a spiral-meander or of a swastika; we can see these forms everywhere, in the friezes around the ceilings, in the «navels» of the ceilings inside ellipsoid framesqas in the house of Agustas in Alistrati, Serrai, and in several mansions of Selitsa (Eratyra, Kozani).

In the representation of an archangel holding the gospel which is in a fresco on the ceiling of the bishopric mansion of Siderocastro (Demir-Isar) we see an awkward imitation of the style of the sculpture in the alcove of Tsirlis' mansion. This looks more like a neo-classic depiction of a winged victory; it is not a convincing representation of an archangel.

In Barzdokas' house, in Eratyra of Kozani, the frieze in the «big room» pictures forests and sylvan life next to double, symmetrical cornucopias which, gradually, turn into garlands as they approach the walls of the triclinium.

Fresco in a house of Tsataltza, in the prefecture of Drama.

In the Vlachic village of Kleisura, we see imitations of frescoes of the mansions of Nevesca. They picture, inside rectangular frames, idyllic scenes, - clearly inspired by western models -, couples walking in forests, pictures like those one sees on the walls of shops in villages.

The frescoes in another house of Kleisura, the house of Annica, are similar in style. One can see a picture of an effeminate Heracles and a lady near a lake with the ever-present swans and, in the background, a row of trees in sharp perspective. These pictures are completed with hunting scenes, trophies inside frames and figures of the Greek pantheon.

The pictures of steamships with paddle wheels and some sails, with the colored gunports, in the house of Caraiscos, in Eratyra, can be seen in the same place of the frieze, in the farthest corner of the ottoman empire: in the house of Haci Sami Efendi in Karaman[315]. In the house of Kefalas, in Tsatalza of Drama, we noticed an example of another current inside the general current of neo-classicism: a particularly descriptive tendency with a sharp linearity of

Fresco in the mayor's house. Kleisura, Castoria.

the pictures where the painter tries to give emphasis to the achievements of mechanical civilization. The

Fresco in Tsataltza, prefecture of Drama.

Fresco in the «Pantheon» of Kanatsoulis' mansion, Siatista.

way of painting the houses is symbolic and the interior spaces intermingle with the exterior, as in the well-

Fresco in the «Pantheon» of Kanatsoulis' mansion, Siatista.

known manuscript of Skylitzis of Madrid[316]. The painter shows a special preference for steamships, railroads and other specimens of the technology of the period. The style reminds us of similar pictures in houses of Asia Minor, as, for instance, in the temple of Kara Mustafa Pasa in Merzefunda (1875) where the painter Zileli Emin, using the same linear technique,

Fresco in the «Pantheon» of Katsoulis' mansion, Siatista.

tries to show his technological knowledge[317] by painting hydraulic works, railroads, and guns.

During the same period - end of the 19th century - there began a tendency to decorate the interior of the domes, in the Athonite phiales, with landscapes, gardens and pictures of cities. Representative examples have been preserved in the phiale of the monastery of Greater Lavra in Athos and in the phiale of the monastery of Prodromos, in Serres, as well as on the fountains of certain mosques[318].

The interior decoration of the house of Petrakis, in Korissos of Castoria, shows, perhaps, the last examples of neo-classicism. Inside circular frames, there are pictures of female figures in western attire, the Genovefa type, surrounded by spiralling meanders. On a panel, there is a picture of a city and a landing party on the quay. The city authorities are welcoming the officers of the ship. It is probably, a copy of a popular lithograph picturing the visit of the leader of a foreign country, or, perhaps, the liberation of Thessaloniki, because the rowboats bear the Greek flag.

The influence of the western rococo was so strong on the art throughout the ottoman empire, and especially in Constantinople, that it became the basic motif around which all the various local tendencies developed and gave these remarkable results. It is an indisputable fact that these foreign influences gravitated to the common melting pot, the center of arts, Constantinople, the capital of the empire and there, the various groups of artisans - which, as we know, visited Constantinople and worked there - communicated in the common influences[319].

From the beginning of the 18th century onwards, the rythmology of baroque-rococo in architectural decoration begins to be more or less generally established - less in the remote towns and villages of the empire.

Apart from the partial «grammar» of rococo in the details of the decoration, it is obvious that the style has been generally assimilated and that ready-made common models are intepreted, in various locations, with sufficient faithfulness, but also with a freedom which permits the personality of the artist and, probably, the local artistic tradition - whose carriers had always been the anonymous popular artists of the various guilds - to intrude themselves[320].

During the turkish occupation, apart from the associations of manufacturers, there were also - especially in the mountain settlements - certain specializations which characterized the whole settlement, such as the builders-masons (Coudareoi), goldsmiths (Kalarytes) and painters (Chionades).

Fresco in Petrakis' mansion in Korissos, Castoria.

In the various painting studios, the apprentices were taught, empirically, by old masters of the art. Thessaloniki was still the most important center of icon-painting, but other centers, where painting was taught, began to appear, as, for instance, Selitsa (Eratyra), Vogatsico, Edessa, in West Macedonia; Chionades, Capesovo and Fortosi, in Galatista, in Chalkidiki, and others[321].

Inside the borders of the vast ottoman empire, the

Fresco in Petrakis' mansion in Korissos, Castoria.

various local guilds of builders and artists, managed to develop and spread the local architectural and artistic traditions while, at the same time, all the various building and decoration tendencies blended into one common spirit. The various local building or artistic groups did not mind crossing the vast empire to work in far away places, thus carrying their local artistic tradition to the most remote corners of the country, and, at the same time, receiving other, local influences. As a matter of fact, Ottoman Turkey was usually open to any local artistic influence and, from the 18th century onwards, it was also open to direct western influences[322]; futhermore, the various ethnic groups were free to develop their architectural and artistic styles.

The accuracy of the copies of the various themes, not only in their entirety (e.g. the developments of the surfaces of the rooms, ceilings, wood panelling) but also in the details (the representations of symbolic landscapes and typical baroque motifs), implies the existence of models; lithographs, copperplates and, definitely, tracing[323].

Among the wood carvings of the rich mansions of Macedonia we can see details in the figures of the motifs and also techniques similar to the familiar temples of the churches of the period, which shows that, probably, the same groups of craftsmen built houses and churches. Furthermore, the construction of the elaborate panels of the ceilings in the houses of Castoria and Siatista, which evince a distinct ottoman influence, proves that these craftsmen also built mosques because, in mosques, decoration with geometric arabesques of small pieces of carved wood and adorned with pearls or ivory was very common[324].

We saw in the previous paragraphs that the theme and the style of the interior decoration was influenced by well-known miniatures of manuscripts, especially of «pilgrimages» of the 16th, and, particularly, of the 18th century; similarly, the decorations of the interior of many official buildings of the ottoman empire evince the influences of ottoman miniatures of manuscripts of the end of the 17th century. Günsel Renda, in a study of his[325], ascertains this influence and the artists' effort to render a likeness of the subject of these miniatures most of which date from the period known as the Tulip Period. The oldest examples are in the manuscript Hamsei Atai (Topkapi R 816) of

1728[326].

The older stylized floral decorations were superseded by the plethoric forms of baroque with the juicy floral motifs, the curved cornices, the imaginary landscapes, the pictures of Constantinople and other big ports of the ottoman empire, evidently influenced by popular models, probably paintings, which circulated in the market places and bazaars of Constantinople, exactly as today one can find cheap lithographs for every taste, picturing Mecca and the Kaaba, and other holy islamic places. We can see the same decoration, copied by popular artists, today, in mosques and in medrese in Thrace and Asia Minor.

From the middle of the 18th century onwards, appear examples of tromp d'oeil paintings, of the western style, in the ottoman interior design[327]. But human figures did not appear before the end of the 19th century[328].

If we compare the arrangement of the decorations of the interior of the Macedonian mansions and the ottoman residences we will find many similarities. But what makes the greatest impression on the visitor is the artistic quality of the decoration of the mansions and the houses of the Greeks of West Macedonia, which is not inferior to the most imposing works of the court of the sultan.

It might be interesting to investigate the phenomenon of the high quality of the work done in the mansions of West Macedonia by local popular painters who had obviously been apprenticed to artists in Constantinople and, later, worked in many public buildings of the ottoman empire[329]. However, before making a systematic study, we must examine each geographical region to get familiar with the material which will help us to make comparisons.

This study of the interior decoration of those houses, must be followed by a systematic comparison, not only with the corresponding examples which have been preserved in Turkey, but also with the tendencies prevalent in the icon-painting of the period[330] because they constitute the only reliable source of our artistic development[331], which can influence our effort to study the origin of our traditions constructively.

On the walls of the «Synodicon» of the monastery of St. John Prodromos of Serres, there is a fresco depicting the palace of Sebrun, near Vienna which was built as a hunting lodge during the reign of

Leopold I and was completed during the time of Maria Theresa (1744). The fresco in the hall of the hegumen must have been painted in 1795, that is, «when the hall was remodelled thanks to the financial aid of Messrs. Tsertsises of Serres. The frescoes were painted by the wonderful painter Nedelcos»[332]. The monks explained that the fresco of the palace showed the association of the monastery with the rich cotton merchants of Serres, who were the «trustees» of the monastery in Vienna[333]. However, in addition to the fresco of the palace and its gardens - the work of the dutch architect van Stekhuen[334], - there is also a landscape of Bosphorus (the palace of Beylerbey) on the SW wall, and another lanscape on the NW wall. Nedelcos, the artist who painted the frescoes, gives some information about his specialty and abilities in an inscription in the dining hall of the monastery (1795) : «*It was painted by Nedelcos, the wonderful and clever painter of cities, ports and every kind of landscape with rococo decorations*»[335]. The painter knew quite well that his style was late turko-rococo, in other words the western - french rocaille style which was fashionable during the time of Louis XV, especially between 1720 and 1750, which came to be known as rococo[336].

Doubtlessly, the influences came through the commercial routes. From the big cultural and commercial centers of Europe, the Greek merchants brought collections of models («cartouches», «lambris») and many kinds of patterns for plaster decorations. M. Kantsoulis believes that the patterns for the decoration of the mansion of Manousis, in Siatista, were bought in Germany because the merchants of Siatista had many contacts there. Most probably the owner of the house himself brought the models and the patterns back from one of his trips to Germany and gave them to the painters[337]. Many themes of this secular painting of the 18th and 19th century were used in churches[338], outer narthexes of «catholica» of monasteries[339], even mosques, as, for instance, the Yokousta djami (Bairaklι djami) (1846) in Samakovo[340].

We have already mentioned the native towns of the popular painters. However how the ecclesiastical and secular painting developed in those remote villages, is still a problem. The explanations given by the painters themselves - mainly, poverty, which made them turn either to stockbreeding or to painting - are not satisfactory. (A painter from Chionades charac-

Fresco in Tsiatsapas' mansion in Castoria.

teristically said: «our place produces only oregano and hares»[341].

The small village of Chionades produced 65 popular painters. When Pagonis finished the frescoes in the church of St. Marina of Pelion in 1802, he wrote

Fresco in the «Pantheon» of Kanatsoulis' mansion, Siatista.

Flowers in the vase, a bird perched on the cypress, the date, 1757, blue and green colors in yellow background.
Gerechtes' mansion.

on the column capitals of the big basilica: «*Made by the hand of Constantine Pagonis of the tribe of Pas-chalades from the village of Chionades*»[342]. The tribe of the artists was sometimes mentioned, as, for instance, in another inscription the «*tribe of Botsareon*» is mentioned.

Painters from many parts worked in the Macedonian mansions. M. Kanatsoulis writes that the frescoes in the «Pantheon» of the mansion of Siatista, which was built in 1811, were painted by Euthymios Efthimiou, a painter from Patra, and it was inspired by Charisis Megdanis' book (Greek Pantheon) published in Pest[343]. Later, painters from Vogatsico, and, among them, the well-known Themistocles Chadjitheocharis, began to appear[344].

It is comparatively easy to distinguish the christian houses from the ottoman houses. Although the models, the themes and the color scale are the same,

there are certain minute details which show the difference. In a turkish room, Constantinople is pictured without churches and crosses; it has mosques and minarets only. And certainly, no priests holding the cross are pictured - like the one in the fresco of Poulkides' mansion in Siatista. In the mansion of an ottoman family, the builder or the painter never writes inscriptions in Greek[345] nor does he put such inscriptions as IC-XC-NI-KA, which we saw in Tsatsapas' mansion; and no priest would ever decorate a transom window and sign it as, for instance, in the mansion of Chadjiyannides (Neradjopoulos) in Siatista which was built in 1755 and has the inscription: «*the priest Moschos was the master artisan*»; no saints, or crosses or double-headed eagles were ever pictured in ottoman houses. Furthermore, no important ottoman mansion has been preserved in Macedonia.

In the 19th century, a period marked by neoclassicism, the Greek houses begin to show distinct external differences due to the prevailing rhythmology and internal differences due to the themes taken from the Greek mythology and the landscapes and monuments of Athens, capital now of the free Greek nation. There are no such pictures in the ottoman residences. There are no pictures of nude deities of the Greek Pantheon. Only, in the mansion of Midat Pasha, in Russe, there are certain neutral romantic representations, such as «Eros and Psyche»[346]. Very rarely were meanders and swastikas used in ottoman houses.

It is possible that all the variations of the form of the meander did not come from the West but also from the East through certain Chinese models which had circulated in Europe[347].

However, even if all the aforementioned differences are absent, a specialist can tell, by a barely perceptible detail, whether the house belonged to a christian or muslim, to a Greek or to a Turk.

*

It is not possible to make a list of the mansions that were built in the 18th and 19th centuries in Macedonia because the most important towns and villages that flourished during that period were destroyed by the Turkoalbanian hordes. But the samples which have been preserved evince the wealth and quality of architecture of the period. The most important mansions have been preserved in Kozani. Parts of the wood carvings of their rooms have been brought to Athens and are on display in the Benakis museum. Another gilded part - similar to the rich temples of the churches of Kozani and Eratyra - is kept in the mansion of Melas in Kato Kifissia and is the richest of the preserved samples.

Some important mansions have been preserved (although in a very bad condition) in Castoria, Siatista, Metsovo, Ambelakia, Veria (the mansions of Naussa and Edessa have been destroyed), in Kleisura, Nymfeo (Nevesca), and very few in Florina, and Pisoderi. These are the last vestiges of the past and are valuable to those who want to understand the social

Fresco picturing Constantinople in Cakir Aga mansion, Birgi, Asia Minor (photo: 1982).

and economic structure during the turkish occupation; no effort should be spared to preserve them so that to be seen by future generations.

These famous mansions of Macedonia are products of the architecture which constitutes a continuation of the Byzantine and were built by local, well-known craftsmen; this became possible only because the rich Macedonian traders had the means and the will to build them. However, those merchants were not interested in building only big houses for themselves; they built schools, churches, supported monasteries, gave financial aid to poor youths who wanted to further their education. Thus, Hellenism, along with the important professional organizations, the elders (community organizations) and of the various corporations and the ever-present church, managed to survive and, finally, become free again.

●

N. MOUTSOPOULOS
THE HOUSES OF THE MACEDONIAN COM-
MUNITIES: 15TH - 19TH CENTURY
NOTES

1. N.C. Moutsopoulos, «Τα 'Δρακόσπιτα' της ΝΔ Εύβοιας. Συμβο-λή στην αρχιτεκτονική, την τυπολογία και τη μορφολογία τους» (The 'drakospita' of SW Euboe. A contribution to their architecture, typology and morphology.) ΕΕΠΣ, Τμήματος Αρχιτεκτόνων της Πολυτε-χνικής Σχολής του Α.Π.Θ. 8. Thessaloniki 1982, p. 421-445.

2. N.C. Moutsopoulos: «Αρχιτεκτονικά μνημεία της περιοχής της αρχαίας Βούρας, Ιστορική και μορφολογική εξέτασις» (Architectural monuments in the region of ancient Vura; an historical and morphological examination), Athens 1981, p. 29-58.

3. N.C. Moutsopoulos:«Αρχιτεκτονικά μνημεία της περιοχής της αρχαίας Βούρας» (Architectural monuments in the region of ancient Vura), op. cit., p. 29-34.

4. A study of the typology and form of the dwellings of the serfs of the turkish timars might be interesting· cf Georgios Chadjikyriakos, «Σκέψεις και εντυπώσεις εκ περιοδείας ανά την Μακεδονίαν (1905-1906)» (Thoughts and impressions of a tour in Macedonia (1905-1906)), Thessaloniki 1962, p. 14 (a description of the inhabitants and the residence of the bey of Dodular, near Thessaloniki. Many of them were duplexes, such as the one which has been preserved in Eleochoria, near Thessaloniki. cf corresponding «two-room houses» of Albania as they are pictured in the book of Franz Baron Nopcsa, *Albanien*, Berlin Leipzig 1925, p. 35, pic.19, p. 39, pic.23 (Kolaj). Huts of settlers (*pareci*) have been preserved in Rumania. Georgeta Stoica: «L'architecture vernaculaire en Roumanie» pub. UNESCO, p. 46.

5. Such as the one that has been preserved in Eleochoria of Thessaloniki which, in the years of the turkish occupation, had been a «ciftlik». Cf. similar types of twin share-cropper's houses in Albania in Faruk Zarshati's «Banesea Popullore në Malësi të Lezhes» (La mansion caracteristique de la Malesie de Lezhe), *Monumentet*, 12, 1976 (p. 183-195) p. 188 pic.II.

6. A. Keramopoulos, «Ανασκαφαί και έρευναι εν τη Ανω Μακεδο-νία» (Excavations and research in Upper Macedonia), *Αρχαιολογική Εφημερίς (Archaeological journal), 1932, p. 116, 117.*

7. A. Keramopoulos: *op. cit., Archaeological journal*,1932, p. 117.

8. Apostolos E. Vacalopoulos: «Ιστορία του Νέου Ελληνισμού» (History of modern Hellenism) *BZ*, Turkish rule 1453-1669. The historical foundation of the modern Greek Society and Economy, Thessaloniki 1964, p. 62.

9. Albanian Vlachs.

10. Kataphygi of Naupactia, Aetolo-Acarnania, Agnanta of Arta, Karditsa, Kozani, Grevena (the Calithea of today) «Λεξικό των Δήμων, Κοινοτήτων και οικισμών της Ελλάδος» (Dictionary of Munici-palities, Communities and Settlements of Greece), Athens 1974.

11. Leon Heuzey, *Le mont Olympe et l' Acarnanie*, Paris 1860 p. 205-206. A.Vacalopoulos: *«History of modern Hellenism*, V II 1, Thessaloniki 1964, p. 81-81. Podari, a name similar to another usual name of villages; Podochori, which, compared to the corresponding Podgorie of slavic villages (meaning the feet of a mountain) might help to find the probable location of the original cell of the settlement, in a geomorphologic formation in a place where the river passes near the foot of a mountain.

12. Eustathios I.Stougiannakis: *«History of the city of Nausa»* Edessa 1924, p. 19 - 20.

13. N.C. Moutsopoulos, «The mansions of the traders of Macedonia» *Proceedings of the Symposium: «Diachronic development of communalism in Macedonia»* 9-11 December 1988, Thessaloniki 1991, p. 356, Cf. Th.Sarantis: «The villages of Grevena according to the codex of the monastery of Zavorda (1692)», «Ημερολόγιον Δυτικής Μακεδονίας», (Almanac of W. Macedonia v.I), 1960, p. 207-212.

14. A. Vacalopoulos: *«Οι δυτικομακεδόνες απόδημοι επί Τουρκο-κρατίας»* (West Macedonia emigrants during the turkish occupation), Thessaloniki 1958, p. 4.

15. I.N. Philimonos: *«Δοκίμιον περί της Φιλικής Εταιρείας»* (A treatise on the Friendly Society, Nauplion 1834) p. 72-73· Cf. collective publication in Armoloi, August 1976, «The groups of craftsmen», p. 7.

16. L. Heuzey, *Le mont Olympe et l' Acarnanie, op. cit.,* p. 45-48, Krystallis «*The complete works»* VI Preface - Introduction - Edition

G.Valetas, Athens 1951, p. 504, A. Vacalopoulos, *Ιστορία του Νέου Ελληνισμού*» (*History of modern Hellenism*) V II 1, Thessaloniki 1964, p. 84.

17. Krystallis «*The complete works*» V I, *op. cit.*, p. 504 «It should be finally noted that the inhabitants of Vlacholivadi have the same names, the same language, the same accent, the same physiognomy, the same apparel, the same occupations, the same customs and habits and the same songs with those of the inhabitants of Samarina and the surrounding villages»· Cf. A. Vacalopoulos , *op. cit.*, p. 89.

18. We mention the mountain villages of the country with an altitude of over 1200 m.: Aghios Athanasios of Pella (1200), Livadites of Xanthi (1200), Magouliana of Arcadia (1200), Pades of Ioannina (1200), Nympheo (Neveska) of Florina (1350), Lower Vermio of Imathia (1400), Kataphygi of Kozani (1400), Pisoderi of Florina (1420), Aetomilitsa of Ioannina (1430), Samarina of Grevena (1420). Pourianos Stavros of Magnesia (1600).

19. N.C. Moutsopoulos: «*Τα Θεσσαλικά Αμπελάκια*» (*Ambelakia of Thessaly*), Thessaloniki 1975, p. 13, and: «*Τα αρχοντικά των πραματευτάδων της Μακεδονίας*» (The mansions of the Macedonian traders), *op. cit.*, p. 357.

20. Helene Antoniades-Bibicou: «Villages desertes en Grèce, Un Bilan provisoire» *Villages désertés et histoire économique XIe-XVIIIe siècle*. Ecole Pratique des Hautes Etudes - VIe Section. Paris 1965, p. 364.

21. G.N. Aikaterinides in «*Νεοελληνικές αιματηρές θυσίες. Λειτουργία - Μορφολογία - Τυπολογία*» (*Modern Greek bloody secrifices. Function - Morphology - Typology*), p. 152, gives important information about the popular beliefs concerning the protection of the settlements. «These are important pieces of information -remark- ably similar- about the ritualistic inauguration of the village, which aims to protect a new-born settlement against evil-chiefly diseases: they yoked two twin calfs together and made a furrow all around the village; then they buried the calfs in front of the entrance of the village. The inauguration was done with two twin calfs yoked together and adorned with silver harness. They made a furrow all around the village, a narrow furrow that completely enclosed the settlement. And where the furrow ended, and the enclosure was completed, they buried the calves alive. And afterwards when they had decomposed, they took them to the church, the priest blessed the remains and then they buried them in the cemetery.» As the time passed, the custom became a legend which no one seriously believed. Outside Tsiraki, a village near Grevena, people used to show two big stones, supposedly the grave of two calfs. Other places, elsewhere, are supposed to be either the graves of the calves or connected, in some way, with the custom. Also, the line that the furrow followed around the village was marked with wooden crosses at intervals ; that is probably why so many Aetolian villages are called «Stavros» (cross) while other «Gainia» (inauguration). According to the custom if something bad happened (for instance, a killing), then the village had to be inaugurated again. The ritual was repeated also in cases of epidemics and always it was centered round the killing of the animals which were supposed to carry the sins or evils of the community away».

22.Eustathios I. Stouyannakis: «*Ιστορία της πόλεως Ναούσης*» (History of the city of Nausa), Edessa 1924, p. 37 and on. The legend of the founding of Nausa (Niausta, Niagusta, Agustos etc.) reminds us of the legend about Carthage recorded by Titus Livius 134,62. About the true boundaries of Nausa, there is a turkish document which Stouyannakis has published along with a greek translation., *op. cit.*, p. 39-42.

23. G. Aikaterinides: «*Ο εορτασμός του Αγίου Γεωργίου εις Νέον Σούλι Σερρών*» (St George's day in the Suli of Serres), *Serraika Chronica*, v.VI, 1969, p. 133, 135 pic.4. Cf: «*Εαρινά έθιμα λαϊκής λατρείας από την περιοχή Σερρών*» (Spring customs of popular worship of the region of Serres), 1*st Symposium of folklore of N.Greece*, Thessaloniki 1975, p. 15 and on.

24. G. Aikaterinides: «*Ο εορτασμός του Αγίου Γεωργίου εις Νέον Σούλι Σερρών*» (St George's day in New Suli of Serres), *op. cit.*, p. 134, pic.3. D. Lucatos: *Πασχαλινά της Άνοιξης* (*Of Easter and Spring*), Athens 1988, p. 138-141.

25. N.C. Moutsopoulos: «Les sgraffites du Pangaion» V. «In memory

of Panayotis A. Michelis» Athens 1971, table LII and: «*Ηράκλεια Σιντική*» (Heraclia Sintiki), *Filia Epi es G.E. Mylonan*, v. IV, Athens 1990, p. 142. Cf. P.K. Yokas, «*Η καταγωγή των αρχαίων Μακεδόνων*» (The origin of the ancient Macedonians), Thessaloniki 1977, p. 100. «The characteristic symbol of the Paeonians which appears on many coins of the Paeonic tribes had various greek names, such as, heliotropion, the wheel of the sun, the eye surrounding the world, the eyelid of the golden day, the all-seeing circle of the sun, the eye of Zeus.».

26. The following account is related to it: «In a case of an epidemic, the elders summoned the inhabitants and ordered an old man to take two black oxen, yoke them together to a plow and make two furrows, in the shape of the cross, from one end of the village to the other; then they buried the oxen and the plow and the epidemic stopped. Outside the village of Papades, there was a cross. That place is called «Cross»; two calves were born to the same mother; then they yoked them to a plow and «crossed» the village; and at that place, they killed the calves and buried them so that neither the plague nor cholera can enter the village». In Euboea, the ritual is more complicated. «When we heard that an epidemic had hit a neighboring village, and if a cow happened to give birth to two claves, the elders of the village would run and gather twelve maidens who would gather cotton and would dress and weave it all in one day. When the cloth was finished, three priests would take the cloth and wrap it round the two calves. Then a young man would take them in his arms and all together would go to four points, outside the village, forming the ends of a cross and they would go all around the village, chanting, and when the calves died, they would burn them and the place would be named «crucifix». Then, no disease would hit the village. It is a good omen if a cow gives birth to two calves». It is said that the village of Damalas, in Troizenia took its name from the calves (damalia) which the inhabitants killed in the middle of the village. The Athenian Colonaki has also taken its name from a related legend. also describes a complicated ritual: «A disease had spread in the village. At that time a cow gave birth to two calves, something that had never happened before. Some people said it was a good omen, others it was bad. The elders came then to decide. They decided to have a divine service and because they believed that the disease had come from the north, they made a ditch in the shape of the cross near the fountain outside the northern side of the village, a place called Kliza. They believed that most of the diseases had come from the caves of the mountains. Before the ritual all the village had fasted for three days, the men separated from the women. On the third day they had the divine service, then they all went to Kliza, the priest with the gospel at the head of the procession, then the chanters holding the icons of the Virgin Mary and St. John Theologus, and after them came the cow with the two calves. The ditch in the shape of a cross was ready. When they reached the place, the priest blessed them and then they killed the calves, dropped them in the ditch, the priest blessed them again and then he blessed the holy water and exorcided all evils. When they got back to the village they had a picnic in the churchyard (the church of St.John). The legend says that the water of the Klizas fountain has the power to cure any disease». G. Aikaterinides, «*Αιματηρές θυσίες*» (*Bloody sacrifices*), p. 156-158. Cf. D. Petropoulos, «*Όσια και Ιερά - Σταυράτα*» (Holy boundaries - Crosses), *Yearbook of the School of Philosophy*, v. XI, Thessaloniki 1971, p. 277 and on.

27. George Ostrogorsky, *Histoire de l'etat Byzantin*, Paris 1956, p. 558.

28. E. Oberhummer «Die Türken und das osmanische Reich», Leipzig - Berlin 1917, H. Gibbons: «The foundation of the ottoman Empire», Oxford 1916. G. Georgiades-Arnakis: «*Οι πρώτοι Οθωμανοί*» (The first Ottomans), Athens 1947. George Ostrogorsky: *Histoire de l'etat Byzantin*, Paris 1956. A.Vacalopoulos: «History of Thessaloniki» Thessaloniki 1983, p. 201.

29. O.L. Barkan: «Les déportations comme méthode de peuplement et de la colonisation dans l'empire ottoman» *Revue de la Fac. Sciences Ec. de l' Univ. d' Istanbul* 11/1-4, 1949 /50, p. 87.

30. O.L. Barkan, *op. cit.*, p. 103 «On comprend aisément qu' un Etat qui avait une telle conception de ses droits et obligations ait pu demander ses sujets de se déplacer en masse quand il estimait

nécessaire».

31. O.L. Barkan: *op. cit.*, p. 110.

32. A.Vacalopoulos: «*Ιστορία του Νέου Ελληνισμού*» (*History of modern Hellenism*) v. I, «Origins and formation», Thessaloniki 1961, particularly p. 108-115, 204-221. And: *op. cit.*, v. II «The turkish rule 1453-1669», Thessaloniki 1964, particulalry the chapter: «The position of the christian rayahs, especially of the agrarian workers, in the turkish-occupied greek regions», (p. 9-43).

33. D.N. Krydes - M. Kiel, «The Sanjak of Evripos 15th-16th c.» (Conditions and features of the developmental processes of towns and villages), *Tetramina* 28+29, (1985), p. 1897-1898: «One category of factors includes the compulsory and intentional relocations of populations by order of the ottoman administration, the other category of factors includes the possibility of relocation of populations from the country to the cities under certain conditions».

34. Omer Lutfi Barkan: «Les fondations pieuses comme méthode de peuplement et de colonisation. Le derviches colonisateurs de l' époque des invasions et de convents (Zaviye)» p. 59.

35. Thanas Kamberi, «Vendbaniment dhe banesat Ishatare në Droppulin e poshtëm (Agglomerations et habitations rurales dans le bas Dropull), *Monumentet 12, Tirana 1976, p. 173, 181.*

36. H. Inalcik «*Suret - i - Defteri Sancaki Arvanid* (*1943-1432*) (Cadastre de Korce et de Pëmet 1431-1432) Ankara 1954.

37. Emin Riza - Pirro Thomo, «Caracteres et traits des agglomerations et de l' habitation dans le XIV-XVIIIe siècles», *Culture populaire albanaise,* 1, 1984, p. 52.

38. Emin Riza - Pirro Thomo: «Culture populaire albanese» 1. 1984, p. 46, 51 Pl. III 1,2, fig. 5.

39. N.C. Moutsopoulos, «Βυζαντινά σπίτια στο Μουχλί της Αρκαδίας» (Byzantine houses in Mouchli of Arcadia), *Byzantina* v. III, Thessaloniki 1985, p. 330 pic. 2, p. 332 pic. 5, 6, p. 334, pic. 7,8.

40. Emin Riza - Pirro Thomo, *op. cit.*, p. 51-52.

41. Emin Piza: «Arkitektura e vendbanimit nënojë të Kardhiqit» (L'Architecture de l' agglomeration urbaine en ruine de Kardhiq), *Monumentet* 17, 1979, p. 116.

42. Emin Riza: *Monumentet*, 17, 1972, p. 116.

43. Emin Riza - Pirro Thomo: «Culture populaire Albanaise» 1, 1984, p. 46.

44. Emin Riza, *op. cit.*, *Monumentet* 17, 1979, table III.

45. J.G.V. Hahn, *Reise von Belgrad nach Salonik,* Wien 1868, p. 181.

46. Emin Riza - Pirro Thomo: *Culture populaire Alabanaise*, 1, 1984, p.46.

47. Emin Riza - Pirro Thomo: *Culture populaire Albanaise*, 1, 1984, p. 46.

48. N.C. Moutsopoulos, «Βυζαντινά σπίτια στο Μουχλί της Αρκαδίας» (Byzantine houses in Mouchli of Arcadia), *Byzantina* v XIII Thessaloniki 1985, p. 323-353.

49. N.C. Moutsopoulos, «Από την Βυζαντινή Καρύταινα» (From Byzantine Carytaina), *A dedication to Tasos Gritsopoulos, Peloponnesiaka* V XVI 1985-1986, p. 145 pic 7-16.

50. Cf. N.C. Moutsopoulos - G. Demetrocallis, *The churches of Geraki* v.I., Thessaloniki 1988.

51. Emin Riza - Pirro Thomo, *Culture populaire albanaise 1*, 1984, p. 46, table II.

52. *Op.cit.*, p. 47, pic 1.

53. Emin Riza - Pirro Thomo: «Caracteres et traits des agglomerations et de l' habitation rurale dans le XIV-XVIII e siecles», *Culture populaire albanaise 1*, 1984, p. 46.

54. N.C. Moutsopoulos, *Churches in the prefecture of Pella*, Thessaloniki 1973, p. 104, 105.

55. Ioakim Martinianos, *Moschopolis* Thessaloniki 1957, p. 26-34. Constantine Skenderis in his «History of ancient and contemporary Moschopolis, Athens 1928» p. 8-9 records the information of J.G. v. Hahn, *Reize Von Belgrad nach Salonik*, Wien 1868, p. 247, that the settlement was founded again by the tribe of Mouzakis, according to the codex of Moschopolis.

56. M.Kalinderis, *Historical notes on West Macedonia*, Ptolemais 1939, p. 5.

57. Ioakim Martinianos, *Moschopolis*, Thessaloniki 1957, p. 61.

58. Cf. *Bulgarian-Greek dictionary* of the Academy of Sciences of

Bulgaria, Institute of the Bulgarian language, Sofia 1960, page 917 words: «pole» and «polja», the plain.

59. Socrate Liacos, «*Η καταγωγή των Αρμάνων*» (*The origin of the Armanes*), Thessaloniki 1965 v. XVI.

60. Ioakim Martinianos, *Moschopolis*, Thessaloniki 1957, p. 35.

61. Ioakim Martinianos, *Moschopolis*, Thessaloniki 1957, p. 35.

62. S. Lambros, «Η Μοσχόπολις και η οικογένεια Σίνα» (Moschopolis and the Sinas family), *NE* (=Neos Ellenomnemon) v.21, 1927, p160.

63. S. Lambros, *op. cit.*, p. 160.

64. Constantine Skenderis, «*Ιστορία της αρχαίας και συγχρόνου Μοσχοπόλεως*» (*History of ancient contemporary Moschopolis*), Athens 1928, p. 10-11: «Moschopolis, in 1750, had 12.000 houses, that is 60.000 inhabitants and 20 splendid churches.».

65. Cf. S. Lambros, NE 21, 1927, p. 161.

66. N.C. Moutsopoulos, «Τα αρχοντικά των πραματευτάδων της Μακεδονίας» (The mansions of the traders of Macedonia)», Thessaloniki 1991, p. 359.

67. Gustav Weigand, «Die Sprache der Olympo-Walachen nebst einer einleitung über Land und Leute», Leipzig 1888, p. 5-7. J.G.v. Hahn, «Reise von Belgrad nach Salonik, nebst vier Abhandlungen zur Alten Geschicte des Morawagebietes», Wien 1868, p. 181 and on.

68. The Albanians call it Bitoja, which means «pigeon», probably from the nearby Pigeon mountains. Others called it by the slavic name of the monastery, «obitel». Finally the greek word Monastery prevailed; the turks confused it with the old slavic name Bi-toli and, combining it with the greek name, called it «Toli-manastir». Pantelis G. Tsallis, «*Το δοξασμένο Μοναστήρι*» (*Glorious Monasteri*), Thessaloniki 1932 (Reprinted 1982), p. 5,6.

69. Pantellis G. Tsallis, *Glorious Monasteri*, p. 85.

70. *op. cit.*, p. 86.

71. *op. cit.*, p. 82.

72. *op. cit.*, p. 83.

73. *op. cit.*, p. 84,85.

74. P.G. Tsallis, *Glorious Monasteri*, p. 85. J.G.v. Hahn in his book *Reise von Belgrad nach Salonik*, Wien 1868, p. 180, writes that, at that time, Crusovo was a city of 2.000 - 3.000 houses.

75. D. Salamagas, «*Τα ισνάφια και τα επαγγέλματα επί Τουρκοκρατίας στα Γιάννινα*» (*Guilds and trades in Yannina during the turkish occupation*), Yannina 1959, p. 18. Cf P. Lambros: «*Περί των εκ Καλαρυτών χρυσοχόων και της τέχνης αυτών*» (About the goldsmiths of Kalaryta and their art), *Cleio* 1887 ar.72. Zach. Papantoniou: «About the goldsmiths of Epirus» *Elefthero Vema*, Dec. 22, 1928. Kyriakos Simopoulos, «Ξένοι ταξιδιώτες στην Ελλάδα» (Foreign travellers in Greece)» v. III 2, 1975 p. 342.

76. F.C.L. Pouqueville, *Voyage de la Grèce II*, Paris 1826, v.II, p. 350, 356. W.M. Leake 1835, p. 274-282. Kyriakos Simopoulos: *Foreign travellers*, v.III, 1975, p. 386 and on.

77. Socr. N. Liacos, «*Η καταγωγή των Βλάχων*» (*The origin of the Vlachs*), Thessaloniki 1965, p. 78.

78. D. Salamagas, «*Τα ισνάφια και τα επαγγέλματα επί Τουρκοκρατίας στα Γιάννινα*» (*Guilds and trades in Yannina during the turkish occupation*), 1959, p. 18.

79. Ioakim Martinianos, *Moschopolis, op. cit.*

80. A.J.B. Wace-M.S. Thomson, *The Nomads of the Balkans*, London, 1914, p. 208, 209.

81. Nicolitsa and Linotopi had been destroyed by the Albanians. Sipischa had also flourished but had the same fate with Moschopolis.

82. S. Liacos, «*Η καταγωγή των Αρμάνων*» (*The origin of the Armanes*), Thessaloniki 1965, v.XVI.

83. See N.C. Moutsopoulos, Kastoria, pub. Melissa», Athens 1989, p. 13.

84. Stilian Adhami, «Les rapports economiques, sociaux et culturels entre Vithkuq et Voskopoje pendant la periode de leur epanouissement», *Monumentet* 17, 1979, p. 79-81.

85. Stilian Adhami, *op. cit.*, p. 80-81.

86. Dukas A.Sachinis, «*Ιστορία της Σιατίστης*» (*History of Siatista*), Athens 1929, p. 9-11. Cf. Almanac of the nome of Kozani, pub. «εκδ. εφημ. *Βόρειος Ελλάς*» (of the newspaper *Northern Greece*), Kozani, April 1930, word: «Siatista».

87. Dukas A. Sachinis, *op. cit.*, p. 12.

88. Athan. Sarantis, «Τα χωριά των Γρεβενών» (The villages of Grevena», *Almanac of West Macedonia.* v.I, 1960, p. 211.

89. G.D. Kanatsoulis - A.N. Stratis, «Η Ευρώπη απέναντι της Οθωμανικής αυτοκρατορίας και η θέσις των Ελλήνων» (Europe against the ottoman empire and the position of the Greeks), v.I (1453-1478) Athens 1940 p. 137. I.E. Karagiannopoulos: «*Η χαραυγή του '21. Γεγονότα και διδάγματα»* (*The dawn of 1821. Facts and lessons*). Speech delivered on the 25th of March, 1965 at the Aristotelian University of Thessaloniki. Kyriakos Symopoulos, «*Ξένοι ταξιδιώτες στην Ελλάδα»* (*Foreign travellers*), v. III, Athens 1975, p. 336 footnote no.1. N.C. Moutsopoulos: «Παραμονές του '21» (The eve of 1821», panegyric delivered on the 25th of March, 1982 (A.V.Th.) Thessaloniki 1982, p. 12.

90. N.C. Moutsopoulos, «Ιστορική σκιαγραφία της Κομοτηνής» (Historical outline of Komotini), *Thracian Yearbook*, v.7, Komotini 1987-1990, p. 170-199.

91. Reaya: the flock, and the collective designation of the non-muslim subjects of the sultan. N.G. Svoronos: «An overview of modern Greek history», Athens 1976, p. 42.

92. N.C. Moutsopoulos, *Kastoria* (Greek traditional architecture) pub. Melissa, Athens 1989, p. 62.

93. Vasilis Demetriades, «*Η Κεντρική και Δυτική Μακεδονία κατά τον Εβλιγιά Τσελεμπή»* (*Central and Western Macedonia according to Evliya Tselembi*), Thessaloniki 1973, p.41, 42, 238.

94. Apostolos Vacalopoulos, «*Ιστορία της Μακεδονίας»* (*History of Macedonia*), Thessaloniki 1969, p. 265 and on.

95. The turkish traveller Evliya Tselembi who visited the region around 1670 gives interesting information. V. Demetriades, *op. cit.*, p. 342.

96. N.C. Moutsopoulos: «Τα αρχοντικά της Σιάτιστας» (The mansions of Siatista) *Yearbook of the Polytechnic School*, V.I, Thessaloniki 1964, p. 36.

97. Gumsel Renda: *Batililasma Dömeninde Turk Resim Sanati 1700-1850*, Ankara 1977, p. 260.

98. A. Vacalopoulos, «*Δυτικομακεδόνες απόδημοι επί τουρκοκρατίας»* (*Macedonian emigrants during the Turkish occupation*), Thessaloniki 1958, p. 26.

99. This is a characteristic passage from G.A. Olivier's *Voyage dans l'empire Ottoman* v.I, Paris 1807, p. 27, 28 about the character of the Greek rayahs: «Les Grecs sont gais, spirituels et adroits: ils exercent divers métiers, font quelque commerce, se livrent a la marine, voyagent dans les divers villes de la côte, s'enforcent peu dans les terres, excepté dans la partie européenne ... Les riches sont instruits, souples, tres intrigans ; ils étudient les langues, n'epargent rien pour être employés comme médecins, comme drogmans, ou comme hommes d' affaires auprés des Turcs qui occupent les premiers places de l'empire...».

100. N.C. Moutsopoulos, *The mansions of the Macedonian traders*, Thessaloniki 1991, p. 361 and on.

101. N.I. Pantazopoulos, «*Ελλήνων συσσωματώσεις κατά την Τουρκοκρατίαν»* (*Greek associations during the Turkish rule*), Athens 1958, p. 5, 6 and: «Κοινοτικός βίος εις την Θετταλομαγνησίαν επί Τουρκοκρατίας» (Community life in Thessaly and Magnesia» Thessaloniki 1967, p. 61.

102. N.G. Svoronos: «Επισκόπηση της Νεοελληνικής Ιστορίας» (An overview of Modern Greek History» *Historical Library*, Athens 1976 p. 43.

103. N.I. Pantazopoulos: «Ελλήνων συσσωματώσεις κατά την Τουρκοκρατίαν» (Greek associations during the turkish occupation» Athens 1958, p. 12.

104. N.I. Pantazopoulos, *op. cit.*, p. 18.

105. N.I. Pantazopoulos, *op. cit.*, p. 18-19.

106. N.G. Svoronos, «*Επισκόπηση της Νεοελληνικής Ιστορίας»* (*An interview of modern Greek history*), *Historical Library*, Athens 1976, p. 40,41.

107. D. Salamagas, «*Τα ισνάφια και τα επαγγέλματα επί Τουρκοκρατίας»* (*The guilds and traders during the turkish occupation*, Yannina 1959, p. 17.

108. Sp. Lambros, «Η Μοσχόπολις και η οικογένεια Σίνα» (Mos-

chopolis and the Sinas family), *NE* 21, 1927, p. 160.

109. T. Katsougiannis, «Περί των Βλάχων των ελληνικών χωρών» (*About the Vlachs of the Greek regions*), B' Thessaloniki 1966, p. 13.

110. T. Katsougiannis: «Περί των Βλάχων των ελληνικών χωρών» (About the Vlachs of the Greek regions) B' Thessaloniki 1966, p. 61.

111. K. Simopoulos, «*Ξένοι ταξιδιώτες στην Ελλάδα»* (*Foreign travellers*) v.III Æ, 1975, p. 335.

112. S. Liakos, «*Η καταγωγή των Αμάνων»* (*The origin of the Armanes*), Thessaloniki 1965, p. 17.

113. Elias Georgiou, «*Ιστορία και συνεταιρισμός των Αμπελακίων»* (*History and guilds of Ambelakia*), Athens 1951, p. 57.

114. N. Georgiades, «Θεσσαλία» (Thessaly), Athens 1880, p. 208.

115. I. Leonardos, «*Νεοτάτη της Θεσσαλίας χορογραφία»* (*Modern chorography of Thessaly*), Pest 1836, p153.

116. A.J.B. Wace-M.S. Thomson, *The nomads of the Balkans*, London 1914, p. 214.

117. Kyriakos Simopoulos, «*Ξένοι ταξιδιώτες στην Ελλάδα»* (*Foreign travellers*), *op. cit*, v.III, 1975, p. 335.

118. Arpad Somogyi, *Kunstdenkmaler der griechischen Diasporen in Ungarn, Institute for Balkan Studies Thessaloniki* 1970, No.121, ar. 15,46.

119. Arpad Somogyi, *op. cit.*, p. 19.

120. Kyriakos Simopoulos, «*Ξένοι ταξιδιώτες στην Ελλάδα»* (Foreign travellers to Greece, v.III 2, 1975, p. 335.

121. V.III 2, p. 205-208.

122. I. Cordatos, «*Ο συνεταιρισμός των Αμπελακίων»* (*The guilds of Ambelakia*), Nea Economia, Athens, September 1948, p.123.

123. K. Koukkides, «*Το πνεύμα του συνεργατισμού των νεωτέρων Ελλήνων στα Αμπελάκια»* (*The association spirit of modern Greeks and Ambelakia*, Athens 1948, p. 81. N.C. Moutsopoulos, (*Ambelakia of Thessaly*), Thessaloniki 1975, p.19,20.

124. Ioannis Cordatos, «Ο συνεταιρισμός των Αμπελακίων» «The guilds of Ambelakia» *Nea Economia*, Athens, September 1948, p. 536.

125. Cf K. Koukkides: «*Το πνεύμα του συνεργατισμού των νεωτέρων Ελλήνων στα Αμπελάκια»* (The association spirit of modern Greeks and Ambelakia), Athens 1948, p. 82.

126. N.C. Moutsopoulos, «*Αμπελάκια της Θεσσαλίας»* (*Ambelakia of Thessaly*), Thessaloniki 1975, p. 18.

127. Stephanos Papadopoulos, «*Εκπαιδευτική και κοινωνική δραστηριότητα του ελληνισμού της Μακεδονίας κατά τον τελευταίο αιώνα της Τουρκοκρατίας»* (*Educational and social activities of the Hellenism of Macedonia during the last century of the Turkish rule*) Thessaloniki 1970, p. 11.

128. N. Svoronos, *Le commerce de Salonique au XVIIIe Siècle.* Paris 1956, p. 122.

129. A. Vacalopoulos, «*Οι δυτικομακεδόνες απόδημοι»* (*West Macedonian emigrants durings the turkish occupation*) Thessaloniki 1958, p. 9.

130. N. Svoronos, *op. cit.*, p. 124.

131. K. Amantos, «Οι προνομιακοί ορισμοί του μουσουλμανισμού υπέρ των Χριστιανών» (Muslim definitions of the privileges of the Christians», *Hellenika* v., IX (9) 1936, p. 103, 141. N.Vlachos: «Η σχέση των υποδούλων Ελλήνων προς το κυρίαρχον οθωμανικόν κράτος» (Relations between the enslaved Greeks and the sovereign ottoman state), *L'Hellenisme Contemporain. Memorial volume* 1953, p. 135. Helen E. Koukkou: «Διαμόρφωσις της Ελληνικής κοινωνίας κατά την Τουρκοκρατία» (Development of the Greek society under the Turkish rule) Athens 1971, p. 27-58 «The first privileges granted to the Patriarchate after the fall of Constantinople».

132. G. Megas, «Η ελληνική οικία. Ιστορική αυτής εξέλιξις και σχέση προς την οικοδομίαν των λαών της Βαλκανικής» (The Greek residence. Its historical development and its relationship to the house building of the Balkans», Athens 1949. N.C. Moutsopoulos, «A contribution to the typology of Northern Greece residence», Minutes of the 2nd Symposium of folklore of Northern Greece» (Epirus - Macedonia - Thrace) Institute for Balkan Studies. Thessaloniki 1976, p. 295-297. Cf. related study on the wide-faced type residence of the region between Strymon and Nestos (Bulgarian regions) by Georgi Kodjucharou in the Bulletin de la Section de Théorie et d' histoire de

l'urbanisme et de l' architecture, of the Bulgarian Academy of Sciences, v19, p. 31-95 with a summary in French.

133. Franz Baron Nopsca, Albanien, op. cit., Berlin and Leipzig 1925, p. 42 pic 26, 27 and, «Haus und Hausrat im Katholischen Nord Albanien», Serajevo 1912, p. 29 pic.14,15 (houses with a wide facade in Toplana and Brebula). Latif Lazimi, «Cardaku në banesën Beratase» (Le tchardak dans la maison de Berat), Monumentet, 11, 1976, p. 173-189. Emin Riza, «Studim per restaurimin e një banese me cardak në Oytetin e Krujes» (Etude concernant la restauration d'une maison a tchardak dans le ville de Kruja) Monumentet, 9, 1975, p. 107-125. Sphresa Prifti: «La habitation scutarine a tchardak (galerie ouverle) sour toute la facade», Monumentet 12, 1976, p. 110 pic. 11, p. 114 pic.5 table I.IV, III, IV showing similarities to the houses of Arta. Cf. A.Orlandos, «Παλαιά αστικά σπίτια της Άρτας» (Old urban houses of Arta), «Αρχείον Βυζαντινών Μνημείων της Ελλάδος» (Archives of Byzantine monuments of Greece), v.II Athens 1936, p. 181 - 194.

134. Georgi Kozuharou, Architekturata na selistata tursko nacelenie po srednoto te técnie na reka Arda», Bulletin de la section de Theorie et d' histoire de l' Urbanisme et de l' architecture, v. XXII p. 226, pic.6, p. 270; Zdravka Maretić, «Analiza na arkhitektonskoto i ruristickoto naslestvo na selata Sbinjista i Sterzevo Zahrozeni so izhradbata na Khms Strezervo-Bitola, Zbornik na Trudobu 2-3 1980/81 p. 169 pic 2 p. 172 pic.5, p. 171 pic.4. Radomir Volinjek - Iasmina Aleksievska «Stara Kyća cardak lija vo seloto Mirkovci» Kusturno Nacledstrovo IX, 1982, Skopie 1984, p. 57-58.

135. Sedad H. Edem, Turk evi plan tipleri, I.T.U Mimarlik Fakultesi 1968 (with many plans of the main cell) and: Turk evi Osmanli domeni (Turkish houses Ottoman period) 1, 1984. Cf chapter «The Byzantine influence» p. 25-27, p. 56-85. Godfrey Godwin, A history of ottoman architecture, London 1971 p. 439-441. Haluk Sezgin, Turquie in the paragraph «Architecture traditionelle des Balkans», Athènes 1992, p. 44.

136. Cardak. A turkish word denoting the half-covered space on the upper floor and which passed into the slavic building terminology. Cf. Dogan Hasol «Ansiklopedik Mimarlik Sözlugu», Istanbul 1975, p. 104. «Bulgarian - Greek dictionary» of the Academy of Sciences of Bulgaria. Sofia 1960, p. 1433. The word passed into Greek, too, but with a different meaning: tsardi or tsardaki, the hut of a shepherd or the shed or lean-to of a gardener, etc. K. Dangitsios, A dictionary of the vernacular, Athens 1967, p. 141. N. Andriotis, «Ετυμολογικό Λεξικό της Κοινής νεοελληνικής» (Etymological dictionary of modern Greek, Athens 1951, p. 265: tsardaki: a hut made of branches or straw, from turk. cardak». G.A. Megas, «Θεσσαλικαί οικήσεις» (Thessalian residences), Athens 1946, p. 13: «tsardaki : thatched hut for sheep.

137. The word derives from the Byzantine term «Toxaton» Louis Petit, Actes de Chillandar, I, 1314, p. 60 : and p. 62: «two buildings, one with a toxaton» 1327 p. 233.
Cf. A.Orlandos: ABME, v IV (4) 1938 p. 201.

138. Doskat. Cf.St. Pavlowitch: «L'architecture vernaculaire en Yougoslavie», L' architecture vernaculaire dans les Balkans, UNESCO p. 15.

139. Cf. N.C. Moutsopoulos, «Πρακτικά του Β' Πανελλήνιου Αρχιτεκτονικού Συνεδρίου» (Minutes of the 2nd Panhellenic Architectural convention), Thessaloniki 1962, Technika Chronica, p. 32, 37. And «Τα αρχοντικά της Καστοριάς» (The mansions of Kastoria), Athens 1962, p. 8,14, and «Τα αρχοντικά της Σιάτιστας» (The mansions of Siatista» PS v.I, 1961-64 p. 97 and «Θέματα Αρχιτεκτονικής Μορφολογίας. Οικισμοί. Αρχοντικά-Μετόχια» (Subjects of architectural morphology. Settlements. Mansions - Metochia. Thessaloniki 1977, p. 137 pic.2, p. 147, 157.

140. Edward Dodwell, A Classical and Topological Tour through Greece during the years 1801,1805 and 1806. «London 1819: «Dinner at Crisso, in the House of the Bishop of Salona».

141. Cf. N.C. Moutsopoulos: «Περιστερά. Ο ορεινός οικισμός του Χορτιάτη» (Peristera. The mountain Settlement of Chortiatis), Thessaloniki 1986, p. 124-173. And: «Σπίτια της Χαλκιδικής» (Houses of Chalcidiki, Athens 1968, pic.8-44.

142. Constantin Dioiketes, Chronique de l'expedition des Turcs en

Moree 1715, published by Nic.Iorga, Bucarest 1913.

143. A. Vacalopoulos, «Η Μακεδονία στα 1715» (Macedonia in 1715) Makedonica, v.11, Thessaloniki 1971, (p. 260-271), p. 260, 262.

144. W.M. Leake, Travels in Northern Greece, v.III, London 1835, p. 253.

145. Jacques Ancel, La Macedoine, son evolution contemporaire, Paris 1930, p. 170.

146. Jacques Ancel: op. cit., p. 174.

147. Edwin Hanson Freshfield, «Some sketches made in Constantinople in 1574», Byzantinische Zeitschrift, v. 30, 1929/1930, p. 519-522 table II. Salomon Schweigern: «Ein neue Reysbeschreibung aus Deutschland nach Constantinopel und Jerusalem», Nürnberg 1639, p. 159, p. 160, pic.125.

148. A study, essentially typologic and, furthermore, in a continuous juxtaposition (comparison) of examples of areas of Greece and Asia Minor is the one made by Anton Bammer: «Wohnen im Verganlichen. Traditionelle Wohnformen in der Turkei und in Griechenland.» Graz 1982, pic.7-49.

149. A plan of the Cinili Kösk, outside the walls of Topkapi saray has been published by Ceral Esad. Arseven, Turk Sanati Tahiri. IX. Fasikul. Istanbul VIII. Fasikul, p. 592 pic.1238, p. 593, pic.1240. From the Great Encyclopedia Pyrsos,» v.23, p. 458: «Cinili Kosk was built in 877 H/1473 and was repaired in 1682 and 1713, after a fire, and, finally, it was turned into a museum by the Rumanian architect Monterano in 1875». S. Eyice, Istanbul: «Petit guide a travers les monuments byzantins et turks.» Istanbul 1955, p. 9 sect.4. O.C. Joja: «Contribution to the study of the domestic stone architecture of Istanbul», Revue des Etudes Sud-Est Europeennes, XI-1, 1973, p. 62, writes: «This Cinili Kiosk, built either in 1466 or maybe, a long time before, is a Byzantine building of Syriac type rather than an Ottoman one, as this type will never be repeated in the whole islamic world».

150. A history of Ottoman architecture, London 1971, p. 137.

151. G.Goodwin, op. cit., p. 136 pic.128.

152. Op.cit., Ayda Arel, «Osmani Konut geleneginde tarihsel sorunlar, Izmir 1982 p. 51, pic 122 . Cf.«La maison turque», BIA No 94 (Supplement), 1985, 10 and on.

153. N.C. Moutsopoulos, «Οι πρόδρομοι των πρώτων Ελλήνων τεχνικών επιστημόνων. Κουδαραίοι, Μακεδόνες και Ηπειρώτες Έλληνες τεχνικοί επιστήμονες περιόδου απελευθερώσεως» (The forerunners of the first Greek technical scientists. Koudareoi, Macedonian and Epirote craftsmen, the first Greek Technical Scientists of the period of liberation), Athens 1976, p. 356, 358.

154. N.C. Moutsopoulos, «Τα αρχοντικά των πραματευτάδων της Μακεδονίας» (The mansions of the Macedonian traders», Thessaloniki 1991, p. 364, 365.

155. N.C. Moutsopoulos, «Καστοριά, τα αρχοντικά» (Kastoria, the mansions). Athens 1962 (with many examples), and: «Μαθήματα Αρχιτεκτονικής Μορφολογίας, Μακεδονική Αρχιτεκτονική» (Lessons of Architectural morphology, Macedonian architechture), Thessaloniki 1971, p. 44-47, and: «Η λαϊκή αρχιτεκτονική της Βέροιας» (Popular architecture of Veria), Athens 1967, p. 64-68 p. 79, tables 46, 47, 68, 70, 80-88, and: «Τα Θεσσαλικά Αμπελάκια» (Ambelakia of Thessaly), Thessaloniki 2, 1975, p. 67-85.

156. N.C. Moutsopoulos, «Η λαϊκή αρχιτεκτονική της Βέροιας» (Popular architecture of Veria), Athens 1967, p. 65, and: «Η αρχιτεκτονική προεξοχή "Το σαχνίσι". Συμβολή στη μελέτη της ελληνικής κατοικίας» (The architectural projection, "the sahnisi". A contribution to the study of the Greek house), Thessaloniki 1988, p. 88.

157. N.C. Moutsopoulos, «Οι ρίζες της παραδοσιακής μας αρχιτεκτονικής» (The roots of our traditional archi-tecture). Proceedings of the Academy of Athens, v.57, 1982 p. 124.

158. Cf. «Λεύκωμα νομού Κοζάνης» (The alamnac of the prefecture of Kozani), 1930, 222.

159. Cf. P. Tsiamis, op. cit., 192.

160. Cf. Macedonica, v.II, Thessaloniki 1941, 52, 394. D. Loucatos: «Τα μαντηλώματα ή ο σταυρός της στέγης» (Mantilomata or the cross of the roof), EOS (ΗΩΣ) 1961, No 44, 36.

161. Cf. N.C. Moutsopoulos: «Σιδερένια μακεδονικά ρόπτρα» (Macedonian iron knockers), «Η τέχνη στη Θεσσαλονίκη» (Art in

Thessaloniki), v.II, 1961, No 1 where related bibliography.

162. Cf. A. Orlandos: «Τα παλιά αρχοντόσπιτα της Καστοριάς» (The old mansions of Kastoria), *Archives of the Byzantine Monuments of Greece*, v.IV, 1938, 201.

163. It is worth noting that even in more recent houses with a plan of the «inscribed cruciform» type, the central cruciform space was still called «doxatos» although there was no arcature.

164. A.Orlandos, in his: «Τα παλιά αρχοντόσπιτα της Καστοριάς» (The old mansions of Kastoria) (p. 201) writes that these kiosks have some connection with the Greek bridal chambers or the Roman tablina.

165. N.C. Moutsopoulos, *op. cit.*, p. 151.

166. *L'habitation byzantine*, Paris 1902, p. 13.

167. «Contributions to the study of the domestic stone architecture of Istanbul», *Revue des Etudes Sud-Est Europeens*, v.XI, 1, 1973, p. 60-62.

168. Ph. Koukoules, «Βυζαντινών Βίος και Πολιτισμός» (*Life and civilization of the Byzantines*) v.IV, Athens 1951, p. 291. K. Amantos: «Γλωσσικαί παρατηρήσεις εις μεσαιωνικούς συγγραφείς» (Linguistic remarks on medieval writers) *Yearbook of the Society for Byzantine Studies*, v.II, 1925, p. 283.

169. The 113rd decree of the Most Wise King Leon. P.G. Migne, 107 p. 652.

170. For Miklosich - J.Muller, *Acta et Diplomata graeca*, v.III, p. 50 (IX, document 1202 refers to Constantinople): building with the groundfloor «heliacos» facing southwards and the upper floor «heliacos» facing westwards.

171. Bessarion: «Εγκώμιον εις Τραπεζούντα» (A praise to Trapezus», *Neos Hellenomnemon*, 13, 1936, p. 189.

172. Ph. Koukoules: «Θεσσαλονίκης Ευσταθίου τα λαογραφικά Χιοναδίτες ζωγράφοι» (Folklorism, by Eustathios the Thessalonian» v.I. Athens 1950 p. 69-70.

173. Theophanes: «Chronography» (Car de Boor) 1, 274. G. Kedrinos (Bonn) 1, 698.

174. Porphyrogennetos: «Περί βασιλείου τάξεως» (About the order in the kingdom) Bonn I, 492, II 15 p. 586.

175. Continuity of George the Monk (Bonn) p. 884: "Then, at baybreak, Life departed in Bucoleon's heliacos..."

176. Porphyrogennetos: «Περί βασιλείου τάξεως» (About the order in the kingdom) Bonn II, 15,p. 586.

177. Zfr. Edw. Warren, «The ritual ordinance of Neophytus», *Archaeologia*, v. 47, p. 22.

178. Fr. Miklosich-J.Muller: v.VI, p. 40 (XII, 1087).

179. Armenopoulos (p. 274) speaks about «heliacos or balcony». K. Amantos, «Linguistic remarks on medieval writers» Y.S.B.S. v.II 1925, p. 282.

180. *Byzantine Life and Civilization*, v.IV, Athens 1951, p.291.

181. Schol. Aristoph.«Equites». D.Meruyh Jones - Nigel G.Wilson: «Scripta Academica Groningana» 675 b. (p. 164) «The railings: The projecting timber members of the building or the balustrades, or any bar made of oak; the ancients called «oak» all the trees, that is why the ends of the branches of a tree were called «acrodrya» from «drys», originally, tree». Many villagers still call the «oak», «dendro» (=tree). Sphekes (published by Duhner) 386: «....

182. It is a copy of a lost document of the end of the 11th century describing the events from the reign of Michael I Ragaves (811-813) to the reign of Constantine IX (1042 - 1055). Andre Grabar-M.Manoussacas, «L' illustration du manuscrit de Skylitzes de la bibliothèque nationale de Madrit. Venise 1979, p. 12,13.

183. Tania Velmans «Le Parisinus grecus 135 et quelques autres peintures de style gothique dans les manuscrits grecs l' époque des Paléologues» *Cahiers Archaelogiques*, XVIII, 1967, p. 218, pic 11, p. 29 pic 12.

184. Maria Theochari, «Ένα βυζαντινό χειρόγραφο του Μυστρά» (Byzantine manuscript of Mystras) *Nees Morphes*, Issue No , March-April 1962 p. 25-28. Summary in English p. 69-71. We meet Manuel Djykandyles in 1362 (6870) as a scribe: «The present book was finished by the hand of Manuel Djykandyles in 1362 (6870) as a scribe: «The present book was finished by the hand of Manuel Djykandyles in the month ... ie. Ind. VI wo». D.Bernardi de Montfaucon,

Palaeographia graeca, Paris 1708, p. 71.

185. A. Orlandos: «Τα παλάτια και τα σπίτια του Μυστρά» (Palaces and houses of Mystras» *Archives of the Byzantine Monuments* v.III, Athens 1937, Général L. de Beylié: *L'habitation byzantine*, Paris-Grenoble 1902, *op. cit.*, Char. Bouras: *Houses and settlements in Byzantine Greece, Settlements in Greece*, published by : «Architectural Subjects» 1974 and: «Architecture in Greece during the 12th c.A.D.» *Bulletin of the Society for the study of Neo-Hellenic civilization and education*, 5a, Athens 1982, p. 94-101.

186. N.C. Moutsopoulos: «Οι ρίζες της παραδοσιακής μας αρχιτεκτονικής» (The roots of our traditional architecture), *PAA (Πρακτικά της Ακαδημίας Αθηνών)*, v.57, 1982, p. 128.

187. Charles Diehl, «Constantinople», Paris 1928, p. 146.

188. N.C. Moutsopoulos: «Το τέλος της μεταβυζαντινής αρχιτεκτονικής» (The end of the post-Byzantine architecture)*Xenia, on the 25th anniversary of the bishopric of Iacovos, bishop of North and South America*, Thessaloniki 1985, p. 366.

189. Zeno, *Decree* 128, Leo, *Novel* 113, P.G.v.107 p. 652, *Basilica*, 58,11,9 (pub.I.D.Zeppos v.V, Athens 1912 p. 265) Ph. Koukoules, «Βυζαντινών Βίος και Πολιτισμός» (*Byzantine Life and Civilization*), v.IV, Athens 1951, p. 327 and: «The streets and the porticos of the Byzantine cities» *EEBS* (=*Επιστημονική Επετηρίς Εταιρείας Βυζαντινών Σπουδών*), v.18, 1948, p. 12.

190. Theodosian Codex», *Basilica* 58,11,9.

191. Ph. Koukoules, «The streets and the "emboloi" of the Byzantine cities». *EEBS, v.18, 1948, p. 12.*

192. Cod.Just. VIII, 10,12, c.Basilica 58, 11c.

193. Ph. Koukoules, «Βυζαντινών Βίος και Πολιτισμός» (*Byzantine Life and Civilization*), v.IV, Athens 1951, p. 292.

194. *Basilica*, 58 II c.

195. *Basilica*, 58, II c v.V p. 265. Zeno, *Cod. Just* VIII 10,12 c.CF. N.C. Moutsopoulos, «Η λαϊκή αρχιτεκτονική της Βέροιας» (*Popular architecture)*, Athens 1967, p. 49 footnote 217.

196. Armenopoulos, «Εξάβιβλος» (*Hexabiblos*), 2,4,56. Ph. Koukoules, «Βυζαντινών Βίος και Πολιτισμός» (*Byzantine Life and Civilization*), v.IV, p.292.

197. E.O.K. = Special Building Specifications.

198. N.C. Moutsopoulos, «Το τέλος της μεταβυζαντινής αρχιτεκτονικής» (The end of the post-Byzantine architecture) *Xenia, on the 25th anniversary of the bishopric of Iacovos, bishop of N.and S.America*, Thessaloniki 1985, p. 371.

199. L.Heuzey, *Excursion dans la Thessalie turque en 1858*, Paris 1927, p. 36.

200. Cf. A.K. Orlandos, «Τα παλάτια και τα σπίτια του Μυστρά» (Palaces and houses of Mystras) *ABME* (=*Archives of the Byzantine monuments of Greece*), v.III, 1937, p. 86 pic. 75.

201. Cf. S. Kougeas, *Peloponnesiaca*, v.I, 195,5 p. 101, pic.4.

202. Cf. Baron Franz Nopsca, *Haus und Hausrat im Katholischen Nordalbanien*, Sarajevo 1912, p. 47 pic.25, p. 49 pic.26.

203. Ed. Dodwell, *Views in Greece*, London 1819 Drawing: S. Romardi, engraving R. Havell. Cf. Place and picture, VI, Athens 1983, p. 78-79 pic.30.

204. H. Holland, *Travels in the Ionian isles, Albania, Thessaly, Macedonia etc during the years 1812 and 1813*, London 1815, p. 149. P. Henri Stahl, «Maisons fortifieés et tours habiteés balkaniques», *op. cit.*, 1979, p. 91-92.

205. N.C. Moutsopoulos, «Τα αρχοντικά της Σιάτιστας» (The mansions of Siatista) *EEΠΣ*(=*Yearbook of the Polytechnic School*), v.I, Thessaloniki 1964, pic.23, 58, 59.

206. N. Bees, «Τα Θεσσαλικά Αμπελάκια» (The Thessalian Ambelakia) newspaper *Proia*, August 29, 1943.

207. Ad. Anacatomenos, «Τα νέα όρια της Ελλάδας, ήτοι τοπογραφικαί και εθνολογικαί σημειώσεις περί Θεσσαλίας» (*The new Greek borders, or topographical land ethnilogical notes about Thessaly*), Athens 1887, p. 118.

208. G. Megas, «Θεσσαλικαί οικήσεις» (*Thessalian dwellings*), Series published by the Ministry of Reconstruction, No 4, Athens 1946, p. 91-105, and: «The Greek house», Athens 1946, p. 91-105, and: «Ελληνική οικία» (*The Greek house,*) Athens 1949, p. 30.

209. N.C. Moutsopoulos, «Τα Θεσσαλικά Αμπελάκια» (*The Thes-*

Fresco on the E. wall of the NW sitting room of Keratsis' mansion in Siatista.

salian Ambelakia), op. cit., p. 70.

210. N.C. Moutsopoulos, «*Τα Θεσσαλικά Αμπελάκια*» (*The Thessalian Ambelakia), op. cit.*, p. 70,71.

211. N.C. Moutsopoulos: «Οι ρίζες της παραδοσιακής μας αρχιτεκτονικής» (The roots of our traditional architecture» ΠΑΑ(=*Proceedings of the Academy of Athens)*, v.57, p. 106,108 where related bibliography.

212. S. Lambros, «Η Μοσχόπολις και η οικογένεια Σίνα» (Moschopolis and the Sinas family) *Neos Hellenomnemon*, v.21, 1917, p. 160.

213. Ioakim Martinianos: «*Η Μοσχόπολις*» (*Moschopolis), 1330-1930*, Thessaloniki 1957, p. 37.

214. Daniel Philippides-Georgios Constantas, «*Γεωγραφία Νεωτερική*» (*Modern Geography*), Vienna 1791, p. 241.

215. Felix Beaujour, *Tableau du Commerce de la Grece*, Paris 1800, p. 272.

216. I. Leonardos, «*Νεοτάτη της Θεσσαλίας χορογραφία*» (*Modern chronography of Thessaly*), Pest, 1836, p. 147,148. N.C. Moutsopoulos, «*Τα Θεσσαλικά Αμπελάκια*» (*The Thessalian Ambelakia,*) Thessaloniki 1975, p. 67.

217. N.C. Moutsopoulos, «*Τα Θεσσαλικά Αμπελάκια*» (*The Thessalian Ambelakia)*, p. 68.

218. N.C. Moutsopoulos, «*Τα αρχοντικά των πραματευτάδων της Μακεδονίας*» (The mansions of the Macedonian traders), Thessaloniki 1991, p. 371-373.

219. Cf. G. Megas, «*Θεσσαλικαί οικήσεις*» (*Thessalian dwellings).*

220. Nicolas Moutsopoulos, «Esquisse des problèmes de reanimation des agglomerations historiques» *Proceedings of the 2nd Symposium of I.CO.MO.S.*, Athens 1979, *op. cit.*, p. 39 pic.6, pic. 41, pic. 8, p. 3, pic. 9, p. 45, pic.10. Semne Carouzou, «*Ναύπλιον*» (*Nauplion*), Athens 1979, *op. cit.*, footnote 12. *An anthology of Greek Architecture*, Athens 1981, pic. 48, p. 81-83.

221. N.C. Moutsopoulos: «*Τα αρχοντικά της Σιάτιστας*»The mansions of Siatista» *Yearbook of the Polytechnic School*, V.I Thessaloniki 1964, p. 86-89 (of the insert).

222. N.C. Moutsopoulos, «Παρατηρήσεις στον εσωτερικό χώρο και τη μορφολογία των μακεδονικών αρχοντικών» (Remarks on the interior and morphology of the Macedonian mansions) *Architectural subjects* 1,1967, p. 151.

223. N.C. Moutsopoulos «Οι ρίζες της αρχιτεκτονικής μας παράδοσης» (The roots of our traditional architecture), p. 120.

224. N.C. Moutsopoulos, *op. cit.*, p. 152.

225. *Op.cit.*, p. 152.

226. N.C. Moutsopoulos, «*Καστοριά*» (*Kastoria*), pub. Melissa, Athens 1989, p. 27.

226a. Files, Documenti Greci No 314 (documents of the years 1695-1699). K.Mertzios, «*Μνημεία Μακεδονικής Ιστορίας*» (*Monuments of Macedonian history*, Thessaloniki 1947, p. 209-255.

226b. N.C. Moutsopoulos, «Τα αρχοντικά της Σιάτιστας» (The mansions of Siatista» p. 72.

227. W.M. Leake, *Travels in Northern Greece*, v.I., London 1835, p. 307,308.

228. F.C.H.L. Pouqueville, *Voyage de la Gréce*, v.III, Paris 1826, p. 77, Ioannis Arg.Tozis: «*Σιατιστινά*» (Of Siatista), *Macedonica*, 2. Thessaloniki 1953, p. 326.

229. N.C. Moutsopoulos: «Παρατηρήσεις στον εσωτερικό χώρο και τη μορφολογία των μακεδονικών αρχοντικών» (Remarks on the interior of the Macedonian mansions) *Architecture in Greece*, 1/1967, p. 154.

230. N.C. Moutsopoulos: «Παρατηρήσεις στον εσωτερικό χώρο και τη μορφολογία των μακεδονικών αρχοντικών» (Remarks on the interior of the Macedonian mansions) *Αρχιτεκτονικά θέματα*, 1 (1967) 150-154 and. *Kastoria, op. cit.*, p. 43, pic.47,59,63.,

231. Angheliki Hadjimihali: *La maison greque*, Athens 1949, p. 37-40.

232. N.C. Moutsopoulos: *Kastoria*, Melissa publishing co. Athens 1989, p. 28, 46, 62, 63.

233. Anastasia D. Diamantopoulou, (The Greek origin of the interior decoration of the mansions of Ambelakia,» *Technica Chronica*, monthly, 9 (1971) 559-597) expresses opinions contrasting with ous;

furthermore, she tries desperately to discover ancient models everywhere. There certainly are greek seeds, for instance, in the residential cell and the form of the ancient triclinium (oda), but not in the baroque-rococo designs and colors of the decoration -which are the work of Greek painters, naturally- but which had previously passed through the melting pot of the capital and had acquired that peculiarly popular orientalized style.

234. Cf. *catma, bina, bagdati, kereste, hayat, sahnis, duvar, hatil* and many others.

235. The wise Turkish architect, proffesor Sedad Hakki Eldem, of the Polytechnic of Constantinople, (*Turk evi osmanli domeni...*) accepts the initiative of the local craftsmen and recognizes essential local differentiations.

236. Cf. N.C. Moutsopoulos, «Οι πρόδρομοι των πρώτων Ελληνικών επιστημόνων. Κουδαραίοι, Μακεδόνες και Ηπειρώτες μαΐστορες» (The forerunners of the first Greek technical scientists. "Koudareoi" Macedonian and Epirote craftsmen) *The first Greek technical scientists of the liberation period*, pub. TEE Athens, 1976, 353-453.

237. N.C. Moutsopoulos, «Τα αρχοντικά της Σιάτιστας» (The mansions of Siatista), *op. cit.*, pic.102-106.

238. A. Orlandos: «Τα παλαιά αρχοντόσπιτα της Καστοριάς» (Old mansions of Kastoria).

239. In Siatista they are called «allfursina». A. Zachos: «Τα καράβια της Καστοριάς» (The ships of Kastoria). "*Μακεδονικόν Ημερολόγιον*" (Macedonian Almanac) 1935, 160.

240. The manner of arrangement of the interior decoration with the wood panelling rising to a certain height in the rooms and the friezes with the floral decorations, the various motifs on the ceilings, the «mousandres» and the «mideria», spreads to a very wide geographical area which begins from the Balkans (the Danube) and covers a large part of N.W.Asia Minor and the near East. Especially, the decorations of the mansions of Nadjis and Tsiatapas have many similarities to the decoration of mansions of Albanian regions. Cf. Emin Riza: «La pièce a reception de l'habitation urbaine albanaise» *Ethnographie Albanaise*, v.13, Tirana 1984, 357,361 (fig 5,10), Pirro Thomo: «Aspects d'unité et de diversite de l' architecture populaire albanaise» *Culture populaire albanaise*, 11e Anné (2), 1982, 106, pic.7, ceiling of a mansion in Argyrocastro, 19th century.

241. A. Orlandos, «Τα παλιά αρχοντόσπιτα της Καστοριάς» (The old mansions of Kastoria)», *op. cit.,* 203.

242. P. Tsiamisis, *op. cit.*, 191.

243. N.C. Moutsopoulos: «Οι ρίζες της παραδοσιακής μας αρχιτεκτονικής» (The roots of our traditional architecture), *op. cit.*, p. 128.

244. Bilingual publication of Turkiye Turing ve Ottomobil kurumu, Istanbul 1973, «The rooms in the traditional Turkish house of Anatolia from the aspect of spatial organization». Cf. «La maison turque», *B.I.A.*, No 94 Supplement 1985 p. 14.

245. Reha Gunay, «*Les maisons de Safranobolu, Turquie* (Publication di Turing et Automobile club de Turquie) Cf.Onder Kucukerman, *Turkish House in search of spatial identity*», Istanbul 1988, p. 43.

246. N.C. Moutsopoulos, «Τα αρχοντικά της Καστοριάς» (The mansions of Siatista) p. 109.

247. A. Sigalas, «Πατριαρχικαί Πράξεις, φερμάνια και άλλα τινά έγγραφα» (Patriarchal decrees, firmans and other documents).

248. In Drakia, Pelion, there is inscription: «1793 Mastrogiorgos djamdjis, Alcibiades Prepis, *Paleo-bulgarica* 2, 1987, p. 23 footnote 28. Cf. C.A. Makris, «Οι φεγγίτες των αρχοντικών από το Βυζάντιο στο Μπαρόκ» (The transom windows of the mansions, from Byzantium to baroque) *Proceedings, 1st Symposium of folklore of Northern Greece*, Thessaloniki 1975, p. 181-182.

249. N.C. Moutsopoulos, «Τα αρχοντικά της Σιάτιστας» (The mansions of Siatista», *ΕΕΠΣ, v.I, Thessaloniki 1964, p. 103-106.*

250. N.C. Moutsopoulos, «Τα αρχοντικά των πραματευτάδων της Μακεδονίας» (The mansions of the Macedonian traders), *op. cit.*, Thessaloniki 1991, p. 379-382.

251. Ruchan Arik, *Batililasma dömeni Anadolu Tasvir Sanati*, Ankara 1976, p. 18-22.

252. Miltos Garides, «New copperplate models for the secular decorative painting during the 18th and 19th c. *Macedonica*, v.22, Thessaloniki 1982, p. 2.

253. N.C. Moutsopoulos, *Ambelakia of Thessaly*, p. 19, pic.19.
254. N.C. Moutsopoulos, *op. cit.*, p. 38, pic 39 pic.40.
255. N.C. Moutsopoulos, *op. cit.*, p. 60.
256. Anna Poshkovska: *Liliana Marvodinova, Mural ornaments*, Sofia 1985 (Bulg.,), p. 306, pic.239.
257. *Mural ornaments, op. cit.*, p. 121.
258. *Mural ornaments, op. cit.*, p. 311, pic.246.
259. *Mural ornaments, op. cit.*,
260. *Mural ornaments, op. cit.*, p. 314 pic 259.
261. N.C. Moutsopoulos, «Τα αρχοντικά της Σιάτιστας» (The mansions of Siatista» *ΕΕΠΣ*, v.I, Thessaloniki 1964, p. 57. Cf. G. Bontas, «Ένα αρχοντικό 230 χρόνων στη Σιάτιστα» (A 230 year-old mansion in Siatista) *Macedonian Life*, Issue No 210, November 1983, p. 43.
262. Divani ilhami, Topkapi Muzesi Kitapligi, H.912. Gunsel Renda, «Betililasma Döneminde Turk Resim Sanati 1700-1850» Ankara 1977, p. 81 pic.9.
263. Gunsel Renda, *op. cit.*, p. 81,231. Topkapi Sarayi: Harem-Cevri Kalfa veya gozdeler Dairesi ust kat Buyuk Odasi.
264. *The treasures of Athos.* Illustrated manuscripts v.I, Athens 1973, pic. 470-498, p. 485.
265. St. Pelekanidis, «Die Kunstformen der Nach byzantinischen Zeit im Nord Griechischen Raum» *Kunst und Geschichte in Sudosteuropa 9*, Internationale Hochschulwoche der Suedst Europa Gesellshaft, Recklingausen 1973, p. 125-136 (republished in *Studies of Paleochristian and Byzantine Archaeology*, 174 IMXA Thessaloniki, p. 456-485.
266. Cyril Mango, «The legend of Leo the Wise» Recueil de travaux (Academie Serbe des Sciences. Institut d'Etudes Byzantines, No 6, Belgrade 1960).
267. N.C. Moutsopoulos, «Τα αρχοντικά της Σιάτιο ας» (The mansions of Siatista), *op. cit.*, pic.83.
268. N.C. Moutsopoulos, *op. cit.*, pic.84.
269. N.C. Moutsopoulos, *op. cit.*, pic.85,86.
270. There is a picture of a stork holding a snake in his beak in the «bas oda» of the mansion of Mehmet Ali Aga in Attalia (1796/97). Gunsel Renda, *Batililasma, op. cit.*, p. 139 pic105.
271. A chained lion is pictured in the mansion of Cratsoulis, in Ambelakia, with the inscription: «year 1797. Lelis the artisans» N.C. Moutsopoulos, «Τα Θεσσαλικά Αμπελάκια» (Ambelakia of Thessaly), *op. cit.*, p. 52, pic. 58, p. 53 pic. 63. Chained lions are pictured in mansions of Philippoupolis, in the gable-like alcove of the house of Nicola Nedkovich (*Mural ornaments*, p. 362 pic .332), in the house of Outsa Velyan Ognen and in the house of Lyutov, in Koprivshtitsa (*Mural ornaments, op. cit.*, p. 362, pic. 311). Finally, chained lions are pictured in the gable of a house of Vitasta, Serres (1866) and in Mesoropi, Cavala.
272. Particularly those kept in the library of the monastery of Vatopedio, in gospels, in various liturgical books, such as No 1081 (K.Efstratiades), or in Codex 129 of the monastery of Xeropotamos, of 1698. *The treasures of Athos.* Illustrated manuscripts v.Iq 1973q pic.438-452qp. 478.
273. N.C. Moutsopoulos, «Τα αρχοντικά της Σιάτιστας» (The mansions of Siatista) *,op. cit.*, p. 59, footnote 1.
274. N.C. Moutsopoulos, «Τα αρχοντικά της Σιάτιστας» (The mansions of Siatista», *op. cit.*, pic.64.
275. Hamsei Altai, *Museum of Turkish and Islamic Works*, Istanbul 1969, pic.126.Gunsel Renda, *op. cit.*, No 1.
276. Kitsos Makris, «Ένα ευρωπαϊκό πρότυπο βορειοελλαδίτικης τοιχογραφίας. Τοιχογραφία της Φραγκφούρτης σε σπίτι στη Σιάτιστα» (A European model of Northern Greek frescoes. A fresco of Frankfurt in a house of Siatista), Newspaper *Vema*, June 25, 1978, p. 4.
277. N.C. Moutsopoulos, «Τα αρχοντικά της Σιάτιστας» (The mansions of Siatista), *op. cit.*, pic.68.
278. M. Garides, «Καινούργια χαλκογραφικά πρότυπα για την κοσμική διακοσμητική ζωγραφική το 18o και 19o αιώνα» (New copperplate models for the secular decorative painting in the 18th and 19th c.), *Macedonica*, v.22, 1982, p. 5.
279. M.Garides, «Καινούργια χαλκογραφικά πρότυπα για την κοσμική διακοσμητική ζωγραφική το 18o και 19o αιώνα» (New cop-

perplate models for the secular decorative painting in the 18th and 19th c., *Macedonica*. v.20, 1982, p. 10.
280. The two-headed eagle is another popular symbolism and adorns many interiors of mansions, such as the triangular gable of the door of a room of the mansion of G.Schwartz (N.C. Moutsopoulos, «Τα Θεσσαλικά Αμπελάκια» (Ambelakia of Thessaly), *op. cit.*, p. 42 pic. 45) and, sometimes the exterior of houses, e.g. the house of Iv. Hadziruskov in Bansc. *Mural ornaments*, p. 145,365, pic.338.
281. Prof.Asim Multu: «Turk evleri» Sanat Dunyamiz, 1,3, 1975, p. 9
282. Reha Gunay, *Gerleneksel Safranbolu Evleri ve Olusumu*, 1981, pic.318.
283. Th. Diacomanolis-Dros. Cravartoyiannos: *«Τουριστικός Οδηγός Φωκίδος»* (*Tourist guide of Phocis*), Amphissa 1968, p. 27. D. Stamelos, «Neo-hellenic popular art», Athens 1982, p. 109.
284. I.M. Hadziphotis, *Tourist guide of Syme*, p. 49.
285. Spyros Kokkinis, «Ιστορικά μνημεία και λαϊκή αρχιτεκτονική στη Χαλκίδα» (Historical monuments and popular architecture in Chalkida), *Archives of Euboen Sudies.* v.XV, 1966, p. 37.
286. Metin And, *Turkish miniature painting. The ottoman period*, Istanbul 1982, p. 36,37.
287. Metin And, *Turkish miniature painting. The ottoman period*, p. 36 Istanbul (Matrakci Nasuh's Beyani Menazil Sefer-I Irakey).
288. Op.cit., p. 37. Cf. Hasim Karpuz, *Turk Islam Mesken Mimarisinde Erzerum Evleri*, Ankara 1984, p169, pic.1.
289. Önder Kuculerma, *Odalar*, Istanbul 1973, p. 42. Rifat Osman'a Gore: «Edirne evleri ve Konaklari» (Turkiye Turing ve Otomobil Kurumu) pic.7-13.
290. Gunsel Renda, *Batililasma, op. cit.*, col.pic.11.
291. N.C. Moutsopoulos, «Τα Θεσσαλικά Αμπελάκια» (*Ambelakia of Thessaly*), *op. cit.*, p. 46 pic.49.
292. *Mural Ornaments, op. cit.*, p. 39.
293. *Mural Ornaments, op. cit.*, p. 231.
294. Gunsel Renda, *Batillasma*, p.85, pic.50.
295. Gunsel Renda, *op. cit.*, p. 87, pic. 53,54.
296. Gunsel Renda, *op. cit.*, p. 102, pic.70.
297. Cf. N.C. Moutsopoulos, «Καστοριά, τα αρχοντικά» (*Kastoria, the mansions*), Athens 1962.
298. N.C. Moutsopoulos, «Το αρχοντικό του Σιόρ Μανωλάκη στη Βέροια» (The mansion of Sir Manolakis, in Veria), Zygos, Issue 56-57, 1960, p147-163. Cf.D. Stamelos: «Νεοελληνική Λαϊκή Τέχνη» (*Neo-hellenic popular art*), Athens 1982, p. 106-108.
299. G. Renda, *op. cit.*, pic.16.
300. Apostolos Ducas Sahinis, «Το αρχοντικό του Νεράντζη Αϊβάζη» (*The mansion of Nerantzis Aivazis*), 1977 p. 17 and on.
301. N.C. Moutsopoulos, «Τα αρχοντικά της Σιάτιστας» (The mansions of Siatista), *op. cit.*, pic.85.
302. N.C. Moutsopoulos, «Τα Θεσσαλικά Αμπελάκια» (*The Thessalian Ambelakia*), p. 24, pic 25.
303. N.C. Moutsopoulos, «Τα αρχοντικά της Σιάτιστας» (The mansions of Siatista», *op. cit.*, pic.90,91.
304. N.C. Moutsopoulos, *op. cit.*, pic.88.
305. Such as the Fates, the birth of Athena, Cronus eating his children, Aeolus, Rea and the Corybands, Pluto and Persephone, the Hesperides, the Sphinx, Pan, Asclepios, Artemis, Hephestus, the Gorgons, Apollo, Chimera, Hermes, the Graces, the Colossus of Rhodes, the Sirens and the labors of Heracles.
306. N.C. Moutsopoulos, «Τα αρχοντικά της Σιάτιστας» (The mansions of Siatista), p. 69, table 74, pic 2.
307. Cf. Gunsel Renda, *op. cit.*, p. 158,159 pic.125-127, p. 244,245.
308. I, I.Touratzoglou: «Γραπτή Αμαζών εκ Νυμφαίου» (The painting of the Amazon, Nympheon) *Athens Annals of Archaeology.* Add.II, v.I Issue 3 (Vol.I fasc 3), Athens p. 307-310.
309. «Η φωνή του Νυμφαίου» (The voice of Nympheon), Issue No 42, March 1978.
310. I. Touratsoglou: «Ο Αρίστιππος του Νυμφαίου, στο αρχοντικό Θ. Τσίρλη» (Aristippos of Nympheon in the mansion of Th. Tsirlis). *Macedoniki Zoe*, 22, March 1968, colored picture.
311. Eudokia Meliatzidou-Ioannou: «Μιλούν οι τοίχοι των αρχοντικών» (The walls of the mansions speak) *Macedoniki Zoe*, Issue 271,

December 1988 p. 32 Cf. N. Loustas, «Ἄρχοντες καὶ αρχοντικὰ Νυμφαίου (Νέβεσκας)» (Nobles and their mansions in Nympheon (Nevesca)) *Aristotelis*, v.35-36, Florina 1962, p. 97-119.

312. Cf. related picture of «Eros and Psyche» in the residence of Midat Pasha at Rouse. *Mural Ornaments, op. cit.*, p. 155.

313. N.C. Moutsopoulos, «Τα αρχοντικά της Σιάτιστας» (The mansions of Siatista), *op. cit.*, pic.89.

314. Family scenes are also pictured in the mansion of Lekow in Panaggurishte of Bulgaria, dated from the second half of the 19th century. *Mural ornaments, op. cit.*,p. 315, pic.253. In the house of Oslekov, in Kopriftitsa, within an oval frame, in the foreground, two women, in local costumes, are spinning, in the center, a baby is sleeping in a cradle, and in the background, there is a picture of a renaissance palace. (Mural Ornaments, *op. cit.*, p. 347, pic.300).

315. G. Renda, *op. cit.*, p. 154, pic.120.

316. A.Grabar-M.Manousacas, *L'Illustration du manuscript de Skylitzes de la Biblioteque nationale de Madrid*, Venise 1979, Pl.XXVIII, XXXI, XXXVI, XL fig.127,128,197,198,203.

317. G. Renda, *op. cit.*, p. 159, pic.126, 127, 245. Cf. Ruchan Arik, «L'art figuratif populaire en Anatolie», *Objects et Mondes*, Turquie. Le revue du Musée de l' homme. V.ZI - Fascicule 1. Spring 1981, p. 14.

318. R. Arik, *op. cit.*, p. 16.

319. N.C. Moutsopoulos, «Παρατηρήσεις στον εσωτερικό χώρο και τη μορφολογία των Μακεδονικών αρχοντικών» (Comments on the interior space and the form of Macedonian mansion houses: *Architecture in Greece*, 1/1967, p. 150.

320. N.C. Moutsopoulos, «Παρατηρήσεις στον εσωτερικό χώρο και τη μορφολογία των Μακεδονικών αρχοντικών» (Comments on the interior space and morphology of the Macedonian mansions» *Architecture in Greece*, 1, 1967, p. 150-154 «Comments on the interior space», *Architecture in Greece*, 1/1967, p. 151.

321. C. Makris, «Η ελληνική λαϊκή ζωγραφική» (Greek popular painting), «Ημερολόγιο Ταχυδρομικού Ταμειευτηρίου 1983» (*Almanac of the "Tachydromicon Tamiefterion" 1983*).

322. Cf. G. Renda, *op. cit.*, p. 265. «It is apparent that the new movement spread both in the royal circles and outside, and non-muslim Ottoman artists also took a great part in this vogue, but there was a unity of approach until the very end of the 19th century in all circles, christian and Muslim».

323. N.C. Moutsopoulos, «Παρατηρήσεις στον εσωτερικό χώρο και τη μορφολογία των Μακεδονικών αρχοντικών» (Comments on the interior space and the form of Macedonian mansions», *Architecture in Greece*, 1/1967, p. 151.

324. Gelal Esad Arseven, «Les Arts décoratifs tures», Istanbul, 1954, p. 44, pic.154, p. 46, pic.164, p. 197,201, 202-205. Cf. C. Macris, «Αρχόντισσα Σιάτιστα» (Noble Siatista), article in the newspaper *To Vema*, June 25, 1963.

325. G. Renda, *Batililasma Doneminde Turk Resim sanati 1700-1850*, Ankara 1977, p. 262 and on.

326. G. Renda, *op. cit.*, p. 36, pic.4, p. 38, pic.5, p. 39, pic.6.

327. G. Renda, *op. cit.*, pic.67, 68, 74.

328. G. Renda, *op. cit.*, p. 264 Dr.Emel Esin: «Sadullah Pasa Yalisi» *Turkiyemiz*, 17, 1975, p. 24.

329. N.C. Moutsopoulos, «Οι πρόδρομοι των πρώτων Ελλήνων επιστημόνων. Κουραδαίοι Μακεδόνες Ηπειρώτες μαΐστορες» (The forerunners of the first Greek technical scientists. Kouradeoi. Macedonian and Epirote craftsmen». First Greek technical scientists of the period of the liberation. Athens 1976, p. 353-453.

330. Cf. A. Roskovska's study, «L'ornamentation des peintures murales, créé par les peintures d'icônes de l'école de Samokov pendant la renaissance Bulgare» *Bulletin de l'Institut des arts*, v.XIII, 1969, p. 115-145.

331. Cf. pictures inside gilt wood frames in the «catholico» of the monastery of Rozinos, near Melenico. *Mural ornaments, op. cit.*, p. 336, pic.275.

332. Arch. Gabriel Countiades, «Σύντομος ιστορική επισκόπησις της Ιεράς Μονής Προδρόμου (Σερρών)» (*Brief historical sketch of the monastery of Prodromos*), Serres 1976, p. 20.

333. Information given by the Most Reverend Constantine, bishop of Serres and Nigrita in a letter (June 9, 1977).

334. Cf. *The Pyrsos Encyclopedia*, v.VII, p. 252.

335. *History of the Greek Nation*, v.XI (1660-1821) Ecdotiki Athinon, Athens 1975, p. 255.

336. Menis Kanatsoulis, «Με αφορμή μια τοιχογραφία στο αρχοντικό Μανούση στη Σιάτιστα» (Occasioned by a fresco in the mansion of Manousis in Siatista) *Macedonica*, v. 24, 1984, p. 191.

337. M. Kanatsoulis, *op. cit.*, *Macedonica*, v.24, 1984, p. 193.

338. For instance, the tympana of the church of St.Marina in Philippoupolis. *Mural ornaments, op. cit.*, p. 94.

339. As in the monastery of Kosiphoinissa on Pangeon, of St.John the Baptist of Serres, in monasteries of Athos and the monastery of Rozinos (Alcibiades Prepis, *op. cit.*, *Palaeobulgarica*, 2, 1987, p. 101, pic.6) and the monastery of Rila in Bulgaria. Anna Roshkovska Liliana Mavrodinova, *Mural Ornaments, op. cit.*, p. 81.

340. Mural ornaments, *op. cit.*, p. 372 pic.348.

341. Kitsos Makris, «Χιοναδίτες ζωγράφοι» (*Painters of Chionades*), Athens, Melissa publ.co. 1981, p. 30.

342. Kitsos Makris, «Χιοναδίτες ζωγράφοι» (*Painters of Chionades*, Athens, Melissa publishing co. 1981.

343. M. Kanatsoulis, «Les peintures des demeures de Siatista aux XVIII et XIXs et les labirants», Paris 1984qp. 115-118.

344. A.Z. Varsamides, «Λαϊκοί ζωγράφοι από το Βογατσικό» (Popular painters from Vogatsico), *Macedoniki Zoe*, Issue No 271, year 23rd, 1988, p. 40-43.

345. N.C. Moutsopoulos, «Τα αρχοντικά της Σιάτιστας» (The mansions of Siatista), *op. cit.*, p. 44 and on.

346. *Mural ornaments, op. cit.*, p. 155.

347. Cf. *Ostasiatische Kunst*, Kunsthaus Lempertz, p. 55, No 2242, a prayer mat, Sinkiang.

The sinaitic «metochi» in Phanari, Constantinople.
(Photo: Prof. Haluk Sezgin)

Vernacular Art in Macedonia

Efthymia Yeorgiadou-Kountoura

The Study of Vernacular Art

It was not until the final decades of the 19th century, under the influence of Romanticism, that the interest of Greek and foreign scholars began to turn to the study of the Greek vernacular culture. This study focused first on the linguistic monuments, and later on the remnants of physical life. The outward forms of this culture were the expression of a traditional way of life during the period of Ottoman rule. As soon as independence was won, they were shouldered aside by the 'cultural imperialasm' of the West as the "ignominious and contaminated heritage of four centuries under the Ottoman yoke".[1]

The cultural traditions of the Ottoman and Byzantine periods conflicted with the ideology of the ruling class and the intellectuals who, imbued with the neo-Classical principles prevailing in Western Europe, looked back with admiration on the glorious heritage of ancient Greece as the only truly 'Hellenic' tradition. They cultivated 'katharevousa' and what might be described as ancestor-worship.

The questioning of the continuity of the Greek nation by Fallmerayer made its contribution to reinforcing the historical awareness of the Greeks and to the rehabilitation of Byzantium. This can be seen in the studies of Spyridon Zambelios, and above all in Konstantinos Paparrigopoulos' monumental five- volume History of the Greek Nation (1860-1874), which documented the indivisible unity of the ancient, medieval and modern Greek nation.

There was a simultaneous shift, too, in the direction of the vernacular language (demotic), first in poetry and subsequently in prose, and fresh interest developed in the study of the vernacular culture. Zambelios had already distinguished between the learned and the vernacular traditions in the history of Greek education. In My Journey (1888), Psycharis gave added publicity to demotic and associated its predominance with the intellectual and spiritual yearnings of a young generation in search of direct and sincere forms of expression.

Periklis Yannopoulos, one of the advocates of the Romantic and idealist spirit early in the 20th century, believed in the creation of a new Greek culture which would stand out for its uniqueness. Thus, he wrote in 1902, "we have the natural world, the vernacular world, the world of slavery, the heroic world, the religious world, the Byzantine world, the perfect world and the mythological world. And all these worlds of ours, each line and each expression of which is singular and peculiar to us and bears no relation to any parallel form of expression, whether of the French or the English or the Italian or the German world, go to make up the world of Greek painting which is our vitals, our spirit, our soul, our blood."[2]

However, it was not until the appearance of Nikolaos Politis that systematic study of vernacular modern Greek culture began. In his work, Politis established folklore studies as an academic discipline which sought out the remnants of the past in the present, following a course in the direction opposite to ancestor-worship and the attempt to revive the past. Politis was behind the formation of the Folklore Archive (1918) and publication of the periodical Laographia ('Folklore Studies', 1909), and he was indirectly responsible for the formation of the Lyce of Greek Women (1911) and the Handicraft Museum (1913).[3]

Aristotelis Zachos and Dimitris Pikionis made particularly important contributions to the study of vernacular architecture. Zachos wrote: "If we turn our attention to them, the architectural models both of these parts [Macedonia] and of the rest of Greece are destined to correct our architectural aesthetics, which have been distorted by the invasion of an art alien to our customs and our traditions. From those models alone a pure Greek architecture could spring."[4] In his Foreword on Vernacular Art, Pikionis noted reflectively, "only an understanding of the laws of art and its patterns will lead you to art".[5]

D. Loukopoulos played an important part in collecting folklore materials from Central Greece. Angeliki Hadzimichali produced a vast volume of work in the field of vernacular art, and represented the ideological attitude of intellectual circles towards the traditional culture. "Greek vernacular art", she wrote, "is one of the most authentic expressions of the soul of the people, and it is the firm foundation beneath all modern Greek

Interior decoration in the Katsoulis house in Siatista.

artistic creation. As we study the features of our vernacular art, we shall come to gain a better knowledge of our race and of ourselves, and then, in accordance with that consciousness, we shall mould a new and truly Greek and patriotic aesthetics and art. That will help in the task of creating our culture out of the real strengths of the nation."[6]

At a later date, Professor Stylianos Kyriadikis made folklore studies a more systematic discipline, while Konstantinos Romaios produced interesting comparisons between the forms of ancient and modern Greek culture.[7]

During the Twenties, a variety of circumstances in the political and social sphere caused a reassessment of vernacular art - and also an overestimation of its importance. While the initial underestimation had proved fatal in terms of the preservation of the material remnants of the vernacular culture, the subsequent shift in attitude - charged first with sentimentality and then with commercialisation - disorientated for many years research and study in the various fields of the art of the Ottoman occupation. It is interesting that during critical periods in Greek history the 'vernacular' has become associated with the 'national' and, as an expression of the ideology of the bourgeiosie, has taken the form of slogans such as 'back to our roots' or 'preserve our traditions'.[8]

In recent years, a new approach to the problems of traditional culture - one based on the principles of ethnography and social anthropology[9] - has become apparent. Although modern studies and publications have made a positive contribution to a more profound knowledge of the vernacular culture, there are still many questions to answer, especially in the field of artistic creation and its processes.

The Significance of the Term 'Vernacular'

The significance of the frequently-used Greek adjective 'lakos', here rendered 'vernacular', is far from clear. It can be used to describe either the forms of expression of an entire people with a shared education and a single way of life, or those of a specific social class.[10]

Here, the term 'vernacular art' is used in the first meaning, that is, as the artistic expression of a people creating in accordance with traditional models, and it refers to the secular art of the Ottoman period by way of

Exterior decoration of the Poulkidis house in Siatista.

contrast with the religious art of that time, which has come to be called 'post-Byzantine'.

In some special cases, such as the paintings which decorate urban houses, the term 'vernacular' art is not entirely appropriate: the craftsmen who produced it may have been men of the people, but the models they applied and the objective in the mind of the owner of the house were far removed from the specifications of vernacular art. As a result, the themes of such decorative painting are confined to views of cities, imaginary landscapes and decorative motifs. By way of contrast, the ecclesiastical iconography of the time was rich in scenes from everyday life,[11] and could be said to have been the artistic creation of the people intended to meet the needs of the people.

The Historical Background

The Church as an institution and the church as a building did much to preserve Orthodoxy during the centuries of Ottoman rule. Furthermore, it maintained the national and social cohesion of the enslaved Greeks and kept alive their links to the historic past.

The privileges granted by the Turks under the treaties

of the late 17th and, above all, the 18th centuries benefited the local communities and the guilds and did much to make possible the growth of commerce among the peoples of the Balkans, especially the Greeks. The Treaty of Karlowitz (1699) set the seal on Turkey's defeat at the hands of Austria, which became a power of importance in the Danubian states and the northern Balkans. The Treaty of Passarowitz (1718) set the terms on which trade between the nationals of the two signatories, Austria and Turkey, could grow, made provision for the free movement of merchants and goods down the valley of the Axios, favoured the development of commercial transactions and removed the restrictions on the use of the ports of Thessaloniki and Trieste. The Treaty of Kutchuk Kainardji (1744) was intended primarily to protect Russian interests, but it also extended many privileges to the Greeks, including religious toleration and freedom of movement as merchants. As a result, by the mid 19th century the Greeks were at the centre of economic and cultural development in the southern Balkans.[12]

Numerous Epirots, Macedonians and Thessalians took advantage of this state of affairs to travel to the large urban centres of the Empire - Constantinople, Thessaloniki, Kavala - and throughout the northern Balkans, Central Europe and southern Russia in search of their fortunes. Most of these men were merchants, but they also included builders, carpenters, masons, metal-workers and professional people, who left their homes on a seasonal basis or for longer stays. As a result, we find builders from Eratyra (Selitsa) and Vogatsiko working alongside Epirots in Constantinople, and the artists of Samarina travelled as far afield as the Peloponnese.

The activities of the Macedonian merchants were of particular importance. The geographical position of western Macedonia made travel to Italy and the rest of Europe easy, and the caravans of the Balkans were operated largely by Epirots and the men of Western Macedonia (Kozani, Siatista, Samarina).[13]

The merchants of Siatista traded with Austria-Hungary and Germany, exporting leather, furs, threat, raw cotton and wine, and importing silk and woollen cloth, glass, china and mirrors. The wealth of Siatista caused it to be called 'flourochori' ('money-town'). The French traveller Pouqueville (1806) describes Siatista as follows: "My amazement was great wen, walking through the market-place with its fine shops, I found well-built houses and enjoyed the sight of a wholly Greek town

Traditional house in Florina.

with an appearance of prosperity and cleanliness which one will find nowhere else in Turkey". As for the people,

Mansions in Kastoria.

The Kanatsoulis house in Siatista.

Pouqueville notes that "there were merchants who appeared to have gained a certain amount of German simplicity from their stays in Vienna, Leipzig and Germany and to have lost the wiliness of the Greek character".[14]

Kozani traded with Germany, Austria-Hungary, Poland and Constantinople, and had developed the market for saffron, cotton cloth and thread. According to Harisios Megdanis, a 19th century scholar from Kozani, the wealthy citizens of the town "competed with each other in the building and decoration of fine houses and in luxurious and courtly living".[15]

Kastoria, whose trade in furs never ceased to flourish, traded with Leipzig, Paris and London as well as Constantinople.

In eastern Macedonia, Serres exported cotton and tobacco to Austria and France, while leather and silk went abroad from Meleniko.

The Greeks who lived abroad organised themselves into communities which were active in culture and intellectual matters. There were Greek schools and prolific publishing houses in Venice, Vienna and Budapest, and Greek newspapers, periodicals and books were to be found everywhere. Many of the Greek emigrants distin-guished themselves in the arts and sciences, apart from trade. These emigrant Macedonians kept up close links with their families at home, often returning to their native villages to settle for good. They did much to further economic and cultural progress in many of the towns and villages of Macedonia. This prosperity caused the creation of a bourgeois class which altered the existing social structure and placed life on a new footing.

By promoting education, advancing the arts and letters and raising the cultural level, the emigrant Macedonians helped to establish a spirit of liberalism which did much to help the cause of liberation from the Turks.

In parallel with this change in the economic and cultural framework, the enlightenment had the effect of moderating the strictness of religious belief, which in turn had a direct impact on the proliferation and flourishing of vernacular art. As the Byzantinologist D. Pallas puts it, "Mystical ecstasy lost its impetus and religion now became a national symbol, a bond, a living tradition, a moral rule. It was no longer a spiritual movement. The search for refinement, for the display of social grace, for beauty, began. A new style prevailed: the 'bourgeois' style which, with the vernacular, heralded the coming of the War of Independence".

It was thus in the manufacturing centres of Epirus, Macedonia and Thessaly, where the new bourgeois class of merchants emerged, that all the sectors of vernacular art - architecture, painting and handicrafts of various kinds - flourished to the greatest extent. Quite apart from Thessaloniki, which had always been an urban centre, the Macedonian towns of Siatista, Kastoria, Kozani, Verria, Edessa, Nymphaio, Serres, Meleniko and Kavala emerged in this role.

Architecture

Apart from the settlements which had survived from earlier times, Ottoman rule in Macedonia saw the building of a large number of new towns and villagers in inaccessible and isolated locations for reasons of safety. Planning was non- existent in these new settlements. Houses were built around the parish churches, and the arrangement of open spaces, roads and paths was as dictated by the terrain and the gradual growth of the settlement.[16]

Scholars of vernacular architecture are not in agreement on whether the houses of Macedonia should be placed in three categories (vernacular, intermediate, mansions, D. Philippidis) or two (vernacular and mansions, N. Moutsopoulos). There is also a tendency for the term 'mansion' to be replaced by 'urban house' (M. Garidis).[17]

Although vernacular houses - structures with a single room for animals and humans - are to be found in almost identical form throughout Greece, evolving into more complex types of house with subdivisions of the interior or additions, the mansion houses are characteristic examples of the secular architecture of Macedonia and its surroundings in the 18th century.

Despite the differences from area to area, caused by topographical, climatic or economic factors, all these houses seem to have a common origin which can perhaps be traced back to the last centuries of Byzantium.

These houses combine the defensive features of stone-built tower-like lower storeys with a lighter and fundamentally wooden structure on the upper floor or floors, which have balconies of various kinds borne on supports. The roof, with its Byzantine tiles, has eaves which may protrude beyond the walls for as much as one or one and a half metres (Sior Manolakis mansion, Verria, 1839[18]). Similar mansions have also survived in Albania and Bulgaria, areas outside the frontiers of modern Greece.

Wood and stone were the principal building materials. The ground floor was built of stone, although

Proprietory inscription on the Manousis house in Siatista, built in 1763.

layers of wooden cross-ties were often inserted. The upper floor or floors and the interior partitions were wooden, using the lath- and-plaster method.

Macedonian houses often have courtyards with high walls shutting them off from the street. Inside the yard were the well, the stone-built oven, the lavatory and other service areas. Such mansions might be L-shaped, in the form of a Greek[19], or square.

The ground floor was used as a storage area, and from it a staircase led up to the mesopatoma ('in-between floor') and the upper storeys.

Where there was a mesopatoma between the ground floor and the upper storeys (as in Kastoria, Siatista and Verria) it was used as the owner's workshop or commercial premises, or might be arranged as the family's winter quarters (winter sitting-room, bedrooms, kitchen).

The upper storey, which gained in area thanks to its extension on supports, was used as summer quarters and contained the main reception rooms.

"The Rape of Persephone": mural in the Kanatsoulis house in Siatista.

The staircase ended here in the parlour or 'doxato', a name originating in the line of wooden arches which decorated it. The parlour was marked by its slightly raised floor, while the rooms that communicated with it often had fireplaces in the centre of one of their outer walls.

A horizontal cornice ran right round the inner walls of the rooms, at the height of the top of the door and window openings. Above this were multi- coloured decorative glass lenses, and this band was also used for paintings of cities, imaginary landscapes or other decorative motifs, usually vases of stylised flowers. Below the cornice were the door and window openings, together with fitted cupboards in which clothes, food or valuables were kept. The remaining areas of wall were covered with wooden panels (with carved or painted decoration) or bore more paintings. Low sofas, covered with brightly- coloured rugs, were placed against the wall on either side of the fireplace.

The mansions of Macedonia and of the Balkans in general were the work of teams of builders, masons and carpenters from the villages of Epirus and western Macedonia and from the area around Skopje in Serbia.

They were organised into guilds known as sinafia or esnaf, and they travelled the Balkans building churches, mosques, houses, bridges and fountains.

According to P. Tzelepis, "the work of these vernacular architects reveals all the care and experience of reflective artists. It shows the faith, love and respect they had for their art. Their virtues gave them a sense of measure which prevented their own personalities from selfishly influencing their work or dominating the building to the detriment of its inherent value. This self-abnegation may mean that the names of the architects have been forgotten, but it gives their work a national importance which has put down roots and become identified with the country's heritage, casting its reflection over the Greek people as a whole."[20]

Paintings

In those buildings which make use of external painted decoration, it extends along the narrow band from the eaves to the top of the lenses or windows, between the windows (Albania, Western Macedonia) or beneath the protruding upper storey. This ensured that the paintings were protected by the roof or by the upper

A mural in the Aivazis house in Kastoria.

floor. Such paintings show imaginary landscapes, trees and birds - usually without any regard for scale or proportion (Western Macedonia) - or purely decorative motifs (Kavala).

The interior decoration of these buildings is of greater interest. In the decoration, the owner's personality, his wealth and his knowledge, his familiarity with the countries to which he travelled, his cultivation and tastes and his views on himself and the world could all be seen indirectly. Such a task was a test of the capacity of the vernacular painter, of his art and of his technique.

Painted decoration usually occupied the area above the corine of the walls, while the lower surfaces were wood-panelled. In other cases, the paintings covered the entire wall surface of the room or staircase. These paintings are incredible in their variety of theme and style: views of cities, imaginary landscapes, scenes from mythology, plant and other decorative motifs are all mixed up with obvious influences from baroque, rococo, neo-Classicism and Muslim art.

Among the most striking examples of secular vernacular painting are the scenes which show imaginary and idyllic landscapes with rivers and bridges, deer and hunters, wild and domesticated animals, fearsome vultures (one of them actually marked "vulture" in the Manousis mansion, Siatista, 1787) and other exotic birds, usually depicted as larger than the trees or buildings on which they perch. All this thematic material is spread out across the walls without perspective or proportional scale - just like a carpet. Astrological symbols, too, were used (Manousis and Maliongas mansions, Siatista). The theme of the sliced water-melon is frequent - apparently it once symbolised the decapitation of St John the Baptist - either by itself or in conjunction with other motifs. The double-headed eagleis a common motif in domestic iconography, as is the bird devouring a snake.

Views of cities were among the favourite themes used in the decoration of houses in Macedonia. A cartographic technique was used in most cases; this style appeared in the 15th century and was predominant in the Greek world until the 19th century, when it was displaced by Western rules of perspective and spatial interpretation. (Among the last examples of the cartographic approach in modern Greek painting are the series of

Interior decoration in the Nerantzopoulos house
in Siatista (1755).

scenes from the War of Independence which Zographos produced for Makriyannis.) In producing these bird's eye views of cities, the craftsmen were following the principles of Byzantine and post- Byzantine art: they not only showed what they were capable of knowing and seeing, but enlarged the things that made an impression on them and removed anything they saw as super-fluous.[21]

Constantinople occupies pride of place in the paintings of this category. It combined the marvellous and the symbolic, and as 'the Queen of Cities' it continued to inspire national dreams in the hearts of the enslaved Greeks. There are panoramic views of Constantinople in numerous houses in Kastoria, Siatista, Eratyra and Ambelakia[22], and still more in houses and mosques now on Turkish soil.[23] The city is usually depicted in such a conventional and stylised manner than if it were not for the peculiar topographical division into three districts it would not always be possible to put a name to it; even Santa Sophia cannot always be picked out. But the

sailing-ships and boats are always there in the sea, and there are fish which the folk craftsmen delighted in showing larger than life size.

In a view of Constantinople from the Poulkidis mansion in Siatista (1752-59), one of the earliest renderings of this theme, the vernacular artist embarked upon a free adaptation of his topic. As Garidis has pointed out,[24] the artist used a copper engraving of Vatopedi Monastery on Mt Athos as the model for the right-hand side of his painting, which shows the main section of Constantinople. This is interesting for the light which it sheds on the type of model used by the painters of the age, and also for the trend to revitalise and enhance the stylised scene which it reveals. In addition, the presence of dragons, seraphim and a priest give the painting covertly national allusions.

In a later depiction of Constantinople in the Kariophyllis mansion, Siatista (1844), the approach is quite different and there is an attempt to portray reality more faithfully and respect the principles of perspective and scale. The painter's concepts have altered under the influence of Classicism and he would seem to be following different models.

The Bosporus was also painted (Keratzis mansion, Siatista), as were other harbour towns (Sior Manolakis mansion, Verria, 1829), with the houses and ships arranged symmetrically and paratactically. The fact that the artist's intention was purely decorative and his concepts non-realistic can be seen clearly in the scene of a city crossed by a river in the Tsiatsapas mansion in Kastoria. The composition is crowned with the familiar sliced water-melon motif (in the position usually occupied by the name of the city), the most important buildings - such as a belfry with a clock - are picked out and the waters of the river are full of fish out of all proportion to the size of the ships.

Apart from cities, the monasteries of Mt Athos were another favourite topic (Manousis mansion, Siatista), and were painted after copper engravings. The monasteries were painted inside 'frames' in the upper band, next to the glass lenses, while other such frames housed the mountains of Macedonia, identified by inscription: "Siniazikos", "Kesavos", "Elympos", "Athon", etc.

The paintings in the Siatista mansions are not confined only to the cities of the East, real or imagined: Western cities such as Frankfurt and Madrid (the Maliongas mansion, 1844) also make their appearance. Could these be indirect testimony to the travels and the cosmopolitanism of the owner? They are certainly adaptations of earlier Western copper engravings which Makris[25] and Garidis[26] have identified. In these paintings, too - as we have already seen - the vernacular artist does not copy his models, simply following them along general lines and enhancing them with features taken from the vast range of traditional motifs.

The stylised landscapes with buildings seen in oval or square frames and identical to those also found on the screens of churches (Keratzis mansion, Siatista, and the screen of the Presentation of Christ in the Temple, Thessaloniki) are of a purely decorative nature. The presence in these scenes of Western aristocrats, identifiable by their clothes, or of Austrian hussars (Maliongas house, Siatista) testifies to their Western origins. There are also numerous 'frames' containing decorative motifs with fruit or flowers and displaying rococo influences. In many cases, the fruit and flowers are of plaster or stucco, in relief. Also present in some cases are Christian inscriptions and abbreviations (IS, XS, NK: Tsiatsapas mansion, Siatista).

On the wall of a corridor beneath the staircase in the Manousis mansion at Siatista is an interesting rendition in the form of a painting of a complex rococo cartouche[27] typical of the period of Louis XV (1720-1750). This was a period when Western influences, and especially those of France, were beginning to penetrate the Ottoman Empire, and they were recorded in the art of the period. This cartouche survived in a number of variations into the 19th century, sometimes containing fruit or - as in the case of the houses of Eratyra - figures.

The winter sitting-room of the Kanatsoulis mansion in Siatista has preserved a rare example of a painting of mythological scenes. In large rectangles on the lower sections of the wall and in oval frames in the upper band are some 20 mythological scenes, each with its inscription: the gods of Olympus, Rhea, Zeus, Aeolus, Asclepios, Dice, the Gorgons, the Colossus of Rhodes, and so on. These wall-paintings are dated with exactness by an inscription over the door of the room: "1811 June 12", and according to M. Kanatsoulis they were the work of a painter called Efthymios or Efthymiou from Patra. There is a connection with a treatise of the period by Harisis Megdanis of Kozani, published in Pest under the title Hellenic Pantheon.[28]

The vernacular artists did not attempt to confine themselves strictly to the ancient style, and they had no hesitation in enlivening their compositions with scenes from the everyday life with which they were more familiar. In the scene showing Aphrodite, the group in the lower part of the picture seems to be an illustration of members of the society of the artist's day, while the musical instruments accompanying the dance of the Muses, the Corybantes and the rape of Persephone are the violin, the clarinet and the drum, as used at the secular feasts of the time.

In other scenes, such as those showing Chimaera or Hermes, the iconographic types used resemble those of religious iconography. The manner in which the figures are depicted is also reminiscent of the post-Byzantine icon-painters, thus reminding us once again of the foundations which the religious and secular painters of the period had in common.

Also of interest are the three portraits on the column capitals in front of the windows of the rooms. One of the male figures and the female figure can be identified with the owners of the house, thus testifying to the tendency on the part of the urban merchant class to seek recognition and social advancement. Similar portraits of the householders are to be found in other buildings (the Keratzis house, Siatista, and the Karanitsios house at Eratya: "the good lady of the house"). It would be even more interesting if the third portrait could safely be identified as the artist.

Portraits of eminent citizens were common during the 19th century, and are found in churches as well as in houses (often among the saved in the scene of the Day of Judgement). They are shown in the clothes of the period, which were an indisputable indication of their social class.

Throughout the 19th century we have abundant evidence of the influence of neo- Classicism, which as an expression of the ideology of the age promoted and imposed models taken from antiquity. Neo-Classicism left its imprint deep on the official art of the free Greek state, and also entered vernacular art in the form of mythological or allegorical scenes and imitations of buildings, statues and decorative elements. Paintings of this kind have survived in Nymphaio, Eratyra, Siatista and Vlasti.

At Nymphaio, the shading technique was used to convey an illusion of the three- dimensional original in pictures of the statues of Classical antiquity or Roman copies of them (Amazons,[29] Aristippus), while ancient monuments such as the Parthenon, the Gate of Hadrian and the Temple of Olympian Zeus were depicted and numerous cupids painted, especially in Eratyra. Guilio Romano's Dance of the Muses adorned houses all over Greece and was also used on embroideries, woven goods and printed textiles in many parts of the country.[30] Early in the 20th century the Greek key appeared as a motif for the frame around paintings.

Scenes from modern history were quite common, too, with the figure of Rigas Pherraios being the most popular (Vlasti, Eratyra).

The scene showing musical instruments in the Karanitsios house at Eratyra is unique.[31] Here a double stylised Horn of Plenty surrounds a series of folk instruments - a drum, a tambourine, clarinets and a bugle - to allude to the householder's occupation.

The symbolic representations connected with the concept of time, including personifications of the four seasons, of day and night or of the four tribes display resemblances to similar themes in ecclesiastical iconography.

We have information to the effect that many of the artists who painted the houses of Macedonia were local men or from nearby districts (Kleisoura, Drosopigi, Vlasti, Eratyra). Their main occupation was icon-painting but they also met the demand for secular paintings. It was not essential that these craftsmen should be talented artists; if they were gifted, that was simply an additional qualification. Some of them had spent a period of apprenticeship on Mt Athos, and manuscript manuals of painting which have come down to us tell us of their techniques.[32] The painters, like the other craftsmen, were organised into guilds and they travelled the towns and villages from spring to autumn painting houses and churches. There is a typical inscription in the refectory of the Monastery of St John the Baptist at Serres: "Painted by the great artist Nedelkos the skilful, painter of pictures of cities, ports and landscapes of all kinds with decoration in the rococo manner".[33]

Painting is the most interesting of all the vernacular art forms, since it gives us a picture - not, unfortunately, always a clear one - of the history of an area or an age.

As we have seen, some progress has been made in the field of models, but our general knowledge of Constantinople and the other cities is too limited to allow us to make the comparative study which would give us an exact picture of things free of ethnic sensitivities.

Vernacular painting had a particular fascination for the Greek intellectuals, poets and painters of the generation of the Thirties, who 'discovered' Zographos and Theophilos. Kontoglou, Asteriadis, Vasileiou and Tsarouchis all drew productively on the themes of vernacular art in their attempt to 'return to their roots'.

Glass Lenses

Glass lenses, which are usually rectangular in shape, rising to the point of a Muslim arch, were located over the windows on the upper floor and were interpolated into the paintings which decorated this band of the building. The lenses acted as a kind of variable addition to the paintings which decorated the house, as the fluctuations in the light passing through them created constantly altering impressions of colour inside the rooms. They also had a practical purpose: when the large windows below, which were not glazed, were covered with

wooden shutters for reasons of safety or because of the weather, they provided the room with light.

Most of the glass lenses to be seen in the mansions of Macedonia are in Siatista, and these are also the most highly decorated examples of their type. Multcoloured pieces of glass fitted into plaster frames formed vases with stylised flowers and geometrical shapes, and these would be flanked by cypress trees and rectangular compartments filled with complex carved patterns.

The shapes, techniques and motifs used for these lenses are reminiscent of the stained glass in Muslim mosques. However, the presence of national and religious symbols (the eagle, the cross, the mounted saint) and the miniature inscriptions in an archaic manner with the names of the craftsmen responsible - usually priests (see the Nerantzopoulos mansion in Siatista, "Moschos the priest, 1755") - bear witness to the Greek nationality of the artisans. Even in the verse inscriptions - difficult of access and harder to read - which can hardly be praised for their linguistic correctness or clarity, we can clearly see the householder's pride in his home and his desire to show off his learning:

Wood-Carving

Wood-carving flourished after the 17th century, and the most outstanding examples of this art, executed under the influence of the European baroque, were initially intended for use in churches: screens, pulpits, bishop's thrones, shrines, stands and doors. When houses for the wealthy began to be built in the 18th century, secular wood-carving became widespread, too. Given that the same craftsmen produced carvings for churches and houses, the stylistic features are shared. Epirus and Western Macedonia were the areas in which most of the wood-carvers originated. Like the other craftsmen, they travelled widely, executing their commissions on the spot or assembling ready- made parts in wood-carving centres.

Secular wood-carvings can be divided into two categories: those which formed part of the interior decoration of houses and portable pieces such as furniture and household utensils.

The ceilings, walls, pillars, arches, cupboards and wall panelling of the mansions were all made of wood, decorated with carvings, paintings or a combination of the two.

Wooden ceilings vary widely in their decoration and, according to the room, could be square or rectangular. Particular attention was paid to the centre of the ceiling, known as the 'heart' or the 'navel'. Here there would be a square, rectangular, polygonal or circular pattern, often carved more deeply than the rest of the ceiling, which was brought out by successive framing patterns and served as the main decoration of the ceiling. Special care was lavished over the 'navel', which was given arabesques influenced by Muslim models, rosettes in relief, stars and even pieces of fruit. In addition to the carvings, the ceiling was often richly painted, with geometric and floral motifs spreading in complex patterns right across the surface of the ceiling.

In some cases, the entire interior of the room would be decorated with wood- carvings (Tsiminakis house, Kozani, 18th century) or with carvings which had then been painted (Manousis mansion, Siatista, 1762).

Doors were wooden and consisted of a single panel, often decorated with plant or geometric motifs.

The fitted cupboards installed in many rooms were used to store bedding, woven goods, clothes and food, along with the household's valuables. Sometimes a series of little niches would be inserted between the cupboards, and smaller objects placed there.

Apart from their functional role, these cupboards are marvellous examples of decorative art, with rhythmically alternating surfaces, a vast variety of decorative motifs and a wealth of colour to add to the atmosphere of comfort and prosperity of the living quarters.

The decorative motifs used by wood-carvers or painters in these cupboards and in the wall panelling -- flowers protruding symmetrically from a vase, suns in human form, stylised architectural landscapes - were common to the carved wooden screens of churches and the decoration of houses.

By way of contrast with the Greek islands, Macedonia and the rest of the mainland could boast very little in the way of portable pieces of furniture: chests, trunks and cradles.

The chest, which, with the clothes it contained, was the central feature in each girl's dowry, would be richly decorated with wood-carvings, inlays or paintings. The long side on the front was usually decorated, while cypress trees, floral patterns, birds, animals and geometrical designs made a more rare appearance on the short ends. Sometimes the chest would be inlaid with mother- of-pearl or lighter-coloured wood. Cypress or cedar wood was usually used for the chests, to give the clothes a pleasant aroma and protect them from moths. These chests were often imported, in which case they were decorated in a different way.

The wood-carving of shepherds produced many interesting examples of the decoration of everyday objects: crooks, distaffs, spinning-wheels, spoons, pipes. The shepherds gave shape to the world of their imagina-

Wooden ceiling in the Aivazis house, Kastoria.

tion by carving superb combinations of patterns with spontaneous taste and the most primitive of tools.

Stone-Carving

During the Ottoman period, carving in stone and marble continued to be in the Byzantine mould and was

Carved wooden distaff.

Silver phylactery depicting St George.

origin, reflected in their Greek names. These were made or repaired by coppersmiths, ironsmiths and tinsmiths, and might be either of beaten metal or forged. Their decorative motifs, carved or more rarely in relief or perforated, were in accordance with Byzantine or Eastern models: rosettes, cypress trees, geometrical patterns, imaginary buildings, pentagrams, depictions of the saints and double-headed eagles. Sometimes the date or the name of the owner or craftsman is added, in Byzantine script.

Metal utensils were sold by travelling merchants or from stalls at markets and religious feasts.

Pottery

Pottery utensils such as jugs and cooking-pots were widely used by the households of the Ottoman period.

The making of pottery developed in areas which had the necessary raw material - clay, in various colours. In Macedonia, pottery was manufactured in Kozani, Florina, Argos Orestiko, Diavata and Nea Karvali.

Macedonian pottery stands out for its simplicity and for a preference for closed rather than open vessels. Sometimes the utensils were left in the natural colour of the clay, while elsewhere they were glazed (faience), especially in the Florina area.

Decorative motifs were plain and were applied by carving or in white paint: simple geometrical shapes, plant motifs, more rarely animal motifs.

However, there were many occasions on which the craftsman's artistic inclination went beyond the purely utilitarian mission of the vessel, and then complete pottery animals or plants would be attached to the handle or body of the jug, or complex spouts would be moulded (Florina, Nea Karvali) after the fashion of similar vessels from Asia Minor. The features of the earthenware produced in Florina were reminiscent of the pottery of neighbouring Yugoslavia, a reminder of the freedom of communication between these areas.

confined to reliefs for the decoration of churches, houses and fountains - that is, to lintels, door-posts, lenses and decorative friezes.

The reliefs built into the walls of houses often contained inscriptions which gave more information than the year of building and the name of the owner, together with decorative symbolic depictions to protect the house and prevent evil from crossing the threshold: crosses, appeals to Our Lady and Christ, masks whose exact significance is a matter of controversy, national symbols such as the double-headed eagle, and plant motifs.

These reliefs were carved by the stone-masons who were indispensable members of the teams of builders who set out each year from Epirus and Western Macedonia and travelled the whole of mainland Greece and the Balkans.

Metal-Working

After the 18th century, metal-working became a significant activity in the towns and villages of Macedonia. As far back as the Byzantine period, Thessaloniki had been an important centre for the processing of copper, and Kozani and Verria also worked metal on a smaller scale. In many cases, metal fittings of various kinds - especially clappers for bells - were worked with particular care and enthusiasm.

A large number of copper, brass and tin utensils were needed for everyday life: coffee-pots, trays, pestles, braziers, jugs, etc., many of which were of Turkish

Weaving - Embroidery

Weaving was the most important domestic craft. The institution of the dowry made a major contribution to its development, as it also did to embroidery, jewellery and furniture-making.

"This form of art", wrote Alki Kyriakidou-Nestoros, "was closely bound up with the family and economic life of the people of Macedonia and Thrace, where we can see it serving not only as a source of wealth but also as a firm component of customs, superstitions and traditions".[34]

Weaving catered for all immediate domestic and occupational needs and the family's requirements in clothing, admirably combining practicality with rich and imaginative decoration. In the areas of clothing and domestic fittings, the variety of materials and techniques used was rivalled only by the wealth of decorative motifs. The creations of this branch of handicrafts - together with embroidered goods - are often of the greatest artistic interest.

Various techniques of weaving were used, depending on the type of material to be produced, and the decoration of each type was determined and dictated by its use. Decoration was also determined by rules common to every country and every period: form, symmetry, rhythm, the arrangement of motifs in bands, and the use of secondary colours.[35]

The designs woven (or embroidered) can be classed either as geometrical or representational, and are the common artistic heritage of each country. Individual weavers or embroiderers could draw on this stock of themes and render their choice in their own way and in accordance with their abilities.

The role of colour in weaving is most important. "The alternation of colour is not simply a matter of changing design; it is much more complex. Yet there is a strict rhythm of colour which is not the same for each colour pattern and is repeated regularly in the composition."[36]

The dyes used were natural, producing deep, harmonious shades which modern chemicals cannot replicate. The plants which grew in each place and the local knowledge of dyeing methods were important in determining the colours of the vernacular woven goods and could be used to trace their geographical origins.

Apart from its significance as a domestic skill, weaving also developed into a craft industry in which male weavers had their part to play. In northern Greece (Macedonia, Epirus and Thessaly) woollen cloth was made for clothing, blankets, rugs, saddle-cloths, etc. The workshops of Siatista and Kozani turned out products made by sewing woven materials together (called 'alfoursina'[37]), and these were noted for the symmetry of their patterns and the harmony of their colours.

Traditional costumes occupy a place of distinction in the folk arts. By way of contrast to male costume, which was largely manufactured, the female costumes of Macedonia (as of the rest of Greece) were richly decorated and highly varied. At first, the entire costume was made at home, while later some of its components - kerchiefs, belts and even pieces of material - were manufactured or bought in the marketplace. Over time, this caused a difference to emerge between the urban costume, which displayed foreign influences, and the

Women of Grevena in traditional dress.

more conservative village costume. The costumes of Verria, Naousa, Kastoria, Siatista, Roumlouki, Asvestochori, Episkopi and Florina are of particular interest, as are those worn by the Sarakatsans.

One of the features common to Greek male and female costume - and, indeed, to the entire Balkan area - was the smock, a very ancient item of dress. In the female costume, this was highly decorated and richly bejewelled. Among the other basic components of the female costume were the jacket, the false sleeves, the cotton coat, the apron and the kerchief, all of which varied in name and design from place to place.[38]

In traditional costume, as in woven goods, colour and decorative motifs are of great importance. Colour was a distinctive mark of class - class which, in the community of this period, was a matter of age and family circumstances rather than social position. According to ethnologists and students of folklore, the decorative motifs conceal

An example of Macedonian silverwork, with an engraved pentacle.

symbolic meanings bound up with the intellectual level of the people. In bridal clothes, in particular, some repeated motifs (cockerels, pine-cones, trees) have been associated with fertility since ancient times.[39]

It would seem that the women of Macedonia were so affected in their dress and vain as to make a bad impression on visitors from Western Europe. Pouqueville, while praising the pies and wine of Siatista, had this to say about the women: "As for the women, I cannot say where they found their model for deforming themselves as they do in the way they dress. If the foreign visitor is amazed by the singularity of the dolmans [...] then he should see the Macedonian women of Siatista, laden down like horses with velvet garments covered with braid and decorated with little pieces of cloth so as to form pictures of various things. A Chinese bridge might form the entire back of one such garment, or a cypress tree, a pavilion or some other objects, always on a large scale, and so a tree and some houses might be seen as respectable dress for a lady. One of our screens would be a fine adornment for these women. Following the fashion of the Jews, they conceal their hair beneath muslin kerchiefs, over which they wear the Vardar band. Attached to this is a red fez in the form of a net horse-blanket falling down their backs. Under this strange headgear they are not, of course, very elegant, since they rival each other in the length of their coverings, and some of them wear it down to their heels. As is the case

throughout the East, the Greek women do not believe themselves properly adorned unless they are wearing the rouge and powder with which they plaster their necks and faces, mixing it with some shiny cream so that one is reflected in the brilliance of their charms. Among these charms is to shed into the heavens a kind of cloud of stars in the form of small pieces of gold; there is no great lady whose collection of cosmetic aids does not include, next to the boxes of rouge and cinnabar, a leaf of gold with which to decorate her face."[40]

The local differences we have already noted in weaving and embroidery also applied to the decorative motifs and colours. According to scholars, the "harsh and grave character of the north Greeks" can be discerned in the embroidery of Macedonia, although influences from East and West can also be discerned.

Embroidered materials were used to decorate the local costume and the home. In terms of the manner of their production, they can be classed as needlepoint, worked over a pattern or in even stitches across counted threads.

Just as there were professional weavers, so, too, the crafts of embroidery and braiding were practised by professionals.[41]

Teams of embroiderers and gold-embroiderers travelled the country executing the gold embroidery work on clothes of all kinds, which accounts for the fact that we can see a uniform decorative approach to this particular art. The embroiderers would draw their decorative designs on to pieces of paper pinned to the cloth (felt, wool, silk, velvet, etc.) and these would then be embroidered in silk, gold or silver thread. The braiders, on the other hand, had settled premises and there they worked their decorative themes in gold wire or thread. The braid technique was used for Good Friday bier covers and church vestments, and for head-coverings and shoes in the secular sphere.

Silver and Gold

Increasing amounts of work in silver and gold were produced in Macedonia for ecclesiastical and secular use during the 17th and 18th centuries. The mining of silver in Chalcidice assisted this process. Although they never rivalled the goldsmiths of Kalarryta in Epirus, there were noted craftsmen working gold and especially silver in Nymphaio, Kozani, Thessaloniki and Serres.

Ear-rings, necklaces, buckles and large, heavy pieces of jewellery with decoration of various types all formed integral parts of the male and female traditional costume. This jewellery set its wearers apart and helped displays of social standing, but it was also a useful investment, being easy to carry and convert into cash.

Carved wooden ceiling in the Vourka house in Kozani.

Indeed, gold and silver coins were attached to some pieces of jewellery.

Carved document case.

The jewellery turned out in commercial workshops does not differ from place to place and shows similarities of technique and decorative approach even when it originates in locations far distant from each other. Beating, wiring and enamelling were among the techniques used.[42]

Nyphaio (Neveska) was a renowned centre for silver-work after the 18th century. The craftsmen from the town, with their little boxes of tools and materials, travelled far and wide, stopping wherever there was work and returning home for the feast of Our Lady on 15 August.

An examination of the different forms of vernacular art (architecture, painting, handicrafts) shows the close relationship between ecclesiastical and secular art and also the shared features of the art-forms in the Balkan peninsula and Asia Minor in the 18th and 19th centuries, under Balkan political domination.

●

EFTHYMIA YEORGIADOU-KOUNTOURA

VERNACULAR ART IN MACEDONIA

NOTES

1. Nikos Mouzelis, "Modern Greek society - aspects of underdevelopment", Athens 1978, p. 323.
2. P. Yannopoulos, "The Greek line", Athens 1965, p. 66.
3. See S. Papadopoulos, "The art of the coppersmith in the Greek village 1900-1975", Folklore Foundation, Nafplio 1982, pp. 12ff.
4. A. Zachos, "Popular architecture", The artist (O Kallitechnis) no. 17, August 1911, p. 186.
5. D. Pikionis, "Texts", National Bank Educational Foundation, Athens 1985, p. 52.
6. A. Hadzimichali, "Greek folk art - Skyros", Athens 1925, p. 5.
7. K.T. Dimaras, "History of modern Greek literature", Athens 1975, p. 439.
8. For more detail, see A. Politis, "Popular culture", Anti, no. 43 (17.4.1976), pp. 44-45. 9. Papadopoulos, op. cit., pp. 32ff.
10. S. Asdrachas, "Popular culture", Anti no. 40 (6.3.1976), p. 43.
11. In the monasteries of Mt Athos, above all, and in other churches the iconographic cycles of the Benedicete and the Second Coming include scenes of revelry and social criticism directly related to the social conditions of the period.
12. For these treaties and their impact on the Greeks, see "History of the Greek Nation", vol. 11, Athens 1975, pp. 36, 50, 53ff.
13. For the emigrant Macedonians, see A. Vakalopoulos, "History of Macedonia 1354-1833", Thessaloniki 1969, pp. 399ff.
14. G. Tozis, "Siatistina", Macedonica 2 (1941-1952) pp. 325, 326.
15. Vakalopoulos, op. cit.. p. 405.
16. For town planning and architecture, see D. Philippidis, "Modern Greek architecture", Athens 1984, pp. 51ff.
17. M. Garidis, "Copper-plate types for secular decorative painting" Macedonica 22 (1982), p. 1.
18. N. Moutsopoulos, "Sior-Manolakis' mansion in Veria", Zygos 56-57 (1960), pp. 11-31.
19. P. Tzelepis, "Folk architects", Zygos (1956), p. 7.
20. P. Michelis, "Aesthetic review of Byzantine art", Athens 1972, p. 154.
21. There are pictures of Constantinople in Kastoria (the Natzis mansion, second half of the 18th century, and the Tsiatsapas mansion, 1798), in Siatista (the Tzonos house, 1756, the Poulkidis house,

1752-59, the Maliongas house, 1844, and the Kariofyllis house, 1844), in Eratyra (the Makris house, 1875-85), and at Ambelakia (the Schwartz house, 1798).

22. Garidis, *op. cit.*, p. 8, note 2, and N. Hadzinikolaou, "Ethnic art and progress", Athens 1982, p. 40, fig. 4.

23. Garidis, *op. cit.*, pp. 10ff.

24. K. Makris, "Steps", Athens 1979, pp. 367-370.

25. Garidis, *op. cit.*, pp. 5-7.

26. M. Kanatoulis, "On a fresco in the Manousis mansion in Siatista", Macedonica 24 (1984), pp. 188-196.

27. M. Kanatoulis, Les peintures murales des demeures de Siatista aux XVIIIe et XIXe s., Paris 1984, pp. 115, 117-118.

28. I. Touratoglou, "Written Amazon in Nymphaion", AAA 1968 (3), p.

29. K. Makris, "Neo-classic influences on Greek folk art", Thessaloniki 1986, pp. 52ff.

30. This wall-painting has been detached (the building to which it belonged having been demolished) and is kept in Eratyra Museum but is not on view. K. Makris, "Frescoes in the houses of Eratyra-Selitsa", Thessaloniki 1986, pp. 15ff.

31. Makris, "Steps", pp. 289-296.

32. "History of the Greek Nation", *op. cit.*, p. 255.

33. N. Moutsopoulos, "The mansions of Siatista", Thessaloniki 1961-64, p. 86.

34. A. Kyriakidou-Nestoros, "Woven materials in Macedonia and Thrace", Athens 1965, p. 1.

35. *Ibid.*, p. 45.

36. *Ibid.*, p. 77.

37. A. Zachos, "Allfoursina cloth pillows, Macedonian Journal" (1935), pp. 159-161.

38. A. Hadzimichali, "Greek folk dress", Athens (n.d.), p. 21.

39. Kyriakidou-Nestoros, *op. cit.*, p. 62 and passim.

40. G. Tozis, "Siatistina", Macedonica 2 (1941-1952), pp. 326-327.

41. "Embroidery and jewellery in Greek folk dress", Greek Folk Art Museum, Athens 1966, pp. 12-13 for the embroiderers and p. 116 for the braiders.

42. *Ibid.*, pp. 18-19.

43. Hadzinikolaou, *op. cit.*, p. 38.

Aspects of traditional culture in Macedonia (19th and early 20th century)

Eleanora Skouteri-Didaskalou

The context

The following pages contain an attempt to identify and to describe from an anthropological point of view some of the features which have shaped the historical particularity of Macedonian culture. The dissection of times and places and the analysis of their organization are an attempt to apply to specific historical data Alki Kyriakidou-Nestoros' proposition for the study of (Greek) traditional culture on the basis of these co-ordinates[1].

The traditional culture which developed in Macedonia within its more recent history is a result of the particular way in which certain central cultural and social elements coalesced into an organic whole. The cultural constants and permanencies which over the centuries had bound together a particular way of life in this area were the warp and the weft of the culture of the 19th and the first half of the 20th century, the canvas on which particular historic circumstances embroidered their changes and transiencies. Changes and continuities in the people's relationships with the land and with nature, in their relationships with their rulers and with each other. Changes and continuities in attitudes and behaviour, in work and play, at home and on the road, in food and in clothing, in the experiences and expectations of the people who lived in this land.[2]

In reality, the practical effects of these changes, whether on a smaller or a larger scale, varied from differential to unexpected to insignificant. Sometimes they were absorbed smoothly into the slow rhythms of accepted ways of life, occasionally surfacing on another level as a break in the pattern creating the conditions for change, which might be a superficial modification or a radical transformation. At other times they appear as abrupt breaks, impose themselves as reforms, or emerge as necessities. In short, these are changes which in one way or another have brought about alterations, upheavals or adjustments to the patterns of life and the cultural infrastructure of the society in question. Nevertheless, to the degree in which the long-lasting central structures absorbed these changes and remained predominant within the particular historical circumstances, the culture of Macedonia was traditional: it was characterized on almost all levels by orality, conformity and conventionality. This is the type of culture Alki Kyriakidou-Nestoros calls "popular culture"; as she says, "it is a popular culture with the same basic structures, (...) it is basically the same culture which organizes daily life in the cities and the villages alike".

It should be noted that the Greek character of this particular traditional culture appears to predominate on all levels, from the "popular" to the "scholarly", and from the official to the ordinary, though in differing degrees and with different effects on the lives of the inhabitants of the region according to their religion, the language or languages they used, their social position, their economic activities, their relationships with the various levels and types of authority, their sex, their level of education, and of course, towards the end of the period (though in a degree which remains to be studied in more depth) according to an inflated "national consciousness and identity".

The dissection of temporal and spatial organization is an attempt to identify certain features of traditional culture in Macedonia, highlighting those aspects which illustrate the particularities of this culture on the level of everyday life. More specifically, then, these aspects of traditional Macedonian culture refer to the various forms by which the daily life of the Christian, and particularly the Greek, populace was adapted to the structural frame of reference which regulated the lives of the inhabitants of that particular area, during the period from the re-establishment of Ottoman supremacy in northern Greece following the founding of the free national states in the Balkan peninsula, to the adhesion and incorporation of this area into the national states which, after the Balkan Wars, divided among themselves the lands of

Peasants from Kampania, the plain of Thessaloniki, early 20th century. (L.Schultze-Jena, Makedonien..., plate XLVI).

Macedonia, Thrace and Epirus. On the level of everyday life, at least, the identity of Turkish-occupied Macedonia (and northern Greece in general) was shaped both by the national identity of the culture of the Hellenic state, which was endeavouring to grow into a European nation, and by its relation to and within the limits of the attempted modernization of the traditional structures of the Ottoman Empire, especially in its European territories.

The systematic incorporation of the land of Macedonia into the Hellenic state (especially on the level of national education and the reduction of local self-government), the shuffling of populations, which was accelerated by the influx of large numbers of refugees after the disasters in Asia Minor, the migrations of rural populations, increasing urbanization and the general economic and political developments, as well as a political ideology and practice which favoured national homogeneity over local cultural particularities and differences, all contributed to a substantial shrinking and the eventual inertia of

Macedonian traditional culture, and its gradual absorption into the dominant formations of the panhellenic "modern Greek culture" of the 20th century.

A. An examination of spatial organization

1. From the environment to territorial organization

Every society organizes its territory, organizes itself within and in relation to it, as it lives on it. Territorial organization means the immersion of the community in its environment - natural, social and historical.

Sometimes, of course, the environment itself appears to restrict the way or ways of life of the inhabitants of a particular region, whose margins of choice in this matter seem to be non-existent. However, even in such cases, the coercions imposed by natural, social and historic conditions are neither absolute nor definitive, since a people's immersion in its

The mouth of the Axios, on the Thermaikos Gulf.

environment means the way or ways by which the people actively adapt to their environment, as they and their relationships are shaped by this dynamic process. From this point of view the environment, including the natural environment, is nothing more than the (more or less permanent, as the case may be) setting for the social and cultural activities of the inhabitants of a given area; the setting in which a culture is worked out, where people live and create, a setting as it is conceived and experienced by those who live within it.

If territorial organization depends on the relationship between man and his natural and social environment, then it is also closely interwoven with the organization of society and with its reproduction, that is, its history. This structural connection between territorial and temporal cohesion is stressed by Fernand Braudel's definition of a culture: that is, that every culture is first and foremost a place where a group of people who speak the same language, and whose inter-communication therefore uses common symbols, develop a certain way of life which, when it

has achieved a degree of temporal permanence, constitutes the culture in question[1].

Our dissection of territorial organization in the traditional culture of Macedonia is restricted to an initial inventory of certain elements. These particular data are related to the permanencies and transiencies of modern Hellenic culture in Macedonia, and refer particularly to the ways in which its agents, the inhabitants of this region, experienced their land as they lived on it, as they travelled over or beyond it, as they used or transformed it, as they conformed to its restrictions or strove to surmount them in order to face new challenges or enter into a new and better life.

2. Organization of the territory of Macedonia

2.1. People and the land: from settlement to the organization of communities

By the final period of the Turkish occupation, the territory of Macedonia had acquired a degree of cohesion based on certain elements which functioned

Megali Prespa Lake.

conjointly, and on the basis of which it is possible to describe this particular place over a particular period. We suggest that the elements which conjoined and shaped the Macedonian territory, while they in turn were shaped within it, were the various units of settlement, the human communities of every type, which wove a web or a network of dense and complex relationships constituting the specific socio- economic conformation.

These units of settlement include: communities (i.e.: villages[2]., towns, cities, conventual complexes, etc.), smaller residential units (sheepcotes[3], huts[4], wharves, mills[5], etc.) and houses.

The organization of built-up and inhabited areas presents phenomena common to most individual regions. On the coasts, for example, the villages were located on heights of land and enclosed within walls, while only sheds and warehouses were left in the port on the shore below. By the 15th century the fertile plains of the hinterland had been organized on a multi-focal pattern. The lie of the valleys between the high mountains, for instance, favoured the growth of villages in groups strung out along the same axis, such

as the clusters of villages in the basin of the upper Aliakmon, and in the valleys and plateaux of mountainous areas such as Siniatsiko, Bourino, Vermion, Holomontas, Pangaion, etc.

The evolution of these settlements varied according to times and conditions and their individual economic bases. Thus, for example, in time of war a village protected by its situation on a height of land could prosper at the expense of its lowland neighbours, while a more accessible village would thrive as a religious, economic and social centre in times of peace. Moreover, family farms meant that the members of this society could be self-sufficient in isolated units, while trade, where it existed, was carried out on a limited scale and, significantly, did not deal in basic necessities but in non-essentials. More systematic employment in agriculture and cottage industries created the conditions in which export trade could flourish and imports (of raw materials and consumer goods) became necessary.

The basic distinction, then, is between mountain and lowland settlements. Mountains and plains provided in themselves the differing conditions which gave rise to different types of settlement: the plains with their smooth expanses of land were ideal for collective habitation, while the broken and uneven nature of the land in mountainous areas favoured settlement in scattered units. In the first instance, the houses and communal buildings (church, coffee house, shops, possibly a school, etc.) were centred in one place, and surrounded by arable land which was parcelled out among the villagers; while in the second, the smaller and naturally uneven plots of farmland and pasture discouraged the growth of villages: each house or group of houses (family or tribal settlements) was located on its own land. But even in these cases, a later phase of development was marked by increased centripetence: the more the settlement developed, the more houses clustered around the initial nucleus. A good example of developent of this type is furnished by the mountain towns of Pindos: Samarina, Perivoli, Avdela, and Siniatsiko (or Askion): Siatista, Eratyra (Selitsa), Vlasti (Blasti), Galatini (Kontsiko). The model of this type of development, of course, was the city of Thessaloniki (a real giant for the age and the area), where the bulk of population growth was concentrated on the old, Byzantine, heart of the city, which seems to have remained within the city walls long after they had lost their defining function. The centripetal development of the city of Thessaloniki was remarkably pronounced, although there continued to be villas and country houses outside the city proper as well as large colonies of refugees on the outskirts.

The steady influx of Turkish settlers onto the plains forced most of the former inhabitants to withdraw to the mountains. This internal colonization continued, with brief interruptions, until the end of the 19th century. Those who remained shared the land (or rather the use of the land) with the Turks; some of these, like the Valaadhes of the Voio villages in the Anaselitsa district, adopted the Moslem faith. Others, such as the villagers of Hasia and Roumlouki on the plain of Kampania, continued to live in their own villages while working as serfs for Moslem or Christian landowners. In both cases, however, political and social changes in the organization of the inhabitants of the land brought about changes in the regular evolution of independent agriculture and the structure of rural settlement. Also included in this category were those villages whose inhabitants had been tenants of monasterial farmlands or Christian landowners before the Turkish occupation: these were permitted to retain their lands upon submission to the invader and reclassification of their holdings under the new system.

The majority of those who moved to the mountains were fleeing areas where Turkish settlement was systematic, such as for example the villages of the broad plain in western Macedonia which extends from Kozani to the lake of Ostrovo, where the influx of Konyars (from the name of the Turkish city of Iconion) led to their becoming known as "Konyar villages" (Konyarochoria).

With the departure of the refugees, the amount of land used also changed. This mass migration, anonymous and extensive, took every conceivable form: it was not only families and small groups that moved, but often entire villages. The internal structures of these groups and their settlements varied

Mt Olympus from the Gulf of Thessaloniki. (A.Goff- H.Fawcett, Macedonia. A Plea for the Primitive. London,1921, p.128).

The valley of the Strymon. (A.Goff-H.Fawcett, Macedonia. A Plea for the Primitive. p.218).

accordingly. When a new settlement was formed gradually, the first families formed a nucleus of "natives", and those who came later, often from completely different areas, settled on the outskirts, forming a dynamic fringe where all comers were welcome. Settlements of this type include Siatista, Vlasti and Grevena, where the diverse origins of their inhabitants, frequently from far-flung areas, are reflected in the division of these towns into different quarters, quite distinct in their architecture and in the occupations and customs, etc, of their inhabitants. When whole villages moved and re-settled in new locations, they usually retained their traditional forms (social and communal organization, customs and traditions, their general way of life, in other words), but adapted to their new surroundings. Typical examples of the retention of local customs are found in various areas of Macedonia settled by Epirotes, Vlachs, Sarakatsani, Karagounidhes from Thessaly, and Greeks from the south, from Mani for example. (A similar phenomenon occurred in this century, with the refugees from Asia Minor, Thrace and the Black Sea provinces who retained their distinct cultural identity when they settled in various urban and rural areas.)

The retention of a distinct cultural identity (which was evinced on many levels, including those of language, customs, dress, manners and social usages) was the result of both internal and external pressures on each group: for example, a language or dialect is not easily abandoned if the general social or cultural framework does not favour inter-marriage or other types of social relationships, such as common celebrations, mutual assistance, neighbourhood, sponsorship, etc, which would bring about changes in social behaviour. Descent from "elsewhere" is recorded in the family and personal names, and in the names of villages and neighbourhoods. For example, the people who abandoned the village of Phourka on Mt Pindos settled in various colonies in Western and Central Macedonia, where they became highly sought-after tailors (they were known as "Phourkiotes terzidhes", or tailors from Phourka); others founded two new settlements, both called Phourka, one in southern Thessaly and one in Chalcidice. In other cases we find neighbourhoods or entire districts called "Epirotika"

"Paezanes", peasant women from Asvestochori.
(Photographic Archives of the Folk Museum, University of
Thessaloniki).

or "Agraphiotika" or even "Gyphtika" or "Gyph-
tomahalas" ("the gypsy quarter"), or more recently
place names prefixed by the word "new". Finally, in
their customs and their dress, their feasts and their
celebrations, these migrants usually retained their
patron saints, their festivals, their foods and of course
the distinctive outer appearance afforded by the costume of their place of origin. A typical example is the
case of the village of Asvestochori near Thessaloniki,
where the original population was augmented late in
the 18th and early in the 19th century by Vlach settlers
from Agrapha. The "natives" called the newcomers
"Vlachs", and they in turn called the local people
"paesani" (peasants, or natives); this distinction was
maintained for many years on every possible level:
different languages, different dress (the traditonal local costume was eventually abandoned for the more
urban Vlach dress), different organizations (the
Paesani founded a philanthropic society called
"Mnemosynon" (memorial), while the Vlach society
was called "The Brotherhood": the two were at length
united under the name "Philanthropic Fraternity" in

1906), and finally, different professions and occupations [6].

The intense demographic activity which followed
the destruction and the systematic evacuation of urban, semi-urban and rural areas from Ioannina to the
district including Darda, Korytsa and Moschopolis
(such as the detruction of Moschopolis in 1769, the
persecutions of Ali Pasha and the Turco-Albanian
beys in the late 18th and early 19th centuries, and the
transformation of entire agricultural districts in
Western Macedonia into chifliks) seems to have
played a particularly important role in shaping the
villages and, on a wider scale, the cultural districts of
Macedonia, especially Western Macedonia. One (extremely general) characteristic of this period is the
constant migration of urban-type populations (merchants, artisans, practitioners of specialized professions) and their re-settling in areas whose
predominant socio-economic structure was based on
land ownership, or rather on land use generally,
whether for cultivation or for other types of exploitation, such as hunting, wood-cutting and animal husbandry. This type of settlement occurred chiefly in
Western Macedonia; but migrants from Epirus (artisans, herdsmen and merchants) settled in every
corner of Macedonia and even in Thrace. This almost
mass migration of Epirote populations and their installation in Macedonia in the 18th and 19th centuries
was accompanied by a similar movement of Vlach-
and Albanian-speaking groups, who settled in many
parts of Macedonia. For example, after the devastation of 1770, the inhabitants of Linotopi, Nikolitsi,
Nitsa, Phousta, Darda Virtianik and Vithokouki scattered, and settled in Vlasti, Monastir (Vitolia),
Krousovon and the Ochrida district [7]. These Vlach
migrations continued, albeit on a lesser scale, until at
least 1912; in 1911, for example, a number of Vlach
families bought a chiflik belonging to a citizen of
Naoussa named Hatzidimitriou, located in the village
of Horopani (now called Stenimachos), where they
settled; Mr Hatzidimitriou's tenants moved to other
farms in the Naoussa district [8].

We have seen that these population movements
generally conformed to certain patterns. The lowland
and the semi- mountainous areas, where the land,
divided into relatively small chifliks worked by tenant
farmers, passed fairly easily from the hands of Turkish
landowners into those of wealthy Greeks or Jews,
especially in the latter part of the 19th century, were
settled by people from economically similar areas: for
example, emigrants from the many tenant farms

Vlach families. (E.Papadimitriou, Old Photographs, Epirus-Macedonia, 1977, p.44)

around Hasia settled on chiflik farms in Tsarsampas (Kozani), in the Servia district, in Chalcidice, in the Gevgeli and Serres districts, etc. In these cases the people either continued to farm land belonging to others, as "ortaksidhes" or "missakaridhes" (share-croppers), serfs or tenant farmers, or, at a later stage, endeavoured to acquire their own land and houses. A typical example is the village of Daskio (formerly Dratsiko or Triatsiko) in Pieria: this area had attracted a number of Sarakatsani herdsmen, refugees from the neighbouring mountain villages, and lowland farmers. When the old settlement was destroyed the inhabitants scattered. Some returned in 1735, when the Turco-Albanian bey who owned the land rounded up as many of the former inhabitants as he could, rebuilt the village and "mirasse ta tapia": distributed the land- titles. The people built a church and settled the boundaries with the neighbouring villages; the bey retained the right to the tithe. Early in the 19th century the villagers purchased their village from the bey "and turned it into an important centre"[9]

The mountainous areas, on the other hand, were settled by farmers and herdsmen from devastated areas on Mt Grammos and in Epirus, who later, from the second quarter of the 19th century, bought from the Turkish landowners property in the villages where they had settled or which they had founded. In most

cases the money was the product of their professional activities as artisans, merchants, carters, etc. In this way they created independent and prosperous villages whose economy was not based solely on raising live-stock or cultivating vineyards, but on an inflow of cash and on the creation of a capital of savings and commercial funds from the seasonal employment of specialized artisans and from the earnings of emigrants and traders. In these cases the co-operative purchase of communal land was followed by com-munal investment in infrastructure, such as fountains and water works, bridges, roads, public buildings, schools and philanthropic institutions. For example, in the second quarter of the 19th century groups of emigrants (farmers and craftsmen) bought from the local Turkish beys the land around the villages Krimini and Rodochori in the Anaselitsa district of Voio (in 1845 the inhabitants of Rodochori amassed enough money "to purchase the village of Radovis-ti"[10]), and effected a number of public works.

Finally, areas where for particular historical reasons there already was an urban nucleus were magnets for city dwellers, who enhanced and in many cases accelerated the development of mercantile centres. Generally speaking, these people settled in places where their possession of certain economic and political privileges guaranteed the necessary condi-

Kavala, from the sea.

century there were three cities in Western Macedonia with a population of 8-9,000 (Kozani, Kastoria and Siatista), while there were several smaller towns with more than 2,500 inhabitants (Florina, Samarina, Grevena, Eratyra (Selitsa), Servia, Neapolis (Lipsisti or Lapsista), Ptolemaida (Kailaria), Kleisoura). Other towns had between 1,200-2,000 inhabitants: Pentalofos (Zoupani), Vogatsiko, Perivoli, Vlasti. This situation remained virtually unchanged until the Liberation. By the beginning of the 20th century Thessaloniki had 160,000 inhabitants, Monastir 50,000, Serres, Kavala and Drama 20,000 each, and Kozani, Kastoria and Siatista about 10,000. The principal mountain communities, such as Vlasti, Samarina, Tsotyli and Pentalofos had populations of from 2,000 to 7,000.

After the Liberation in 1912, the remote mountain towns (Eratyra, Samarina, Vogatsiko) stopped growing, and their native and refugee populations moved to urban and semi-urban centres on the plains, or emigrated to target areas abroad, chiefly in America and Australia and later in Western Europe.

Kastoria: in the old city.

tions for the "free" exercise of commercial and economic activities and, of course, for cultural, social and communal life, such as, for example, Kozani, Siatista, Selitsa, Vlasti, etc. The concentration of the population in urban centres, and the installation of merchants, technicians, craftsmen and artisans who formed powerful guilds, all contributed to the rapid (by the standards of the age) development of these centres. An interesting example is furnished by Kavala, where the inrush of settlers and the extraordinary development of trade and commerce in the second half of the 19th century spurred the merchants and craftsmen to found new neighbourhoods outside the old city limits[11].

To complete our description of the demographic situation, it is well known that by the end of the 18th century the population of the cities and towns of Macedonia had grown to such an extent that local production was no longer sufficient either to feed or to employ their labour forces. For example, by the end of the 18th century Thessaloniki had approximately 90,000 inhabitants, Serres 30,000, Edessa (Vodena) 12,000, and Veria 8,000. By the end of the 19th

*Vlachs from Samarina: (a) Watchman dressed
as a brigand, with his lamb (b) Boy with coat
and overcoat. A.Wace-M.Thompson, The
Nomads of the Balkans, 1914, plate XI,I).*

2.2. The land and the people: from survival to organized production.

The complementary nature of the units of production which was typical of Macedonia during the period of Turkish rule (as it was of the Balkans in general)[12] was based on a distribution of labour which led to the specialization of production on a geographical basis. The principal divisions were: agricultural cultivation, animal husbandry, artisanal enterprises, arts and professions, and transport (transit trade).

Interchanges among these sectors were effected by a barter system, but also by means of money: by the end of the 17th century the traditional society was systematically and increasingly engaged in the commercialization of production and the monetarization of the economy.

Although certain areas focussed, permanently or temporarily, on a single productive sector (for example, the extensive cultivation of cotton and silk in the Serres district[13], the systematic raising of livestock by Sarakatsani nomads and Vlach semi-nomads, and the systematic tobacco farming in the villages around Giannitsa and in Eastern Macedonia), while some centres enjoyed a diversity of production (for example, the Thessaloniki area had not only extensive farming, but also industries and a lively transit trade), production was basically agricultural, and took place within production units which supplied their own wants as well as the market.

Until the final years of the Turkish occupation, the economy remained fundamentally agricultural, based on farming and animal husbandry. The principal crops were cereals (wheat, oats and maize), cotton, tobacco, olives (in Chalcidice), and grapes. The exclusive raising of livestock occurred only in certain areas of Eastern and Western Macedonia, and was largely the province of nomadic and semi-nomadic populations.

Agricultural production furnished local industries with their raw materials: wool, cotton, silk and linen. This meant that many branches of industry, and especially the cottage industries, were dependent on agricultural production. The driving force behind the cottage industries, in which as a rule the whole family participated, were the women. Weaving was the major occupation, as it served to supply many of the family's needs. Gradually some of this family production

*Florina, home from the fields. (E. Papadimitriou, Old
Photographs, Epirus-Macedonia, 1977, p. 74).*

Tobacco farmer's house. (E.Papadimitriou, Old Photographs, Epirus-Macedonia, 1977, p.86).

began to be sent to market; this occasionally resulted in a full- fledged business, all of whose production was destined for sale. The Vlachs of Samarina are a good example of this: Vlachs from the mountainous areas of Grevena came down to the fair of Agios Achillios in Grevena, and other fairs in the area, to sell their "velentzes", a type of heavy blanket. Many Vlach families, indeed, abandoned herding entirely, and turned to crafts and commerce[14] instead. The case of Serres is even more interesting: extensive cotton cultivation on the plain which the Turks called "altin ova" (the golden plain)[15] led to the development of powerful weavers' guilds and to a broadening of trade; the market which was held every Tuesday in Serres was a large scale cotton market. Central and Eastern Macedonia (as well as neighbouring Thrace) enjoyed similar growth from the middle of the 19th century on, as a result of the intensive cultivation of tobacco.

Economic development coincided with urban

Women weaving in Avdela (1906 photograph by the Manakis bros.). (Chr.Christodoulou, The photogenic Balkans of the Manakis brothers, 1989, p.31).

Typical example of a Western Macedonian ceiling. The N.Vourkas house, Kozani.

development, the monetarization of the economy, the modernization of technology and the Europeanization of customs and attitudes. A typical example comes from Eastern Macedonia, where the villagers from around Serres called the city-dwellers "Frangi" (Franks, Europeans) because they wore European clothes ("frangoforemeni") and had adopted certain European habits[16]. In Western Macedonia, Siatista was known as "Florochori", while a little farther north the Greek- speaking villagers called the Vlach town of Kleisoura "Cosmopolis"[17]. The city of Naoussa shows how far this development could go. Naoussa enjoyed the privileges of its status as a domain belonging to the Valide Sultana, or Queen Mother; and during the 18th century it knew an extraordinary period of growth. It was destroyed by the Turks in 1822, but by the end of the century was once again flourishing. It was one of the most important commercial and industrial centres in Macedonia, with systematic production of silk, hydro- and steam-powered spinning mills, and gold- and silver- smiths, as well

as the hub of a prosperous agricultural area producing wheat, barley, maize, rice, grapes, wool, silk and dairy products[18]. In many cases, however, specialization resulted in only very modest development. For example, the master craftsmen (masons, woodcarvers and painters) from the Mastorochoria (literally, artisanal villages), mountain villages in Western Macedonia such as Zoupania and Kastanochoria, who had skilled labour to offer on a wide and growing market, had indeed managed to break free of the poverty which was a consequence of the location of their villages, but were unable to lead these villages to a more urban type of development. On the other hand, there were urban centres which had specialized in certain industries but which never managed to go beyond a very basic level of development. The town of Eleutheroupoli (Pravi) on Mt Pangaion is a case in point: although it was the principal town in its district and a metropolitan see, it was surrounded by marshes which, until they were drained in the first quarter of the 20th century, covered the entire (now lush) plain, and its inhabitants had no other source of income than their tanneries and shoe manufactories. Neighbouring Megarropi was also a single industry place (weaving) which never developed into anything more than a small town[19].

The factors which caused certain settlements to develop did not always work in the same way. Some places which became centres of local agricultural production, such as Argos Orestikon (Chroupista) in Western Macedonia for example, were still unable to reach beyond their immediate environs. There were towns which were centres for a wider agricultural area, towns whose population was principally Turkish, such as Kailaria (Ptolemaida), Giannitsa and Drama in Western, Central and Eastern Macedonia respectively, but which yet remained rural, provincial places[20]. The case of Gevgeli was completely different: its rapid growth was entirely due to its specialized production. By the late 17th century the inhabitants of several hamlets such as Goumenissa, Griva and Karpi (Tserna Reka) had been relieved of their obligation to pay municipal taxes in return for their labour at "batanisma", the repeated washing of the heavy woollen fabric used for the uniforms of the Janissaries, which was one of the steps in its production[21]. The inhabitants of the tiny village of Gevgeli[22] raised silkworms and spun silk thread, mainly for their own use. The construction of the railway from Thessaloniki to Skopje in 1872, followed by that linking Thessaloniki with Europe (1888), contributed to the rapid development of the village, which became not only a central market for the agricultural produce of the whole area, but a specialized market for silk cocoons: more than one million cocoons passed through the market of Gevgeli every year in June and July. In 1887-1888 a small silk manufactory employing local female labour was built, followed in 1900-01 by a larger factory, which belonged to the Sultan and was equipped with the latest machinery. The number of women employed increased dramatically, both through the temporary engagement of 60 labourers from the model manufactory at Proussa and the subsequent formation of skilled local workers. In 1895 the Rezi tobacco cutting factory was founded by the Tobacco Monopoly, followed in 1900-01 by the large Erzok factory which handled all the tobacco produced in the entire area. The case of Gevgeli is interesting, but it was not the norm. Industrialization was generally connected with already developed urban centres whose substantial populations provided a supply of cheap labour and where in turn industrial and commercial development contributed to encouraging migration to the cities. In larger communities, which garnered the agricultural production of a wide area and sent it on to important markets at home and abroad, places like Veria, Naoussa, Kozani, Melenikon, Kavala, Serres, and of course Monastir and Thessaloniki, agricultural production, in conjunction with the growth of local industry (often quite substantial by the latter half of the 19th century) and the expansion of commercial networks, provided a solid foundation for their urban development[23].

As markets developed, the distinction between small industry and cottage industry became less and less clear. Until early this century a substantial proportion, larger or smaller according to area and living conditions, of basic necessities (food, clothing, housing, tools, utensils, etc) was provided by domestic or

Samarina: the priest and his family at a festival.

Transport by ox-cart. (E.Papadimitriou, Old Photographs, Epirus-Macedonia, 1977, p.73).

cottage industry, which remained chiefly the province of the women of the household, rather than the men. Nevertheless, in fewer and fewer cases was clothing, even the most important garments, such as wedding dresses, made at home from untreated materials; the old home made tools were replaced by purchased ones, hand made (or sometimes factory made, such as Italian scythes in the 19th century), as were furnishings for home and workshop. On the other hand, changes in the way certain basic foodstuffs like bread[24] and dairy products, as well as other items such as legumes, vegetables, rice, cereals, fruit, salt and spices, were supplied, stored and used, introduced changes in the organization of household labour, and also in diet and life style, especially in the cities. Finally, household utensils were more and more often made of metal, and thus purchased from local markets or foreign sources, while wood was introduced into the house in the form of purchased or imported wooden furniture[25].

The growth of industrial production, artisanal and peripatetic, as well as of cottage industry and agriculture in some cases, was linked with the development of guilds. Old corporations were reorganized in the old (Byzantine) centres, while the newer cities, towns and villages developed new types of corporation. In the 18th and 19th centuries, professional guilds and associations of craftsmen ("esnafia" or "koumpanies" or "roufetia") were a powerful factor in the way communities grew and were organized, and in the political and economic life of the cities and towns of Turkish-ruled Macedonia, especially in the larger urban centres of Thessaloniki, Monastir, Serres, Kavala, Kozani, Edessa and Veria. In the smaller communities the cottage and artisanal industries were almost a constituent feature of the town itself, which in fact functioned as a sort of co-operative. For example, in Agion Pneuma (Serres), most of whose inhabitants were small independent farmers, a farmers' guild ("esnafion tsiftsidhon") had been formed as early as the mid 18th century, which made an important contribution to the evolution of the life of the community. There were also farmers' guilds in the neighbouring villages of Ano and Kato Kamenikia[26]. The villagers of Krokos (Goblitsa), near Kozani, were mainly employed in the cultivation of the precious crocus; those of Skotina (in the district of Naoussa) made carding tools (which they sold themselves at central and local fairs); the people of Arkoudochori, Phytia (Tsiornovo) and Marousia were wood-cutters and charcoal burners. The citizens of Naoussa were organized into guilds representing a variety of trades, such as gunsmiths, cutlers, curio-makers, dyers, silkworm growers, and, most important of all, weavers of woollens, silks and linens, such as the famous "havlia" towels[27]. There were also a substantial number of guilds in neighbouring Edessa, in Kozani, and of course in all the larger cities in Macedonia: Kastoria, Melenikon, Serres, Kavala, Monastir and Thessaloniki [30].

The concentration of people in urban centres both in the mountains and on the lowlands, as well as in the mountain villages, exacerbated the problem of food supplies. From the middle of the 18th century to the beginning of the 20th (with an interruption in development and a local economic crisis during the period of the Revolution and the founding of the Greek State (1821-1830), while the repercussions of the various international political and economic crises were felt even in the most remote mountain hamlet), food and clothing requirements were only partially met by production for home consumption. Trade[31], at first rudimentary and limited to open air markets, steadily covered more and more of the people's needs in raw materials, food, clothing, tools and "luxury" items. A dense transportation network served the whole of Macedonia, following roads and footpaths, over mountains and rivers, across marshes, lakes and plains. Merchants, pedlars, muleteers, seasonal labourers, artisans and travellers all used this network, carrying with them assets of every description: goods, services, labour, knowledge, innovations, techniques. The retail merchants were the catalysts which kept this whole traditional society working as it slowly moved towards modernization. Trade turned Macedonia (and northern Greece generally) into a market for consumer goods from the factories and workshops of the West, while at the same time making available to European markets the area's own products and, particularly, its raw materials: cotton, yarns, wool, leather and hides, dried fruit and nuts, wood, tobacco, etc. Meanwhile, the cities of Macedonia were establishing trading houses in Western, Central and Eastern Europe. Small and medium scale commerce was principally carried out by Greek traders, while large scale trade was in the hands of European trading houses, in accordance with the Great Powers' policy on trade and commerce with the Ottoman Empire. Together with the craftsmen and the skilled artisans, these merchants constituted a solid middle class foundation for the cities of Macedonia.

Commerce and crafts became sources of wealth and easy affluence. Throughout the 19th century (and with increased intensity early in the 20th century), a portion of the capital accumulated in this way was invested in public works for philanthropic and educational purposes. But most of the profits from industrial and commercial activity, both at home and abroad, as well as from savings[32], banking and money-lending, were (re-)invested (especially in the cities) in the industrialization of artisanal and domestic production and in the expansion of commercial activities. Finally, a smaller share of these profits went towards the purchase of land. Such investors were mainly Greek and Jewish businessmen.

The patterns which appeared in the acquisition of land for agricultural exploitation are significant. In lowland and semi-mountainous areas wealthy Christians (for the most part) bought large tracts of land in agricultural communities. For example, by the middle of the 19th century the villages Choropani, Ano Kopanos, Giannakochori, Marina (Tsermarinovo), and Monospita, on the plain which lies between Edessa and Naoussa, had been acquired by wealthy Christian landowners from Naoussa[33]. At the turn of the century there were approximately 10,000 hectares (25,000 acres) of farmland between Naoussa and the Lake of Giannitsa (13 large chifliks), of which 1/25 belonged to Greeks, 1/20 to Vlach speakers, and the remainder to Turkish landowners; while of the approximately 2,000 hectares of farmland around Veria, 1/20 belonged to Greeks, a small fraction to Jews and the rest to Moslem citizens of that town. To the southeast, between Veria and the lake of Giannitsa, there were 13,000 hectares of farmland (23 chifliks), of which 1/5 belonged to Greeks, a small fraction to Jews and the rest to Moslems. South of Veria towards the Aliakmon there were 10,000 hectares of farmland (19 chifliks), of which 2/3 belonged to Greeks and 1/3 to Moslems. Finally, in the mountainous area between the Aliakmon and Edessa (Mt Vermion), there were 30,000 hectares of farmland with 26 dependent villages (of which only 3 were inhabited, 20 having been abandoned and the remaining three serving as summer quarters for Vlach herdsmen), of which 1/4 belonged to Greeks, 1/8 to Vlachs and the remainder to Moslems[34].

The geographical area of Macedonia is divided [35] into three distinct regions: the eastern region, with its extensive single crop cultivation; the central region, with Thessaloniki at the heart of a fertile plain; and the western region, with its flourishing mercantile towns, its market gardens and fields of cereals on the banks of the Aliakmon, and its flocks of animals in the mountains (the Vlach villages on Mt Pindos, and the Sarakatsani around Florina and Monastir).

In the fertile plains, areas such as Eastern Macedonia, Kampania and Roumlouki in Central Macedonia, or Karagiannia and Hasia in Western Macedonia, where the land belonged to large and more modest landholders (Turks, and, after the middle of the 19th century, Jews and Greeks), to the throne, to charitable institutions or to monasteries ("vakoufika" lands or villages, monasterial farms), there was extensive single crop cultivation. An example of this is furnished by the cultivation of cotton in the densely settled and heavily populated plain around Serres, which Beaujour described at the end of the 18th century in the following words: "The entire plain has been turned over to the cultivation of cotton; it is covered with nearly 300 villages which, seen from the heights of Mt Kerkini, appear to touch one another and suggest the impressive spectacle of one endless city..."[36] In the semi-mountainous areas, however, where the soil was poorer and the land was cultivated by smallholders, the farms were planted, either concurrently or sequentially, with a variety of crops, to be consumed locally or used to pay taxes (such as the tithe) in kind.

However, in spite of such extensive farming, Macedonia was also an area of large and populous cities: nearly one third of its population were city dwellers. From the time of the Treaty of Passarowitz (1718) until the Liberation the cities grew steadily, while on the contrary, in certain areas of the countryside the farming communities were being eroded by internal and external emigration and groaning under the weight of heavy taxation and arbitrary actions and exactions.

The principal cities of Eastern Macedonia were the commercial port of Kavala and the prosperous city of Serres. From the centre of Macedonia Thessaloniki, second city in the Empire (after Constantinople), shed its lustre over the entire Balkan peninsula. Western Macedonia, besides Monastir in the north, boasted several smaller cities, including Kozani, Siatista and Kastoria, which were all busy provincial centres with flourishing commercial and artisanal activities. A bustle of a different sort characterized the mountain villages of Voio, Kastoria and Florina: organized into professional guilds (kompanies, esnafia or roufetia), their men criss-crossed the Balkans selling their skilled labour as builders (koudarei), sculptors (pelekani), wood-carvers (tagiadori), gold- and silversmiths (koemtzides).

Chalcidice was in a category of its own, for, besides Mt Athos, there were two large "federated" groups of villages: one was the twelve "Mademochoria" clustered around Arnaia (Liarigova) and the silver mines: these included Siderokapsa, Galatista, Vavdos, Ravna, Stanos, and Ierissos; the other group were the fifteen Hasia or Hasiochoria located farther south, in the mining district centred on Polygyros.

2.3. Experiences of the land: wayfarers and nomads, travellers and exiles, emigrants and refugees

Wars, agriculture, trade, intermarriage, and the movements of nomads all follow their own rhythms. Brigands and pedlars, brides and grooms, labourers,

The Pasha's Bridge over the Aliakmon River, near the village of Mesopotamo (Giangova), links the district of Grevena with the district of Kozani.

master craftsmen and their apprentices, herdsmen and soldiers, all move from one place to another, from one job or type of employment to another. The population of the area and during the period under consideration (but this is true of the Balkans in general over a vast period of time, from the neolithic revolution right up to today) was exceptionally mobile.

These migrations, some more cyclical than others, reached their peak at two "critical" periods of the year: the feasts of St George and St Demetrios (especially for the nomads and the herdsmen) were considered the turning points of the year, marking the beginning of the summer and the winter periods respectively. The farm labourers (male and female) left their houses in the spring to serve on the chifliks of their masters until the reaping and threshing were finished, or to cultivate tobacco or collect the silk- cocoons (kseklaroma), and returned home late in the autumn. From then until the feast of St George navigation (fishing and transit shipping), overland haulage by mule train, the peregrinations of the craftsmen, and epidemics (malaria in the marshes of Giannitsa and Ptolemaida and the lakes of Central Macedonia), all subsided. The herdsmen kept their flocks in winter quarters on the plains, and the Turks suspended their bellicose operations. The advent of summer set everything in motion once again. And the height of summer was the best time for weddings and fairs, especially around August 15, the Feast of the Assumption.

The other type of displacement, with its own experience of the land, was that which related to the growth and decay of settlements, the kind of migration which is the result of poverty, oppression and misery, of natural disasters (earthquake and tempest), of war and invasion, of epidemic disease (malaria, cholera, plague). The uprooting of populations, which we usually refer to as internal emigration, was a phenomenon which continued with only brief interruptions until well into this century, culminating in the exchanges of populations and the influx of refugees from Asia Minor, the Black Sea provinces and Eastern Thrace.

These were the two types of mass migration; there were also movements of individuals or groups "abroad": communities in Vienna, Trieste, Venice, and later America and Australia. There were also longer term migrations of artisans and labourers, who moved to cities within the Empire to work as bakers, tilers, builders, gardeners ("bahtsevanides"), tailors, etc.

After about 1850 the trend to urbanization became more pronounced: the peasants slowly left their villages for the cities, settling in "popular" neighbourhoods, in shanties, in illicit housing, under the walls, and (after 1930) in working class flats.

3. Forms of spatial organization in traditional Macedonian society

3.1. Dwellings and dwelling-places: rural and urban structures

The house, the household, the family. In traditional Macedonian society, in modern times, the household meant the members of one family who lived together. Depending on the size and type of family (whether a nuclear family, i.e. one or two parents with their child or children and one or more grandparents or other dependent family members; or an extended family, which usually meant the parents with their married children (usually sons rather than daughters) and their children, and any other dependents), the household could include one or more "families". As a rule, in rural areas and among the lower classes at least, all the members of the family worked to ensure the survival of the household: men, women and children, old and young alike, all contributed in whatever tasks fell to each one's lot. The farm work was shared by all; but beyond that, the women did the housework and (usually) domestic craft;. the men looked after the animals; the children helped wherever they could (even when they were attending school); and the elderly helped to look after the children and did whatever else they could. Artisanal workshops (and later factories) employed both men and women, as did agricultural operations requiring seasonal labour. For example, farm labourers, both male and female, covered wide tracts of territory during the harvesting season; while artisans, craftsmen, merchants and muleteers travelled to more distant places.

A household could have a permanent or semi-permanet home, or it might migrate systematically. There were permanent installations of varying sizes in the cities, towns and villages; there were semi-nomadic settlements of people, such as the Vlachs of Pindos, Vermion and Eastern Macedonia, who moved between the mountain hamlets where they grazed their flocks over the summer and the scattered, temporary installations on the lowlands where they spent the winters; and there were the mobile installations of nomadic populations of herders, such as the Sarakatsani[37], who travelled pre-determined routes, setting

Nymphaio (Nevesco), from the SE. (A.Wace-M.Thompson op.cit., 1914, plate XXIV,I, The Nomads of the Balkans (Greek translation) 1989, p.328).

up their huts ("kalyvia") along a network of temporary sites, or nomads like the gypsies who travelled in small or large groups, working (usually for short periods) as farm labourers in agricultural areas where there was a demand for cheap labour, or as craftsmen (usually in metalwork, as tinkers or smiths, but also as musicians) as they moved from village to village and from fair to fair: sometimes these artisans settled with their families in localities where there was a demand for skilled labour.

The village. There were two main types of village: a) chiflik or metayer villages (kolligiko chorio or chorio-chifliki), such as those around Eleutheroupolis; and b) free villages or autonomous communities (kephalochoria), such as the villages on Mt Pindos, or those of the hill country of Anaselitsa (Voio).

Sometimes, under more or less violent conditions (arbitrary occupation, debt, economic difficulties, poverty, famine) free villages degenerated into chiflik villages; while in other cases the tenants of a bound

village were able, either as a group or individually, to redeem, partially or entirely, their land and their houses.

Groups and clusters of villages. These are also of two types, depending on the type of settlement composing the group: a) metayer villages (kolligika choria), such as, for example, the Hasia villages in the Grevena district, the "Graikochoria", 50 Roumlouki villages on the Kampania plain near Thessaloniki, or the "Darnakochoria" in the Serres region; and b) free villages, such as the "Mastorochoria" or "Zoupania" in Western Macedonia, or the "Mademochoria" in Chalcidice.

The city. Regardless of their size and population, we distinguish between two types of cities: a) the autonomous communities which fulfilled the functions of a city: the population of such urban settlements was usually purely Greek, or at least with only a very small foreign element intermixed with the majority, as was the case in Siatista, Kozani, Edessa

Kastoria, the lake and the city, early 20th c.) (L.Schultze-Jena, Makedonien..., plate LXXI).

before the 1822 catastrophe, etc; and b) the independent city or urban administrative centre, which usually had a mixed population, as for example Grevena, Servia, Kastoria, Veria, Kavala, Melenikon, Serres, Thessaloniki, Monastir.

Autonomous and self-sufficient units (residential and non-residential). We can distinguish, among others, the following units: a) farms (tsiflikia); b) monasterial farms (metokhia); c) monasteries; d) herdsmen's huts (kalyvia) and rough shelters (exochika) for the migrant seasonal agricultural labourers (ksomerites): these were made of rushes, branches, reeds or drystone, with a hearth and a raised platform, or divan; e) lean-tos (tsardakia) and watch-towers (dragasies) for the guards set to protect the vineyards (dragates); f) stables, sheds and pens for animals; g) mills, usually wind or water driven: these include special watermills for the preparation of woollen fabrics; h) inns; i) quarries, mines, salt pans, limekilns, potteries, etc.

3.2. The house

3.2.1. House and household

"Private" buildings, whether or not owner-occupied, were used for both residential and productive purposes. These buildings represented the material reality of pre- capitalist ways of life.

Houses and settlements, of course, recorded and reflected economic and social relationships. The house, from this point of view, contained that autonomous and self-sufficient unit, the household. The structure of the house demonstrated the position of the family within the socio-economic system,

whether it was a small rural family of 4-6 members (father, mother and children), a large household with workmen, fosterchildren ("psychopaidia", or "children of the soul") and servants, or the typical 19th and 20th century bourgeois family, with its maidservant.

While the prosperity of the master of the household was reflected in his handsome house, the reception rooms ("kali ontades"), the luxurious furnishings, the well stocked cellars and the smoking chimneys proclaimed the mistress of the establishment a good housekeeper. On occasions such as holidays or weddings, both husband and wife would do their utmost to display their affluence to the whole community.

In the free villages and those communities which enjoyed privileged treatment from the Turkish authorities, decoration was not limited to the inside of the house but embellished the exterior as well. Nevertheless, these imposing houses combined social ostentation with safety measures: they were both monument and fortress, with small windows reminiscent of loop-holes, barred doors, wickets, few openings on the ground floor, inner courtyards, high walls, etc. The phrase "my home is my castle" was a literal expression of its double function - for those who could afford such a house.

Building and blessing the house

The hearth ("parastia", "stia", or "estia") was the heart of the house, which had as many rooms as circumstance and necessity dictated. Outside there were a courtyard and various outbuildings: bakehouse, wash-house, well, etc. Animals were housed either in separate stables or sometimes in the main building itself.

Spatial arrangements were essentially functional. The sitting room, the cellars and storerooms, the wine-press ("poustavi" or "patitiri"), the wooden cupboards ("messandres" or "doulapes"), the loom, the kitchen, the covered verandas ("hagiati"), made the inside of the house comfortable and practical; the "kalos ontas" was only used for festivals and holidays. There would be few actual pieces of furniture, but a plethora of rugs and carpets, tools and utensils, which constituted the household furnishings. The houses were lit by torches, lanterns, and later gas-lamps.

A variety of construction techniques were used for the walls: a) stonework cemented with lime mortar or mud; b) lath-and-plaster work ("bagdati"): a wooden framework was filled with cane or laths and plastered over with lime mortar; c) infilling ("tsatmas"): a

Family in Avdela (photograph by the Manakis bros). (Chr.Christodoulou, The photogenic Balkans of the Manakis brothers, 1989, p.18)

Interior of the Mertzos house in Nymphaio (Neveska)

framework of wooden beams ("kerestedes" or "dokaria") was filled in with bricks, broken tiles and chipped stones and pebbles; d) a row of wooden beams lashed together with flexible rods and plastered over with mud; e) drystone, and f) sun-dried bricks ("plithia") of red clay. The roof was built of wooden beams ("grinties") covered with slate or tile, and was either gabled or of the pyramid type.

Construction: the builders

Houses were built by master craftsmen organized into groups (guilds, roufetia, esnafia or kompanies). They would set out from one area in bands or gangs; they were builders (those from Western Macedonia were called "koudharei" and those from Thrace "dulgheridhes"), plasterers, sculptors in wood or stone ("pelekani"), wood-carvers ("tagiadori"), carpenters, painters, roofers, etc. The master-builder was the head of a band of professional builders, apprentices ("mastoropoula") and assistants ("tsirakia"). Especially renowned were the koudharei from Vourbiani and Pyrsogianni, near Konitsa, the koudharei and pelekani from the "mastorochoria" of Voio (the "Zoupania") in Western Macedonia, the dulgheridhes from Souphli and Adrianople in Thrace, and the painters from Hionades in Epirus. All these master craftsmen built, sculpted and painted the houses and the mansions of Macedonia and the rest of the Balkans. They worked on communal and public projects (churches, roads, bridges, fountains, squares), or for private clients, well-to-do and wealthy householders. The contract below refers to the building of a house in the village of Dolos (Vythos), in the district of Kozani, by eminent local builders[39]:

"The under-signed architects Kostas Tzoumanis and Kostas Tsioumas concluded the following agreement with Demos Tsiotsios:

The architects promise to build a two-storey house for Demos, they will provide all the stone and slate necessary. They will build three sculpted doors and one sculpted cornerstone; the other door and window frames will be plain. Also the upper corner stones will be shorter; the under-signed will build the doors and the windows, they will plaster it and roof it and deliver it in good condition. They will also build a chimney for the stove, cut into the stone wall. Demos promises to pay at a rate of 3 1/2 piastres a yard; from the foundations to the upper storey the walls will be 75 centimetres thick at the bottom, the others will be 75 or 70 or 65 centimetres thick. The owner promises to deliver to the site earth for the

mortar, and water; the architects will dig the foundations, and Demos promises to provide them with dinner and supper, and to make the tools for the workmen, and to give them gun-powder, and the iron tools he will provide himself. Wherefore is this present drawn up for the security of both parties, and is signed below.

1890 April 16 Dolos.

The architects received in earnest two Turkish pounds: 214 piastres.

(signed: the architects, the owner, the witness).

the chimneys above are to be built by the builders and are to be calculated by the yard.

(On the back of the document) we received a further 10 (ten) Ottoman pounds.

1890 May 10 paid to (signatures)"

Less affluent farmers and those who lived in the poorer neighbourhoods of the cities usually built their own houses. The farmer prepared all the materials: stone, wood, mortar, bricks. The whole family worked on the house, and friends and neighbours would lend a helping hand. This tradition of mutual assistance and cooperation was encountered all over Macedonia. On the island of Thasos, "when someone wanted to build a new house he would go to the mountain to cut the timber ("kereste"). On Sunday all his friends and relations would go with him to bring the kereste down. His wife would prepare fritters, and when they came back to the house she would set them down to eat, and she would also offer them raki"[40].

In certain cases, houses were built by order of the landlord (the bey, the landowner), employing builders from the village. Such houses, land and buildings both, belonged to the landlord, and were usually shoddily built: an example of this are the houses of the Roumlouki.

Traditions associated with the blessing of a new house

These are generally very similar. The central figure was the householder (the "master" of the family or household). It was to him that services were rendered, either for wages, in the case of professional builders, or in exchange for similar services to friends and relatives. In return the householder offered gifts, which originally were probably functional in nature (payment in kind), but later were merely symbolic. The offering of such gifts was known as mantilomata, kerasmata and bahtsisia (offerings of kerchiefs, treats and gifts of money), and occurred at principal points during the construction of the house: the laying of the cornerstone (treats and a dinner), the placing of the

Herdsmen's huts in Eastern Macedonia. (E.Papadimitriou, Old Photographs, Epirus-Macedonia, 1977, p.110).

roof-tree, and, most important of all, between the laying of the final roof beam and the commencement of the tiling: "to kremasma ton mantilion" and "richnoun ta bahtisia" (hanging the kerchiefs on the roof as a banner, and offering gifts of money). When the house was completed there were more treats and a dinner. This is a description of the customs pertaining in Krimini (Voio)[41]:

"Before the cornerstone is laid, the site is blessed. The cornerstone, which is inscribed with the date of construction, is posed on the east side of the foundations and a coin is placed underneath. Beside it is a bottle of holy water for the blessing. The master of the household offers a dinner to the builders in honour of the happy occasion. When the walls are complete and the roof is ready for tiling, "richnoun ta bahtisia" (gifts of money are offered). The builders raise on the roof two crosses of wood, and string a length of rope between them. The household and their relatives offer their gifts, which are usually shirts, socks, kerchiefs. The master-builder takes each man's gift, hangs it from the rope and, while the other builders pound their hammers on the roof beams, exclaims melodiously "The gift that Master Thomas has offered out of love for the workmen is most welcome. May God grant him his heart's desire; may his children live; may he live to enjoy them. As the flowers on the mountains and the grass of the plains, even as the grass in the valley of the Vardar, so numerous may be the blessings the Lord showers on him. We thank him for his gift."

3.2.2. Typical styles of houses

(a) The huts of the nomads

Example: the "konakia" (dwellings) of the Sarakat-sani of Florina[42]

"...Northeast of the village of Pisoderi, on the heights of Vigla, as this mountain is generally called, the Sarakatsani shepherds have erected their huts [...] Since 1926 they have been coming to Pisoderi from May until the feast of Aghios Dimitrios. During the winter some of them return to Polygyros in Chal-cidice, where they generally live in rented houses (for, as a Sarakatsani woman told me quite frankly, they do not want to buy houses and live always in the same spot, because "the climate might not suit them": they want to be free, to move from place to place: "we are still tent-dwellers (skinites)", they told me); some of them, though, do own houses. Others move to Kilkis (ta Kirkitsia). Thus during the winter they are ligous-tari as they say, (they live in small groups); while in the summer kanoun ta kolligia (they gather in vil-lages). [...] These Sarakatsani are known as Kas-sandrini, to differentiate them from those who come from Thessaly or Morea, who in fact do not consider the Kassandrini as real Sarakatsani.

...In 1937, the year the survey was made, of the 18 huts the twelve were conical "with a hood" (me kat-soula), while the remaining six were square [...] Both men and women work on the construction of these huts, which are made of branches. (The men cut the branches, the women carry them, and both together

they put up the huts) [...]

(a) Huts with katsoula: To build these, they first clear the ground where the hut is to be erected, and they plant in the earth 30 or 40 long, straight, flexible wands in a circle [...] these form the framework of the hut. The convergent upper ends of these wands are joined to give the hut a more or less conical shape. Then they weave branches through the uprights, and cover the whole construction with straw. Finally they place the katsoula, which is also made of straw, on top. These conical huts have no windows; they receive light only through the opening which serves as a door. The fireplace is located in the middle of the hut. Near the larger, main hut they build a smaller one for clothing and household goods.

(b) Square huts: These have ridged roofs. To build these, three parallel rows of (usually) three upright forked poles (fourkes, or forks) are erected. For the middle row [...] taller poles are used. Upon these is placed the rafter (kavallaris, or rider), that is, the long, horizontal ridge pole; long beams are also placed on top of the other two rows of poles, "and the framework of the roof is filled in with kaproulia and hartoma (wooden construction), and covered with straw, while the walls are covered with woven branches". The huts are divided (by a wall of branches) into two parts, the main part, where the family lives, and a storeroom [...] In the main room the fireplace, which they call the gounia (corner), built into one of the shorter walls. On either side of the fireplace are the kathisma (low stone seat) and kathismata, or settles (narrow wooden benches fixed to the framework of the hut). On the

Serf's cottage on the Bardovtse chiflik, in the northern Axios valley, early 20th c. (L.Schultze- Jena, Makedonien..., plate LXIII).

The "low house" of tenant farmers in the villages of the Roumlouki and the Graikochoria, early 20th c. (L.Schultze-Jena, Makedonien..., plate LXXI).

kathisma beside the fireplace are placed woven cushions. These. together with a few cooking utensils on wooden shelves fixed high on the walls of the hut are the only furniture and the only decoration of these dwellings. For beds they place branches (batses) on the ground and cover them with velentzes. A small area in front of the hut is enclosed by a fence and serves as a courtyard. This is where the kathismata are placed. Another enclosed area is used for washing and cooking. A small bahtsedaki (kitchen garden) behind or beside the hut, some upright poles or branches to protect the washing, and the woodpile complete the establishment [...] Within the encampment there are three bake-ovens for the use of all the families..."

(b) The houses of the tenant farmers (kolligi)

Example: House and grounds (binias and spitotopos) in the Roumlouki villages[43].

Single storey ("level" or "low") houses were the norm; less common were two storey ("tall" or "raised") houses. Each house was built on its own grounds: a plot of land, with out-buildings, enclosed by a fence (plokaria).

The main house and the out-buildings (store-room and cabin or bake-house or flour-shed) were in the middle of the plot of land. The family slept in the main house, but worked and ate and spent most of the day in the cabin; they might even sleep there too, on occasion, or sometimes in the barn. The cabin was divided into separate rooms; there they kneaded and baked their bread, worked at the loom, and stored their wheat, flour and other produce. The straw for the animals was stored in the barn, and the livestock slept in a shed. On the grounds there would also be a threshing-floor, a flower garden and a vine-arbour. The main house would have three or four rooms with hard earthen floors; only the central room with the hearth might be panelled with boards. The chimney was built in. A typical feature of both the house and the cabin was the ambrosti, a kind of ante-chamber where most family life was lived.

All the buildings were built in the same way: heavy timbers (kerestedes) formed the framework; the spaces were filled in with mud and straw, and then plastered. The roof was made of rushes from the marsh. These rushes were also used for the matting which covered the floors and the walls to draw the damp.

Within the house were kept utensils, some small pieces of furniture (the baby's cradle, some stools, the strosses "covers, carpets", the soufras "a small. low, round table or pastry-board" or the sini "a round metal tray used as a table" and the family's clothing heaped in youkia "piles of clothing". Tools and everyday utensils were kept in the cabin. Some houses had a chest to hold the family's wardrobe and treasures.

The house was usually shared by two or more

families (the parents with their married sons), and was often divided to accommodate this extended family.

Example: The houses of the koligi and the dwellings of the landowners on the chiflik of Meliki (Roumlouki)[44].

"The chiflik of Meliki covered a total expanse of 33,269 old Turkish stremmata (i.e. 2,481 hectares, or 6,130 acres); it consisted of arable land with small areas of forest and pastureland, which were also susceptible of cultivation. It belonged to Gioumni Effendi, and after his death to his six heirs. Subsequently the farm was purchased by a family of landowners, and by some smallholders from the village. A small part reverted to the National Bank as exchangeable land [and in 1929 was distributed to landless farmers].

...Until 1902, when the first parcels of land in Meliki were sold, the land and buildings belonged to the beys [...] The beys furnished the seed and the land, and the Greeks worked on the land in return for 50% of the harvest. Of this the beys took 10% for municipal tax and a further 2% for the so-called monafi; the remainder they shared with the tenants (koligi) [...] The koligi did not always occupy the same houses, but every August, after the wheat was harvested, they were moved around: those who were most faithful and worked the hardest were given houses in a better, more central location in the village [...] The rayah (non-Moslem subjects of the Turkish Sultan, peasants) did not only work on the farms, but also practised the trades of kyradji (muleteer), arabatji (owner of large mule trains) [sic], tsambazi (dealer in livestock), and many others, but always under the surveillance of the bey [...] Fayik Pasha, the eldest son of Gioumni Effendi, lived at Betolia (Monastir). Once he visited his chiflik at Meliki, and when he saw the old bell-tower of the church of Agia Paraskevi which was built in 1809 [sic] and saw that it even had a cross on the roof, he was so furious that he ordered a mansion (konaki) to be built five metres taller, and a crescent to be placed on the pinnacle. And so the rayah of Meliki assembled and built a strong konaki, a four-storey mansion 25 by 12 from which you could see all over the plain, and which was burned down by Katsampas on June 29, 1910; at that time it belonged to Hatzikos who had bought it from Fayik Pasha, and it was located on the site where our primary and high schools are today."

Example: Share-croppers' houses near Melenikon.

[The following is the description of the house of one of the eleven ortaksidhes (that is, mesiakaridhes) (share-croppers) who lived and worked on one of the chifliks belonging to the Community of Melenikon in the second half of the 19th century. The description is taken from the Ktimatologhion tou Kinou tou Melenikou (Land Register of the Community of Melenikon), probably from 1872][45].

"The house of share-cropper Stamati Giannou: A house with a barn, the door opening onto the courtyard and another outer door from the adjoining tsardaki (hall). There are three ontadhes (rooms) above the tsardaki, of which one is large and has a hearth. The tsardaki is square with 16 posts all around, 3 in the middle and 5 towards the rooms. Under the ground floor there is a store-room divided into six parts with a capacity of six hundred esmakia. Below there are vegetable gardens belonging to the same property; above is the road, beyond which are the houses of five other share-croppers. On one side is the Sfogarovo hollow, and on the other are vegetable gardens, threshing-floors and barns belonging to this property (that is, to this Community property), which are therefore registered..."

(c) Fishermen's houses

Example: The houses in the Prespa villages[46]

"The first houses here were oblong, built of sun-dried brick and roofed with straw or reeds. They were separated into two parts, one for the animals and one for the people. Between them was a partition made of reeds [...] Many of these houses had no hearth; they lit their fires in the middle of the floor, and instead of a chimney there was a hole in the roof to let the smoke out [...] Over the fire they suspended a cauldron which they used for cooking [...] The houses had two openings in the front, which served as windows. They opened them by day to let in a little light and then closed them again [...] In the middle [...] towards the animals' side of he house was the door. Outer door, inner door, it was one and the same, for everyone and everything. It was made of pieces of wood hastily nailed together cross-wise. They cut down reeds, which they arranged carefully and then covered them with mud. Others, who knew more about carpentry, cut poplars and hewed thick planks, which made for a more solid construction [...] Gradually the aspect of the houses changed [...] They came to have two storeys. Several of them had two divisions below, one for the animals and one for a storeroom [...] The upper storey had two rooms with earthen floors, or sometimes they laid down straw matting. The windows were tiny, just big enough to admit a few rays of sunlight. It was dark inside, and there was practically no fresh air [...] Since 1900 when they started emigrating to America and Australia, life has been different. Now, in the place of those dark houses, once they had torn down all the old ones, they are building those lovely country style houses, with every modern convenience..."

(d) The typical ploughman's house (zevghitospito or patospito in Western Macedonia and the area of Elassona)[47]

"The ploughman's house, the oldest and simplest type of one room dwelling in Greece, particularly in the villages, was a familiar sight in Thessaly and in Western Macedonia. In Thessaly it was called tou zevghosp'tou (the ploughman's house) or ou patosp'tous (the low house, the earth house), and in Western Macedonia tou patosp'tou [...] They were usually square built, of stone and mud, measuring about 4 metres wide by 10 long, inside. The front, one of the longer sides, that is, was usually built facing south, or,if that were not possible, facing east. The house was partitioned into two separate areas: to the west stoun patosp'tou and to the east stou spit' i onta [...] If the ground sloped away to the east they would build an underground room under the onta. called the patouma (floor). In such cases the ontas would be raised a few steps above the level of the patospito, to give more head room to the "floor" beneath [...] These buildings usually had only one door, in the middle of the south wall [...] However, a second door was sometimes opened in the north wall, directly opposite the main door [...] this was known as the thyropoul' or portopoul' (little door) [...] Between the patospito and the ontas was a low wicker-work partition, covered with plaster or filled with tsatmas (bits of broken brick, tile, stone, etc), running the whole width of the building, with a passage left open into the onta [...] Many farm families put their ambar' on it: this was a rectangular wooden chest with two pouring spouts (matia, or eyes), used for storing flour [...] The house or ontas: the ontas was lit by two windows in the eastern wall [...] For security at night and protection from cold in the winter, there was a one-piece wooden shutter (kanat') on the inside, which closed by means of two forged hinges (krikeles). There was no glass. In the winter they would leave the shutters partially open to allow a little light to enter while still protecting the room from cold and snow. They would often cut windows in the north and south walls as well [...] For cooking, and for heating the house in the winter,

a fireplace (tzak') was built into the east wall. While this wall was being raised they would leave a rectangular opening in it [...] Over this they would shape an open pyramid, which narrowed as it neared the top of the wall: this housed the chimney (to outzak). The inside of the fireplace, the pyromakhos, was lined with red clay. In front of the fireplace was an apron, or hearth (parastia), finished with slate, and with vertical slabs of slate on the sides (magoules, or cheeks) to protect the surrounding area [...] The hearth was surmounted by an inclined, rectangular construction of wood and mud, to cover the top part of the fireplace. At the base of this hood a sort of mantelpiece was left, (to boukhari), where in earlier years the lanterns were set and in more recent times the gas lamps [...] In the winter the room was lit by torches or small oil lamps [...] The furnishings of the ontas were rudimentary: o trapezous (a low table), i arkla (cupboard) and the spitomazouma (household gear). Instead of beds they merely laid out a large mattress filled with straw or corn husks (stromatsa), and in winter mattresses of goat-hair (ta saismata) [...] Cooking was done on the fireplace [...] For baking bread and pies they used a shield-shaped covered metal tray called a gastra, which when not in use hung from a hook, the gastrologo. The patospito, which occupied the western half of the building, was used to stable and feed the animals (from a manger), store the grain and house the loom [...] The roof was generally squared, occasionally ridged [...] The hayati (covered veranda), which was always placed on the long, southern side of the house, served as a summer house for the peasant families. There they sat during the day and there they slept in the summer, on built-up wooden or earthen beds (krevata or anakhoma). The animals also spent the day there [...] The veranda was roofed with slate, tiles or rye straw (vrizamies), like the house itself. The oven was often built on the veranda, and the loom set up there for use in the summer. Such were the houses of the poor peasants, who were kept in abject poverty by whoever happened to be in power, such poverty that the dowries of their daughters could fit in a bag and a sack tossed in a corner (angonia) of the room".

(e) A typical house in the "free" villages

Example: From peasant hut to wealthy mansion in Krimini (Voio)[48]

"Around the houses are grounds, in which are disposed the courtyard and the gardens. This area is surrounded by a wall two metres high, surmounted by large stone slabs which are set in place by special masons in such fashion that they shed the rainwater. At the edge of the courtyard are the household out-buildings: the cook-house, the stables, the barn. In the courtyard there is also the well which supplies water for the family and the fruit trees. The yard has a double door made of thick planks, secured by a heavy wooden or iron bar. The houses are two-storied, with stone walls and wooden roofs mounted on beams (grinties). These beams are wide and thick: they were probably hewn from the large trees with which the region is amply provided. The double door of the house is made of heavy planks and secured by a solid wooden bar. Next to the entrance are a small area (the patospito), the cellars and the stables, which at a later period were built outside the house. On the south side of the house there is a small later addition, a room (the soba), where the family spend the winter. A wooden staircase leads to the second storey, with the hayati (hall) and two or three rooms. The floor is wooden, and sealed with a layer of mud mixed from red clay. There is no ceiling; the small windows have no outside shutters, but wooden kanatia (one-piece wooden inside shutters) which are closed at night and when the weather is bad. The fireplace is built into the wall and has a boukhari (a sort of mantelpiece). Inside the fireplace hangs a chain for a ghioumi (copper water jar) or a kakavi (cauldron) of water. The furnishings are simple. Small bundles of rye straw tied together form the mattresses placed on either side of the hearth. On these are laid thick saismata of wool and goat-hair, while others serve as blankets. There are cupboards (messandres) built into the walls for the bedding. In the cellar we find the wine-press (poustavi) where the grapes are pressed, the kados (cask) which holds two thousand oka of must (approximately 2,560 kilos), vaenia (barrels) of wine, ambaria (bins) of grain, kioupia (jars) of pickles, tubs of cheese and salt-packed foods, earthenware jugs for wine, earthenware plates (missoures) for food, wooden spoons (papaditses), tsiotres (wine-flasks), and all the family's tools.

The houses which were built towards the end of the 19th century are elegant, spacious, comfortable and finely furnished. The grounds are ample, enclosed by a wall built of stone and mortar. The courtyard is paved with smooth flagstones. The rooms are large, with wooden floors and ceilings and wide windows. In some houses the ceilings are carved around the edges, while others are painted with scenes from the life of the family and the village. The timbers supporting the floors and the roof are of poplar. The rooms,

especially those on the ground floor where the family spends the winter, have fireplaces in the centre of the wall facing the door; these are built of massive slabs of stone, smooth or carved.

Every house has a "good" room upstairs, to receive visitors whenever there is a celebration in the household. The floor of this room is covered with a multi-coloured woven kilimi (pileless carpet); and there are divans with red velentzes, embroidered pillows woven on the loom, and cushions in the corners.

The houses have loop-holes overlooking the entrance, and iron grilles on the windows; some have terraces and some balconies."

Example: The house of a wealthy family in Vogatsiko (Western Macedonia) [49]

"The people of Vogatsiko, being for the most part professional builders, did not only work abroad, building mansions for strangers: thay also built their own.

The traditional houses usually have a walled courtyard in front, where various out-buildings such as store-rooms, stables, ovens etc. are located. The courtyard has a double door, so that the beasts of burden with their various loads can pass through. Here, many houses have a well in the courtyard, for the village is located in a dry place and must rely on the underground water which comes down from the mountains, at a considerable depth, too.

These old houses were built entirely of stone, limestone, with walls nearly a metre thick. They have two storeys; the cellar and the store-rooms, etc. are on the ground floor, as well as a stairway leading to the floor above. There are no large windows, just one or two small ones; these close by means of a thick inside shutter which fastens with an iron bolt for safety. In order to be able to watch the road and the courtyard, there are loop-holes at intervals, that is, narrow slits 5 to 10 centimetres wide by 50 centimetres high.

The roof is made of wood on a framework of grinties (beams), which are very thick. The door is a double one, made of thick planks and secured on the inside by a long, heavy piece of wood fastened by a metal bar. The fireplace is built into the wall; above it is a mantelpiece (boukhari) on which there are always a mirror and a hurricane lamp to light the house at night.

Within the fireplace there is a chain with a hook, from which can be hung the gkioumi or the kakavi with the water to be heated.

Interior of the Sapountzis house in Kastoria. (Gallery of Greek Folk Art. Volume I. Mansions in Kastoria, Collection of Greek Popular Art, 1948, plate 30).

Messandres (cupboards) are built into the walls to hold the heavy covers (quilts, blankets, rugs). In the cellar are the wine-press (poustavi), the flour-chests, the jars of pickles (peppers in vinegar), the tubs of brine, the wine, and all the household equipment: the farmer's tools and the housewife's cooking utensils.

Every house has a kripsana (yizba), a secret hiding place for precious objects. The hall is spacious, with a raised dais on each side where they spread the mattresses; these were filled with corn husks and covered with flokates velentzes (thick blankets) woven by the mistress of the house. On festive occasions they bring out the many-coloured kilimia, woven in various patterns, with Greek keys and geometric figures, and spread them on all the floors. All the windows had curtains of woven cloth, white, with a border of home-made lace, made of silk thread, often coloured. The guests would sit tailor-fashion on the divans, seated on thick blankets. There, that was how the houses were in the 19th century. Those old mansions, with their heavy, luxurious furnishings, were pillaged and burnt by the Turks in the horrors of 1912."

Example: The house of a wealthy family in Kolindros (Pieria)[50]

"In olden times it was the custom in Kolindros for the father to build a new house for each of his children, when they began to move away from home. The first thing to do was to locate a suitable plot of land for building. Then they had to assemble all the materials (stone, posts and planks hewn out of huge oak logs, lime, and Byzantine tiles), before the foundations could be laid. The foundations would be blessed; and they also used to observe the old pagan custom of killing a cock and pouring its blood on the foundations to strengthen them. Then the work began, under the supervision of the master-builder; his workmen were at one and the same time masons, and carpenters who could build the wooden parts of the house (doors, windows, floors, ceilings, roof) and plasterers who made the inner partitions, and did the plastering and the whitewashing. When they were ready to put the roof on, they raised a cross from which they hung the gifts offered to the workmen by the master of the household and his relatives: these included servetes (kerchiefs, scarves and towels), tsourapia (socks), lengths of cloth, etc. With each gift they chanted the phrase "We welcome the peskes (gift, offering) of...". The house was built according to one of two traditional styles. The first type was a one or two storey house either entirely built of stone or with the ground floor and the first floor of stone and the upper floor having a wooden framework which extended out over the stone wall. This extension was supported by brackets (ta fourousia), and formed a sort of elongated balcony. This adjunction made the house bigger and brighter, and gave it a broader view. The second type of house had, instead of protruding balconies, one or more recessed covered porches (hayatia). Often the brackets supporting the balconies [...] were of carved wood and very decorative. The wooden framework of the upper floor followed the tsatmas system: it was filled with mud and bits of pumice-stone, and plastered inside and out [...] The ground floor was much taller than the other floors; the storerooms (ambaria) were located there, and the tubs, the loom, the hay-lofts, the stables and the hen-houses, and the toilet. The ground floor entrance to the house had a wide double door of oak reinforced with broad-headed nails; each section had a large hinge and a koraka (door-knocker), and it was secured by means of an iron or wooden bar. A wooden staircase led to the first floor, which had one room, the everyday sitting-room, plus the kitchen, the larder, and the kneading room; while on the second floor there were a hall for raising silkworms and for dances and parties, two or three bedrooms and the kalo ontas (reception room). Every room had its fireplace (if there was no hearth in the reception room they would place in it a brazier of copper or bronze), its gelevia or panorafia (high shelves), its messandres (cupboards), its arched recesses with their single shelf, its windows with their kanatia (and in older times a grill, or kafasi), its plain or sculpted doors and its tables [...] its seats (chairs or stools), its high or low minteria (wooden dais) [...] its berdedhes (curtains) [...] its locally made kramia (bed-spreads) or its kilimia made in Larisa, its bouro (a bureau, a chest of drawers, upon which were set a lamp, some photographs, etc.),

its pictures on the walls [...] In one of the rooms there would also be the shrine with the family's sacred images, the censer and the votive lamp, while another would have the sentoukia (chests) which held the household treasures.

Some of the family's utensils were of copper: kazania (cauldrons), tzentzeredhes (cooking pots), ghavathes (shallow bowls), kanates (jugs); some of wood: pinakia (plates), tsotres (wine-flasks), hoularia (spoons), pirounia (forks), goudhia (mortars), pinakotes (bread-boards), skafes (kneading-troughs); some of leather: koskina (sieves); and some of tin..."

Example: The house of a wealthy family in Kleisoura, Western Macedonia[51]

"The earliest houses in Kleisoura were small, low, single storey buildings, enclosed by high stone walls with a heavy oaken door which was closed at sunset and secured with a thick oaken bar reinforced with two bands of iron [...] They were built of thin slabs of stone, suitable for roofing. These houses usually had three rooms, a kitchen, and a hall which was paved with square or rectangular flagstones in the part towards the main door. Of the three rooms, one was called the kathimerino or himoniatiko (the sitting-room, or the winter room); it was quite large, with a big, deep fireplace and a platform in front covered with a special paving-stone (ountzeri); it also had cupboards for the things they needed every day for eating and sleeping [...] The second room was the reception room (odai-basi, literally, "man-in-charge-of-rooms"), where guests were received on holidays and festive occasions; it had wooden divans called menteria, and sofas or chairs opposite; it was ornamented with a large mirror, rugs for the divans (minterliki), fine curtains, icons, a wall clock, photographs, etc. The third room was called "the hearth room" [...] it usually faced west, and served as a summer sitting-room. In both this room and the winter sitting-room there were platform beds on either side of the fireplace, raised about ten centimetres above floor level, with straw mattresses covered with kilimia or velentzes in the winter. This is where the family slept, with velentzes for coverings, and, when the weather was very cold, thicker, heavier blankets called tserghes. The hall usually faced north, and had a divan and chairs or stools on either side; this was the room where visitors were received on Sundays and weekdays in the spring and summer. The windows in the hall and the other rooms were always protected with iron grilles, for safety reasons. Below the hall and the other rooms were the cellars, usually three in number, dug deep into the earth so that various kinds of foodstuffs could be kept fresh in summer and winter alike. The kitchen was also nicely arranged, with cupboards and many shelves for all the cooking utensils: saucepans large and small, baking tins, round trays, frying pans, plates and glasses, knives and forks, etc. [...] The sink was carefully built so that the dirty water ran out away from the foundations; it was lined with a special stone, thick and smooth; underneath and to one side was a wooden shelf to store the water jars, three or more of various sizes, used to bring water from the tap. On one side there would be two ovens, a large one for bread and a smaller one for pies and roasts, built by a professional oven-maker [...] Every house had a stable with a hay-loft in the courtyard, built away from the road; there was also a hen-house in it [...] Most houses also had a wash-house, outside, near the stable [...] For illumination, in the 16th and 17th centuries they used torches, in the 18th oil lamps (burning common or spermaceti oil), while in the 19th century they used coal oil [...] After 1700 they began to build two storey houses; and between 1800 and 1880, when Kleisoura was at its most flourishing, imposing three storey mansions were built, to plans and using materials that made them extremely solid and luxurious. The walls of these houses were of chiselled blocks of stone, without mud but worked with lime mortar; on all sides there were loop-holes for defensive purposes and to fight off bandits [...] As for the masons, those from Zoupani and Kostarazi were generally preferred. The disposition of the rooms, the cellars and the other facilities was the same as described above..."

(f) Houses in urban areas

Example: Town houses in Melenikon[52].

The houses in Melenikon were for the most part built on the edge of the ravine. Because of the steep inclination of the ground, they were much higher on the ravine side than on the other.

"The entire first floor, which was usually windowless or in rare instances had a few very small windows, served as a storeroom. From the outside, the upper storey was remarkable for the number of its windows. The whole building, although without a trace of external decoration, created the same sort of impression as the monasteries of Mt Athos; it looked rather like a castle.

Admittance to this traditionally designed building was through the great front door, which was secured on the inside by a wooden bar called a perati. The inner door would then be opened. This inner door led into the large - usually excessively large - central hall, or sala, around which were disposed the various rooms.

In most wealthy houses there was a railed dais (exedhra) in this central hall. This raised platform was originally designed (going back to the Byzantine epoch) to allow noble guests to watch the performance of the dancers and mimes on the floor of the hall.

In certain houses, wooden pillars reached from this railing to the ceiling: at one time curtains may have been hung between them. The various rooms of the house were disposed on three sides of the central hall, and were called: 1) ou kalos or ou megalos nountas (reception room), 2) ou himoniatikos ou nountas (winter room), 3) ou kaloukrinos ou nountas (summer room), 4) i zimoutiki (kneading-room), 5) tou killari (larder), 6) tou maghirio (kitchen), 7) tou anangeou ("the necessary room", the W.C.)

In the large room and the winter and summer sitting rooms there were minteria, approximately 60 centimetres high by 50 wide. Those by the hearth were often broader, as much as 1.5 metres wide. Built into the walls was the missandra or roukhouthesi (cupboard), and there were shelves on the walls in the corners. The fireplace, or outzaki, was built into the wall..."

Example: The old houses in Serres[53]

"...The Zaparas house is of particular importance in the study of popular housing, for it recalls a type well-known in Macedonian architecture: the house built to a ground plan in the shape of a . The ground floor entrance opens into a hall which leads to the five auxiliary areas on this level. From this hall a staircase leads to the upper floor, where the principal rooms of the house are located, the sitting rooms and the reception room [...] One turning of the staircase leads to the sun porch (hayati) on the upper floor. In our older examples, this sun porch was always open, as it is in the present case; later, however, we find it closed in with windows, with their familiar wooden railing and dark shutters (kepengia) and their fanlights above, those small bright windows common in Byzantine times and often brought from abroad. On the northwest side of the sun porch there were three rooms in a row, the middle one being the smallest. In older houses, such as those we have looked at in Kastoria, Veria and Ampelakia, this room was not enclosed, but

Tsetsapas (or Tsiatsiampas) mansion in Kastoria. (Mansions in Kastoria, op.cit., plate 30)

open to the sun porch. In other cases this central area was one or two steps higher than the rest, and was often separated by a wooden trivilo (railing), which gave it a certain air of formality.

In the Zaparas house, the northeast room is the only one where the fireplace balances the window, in the traditional fashion [...] The particular care displayed in the windows and the wooden doors (dabladhotes portes) indicates the prosperity of the master of the house, and is a good example of popular Macedonian architecture during the years of Turkish rule, and in particular of the -shaped building [...] Along with another local mansion, the house belonging to Sophia Kyriakidou, which exemplifies a further development of this type (the shape has longer wings on the ground floor, which extend in four directions on the first floor, forming an H), it constitutes an excellent example of the evolution of Macedonian architecture from the middle of the 19th to the beginning of the 20th century..."

(g) From town houses to mansions

The "mansions" of the Balkans (and especially those of Macedonia) are a special type of dwelling, as distinct in construction as for the life style they offered and the social values they expressed or imposed. Although wealthy and luxurious houses had of course existed before the 18th century (some indeed since

Byzantine times), the houses generally designated as archontika (mansions) are a product of the tremendous changes that occurred in the 18th and 19th centuries, reaching their peak in the second half of the latter. Merchants who had made their fortunes (most probably somewhere in Central, Western or Eastern Europe) would return home to their own village and build a mansion, large or small. These mansions were thus built in a variety of settings, in cities, towns and rural areas alike. Many imposing "public" buildings were also erected during this period, both to enhance the community and to display the generosity of the archontes (wealthy community leaders): these included handsome fountains, schools, churches and bell towers (after the second quarter of the 19th century), roads, bridges and public squares. This meant that much accumulated wealth was poured into buildings which stood out among the more traditional buildings. Fine materials (both local and imported), famous masons, renowned for work all over the Balkans, and a choice site: all were carefully selected to endow the building, whether private or public, with an air of "quality" and to demonstrate the gentility of the builder.

A residential mansion was not merely a statement; it was also perfectly functional: house, warehouse, stable, shop, office, workshop. From this point of view the archontika constitute a particularly complex case: on the one hand they mark specific historical changes, while on the other they take their place and continue to function within the framework of tradition and by its rules.

In point of style the archontika had many common characteristics as a class, as well many differences in comparison with more ordinary houses, so that they can, as a class, be contrasted with such "ordinary" dwellings. Of course, between the poor peasant hut and the wealthy town house and the mansion there are many intermediate types. There are, for example, imposing residences which can be called neither mansions nor "ordinary" houses. Again, the archontika themselves have different styles. In Kastoria, for example, the floor plan of such houses is square, while in Siatista it is L-shaped; but since both types display similar lay-outs and external architectural features, and share common structural characteristics, they are considered as belonging to the same category. Then there are the mansions in Veria, where the exiguity of the terrain imposed an inversion of the typical orientation and arrangement of the buildings. Narrow lots meant that auxiliary areas such as the oven, well, fountain, store-rooms, etc. had to be squeezed into the inner courtyard. From this courtyard an external stair led up to the second floor. The veranda on this level was at the back of the house and often covered a portion of the yard. The front of the house had was almost entirely blank: it displayed only a few small windows and a barred door. The Verian mansion, in other words, could be called introspective. This same attitude characterized not only individual houses, but even entire city blocks, where all the houses faced inwards onto a sort of inner square (which might occasionally contain a church). These blocks of houses, where the outer walls of the buildings formed an enclosed square, often constituted separate walled neighbourhoods (mahaladhes), self-contained and self-sufficient.

It is certainly possible, however, to speak of the "typical Balkan mansion", to which Veria constitutes an exception. And although there are no longer many examples of this type of building, there are still many of the older ones, in Veria, Kastoria, Kozani, Siatista, Edessa, on Pelion and in Ampelakia, in Adrianople and Philippoupoli, in Serres, Melenikon, Kavala, Monastir and Thessaloniki. Similar buildings can also be found both as isolated examples in various places (Nymphaion, Vogatsiko, etc.), as well as concentrated in small communities of professional builders (e.g. in the "Mastorochoria", Zoupania, Rodochori, Krimini, etc.), where the masons built houses for themselves which looked like small mansions, but of course could not compare in affluence and luxury with the great houses of the wealthy merchants, landowners, businessmen and mariners.

In Veria, the celebrated archontika of Sior Manolakis, Rakhtivanena and Vikelas no longer exist; the Sapountzoglou house, however, is still standing. Kastoria still has its great mansions "freely" built in the midst of well-treed gardens: the Natzis, Tsiatsiampas and Papaterpou houses, for example. In Siatista the Manousis, Kanatsoulis, Poulkidis and Tzonos mansions, among others, still exist.

Example: the oldest form of mansion. The Bampoura archontiko in Melenikon[54]

(This house was known as "the big house" or "the clock house", because of the large clock on its tower).

"The only private house we know of which dates from the Byzantine period is the mansion in Melenikon. This house, "the big house", as the townspeople call it, was built in the middle of the city, on a rise from which it dominates the surrounding

Manousis mansion in Siatista.

area, possibly in the 12th but more likely in the 14th century, judging by the decoration of the facade. It is a square building, 17.6 metres on each side, reinforced with a high tower and built for defense, although it has never been anything but a dwelling-place...

The house is built of small blocks of stone and bricks set in very simple geometric patterns. The tower served as a vigla, or watchtower, and for defensive purposes; it was built of wood, and most of it is of much more recent construction: only the lower portion is of stone and brick and contemporary with the rest of the house.

The house has a ground floor and two storeys on the main facade, and two storeys at the back: this was necessitated by the steep declivity of the site. The windows are rounded at the top, and measure 1.1 metre high by 1.15 metre wide. The number of windows is not the same on each side; one side, indeed, is completely blank. Inside there is a large central hall paved with hexagonal flagstones measuring 20 cm a side, which reaches right to the roof of the building, and ten rooms, five per floor. These rooms all open on to the central hall as well as communicating with each other. The room to the left of the entrance is relatively elegant, with a new Turkish-style wooden ceiling; next come some bedrooms and to the right a kitchen, all very poor and terribly dilapidated.

The second floor is uninhabited, and used only for storage. It is reached by means of a ladder leading into a wooden attic supported by two wooden posts. The inner partitions have been altered since the house was first built, as has the lower portion of the facade, which has undergone repairs. But the general disposition of the rooms has probably not changed. A stone staircase used to lead up to the part of the house which today is used for storage: the base of it is still visible [...] The walls of the rooms on this floor have deteriorated to such an extent that it is now impossible to be sure what they were used for. They may well have been women's quarters, store-rooms, and cabinets. A shallow staircase led up to the front door, which was guarded by the tower.

The Melenikon mansion, which for the moment is unique of its kind, is in no state to astound us by its luxury and its age; but it is still of great interest, as an example of a hitherto unknown type of house, belonging to a wealthy provincial gentleman or a prosperous citizen of a border city".

Example: An introduction to development in Moschopolis (destroyed in 1769)[55]

"In Moschopolis we can follow more closely the various stages of architectural development, from Konstantas' sixteen primitive huts, which formed the original settlement, to the marvellous mansions of the more recent past [...] The wandering nomadic herdsmen and tent-dwellers needed somewhere to settle permanently. A gentlewoman built huts for them in a sheltered spot on the Obar plateau, a protected site enclosed on all sides, facing east and watered by three streams, which looked like a vast sheepfold. These primitive huts, at an altitude of 1200 metres, were of immense benefit to the noblewoman's flocks and their herdsmen, and lasted for 100 years, with many improvements and additions. Over the years these huts gradually became little stone houses, with fireplaces against the terrible cold of those parts, and roofed with slates which they cut and carried from the abundant nearby quarries; with sheds for fodder for the animals, and ovens, and possibly other auxiliary rooms as well, beside the first. When Moschopolis moved on to the second stage of develop-

ment and became an industrial centre, then architectural structure changed too, but without losing its original character. The preparation of woollens requires larger and more secure houses. The old shepherds' huts became safer and more spacious. Another storey was added, and more rooms, while the family continued to use the ground floor. The house was protected by loopholes. We have now reached the second stage, the urban stage, which serves industrial purposes while at the same time affording increased comfort to these wealthier families. Decorative features begin to appear in various parts of the house. In the third and final stage, the age of general economic prosperity, when Moschopolis became a major banking and commercial centre as well as an industrial city, the economic capital of Epirus and Macedonia, the architectural aspect of the city changed again, reflecting the affluence of its inhabitants. Decorative features enhanced the buildings, and architecture became a both a science and a means of aesthetic expression. A third floor was added to these houses for the reception of visitors and guests for solemn celebrations and official occasions. More rooms were added, including verandas and covered colonnades, and works of art put the finishing touches to the exquisite interior decoration of these houses, which had by now taken on both the name and the aspect of archontika. The courtyard has expanded to include a garden, with a fountain in the middle. Summerhouses and other small structures frame the courtyard, creating a very pleasant overall appearance. Finally, the influence of their European travels, especially to Venice and Austria, was evident in the exterior and to an even greater extent the interior decoration of the houses of these wealthy merchants.

The town house was the product of Moschopolis' second phase of development (1600-1700), and the archontiko of the third, during which architecture reached its fullest flowering, but always within Macedonian tradition. Venetian and Austrian influence was minimal, and affected only details. The popular character of architecture continued to be manifest and to be enriched, but was always grounded in local tradition. The builders and craftsmen who designed and built these houses grew steadily in expertise, and in time became highly sought after throughout the Balkan region, carrying their skills to every corner of the peninsula. The masons' guild of Moschopolis was said to be one of the largest and wealthiest. The allied art of wood-carving developed in tandem with architecture, and this period has left remarkable monuments all over Epirus, Macedonia and the Ionian islands. The designs of these works, which are to be found in houses, churches and ornaments as well as in the woodcuts illustrating the works of local publishers, together with the delicacy of their execution, indicate that by the final stage in the development of the city this art form had achieved an enviable position as a form of popular expression. Other crafts also developed during this period, including those of the goldsmiths and the coppersmiths, whose guilds were also among the most important in the city. With the collaboration of these other crafts, then, popular architecture in Moschopolis was able to create its famous archontika and its splendid churches, unique in Macedonia for the perfection of their construction and their carved wood decoration. It must be remembered that architecture requires both a high degree of affluence and a body of expert technicians capable of executing the details of the decorative designs. When wealth is joined to technical expertise, then the product is the wonderful archontika and the splendid churches of Moschopolis.

Let us now take a closer look at things: From the outside the town houses and mansions of Moschopolis were nothing special to look at; this was out of fear of the Turks, who regarded any sign of affluence among their subjects with envy and aversion. In order to avoid criticism and penalty, then, the citizens of Moschopolis did not, like those of other areas, decorate the outsides of their houses. The two-storey town houses, of which the inimitable Vilaras has given us a marvellous description of the manner of their construction in Giannina [...] as well as the three storey archontika, were on the outside perfectly plain. The ground floor was built of large blocks of stone, of irregular shape but cleanly cut; there were two or four loop-holes on the front. A domed entrance led inside to the domestic quarters: kitchen, wash-house, wood bins, larder and other necessary areas. Most houses in Moschopolis did not have a courtyard, with the main door separate from the house itself, a kind of outer door. The front door was in the middle of the ground floor, as appears from the 1767 engraving and from the reminiscences of our elders [...] There were however some houses that did have both a garden and a garden door. Inside, a wooden staircase led up to the second floor, and those houses that had a garden had an outside stone stair as well. On the second floor there was a wooden-pillared solarium (liakoto or krevata) facing south, bedrooms, a maid's room, a bath, and large cupboards; but the most important room was the reception room, a large room with a fireplace and a balcony, with divans all around, and with at least three arched windows looking on to the street. If the house had a third storey, then it was used for receptions, and contained a large room with windows giving on to the balcony, and a solarium on the south side flanked by other rooms. The roof was covered with slates of various colours, cut from the abundant quarries of the village of Poleni [...] How this stonework must have embellished the appearance of these houses, and even more so the churches! At sunset Moschopolis must have looked magical, like a fairy tale city. Unfortunately we cannot know exactly what these houses looked like at the height of their glory, and to what extent they maintained the traditional Macedonian type. But since there were buildings with forty rooms, like the Hellenic Academy, or even with twenty and thirty rooms, their structural character must certainly have changed..."

Example: Archontika in Siatista[56]

"...The mansions of Siatista, thirty or so in number, built 200 and more years ago when Siatista, secure on the untrodden heights of her mountains, was at the peak of her prosperity, present one of the most perfectly evolved forms of domestic architecture in the country. The feast-loving gentry, scorning the poor and plain, poured their wealth into decent dwellings fulfilling the requirements of a superior and luxurious lifestyle. It was they who afforded the craftsmen among the populace the opportunity and the means to exercise their dexterity and to develop their natural taste.

All the archontika in Siatista are built to the same plan, and with virtually the same interior disposition. All arose out of the same desire for elegance; all impress the visitor by both their size and by the spaciousness and luxurious decoration of their interiors. They are imposing buildings of two or three storeys, with high stone walls around their gardens and loop-holes carefully positioned for defence in hours of danger and against Albanian invasion.

As a rule these houses are built facing south; and a portion of the facade will project somewhat, in order to afford lateral protection to the double oak door, which is also guarded by loopholes in the wall on either side.

On the ground floor there is an inner, paved courtyard, the mesia, with two staircases, of which the one on the right leads up to the first floor, called the anoi. All the rest of the ground floor is occupied by storerooms (magazia), and by the katoi, or cellar, with

Nerantzopoulos mansion in Siatista.

the wine-press, wine barrels, jars and other household necessities. Mounting the right-hand stone staircase, we come to an open passage, protected by a railing, which surrounds the inner courtyard on three sides like a hanging balcony. On to this passage open the rooms of this floor, which occupy its four corners. These are known as the winter rooms, for it is here that the family spend the winter. Between the rooms on the north side a broad space is left open; this is the solarium (iliakos), and its two or three windows afford considerable light to the room. The floor of the solarium is raised a step or two above the level of the corridor, from which it is often separated by a handsome wrought iron railing and slender columns which meet overhead in a delicate arch. The walls are lined with panels of wood (pharsomata) decorated with colourful paintings, and the ceilings are ornamented with wood-carvings. It is doubtless the most beautiful room on this floor, and is used for the recreation of the family and their guests on holidays. The name "solarium" indicates that this room was originally

open to the sun, as is the case in similar old houses in Epirus and Thessaly, where the mesia is not closed in front by a wall, thus giving the building the shape of the letter .

The disposition of the rooms on the second floor is like that of the first, with the exception of the mesia and iliakos, which on this floor form a large hall with projections (ksepetakta) on the north and south sides, and with rows of windows. With its elegant reception rooms and the abundance of light afforded by its gabled double windows, this floor is the handsomest and most imposing part of the whole house, and is used for the festivals and ceremonies of family and social life. The upper row of windows, which are reminiscent of the lights of Byzantine palaces, are of stained glass and bear superscriptions with metred epigrams. These windows are not merely decorative but also functional, for they afford light to the room when the lower windows are shuttered. Here too the walls are for the most part panelled and decorated with brightly coloured paintwork; between these painted wall panels and the carved wooden decoration of the ceilings, this floor furnishes a good idea of the affluence and the luxury which surrounded the wealthy art-loving gentry of Siatista..."

Example: Townhouses and archontika in Veria[57]

"It is well-known that the best examples of our popular architecture are in Macedonia [...] We in Veria are daily witnesses to the death and disappearance of the last traces of our architectural tradition. Already the most remarkable of our mansions, those belonging to Vikelas (Kanakis), Raktivan (the Raktivanouda) and Sior Manolakis have been demolished [...] We did however have the opportunity to study the third of these [..] Sior Manolakis' house occupied the northern part of the lot. On the ground floor, in order, beginning from the northeast, were the hay barn , the stable, the kneading house and a kitchen. To the south a row of dherekia (wooden beams) support the hayatia on the mezzanine. The front door is on the eastern facade and is decorated on the outside, like all the doors in Veria, with broad-headed nails. It is secured on the inside with a peratis or ambara (bar) and a mandhala (wooden lock). There used to be another door, a service entrance, which was sealed up at a later date. Beside the door, on the inside, was the water tap. On the western side was the kitchen, and next to it, two or three steps higher, the tzamakia (glass-panelled veranda). Next to the veranda was the library, and in the northeast corner a linen closet and

The Villa Allatini in Thessaloniki. Designed by Italian architect Vitaliano Poselli for the Alla- tini family, it has housed the Military Hospital, and the University of Thessaloniki (1926). Today it houses the Prefecture of Thessaloniki.

the WC. From the southern hayati on the mezzanine, a wooden staircase led up to the first floor, where the kalos ontas (reception room) projected outward towards the street, with a broad balcony overlooking the interior courtyard [...] This reception room received light from three sides. In the north wall there are two casement windows flanking the mantelpiece; four Byzantine type windows (arched openings) low on the eastern wall enabled the occupants of the room to watch what was going on in the street below. These windows were unglazed, but had shutters which could be closed. Each of these openings was surmounted by a small window framed in plaster [...] The western wall contained built-in cupboards, with panelled doors painted with floral scenes [...] The walls of this room were veneered in wood painted in pastel colours. Above the lintel and running all around the room was the gilvi (in Vlach, poltsa), a small shelf or ledge which in winter held quinces and pomegranates.

The murals in the onta of Sior Manolakis' house are of considerable artistic value, and link the Veria district with corresponding decorative trends in Kastoria and Siatista at the same period (early 19th cen-

tury)...

From time to time wanderings bands of builders would build in Veria houses similar to those we have seen in Kastoria and Siatista. The houses that are truly representative of the district, however, are a distinctive local product of popular architecture, and constitute a type the evolution of which can be followed from its origins in the smooth-fronted peasant cottage, to the addition of the over-hanging front porch, the typical Macedonian hayati on the ground floor and the eventual repetition of these features on the upper floor as well...

Macedonian architecture is, to a great extent, based on the use of wood. In Veria, however, wood reaches its apotheosis..."

Example: The "villas" of Thessaloniki[58]

"Early in this century, the wealthy merchants of Thessaloniki - Greeks, Jews, Donmeh (a local Muslim-Jewish sect), Franks and Levantines - began to build handsome houses for themselves along the shore outside the eastern, Byzantine, city wall. Before 1900 these houses did not reach beyond Allatini - a district

The old main building of the Aristotelian Univer- sity of Thessaloniki (now the Faculty of Arts). Designed by Italian architect Vitaliano Poselli, it was built on the site of the demolished eastern wall in 1886 to house the Idadie Turkish High School, and later the 2nd Military Hospital.

of small fish restaurants and boat builders until the extension of the new waterfront boulevard. By the time the city was liberated in 1912, a neighbourhood of an entirely new type had grown up, encompassing the area from the White Tower to the Depot (the tram sheds) and from the waterfront to the streets today called Vasileos Georgiou and Vasilissis Olgas. Nestled in carefully tended gardens, these mansions, intended for the summer use of the wealthy, quickly became permanent residences once the horse-drawn tram line was installed.

After a fire in 1890 destroyed the whole centre of Thessaloniki's Jewish quarter, the subsequent rebuilding followed, as was natural, the classical models of that age. The neo-classical style Govern-ment House was built in 1891. The same period also saw the construction of two new hospitals, the Municipal Hospital, which stood in a pine grove and whose its fantastic fountains, reminiscent of the work of Spanish architect Antoi Gaudi (1852-1926), still exist, and the Hippokrateion Hospital, the old main building of the University, the barracks, the 3rd Army Headquarters, several Ottoman houses along Hamidie Avenue (now called Odos Vasilissis Sophias or Eth-nikis Amynis), and many other buildings for the Greek community, which, for several reasons, always displayed a marked preference for the neo-classical style, which was of course the traditional national architecture of Greece.

There was, however, another movement which influenced the architecture of these new mansions,

particularly in the area under discussion, and this was the architectural style known as Art Nouveau, which came to express the period from the turn of the century until the First World War. The essential characteristic of the new "Belle Epoque" style was the attempt to legitimate the dynamic curve, a concept completely removed from the grammar of historical architectural order and in absolute opposition to the syntax of neo-classicism. The new style was influenced by vague floral impressions, entirely cerebral, with no attempt at realistic rendition of form. The prevailing mood is purely decorative. The unfurling and the contraction of curved lines, and their opposition to certain straight ones, constitute the principal charac-teristics of this new style which marked some of the most interesting buildings in the part of Thessaloniki which extended from the eastern wall to the Depot.

Art Nouveau was the expression of that carefree period known as the Belle Epoque, the period which ended with the outbreak of the First World War. This architectural movement, however, which in the end vanished without leaving a significant mark on the history of architecture, did have a more profound intention, and that was the rapprochement of Ar-chitecture with the other Arts. This is what is behind the unceasing striving to use materials in a purely decorative (one is tempted to say two-dimensional) manner; a good example of this is the Villa Adhosidhi, known as the Old Kivernio (Governor's Mansion) and now housing the Macedonian Folklore and Ethnologi-cal Museum, with its use of coloured glass in the

The Villa Mordoch in Thessaloniki. Designed c.1905 by Paionidis for Turkish commander Seifoulah Pasha. Today it houses Municipal Offices.

Silver snuff box (Folk museum of the Aristotelian University of Thessaloniki)

windows, enamel, pottery, wooden appliques, carved stone, cast iron brackets for the balconies, wrought iron grilles, and several other materials. The variety of shapes in windows and doors, the impression of grace and lightness of Thessaloniki's suburban mansions, often achieved by the use of the cheapest of materials, is particularly marked in their architectural aspect. Here there is no attempt at serious Style, but on the contrary a desire to create affable and charming buildings expressive of (and in this they are perfectly successful) the optimism of a class of citizens who had climbed to a higher economic and social level...

It was, of course, impossible that all the mansions in this area should conform to one single architectural style, for the simple reason that the district where they were built was a battleground of conflicting interests and ideologies: they were the fruit of an era which was seeking to express itself.

Some of the most noteworthy mansions of this area were those belonging to the Hatzilazarou family, to the Abbott, Rongotis, Kapantzis and Harisis families, and the Fernandez "Casa Bianca" and the Depot, these last two being the work of Levantine architect Pietro Arrigoni..."

3.3. Settlements

3.3.1. Settlement and community

The structure of Macedonian settlements

The settlements of the Macedonian region, regardless of their mythological or historical founding and independent of their evolution, display certain struc-tural characteristics which evince their "neighbour-hood" nature, in terms of oral tradition. The social relationships recorded in the ways in which the territory was organized in Macedonian settlements were associated with daily life, and were direct (i.e. "oral") relationships, relationships affecting all members of the community, and finally, relationships which had specific social significance within the limits of each specific community.

From this aspect we can distinguish between two types of settlement which are radically different in the nature of their social life. On the one hand there are all those settlements whose functional existence was defined and limited, both in extent and in character, by factors which were not part of the social life of the inhabitants of the settlement in question. For example, the chiflik farms never acquired the character of a community, even when they boasted a considerable number of houses inhabited by farm labourers: the physical organization of these settlements did not favour - in some cases did not even permit - any social life among their inhabitants. There was nowhere for the people to congregate: no church, no square, no coffee shop, no shops, no fair or market or festival; the centre of their universe was the manor house, and their lives were divided between their long exhausting hours in the fields and the humble walls of the houses which provided shelter, permanent or temporary, for their families. In Northwestern and Western Macedonia there were a large number of settlements of this type, where the overwhelming economic functions of the people limited in the extreme their social functions. The structures of these settlements were generally fixed and unchanging, while the attention of their human population was constantly turned outwards, even when leaving was impossible or actually prohibited: in search of a better house, better living and working conditions, in search of a basic social life.

The chiflik villages of the tenant farmers and share croppers constitute a significantly different version of this type of common settlement. In these villages, especially in the 19th century and often on the initiative of the landowner, certain fundamental changes occurred. For example, a church would be built, or an old chapel restored; around the manor house gathering places wouldbe built, shops appear, or ceremonies, festivals and customs in which all took part would be reinstated.

The second type of settlement were those which invested their future in their social life: hamlets, villages, towns and cities. The observations which follow regard this second type of settlement, and attempt to trace certain points relating to the anthropological character of social life.[59]

Continuity in settled areas[60]

Although the name of each settlement to some extent indicated its morphological or historical relationship with the land, its actual location, that is, the specific place it occupied, was reinforced by traditions which dwell on its native identity. In many places, for example, there is a tradition that, when the village was founded on its particular site, in order to give it a solid foundation and protect it from illness and disaster, the first inhabitants ploughed all around the site or encircled it with shrines. In Megalochori (Serres), for example, local tradition says that when the village was founded, in order to protect it from all harm, "they took two twin first-born children, two twin calves and two ploughs from the same smith; they yoked them up and ploughed all around the village..."[61] Similar traditions relating to the founding of villages are found in other areas as well. For example, in the village Promachi (formerly Blachovo) in the Almopia district (Pella), the people recount that "when people from Gramali came here and settled in the village, they yoked up twin oxen and ploughed all around the village, and declared that from that day forward nothing could move the village from its site. And that is just what happened. Our village is still in the same place. Tradition says that because the village was ploughed, no one who leaves the village will succeed in life, wherever he may go. This is still believed today, and that is why no one from our village ever leaves".[62]. An interesting variant on this tradition is the story of the founding of Naoussa by Gazis Evrenos, "to whom the Sultan granted, in fulfilment of his request, as much land as could be covered by a buffalo hide on which to found a city which would belong to the Queen Mother. The general cut the hide of a beast into a long thin strip, and with it enclosed the site where the city was to be built. Another version says that he erected four poles of plane wood at four points and stretched the strip of hide around them. These poles took root, and eventually grew into the towering trees which until recently marked the four points of the compass at the edges of the city."[63]

The boundaries of a settlement were marked by two concentric circles: (a) the oria, or landmarks (that

Landmark marking the boundary between Epirus and Macedonia. (E.Papadimitriou, Old Photographs, Epirus-Macedonia, 1977, p. 7)

is, the iconostasia: miniature rural shrines with an icon and a votive lamp; or iera stavrata: sacred landmarks bearing a cross; or vakoufia: pious foundations), the chapels, threshing floors, fields and vineyards, woods and mills (water and wind mills, mantania or dristeles or nerotrives "wool washing machines" marked the outer circle, the outer perimeter which visibly enclosed the village within its boundaries. The walls of the cities with their gates, like the tangible thread that bound the vakoufia as they stood at the points of the compass or on the roads or at the crossroads leading to the village, both separated and protected the settlement from its neighbours and from the outside world in general, dangerous because unfamiliar, unknown. Near the village landmarks and at frequently travelled crossroads were the inns and open air coffee shops which served travellers and passers-by. (b) The second circle was that marking the built-up and inhabited area of the village. On the edges were the smithies, the tanneries and any mills that were not in the outer circle. In the centre were the public areas: the village square, the church, shops and workshops, coffee shops, the fountain. Larger settlements were subdivided into neighbourhoods, each with its own centre and its own outer limits to separate it from neighbouring quarters.

The landmarks (of all kinds) were reaffirmed at regular intervals, or whenever necessity imposed. For example, on the feast day of the master of the household, the whole house celebrated; on the feast day of the saint to whom a church was dedicated, the whole parish celebrated; on the feast day of the patron saint of a city, the whole city celebrated. Another form of affirmation of landmarks were the various festivals or ceremonies or gatherings in which the whole village or parish participated: for example, rougatsaria (or mummers, a Twelfth Night ritualistic parade in which groups of young men and boys go from house to house around the community asking for money, roga), kalanda (carol-singing), fani (Twelfth Night or carnival ritual fires), carnival pageants and fancy dress parades, St John's Day bonfires, klidonas (a St John's Day custom of telling fortunes; young girls tie their trinkts into a jug, leave it out overnight, and next evening they guess their future as to their marriage), kounies, weddings, funerals, memorial services, pronouncing of blessings, banquets, dances and games, harvesting and other agricultural labour, vigils, laundering, discussion and gossip, work and play. The regular blessing of the landmarks assured the renewal of their force. Litanies, processions carrying sacred images or the Epitaphion (an embroidered cloth representing Christ in the tomb which is carried around the village or parish on Good Friday), the stavroma ton dendron (a ceremony of protection during which the priest sanctifies carefully chosen trees around the village so as to mark the sign of the cross enclosing the settlement and exorcising dangers), the lighting of candles or votive lamps in the shrines, blessings, perizosimo (a ritual encircling of a house, church or settlement), and various other practices of a religious (or magical) nature renewed and reinforced the potency of the landmarks. For example, the local tobacco growers who live in Neo Souli (formerly Soubaskioi), one of the Darnakhochoria (a group of settlements in the area of Serres), make a long procession on the feast of St George after church. The procession sets out from the chapel of St George in the cemetery outside the village, and proceeds in a circle around all the outer landmarks; at the four cardinal points of the compass the procession stops, and the priest says a prayer and "ypsoni" ("elevates"), that is, he places bits of the consecrated bread in a hole in the trunk of the tree marking that place. According to tradition "the object of this circular procession, in the minds of the faithful, is to pray for a good harvest and for protection against all evils, especially hailstones [...] The procession of icons for this same purpose, that is, to ward off specific dangers in the district of Serres, is usually carried out during the week following Easter, and especially on the Thursday, as for example in the villages of Ano and Kato Orini, where a bull or a sheep is also sacrificed in a public ceremony"[64]. In Western Macedonia, in the village of Aghios Georgios (formerly Tsourkhli), in

the Grevena district, the villagers relate how "shrines were placed all around the village, and thenceforth illness never visited the village again [...] Our village is encompassed all around by the Saints".[65]

The periodical or circumstantial or permanent (re)statement of the settlement's boundaries aims not only at the strengthening of the landmarks, but at the reaffirmation of the identity of the settlement on the land. It is characteristic that in certain areas it is customary to draw a plough around the village in order to ward off epidemic disease. For example, in the village of Palaikomi (district of Serres), "according to tradition [...] when plague threatened the village they would dig a trench all around the village with twin calves"[66] This type of encirclement, which renews the strength of the village landmarks, both records the site of the village on the land, and reinforces its continuity in time.

The same function of identification and continuity in time and space is also achieved by the centre of the village (or neighbourhood). In Christian communities, the church (or the mosque, in Moslem areas), the square, and public facilities such as fountains, wells and shopping areas are a material and symbolic continuation of the houses of the families that make up the community (or parish, neighbourhood, quarter, etc). It is characteristic, for example, that a community celebrates every year the feast day of the church (or chapel, or shrine) around which it grew up (or thinks it grew up). Often there will also be a tradition justifying the construction of the church on that particular spot: for example, that the saint led their ancestors to that place, or protected them from some danger, or that a miraculous icon was found there or water gushed forth from that place. Even in cases where the church in question is located outside the boundaries of the village (in the cemetery, for instance), and is not the physical centre of the settlement, it is still the spiritual centre of the community.

Separate neighbourhoods (quarters, districts) usually correspond to the local parishes. In a settlement with a mixed population there are usually two or more quarters, each with its church or mosque, inhabited by those of the analogous nationalities or faiths. These quarters were often directly or indirectly named after those who lived in them, as for example Kassaba and Varossi in Grevena, or names like Gyphtomakhalas or Tsingomakhalas (Gypsy-quarter), Frangomakhalas (European quarter), Ipirotika (Epirotes' quarter), Agraphiotika (the quarter of those from the Agrapha mountains in Thessaly),

The central market in Serres (the Orta Tsarsi, with the Bezesteni in the background). (V.Tsanakaris, Picture history of Serres, 1991, p.33)

The "Bezesteni" in Thessaloniki.

Tourkomakhalas (Turkish quarter), etc, which are found in many places; or the Metsovit makhalesi and the Skamnelit makhalesi in Moschopolis, named for settlers from Metsovo and Skamneli, while the Arnaout makhalesi was the Albanian quarter.[67] In large settlements, and especially in the cities, the various neighbourhoods are usually named for the parish church or local mosque, or for an activity identified with that district, such as for example "t'Albanaria" (farriers' quarter), "ta Tabakaria" (tanneries), "t'-Argastroudhia" or "ta Magazia" (workshops), "to Khani" (the inn), "i Agora" (the market-place), "to Pazari" (the bazaar), etc. Neighbourhoods may also be known by the name of a prominent local family, like "Gkitsadika", in Kolindros, called after a well-known local family, the Gkitsadhes.[68] Neighbourhood names in Thessaloniki reflect the primordial role of the churches in the topological organization of the city.[69] In smaller places the principal church and the area immediately around it served not only for purposes of worship but as a central location for many other social and economic functions, e.g. weddings, ceremonies, religious and commercial fairs, markets, signing of contracts, community events, and many other such activities; while elsewhere certain social events might be held in other suitable locations, such

Provincial Turkish manor house: the "konaki" with its strong walls and towers, on the Bardovtse chiflik. (L.Schultze-Jena, Makedonien..., plate LXV).

as recreation centres, coffee shops, promenades, fair grounds, dance halls etc.

In central communities and in the cities, however, each sector of the economy had its own quarter where most of its practitioners were located: for example, ta Tabakika (the tanneries), ta Khalkeia (the copper-smiths'), i kapnapothikes (the tobacco warehouses), o Mikhanes (lit. the engine, i.e. the factory)[70], o Kir-hanas (the dye-works)[71] Mili (the mills), to Ydragogeio (the aqueduct), i Vrisi (the water-tap), to Sintrivani (the fountain), i Skala (the wharf), i Bakhtsedhes (the Market-gardens), and of course, the primary site for economic transactions, i Agora (the market-place) also called to Pazari (the bazaar), to Tsarsi (the market-hall), or to Bezesteni (covered market).[72]. The market usually occupied a central location in the settlement. In large places it occupies permanent installations arranged according to various sub-divisions, such as craftsmen's workshops, warehouses, oil-dealers, the fish market, butchers' shops, etc. The market was not only the centre of its own community, but also the centre of a much wider surrounding area. The markets in central towns and

cities, the bazaars held on given days of the week, and the great annual commercial fair permitted a large number of merchants, pedlars, producers, artisans, craftsmen and, of course, buyers to conduct transactions on a more or less regular basis, while merchandise moved in a dense network of local markets. For example, the market at Moschopolis: "The city market with its large treed square, its many handsome fountains, the shops and workshops all around and particularly its lively movement gave the impression of a market in a large European city. Commercial fairs were held there several times a year, and people came to shop from towns and villages from neighbouring districts of Macedonia and Epirus, as well as nomadic tent-dwellers and Vlach herdsmen from mountain regions [...] In time Moschopolis became the centre of all commercial activity in Epirus and cast even Giannina into the shade".[73] "Moschopolis was a hive of commercial activity. people came from many places to buy goods. From Delvino and Droviani they came two or three times a year to buy local merchandise, including the kind of flokates (shaggy rugs) still known as "Moschopolis flokates" and which are referred to in the wedding song which tells the bride:"...and I brought the groom's Moschopolian flokata".[74]

3.3.2. Typical kinds of settlements

(a) The chiflik village

In the chiflik village "...the tenant farmer was as a general rule employed to cultivate a single crop, usually cereals; he also had the right to raise a few animals, both large and small, for himself, without being obliged to share the revenue from these beasts with his landlord. In the low mud huts provided by the landlord, almost underground , wretched and filthy, they nevertheless managed to garner enough for a biologically sufficient if not a varied diet, able, in conjunction with their physical labour, to maintain them in health and vigour, insofar as the climactic conditions, especially in marshy districts, permitted [...] The settlements of the kolligi were composed of low mud huts clustered around the landowner's two-storey house, huddled on lower ground so as to be under the landlord's eye; they were wretched communities, with no private courtyards, no horizon, no room to breathe [...] There was no market-place, and the sullen villagers met only in the churchyard; even the tiny village shop belonged to the landlord or to one of his men..."[75]

Example: The farm (the chiflik settlements Palikoura and Bardovtse in Northwest Macedonia)[76]

The houses of the peasants (serfs, tenant farmers) were provided by the landowner (bey, aga, chiflik owner), and were usually situated near the fields. In construction they were hastily-built, shoddy and insanitary: reeds or brushwood woven together formed a conical or square hut with a ridged roof. Sometimes they were raised on stilts for protection from animals, water and mud. Some were built of drystone and tsatma (a wooden frame filled in with bits of stone, tile, etc). They were usually single-roomed dwellings, with or without a stable; they were built in a tight circle or around three sides of a square, each touching the next, and facing inwards so that their backs formed a sort of protective wall. There were no public areas. The natural "square" formed by this arrangement was an open common for the use of man and beast. The barns were located in another area altogether, towards the edge of the property, and were more solidly built than the peasants' huts, in order to protect the crops

from any form of danger (from the peasants, from thieves, from bad weather). The landowner's or overseer's house also stood somewhat apart. Usually built on a hill, it would be a stout, well-built, two-storey tower of a house, sometimes richly enough furnished to be reminiscent of a Turkish city mansion. These houses often served the gentry as summer residences. Others were more warlike in appearance, with strong high walls, loop-holes and angular towers, gates and guards, just like a fortress. There were many such chifliks and konakia in Western Macedonia.

Example: The chiflik villages of the tenant farmers of the Roumlouki[77]

According to a description given by N.Th. Schinas (1881-1886)[78], there were in this region several settlements (40 or 50 villages) inhabited principally by Christian Greek (with very few Turkish or Bulgarian) farmers, which were thus known as Ouroumlouki or Roumlouki (lit., the land of the Rumi, i.e. Romii, Greeks) or Grekochoria (Greek villages). These communities were small chiflik villages belonging to powerful landowners (Turkish beys), which contained as a rule from 10 to 80 peasant families, with the exception of the central village of Gida (today called Alexandria), with 130 families, a church and a boys' school.

"All the villages of this Ouroumlouki, lacking watermills, have their grain ground in the villages Voudistra and Obar, which lie to the north of the lake of Loudias (lake of Genitsa), for every attempt to build a watermill in the village of Niselouda has proved fruitless, on account of the flooding of the river Aliakmon; they also have horse-powered mills, or they go to the mills of the villages between Vodena (Edessa) and Genitsa...

"With the exception of three villages (Kolakia, Valmada and Giantsida) as well as the Ottoman village of Mustaphac, all the rest are chiflik villages with few resident Greek families [...] The inhabitants of these villages are very hard-working, and very abstemious in their diet, taking neither wine nor meat [...] [Most are farmers] but many, including those of Kolakia and Karya, are fishermen (yuvarites) [...] and well-acquainted with the rivers and the entire coastline..."

According to A. Hatzimihali (1931)[79]: "Scattered over the plain of Thessaloniki beyond the Loudias River (Kara Asmak), with the lake of Giannitsa to the north, the mountains of Veria to the east and the foothills of the Pieria mountain range (Flambouro) to the south, some 50 or so villages large and small (49 are named) constitute the Roumlouki or Ouroumlouki, which is cut in two by the Aliakmon. This name was applied to it by the Turks, and means "place of the Greeks" (from rum, meaning Greek, and luk, a possessive suffix). Almost all these villages lie on the lowlands, and are well-watered by the Aliakmon. During the years of Turkish occupation even the largest of them (Gida, Korphi, Meliki) were chifliks belonging to wealthy landowners. Although these landowners were for the most part Turks, the population of these villages was always and exclusively Greek: no Turk ever settled in the Roumlouki.

The inhabitants of these villages are farmers, ploughmen and herdsmen; a very few practise small crafts. They are all hard-working farmers who cultivate the fertile and productive land, which is why their livlihood is abundant. They live simply, however, and have virtually no communication with other villages. This is the life they have been used to since the days when they were koligi, with no property of their own, the land they worked belonging to the aga. The land being rich, their animals (horses, sheep, buffalos and curly-horned cattle) [...] are well-fed. Their roosters are of a special breed, tall and plump, with white feathers and a loud, long-drawn-out crow.

The people of the Roumlouki rarely go to Thessaloniki. Their trading is done once a week in Veria, which is the capital of the district..."

Example: Farms belonging to religious communities in Chalcidice (chorio metochi): Athytos

According to N.Th. Schinas, in 1887[80] "the village of Atheton (today called Athytos) was inhabited by 120 Christian families, and had a church, windmills, watermills and boats..."

Adolf Struck wrote in 1903 that "at the beginning of the century [Athytos had] 120 houses, and its inhabitants [were] dependents of the religious community of Aghios Pavlos..."[81]

A study by N. Moutsopoulos (1976)[82] reports that in Athytos "the village church, Aghios Dimitrios, was built in 1857, according to an inscription in the sanctuary. Of the houses recorded and those which bear an inscription, the oldest was built in 1864. It is a two storey building, with a long facade, with a wooden varanda and an outside stone stairway. The other buildings are registered in the years 1876, 1889, 1891, 1898. The church on the waterfront dates from 1885. There used to be a dye-works in the village (1884), which served the whole region: it is still

standing. There was also a pottery which produced lovely terra cotta jugs. Now there are three or four potters who have abandoned their craft for farming [...] The village is divided into different neighbourhoods, each one inhabited by a single family [...] The older families are almost all farmers, with a few who raise livestock. Many years ago they raised silkworms; they roasted the cocoons andsent them to Thessaloniki. There were certain women in the village who produced silk thread by boiling the cocoons in cauldrons; the silk they produced was used by the women for their dowries [...] The region is rich in limestone, which masons from Albania and Skopelos used to build the older houses..."

(b) Head villages and "free" settlements

Example: The Mademochoria (mining villages), the Hasikochoria (choice villages), and the marsh villages of Chalcidice

The Mademochoria

A.E. Vakalopoulos says[83]: "According to descriptions furnished by the English traveller Urquhart (1839), by the third quarter of the 18th century the villages around the silver mines of Sidirokapsa (the Byzantine Sidirokausia) had already formed a federation known as the Mademochoria, with its capital at Liarigovi (Arnea), for the purpose of exploiting the silver mines. 1775 saw the creation of a federation unique in the history of the Greek community, an association of villages inhabited by miners and other labourers [...] According to Urquhart, it included 12 large villages and 360 smaller ones [...] the second number is perhaps somewhat doubtful [...] This cooperative was recognized and confirmed by edict [...] The inhabitants of these villages were under the jurisdiction of the madem emin, that is, the manager of the mines, who held the reins of civil and police power, but was not entitled to intervene in the internal administration of the federation [...] Those who worked in the mines were exempt from all other taxes [...] Each village in the mining federation had its own separate communal administration; but each chief village elected a representative who together with his colleagues from the other principal villages formed the twelve member governing committee of the federation [...] According to French traveller Cousinery's description of Liarigovi (early 19th century), this central community had approximately 400 houses [...] and furnished 100 miners a year [...] Their wages were so low that the other communities levied subscriptions to relieve their families. The mines manager kept close watch over the extraction of the ore and the payment of the daily wage, and he seems to have oppressed the miners to such an extent that they were only with difficulty able to feed their families [...] This means that the Greeks were not entirely free, as Urquhart insisted [...] The twelve principal towns of the Mademochoria in the mid 19th century were: Galatista, Vavdos, Ravna, Stanos, Varvara, Liarigovi, Novoselo, Mahalas, Isvoros, Horouda, Revinikia and Ierissos. The capital of the community was Mahalas..."

According to N.Th. Schinas (1887)[84]: "The section of the Mademochoria on the peninsula of Chalcidice [consists of] nine villages, instead of twelve as was the case in the past" (that is: Liarigovo (Armaia), Erissos (Ierissos), Varvara, Gomati, Mahalas, Novoselo, Revenikia, Paliochori and Horouda). "North of the village of Mahalas lie the ruins of the village of Horouda [...] The road thence, after traversing a small wood, passes by the lonely tower and manor house of the said Madem aga on the right..." (page 518) About the two largest villages he says "...Liarigova has 400 families, living in 227 fine houses, some of which are two-storied; it has a church, two bake-houses, 40 shops, 10 inns [...] and six water taps with abundant water. The people are friendly, and by profession are chiefly mule drivers and beekeepers; a few are merchants, and the women weave beautiful woollen carpets. A market is held every Saturday..." (pp 517-518) and "...The town of Erissos [...] is inhabited by 275 families who live for the most part in poor, single storey dwellings. The people are mostly fishermen, and own about 200 fishing boats [...] some of the men grow fruit, cereals, cotton, sesame and legumes. The town has 20 businesses (of which 7 are coffee shops and 5 are shops), a wretched church, the foundations of a school, 4 ordinary smithies and 4 inns..." (page 521).

The Hasikochoria or Hasia

According to A.E. Vakalopoulos[85]: "...Northwest of the Mademochoria are the 15 "free villages", [...] situated on the "mild mountains", as they call the cultivated slopes of the region that extends to the Gulfs of Toronaios and Thermaikos [...] Each village has its own leaders [...] and councillors which it sends to Polygyros (a town of 600 families) to the seat of the Aga who has leased the revenues from the Porte [..] With the exception of the Turkish chifliks and the monasterial farms belonging to Mt Athos, all the rest of the land belongs to the Hasikochoria. This region has excellent pastureland, and fields which produce an abundance of wheat of the highest quality, cotton, honey, wax, etc. Silkworms are also raised here, especially in the two principal towns of Polygyros and Ormilia".

This is what Schinas has to say (1887) about Polygyros[86]: "...A river flows through the town, dividing it into two districts, one on each bank; the district on the far shore has few houses, but these are fine, country manors, and they are linked to the near bank by a wooden bridge. Above.them is the Siminaris water-mill [...] These houses now number 393, and house that same number of families; the number of families fell sharply during the Revolution of 1821 and that of 1854, at the time of Tsam Karatasos, when all the leading citizens of the town were slaughtered [...] It is the capital of the province, and the principal town of the "Hasika" district. The governing class and the kaimakaki live there; it is also the seat of the bishop of Kassandreia. In the middle of the city is its only church, which is dedicated to Saint Nicholas and has a number of icons of rare artistic value. In front of the church is a straight paved road which also serves as a market-place; it has 25 businesses along its length, both grocers' and other shops, and 10 inns [...] there are also a similar number of farriers and a private oven. The city has a good and complete school system [...] with a total of some 300 students. The citizens of Polygyros are Christian Greeks; they are industrious and restrained, but hospitable too, and they devote themselves to their fields, bee-hives and vineyards; those who have mulberry orchards raise silkworms, and there are also olive groves. These providing sufficient revenue, the people do not engage in more extensive trade, although many of them are both wealthy and enterprising. The community is presided over by an alderman and the ikhtiar mizlisi [...] The women [...] work at weaving and oil-pressing; with the exception of shoes, all the rest of their trousseau, together with furniture and utensils, they make themselves [...] Besides the water-mill which is in the city, and 7 others in the surrounding area, there is also a windmill, which, though, is rarely needed; there are also a suficient number of oil-mills and 5 permanent oil-presses..."

The 12 Valta villages

A.E. Vakalopoulos says[87]: "There is a small group of villages in the Kassandra peninsula centred on

Valta, which is the seat of a Turkish voevodhas (administrator). Of these the principal ones are Athytos, Valta, Phourka, Kalandra ana Aghia Paraskevi. The people there cultivate the same products as they do in the Hasikochoria, but they also have lots of small boats and dories. At the beginning of the 19th century [...] 700 families lived in Kassandra, of whom 600 were smallholders and the remaining 100 were tenants of monasterial farms belonging to Mt Athos. They had 500 ox-drawn ploughs and 700 head of oxen, besides cows, horses, and flocks of sheep and goats numbering 20-30,000 beasts; all this wealth was distributed equitably among the people..."

Schinas wrote (1887) of Valta[88]: "...a village of 150 Christian families, 2 churches, 2 inns, 5 grocery and coffee shops, and in the centre of the village a magnificent plane tree with a fountain under it."(Re Athytos, see above)

Example: Island and seashore settlements. The villages on the island of Thasos

Thasos in the 18th and 19th centuries (according to travellers' descriptions quoted by A.E. Vakalopoulos[89]: "...the island (was a fief of Kapoudhan Pasha, and it paid him an annual revenue of 30 pounds, more that is than any other island in the Cyclades or Sporades), until as late as the beginning of the 18th century had 7-8,000 inhabitants in 12 or 15 villages (some of them coastal), considerable revenue and a certain amount of trade, according to French priest Braconnier who visited the island in 1707 [...] The island produced [wine, oil, wax, considerable quantities of wood, and cochineal for dye]... Fear of pirates had gradually driven the inhabitants from the coast to the interior of the island. There, in isolated places with lush vegetation, or behind inaccessible and precipitous rocks they built their villages. This was Thasos until as recently as the mid 19th century [...] The two villages farthest away from the coast were also the biggest during the years of Turkish occupation; these were Theologos, or Tholos, as the Turks called it, which was the capital of the island until the early 19th century, and Panaghia. Theologos had (and still has) the most land. The site where the village is today was probably settled by refugees from Constantinople after it fell to the Turks, as well as people from the villages in the northeastern part of the island who fled to the interior.

Panaghia seems also to have been built in fairly recent times. Oral tradition says that it was founded 300 years ago on its more remote location; and indeed,

the oldest houses, or rather the oldest quarter, was built 300 years ago on the slope of Mount Pyrgi which faces inland and is hidden from the sea. The seaward slope was settled much later, probably in the 19th century, and is still called Kolitzidhes, after the officials of the customs station there, who watched the sea for approaching ships. Many of the inhabitants of Panaghia must have come from the port of Limena, which emptied rapidly during the 18th century. Fear of pirates drove the people to the hills, coming down to their fields only to cut the hay, gather the olives, sow the wheat and other summer crops, and to harvest. At sunset they would return to their hill villages for the night [...] These communities maintained watchtowers (viglaria) on the coast, manned by paid watchmen [...] who sounded the alarm in time of danger [...] This irregular situation lasted until the middle of the 19th century... Towards the end of the 18th century the islanders, who according to the French consul in Thessaloniki, Cousinery, numbered no more than 2,500, lived in 7 villages built in isolated places [...]The governor of the island was a voevode, who was replaced every year and who had a suite of 7 or 8 men [...] The people of Thasos were free to cut timber and to export sizeable quantities of firewood. The income was deposited in the community treasury and constituted a fund for the payment of taxes..."

N.Th. Schinas described the site (1887)[90]: "On the northeastern tip of the island [...] is a small man-made harbour, o ormos tis Panaghias (Mary's bay); the governor's mansion is on the western shore, and since the eradication of piracy the governor spends a short time there each year. The settlement lies between the ancient port [...] and the ancient wall; this ancient city of Thasos was once inhabited by 20-30,000 people [...] The village of Panaghia lies on a pine-clad hillside, invisible from the sea, and is traversed by a river of the same name. It has 1,900 inhabitants [...] and has some 50 shops and coffee houses, 2 churches, a school and many springs, of which the best is that which rises near the roots of the plane tree..."

The village of Theologos is in a ravine [...] hidden from the sea, it lies in a dense forest of walnut, mulberry, plum, peach and other trees. Its houses, although they have two stories (the ground floor serving as a stable), are roofed with the branches of trees; they extend along the right bank of the river of Aghia Vasiliki which runs to the south of the village [...] Its 2,225 inhabitants are hard- working people, whose principal food is corn meal mixed with rye; they live in two adjacent neighbourhoods, each one constitut-

The market in Samarina. A.Wace-M.Thompson, op.cit., 1914, plate VI (The Nomads of the Balkans, Greek translation 1989, p.310).

ing a separate community: the one is known as Upper Theologos, whose inhabitants worship in the church of Aghia Paraskevi, the other as Lower Theologos, where they worship in the church of Aghios Dimitrios. There are three more churches within the town itself, and others in the surrounding district; there are also two schools, 18 shops of different kinds and 2 ovens for baking bread. The water supply comes from springs [...] On the far bank of the river are the ruins of a stone tower around which a century and more ago, when it was the seat of the governor of the village, there was a Turkish quarter of which all trace has now disappeared, since ... no Turk has lived on the island for many years...From its vineyards on Astris bay the village produces the finest red wine, which costs 45 lepta an oka; it also exports oil, honey, wax, tar, pitch, pine bark, pine-wood, firewood, and wood for ship-building; it grazes large flocks of goats, oxen and cattle, and keeps bees; it also produces for domestic consumption peaches, plums, apricots, pomegranates, etc..."

The mountain village: the Vlach village of Samarina, on Pindos[91]

"Seen from afar, the village does not look like a continuous mass of houses, but rather like a chain of more or less separate groups of houses scattered over a gentle slope. This impression is reinforced by the fact that almost every house has its own garden. Although the lower town, the part around the market, is more homogeneous, the rest of the settlement is broken by empty spaces where there are neither houses nor gardens [...] One peculiar aspect is the fact that the village's four churches are all on the outskirts. This may be a result of the old Turkish edict that no churches were to be built within the villages [...] Lower down the valley there are various kinds of mills, both flour mills for grinding grain, and mantania for pounding the woollen material they make in the village [...] Samarina has some 15 canals in the various neighbourhoods, and so the people do not have far to go for water [...] At the main entrance to the village there is a stream with a wooden bridge; before the bridge there are two shops, a smithy and a cutler's. After the bridge, on the left, are two tailors' shops [...] then several general stores, where they sell lead shot, cottons, aniline dye, mirrors, silks and soap. The road narrows after that, and we reach the middle of the village, known as to Hani (the inn). This is where the market-place is, and the village square. It forms a rough triangle, 95 metres long, and is paved with cobblestones. In the middle are a large willow and a small cherry tree. Around these trees there is a low stone wall on which the muleteers expose the goods they bring back from their travels: from Sorovits (Amyntaion), lamp oil; olives from Volos or Avlona; red wine fron Siatista; vegetables (such as onions, peppers, eggplant and beans) from Tsotyli; fruit from the villages on the foothills of Pindus, wheat from Kozani and Monastir [...] The central coffee shops and grocers' are found in Hani, as well as the old inn [...] As the centre of the village, Hani is of course the place where all roads (from Grevena and Giannina) meet..."

Example: the mountain town (Lakkovikia, on Pangaion)[92].

"In a small, shallow declivity on Mt Pangaion, a valley rather than a ravine, just where it begins to descend towards the Strymon River and the Gulf, in a lonely spot among a tumble of small, bare hills, [...] lies our town of Lakkovikia [...] To the northwest of the town, on a height of land, is the windmill, which was built by the villagers many years ago, and later purchased and repaired by two brothers from the Hatzopoulos family of Kymi, on the island of Euboia. This windmill, now in perfect working order, is of immense benefit to the villagers who, without even a water-mill, had formerly been obliged to go down to the water-mills near Orphanos or below Provista (a tobacco-growing village on a marshy site low among the foothills on) to grind their grain [...] Encircled on all sides by hills, some high, some lower, the town does not lack splendid, romantic and enchanting views [...] it has, spread out before it like a brilliant green carpet, the entire broad plain of Draviskos, Serres, Demir-Issar and Nigrita which lies between the mountains Pangaion, Menikio, Veles, Kourtsa and the lower range of Nigrita [...] it also overlooks the city of Serres, whose windows reflect the early rays of the rising sun, setting the city alight with the glitter of gold. From that height one can see a number of

villages, large and small [...] On account of its location only a few fruit or other trees ornament the town itself, namely willows, poplars, oaks, plum, apricot, apple, fig, pomegranate, peach, quince, pear, walnut, almond, mulberry, plane, elm, etc; there are also several plants and bushes with local names. But even beyond the town we do not find the abundance of woods and trees typical of all the villages on the northeastern and southern slopes of the mountain [...] Because the soil of the town is bare, rocky, and extremely uneven and abrupt, and the arable land nearby is not sufficient for all, the farmers are obliged to walk for two hours every day to the place where they have their fields [...] Not very long ago, as the old men relate, all the hills around the town, indeed the whole region, was green and dotted with woods and vineyards [...] The town brings its drinking water from a considerable distance, by earthenware ducts across the hills of Pangaion; these feed five taps in the town. In time of drought, however, there is no longer enough water to reach the town, which must then fall back on the two wells with which it is blessed...

The whole town musters some 400 houses and more than 2,028 inhabitants, of whom 1012 are men and 1016 women; it is the third largest town on Pangaion. Its houses are built of stone and are set very close one to another; the streets are narrow and uneven. The town has been divided from the beginning into three districts [...] Apart from the original inhabitants, there are many immigrant families of Greek- speaking Vlachs and Albanians who moved to the town from Epirus, Thessaly and Albania early in this (19th) century, and who enjoy virtually the same rights as the natives...

The little church of Aghios Athanasios lies just to the west of the town, and was there of old; it was rebuilt in 1843 [...] the chapel of Profitis Ilias (the Prophet Elijah) lies outside the town, to the north [...] it was built in 1866, and every year on July 20 a great festival is held there. In the middle of the town is the chapel of Aghii Theodori; according to the date on the altar, it was built in 1662...

Approximately three quarters of the townspeople are farmers, the remainder being merchants, grocers, tailors, shoemakers, smiths, saddlers, farriers, shepherds, weavers, dyers, etc. Besides their household duties, the farmwomen help in the fields, the others work at spinning and weaving, and other such occupations. Although the fields lie so far from the town, the soil is rich and very fertile. It produces the finest wheat, barley, maize, oats, rye, cotton in

Thessaloniki, view of the city looking towards the sea, early 20th c. (L.Schultze-Jena, Makedonien..., plate LXXXVIII)

abundance, excellent wine, legumes, sesame, aniseed, etc [...] The main crops are wheat, wine and cotton, which are o traded to neighbouring cities. Sericulture is virtually non-existent, for want of the proper trees for feeding the silkworms. Further, the lack of water means that vegetables cannot be grown, but fortunately these can be brought in from elsewhere [...] Every Sunday morning a small market is held..."

c) The city

During the final period of the Turkish occupation, there were in Macedonia a profusion of cities, towns and boroughs; there were also villages of varying sizes which displayed certain urban characteristics. In these settlements urban functions were transformed with astonishing rapidity. From one point of view, the cities in Macedonia conformed to the general type of the Balkan city: let us take a closer look at certain more or less particular aspects of the Macedonian city.

Thessaloniki (18th to early 20th century)

Most of the familiar sources of information on the history of modern Thessaloniki[93] are in agreement as to what gives it its character as a city: its historical continuity of form and feature, and the density and complexity of the relationships which hold it together as a city while at the same time engaging it in a wider network of relationships and procedures of change.

These characteristics are clearly and concisely outlined in this description taken from "Modern Geography" (1791)[94]: "Salonika, Thessaloniki, is now the metropolis of Macedonia; it is an ancient city, celebrated, extensive, populous, very beautiful, and a bustling centre of commerce, situated on the eastern shore of the head of the Thermaikos Gulf, with a fine harbour; part of the city lies on the flat land and part on the hills. It was founded by Cassander, Philip's son-in-law, and named for his wife, Thessaloniki; earlier this area had been known as Thermi [...] It is inhabited by Greeks, Turks and a large number of

Jews, most of whom came here when they were expelled from Spain. It has the honour to be the seat of a Metropolitan, who has a number of bishops under him and who lives within the fortress, as do all the Greeks, and who exercises his religious functions somewhat more freely here than in other places. The Christians have their churches, and the Jews their synagogues. There is also an Armenian community, and consuls from various places..."

The city had already crossed the threshold of modernity, in its own special fashion, early in the 18th century. Its size and grandeur recall (on a smaller scale, of course) that great centre of European civilization, Rome. Barskij, a Russian traveller of the first half of the 18th century, noted[95]: "The houses are all of stone, with tiled roofs; but their style is ugly and terribly out-moded. While there are some wealthy mansions, they are nothing like those in Italy. In Italy they have five stories and countless rooms, whereas here they are few in number and never have more than three stories. The fame of the city does not reside in its beauty or in its fortifications, but in its antiquity and its land and sea communications. People come to Thessaloniki from Constantinople, Egypt and Venice, by merchant vessel from England and overland from the continent. Germans, Vlachs, Bulgarians, Serbs, Dalmatians, people from every part of Macedonia and the Ukraine, wholesalers and pack merchants, they flock into the city bringing merchandise of every description. Every year ships arrive from France to load grain. The population includes Greeks, Turks, Jews and Frenchmen [...] The Jews of Thessaloniki are very wealthy, and all buying and selling, by barter or cash, passes through their hands. Except for the poor, they all wear long black robes, and a red cap as required by law. Their tongue is Spanish [...] Water flows fron fountains in the Turkish mansions and in the principal streets. The walls (of the houses) are wooden, plastered but unpainted, and the roads are paved, but unevenly..."

According to Jesuit missionary Souciet (1735)[96], the city "...is two leagues in circumference. Two thirds of its area are occupied by buildings, and the rest by gardens. The Turkish gentry have built their mansions on the higher ground. Most of the Greeks live at the foot of the encircling hills. The wealthier among them have magnificent houses built in the Turkish style. The Jews occupy about one third of the city; they live in the lower part, around the market and by the seaward walls. Most of them are so poor that they live in houses open to the four winds and without glass in the windows. Weakened by malnutrition and insalubrious housing, the Jewish population is decimated by every epidemic, including the plague [...] The streets in the lower part of the town are narrow, ill-paved and filthy. In the centre, where the market is, the streets are roofed over with planks, and are thus very dark. In the summer, however, they do remain cool. In that district there is a large solid building with seven domes, called the bezesteni; this is where the linen drapers have their shops, and the sellers of silks and muslins [...] The city has four or five inns, which are all large buildings with several wings and many rooms."

The description of French traveller Sanini in the same century strikes a similar note[97]: "Narrow, unpaved, crooked streets, wretched houses. The people live in the blackest despair. The city looks much better seen from afar [...] The wooden houses catch fire readily [there follows the description of a big fire]. In the harbour ships load large quantities of the products for which Macedonia is famous throughout the West: tobacco, excellent wools, silk, wax and honey. But the populace suffers from fevers. The marshlands between the city and the Vardar river (Axios) have become a source of contagion and epidemic disease which are massacring the population". Towards the end of the century, Pisani[98] completes this picture of an "oriental- European" city: "The Turkish buildings in the city are made of wood and painted red, with the lower level black. Beneath the eaves and at the corners gold letters spell out verses from the Koran. The houses have verandas or terraces, and courtyards with many cypress trees [...] Most streets have wooden roofs, which is very unhealthy, for the air cannot circulate beneath them...".

Felix de Beaujour[99] expresses a different opinion (1800): "This city, seen from the roads, resembles a half moon, or semi-circle, with its diameter along the waterfront [...] Thessaloniki faces south: the houses, built in tiers like an amphitheatre on the slopes of the hill, with cypress-filled gardens all around, present a pleasant scene from afar. But when one enters the city one is astonished to find nothing but narrow, crooked lanes, shoddily built houses, not one single square, not one paved crossroad. Thessaloniki may be one of the finest of Turkey's cities, but it looks more like one of our villages..."

The countryside began just outside the city: gardens, forests, fields, but mud and marsh as well.

Ενδυμασίε Θεσσαλονίκης
Ελλάς

Jews in Thessaloniki, from an old post card.

Within the city, especially in the poor quarters, the filth, the crowding, and the penury combined to create a sense of suffocation: muddy streets, open sewers, darkness and damp were an invitation to every kind of disease. Several streets, central ones for the most part, as well as the older channels, were paved with cobblestones.

At about this same time a chronicler who has become known merely as "Anonymous" penned these few lines describing the city[100]: "The ruins of two old forts by the sea and two more farther inland. A strong fortified wall runs all around the city. The houses are wooden, red-painted except for the area just under the roof, which is black. Most of the streets have wooden roofs to protect them from the heat, but which, however, also prevent the air from circulating freely. Some streets are full of pigeons, storks, sparrows, magpies and crows, as well as cats and dogs. No one dares harm these animals for fear that the Turks will punish him as a murderer. The shops are secured by a simple latch, for there are no thieves".

By the end of the 18th century the Turkish houses began to change, a process which continued throughout the 19th century: "The houses of the Donmeh (a sect of Muslim Jews in Salonika) are built differently [...] For the most part wealthy merchants, in some sort the flower of the Jewish community in Thessaloniki, they occupy a more developed, more commercial level. Their back yards are not used for growing vegetables, but only for flower gardens [...] Neo-classical influences on the decoration of many of their houses, [together with] the sage symmetry imposed by the traditional Balkan house, with its sakhnisia, its overhanging covered balconies; the corner posts and the roof beams are fluted, and the areas just under the roof and over the windows are decorated with plaster ornamentation in a supposedly classical style..."[101]

In the 18th and 19th centuries the Christian quarters were centred around the principal parish churches or other monuments. The best known of these districts were the Kamara (around the Arch of Galerius), and those around the churches Aghios Dimitrios, the Acheiropoiitou, and Nea Panaghia.

In the middle of the 19th century English traveller Mary Adelaide Walker was impressed by the size of the city's population. "The population of Thessaloniki," she wrote in 1860[102]., "which is a mosaic of nationalities and tongues as are most oriental cities, consists mainly of Turks, Jews and Greeks, as well as many people from adjacent countries: Albanians, Bulgarians, Vlachs, Ionians, mountain people from Pindus and islanders from the nearby archipelago, some Europeans (which means English, French, German and other "Franks"), and a sizable number of gypsies who are no longer nomadic but have settled in the part of the city designated for them; they are the recognized blacksmiths and tinkers [...] The Jews are the

The Villa Kazantzis (detail).

most important sector of the population. They control, with the exception of one extremely wealthy Anglo-Levantine family of merchants (she probably means the Abbot family), virtually all trade and industry in this the third commercial centre of the Empire. Their fortunes are vast, but despite this their outer appearance, as well as that of their houses, is poor and dirty, for they hope in this way to escape the greed of their voracious Turkish rulers [...] Their "aristocrats" occupy a higher place in society here than do their brothers in Constantinople; this is to a great extent owing to the elegance of their women [...] Walking down the streets, especially in the market area, one often encounters persons whose appearance is somewhat startling at first. They wear the long kaftan and white turban of the Moslems, but one glance at their faces leaves no room for doubt but that they are Jews. These are the Donmeh, or Mammin, followers of Shabbetai Tzevi [...] a peculiar sect. They never intermarry with either the Turks or the Jews, and of course certainly not with the Christians..."

Towards the end of the 19th century the mansions of the wealthy - whether Greek, Turk, Jew or "Frank" - began to occupy the area beyond the Tower[103]: "This is a region of manor houses and country villas, built by the wealthy merchants of Thessaloniki; it extends

from the White Tower to the Depot along the eastern shoreline and the road running parallel to it, which today is called Vasilissis Olgas and Vasileos Georghiou [...] Initially these mansions were built as country houses, but with the construction of the tram line they gradually became permanent residences. Between 1894 and 1912 nearly one hundred such mansions were built [...] 27 of which were Greek archontika..."

By the turn of the century Thessaloniki had a number of neighbourhoods which were not unlike some found in European cities: upper class districts with mansions and villas, and lower and middle class neighbourhoods with carefully tended two-storey houses set in gardens behind tall trees. Life in the city and the life of the city marched along together, interlaced, following a complex double rhythm: the beat of modernity, which regulates life according to the unforgiving pressure of time and money; and the rhythm of tradition, where the changing seasons are marked by the feast of Aghios Georgios in the spring and the feast of Aghios Dimitrios (patron saint of Thessaloniki) in the autumn, where the passing of the lamplighter marks nightfall and daybreak and the hours are announced by the pasvantis with his rod. A world where news is communicated by newspaper and town-crier, where gossip and the affairs of the day pass from house to house and from ear to ear.

This was Thessaloniki at the confines of history, the Thessaloniki of 1912, the city before the Great Fire of 1917. "...It is a city of contrasts" wrote French Byzantine scholar Charles Diehl[104], "the broad quays set off by European style buildings which developed all along the harbour, and the elegant villas to the east which form the district of Kalamaria, contrast sharply with the heart of the city, with its narrow ancient streets like the one which crosses the city from side to side along the line of the Via Egnatia, and on the hillside the picturesque wooden houses of the Turks [...] Despite all this it is a charming city. To the traveller arriving by sea it appears like an amphitheatre climbing up the sides of the mountain, encircled by its ancient walls, crowned with domes and minarets, dominated by the imposing presence of the Acropolis with its time-gilded walls..."

The cities and the countryside of Macedonia

The study of this region is rendered particularly interesting by the sharp differentiation between types of settlements: in the 18th and 19th centuries there were cities and towns with modern cultural systems

SALONIQUE. — Incendie. — Les quais. — 19 Août 1917 (7 h.).

The Great Fire of Thessaloniki

arising chiefly out of economic prosperity. The cities which, in their periodical, one might almost say circumstantial, prime boasted wealth and power, still belonged to an environment of agricultural poverty, where the land did not always yield its fruits because the torrents that rushed headlong down the mountain slopes buried the valleys under a layer of mud. Malaria and the uncertainty of the harvest restricted the efficacity of common enterprise. Relationships between the city and the countryside were governed mainly by the exploitation of production. The markets of Kozani, Kastoria, Servia, Velvendo, Ptolemaida (Kailaria), Neapoli (Lipsista), Florina, Edessa, Naoussa, Veria, Serres, Kavala, Melenikon, Thessaloniki, Monastir and other cities and towns throughout Macedonia gathered in the produce of the surrounding countryside, furnishing the peasants in exchange with essential items and "luxury" goods. This relationship between the Macedonian countryside and its cities was to some degree one-sided: the city, which served both as market-place and as middleman, became steadily richer and more influential at the expense of the rural areas. At the same time city life, and the mere idea of "the city", served

Veria, the entrance to the city, early 20th c. (L.Schultze-Jena, Makedonien..., plate LV, above).

The view from Edessa, early 20th c. (L.Schultze-Jena, Makedonien..., Plate LV, below)

as cultural models which shaped ever more markedly the life of the countryside.

As commercial centres the cities were, to a certain extent, free of the land and its economic constraints. They developed their own "laws", which differed in varying degrees from the traditional "laws" of the

Thessaloniki, the Fountain (Sintrivani)

rural areas. The guilds and corporations, which were organized by the merchants and artisans in particular, achieved far more than they expected in the orientation of the socio-economic life of the city.

Nevertheless, the various urban functions of the cities did not necessarily afford them an air of modernity. The fundamental characteristic of the Macedonian city was collectivity: the city was the crossroads of traditional society, the source of its strength. The authority of the city - economic (with its markets), religious (with the seats of metropolitans and bishops), cultural (the city provided models to be

This relationship between the city and the countryside retained its essential characteristics even after the progressive transformation of the larger Macedonian cities, gradual from the middle of the 19th century and ever more rapid by the century's end: the industrialization of part of the process of production and the introduction of technological innovations marked changes which affected all sectors of social and economic life. For example, starting in the 1870s Thessaloniki developed a network of rail links. Gas first began to be used early in the 1890s. 1893 saw the first horse-drawn trams. In 1899 the first houses ac-

Typical representation of the Prophet Elijah; the inscription reads "the chariot of the sun". The feast of the "saint of the mountains" is observed on July 20. Silver phylactery. (Folk Museum of the Aristotelian University of Thessaloniki).

copied, organized education, etc)- diminished on all levels the deeper into the countryside it spread. In the pre-industrial and proto-industrial systems, the city functioned as an administrative centre for agricultural production, as a market-place, and at the same time as a centre of state authority (e.g. Thessaloniki, Serres, Kastoria, Kavala, etc). Nevertheless, there were areas where the city's sole function was that of broker for transit trade (Siatista was such a city). In both cases, however, the city served as a liaison between its surrounding area and the international market.

quired running water. In 1902 the first quay in the busy harbour was completed. Improvements in transport and communications facilitated acceleration of social and economic functions. European clothes became the norm for urban wear, more and more purchased provisions were found in city kitchens. Amusement and recreation halls, theatrical performances (and early in the 20th century the cinema) attracted spectators from all classes and all social strata. The world of the Macedonian city, "wearing its traditional dependence", entered upon a new way of life.

B. An examination of temporal organization

1. Cyclical time and linear time

"Paliouglias, the old castle, has been there since the days when the Greeks fought with bows and lived for four hundred years before they lay down and died", they used to say in the village of Paliokopria (district of Grevena).[1]. "Every year on the 20th day of "the Reaper" (July), when we had our feast day, a deer would come, and we used to wait for it [...] But one year when it arrived it was all of a sweat, all worn out, and we cut it down there and then..." recounted the people of Aimilianos (Grintadhes) in the same area.[2]. "Until the time of Ali Pasha the Valladhes (islamized Greeks) were Christian..." they maintain in many villages in the province of Grevena.[3]. "Ap' t'Ai Giorgiou st'Ai Dimitriou" [from St George's Day (April 23) till St Dimitrius' Day (October 26)] was how the peasants of Macedonia measured the duration of a lease, a labour contract, or the season spent working abroad. "Irti Stavros, stavrouni ki sperni" [It is the Feast of the Cross (the Elevation of the Cross, September 14), time to cross yourself and start sowing], the farmers of Drimos (near Thessaloniki) used to say when sowing time came round.[4].

In the Serres "Chronicle of Papasynodinos"[5] we read: "1600. Monday, September 21. I, Papa-synodinos, was born. That is what my father, Father Sideris, told me, for he had it written down in his notebook [...] 1617. Sunday, November 9th. I, Papasynodinos, was married to Mistress Avrabakina by Father Timothy of Serres [...] 1621-22. There was great hunger throughout the land, and in Macedonia wheat sold for 160 farthings an oktari, and millet for 130 [...] 1638. And once they had destroyed this Manolis, the whole village was destroyed, and they left, and the houses remained empty... For as the old people say, "The good build and the evil destroy..."

Finally, in the "Chronicles and Notes" we read[6]: "In the year (7177=)1668, on the twenty-first day of the month of December, Sultan Meimetis arrived from Veria and stayed in the house of the Emin Meimet aga; and the kaimakami stayed with Pekir Effendi, and their followers in the houses of the Greeks and the Turks. And they stayed for eighteen days, and they returned again to Larisa. And what the people suffered from being chased out and other unbearable burdens, from the disorder brought by the king, cannot be described, for they even brought their wives". A little farther down we read: "In the year (7182=)1673, and on the twenty-fourth day of September, Pekir Effendi died and went to the place

*Winter. Wall painting in the Kariophyllis house in Siatista.
(Photograph by E.Georgiadou-Kountoura).*

where the devils are shod, and to hell-fire and damnation, and Veria lost a great and honest judge".

Years, months, dates, periods of time, events, memories, traditions recounting who they were and where they came from. "As the old people say" and "stories our grandfathers used to tell", landmarks in people's lives, the cycle of their labours, their travels and their wanderings, their sufferings and their joys. In other words, human experiences in place and in time.

From the preceding examples it is clear that the way in which people in the traditional Greek society of Macedonia organized their experiences (that is, their everyday lives) in time was both practical and symbolic. As A. Kyriakidou- Nestoros says: "Time, in the popular mind, is not an abstract, mathematical concept; it is what it contains, the experiences it embraces. November is Sporiatis, the Sower, because that is when they sow; June is Theristis, the Reaper, because that is when they reap; July is Alonaris, the Thresher, because that is when they thresh. The experience of time is principally work and its content principally food: when they say "we had a good year", they mean "we had a good harvest".[7]. What does "time is what it contains" really mean in the traditional civilization of Macedonia? How were the experiences of the people organized in that specific place at that specific time? Within what framework was the passage of time actually lived?

In the context of daily life, time is fundamentally practical and symbolic, in the sense that for its expression partial, specific and disconnected (or even contradictory) categories are used, according to circumstance; while on the contrary, established arrangements for the expression of time employ clear, coherent and abstract categories from the domain of the theoretical and scientific concept of time.[8]. Thus, for example, time in the agricultural year is natural and cyclical (that is, a cycle of successive, repeated - at more or less regular intervals - tasks which follow the rhythm of the seasons), because it is practical: the rural year is not organized on the basis of an abstract, distant knowledge of nature, but on the basis of specific practises and operations in relation to nature. In the ecclesiastical calendar, on the other hand, while time is of course cyclical and repeated (it is organized around a cyclical sequence of feasts and rituals connected with the religious life of the people, the Christian community in this case), it is also an instituted year, because it is the result of the abstract and conscious procedure which considers time as a whole and gives it shape (the calendar of holy-days) in the form of rituals. Finally, although the lineally continuous time of the calendular and historiographic concept is of course theoretical, abstract and scientific, when it is used within the context of traditional apprehension it ceases to be distant and objective: it becomes subjective and acquires specific content; for example, specific dates and indefinite temporal categories ("in the olden days", "in the

time of the Greeks", "when so-and-so died", "the day it hailed", etc) are all used in exactly the same way, for they refer to the particular past and to particular landmark events in the lives of particular people who have an immediate, practical connection with the life of the speaker.

In the daily life of Macedonia during the years of the Turkish occupation, when oral means of communication combined with written (the latter remaining auxiliary to the functioning of society and being absorbed by the logic of oral tradition[9]), the two ways of defining time were confounded: practical knowledge drew on and influenced formal knowledge to the same extent that the relationship of man to the land was not dependent solely on his direct contact with nature, or solely on his own actions and behaviour, but on the institutions and the mechanisms appointed by the various authorities.

Temporal organization in the traditional society of Macedonia also signifies spatial organization: people are living somewhere while they are living their history. The organization of time and space establishes them as a continuous and cohesive whole; and, like continuity in space, continuity of time does not necessarily imply a linear sequence. Continuity in space is established not only materially but also symbolically; place, irrespective of the partial material or symbolic interruptions which characterize it) exists circumstantially on the level of ritual behaviour and symbolic thought. Place is organized into units, parcelled out, divided, reconstituted, while people are living in it and in relation to it. In the same way continuities in time are defined both materially and symbolically: time flows, but the seasons pass and return in their established sequence; the years pass for the individual, but for the generations which follow one another the pattern is always the same; men are born and die, but the life of the community goes on; innovations

Spring. The plain of the Strymon, Eastern Macedonia (A.Goff-H.Fawcett, Macedonia. A Plea for the Primitive, 1921, pp 80, 128,218)

appear, but in the degree to which they are absorbed by the rhythms and forms of the prevailing way of life of society, this society remains fundamentally traditional.

It would appear that despite the use of writing and the calendar and despite the (limited) presence of the historiographic concept, the relationship between life and time remained traditional. Time was considered cyclical, recurrent, organized into standard forms, periodic, conventional, specific. In the examples offered at the beginning of this chapter, the use of dates in the diaries (Enthimisseis, literally "reminders", notes written on the margins of holy books as reminders of events which impressed) kept by certain educated people (i.e. clergymen) did not make historical time any more specific than does the phrase "long ago, when...", which is used in traditions interpreting the founding or the history of a settlement, a family or an individual. The year 1662 was the year of the great famine for the people who lived it or who in one way or another experienced its consequences, just as the end of every winter is a period of anxiety for the farmer who, having experienced hunger and knowing that it is dependent on the weather, lives through the testing time of the natural year. The reminders we spoke of do not record abstract history, they do not produce theoretical reasoning; they record actual experiences in the same fragmentary way that men live their daily lives. This however in no way implies that people's lives are unorganized and accidental; people's individual and social lives are shaped and moulded within recurrent and conventional patterns which permit men to survive within the context of their specific society.

2. Constraints of time within the traditional society of Macedonia

2.1. Natural (or ecological) and social (or structural) time

In the traditional Greek society of Macedonia, time was organized according to patterns which defined, directed and circumscribed the lives of the people who made up that particular society.

The traditional constraints of time obey the same logic as the constraints which governed spatial organization in traditional society. Just as spatial organization depended on the relationships between man and his natural and social environment, so temporal organization depends both on natural environment (nature and the changes observed in the natural course of things), but also on social environment: the measurement of time imposed by the religious or ecclesiastical, political and economic authorities.[10]. The concepts of time and place, therefore, are closely interwoven. Nevertheless, time in traditional society is essentially ecological or natural time[11]: every recognition and measurement of time is rooted in the changes which occur periodically in nature and in the way in which men in their social groupings deal with these changes. The recognition of ecological time, and therefore its organization, is restricted to what concerns the life of the community or the group within the annual cycle, and is thus by its very nature incapable of distinguishing longer periods than the year with its seasons. Seasonal, lunar and solar changes recur year after year; day regularly succeeds night. Ecological time,

The landmarks of the year: Saint George and Saint Dimitrios. Double silver phylactery with images of the mounted saints in relief on both sides; the inside contains a wooden miniature, (Folk Museum of the Aristotelian University of Thessaloniki).

therefore, is cyclical both literally and metaphorically. Ecological time is based on the year. The rhythmic alternation of tasks, the rhythmic movements of the people, are a response to the fundamental distinction between summer and winter.[12]. The concept of seasons is more a consequence of social activity than of the meteorological differences which characterize the seasons.

In traditional Macedonian society, the ecological rhythm of the year was translated into a social rhythm; and the antithesis between the ways of life at the end of the winter and the the summer seasons constituted the two poles for the recognition of time and the organization of daily life: t'Ai-Giorgiou kai t'Ai-Dimitriou [(the feasts of) Saint George (April 23) and St Dimitrios (October 28): April was also known as Aigiorgitis, and October as Aidimitriatis] were the two landmarks of the year. In a more general fashion, too, the solstices and the equinoxes marked the critical phases in the life of the countryside and of rural society.[13].

The civil year, the ecclesiastical year and the economic year were built around the natural calendar; and from this point of view their organization was also cyclical, rhythmic and recurrent. The ecological, the ecclesiastical and the civil years overlap. The old tefteri (ledger) of the Monastery of Aghii Anarghiri in Kastoria records that: "[1808-1812]...a schedule was drawn up of our community's debts to the most illustrious Beys, and every year at the feasts of St George and St Dimitrios a portion was paid..."[14] Social, economic and civilian signposts (dates, financial arrangements for the repayment of debts, civilian relationshiops), natural signposts (the two turning points of the calendar year, the beginning of summer and the beginning of winter), and religious signposts (the two mounted saints whose presence guarded the initiation of economic activity for all the Christians in the Balkans) manifest at different levels the same relationship between man and time.

The life of the community also followed the rhythms imposed by nature, since social and community activities were "measured" and organized on the basis of the natural and the ecclesiastical year. For example, the hours of work and repose followed the rhythm of day and night; and when on occasion work had to be done at night, as was often the case with the stripping of the corn, or with weaving, then it was called ksenichti, working all night through. The days of labour were interrupted by Sunday, the day of rest. The craftsmen who went abroad to work left in the spring, at the feast of St George, and returned in the autumn, at the feast of St Dimitrios. The herdsmen scattered at the feast of St Dimitrios to spend the winter on the plains, and gathered again on the high summer pastures at the feast of St George. Farm labourers poured into the fields and plains for the season

of reaping the grain and harvesting the cotton and tobacco, and returned to their villages to plough and sow their own fields. The periods when the people were assembled in their own communities were the times for feasts, festivals and weddings; but there were also major festivals to mark the passage from one season to another in the natural and agricultural year: Christmas (with the Twelve Days) and Easter, Megali kai Mikri Sarakosti (Great and Little Lent, the 40 day periods of fasting before Easter and Christmas respectively), tou Evangelismou kai tou Ai Gianniou (Lady Day, March 25, and St John's Day, June 24), St George's Day and St Dimitrios' Day, tou Stavrou (feast of the Elevation of the Cross, September 14) and tis Panaghias tis Polysporitissas (Our Lady of the Seed-time, or the Presentation of the Virgin Mary, November 21), tou Aghiou Tryphona (St Tryphon's Day, February 1) and tis Aya-Varvaras (St Barbara's Day, December 4).

And in human life, too, human life which follows the biological cycle, the rhythms of nature, with its ages and generations and particular social categories, distinctions are made on the basis of one's status within society: married/single, old/young, adults/children, fathers/sons, women/maidens, mothers/daughters, etc. This type of social time measured and defined individual lives within the framework of a particular society, just as the organization of labour on the basis of the distinction between work and leisure, with feasts and festivals to mark the passage from one stage to another, defined social time within the life of the community.

Nevertheless, whether it was for the marking of the agricultural year, or for the organization of economic activities, or for the marking of their individual biological and social lives, or for their perception of the past and their own history, the people of Macedonia's traditional society, as is of course the case with all traditional societies, were not seeking precision.[15]. The constraints of time which ordered their daily lives owed their form more to the power of tradition and its immediate links with nature, than to the abstract constraints of the clock on the wall.[16].

2.2. The rhythms of labour and of social life

In the traditional society of Macedonia, work patterns followed natural patterns. For example, the working day lasted from sunrise to sunset, not only for the farmer but also for those who worked at crafts or in industry, commerce and transport. Time was calculated by means of natural signposts. In Chalcidice[17], for example, to name the various hours of the day or the seasons of the year, they used to say: "varisi i ilious" (the sun has struck, i.e., has risen), or i ilious gioma (the sun is full, i.e. it is noon), or "the sun is three crutches high"

Moonrise over Mt Pangaion.

or "twice a man's height", or "the sun reigns in splendour" i.e., the sun is setting. They also used social signposts related to their temporal content: for example, "with the cows", which meant when the cows came home from the pastures, or "at the priest's hour" (at the hour of the Angelus), or "at suppertime" or "after supper"; or they used words like "the Reaper" and "the Thresher", for June and July, or phrases like "the month of St Nicholas and Christmas", for December. Then too they sometimes used terms and signs drawn from the abstract and scientific measurement of time, as when they used "mid-week" for Wednesday, or used the official names of the days and months or used abstract concepts for periods of time, words like hour, day, week, month, year, etc.

The sequence of labours connected with the "natural" economy (agriculture and stock-raising) supplied the yardstick for the measurement of time. Natural alternations such as day and night, summer and winter, were used as reference points for the recognition and the organization of time. Ecological time was thus also in reality social time, for it reflected the relationships of man with his environment; and ecological rhythms were translated into the social rhythms of the annual cycle of

agricultural occupations: the end of the summer meant winter quarters for the flocks and preparation of the land (sowing, cultivating, harvesting, storing) for the crops. The sequence of procedures was interrupted by the feasts and holidays which marked the passage from one occupation to the next. From this point of view, the annual cycle of holy-days and the annual cycle of agricultural tasks were the two faces of the same cyclical system of measuring time.

The natural patterns for measuring time applied equally in urban and rural areas, whether the passing of time was measured by the sun itself or by cock crow or church bell, by the town crier announcing the hour or the lamp-lighter lighting the street lamps, by the clock on the tower or the watch in one's pocket.[18].

In Serres, for example, in the marble-paved courtyard of the Eski-Tzami, with its cypress trees and marble fountain, "in a small room on the ground floor there were two large wall clocks of great accuracy [...] which functioned by means of a pendulum. One was regulated "a la Franga", showing European time with noon at twelve o'clock, and the other "a la Tourka", that is, on the old Byzantine system which showed twelve at sunset. The life of the city was arranged on the basis of the old

To the sound of the bell. (Mt Athos, photograph by Mytilini photographer S.Houtzaiou). (Photographic archives, Folk Museum, University of Thessaloniki)

By the light of the lantern. (Mt Athos, photograph by Mytilini photographer S.Houtzaiou). (It was probably taken in Mytilini, but the photographer did also work in Northern Greece). (Photographic archives, Folk Museum, University of Thessaloniki)

When the cock crows. Wall painting from the Nantzis mansion in Kastoria. (Gallery of Greek Folk Art. Volume I. Mansions in Kastoria, Collection of Greek Popular Art, 1948, plate 26).

Byzantine system. The shops closed at sunset, the covered market closed its doors at sunset, the grocers and chemists at "one o'clock in the evening", that is, one hour after sunset, winter and summer alike. The word midnight always meant the same thing, namely six hours after sunset, whatever the season. The morning hours and the beginning of the working day fluctuated in accordance with the season [...] The only exception was the timetable of the train from Thessaloniki to Constantinople, which followed European time [...] When Turkey was expelled in 1912 [...] European time, which

The market in Serres, the Bezesteni, the Eski Tzami and the Clock Tower. (V.Tsanakaris, Picture history of Serres, p.33)

put twelve o'clock when the sun was at its highest, was applied everywhere. This caused great dissatisfaction, especially among the elderly who had all theirlives been accustomed to the old Byzantine system of telling the time...".[19]

In Melenikon, the archontiko of the Bampouras family was known to the local people as "the great house" or "the clock house", "because at one point [...] its tower was embellished by the adjunction of a large clock. This clock is no longer there. The rhythm of its striking, the pulse of Melenikon, has ceased. The tower itself may have fallen too...".[20]. The old quarter to the west of Varosi in Serres was called Ora (hour, time), because of the tower that used to stand there (before the city was plundered and set aflame by the Bulgarians in 1913), with its great clock which struck the hours.[21]. As P. Pennas noted: "This municipal clock [...] must be a relic of Byzantine years. In any case, Robert de Dreux, a French Capucine monk, saw it (and was greatly impressed by it) when he passed through Serres in 1668: "...But what I found most remarkable about the city of Serres was that in the centre there is a certain clock, built like a square tower, with a huge bell which rings out the hours in the European fashion, that is, beginning at midnight, just as we do. This is worthy of remark because, as far as I am aware, there are no municipal clocks

anywhere in Turkey, and furthermore, the Turks do not calculate the time as we do, beginning at midnight, but as do the Italians, who count the first hour with the setting of the sun...".[22]. This clock, however, Pennas continues, "if I remember correctly, sounded the hours in the Turkish fashion during the final years of the Turkish occupation, and not in the European style as de Dreux says. Furthermore, his statement that there are no other municipal clocks is deficient in historical accuracy, for travellers (such as Lucas in 1712) have mentioned clocks in Drama and Philippoupolis. The village of Angistron in the district of Serres also has a clock, similar to the one in Serres, which is still working today, and which, as I was able to ascertain [...] dates from the Byzantine period and was merely repaired by the Turks in the 18th century. It consists of a square stone tower [...] culminating in a wooden room [...] housing the huge clock mechanism which, however simple and primitive it may be (for the usual metal spring is here replaced by a coarse rope with two stones hanging from it), sounds the hours with wonderful accuracy by means of the great bell which hangs there ...".[23].

The use of clocks, nevertheless, (and this includes the pocket watches which adorned the dress of up-to-date city dwellers), would not signify a radical change in the traditional conception of time until their rhythmic striking began to measure, on the basis of an entirely arbitrary system of temporal organization, all aspects of human life.[24].

2.3. The role of time in customary behaviour

In traditional Macedonian society the calendar was a cyclical sequence of activities in which daily practices alternated with ritual practices. In reality, the passage of time was a succession of occupations, where feasts and festivals, customs and ceremonies, marked the passage from one type of activity to another, from one daily routine to the next. The interval between two ordinary given periods was only a different period of time; for example, between two weeks there was a Sunday, between two months there was the first of the month, between two years there was New Year's Day, between two seasons there were feasts and festivals. Analogous phases and passages were evident in the life of the community. For example, the various stages of human life corresponding to age and status succeeded one another regularly, and the passages from one to another were marked by the appropriate traditional rituals and ceremonies: birth (customs associated with birth and baptism), coming of age, marriage, the arrival of children, old age, death. Each person passed through all these stages, living them in accordance with his or her sex. And the life of the community passed from one year to the next or from one harvest to the next or from one festival to the next. Time, then, for man in traditional society, consisted of phases and of the passages from one phase to its successor.

The confines, of course, both material and immaterial, real and symbolic, concrete and abstract, were always considered dangerous, sacred. Just like the physical, land boundaries, so too the temporal confines, the fatal moments of passage from one phase to the next, were always protected by means of ceremonies to ensure transition and continuity. These ceremonies, which Arnold Van Gennep has called "rites of passage".[25], aim at the safeguarding, reproduction and stability of society on three levels: the individual, the social and the natural. These three interact: the individual in society, society in nature, nature as society defines it, nature as the individual lives it. The underlying pattern in all rites of passage follows a pattern of internal temporal organization[26] in three phases: separation, passage (or transition), and incorporation.

Customary behaviour characteristic of Mace-donian rites of passage, which was not very different from analogous ritual behaviour in other parts of Greece, related to actions and operations concerning:

a) Ceremonial dress (at weddings, births and deaths), and ceremonial costume (for example, roughatsaria,

Wooden miniature with scenes from feasts of Christ and Our Lady on both faces; the miniature is en- cased in a double silver phylactery (with images of the two mounted saints). (Folk Museum, University of Thessaloniki).

koudhounadhes, perperouna, carnivals, etc. These were groups of lads or mummers with bells or boughs: on New Year's Eve and New Year's Day groups of men and boys armed with bells went about making the night hideous, presumably in order to frighten away the evil spirits; or bands of male mummers, numbering up to twenty characters, such as the bride and groom, the Arab, the Bey, old gaffers and grannies, warriors, the doctor and the midwife, devils, bears and goats, would parade and perform rituals on New Year's Day or on Twelfth Night. The perperouna was a springtime rain charm, named after the girl who performed the principal part.) Sometimes ceremonial dress involved reversing roles by age or sex: for example, men dressing as women, wearing clothes inside out, or dressing a baby in his father's shirt. Ritual disguises were customary during the Twelve Days of Christmas (December 25-January 6), the Carnival before the Easter Lent, the smaller carnival before the Christmas lenten period, the Feast of Lazarus (Lazari and Lazarines), St George's Day (Ai Giorgis, wreaths of May), and others.

b) Ceremonial actions, such as the great or double Easter dance, the bride's dance, shaving the groom, washing the bride's hair, exhibiting the dowry, blessing the waters, memorial services, leaping the fire, etc. These ritual actions may be specifically related to ritual,

The Sarakatsani of Macedonia:Baby's cap from Servia
(Collection of the Peloponnesian Folk Institute).

offered at memorial services), aparkhes (an offering of the first crops), May garlands, etc.

e) Sacrifices, such as the sacrificing of an animal (kourbani, as it was called) or the offering of the first fruits of the harvest,

f) Feasting and gifts. These included banquets, treats, offerings of first-fruits, gifts of money, the bounamadhes (gifts) offered to guests, mummers, kalantadhes (carol singers, usually children) or Lazarines, and offerings made to those who performed services (e.g. mantilomata, gifts of kerchiefs).

g) The exchange of gifts, such as the mantilomata; the koulikia and sinia (wedding gifts laid on large round trays called sinia carried around among the guests) at weddings; or the riksimo (the "tossing" of a special gift) which the godfather offered his godchild at the christening, and the martiria (tokens offered by the godfather to those witnessing the baptism) he offered the guests.

Verbal behaviour was connected with:

a) Ritual songs, such as those sung at weddings (by the bride, the groom, the bride's mother) and at funerals and memorial services (dirges); and those sung at various ceremonies and festivals, such as carols, Easter hymns, the Good Friday lament, the songs that accompanied the Easter dances, songs sung for St George's Day (t'aigiorgitika), for the coming of spring (ta chelidhonismata, or "swallow songs", sung by groups of children on March 1st), for the Feast of Lazarus (ta lazariatika, sung by groups of girls and/or boys of the same age), for the Feast of the Dead (ta rousalia, sung either on the Saturday after Easter or on the Eve of Pentecost), and the tragoudhia tou fanou, satirical songs sung around the bonfires on the evening of "Cheese-Sunday", just before Lent; and

b) proverbs and proverbial speech, standard wishes, incantations, and the advice and admonitions that accompanied ritual actions and operations.

Although rites of passage covered the crossing of all sorts of temporal and spatial boundaries, there were, nonetheless, certain amomg these which were of particular importance in the life of the individual or of the group. Chief among these were the customs connected with the arrival of the New Year (that is, the assurance that life will continue), the customs connected with festivals (that is, the re-affirmation of the identity of the group and the renewal of the links binding its members), and finally, the customs connected with weddings (that is, the safe-guarding of the permanence of the structure of society on the level of the home and the family). The customs connected with the New Year (which have been thoroughly studied by N.G. Politis, G.A. Megas, D. Loukato, and A. Kyriakidou-Nestoros, who included among their examples facts and information about north-

often derisory, imitation of landmarks in human, social or natural life. Examples of this are the "blessing of the waters with devil-water", in which the roughatsaria (Twelfth Night mummers who go around the houses asking for money) mock the priestly blessing of the waters which takes place at the Epiphany), the "wedding" of the monk and the maiden, the "birth" of the monk and his "death", etc.

c) Symbolical actions, such as the pantrema (wedding) of the fire, the cutting of the New Year's cake, the smashing of the pomegranate (for luck), making the sign of the cross, spitting (to ward off bad luck), insulting and offensive gestures, ritual spring-cleaning, etc.

d) The making of symbols, such as Kyra Sarakosti ("Lady Lent"), i chelidhona (the swallow), the koulikia (special wedding loaves), the drakos (a cross symbol made with the first stalks to be harvested), koliva (a dish

The Feast of St John in Samarina: girls gathered at the Papazisis tap for the "klidhona". A. Wace- M.Thompson, The Nomads of the Balkans, 1914 plate XX, Greek translation 1989, p.324, I.

ern Greece) are fairly similar throughout Greece. Wedding rituals, on the other hand, and local or regional gatherings to celebrate festivals, are far more varied (at least superficially), probably because, through their own manner of social reproduction (i.e., in the special value attached to traditional wedding customs) and in the regular affirmation of their own community (through the special significance of their own local festival), people strive to invest their identity in their history and their home.

3. Forms of organization of social time in the traditional society of Macedonia

3.1. The Macedonian wedding as a system of family organization

3.1.1. The place of marriage in social life

The various preparations and ceremonies carried out before and during a wedding (match making, invitations, washing the bride's hair, exhibiting and transporting the dowry, baking the special breads, ceremonial dressing, the songs and dances, etc) constituted a particular traditional formal ceremonial, which determined the social position of the two families united and of the new family unit created within society by each marriage. The whole procedure established the family status (financial and social), the social solidarity and the socio-economic security of the newly-formed couple. It is clear that the nature and the specific form of these ceremonials in each instance, that is, how lavish and how well organized they were, established within the traditional society of Macedonia the particular social identity of each new social unit. This explains phrases like timimenos gamos ("honoured" or "dignified wedding"), kala stephana (a

wish for "good marriage wreaths", i.e., a good match), megalos gamos (a big wedding), gamos me ta kala spitia (marrying into a good family), simpetherio me tzaki (marriage arranged with a "hearth", i.e. a distinguished family), etc.

The ideal of the traditional Macedonian family was complete self-sufficiency on the level of physical reproduction as well as on the economic level. Nevertheless, the physical agents of reproduction within the group, the women, were in an ambiguous position, for although their "femaleness" bound them to their own homes, they could not reproduce within the family where they were born without violating the law of virginity in their father's house or the prohibition against incest. In traditional Macedonian society (as in other societies) every woman had the right to two different existences, that of a maiden in her father's house and that of a wife (and mother) in her husband's; spinsterhood was an abnormal state to be avoided at all costs. Wedding customs underlined both states, with the weight on the woman's reproductive role. These customs aimed at protecting the bridegroom from the "binding" (by magic spell) of his reproductive abilities: customs such as the dance in the iron baking pan to protect him against "spells", the binding of his waist with a sash woven and embroidered by the bride, as well as the various songs and other adjuratory actions. Another series of customs symbolize the bride's worthiness ("a capable girl") and modesty (silence, respect, reverences, hand-kissing, veiled face, etc) and thus her moral qualities.

In most cases the bride was the mobile element in the marriage (it was the bride who went from her father's house to her husband's or father-in-law's); thus although she symbolized the hearth of her father's house, it was her lot to go as "a stranger to a strange house", except in

Wedding couple in Samarina (photograph by the Manakis brothers).

those cases when the couple remained with the girl's parents.

The bride who moved from her old home to her new was infallibly accompanied by her trousseau, regardless of its quantity, quality or kind. It was known by several names: ta pragmata" (her things), her clothes, her dowry, ta goutia or ta kala (her possessions, her goods); and it was composed of household goods or spitomazoma (bed-clothes, clothing, household gear, and sometimes furniture). Often, especially in "urban" areas, the dowry was supplemented with cash (trakhoma, nakhti) and with land (a house, fields, vineyards, orchards, etc). In some cases a special contract was drawn up, affecting one or other of the parties. The trousseau declared the status of the family who furnished it and of the person or family who received it. It was an act of ostentatious consumption, just like all the other expenses that were judged necessary for a "good wedding". The prikia (trousseau) yikos or yuki or daros or templo (pile of clothing and bed-clothes) or nifiatiki kasela (bridal chest) demonstrated the industriousness of the bride and the

prosperity of her family. The ceremonial removal of the trousseau and its exhibition exemplified the competence of the bride in household matters. But there were also other customs and ceremonies which stressed the introduction of the bride into her new house: she sat veiled beside the hearth; she bowed to the hearth; throughout all the ceremonies she faced inwards, towards the house; and in the house she remained beside her mother-in-law or sponsor, always silent, modest and willing.

Beyond the ostentation and the symbolism of the trousseau, the bride's belongings were also of practical value, both on the social level (a portion was offered to the participants according to their services) as well - and even more importantly - as on the economic level, for these objects constituted the solid foundation on which this new social unit could reproduce.

The social organization of rural society, and of traditional "urban" society as well, was built on the continuity (that is, the reproduction) of the productive unit, the family. The principal concern, then, of the community was the unimpeded issue of this procedure: all the customs and institutions associated with weddings (before, during and after), the lengthy period required by the whole procedure of institutionalizing reproduction (the logosimadho: a token exhanged as "a word of troth", the engagement, the wedding, the trousseau and dowry, the marriage contract), in general all the established conventional behavioural systems connected with the exchange of wedding gifts and donations, and all the rituals connected with the fertility of the bride and groom and the "good foundation" of the new household, tended to this end.

3.1.2. The structure of the solemnization of marriage: its temporal and spatial organization[27]

Although weddings were held in all seasons, certain times of the year were preferred while others were prohibited by the church or by society (through various superstitions). In Macedonia generally the preference was for the autumn, especially St Dimitrios' Day, and the winter; in Kataphygio (on Mt Olympus) people preferred the summer, as did the Vlachs of Pindus, who celebrated mass weddings in the churches of their mountain villages on August 15th (the feast of the Assumption of the Virgin Mary). Weddings were forbidden during periods of fasting (Christmas and both lenten periods), while certain other days and festivals were generally avoided, as "bringing no good": Tirini, for example, (Cheese-Sunday), the day before Lent, was avoided because those wedded on that day were sure to be tormented: the misunderstanding comes from the term tirini, meaning made of cheese, which sounds like the verb tiranieme, meaning to be tormented; Monday

Wedding in Samarina: Bringing the bride from her house on horseback. A.Wace-M.Thompson, The Nomads of the Balkans, 1914, plate XVI,2. Greek translation 1989, p. 320, 2)

Wedding in Samarina: The "wedding pies" (called "boubgala", it was probably a custard pie). A.Wace-M.Thompson, The Nomads of the Balkans, 1914 plate XVIII,1. (Greek translation 1989, p.322, 1)

Wedding in Samarina: Outside the groom's house, the dance of the bride and groom. A.Wace-M.Thompson, The Nomads of the Balkans, 1914, plate XVII,1. (Greek translation 1989, p.321)

(Dheftera: literally, second, or doubled) was a bad day, for a marriage solemnized on that day was apt to be "repeated"; Tuesday was a very unlucky day, for it was a Tuesday when Constantinople fell to the Turks; Wednesday was bad, for Christ was arrested on a Wednesday ("everything went wrong for him, even his wedding was on a Wednesday"); Friday was considered dangerous because it was the day of the Crucifixion.

"Joy" was generally linked with the Lord's Day, Sunday, and this was the preferred day for the solemnization of marriages: that is, for transporting the bride and her trousseau, and for the blessing; for in reality a wedding was a very complex procedure, which began with the match-making and was not completed until 1-3 weeks had passed after the ex-

Wedding in Samarina: The bride and groom with their attendants. A.Wace-M.Thompson, The Nomads of the Balkans, 1914, plate XVII,1. (Greek translation 1989, p.321).

A couple from Perivoli. (Chr.Christodoulou, The Photogenic Balkans of the Manakis Bros, 1989 p.25).

change of wedding wreaths.

It was not only the two families and their relatives who participated in the wedding festivities, but the entire village. The kalesmata, that is, the invitation to attend a wedding, was a symbolic act of particular importance for social (and economic) relationships within the community. This is evident in phrases like: "we invited them to our joy", "we invited everybody", "are we to invite all the world?", "we kept inviting people till nobody was left uninvited", and in songs like "Zidhros' song", or the one from the border country called "Dighenis Akritas goes uninvited to the wedding".

The whole community participated both in the wedding itself and in "dowering" the young couple with money, food and gifts. Although these gifts might often be of little intrinsic value, they always had symbolic significance: shepherds, for example, would offer samples of their handiwork, such as distaffs, sock needles, wooden cups, spoons and vessels, etc. Besides the friends and relatives invited as guests, there were also a certain number who had specific functions to fulfil: the sponsors, the attendants (the groom's kinsmen and particular friends), the woman or persons acting as "inviters", the gambrostoli (the groom's wedding procession of friends and relations), the psiki or sympetherio (the parents of the couple), the nyphostoli (the bride's wedding procession of friends and relatives), and the midwife.

Matches were made between families belonging to the same group (with respect to residence, race, religion and socio-economic level). The theoretical ideal was endogamy, marriage within the limits of race or tribe ("better a cobbled shoe from your own back yard"), although the opposite, marriage into a higher class, was often sought ("seek a bride of rank", "seek a bride of family").

Essentially, match-making took place between two opposing groups. From this point of view, the role of marriage was to seal an alliance between two (effectively or potentially) antagonistic groups with no previous bond of kinship or "connection" by marriage. Marriage with a stranger was avoided, however, unless he had settled in the village. The rivalry between the two families was manifested through various wedding customs, such as who would host the most splendid banquet, offer the most expensive gifts, or invite the most guests. For the Vlachs of Kirli-kioi (district of Serres) the rivalry began on the Friday before the wedding and applied to absolutely everything, from wood-chopping and bread-baking to feasting and drinking.

One of the salient features in the attitude towards marriage was the dominant concept that the bride was carried off, or stolen away, form her father's house by the groom and his family. Everything tended to support this theme: the bride would take leave of her home by saluting the house and the hearth; she would also take leave of the graves of her ancestors; as she left the house her family would pour out three vessels of water, as if she were leaving on a long journey; she would kick over and spill, or break, a glass of wine (a traditional leave-taking gesture), etc. Sometimes there would even be a symbolic acting out of the abduction of the bride by the groom and his friends (in the Roumlouki, such abductions were real, and were perpetrated to avoid the heavy expense of a proper wedding). This concept is behind the songs sung by the two sets of parents on their meeting:

"My dear daughter, a message has come to you from your mother-in-law: My dear maid, arrange your trousseau and your gifts prepare. I have arranged my trousseau and my gifts I have prepared. My bridal pillow still remains, but I shall soon finish it."

"Turn me out, my mother, send me far away to foreign parts, That I make sisters of strange women, and foster- mothers of foreigners, That foreign women may wash my linen, and my best clothes. O my mother, tend my dear plants well!"

"I leave a "farewell" to the village, a "farewell" to the brave lads, And to my mother I leave three vials of poison, One of which to drink at morn, the other at mid-day, The third on which to sup at eve, and lay down sleep."

"In the centre of the courtyard a partridge stands and speaks, Where are you brothers? Come here that you may send me forth! And do not fear tender one, we

are all round about and all fire our muskets."

"Curse on you, my mother, on you and your negotiations, that you sent for strangers to come and take your child, to take your wealth and fortune, to drink your wine."

"They have you, they have seized you, my beautiful one! They have taken you to foreign lands, my darling, to foreign lands and distant. For what cause, mother, have you driven me from my home? I have not driven you forth, my girl, for I send you to your home and to your household."

"Come, good gossip, what evil do I do, that you should send the hawk to take my partridge away from me, and my parish is disgraced and yours is adorned."

"O you fellow mother-in-law, what harm have I done to you, to send your eagle To snatch away my dear bird and to rob my courtyard of its beauty?"

"From the courtyard a maid is missing and from the parish one is missing, and from her mother one is missing, and from her brothers one is missing."

"Your village we have trodden, your maiden we have taken."

"Come forth, O mother of the groom and the bride's mother-in-law, To see your eagle what a partridge he is bringing home! She cannot be seen for gold and pearls, she cannot bend for brocade of gold!"

One of the most characteristic gifts the bridegroom offered the bride was a pair of shoes. This was to "facilitate", and symbolically to protect, the passage of the bride to her new state; and this is why the breaking of an engagement (of any kind) is expressed by the phrase "She handed him his shoes".

This change of identity had to be protected against ill-wishing and the evil eye: for this reason the bride wore a veil, the bridal bed was prepared in another house, or the bride slept for one or two nights with her mother-in-law, her godmother and her "guardians" (in Kastoria, for example, the midwife). Further, the colour red was largely used to guard against evil (in many places, the traditional wedding dress was predominantly red: this was the case in the Ventzia (a group of villages south of Siatista) of Western Macedonia, or in the older wedding costume of the Sarakatsani, in the wedding chemises, etc.) A change of identity, especially for a bride, also meant a change of dress, of external appearance. The method used was a code that "signalled" the change. This symbolism reached its peak in the various bindings that were worn: girdles, sashes, kerchiefs, embroidered and metal belts, and headdresses. In the Roumlouki, for example, the unmarried girl wore a simple head-scarf (tsemperi), the bride her katsouli me foundes (bridal toque with specially arranged tassels and adorned with

The tasselled wedding coif worn by brides and newly married women in the Roumlouki. (Tradition has it that Alexander the Great honoured the valiant women of the region, who fought for Macedonia, by permitting them to wear this magnificent headgear) (A.Hatzimichalis, Greek Folk Art. Roumlouki - Trikeri - Ikaria 1931, p.22).

artificial flowers and jewellery; the katsouli was the head-covering forming the base of the bridal headdress, and was worn even in bed); the young married woman wore the katsouli, and the elderly wore two mafessia (scarves), one over the other.

3.1.3. Examples of wedding ceremonies in Macedonia

Village weddings and city weddings

Example: The cycle of matrimonial ritual in the Roumlouki[28]

"The boy, the child, must learn from earliest youth to work in the field and in the fold, in the byre with the cows and in the pen with the sheep; and the girl must learn to keep house and to weave [...] The bridegroom purchases his bride, she is bought, and the price is heavy, he must dig deep into his pocket [...] Boys from the same village make the best husbands; they already know them, and that way they can be sure of their future. But they do also arrange marriages with boys from other villages [...] If the parents are not willing [...] the young man suggests i fevga or to klepsimio (elopement or capture), that is, he steals the bride away and takes her to his father's house. (He steals her when she goes to the tap for water), that is why this tap is called the abduction-tap. As for the bride's clothes, after five or six days they send the match-maker to demand them from the girl's father; he is obliged to hand them over, as long as he is paid for the mother's milk the girl drank as a baby...

Even when there is no abduction the groom is required to pay the bride's father for her mother's milk, in proof that he has bought her. In other words , he has purchased an object which henceforth belongs to him [...] A man who abducts his bride does not have to pay the kaparo (earnest- money) which is normally paid for the bride when a betrothal is concluded. The usual wedding customs, the dancing and the feasts, are also foregone in such cases [...] The parents of the young couple, the sympetherika, have nothing to do with the wedding celebrations, and all contact between them ceases with the betrothal of their children [...] If the match "takes", the match-maker commences the negotiations between the groom and the bride's father; for his trouble the groom offers him a new pair of shoes. First of all the groom must pay for the mother's milk; and then he gives the bride 8 or so gold coins, of the best quality he can afford, to wear on her manglikoutari (a special head ornament of silver chains decorated with coins worn by all brides and married women). Then he sends her the manglikoutari, the chain for her bodice, the skalomangaro me tous paradhes, ton toka, ta paphilia, ta bilitzikia, ta tsourakia, ta dhaktilidhia (bridal jewellery and ornaments of all sorts: silver chains with hooks and coins, necklaces, pins, buckles, bracelets, rings), as well as the bride's stolisia or takimi (bridal outfit), including the chrysokontoso (waist-coat embroidered with gold), the broumanika (heavily embroidered sleeves), the sigouni (sleeveless coat) and the katife saghia me ta dhak'tla (velvet sleeved coat embroidered with finger motifs) made of cloth woven by the bride herself on her loom [...] All contact is through the match-maker, whether oral or, as is more usual, in writing, the better to remember what has been agreed. The girl always furnishes all the woven goods, the work of her loom, as many items as she can; when there is a formal betrothal she must try to make a good showing. This trousseau includes ta zounaria (belts and sashes), i phoustes (skirts, which she begins preparing at the age of fifteen), ta

katastaria (underwear), ta poukamisa (chemises), ta skoufounia (socks), as well as the cloth for the saghiadhes (sleeved coats) and the kontosia (waist- coats) which the bride sends to the seamstress to be paid for by the groom. There are also ta velentzia (heavy woollen blankets), ta khremia (mats and carpets), ta sentonia (sheets), ta proskefala (pillow-cases) i tourvadhes (bags), ta sakia (sacks), mesales and petsetes (tablecloths and towels), etc. If the groom chooses a poor girl for his bride, then he sends gear of his own, that is, cotton and wool for her to weave her clothes and whatever is required for the household. A wealthy bride must have at least 10-12 new sets of clothes [...] The groom sends the match-maker to the girl's house with the engagement ring [...] From the girl's house the match-maker receives an engagement ring for the groom, as well as her gifts (a woven chemise for her mother-in-law, a suit of under-clothing for her father-in-law, socks and towels for the groom, and kerchiefs for his brothers and sisters. Guns are fired both at the bride's house and at the groom's [...] Celebrations begin in both houses, to the music of drums and clarinets. [Visits are paid and gifts are exchanged; for example, they bring the bride the chest containing the gifts from the groom, etc).

The groom selects his sponsor, his nounos, and informs his fraternal friends, ta bratimia [...] The sponsor is the most important personage at the wedding; he organizes the groom and his friends, [...] as well as the daftsarei, relatives chosen to act as messengers, so to speak. The sponsor selects a nona, his wife or sister or some other female relative. She too has certain obligations.Among other things she must buy the material for the bride's coat (antiri) and for the red khlambouro or flambouro (pole or standard with a banner) which the sponsor will hold during the wedding ceremony. The groom's friends make their owm banners with blue or yellow kerchiefs. These banners are long poles with kerchiefs nailed to them like flags. At the top of the pole is planted an apple, quince or peach, with basil leaves all around. But the king of the wedding is the groom, because "it is his wedding and he is making a splash".

Weddings are always celebrated on a Sunday, and the preparations last all week. The klouthia, as the people of the Roumlouki call the various customs which precede a wedding, begin on Friday. Both families send out their invitations. This is done three times: Friday morning the male relatives announce the wedding, Saturday morning the maidens, and Monday morning, after the wedding ceremony, it is the turn of the midwife. This signifies the man, the maiden and the woman, respectively. The girls assemble at the groom's house na anapiasoun ta kaniskia, that is, to knead the dough for the special bridal bread as well as for all the bread that will be required for the wedding feast. On Saturday morning the bride first washes her hair, and then arranges her trousseau in the trunk the groom has sent. [A special loaf is sent to the sponsor, at the groom's house, as an official invitation to the wedding. At the groom's house, in the meantime, the musicians play while the groom is shaved, and 4 or 6 young girls dance for him, two by two. The groom is shaved by a young married man, while a couple, boy and girl, hold the towel and the basin. Then the groom changes into his wedding clothes. Accompanied by the musicians, he sets out to meet his sponsor and his friends, for the celebrations at his house]. In days of yore the procession would pass by the house of the aga or governor, where the musicians would play and gifts would be offered them.

On Sunday morning, the messengers, who are close relatives of the groom, take a bottle of wine, some raki and a wreath-shaped loaf and go to fetch the groom's friends. These are dressed in their best clothes, carrying their banners [...] If the bride is from another village, they set off earlier. In the meanwhile, the bride is being prepared. She is seated on a straw mat, which has been placed over the iron plough strap so that she will have the strength of iron. Three young married women pass the strap three times around the bride's body, to protect her from evil and to make her as limber and as strong as the strap. They dress her in her wedding clothes, all except for her sash and shoes, which are put in a sieve with rice, sweets and other good things [...] The two messengers announce the approach of the groom, who, accompanied by the nounos, the nouna, his friends with their banners, and the musicians, has come to fetch the bride. (His parents wait at home.) The nouna, richly dressed, carries a sieve wrapped in red silk and full of sweets and flowers [...] The bride's father steps out of the house to welcome the groom, followed by her mother and their closest relatives. They salute each other three times on both cheeks, but without embracing [...] The women enter the house to greet the bride, some staying in the yard to admire the trousseau. [One of the bride's relatives passes around the groom's waist the sash the bride has woven for him. The trousseau is loaded into the carriage, which first follows the bride to the church and then continues towards the groom's house. A carriage takes the bride to church; in earlier days, she would have ridden to church on a white horse.]

When the bride steps out of her father's house, she is greeted three times by the eldest of the groom's friends, who then takes her in his arms and, facing eastwards towards the sun, lifts her on high three times [...] The bride has the skirts of her coat turned down, and her face covered with a white veil reaching to her waist. She bows three times to the sun, making the sign of the cross over and over again [...] then she takes the consecrated bread and breaks it in two, tossing one half on to the roof of her house; the other piece she hides in her bosom, to put in her husband's flour chest for luck. She is showered with grain and rice [...] Without looking towards the bride's house, the groom throws his hatchet behind him three times [...] Three times on the way to the church the bride bows to the groom [...] Upon her arrival in front of the church, she again bows three times to the sun [...] In the middle of the church, displayed on a blanket, are the silver vakoufika stefania (community owned wedding-wreaths, used only in the church during the wedding ceremony) [...] During the ceremony the nounos covers both bride and groom with a silken cloth [...] When they return to the groom's house, the groom and the nounos are the first to enter. One of his first cousins sweeps the pathway to the house with the oven cloth, so that the bride may enter without stumbling. The bride bows to her husband's parennts and relatives, and offers them various gifts. She then enters the house and makes the rounds of all the rooms, looking for the ploughshare (which is hidden behind the door). At the feast the bride tastes nothing, except for three mouthfuls accepted from the hand of the nouna. In the meanwhile, the bride's family are at home, weeping and wailing. After the feast, only the close relatives remain behind. The newly- weds dance their first and last virgin dance, led by the nounos with his banner. The couple then bow three times to the sun, and are showered with rice. The three banners are set up on the roof of the house, where they will remain for three days. The couple retire; two hours later the midwife brings out the proofs of the bride's virginity, and displays them in the village.

On Monday morning the bride rises first, to sweep out the house. [She then helps her parents-in-law to wash, and boils the coffee in its little pot. Her mother-in-law ceremoniously shows her around the house, after which they tidy up]. The midwife takes the bride's headdress and, carrying it with her, makes the rounds of the village inviting the guests [...] She then returns the headdress; the bride puts it on over her coif, and proceeds to adorn herself with her gold and tassels and all her various ornaments, to receive her guests. The women who come to help must be young, and there must always be an odd number (3,5,7, etc). They prepare pies [...] they bring more pies from the houses of the nounos, the groom's friends, etc, for Monday's feast is the biggest of all [...] On the third day the women go to the tap to wash the pots and other household utensils [...] There then follows a series of dinners designed to reconcile the two sets of parents; these are held quietly, with only the closest family members present, and without music or dancing. The first is given by the father of the bride, one week after the wedding [...] This will be the first time the bride has returned to her former home. The next Sunday, the groom invites his wife's parents; and on the third Sunday the nounos invites the young couple with both sets of parents..."

Example: A wedding in Lakkovikia, on Mt Pangaion[29]

"...Every wedding is preceded by a betrothal, which is usually arranged by friends or relatives. The promoter of the marriage is known as a match-maker. During the betrothal the groom sends the bride a ring, gold coins, and other gifts; he also offers gifts to all the members of her family. The bride returns gifts of equal value to the groom and his family. The groom does not offer his ring in person, but pays a formal visit to his father-in-law's house with others on another occasion. All these visits, during which gifts are exchanged, are called by us chirophilimata (kissing the hand).

The length of the betrothal is not fixed; all contact between bride and groom is strictly forbidden during this period [...]

The following wish is expressed to the young couple: "in health the kerchief (or the dress)".

One week before the wedding the invitations are sent: that is, gifts are dispatched to the bride with the request that she make herself ready. The wedding preparations are usually begun on a Thursday evening, with the arrival at the home of the bride and groom of women and unmarried friends and relatives to begin kneading the first bread [...]

On the following day (on Friday, that is), the women and maidens come again to complete the preparations for the wedding. Afterwards the bride or the groom, with other young men and maidens, and with three newly married women, cut the first bread and eat it. Also on that day they display the trousseau, which consists of various pieces of furniture, copper vessels and the like, and which virtually all the women of our town go to inspect. An old woman stands by the trousseau to guard it until Sunday, when the sponsor (koumbaros, or nounos) rewards both her and a number of youngsters each holding a pillow. The trousseau is relinquished to the groom's family by the bride's father or mother.

On Saturday at about the tenth hour a long procession accompanied by musicians and with great pomp carries substantial gifts to the bride and her relatives, including the bridal costume; this is called pothesis. (Among our people, the bridal costume is the gift of the groom's father, but among those from other places it is provided by the father of the bride.) Towards evening, two or three friends of the bride or groom, parastolia or parastekameni (followers or helpers) as they are called, with

or without musical instruments, carrying a bottle of wine or raki, go around to all the families who have been invited and summon them to the banquet and the dance which is to follow. Everyone dances while waiting for the guests to assemble. Then comes the feast, after which various songs are sung; these are known as banquetting songs...

On Sunday morning the inviting continues in the same fashion The groom is shaved, and dons a splendid costume. Meanwhile, at the bride's house, the following scene is taking place: young maidens, friends and relatives of the bride, comb and braid her hair to the accompaniment of their singing, while her relations shower her with silver coins, which are collected by the maidens who attend her throughout the ceremony, and are known as zimostres (kneaders). Then they dress the bride in her wedding dress and, away from the other people, cover her head with a golden veil which hangs down to her knees both before and behind; also with a transparent red veil, although this is now quite rare. When she is dressed, she slowly but gracefully kisses the hands of her attendants, before taking her place in front of one wall of her room, which has been decorated for the occasion with a rich and splendid carpet surmounted with seasonal flowers, often including ivy for prosperity. This is called the nymphostoli. When all the guests invited by both the bride and the groom have assembled, and when everything is ready, the wedding procession leaves the groom's house, led by the musicians, and, having stopped to collect the nounos, who carries in his hands a bowl full of wine and decorated with flowers and rings of bread, arrives at the bride's house. There, some people continue the old custom by which the bride's attendants close the door to the groom and refuse to admit him to the presence of the bride until he has offered them gifts; in other houses this custom is no longer observed, and the groom is conducted immediately to the bride, where he is offered a glass of wine by her sister or some other female relative, who also ties around his neck a handsome kerchief with which she gives him a smack. From the bride's house the procession moves on to the church; the bride, with tear-filled eyes, leaves her room making the sign of the cross. When she reaches the head of the stairs, she touches her forehead three times to the ground before starting down; then with her right foot she kicks over a glass full of wine, and sets off, leaning on the arms of maiden friends and relatives who sing as they go, and accompanied by all her guests, called also boughtzianidhes, some of whom may carry long spits threaded with pieces of meat. The bride walks very slowly and modestly, with downcast eyes. This modest and dignified pace is called kamaroma. A few years ago both bride and groom would proceed to church on horseback. Often on

The wedding of Giannis and Anastasia Manakis in Monastir (1922). (Chr. Christodoulou, The Photo- genic Balkans of the Manakis Brothers, 1989 p.44)

her way to the church, and again from there to the groom's house, the bride would kiss the hands of many of those who were gathered along the way. I shall pass over the ceremony in the church. From the church the bride is accompanied by the relatives of the groom, but she continues to walk slowly and modestly..."

More recent features of the traditional Macedonian wedding (late 19th and early 20th century)

Wedding rituals retained their traditional characteristics even in more up-to-date urban centres. The dangers, the uncertain future, and the sense of insecurity which haunt every newly constituted household do not permit the abandonment of habits and attitudes established by tradition through ancient customs and conceptions of marriage, and which guide the young couple in their social life along the safe path of the old ways. From this point of view, the changes encountered only affected certain features and customs, not the wedding ritual as a whole.

Perhaps the most important change was in dress. Men, especially those from the middle and upper urban classes, had abandoned traditional dress and adopted

European fashion; their wedding garments too were European in style. Many old wedding photographs show the groom in European dress and the bride wearing the old traditional costume. At a later stage, the bride's dress too began to change, even though it was generally accepted as the most traditional of women's costumes. In Melenikon, for example, the groom sent his bride an "Aspri Fouriskhia" (white dress).[30]. This fashion was followed, although much more slowly, of course, by many women in the provinces; and thus the colour of the bridal costume changed (in areas where it had traditionally been red it became white, as in Melenikon, for example, where "in the olden days the bride didn't wear a veil and carry flowers, but she wore a red headdress"[31]). In some instances the bridal costume was modernized, or even abandoned entirely for a white European style dress with a veil. In any case, changes in nuptial attire were more a reflection of the general modernization of society, rather than of changes and modernization of the celebration of marriage itself, for European costumes were worn by people who still obeyed the ritual patterns of tradition.

Another significant change affected the type of wed-

Epiphany in Avgerinos (Konstantziko) Voiou, Western Macedonia, in 1902. (Photograph from the collection of G.Glykerou,
published in the 1980 Calendar of the Avgerinite Cultural Association in Thessaloniki).

ding gifts. The urban habit of dowering one's daughters with money and land slowly spread to other areas where this was not traditional. Nevertheless, the trousseau remained the fundamental feature of the dowry, for the exhibition of the bride's trousseau still mirrored social perceptions of family status.

In many cases the method of inviting one's guests also changed. The trend (which developed late in the 19th century) towards sending handwritten or printed wedding invitations reflects a more general change in conceptions of social intercourse. Writing consecrated a system of remote and closed choices, which replaced the old, open system of social relationships in which the traditional attitude that a wedding was the affair of the whole community could flourish. In some cases attitudes and habits were confused. In Kleisoura, for example, towards the end of the 19th century, the custom was to send "young relatives of the groom wearing pistimalia (long sashes) offered by his mother around their waists, and accompanied by musicians, to deliver the wedding invitations to all the relatives, friends and acquaintances

on their list; and last of all, a child with both parents still living, preceded by the musicians, would take the biggest invitation to the bride. This was printed on white paper, measuring 60 x 50 cm; it had a coloured picture of a young couple holding two wreaths, and above, two cupids with a heart between them, on which were inscribed the three initials of each of their names...".[32]

The contents of an official invitation from Kleisoura, dated 1896, clearly demonstrate how traditional Macedonian society was wavering between tradition and modernity:

"...Inasmuch as you are aware that tomorrow, Sunday, the 29th day of this month, shall take place by common decision and agreement the marriage of our son Konstantinos to your beloved daughter Maria, we beg that, having adorned and arrayed our beloved daughter-in-law in accordance with our customs and usages, you may have her in readiness at four o'clock, for at that hour we shall dispatch the ceremonial procession to escort her to the church for the solemnization of the marriage. With all good wishes we remain...".[33]

3.2. The festival as a system of communal organization in Macedonia

3.2.1. The place of the festival in social life

The festival was a festal public gathering held at regular intervals (every year, every three years, every five years, etc), in a particular (usually open) place, in honour of some saint or some ecclesiastical celebration. In ancient Greece, the term meant a great feast, or an important religious assembly. Such gatherings were dedicated to a particular god, were held in sacred places, and were accompanied by sacrifices and other religious rites, by feasts, games, contests, dancing and singing. Both the word and its meaning were retained in traditional society into modern times, the only difference being that the occasion honoured some Christian saint or celebration, and churches and chapels replaced the old temples and sacred groves.[34]

The festival was the quintessential social occasion: the community or group (neighbourhood, parish) which was celebrating was identified with its festival, with the moment of the festival, for that was when the social relationships constituting its "us" acquired their fullest significance. "Festival" was also the name given in some localities to the major Christian feasts: for example, in the village of Mikri Volvi (district of Thessaloniki), "the three festivals" meant Christmas, New Year's Day, and Epiphany.[35] The word festival, however, also carried the more general connotation of joy, holiday, celebration, that which permitted people to escape from the rigorous discipline of everyday life. In many instances, in fact, the word acquired a negative aura, indicative of inappropriate and unseemly indifference and frivolity. Phrases such as "Is this a time for festivals?" or "He/she is only good for the festival" indicate that in traditional society celebration is strictly controlled and is obedient

The festival of the Panaghia in Avdela, the second day.
(Chr.Christodoulou, The Photogenic Balkans of the Manakis Brothers, 1989, p.21).

to social rules which define precisely where and when a "festival" is appropriate.

These festivals had two characteristic features:

a) A specific gathering place hallowed by tradition. This place had some distinctive physical feature (a hill, eminence, cave, fountain, spring, lake, river, tree or grove, headland, etc), and this natural distinguishing mark was further accented by the construction of a temple, by the levelling of a certain area (threshing floor, fair ground, dancing floor), the planting of trees, or the construction of a fountain, a pool, or something along those lines.

b) A fixed time for the gathering, again traditional. The particular point in time at which the festival took place, which might be from one day to a month or more, traditionally coincided with some religious celebration, and the church would be dedicated to the saint or occasion in question. The time of the festival was a communal time: the festival of the patron saint (or saints) of the community was a time of festival for the whole community, which was closely identified with its patron. This communal and religious occasion, when church and community celebrated together, became a widely known reference point. For example, the festival of Our Lady of Liokali in Katakonozi, a northern suburb of Serres, which was held on September 8th (Our Lady's birthday), was known throughout Eastern Macedonia. "The drums of Liokali have sounded", was a phrase commonly used to mean "Time to set to work"; it was the signal to set about the serious business of the autumn season..[36]

In each community the time of the festival came at a time of crisis in its particular economic and social situation. The festival itself, therefore, occupying as it did a specific time and place, served as a signpost to mark the passage from one state to another. This is why it is considered as a rite of passage, that is, a ritual of regular alteration in the life of the community, for it signified the sacred, the hallowed in place and time, in contrast to everyday life.

3.2.2. The complex nature of the festival

The festival is a three-dimensional phenomenon, combining religious, social and economic aspects. None of these aspects, however, can be isolated from the others; on the contrary, none could exist without the others; they are interlinked and reciprocally reinforcing. There are however certain exceptions, cases where one aspect tends to overshadow the others, where the festival tends to become uni-dimensional, as in the case of a festival which turns into a trade fair, a livestock fair, a bazaar, when its very nature and function are radically transformed.

As a social phenomenon, the festival has its roots in

Horseback procession of men from Siatista, taking their red blankets to the fair at the festival of Our Lady (Assumption Day, August 15) at the Monastery of the Assumption near Mikrokastro (Tsirousino), in the district of Kozani. This important festival attracted people from all over Western Macedonia.

the land (the place) and the agricultural (and by extension the general productive) cycle. The festival determines the place, the specific position of the community, and its place in the specific annual cycle, the date of the festival which is constantly renewed and recurrent.

As a religious phenomenon, the festival is rooted in a metaphysical conception of place and time, which establishes the hallowed place (fair ground, church building, procession, church service) and the hallowed time (the feast day of the local saint). It establishes the time of the festival in contrast to the time of work, and the extraordinary (the hallowed and sacred) in contrast

Men's dance at the festival of the Ascension Day in Samarina. A. Wace - M. Thompson, The Nomads of the Balkans, 1914, plate IV. (Greek translation 1989, p. 308, 2).

to the ordinary (everyday life).

As an economic phenomenon, the festival is characterized by a form of (initially rudimentary) exchange and redistribution of wealth (goods and money), with the payment of vows, donations, offerings, auction , community banquets, etc. A form of interchange which was occasionally transmuted into purely economic and commercial transactions.

The congress of all the members of the community in one place at one time, under strictly predetermined circumstances, with an established procedure, both affirmed and confirmed their cohesion and their sense of community, and promoted their unity. The individual is identified with the group, and the group with itself, in a series of typical (ritually predetermined) contacts in a demonstration of the socially correct: friendship, cooperation, hospitality, peace, and in general all the positive values approved by the community. The festival was an outward manifestation of "us" as opposed to "them", the others; it was the occasion for the strengthening of community relationships with individuals and other communities as units, and finally, for the resumption of the obligation to preserve communal, and to extend inter-communal, relationships.

For one particular moment in time, the community which was celebrating its festival became the centre, the pole of attraction, for the mass mobilization of all the surrounding communities. However extensive the district might be, for that one moment it had one common centre. Each community in turn could become a centre of attraction. During the festival the social identity of each participating community was highlighted: those from each different place were quite distinctive in their local costumes. And when a festival was adopted by more than one community (as was the case, for example, with the festival of Our Lady of Tsirousino, near Kozani), which happened when it was held in a sacred spot on the confines of different communities, in a monastery, or in plcae like a hill, a mountain chapel, a riverside, etc, then attendance and rivalry in offerings were heightened.

The festival was the prime socio-economic event in the community..[37] Its most picturesque moment was probably the gathering of the traders and pedlars, with merchandise of every description, at the site of the festival in hopes of selling their wares. These festivals provided a most effective system for the exchange of goods on the domestic market, at least within the limits of each district. Almost all festivals had a fair as well, even if only a small one. Often the very word "festival" was used indiscriminately to mean "fair", from the small weekly fairs which later became mere bazaars, to the large annual trade fairs. And precisely because the mer-

Wooden spindle head. The lower part depicts three women dancing, and the top a woman holding a baby. (Folk Museum, University of Thessaloniki).

cantile element tended to overshadow the religious, the Church often laid down specific rules for the functioning of trade fairs in distinction from the religious festivals. The confusion between bazaar and festival/fair is considerable. Although some festivals were actually called bazaars, because the mercantile element was never entirely predominant the word "bazaar" should be reserved for the regular periodic market, large or small. Furthermore, even today, when the concept of economic worth seems to have acquired a life of its own, within traditional society all phenomena and codes of behaviour still retain their triple nature: social, economic and religious.

The festivals, then, were places for exchanges and transactions, but they were first and foremost places for establishing social relationships, for ceremonial and celebration. These gatherings were highly convivial. The crowds of people who flocked in needed to be housed and fed, for the festivals lasted several days; and so tents and booths were set up: in ancient Greece, in fact, the verb "to pitch tents" came to mean "to celebrate a festival", and the same was true in more recent times.

One of the greatest local festivals was held in Thessaloniki. The feast day of its patron saint was the occasion for a tremendous popular gathering and for a revitalization of the local economy with an influx of goods and money. Into Thessaloniki for the Feast of Aghios Dimitrios "came not only those from the nearby villages, but hosts of people from every place and of every race: Greeks, Serbs, Bulgars [...] from as far away as the Danube [...] They came from Italy and Spain and

France and Asia, and from other places too..."

The festival was a ritual popular gathering, and it featured: religious ceremonies (a procession, vespers, veneration of the icons, liturgical services, blessings, blessings of homes, etc), collections, payments of vows, auction sales, banquets (with all contributing and all sharing), sacrifices (to kourbani, or "animal sacrifice", was an offering by a group, and individual or a family in which the whole community shared), special dances (such as "dancing the cup"), singing and dancing generally, games (tug-of-war, wrestling, running races), and special rites, such as the representation of St George killing the dragon.

3.2.3. Fairs and festivals in Macedonia

Typical religious festivals

The festival of Aghia Paraskevi (July 26) in Kolkhiko (Balaftsa), district of Thessaloniki [38]

"[The custom described below is indigenous to Balaftsa, a village lying to the northeast of Thessaloniki at a distance of about four hours. The village is inhabited by 65 families, of whom 20 are independent, and the others are tenants of the chifliks...] On July 26, feast day of Aghia Paraskevi, the village celebrates. The people exchange visits; wandering musicians entertain from house to house; and towards noon everybody, villagers and visitors alike, for many people come in from all over the district on this occasion, proceed with their wives and children to a verdant spot outside the village. This is the site of the chapel of Aghia Paraskevi, and the people wait around under the shade of the trees until all have arrived. Nearby, food is cooking in large kettles suspended over fires, for the meal which they will all share. When everyone has come, the church bell summons them into the little courtyard, where the priest in his stole conducts a short service; then the swarms of villagers sit in groups in the courtyard of the church and eat the food which has been prepared. The cost of this meal is borne by the coffers of the community [...] After dinner, community officials, who have procured a copious supply of watermelons, which because of the abundant production in that area are there sold at very low prices, go around to each of these groups and auction off their watermelons for the benefit of the church. These are sold at extravagant prices. In the same way various handicrafts from the village are also auctioned: towels, sheets, kerchiefs and handkerchiefs, all embroidered and all offered to the church. These too are sold at very high prices..."

The tradition of the festival of the Prophet Elijah (Profitis Ilias) at Grintadhes, in the district of Grevena[39]

"Every year on the 20th day of the Reaper (July),

[sic], when we had our festival, a deer used to come on that day, and we used to lie in wait for it, and we killed it and cooked it in a cauldron. And everybody who came for the festival took a piece and ate it. But one year it came all in a sweat, all worn out, and we cut it down right then, because it was late in coming. And since that day it has never come again".

Ta kloubania t'Aghiou (sacrifices to the Saint) on the island of Thasos [40]

"In the olden days they used to make sacrifices to the Saint. Great and small alike would gather to feast in honour of the Saint. They would sit down several families together, friends and relatives. If two families had quarrelled, on that day they could make it up. One family would send the other a dish of food, and the other would reply with a jug of wine, they accepted each others gifts and so they were reconciled..."

Example: The kourbantzidhes (those offering an animal for sacrifice) of Saint John, in Angista (Serres)[41]

"On the Feast day of St John (January 7) the priest brings the icon out of the church; whoever wants to help in the kourbani puts his hand on the icon. This is a promise to the Saint, and everybody knows that next year these will be the kourbantzidhes. After Christmas the kourbantzidhes go around the village collecting offerings of wheat. This is auctioned [...] and the money is used to buy a cow, oil, and whatever else is necessary to cook it. At the same time they also collect bligouri [cracked wheat] and wood [...] On the day of the Epiphany, after the diving for the Cross, the cow is slaughtered in the courtyard of the church, and the meat is put on to boil that afternoon with the bligouri; the cooking continues all night. The next day, St John's Day, one of the kourbantzidhes takes a plateful of the cooked meat into the sanctuary, where it is blessed by the priest. The same man then returns the meat to the pot with the rest. As soon as the service is over, the meat is distributed. Each villager comes up in turn and takes a platter of food, enough for all the members of his family. This meat is considered blessed..."

Example: The stockherders' festival of Aghia Paraskevi in Dhotsiko (Grevena)[42]

"The custom of the public sacrifice of goats and lambs to ward off evil, or in thanksgiving to the divine, is indigenous to this region as well. Of all such ceremonies the principal one is that held in honour of Aghia Paraskevi, on July 26. On that day, with due reverence and to the accompaniment of folk songs and dances (even today) on the hill above the village of Dhotsikon where the church of Aghia Paraskevi is situated, the ceremony is performed. The festival of

Aghia Paraskevi is an important one for the stockherders; and all the shepherds, herdsmen and cheesemakers flock to it. After Divine Service, there is a blessing in the courtyard of the Church, after which they commence the preparations for slaughtering the animal [...] There is a written tradition about this custom which says: In our village we venerate Aghia Paraskevi. On the heights above the village is the Saint's church. She has several times saved our village from destruction by the Turks. Once upon a time the Turks were intending to destroy the village. In order to reach the village, they had to climb the hill where the church is [...] The day before, Kapetan Loukas came to our village, and told us that he had had a dream, that the Saint had told him to go up to the heights and barricade himself in there to prevent the Turks from reaching the village. And that is what happened. He went up, he built himself a barricade, and when the Turks came they fought ferociously, but they were defeated. Since that day we have celebrated the Saint's favour. The congregation slaughters a goat, and the whole village gathers at the church. In the olden days a deer used to appear from the forest on the day of the festival; it would stand apart, and the priest used to slaughter it himself; then the people would cook it, and everybody ate. Today we slaughter a goat. This year, too, someone offered a goat; the Congregational Committee slaughtered it and cooked it. Afterwards the villagers formed three large groups. Everyone in turn came up and took a piece of meat, and we all ate together. The hide was auctioned".

Example: The kourbania at the festival of St George in the village of Aghios Athanasios (Pella)[43]

"In the village of Aghios Athanasios (Pella), the Feast of St George (which signals the beginning of summer) has acquired a particularly pastoral character. For this reason, until a few years ago the shepherds would offer as a sacrifice (kourbani) lambs, which were slaughtered on the day of the festival, and the meat shared by all who came. Also, on the eve of the festival the ewes were milked for the first time. Before the milking, every household lit a bonfire of dung in front of the door. That evening, while they were decorating their doors with flowers, they would take cowdung and make three crosses on the door..."

Example: The festival of Aghii Anarghiri in the village of Nisi (Pella)[44]

"The Aghii Anarghiri are revered here, too, as doctors, according to the Church; in the village of Nisi there is an old chapel dedicated to them. On their feast day, July 1, a goat which has been purchased with church funds is slaughtered there at the time of the divine service. This goat is roasted on a spit, outside the chapel.

Festival in the village of Emmanouil Papas, in the district of Serres, before the war.

Youngsters of 12 to 20 years of age carry the pieces around to be auctioned; whoever bids the highest sum takes his piece. Part of the animal is kept by the commissioners, who divide it into small portions and share it among all the families of the village. This distribution is consecrated to the health of the village. The Aghii Anarghiri are considered as protectors of children. If an epidemic should happen to attack the children, we say that we must have forgotten the Saints, especially if it happens that the sacrifice did not take place".

The adaptation of fairs and festivals to the needs of economic relationships

Example: To isnafi ton abatzidhon (the guild of the makers of heavy woollen cloth) at the festival of the Monastery of the Baptist, Serres[45]

"...The conduct and the supervision of the festival of the Monastery of the Baptist (Moni tou Timiou Prodromou) has for as long as anyone can remember been in the hands of the guild of the abatzidhes, the makers of heavy woollen cloth. This monastery is renowned for its patriotic activity, its internal administration, its library, and its wealth of animals, lands and treasures [...] At about 9 o'clock in the morning on the eve of the festival, the mules belonging to the monastery would go down into Serres and stand outside the covered market, where the shops of the wool merchants used to be. The abatzidhes were waiting for them; after hanging huge bells around the necks of the mules, they mounted them and set off for the monastery, to the deafening sound of the bells, which was augmented by the bells hanging outside all the shops, which were being rung by the shopkeepers [...] to speed the wool merchants on their way. When the procession arrived at the monastery, its seven bells were rung melodiously, and all the monks lined up to welcome the guild. After a short pause for the traditional refreshments (Turkish delight, coffee, raki), the wool merchants assumed their functions [...] Among other things, there were huge cauldrons of chick peas, which were distributed to the people, with bread, for their evening meal. The people flocked to the festival in great numbers, from Serres and the entire region, bringing a wealth of gifts for the monastery. [There followed vespers and an overnight vigil, and in the morning the service was conducted by the Metropolitan of Serres]. At about noon the festival ended with a banquet in honour of the wool merchants, held in the great hall and attended by the Matropolitan and the officers among the monks. Then they all returned to the city, led by the guild members on their mounts [...] holding the alabassia (fruit grown at the monastery) which they traditionally bought at the festival [...] The

people of Serres were accustomed, that afternoon, to go out to the coffee houses in the countryside to greet the return of the procession by ringing the bells hung up around the coffee shops in answer to the bells carried by the mules.."

Example: The tradition about the tanners' guild and the icon of Our Lady of Rouznou, in Melenikon[46]

"Once there was a queen called Rosa. She had a dream, and she built the monastery of Rouznou. The icon of the Panaghia (Our Lady) was up in a tree. All the guilds came to try to get it down, but only the tanners were able to lift it. And from that day to this only the tanners carry the icon".

[The tanners' guild of Melenikon was entrusted with carrying the miraculous icon in the procession which was held on the Birthday of Our Lady, on September 8].

The emphasis on ritual and religious activities:

Example: The popular celebration of the Feast of St George in Dharnakochori Neo Souli (formerly Soubaskii) in the district of Serres[47]

[A description of the 1965 celebrations]: "The folk festival of St George takes place on the day after the religious festival, that is, on April 24 (or the second day after Easter). After Divine Service in the central Church of the Assumption, the priests and the people proceed to the chapel of St George, which is located a little way outside the village, at the site of the cemetery. A blessing is pronounced, and milk and Turkish delight are distributed. Then a procession is formed, led by the village priest on his mount. He is followed by two youths carrying a sounding-board made of old wood, and then others carrying bairakia me spaleta (banner standards with colourful kerchiefs). Behind them, in a long line, come the children carrying the icons which they had received from the church several days earlier, and which they had placed on the shrines in their homes. The beat of the sounding-board accompanies the procession as it moves in a circle around the boundaries of the village fields. [There follows the description of the oblation to the landmarl. trees at the four points of the compass, and the circling of the chapel by the procession, with songs and special dances]. When the last dance has been completed [...] there isa representation of the miracle of the slaying of the dragon [...] A youth from the village, dressed as St George, with a red mantle and a spear in his right hand, appears on a white horse and rides through the assembled multitude towards a nearby spring, which is meant to represent the lair of the dragon which blocked the village water supply. When he reaches the spot, the water, which has been made ready in a small reservoir, is released to run freely into a nearby watercourse [...] After that, in the Church of the Assumption whence the procession started out, the priest blesses those who carried the icons. The festival is concluded with games and races..."

The festival as social gathering:

Example: The festival of Liokali, and the other festivals in Serres[48]

"In the city of Serres, beyond the torrent in the north part of the suburb known as Katakonozi (that is, the area of the Cantacuzenes, the imperial Byzantine family), was the church of Panaghia tis Liokalis (Our Lady of Liokali), commemorating Our Lady's Birthday. This church [...] belongs to the monastery of (Panaghia) Kossinissa or Ikossifinissa) on Mt Pangaion.[49]. It was burnt to the ground by the Bulgars in 1913 [...] Its festival on September 8 was celebrated every year by great numbers of people, for, apart from the citizens of Serres, the people flocked in from all over the surrounding area. Countless numbers of small traders, selling toys, jewellery, sweets, and small items of all sorts, lined the large courtyard of the church, crying their wares to the pilgrims [...] The festival of Liokali was famous throughout Eastern Macedonia; it was a joyous occasion which marked the beginning of the serious labours of the autumn season. The phrase "the big drum of Liokali has sounded" was equivalent to "it is high time we set to work", for this was the time of year when the children went back to school and their parents set about their preparations for the winter.

Aside from the festival of Liokali [...] other major festivals in the region were: 1) July 27: the festival of Aghios Panteleimon of Gazoros (Porna); 2) August 29: the festival of the Monastery of the Baptist; 3) and 4) September 14: the festivals of the Cross at the chapel of Vysani and the village of Koula (Palaiokastron); and 5) October 26: the festival of Aghios Dimitrios at Provista (Palaiokomi). Even today these festivals are attended by vast numbers of people from the city of Serres and the neighbouring villages [...] During the official religious festivals, assorted troupes of acrobats (tsambatzidhes) attract the attention of the pilgrims with their spectacular performances; they then ask for the favour of a few coins. Before the Balkan Wars a number of travelling circuses used to visit the city from time to time, well equipped with clowns, monkeys, savage jungle beasts, trained horses, all performing to the music of a band. These shows usually set up their tents at "Khilia Dentra" (The Thousand Trees) [...] These spectacles were worthy of attention, and all the schools used to visit them so that their pupils might see the beasts of the jungle and the other animals".

Examole: The festival of Panaghia tis Makryrakhis at Kolindros[50]

"...August 15: free from care, their agricultural labours almost over, the peasants prepare to set out on the great pilgrimage. Fasting, in accordance with the custom of the church, they will go to the Panaghia tis Makryrakhis (Monastery of the Assumption in Pieria) to share in the holy communion. A whole stream of people are headed for the monastery, walking, riding, or drivimg their carts. Pilgrims from all over, from the cities and the most remote villages. Girls in their colourful dresses, with their embroidered aprons and their new petticoats which with every movement afford glimpses of ribbons and lace, with the gold jewellery of their age, the ducats and the florins which glisten in the light and in the shadow. And the young men, in the native costume of their homes, with their brightly coloured sashes and their fezzes tipped flirtatiously to the side, "mangika, ghia to assikliki"..[51] And everyone carries a candle and pays a vow to Our Lady. Among them stand out the wasted faces of the ill, and of others, lying in their carts, or huddled on the backs of their horses and mules, who have come pray for the favour of Our Lady and to find health. All these people [...] are housed for the night in the 150 cells of the monastery's three-storey guesthouse, after they have been blessed, have drunk of the holy water, and have left behind something of their own, an item of clothing, a few hairs from their head, a bit of ribbon, and have lit a candle to the Virgin. After vespers begins the all-night vigil, which is attended by the grown men, the elderly and the ill. At dawn the bells ring out, summoning them to the service [...] After which they all flock back and settle down to eat [...] Then begins the singing and the dancing [...] and to bring the festivities to a close they perform the mime dance "Pos to trivoun to piperi tou diavolou i kalogeri" (How the devil's monks grate their pepper), and such dances as the zeibekiko, the karsilamas, and the khasapiko [...] And with the setting of the sun they make their preparations for departure..."

French archaeologist L. Heuzey gives us an interesting description of this festival in 1858[52]:"...The Panaghia of Makryrakhi is an episcopal convent in the See of the Bishop of Kitros, but it is famous throughout the land. A happy chance took us [there] on a festal day. Pilgrims from all the scattered villages had gathered in the ancient Pierian forest. The wooden corridors of the three-storey building surrounding the inner courtyard on three sides were swarming with people, so many it made one dizzy to contemplate them. Their heads were decorated with cyclamens and a kind of crocus that blooms in Pieria and on Mt Olympus at that season. The ground was covered with long, low tables, around which they sat, tailor-fashion. Among the variegated crowd of peasants it was

The Edessa barbers' guild at the festival at Aghia Triada.

easy to pick out the citizens of Kolindros, with their dignified manners and their rich attire, trimmed with fur..."

The festival as trade fair

Example: The Kervani, the large annual trade fair in Serres[53]

"...Besides the weekly market in Serres[54], which is always busy and animated, there is now a large annual trade fair known as the Kervani[55], which has in fact grown up in response to this very lively commercial activity. Right up until the final decades of the previous century the Kervani trade fair was a major social and economic event for the city of Serres, for it attracted a host of merchants from every country, as well as from the entire surrounding region, and all of Macedonia and the Balkans, who came to take advantage of the lower prices offered by the dealers there to stock up on all the imported and local goods displayed for sale [...] The Kervani trade fair [...] lasted for approximately two weeks [...] Now, at the beginning of this century, changes in social and commercial practices have reduced the

Kervani to a memory, to the name of a huge square block of two-storey buildings, with shops at street level, enclosing a spacious courtyard. This complex is located on the left side of the western gate of the great covered central market known as the Orta Tsarsi (Central Market) and was, apparently, the epicentre of the trade fair and exhibition, from which it derived its name [...] Until it was burned down in 1913, the block of buildings in Serres known as the Kervani housed, at street level, splendid shops entirely European in style, shops selling men's and women's wear, toys, sewing machines, and a host of other things, both items of apparel and household goods..."

Example: The festival of the Monastery of the Holy Trinity (Moni tis Aghias Triadas) in Edessa

"The Monastery of the Holy Trinity celebrates the Feast of Pentecost with great pomp [...] Since many young people gathered at the monastery on the day of the festival, there were also many betrothals then and many abductions. Wandering sweet-sellers sold halva made of semolina, choice revani (one master baker, the famous Gaz-Dimitris of Edessa, sold his revani wrapped in leaves of wild mallow), and a kind of revani made from Edessa's mulberries. There were also musicians, who entertained the people all day, pedlars selling their wares, etc. The people of Edessa, and others who came, also offered gifts to the monastery, sheep and various goods, and, especially on the part of those from Edessa, branches loaded with silkworm cocoons, for it was customary in those parts for silk-growers to present to the monastery the mulberry branch which was heaviest with cocoons, that their production might prosper [...] On that day a blessing was pronounced from the hollow of an old walnut tree which grew in the courtyard of the church. They would set up a pavilion by the walnut tree for this purpose [...] In the courtyard there was also a huge bake-oven, which was busy for days beforehand baking bread and pans of food to feed all the pilgrims on the day of the festival. It used to be the custom, and still is, for the grocers' guild to celebrate on that day [...] all the grocers would go to the monastery, attend the service together, break bread in memory of their departed colleagues, and after the service, spend the rest of the day in the courtyard of the church at the festival. Even today the grocers of Edessa follow this tradition, but not quite as faithfully [...] All the guilds had booths on the western side of the monastery, built at their expense, and on the feast day of their patron saint they would go with their families to the monastery, attend divine service and, when they had discussed their professional problems,

and their wives had cooked, they feasted and amused themselves, and in the evening they returned to their homes..."[56]

The following note appeared in a newspaper in 1919: "On Monday last, the 27th day of this month (the feast of Pentecost, May 27), the Monastery of the Holy Trinity, which is situated below our city in a lush, green, romantic setting dotted wih trees, celebrated with unusual magnificence the anniversary of this Feast, in honour of which, on the eve of the day, there congregated at the monastery a host of people from all the villages in the district, as well as from Karatzova, Giannitsa, Naoussa, and even from Florina. Because of the war and the difficulties consequent upon it, the festival has in recent years lacked the splendour which the tremendous affluence of people in this first post-war celebration this year conferred upon it. There were village women in all the beauty and colour of their local dress, there were pious merry-makers from the most remote villages, and Boy Scouts from Florina, Giannitsa and Naoussa, all passing their time in jubilation and spiritual delight. The band of the Philanthropic Society played several musical selections, and the sellers of sweet-meats and refreshing drinks did a roaring trade. When the festival was over, the happy crowds began to depart, eager to return next year, when we are persuaded that the festival will be more magnificent than ever".[57]

People from Edessa at Aghia Triada. In the background are the holy water basin and the old plane tree.

ELEONORA SKOUTERI-DIDASKALOU

ASPECTS OF TRADITIONAL CULTURE

IN MACEDONIA

NOTES

The context

1.Alki Kyriakidou-Nestoros elaborated this proposition in her lectures. See also her studies: "Popular culture" ("Popular and literary tradition" and "Sources of popular culture in the Turkish period"), in "Greece-History and Culture, Thessaloniki 1981, pp 264-278 (in Greek); "The theory of Greek folklore. A critical analysis", Athens 1981 (in Greek), as well as certain articles published in "Studies in Folklore", Athens 1975.

I followed the same general approach to (traditional) culture in my lectures at the University of Thessaloniki and at the Tour Guide Training School of the Greek Tourist Board (EOT): (see "Notes on Greek folklore and folk art", Thessaloniki [polygraph edition for the local EOT School, 1979], and "Folklore and social history. Approaches to modern Greek traditional society (the example of Northern Greece in the final decades of the Turkish imperium), University notes, (University of) Thessaloniki, 1985).

2.These terms are used on the basis of historical research as defined by the studies of the historians of the "Annales" cycle (e.g. L.Febvre, M.Block, F.Braudel) and of British social historians (e.g. E.Hobsbawm, E. P. Thompson, R.Samuel), as well as in similar approaches to historical research in Greece.

3.See "Sources of popular culture in the Turkish period", *op. cit.*, p. 272. She explains further: "Daily life is characterized by [...] standardization which is the distinctive sign of what we call "traditional cultures", which function principally on the basis of oral communication among their members; oral speech as a means of communication, and memory as its repository, to a certain extent impose a way of life in which reality is faced conventionally. [...] From this point of view traditional culture is a system of conventions transmitted from generation to generation [...]", pp 271-272. In this text (and in her introductory text "Popular and literary tradition", *op. cit.*, pp 264-268), Mrs A. Kyriakidou-Nestoros uses the term "popular" to describe the culture which in earlier texts she had characterized as "traditional". As it also appears from the above comparison, Mrs Kyriakidou- Nestoros uses the two terms interchangeably, although with the word "popular" she stresses the cohesion which governed (Greek) culture in the Turkish period on the level of daily life, where the relationship city-village was complementary and pre-supposed, as she notes, "a common cultural stock which was cut off by the establishment of the independent Greek state, as happened in most cases of newly established national states" (p. 267). In her view, the term "popular" "expresses precapitalistic methods of production, with the particularities which appeared in the Ottoman Empire, at the other end of the scale from the European system as it was on the eve of the industrial revolution" (p. 267). She does recognize, on the other hand, a distinction between popular and literary tradition during the Turkish period on the level of language and law.

A. An examination of spatial organization.

1.See Fernand Braudel "L'apport de l'histoire des civilisations", in "Ecrits sur l'Histoire", Paris 1969 (Flammarion), p. 292:"A civilization is, first of all, a place, a cultural region, say the anthropologists, a dwelling-place. Imagine within this dwelling-place (which may be more or less extensive but can never be excessively restricted), a mass of different goods, from cultural elements (such as the shape and material of the houses, their roofs, but also the art of tattooing and a dialect or a group of dialects and their cooking preferences and a special technique or a manner of perception or a way of making love, or even the compass, paper, and the printing press). The first signs of cultural cohesion are the regular arrangement and the frequence of certain elements and their ubiquity within the framework of a specific area. If this spatial cohesion is seconded by temporal continuity, then we call the whole, the entire repertory, a civilization or culture. This whole is what we recognize as the civilization in question..." (Literal translation [from the Greek translation], with my italics). See also Ai Kyriakidou- Nestoros' free rendering of the same definition: " culture is first and foremost a place (and not an idea). In this place a group of people who speak the same language (and, therefore, communicate among themselves using the same symbols), develop a certain way of life. When this way of life has continued for a certain length of time, has acquired a history in other words, it cystallizes into a certain shape, which expresses the by now definite and stable structure of its divers elements...". See "Folklore and Humanistic Studies", university notes, (University of) Thessaloniki, 1980, p. 37 (in Greek) (my italics).

2.For the term "village" ("chorion"), see the detailed study by Angeliki Laiou-Thomadaki. "The agricultural community in the late Byzantine period", Athens 1987, pp 44-100 (and especially pp 58-94) (in Greek).

3.Stables and sheep-folds were often used as dwelling-places for the herdsmen. These places, nevertheless, were usually places for work, and not for family installation and social life; they cannot thus be called places of installation (regardless of the permanence or the duration of their habitation), or settlements, in contrast, for example, to the monasteries.

4.These "huts" constitute a special case. "Huts" was the name given to the nomadic or semi-nomadic settlements which housed the Sarakatsani and Vlach herdsmen (see also below). The name was also applied to the rough lean-tos (of boughs and branches) which supplied the farmers and herdsmen with temporary shelter when they were working at a considerable distance from their permanent homes. These huts occasionally developed into permanent houses. A number of settlements have a tradition that in their area there were originally only a few "huts" (whence the place name "Kalivia"), which were taken over by the original inhabitants or by refugees from distant areas.

5.The mills also constitute a special case, for they were usually located beyond the boundaries of the villages and so, although the millers and their families did live there, could not properly be called settlements. The term "mill" usually designated a flour mill, which ground all types of grain. It might be powered by hand, water, or wind, and later by engine. The machines which washed the heavy woollen fabrics were also known as water-mills. And finally, the olive-growing areas, such as Chalcidice, also had oil mills. For a glossary and a detailed description of flour mills, see the article by Dim. V. Ekonomidis "Greece's traditional flour mills", in the Annals of the Greek Folklore Research Centre, 25, (1975-1978), pp 150-241 (in Greek).

6.See Ch. G. Tsekos, "History of Asvestochori", Thessaloniki 1957, esp. pp 27-32, 38-42 (in Greek). According to the author, the original settlers of the village of Nichori (Neochorion), later called Asvestochori (Kirets-Kioi) because of its production of lime (in Greek "asvestos"), were "Paisvantidhes" from southern Greece (Mani) who had been brought to this forested mountain area as sentinels ("The Five Koulies (sentry-posts)" and "The captain's watch tower"). Compare also St. p. Kyriakidis' review in "Makedonika" 4, (1955-60), pp 615 517 (in Greek).

7.See Z.Tsiros, "Vlasti (formerly Blatsi)" (in Greek), Thessaloniki 1964.

8.See A. i zaferopoulos, "Imathia, (tourist guide)", Thessaloniki 1981, p. 81. Refugees from Stenimachos in Eastern Romylia settled in the village of Horopani in 1923.

9.See E. Stefanopoulos, "Daskion (Pieria): History and Folklore",edited by A.M.Tzaferopoulos, Veria 1972 (in Greek).

10.See generally Ph.Papanikolaou, "History of Krimini", Thessaloniki 1959, and "Language and folklore in the province of Voio", Thessaloniki 1973, by the same author (in Greek). See also D. Gavanas, "Rodochori (Voio)", Kozani 1974 (in Greek).

11.See S.Romanias, "Kavala then and now", 3rd edition, Kavala 1972, pp 32-33 (in Greek), in which the author publishes an exceedingly interesting petition from the citizens of Kavala in 1864. The petition reads:"The under- signed faithful Christian citizens of the Macedonian city of Kavala ... with regard to the steamships which put into our harbour, increased trade has brought an increase in the number of merchants who seek to rent lodgings for their families, but since we live within the walls of the castle, our houses are small and cramped... we have sought permission... to build houses outside the enclosure of the castle, as well as workshops that we may have space in which to work, but... When Your Government accepts this our petition, the city will grow and become more beautiful, the government will benefit by the sale of properties in areas now unexploited, the value of the tobacco we produce will be increased and the revenue from the export tax on tobacco will be multiplied a hundredfold..." This petition was accepted, and the Greeks were given permission to build houses and workshops outside the walls; the Christians promptly built a church, thus founding the parish known today as Aghios Giannis.

12.See generally "The economic structure of the Balkan countries (15th-19th centuries)", Introduction-selected texts by Spyros Asdrakhas, Athens 1979 (in Greek).

13.For the intensive cultivation of cotton on the plain of Serres see Traian Stoianovich, "Land tenure and Related Sectors of the Balkan Economy, 1600-1800", Journal of Economic History, 20 (1960), pp 234-313. See also Natalys Petrovich, "A Miscellany of Folklore from Serres", in Chronicles of Serres, I (1953), 144 (in Greek).

14.See A. J. Wace - M. S. Thompson, "The Nomads of the Balkans. An Account of Life and Customs among the Vlachs of Northern Pindus.", London 1914 (esp. pp 39-59,69-99,129-145).

15.p. Pennas, "History of Serres from its capture by the Turks to its liberation by the Greeks, 1383-1913", Athens 1966, p. 357 (in Greek), where note (1) reads: "Speaking of the plain of Serres, the Turks used the phrase Serres ovasi altin yiovasi, that is, the plain of Serres, land of gold, both metaphorically and literally."

16. p. Pennas, op. cit., pp 357-365, 375-378.

17. Kleisoura was inhabited by people originally from Moschopolis; their wealth came from trade and from cartage (mule trains) within the Ottoman Empire and in Europe. For the term "Cosmopolis", see F.-C. and H-L. Pouqueville, "Voyage de la Grece" (2nd edition), Paris 1826, vol.2, p. 23.

18.See particularly M.W. Leake, "Travels in Northern Greece", vol.3, London 1835, pp 284-288, and N.Th. Schinas, "Notes of a traveller in Macedonia, Epirus, the New Frontier and Thessaly", Athens 1886, p. 167 (in Greek).

19.See N.G. Philippidis, "Makedonika", in "Parnassos", I (1877), pp 286-302 (in Greek); and generally Asterios Gousios "The Land of Mt Pangaion. The landscape, habits, customs and language of Lak-koviki", Leipzig 1894 (in Greek).

20.Thus, despite the fact that industry and industrial technology (the use of special machines and tools and trained personnel, and the creation of special sites and conditions for mass production) began to appear in Macedonia in the second half of the 19th century, this development was nevertheless slow. With the exception of large cities like Thessaloniki and Monastir, the use of machinery penetrated the processes of production on the terms dictated by the traditional character of Macedonian culture. An example of this mentality comes from Melenikon, which had a distillery (publicly owned, according to the Land Register of the Commune of Melenikon for 1872), which was known to the townspeople simply as "the Machine" (see p. Pennas, "Contribution to the history of Melenikon", in the "Chronicles of Serres", 5 (1969), pp 94-95. In Greek). Compare also the case of the dye works for silk thread and cloth at Rapsani, which the people referred to as "Kyr- Hanas" ("Mr Dye"), from the Turkish word for dye (see K. Chrisohoou, "Traditions, songs, proverbs and tales from Rapsani", a collection of folklore material, registered as number ..505 at the Folklore Archives of the University of Thessaloniki). Moreover, despite the moderization of the mills, these remain, in traditional apprehension, "the haunts of devils, demons, imps, sprites and all sorts of evil spirits" (Compare also the lectures of Alki Kyriakidou- Nes-toros at the University of Thessaloniki "Folklore and Technology: An

analysis of traditional Greek culture on the techno-economic level").

21.I.Xanthos, "The history of Gevgeli and the patriotic activity of its citizens and the people of the neighbouring villages", Thessaloniki 1954, p. 13 (in Greek).

22.See Xanthos, op. cit., pp 17-18; and B. Gounaris, "Social and Economic Change in Macedonia (1871-1912): The Role of the Rail-ways, PhD Thesis, Oxford University 1988, p. 179 (esp. re agricultural and industrial production in macedonia see chapters V and VI).

23.Considerable information about these changes is afforded by con-temporary photographs (late 19th and early 20th century), such as those in the invaluable collection of the Manakis brothers. (See Chr. Christdoulou's study, "The photogenic Balkans of the Manakis brothers", Paratiritis Press, Thessaloniki 1989), (in Greek).

24.Assorted descriptions of cities and towns in Macedonia mention a fairly large number of bake-houses or ovens, which furnished bread and other baked goods not only to public institutions, such as the army, but also to private houses (see N. Th. Schinas, op. cit.).

25.By the second half of the 19th century houses in the cities of Macedonia (especially those of the more affluent citizens) were furnished with furniture and utensils either imported or supplied by local industrial and artisanal production. These furnishings were no longer merely the mirrors, chests and beds of an earlier age, but also included tables, chairs, sideboards, cabinets, bureaus, etc. See for example Natalys Petrovich, op. cit., p. 115. Compare also "The urban Greek house in Thessaloniki, 1880-1912 (Exhibition guide), Folk and Ethnological Museum of Macedonia, Thessaloniki 1985.

26.See D. S. Samsaris, "The community of Aghion Pneuma (district of Serres) under Turkish rule", Thessaloniki 1971 (esp. pp 58 ff), and "Contribution to the History of the Community of Emmanouil Pap-pas", Serres 1970, by the same author (in Greek).

27.E.I. Stougiannakis, "History of the city of Naoussa, from its foundation to its destruction in 1822 (from an unpublished sketch by D. Plataridis, Thessaloniki 1976, note (1) on pp 63-64 (in Greek). For the interesting case of Naoussa, where artisanal crafts evolved into industry particularly in the field of spinning and weaving, see Nikos Kalogyrou and Michalis Nomikos, "The Macedonian city of Naoussa: from the autonomous commune of the Turkish imperium to the modern Greek industrial city", from the Acts of the International History Symposium: The Modern Greek City - Ottoman heritage and the Greek state, vol. 1, Athens 1985, pp 257-271.

28.For the guilds and typical urban professions, see Kon. Stalidis, "Guilds and professions in Edessa during the period of Turkish rule", Edessa 1974 (in Greek).

29.See Michail Kallinderi, "The guilds of Kozani in the Turkish period", Thessaloniki 1958, and "The guilds and the Church in the Turkish period", Athens 1973 (in Greek).

30.See generally N. Pantazopoulos, "Greek associations during the Turkish period", reprinted from the magazine "Gnoseis", Athens 1958 (in Greek).

31.See the relevant article by Traian Stoianovich, "Conquering

Balkan Orthodox Merchant", Journal of Economic History, 20 (1960), pp 234-313.

32.Specific examples of the purchase of land by small farming families are instanced by K. Th. Karabidas in "Agrotica, a comparative study", Athens 1931 (photographic reprint 1978), pp 211-232 (in Greek), which details extensive information about cases of gradual purchase of land in villages near Florina early in the 20th century (and particularly after 1909), with capital coming principally from remittances from emigrants to America.

33.E. Stougiannakis, "The Macedonian Calendar of the Pan-Macedonian Society", 4 (1911), pp 144-145 (in Greek).

34.For land ownership in the districts of Naoussa, Veria and Edessa, see G. Skleros, "Modern Greece", Alexandria 1913, pp 125-127 and 128-130 (in Greek).

35.See V. Sphyroeras, "Review of Hellenism by region", in the "History of the Greek Nation", vol. 11 (in Greek) (esp. pp 189-204 and 218-211). See also Felix Beaujour, "Table of Trade in Greece under the Turkish regime (1787-1797). See esp. the topographic description of Macedonia on pp 35-42 and the details of its agricultural and industrial production on pp 54-95, 134-149, 152-165.

36.See F. Beaujour, op. cit., p. 54.

37.In her study "The huts of the Sarakatsani", (Annals of the Folklore Archives, 6 (1950-1951) (in Greek), which was based on a local expedition to collect folklore material, Maria Ioannidou-Barbarigou says of the distinction between the Vlachs and the Sarakatsani: "A Vlach from Samarina told me the following significant things. The Sarakatsani do not have villages; they spend the summers on the mountains and the winters in their winter quarters. The Vlachs are different, they do have a permanent base. Thus it has been since the world was made. They speak good Greek, they don't even know Vlach..." (p. 233, note 2) It is clear that these definitions, which stress the perception of native origin (emics), are based on the difference between nomadic and semi-nomadic ways of life and survival; the differentiation with respect to language (Greek and Vlach) is an additional informative element.

38.It appears, nevertheless, that small families were the rule at that time, that is, nuclear families of parents with their unmarried children and occasionally some other dependent. It is significant that the migrant families of the 19th century were all of this type, as I pointed out in my presentation to the Congress of the Modern Greek Studies Association, at Anatolia College, Thessaloniki, in June 1989, entitled "Stranger, what is your home? The concepts of community and emigration in Northern Greece in the 19th century". For the predominance of the small rural family during the later Byzantine period in the agricultural areas of Central Macedonia at least, see Angeliki Laiou-Thomadaki, "The rural community in the later Byzantine period", transl. A. Kasdagli, Athens 1987.

39.Nikolaos Moutsopoulos, "The precursors of the first Greek professionals: The Koudarei of Macedonia and the Maistores of Epirus", reprinted from the pamphlet entitled "The first Greek professional craftsmen, at the time of the Revolution", produced by the Technical Chamber of Greece in Athens 1976 (in Greek) (the charter is published with a detailed commentary and bibliography on page 25).

40.For the forms and the distribution of these traditional customs throughout Greece, see D.A. Petropoulos, "Customs of collaboration and mutual assistance among the Greek people", Annals of the Folklore Archives, 5-6 (1934- 1944), pp 59-85. The description of the custom of reciprocal assistance in the building of houses was taken from the invaluable unpublished collection of school-master Nik. D. Argyriou entitled "Folklore of the isle of Thasos", page 18 of the manuscript (in Greek).

41.See Photis Papanikolaou, "Language and folklore of the province of Voio", Thessaloniki 1973, p. 227 (in Greek).

42.M. Ioanidou-Barbarigou, "Huts of the Sarakatsani", Annals of the Folklore Archives, 6 (1950-1951), pp 231-244 (in Greek). The material was gathered from Sarakatsani in the Pisoderi region during the course of a folklore expedition to the site carried out by the author in August 1937. Her observations are supported by a considerable bibliography, and deal with the style of the Sarakatsani huts, which were built of more solid materials for their more permanent summer habitations; the author postulates that this is the reason why the Kassandrini Sarakatsani of Florina are not considered real, nomadic, Sarakatsani. She supplements her observations with a description of the Vlach huts in the Mantoudi district of Northern Euboia.

43.Resume of the detailed description in Angeliki Hatzimichali's "Greek popular art. Folk art in Roumlouki (Macedonia), Trikeri (Thessaly) and Ikaria (Aigaion), Athens 1931, pp 26-32 (in Greek).

44.See G. D. Karagkiozopoulos, "The history of Meliki", Athens 1970, (author's typewritten edition), pp 7,9-10 (in Greek).

45.See p. Pennas, "Contribution to the history of Melenikon", Chronicles of Serres 5 (1969), pp 89-128 (in Greek), which reproduces extracts from the Land Register of the Commune of Melenikon, estimating their date as 1872 (the Charter or Administrative System of the Commune of Melenikon had been adopted in 1813). The quotation is from page 102.

46.See Lazarus Vapheidis, "The beauties of lake Prespa", Athens 1940, pp 72-76 (in Greek).

47.See Argyris Kountouras, "Ploughmen's houses in Krania (Elassona)", Perraivia, 1 (1983), 14-20 (in Greek).

48.From Photis Papanikolaou's description in "History of Krimini", Thessaloniki 1959, pp 92-94 (in Greek).

49.Andreas Koromilis, "Vogatsikon: Its History and Folklore", Thessaloniki 1972 (in Greek).

50.Kleopatra Polyzou-Mameli, "History of Kolindros", Thessaloniki 1972, pp 221-225 (in Greek).

51.M. Papamichail, "Kleisoura, Western Macedonia" (publisher's manuscript) 1972, pp 28-32 (in Greek).

52.Petros S. Spandonidis, "Melenikos, the dead Macedonian frontier", Thessaloniki 1930 pp 100-103 (in Greek).

53.N. Moutsopoulos, "Two old houses in Serres", Chronicles of

Serres, 4 (1961), pp 275-295 (in Greek). In this study (as in some of his other fundamental studies of popular architecture), the author develops an extensive comparison of certain structural features of these houses and of similar houses in Kastoria, Veria and other regions in Northern Greece.

54.The description comes from "L'habitation Byzantine", Paris 1903, by the French general De Beylie, as cited (in her own translation) by L. Christomanou-Kalinsky in her article "The Bampouras mansion in Melenikon", Chronicles of Serres, 1 (1953), pp 181-185.

55.Phanis Michalopoulos, "Moschopolis, the Athens of the Turkish regime 1500-1769", Athens 1941, pp 30-33, (in Greek).

56.Georgios A. Megas, "The mansions, songs and musicians of Siatista", Athens 1963 (in Greek).

57.Extracts from N. Moutsopoulos' study, "The popular architecture of Veria", Athens 1967 (esp. pp 21-22, 83-85, 88-89) (in Greek). (See also the extensive bibliography attached to this edition, as well as the drawings and photographs).

58.Extracts from N. Moutsopoulos' preface to "The mansions of Thessaloniki", published by the Macedonian Arts Society "Techni", Thessaloniki 1976.

59.The political and economic nature of village life in Turkish-ruled Macedonia is treated by other authors as well in this volume.

60.See generally the views of Alki Kyriakidou-Nestoros on spatial organization in her two fundamental articles: "Landmarks, or the logic of the Greek landscape" and "Spatial organization in traditional cultures", Studies in Folklore, Athens 1975 (in Greek).

61.According to information from the folklore collection of Aspasia Petsa, 1954 (the Athens Academy Greek Folklore Research Centre), registered as K.. 2060, page 11, (as referred to by G. Aikaterinidis in "Celebrating St George's Day in Neo Souli (Serres)", Chronicles of Serres 5 (1969), pp 142-143 (note 3).

62.This traditition is recorded by Geo. K. Spyridakis, "Exposition of folklore research in the prefecture of Pella", Annals of the Folklore Archives, 13-14 (1960-61), p. 383 (which refers also to the manuscript register of material, .A. 2394, 1961, page 222-223) (in Greek).

63.See E. I. Stougiannakis, "History of the city of Naoussa", pp 37-41, which reproduces the text (in Turkish, but with Greek characters), and the translation of the part of the edict dealing with the boundaries of the city.

64.According to information contained in "Celebrating St George's Day" (G. Aikaterinidis), (pp 129-160, and esp. pp 134-142); and the extensive bibliography on the subject. Compare also G. N. Aikaterinidis, "Folk mission to the villages of the district of Serres", Annals of the Folklore Archives, 15-16 (1962-1963), which refers to his manuscript notes: A.E.271, A.E.2762, and A.E.2763 in the Folklore Archives (now the Greek Folklore Research Centre) of the Athens Academy, as well as to the older study by Georgios A. Megas, "Tradition and illness", Laographia, 7 (1927), pp 465-520 (esp. pp 489-490) (in Greek).

65.This tradition is recorded by Angelos N. Deuteraios, "Exposition of folklore research in the district of southern Grevena", Annals of the Greek Folklore Research Centre, 18-19 (1965-1966), p. 322, which refers to the manuscript register of this material, registered under GFRC 3027, p. 231 (in Greek).

66.According to G. N. Aikaterinidis, who recorded this tradition in 1963 (op. cit., note 3 to pp 142-143, which refers to GFRC2761, p. 419).

67.Phanis Michalopoulos, "Moschopolis", op. cit., p. 11.

68.Polyzou-Mameli, op. cit., pp 97-98.

69.See too the interesting study by Vasilis Dimitriadis "The Topography of Thessaloniki during the Turkish period 1430-1912", Thessaloniki 1983 (in Greek).

70.That is, the distillery in Melenikon: Pennas, "Contribution to the history of Melenikon", pp 94-95 (f. 20).

71.That is, the site of the dye works for silk thread and cloth in Rapsani (f. 20).

72.That is, the covered market. In Greece, according to A. Orlando, there remain only two covered markets: the Bezesteni of Thessaloniki and the famous Bezesteni of Serres. In Serres, according to the Chronicle of Evligia Tselempi, "besides the two thousand shops, there were nine Bezestenia with domed and leaded roofs, four with iron gates". According to the Chronicle of PapaSynodinou (1630), there was only one Bezesteni, that which is still standing. See Petros Th. Pennas, "History of Serres 1383-1913", Athens 1966, pp 515-517 (in Greek).

73.Michalopoulos, "Moschopolis", pp 13-14.

74.K. Skenteris, "History of Moschopolis", Athens 1928, p. 54 (as noted by Michalopolis, op. cit., p. 12) (in Greek).

75.From Karavidas, op. cit., pp 114-115. See also his general observations on the chifliks and tenant farmers of the Balkans, p. 111 ff.

76.See the detailed description of the chiflik villages of Palikoura and Bardovtse, in the northern sector of the Axios valley, in L. Schultze-Jena, "Makedonien. Land- schafts- und Kulturbilder", Iena, 1927, pp 140-146, 146-150.

77.See generally the analytical descriptions of the plain of Thessaloniki and its villages in Schultze-Jena, op. cit., esp. pp 104-130, which include plans, diagrams and photographs.

78.N. Th. Schinas, "Notes of a Traveller", pp 176, 202-208. The settlements referred to are Mylotopos (Voudrista), Anavissos (Obar), Nisi (Niselouda), Halastra (Koulakia), Valmada and Kymina (Giantsida).

79.A. Hatzimichali, "Greek Folk Art", esp. pp 23-26. The settlements referred to are Alexandria (Gida), Koryphi (Korphi) and Meliki (Melik).

80.See "Notes of a Traveller", vol.3 Athens 1887, p. 538.

81.As noted by N. K. Moutsopoulos "Athytos Chalcidice. Programme for revival and beautification", Thessaloniki (EOT) 1976, pp 77-78 (in Greek).

82.N. K. Moutsopoulos, "Athytos Chalcidice", pp 78-80.

83.See Ap. E. Vakalopoulos, "History of Macedonia", pp 506-512. See also pp 540-581 where he describes the situation in Chalcidice in the pre-revolutionary period and during the 1821 Revolution, as well as the situation after the violent repression of the revolutionary movements and the destruction of many settlements in the area, namely Arnaia (Liarigovov), Petrokerasa (Ravna), Neochori (Novoselo), Stageira (Mahalas or Kazantzi Mahala), Stratoniki (Isviros), Megali Panaghia (Revenikia).

84.See "Notes of a Traveller", vol.3, 1987, pp 490, 517- 521, 826-833.

85.A. E. Vakalopoulos, "History of Macedonia", p. 513.

86."Notes of a Traveller", p506-509.

87.A. E. Vakalopoulos, op. cit., pp 513-514.

88."Notes of a Traveller", op. cit., p. 534.

89."History of Macedonia", op. cit., pp 297-300,313,315 (see also ref.1, note 83, on the Revolution in Chalcidice and Thasos).

90.N.Th. Schinas, "Notes of a Traveller", vol.3, (1887) pp 850-852,860-864.

91.A.J.Wace-M.S.Thompson, "The Nomads of the Balkans", pp 39-42 (free rendition).

92.Gousios, "The Land of Mt Pangaion", pp 25-37. The village in question is Demir-Isario.

93.See generally T.L.F.Tafel, "De Thessalonica eiusque dissertatio gepgraphica", Berlin 1839; Michail Hatziioannou, "Description of the City of Thessaloniki", Thessaloniki 1880; p. Risal [Iosif Nehama], "La Ville Convoitee: Salonique", Paris 1917 (1st ed. 1914); N. Svoronos, "Le commerce de Salonique au XVIIe siecle", Paris, 1956; A.E. Vakalopoulos, "History of Macedonia"; Kostis Moskov, "Thessaloniki 1700-1912: Examination of the commercial city", Athens 1973; Nikolaos Moutsopoulos, "Thessaloniki 1900-1917", Thessaloniki 1980. For the last phase of the traditional history of the city, see Aleka Karadimou- Gerolympou, "The reconstruction of Thessaloniki after the fire of 1917", Thessaloniki 1986. All these important studies on the modern history of Thessaloniki have extensive bibliographies. See also (a), re housing in Thessaloniki at the turn of the century, the publication of the Folk and Ethnological Museum of Thessaloniki, "The urban Greek house in Thessaloniki" (this edition accompanied an exhibition organized by the Museum in 1985); and (b), re the initial phase of industrial development in the city, the Guide which accompanied the exhibition organized by the National Industrial Development Bank in 1987 on the topic "Early Industrialization in Thessaloniki (1870-1912) (org. by V. Kolonas and O. Traganou-Deligianni); and (c), the pamphlet "Thessaloniki and the National Bank, 1913-1940", published in Thessaloniki (1989) on the occasion of the exhibition organized by the Cultural Centre (Northern Greece) of the National Bank of Greece.

94.Daniil Philippidis, Grigrios Konstantas, "Modern Geography (On Greece), arranged by Aik. Koumarianou, Athens 1970, pp 132-133.

95.As noted by Kyriakos Simopoulos, "Foreign travellers in Greece, 1700-1800", vol.1, Athens 1973, pp 109-110 (in Greek).

96.Simopoulos, op. cit., pp 175-176.

97.Simopoulos, op. cit., pp 423-424.

98.As noted by Moskov, op. cit., p. 20.

99.Beaujour, op. cit., pp 42-43.

100.As noted by Simopoulos, op. cit., p. 496.

101.Moskov, op. cit., p. 20.

102.See Mary Adelaide Walker, "Through Macedonia to the Albanian lakes (Ochrida and Maliki), (Greek translation by K. Pyrza, Thessaloniki 1973, pp 31-32 and 34).

103.Moskov, op. cit., p. 26.

104.As noted by Moutsopoulos, "Thessaloniki", p. 49.

B. An examination of temporal organization.

1.See Dim Loukopoulos, "Folklore Miscellany from Macedonia", Laographia, 6 (1917-1918), p. 115 (no.4). Similar traditions are found in divers regions. Compare N.G. Politis "Studies on the life and language of the Greek people. Traditions", vol.1-2, Athens 1904; St. p. Kyriakidis, "Greek giants", Calendar of Greater Greece, Athens 1926; I. Th. Kakridis, "The ancient Greeks in modern popular tradition" (translated from the 1st German edition of 1966), Athens (National Bank of Greece Educational Institute) 1989 (3rd edition); and A. Kyriakidou-Nestoros, "The ancient Greeks in modern Greek tradition", Studies in Folklore, Athens 1975, pp 204-213. (In Greek).

2.Loukopoulos, op. cit., p. 114 (no.5).

3.Loukopoulos, op. cit., p. 117 (no.9).

4.Mich. Slinis, "Rural customs in Drimos, Macedonia", Laographia, 12 (1938), p. 92 (in Greek).

5.See "The Serres Chronicles of Papasynodinou", edited by Petros Pennas, Chronicles of Serres, 1 (1938), pp 27-72 (in Greek).

6."Chronicles and notes", (edited by N.V.X., accordin to the cover and the last pages, under no. 547 (formerly 567) of the Codex of the Library of the Hagiographic Institute in Constantinople, under the title "Rhetorical and epistolary types", Bulletin of the Historical and Ethnological Society of Greece, 4 (1982), p. 695 (in Greek).

7.Alki Kyriakidou-Nestoros, "The twelve months in folklore", Thessaloniki 1982, p. 6 (in Greek).

8.The concept of practical perception (as opposed to literary or scientific or theoretical perception) is proposed by Pierre Bourdieu: sens pratique, sens savant. See e.g. Boudieu, "Le sens pratique", Paris 1980.

9.See generally A. Kyriakidou-Nestoros, "Sources of popular culture under the Turkish regime" in "Greece: History and Culture", Thessaloniki 1981, pp 269-278 (in Greek).

10.Compare J. Le Goff on the perception of time in western mediaeval society: "temporal reality is a multiple of time" (see "La Civilisation de l'Occident Medieval", Paris 1965, p. 223). Le Goff distinguishes between three types of time, all related to natural time: rural time (temps rural), seigneurial time (temps seigneural), and religious and clerical time (temps religieux et clerical).

11.The term ecological time belongs to anthropologist Evans-Pritchard, as does the term structural time. See E.E. Evans-Pritchard, "The Nuer. A Description of the Models of Livelihood and Political Institutions of a Nilotic People", Oxford 1940 (esp. pp 94-138).

12.See M. Nilson, "Primitive Time-Reckoning", Lund 1920. See also M. Mauss, "Essai sur les variations saisonnieres des societes Eskimos. Etude de morphologie sociale", L'Annee Sociologique, 9 (1904-1905), pp 39-132.

13.With respect to the organization of time on the levels of production procedures and the world theory relating to the popular and ecclesiastical calendar of feasts, the traditional society of Macedonia is sustantially the same as traditional society in the rest of Greece: the various individual customs and traditions may differ, but their logic and structure remain the same. In this context see Alki Kyriakidou-Nestoros, "The twelve months", as well as "Time in oral history", Mitis, 2 (1987), pp 177-188 (in Greek) (reprinted in Contemporary Topics, 35-36-37 (1988), pp 233-238). See also G.A. Megas, "Greek festivals and popular religious customs", Athens 1963 (in Greek); and Dimitrios Loukatos, "Christmas and Holiday Rites, Easter and Spring Rites, the Rites of Summer, the Rites of Autumn, Supplementary Winter and Spring Rites", Athens 1979, 1980, 1981, 1982, and 1985 respectively (in Greek). See also Vasilis Apostolopoulos, "The organization of time", in "Greece-History and Culture", vol.5, Thessaloniki 1981, pp 306-323 (in Greek); and Stelios Papadopoulos, "Time in traditional society", Contemporary Topics, 35-36-37 (1988) pp 239-242 (in Greek).

14.Pantelis Tsamisis, "Kastoria and its monuments", Athens 1949, p. 41 (in Greek).

15.For a similar perception in traditional French society, see Lucien Febvre, "Le probleme de l'incroyance au XVIe siecle", Paris 1942 (2nd edition 1968, pp 365-371).

16.For the place of the clock in western culture, see Carlo Cipolla, "Clocks and Culture, 1300-1700", London 1967, where he contends that the clock, which was the prototype of all precision instruments, influenced the nature and the quality of life to such a degree that it provoked radical changes in attitudes and ways of life.

17.Data from the invaluable unpublished Mavroudis Papathanasiou collection of folklore material, "Collection of Folklore and Linguistic material from Chalcidice" (Society for Macedonian Studies, collection no. 1854, manuscript pp 113-114) (in Greek). Extracts from the collection have been published in the periodical "Chronicles of Chalcidice".

18.See Beaujour, op. cit., p. 176, where he records that in Thessaloniki 30 dozen English (pocket) watches were sold annually at prices ranging from 80 to 120 piastres, 300 dozen in Constantinople, 400 dozen in Smyrna, and 30 dozen in Morea. Beaujour observes that "consumption of watches was bound to be considerable in a country with no sun dials or public clocks, and where the hour of prayer had to calculated with precision five times a day..."

19.See Natalys Petrovich, "A Folklore Miscellany from Serres", Chronicles of Serres, 1 (1953), pp 113-114 (in Greek).

20.See Christomanou-Kalinsky, "The Bampouras mansion", pp 184-185.

21.Petrovich, op. cit., p. 114.

22.Pennas, "History of Serres", p. 518.

23.Pennas, op. cit., p. 519.

24.See the article by E. p. Thompson, "Time, work- discipline and industrial capitalism", Past and Present, 38 (1967), pp 58-97.

25.A. Van Gennep, "Les Rites de Passage", Paris 1909.

26.See above, note 13, for relevant bibliography.

27.Regarding the structure and the function of marriage in traditional Greek society, see my studies "On Greek Dowry. Spatiotemporal Transformations", PostGrad Dipl. Thesis, University College, London, 1976; "The "signpost" function of wedding ritual", in "Semiotics and Society", edited by K. Boklund-Lagopoulou, Athens 1981; and "The dowry, or, On the hunter mentality of the modern Greeks", The Citizen, 55 (Nov. 1982), 56 (Dec. 1982), 57 (Jan.-Feb. 1983). See also the reprints of the last two in "Anthropologics on women's issues", Athens, 1991 (2nd edition) (all in Greek).

28.See Angeliki Hatzimichali, "Greek Popular Art, Roumlouki-Trikeri-Ikaria", Athens 1931, pp 103-127.

29.See Asterios D. Gousios, "The Land of Mt Pangaion, Landscape, customs and language" (Leipzig) 1984 pp 55-62.

30.p. Spandonidis, "Melenikon, the dead Greek frontier", Thessaloniki 1930, p. 115 (in Greek).

31.p. Spandonidis, op. cit., p. 115.

32.M. Papamichail, "Kleisoura, Western Macedonia", Thessaloniki 1972, p. 40.

33.M. Papamichail, op. cit., p. 41 (my italics).

34.See Martin Nilson, "Greek popular religion"; also Alki Kyriakidou-Nestoros, "Landmarks and the logic of the Greek landscape", in Studies in Folklore, Athens 1975, pp 15-40 (in Greek).

35.G. Alexandris, "History and Folklore of Mikra Volvi" Thessaloniki 1963 (collection of folklore material in the Folklore Archives of the University of Thessaloniki (no.....161), p. 22 (in Greek).

36.Natalys Petrovich, "A Folklore Miscellany from Serres", Chronicles of Serres, 5 (1969), p. 149 (in Greek).

37.For the economic significance of festivals and the function of merchants and markets under the Turkish regime in Macedonia, see N. Svoronos, "Le Commerce de Salonique", the texts of N.G. Svoronos ("From 1453 to 1821: Administrative, social and economic developments", pp 354- 385) and I. Koliopoulos ("From the Greek Revolution to the Liberation: Administrative, economic and social developments", pp 484-492) in the volume "Macedonia, 4000 years of Greek history and culture", edited by M. V. Sakellariou, Athens 1982 (in Greek). Also the articles in the volume "Modernization and industrial revolution in the Balkans in the 19th century", Athens 1980, the articles in "The economic structure of the Balkan countries (15th-19th century), ed. Sp. Asdrahas, Athens 1979, as well as Asdrahas' research topics, "The Greek economy in the 18th century: subjects and postulations for research", in Questions of History, Athens 1983, pp 224-233 (in Greek). Compare also the paper by E. Voutsopoulou, "City and trade fair", in the Acts of the International History Symposium - The Modern Greek City: Ottoman Heritage and the Greek State", vol.2, Arthens 1985, pp 439-442 (in Greek).

38.See An. Lazarou, "The Christian common repast", Laographia, 4 (1912), pp 306-307 (in Greek).

39.Dim. Loukopoulos, "A Folklore Miscellany from Macedonia", Laographia 6 (1917-1918), p. 115 (no.5).

40.From school-master Nikolaos D. Argytiou's invaluable unpublished collection of folklore material, "Folklore from the isle of Thasos" (the information comes from p. 16 of the manuscript) (in Greek)

41.See Th. Nounis, "From the customs of the Twelve Days in the village of Angista (district of Serres) (1962), collection of folklore material in the Folklore Archives of the University of Thessaloniki (no. .A...44), pp 1-2 (in Greek).

42.Angelos Deuteraios, "Exposition of folklore research from the southern Grevena district", Annals of the Greek Folklore Research Centre, 18-19 (1965-1966), pp 326-327 (which refers to the manuscript register of folklore material, no. ..3027, 1966, p. 167 (in Greek).

43.Georgios K. Spyridakis, "Exposition of folklore research from the prefecture of Pella", Annals of the Folklore Archives, 13-14 (1960-1961), p. 378 (which refers to the manuscript register of folklore material, no. ... (..) 2394, 1961, p. 158-159 and 177-178) (in Greek).

44.Spyridakis, op. cit., pp 380-381 (manuscript pp 17-19).

45.Chr. Christidou, "The festival of the Monastery of Timiou Prodromou", Macedonian Diary, 1959, pp 159-160 (in Greek).

46.Spandonidis, op. cit., pp 86-87.

47.See the analytical description in Georgios Aikaterinidis' "Celebrating St George's Day at Neo Souli (district of Serres), Chronicles of Serres, 5 (1969) pp 129-148 (in Greek). (This study is based on material collected by the researcher, who also filmed these customs during his expedition to the area in 1965).

48.Petrovich, op. cit., pp 149-150.

49.In this rich and powerful monastery on Mt Pangaion "on the eighth day of September a magnificent festival is held, which is attended by people from many areas, who come to venerate the august icon of Our Lady, each one paying her his vow...". See Asterios Gousios, "The Land of Mt Pangaion, p. 16 (in Greek).

50.K. Polyzou-Mameli, "History of Kolindros", pp 204-207 (in Greek).

51.All the young men and unmarried girls gathered at this festival, making it, like all festal occasions (weddings, celebrations, gatherings), a regular marriage market: promises were exchanged and matches concluded. Kolindros had another festival, too, the Feast of the Cross on September 14, which was celebrated at Aghios Athanasios (Kapsalo), and where even more marriages were arranged. See Poluzou-Mameli, op. cit., pp 203-204. It is typical of communities where the men leave to work abroad, and of semi-nomadic communities, that when the community re-assembles at the beginning of the summer season in its mountain village, the great annual celebration (like all festal occasions, in fact) is also the occasion for the conclusion of contracts of all kinds: marriages, apprenticeships, partnerships, etc)

52.L. Heuzey, "Le Mont Olympe et l'Acarnanie", Paris, 1860.

53.Pennas, "History of Serres", pp 366-368.

54.The weekly market in Serres was held every Tuesday.

55.According to Pennas, op. cit., pp 367-368, the Kervani in Serres took its name from the building which housed the trade fair, the Kervani, and which was a typical example of the institutions known as "Kiarvan-seraya" (Caravanserai), the inns common all around the Balkans during the period of the Ottoman occupation. This public building, which was composed of 4 square buildings with stables and bed-rooms arranged around a large inner courtyard, welcomed travellers and merchants, the Kiarvan, more commonly known as caravans.

56.See Konstantinos G. Stalidis, "Aghia Triada, Edessa" Edessa 1977, pp 57-59 (in Greek). The quotation at the end of the description comes from K. I. Sivenas, "A description of folklore in Edessa during the Turkish period", Thessaloniki 1974, p. 25 (as per K. Stalidis).

57.The newspaper "Edessa", issue no.11, June 1, 1919, (as quoted by Stalidis in "Aghia Triada, Edessa", pp 57-58).

Macedonian Emigrants in the Balkan Peninsula

Ioannis Papadrianos

Issues of Macedonian Emigration

Categories and Causes of Emigration

The years of Ottoman rule in Macedonia were marked by the historically important phenomenon of emigration. Many inhabitants abandoned their Turkish-dominated homeland and settled in various parts of the Balkan peninsula, particularly in the Northwest, and in Central Europe. Out of these two broad areas, the former, northwestern Balkans, are of particular interest for the history of Macedonia, since it was there that compact Macedonian settlements were to be found. For this reason, it is with these Greek outposts that the present chapter is primarily concerned.

Macedonian emigrants to the northwestern Balkans can be divided into two large categories: those who emigrated to the regions north to Belgrade and those who settled in the region south of the Serbian capital in the purely Serbian provinces. Various causes contributed to this division; in the case of the early emigration movement after the fall of Constantinople, historians remark the following: the inability of the mountainous, wooded and largely isolated regions to sustain the numerous population who had taken refuge there, fleeing Ottoman oppression; the lack of security in the northern Greek regions, an acute problem by the beginning of the 17th century; the development of economic relations between the West and the Orient, which accelerated after the historic treaties of Passarowitz (1718) and of Belgrade (1739); the decrease in the population of the Hungarian provinces of the Habsburg empire.[1] One should also add the destruction of the prosperous city of Moschopolis in 1769. Its inhabitants emigrated to the northwestern Balkan lands reinvigorating the existing Greek communities.[2]

Two main factors contributed to the second emigration movement, which began around 1804 and had reached its peak by 1830: the opportunities for economic advance afforded in the newly semi-independent Serbia and the failure of the revolutionary movement in Macedonia in 1821-1822. The suppression of the revolt was followed by the familiar pattern of extensive slaughter, plundering, enslavement and a reign of terror. This unbearable state of affairs forced many Macedonians to abandon their homelands and to scatter to every corner of the Balkans. Many took refuge in the towns and villages of Serbia.[3]

The Course of Emigration

As it is the case today with Greek emigrants to Canada, the USA and Australia, at that time Macedonians and other Greeks emigrated to places offering suitable opportunities for commercial and other related activities. They settled mainly along the important highways and waterways. Therefore, very few emigrated to Bosnia-Herzegovina and Western Serbia, while most of them settled in the urban centres along the Morava and Danube rivers.

Initially, emigrants were exclusively males, and

A view of Berlgrade and Zemun in 1808. Watercolour by Franc Jasche.

they usually moved in groups of 5 or 10 persons. They should normally be at least twelve years of age, but there were exceptions. Thus, the important emigrant Dimitrios Anastasiou-Saboff from Naousa followed other Macedonian merchants away from his hometown at the age of six. On their way, the groups split up and its members settled down in places they believed to offer the best opportunity. Members of the same family were often separated. Thus, of the three Karamatas brothers, from Katranitsa of Western Macedonia, one stayed in Zemun (Semlin, *Semlino* in Greek), the second moved to Pozun (Pressburg), and the third went to Leipzig. Members of the Spirtas family from Kleisoura were to be found in four different cities: Kovilj, Ruma, Sisak and Vienna.

The male emigrants left their families behind, in their Turkish-occupied homeland. At least until the destruction of Moschopolis in 1769, they normally did not intend to settle permanently abroad. Yet matrimonies in their adopted countries were not uncommon with the result that some were accused of bigamy.[4]

Identity and Ethnic Consciousness of the Macedonian Emigrants

A worth considering aspect of the phenomenon of Macedonian emigration is the collective identity of these emigrants as manifested both in the way they identified themselves and were defined by their host-populations. Apart from Greek-speaking emigrants, many were Vlach-speaking, the descendants, probably, of native latinized populations; they spoke a Latin idiom akin to Romanian. They were called *Koutsovlachs* in Greek, *Aromunen* in German, *Cincari* by the Serbs. These Vlach-speaking emigrants called themselves Greco-Vlachs or Macedonian Vlachs. So, the Greek school association of Zemun bore the title 'Community of the Romans and the Macedonian Vlachs'.

Quite indicative was the title of a similar association of Koutsovlachs in another city near Zemun, Novi Sad (Neusatz) of Vojvodina: *Communitas Hellenica* or *Graeca*.[5] Furthermore, sources refer to Macedonian and other emigrants from the Greek lands by simply using their country of origin, Macedonia or 'Turkey'. 'Ottoman subjects' was a term applied to all emigrants from Greece until the middle of the 18th century, when the Austrian authorities began to press them to take up Austrian citizenship.[6]

Irrespective of their spoken tongue, Koutsovlach emigrants from Macedonia proved by their deeds that they clearly aspired to a Greek identity. They appeared proud of their Greek origin, they often referred to a glorious Greek past and commemorated the illustrious men of Ancient Greece and the Holy Fathers of the Church. Moreover, they contributed to the struggle of the subjected Christian Orthodox populations to liberate themselves from the Ottoman yoke and retained a keen interest in the affairs of Greece after its liberation. Shops belonging to Koutsovlach emigrants were decorated with pictures of Greek heroes and personalities. Thus, in Zemun, a Koutsovlach had placed right in front of his store a life-size picture of King Otto of Greece in national costume (*phoustanella*). In Belgrade another Koutsovlach had named his liquor store after Georgios Karaiskakis, complete with the picture of the hero of the Greek War of Independence.[7]

The Centres of Immigrant Macedonian Communities

In Serbian Provinces

Starting from the south and moving towards the northern Balkan regions, one comes across the first Greek community established in Serbia in the town of Niš. This community, which at the time of its greatest prosperity (mid-19th century) numbered some 50 families, consisted of persons who had come mostly from Kleisoura and Siatista of Western Macedonia, and Agrapha of Central Greece. Some of these families managed to achieve outstanding wealth and social eminence. The famous mansion of the Christodoulou family was comparable to the residences of the Serbian ruler Milos Obrenovic in the cities of Kragujevac and Belgrade.[8] The Macedonians, as well as the other Greeks of Nis were known to the Ottoman authorities as politically involved; in 1821, the Turks hang the Greek priest Georgios and three prominent members of the community in order to deter the population from participating in the Greek Revolution that broke out that year.[9]

North of Niš, the Serbian city of Kragujevac is located in an area suitable for the development of commerce. For this reason, during the second decade of the 19th century, several Greeks from Macedonia (Siatista, Selitsa, Pisoderi, Milovista, Gopesi, et al.) settled in the city and engaged primarily in commercial activities.[10] It is worth mentioning that the first brewery in Serbia was established by the Macedonians of Kragujevac. The Greek element of Krugajevac was generally peaceful and law-abiding. The records of the law courts of the city contain very few cases involving Greeks sentenced for offences.

Significant Macedonian communities were also to be found in the Serbian towns of Krusevac, Valjevo, Pozarevac, Smederevo, Belgrade and in other, smaller places. In Pozarevac (Passarowitz), the Greek community numbered some 23 families. Its members originated mainly from Macedonia (Selitsa, Siatista) and Epirus (Artsista and elsewhere). The Macedonians and other Greeks had first come to Pozarevac as Turkish subjects. Later, when they had the choice, they prefered Greek citizenship to Serbian.[11] The

The Greek Church of the Birth of Virgin Mary in Zemun.

Greeks of Smederevo were mostly Macedonians. Although their number was small, they achieved such prominence to the extend that official documents of the local authorities were written in Greek; they also acquired their own cemetery, no small achievement at that time.

The most important, however, community established by Macedonians and other Greeks in Serbia was the community of Belgrade. The Greek immigrants in that city originated from Ioannina, Serres, Katranitsa, Thessaloniki, Kastoria, Velvendos and, mainly, from Kleisoura, Siatista, Blatsi (Vlasti), Moschopolis, Selitsa (Eratyra) and Melenikon. Regarding the number of Greeks who lived in Belgrade, two sources can be relied upon: according to the first, which dates back to mid-19th century, there were 109 Greek families in the city or, on a presumed number of 5-6 persons per family, 435-535 persons. According to the president of the Greek community of Belgrade in the early 1930s, Christos Argyris, the community by then numbered 300 persons, not including the numerous Jews from Macedonia who had emigrated to Belgrade as Greek citizens.[12]

Settlements in the Balkan Provinces of the Habsburg Empire

North of Belgrade and, more specifically, just after one crosses the Sava river, lies the picturesque town of Zemun. Under Habsburg domination since the 17th century, the city soon grew into an important commercial centre thanks to its position and the privileges granted to it by the Austrian emperors. Its significance attracted Macedonians and other Greeks and led to the establishment of one of the most important Greek communities with a rapidly increasing population. While in 1764 the community numbered 200-250 persons, by 1835 it had swollen to 1,000 or 1/9 of the city's total population.[13] With regard to the origin of the Macedonians and the other Greek inhabitants of Zemun, a valuable source for the first half of the 19th century is the so-called 'Book of the Commemorated Deceased' of the church of the Birth of Virgin Mary; it records 318 persons coming from various parts, mostly Macedonia as well as Epirus, Thessaly and Albania. The majority of these immigrants, 79, came from Kleisoura in Western Macedonia, and considerable numbers from Blatsi, Moschopolis, and Melenikon.[14]

Zemun borders on the province of Srem, whose name is derived from the Byzantine town of *Sirmion*. In this region Macedonian communities were to be found in the cities of Sremska Mitrovica, Vukovar, and in Sremski Karlovci, the religious centre of all Christian Orthodox (Greeks, Serbs, etc) living in the Habsburg empire. The Greeks of this province had emigrated from Katranitsa, Blatsi, Kleisoura, Verria, Kozani, Siatista, Kastoria, Naousa, and, in particular, Moschopolis.[15]

Many Macedonians and other Greeks had settled in the Banat, particularly at the cities of Pancevo and Vrsac. Macedonians constituted the majority of the settlers in these cities but many other Greeks from Thessaly, especially from Ampelakia, were also active in that former Hungarian province.

Among the Greek communities in Backa, which, together with Srem and Banat, constitute present-day Vojvodina, that of Novi Sad was by far the most important. Most of its members were emigrants from Western Macedonia, primarily dealing with fur trade.[16]

At an early stage, the rich region of Croatia drew the attention of Macedonians and other Greeks who established very important communities in Slavonski Brod, Karlovac, Osijek and Zagreb. Among the Macedonians of the Croatian capital, as it will be seen later, Dimitrios Dimitriou (1811-1872) of Siatista was the most eminent.[17]

Economic activity

Commerce

Commerce was the main occupation of Macedonian and other Greek immigrants in the northwestern Balkan lands –and they excelled in it. This seems to explain the fact that in the region of Srem, the word *Grk* (Greek) became a synonym to merchant. In this region, there is also a village named Grk, probably after a local Greek merchant. Even today, the high street of many villages in Srem is called *Grcka ulica* (Greek street).[18] Finally, Greek merchants may be divided into three categories: commission agents, wholesale merchants, and small traders and peddlers.[19]

The important role of Macedonians in the development of commerce in the cities where they established themselves is evidenced by the cases of Belgrade, Zemun and Novi Sad. The Macedonians of Belgrade were able to control Serbian foreign trade completely, at least until the 1870s, when they began to face the strong Serbian competition. Among the most important Greek firms were those belonging to Ilias and Nikolaos Kikis, Simos Basias, Evangelos Thomas and the Lazaridis and Zachos families.

Thanks to the activity of its Macedonian and other Greek inhabitants, Zemun developed into an important commercial centre. The Greeks of Zemun were mainly into transit trade, and came to be known as *speditori* or *commissionari*. In order to promote their business interests, they formed an association, named 'Brotherhood of the *speditori* of Zemun'.[20]

Due to the activity of the Greek merchants, the products of the Ottoman Empire and the Near East in general were channelled to Central and Western Europe via Zemun: the famous rags and carpets of Persia and Moschopolis, paprica and spices, the renowned wines of Cyprus, Siatista and Naousa, furs from Kastoria, raw cotton from Serres and Veles, the famous dyed and white yarn from Ampelakia, leather from Macedonia and the Levant, silk from Thessaly, textiles from the looms of Naousa, the *alaca* cloth from Kozani, tobacco, salt, etc.[21]

The transportation of merchandise relied on caravans and riverboats. Owing to the nature of the means of transportation and the various hazzards of the journey, caravans, for covering long distances, depended on stations along the way, the so-called *karavanserais* and *hania* (inns). The former were normally large buildings with spacious, square courtyards and a fountain or cisterns in the middle. Lodgings and mews surrounded the courtyard. The *hania* were usually smaller and simpler constructions, located at prominent positions near springs or running water. The *karavanserais* and inns of the Balkans were almost exclusively in Greek hands.

The caravans usually advanced at the rate of 8 hours a day. They were escorted by armed guards and muleteers (normally one for five mules) who took care of the animals and catered for the travellers; when the caravan reached a station, they unloaded the packs and stabled and fed the animals while the guards took over as night watch.

The importance of the caravan for the economy of the Balkans and Central Europe can hardly be underestimated. It was the means through which the precious merchandise of the Levant reached the peoples of those lands; on its way back, the caravan carried to isolated and otherwise inaccessible areas both

Wheet cultivation in the Serves district.

A coutry woman threshing with a wooden yoke pulled by a cow and a... donkey.

material and cultural products of the West, thus contributing to the development of a new cultural awareness.[22]

In addition to transit trade, the Greeks of Zemun also specialized in livestock trading. The Karamatas family, from Katranitsa of Macedonia, were particularly successful in that field, trading animals, especially pigs, from Serbia to the major markets of Budapest, Vienna and Leipzig. A symbol of wealth and prestige, the Karamatas family splendid mansion, where, among other personalities, its owners entertained the imperial couple of Austria in 1817.[23]

Other Trades

Apart from trade, the Macedonian immigrants also engaged in other business related to commerce, such as financing and banking. Of particular importance was the financial undertaking of the Darvaris family, immigrants from Kleisoura, seated at Zemun, before moving, at the end of the 18th century, to Vienna. Another family from Kleisoura, the Spirtas, distinguished itself in banking at the turn of the 19th century. All couriers carrying correspondence and cash from Constantinople to Vienna and *vice versa* always stopped at the Spirtas bank. There is a characteristic description of the way money was packed and despatched from the Spirtas headquarters: "The coins, which were always gold, were spread on strawmats where they were washed. Then, when they were clean enough, their quantity was estimated –they were never counted but put on the scales. After being weighed, the coins were shovelled into small barrels, which were then placed in large sacks. The sacks were sawn and then carefully sealed. Finally, they were loaded on carts which would carry them to their

The frontispiece of the imperial decree, whereby Dionysios Papagiannousis Popovic, the Greek Metropolitan of Belgrade, was raised to the ranks of the Habsburg nobility.

destination".[24]

During the 19th century, other banks, besides Spirtas', prospered in Zemun; the bank of Theodoros Soutaris of Moschopolis, of Panayotis Morphis, an immigrant from Katranitsa, and that of the Petrovic family from Blatsi. It was common practice for these establishments to lend money to new Greek merchants at a small rate, often without signing any promissory note, but simply relying on the recipient's word of honour. However, in 1867, the authorities established a national savings bank, effectively curtailing the financing ability of private banks.[25]

Shipping was a further occupation of the Greek immigrants. Some made a living by transporting cargoes in their riverboats up and down the Danube and its tributaries. Big merchants sometimes had their own fleet for their needs. Konstantinos Hatias, an emigrant from Melenikon, owned four ships, by which he transported from the Banat to Zemun loads of barley and timber for his brewery, and corn for his flourishing pig-farms.[26]

During the 19th century, the Spirtas bankers were also the biggest Greek ship-owners, being in possession of 13 cargo boats and a steamboat named *Archimedes*. Among their cargo vessels, *Macedonia*, which transported merchandise up and down the Danube and Sava rivers, stood out not only for its name, reminiscent of its owners' land of origin, but

19th century mill-machine; its introduction has radically changed the economical and social life of Macedonia.

also for its cost, at 12,000 florins –a huge sum by contemporary standards.[27]

In addition to commerce, transport and related ventures, Macedonian immigrants also distinguished themselves in various trades. They showed a clear preference for those satisfying essential needs; they became tailors, shoemakers, furriers, silversmiths, painters, bakers, confectioners etc. The guild of Macedonian silversmiths of Novi Sad became famous in the South Slav lands. The confectioner Antigonis Papatzortzis, an immigrant from Serres, was the officially appointed purveyor of confectionery to the Serbian court.[28]

Next to commerce, inns and cook-shops constituted the most profitable occupation, attracting many Macedonian and other Greek immigrants. According to G. Weigand, the Greek inn-keeper was a familiar feature in most places formerly under Ottoman domination. Most of the cook-shops located along the main roads of Serbia as well as along the main route to Constantinople were Greek-owned.[29] In the Balkan provinces of the Habsburgs too, Greeks owned the best inns, cafés and eating places. Already in mid-18th century, three of the best places providing bed and food at Zemun belonged to Greeks: to the already mentioned Karamatas and Hatias, and to Nikolaos Roussis of Moschopolis[30]

It has been already mentioned that the first brewery in Serbia was established by Macedonians at Kragujevac. That was also the case at Zemun. Its owner, Hatias, came to be called 'Pivaros" from *pivo*, the Serbian word for beer. The brewery and its many other concerns gave the Hatias family immense wealth and prestige. One of its offsprings, Joseph, grandson of the founding father Konstantinos, married the niece of the Serbian ruler Milos Obrenovic, Jelka.[31]

Intellectual life

Religion

In order to better understand the religious life of the Macedonian immigrants in the northwestern Balkan lands, one has to take into account an important distinction: the Orthodox population living north to the Sava river, in Habsburg territory, were under

The premises of the educational-culture centre of Zemun, built at exactly the same location where previously stood the Greek and Serb school of the City.

the jurisdiction of the diocese of Karlowitz (Karlovac), while those of the southern, Serbian regions were directly under the Patriarchate of Constantinople.

From the start, Macedonian communities tried to get the permission of the local authorities to build their own places of worship, or, at least, to attend service in Greek. Despite some initial reaction, the immigrants, as their economic and social influence grew, achieved their demands.

Of particular interest is the religious life of the Greek immigrants of Zemun, since it was closely associated with that of the other Orthodox communities of the town, the Bulgarians, the Romanians and, particularly, the Serbs.[32]

The first known Greek-Orthodox church at Zemun was that of St Nicholas, completed in 1752. Later, the Orthodox community acquired a second temple, the church of the Birth of Virgin Mary, built in 1780. Among its priests, Konstantinos Rakintzis, who

served from 1804 to 1835, distinguished himself as a man of letters and was also appointed as a teacher to the school of the Greek community.[33] Particularly active in religious affairs was another Greek immigrant of Zemun, the soap manufacturer Theodoros Apostolou from Thessaloniki, who succeeded in getting the permission of the Austrian authorities to build a chapel at the city's lazarette dedicated to the Archangels.[34]

Relations in the religious field between the Greeks and Serbs of Zemun had been harmonious until 1794, when a heated dispute broke out. Early in that year, the Archbishop of Karlowitz, Stevan Stratimirovic, intervened to appoint a committee, consisting of 12 Serbs and 6 Greeks, to deal with religious and educational matters affecting the city's Christian Orthodox population. Liturgy in Greek was to be conducted every other Sunday and on important holidays, such as St Demetrius' Day, Sts Constantine's and Helen's, Easter, the Monday of the Holy Spirit, and on the second day after Christmas. This practice lasted until the First World War.[35] In Novi Sad a similar dispute over service language broke out towards the end of the 18th century. Finally, the Greeks persuaded the Austrian authorities to permit them to perform their religious duties at the St Nicholas church in Greek too, at least until 1848-1849. In Ćakovo, the native town of the great reformer of Serbian education Dositej Obradović, service had always been conducted in Greek. Even today, there is a custom of Ćakovo to chant "Christ is risen" in Greek. In Vrsac, the religious life of the Greeks centred around the church of St Nicholas, the founders and benefactors of which had been Greek immigrants. At the Orthodox temple of Smederevo school boys and girls read the *Apostle* in Greek until 1850.[36]

Service was conducted in Greek at the Belgrade Cathedral, the internal decoration of which had been financed by Macedonian and other Greek immigrants; as a result, the church looked quite similar to the Greek churches of Venice and Trieste. The See of Belgrade was fortunate to be headed by distinguished prelates, among whom one should note the Macedonian Dionysios Papagiannousis-Popovic. He was born Dimitrios at Servia of Western Macedonia. Still very young, he was ordained at Kozani, where he attended the local school known as *Stoa*. Its famous master, Kyrillos from Agrapha, appointed Dimitrios his successor. Later, after the school closed, Papagiannousis had to work as private instructor before moving to Constantinople, where he rose to high positions in the hierarchy of the Eastern Church. In 1783 he was appointed Metropolitan of Belgrade with the name Dionysius. From his new position, he worked hard to improve the spiritual level of his Orthodox flock and to neutralize the effect of Uniate propaganda. As it was customary, Dionysios serbianized his last name into *Popovic*, a surname common among Greek immigrant families.

The period between 1788-1789 was a difficult one for the Macedonian prelate. In February 1788, Austria, allied to Russia, declared war on Turkey and a year later the Austrian commander-in-chief Laudon besieged Belgrade. The siege was protraced while the Turks threatened the city's Christians with reprisals. At that crucial moment Dionysios played a crucial role in the eventual surrender of the Turkish garrison. There is a story of the prelate, with the help of 17 of his fellow immigrants from Kozani, copying the keys to the gates, inebriating the guards and leting General Laudon in. His attitude was duly appreciated by the Austrian emperor Francis II, who, in 1790, appointed him bishop of Buda. For the same reason, seven years later, Popovic and his son, Euphronios Raphael, were raised to the ranks of nobility. Dionysius remained at the head of his Orthodox flock in Buda for almost 40 years, until his death in 1828.

Education

In addition to their religious concerns, Macedonian immigrants displayed particular interest in education; this evidenced not only their desire for professional advance but also their interest in and respect for Greek tradition and culture. Wherever they established their closely knit and prosperous communities, Macedonian and other Greek immigrants built their own schools and staffed them with able teachers. Otherwise, they hired private instructors, most of whom possessed no formal education and were not suitable for the job; usually, they were either parish priests or educated tradesmen or even adventurers.

Very little is known about the Greek schools south of the Danube and Sava rivers; there is no information as yet regarding their curriculum and regulations, their teachers and number of students. More revealing are the sources on the Greek schools in the provinces of the Habsburg Empire. In Zemun, the first Greek school opened as late as 1794. Until then, the Greeks either employed private teachers or sent their children to a school common to all Christian Orthodox. From 1740 to 1754 the priest Theodoros Stergiadis served as the principal private instructor in both Greek and Serbo-Croat. After 1754 Georgios Spidas of Moschopolis is mentioned. He must have taught until 1776, and then he was succeeded by Konstantinos Kopanos who remained in that position until 1785. The afore-mentioned probably taught in both Greek and Slavonic as it is evindenced by a Greek-Slavonic primer, printed in Venice in 1770 at the expense of the Zemun community.[38]

Dimitrios N. Darvaris is mentioned as the last private instructor. He was born at Kleisoura in 1757, the son of an emigrant to Zemun. As soon as he reached Zemun in the age of twelve, Darvaris began to attend the German and Slav schools of the city. Thus he became fluent in German and various Slavonic languages, primarily Serbian. His main instructor in the later was the Serb Timotej Jovanovic. He also attended the Latin-Slavonic school of neighbouring Ruma and then went on to Novi Sad, Bucharest, Halle and Leipzig, studying Literature and Philosophy. Darvaris returned to Zemun in 1785, where he began to give private lessons. He devoted himself to the education of the young Greeks of Zemun, some of whom became teachers themselves and carried on their teacher's work –among them many Serbs. Yet, in 1795, Darvaris left Zemun and moved to Vienna, where he died in 1823. By his will he bequeathed his numerous publications to the Greek schools existing in the provinces of the Habsburg Empire.[39]

The school of the Greek community of Zemun, appropriately named 'Ellinomouseion', soon became famous. Not only Greeks, but also Serbs, Hungarians and Germans of Zemun, Belgrade and other cities sent their children there. The Serb scholar Sreten L. Popovic wrote: "The Ellinomouseion of Zemun was superior even to the Greek school of Belgrade, serving for the youths of many Greek and Serb families as a kind of institution of higher education".[40] Indeed, in 1802, a few years after it was founded, the school had 88 students of both sexes. Among its graduates one should note Ilija Garasanin, the greatest political figure of 19th-century Serbia, and the famous Serb poet Sima Milutinovic-Sarailija.

A number of scholars from Macedonia were among the most eminent teachers of the school: Ioannis Tourountzas of Siatista (1806-1810), brother of Theocharis, the colleague of Rigas Pheraios; Dimitrios Birdas from Velvendos (1822-1823), who came to Zemun as a result of Turkish oppression in his native land following the Greek Revolution. After teaching at Zemun for two years, Birdas went on to Pest and then to Vienna where he studied medicine and became a distinguished physician.[41]

In 1830, the scholar Euphronios Raphael Popovic, the son of Dimitrios Papagiannousis, later Bishop Dionysios, started teaching at the Ellinomouseion. He had studied in Sopron and Saropatak in Hungary, and in Vienna. After his graduation, Euphronios devoted himself to the education of the Greek youth in the lands of the northern Balkans and Central Europe. Before coming to Zemun, he had taught in Pest, Vienna, and Temesvar (Timisoara). He stayed in Zemun for seven years and became director of the school. He was particularly concerned with the tendency of many Greek youths to leave the Museum for German schools. Therefore, he appealed to the patriotic feelings of their parents and at the same time introduced German into the curriculum of the school. It seems that the results were rewarding.[42]

Yet decline in the long run proved inescapable. The Ellinomouseion of Zemun closed in 1876 because of lack of students. There followed a protracted dispute between Greeks and Serbs about the property of the school, which was only settled in 1906, on the initiative of the then president of the Greek community Georgios P. Spirtas. As a result, the Serbs were handed the school fund, which amounted to a handsome 100,000 florins.[43]

A Greek school existed in Novi Sad since 1780. Its first known teacher was Thomas Panagiotou who was hired in 1782. One of its most active and methodic members of staff was Georgios Vellianakis who taught from 1805 to 1842 and served as schoolmaster. He introduced a more systematic approach and prepared the teaching material himself. In the end, however, he became so embittered with the Greek community that by his will, written in Serbian, he left nothing to the Greek school. In 1806, in addition to Vellianakis, we find the deacon Anthimos of Trikki (Trikala) teaching at the same school. Anthimos was probably acting priest of the community.

From 1848 onwards, the school of the Greek community of Novi Sad became a private institution of secondary education attended by both Greek and Serb students. Among its many Serb graduates, it was Dejan Subotic, who later became a general in the Russian army and governor of the Russian provinces in the Far East. The school finally closed in 1870 and five years later its assets were donated to the Serbian secondary school of the city, subject to the condition that Greek would be part of the curriculum *in perpetuum*.[44]

In Zagreb too, the Croatian capital, Macedonian immigrants sustained Greek education: in 1823 we find Ioannis Pelopidas teaching at the Greek school, where the curriculum included Greek, Latin, Old Slavonic, Serbo-Croat, and German. In 1816 the wealthy Greek merchant of Zagreb, Anastasios Theodorou, bequeathed to the school 200 florins. In 1821, the Greeks of Vrsac, induced by the outbreak of Greek Revolution of that year, asked permission to open their own school. A year later, the town council gave its consent. The shool came into being largely thanks to a contribution of 1,500 imperial ducats by Dimitrios Zaimis, great benefactor of the community. His generous support enabled the Greek school of Vrsac to funtion until the end of the 19th century.

Important Greek schools also existed in Serbia. Already in 1718 a school of the Greek community functioned in Belgrade under the aegis of Bishop Mose Petrovic. Yet, for the next century, no further information is available. After 1818 various names of teachers are known, notably the scholar Georgios Evangelidis from Thessaly, Ioannis Misiou, teacher of the Athens University, Professor Stephanos Koumanoudis, Georgios Zachariadis, and Anastasios Theodorou. From the latter's title as *Philosopher and Trustee of the Schools in Serbia* it may be surmized that Greek schools existed in other Serbian towns too.

At that time (1830s), 20 boys and girls studied at the Greek school of Belgrade. In 1847 a second communal school opened with 37 students. Two of the names of its teachers survive: Georgios Kleidis of Kozani and Jeftimije Avramovic. A clear sign of a competitive environment and of the Greek immigrants' zeal for education was the opening, a year later, of a third, private school, based on the method of the great British educator Lancaster. Ten years later, in 1858, a second private school was added; its most important teachers were Euthymios Gerasis, Zographos or Zographidis, and Pipis. Vladan Djordjevic, prime minister of Serbia, was among its alumni; the school, was forced to close in 1884.

More is known about the Serbian elementary school of Belgrade, where Greek was also taught. From 1828 to 1832 its teaching staff included Konstantinos Zachos, first grade, Michael Nikolic of Resna, second grade, and Thomas Sollaros, third grade.[45] In addition to the three-year elementary school, there was a Serbian gymnasium, where courses in Greek were also available. Among its Greek teachers, the eminent Macedonian scholar Panagiotis Papakostopoulos from Velvendos served for 18 years with distinction. Apart from his teaching qualifications, which included a thorough knowledge of both Greek and Serbo-Croat, Papakostopoulos' career owed a good deal to his decency, modesty and kindness which won him the students' love and affection. Many of his Serb students learned Greek and translated several Greek books into Serbo-Croat; among them, the great literary and political figure, Svetomir Nikolajevic is a characteristic example. Nikolajevic published the first monograph on Rigas Pheraios, the Greek visionary of Balkan solidarity and cooperation.[46]

Regarding Greek schools in the other towns of Serbia, the one at Sabac was founded in the second half of the 18th century and functioned until 1870. The eminent scholar and educator Stephen D. Popovic, of Greek origin, studied there. In the early 1820s, after leaving Zemun, the Greek scholar Zachariadis came to Sabac as a teacher. He served at the Serbian school, where he completed two voluminous manuals of Slavonic grammar.[47]

In Smederevo, where there was a strong Macedonian community, it appears that Greek was taught from an early stage. By 1820, a Greek private instructor, Savvas Ljotic, is mentioned as teaching Greek the offsprings of wealthy Serbs. In 1824, the town council reported to the Serbian ruler Milos Obrenovic that a certain Greek priest, Theodoros from Selitsa in Western Macedonia, had arrived, and that certain Greek merchants of Smederevo had agreed to employ him as teacher of Greek. With regard to the school of the Greek community, Konstantinos Popovic is first mentioned in 1827 as teacher, and, two years later, Konstantinos P. Athanasiou. In 1867 a Greek private school opened too. Greek remained as an optional course at the Serbian elementary school of Smederevo until 1870.[48]

The Karamatas mansion in Zemun, where the imperial couple of Austria was once received.

Social status

The Macedonian and other Greek immigrants of the northwestern part of the Balkans, through their hard work and entrepreneurial spirit, in a relatively short time amassed great wealth. Their affluence contributed to their social advance; they came to be regarded the bourgeoisie of their host countries. According to Yugoslav researchers, the Serbian markets were in Greek hands; the upper crust of Serbian society, both materially and culturally was Greek-speaking. As the Serbian scholar Dragutin Ilic put it, the Greeks were to that society what "the salt is to bread"[49]. The most impressive mansions of Zemun,

Belgrade and other towns belonged to Greeks. The pseudo-gothic Spirtas mansion still stands at Zemun, today hosting the city's museum.[50]

The Macedonian immigrants served in their host countries as bearers of Greek tradition and culture. In the minds of the local population the Greek came to symbolize something lofty and attractive. For a while, Greek was the language of the local upper class. Commercial correspondence was carried in Greek, books of account and last wills were written in the same language, which had come to be regarded as a requisite for high positions. Alexios Karadjordjevic, son of Karadjordje Petrovic, the dynasty's founder, had a Greek teacher, the scholar Konstantinos

Rhodophoinikis. His family's arch-rival, Milos Obrenović, also employed a Greek private teacher for his children, Konstantinos Ranos.[51]

However, during the 19th century a reverse tendency started to spread, manifested in the keen interest on the part of the Greeks in Serbo-Croat, since their best customers were Serbs. This is reflected in the proliferation of bilingual dictionaries and grammars, starting in 1803 with Zachariadis' voluminous *Lexikon Romaio-slavonikon*.[52] In 1845, Georgios Kyridis from Kozani and Euthymios Avramović, teacher of the Greek school of Belgrade, wrote a concise Greek-Serbo-Croat method. In 1846 Avramovic wrote a Greek handbook for Serb students of commercial schools, while a similar venture was undertaken in 1863 by Nikolaos Giannakidis, teacher of the Greek school of Novi Sad.

The influence of Macedonian and other Greek immigrants on the social life of the Serbian capital was quite percetible. Local newspapers had special columns reporting news from Greece; Milos Obrenović, although not particularly pro-Greek, accepted as sons-in-law two members of immigrant families from Western Macedonia, the Hatzibakis and Nibakis. Two of his nieces married Greeks too, Konstantinos Iosiph Hatias, as already mentioned, and the rich Greek merchant of Belgrade Giannaki Germanis.[53]

A long line of Greek benefactors, scholars, scientists, politicians and public functionaries distinguished themselves in the northwestern Balkans. Among the great benefactors, the case of the Macedonian Konstantinos Mantic is most telling: he bequeathed to the city of Smederevo 200,000 dinars. Another Macedonian, the merchant Evangelos Thomas endowed nearly half his fortune in the Belgrade Chamber of Commerce to provide for the education of both Greek and Serb youths. Nikolaos and Eugenia Kikis from Kleisoura founded a hospital, which they donated to the 'Merchant Youth of Belgrade'. The Anastasijevic, emigrants from Moschopolis, donated to the Serbian state a building which was to house later the University of Belgrade. Simos Basias, from Kleisoura, set up a fund for poor students of that University with 100,000 dinars. Maria Triantaphyliou left half her property to the Serbian

'*Matica Sprska*' institution of Novi Sad. Harisios Moukas bequeathed large sums to the schools of his native Kozani as well as to the Serbian schools of Šabac.[54]

Three of the ablest mayors of Zemun were Greek immigrants from Western Macedonia: Ioannis Kalligraphou or Kyritsas, from Vogatsiko, Konstantinos Athanasiou Petrovic, from Blatsi, and Panagiotis Morphis of Katranitsa.[55] In Belgrade, Konstantinos Koumanoudis, cousin of the Athens University professor, served as mayor and, later, as Minister of Finance of the Serbian government.

Macedonian immigrants were also active in politics as well as in the cultural field. The most eminent of these figures, Dimitrios Dimitriou, whose family had immigrated to Zagreb from Siatista in 1790, was born in the capital of Croatia in 1811 and

The impressive tomb of the Spirtas family at the Zemun cemetery.

died at the age of 61. He studied philosophy in Zagreb and medicine in Graz, Vienna and Padova. Yet Dimitriou would never practise; instead, he chose literature and theatre as his main occupation. He wrote a series of short stories, plays and lyrical poems and at the same time worked for the evolution of the Croatian theatre. In 1843 he was acquainted with the Croat nationalist Ljudevit Gaj, leader of the 'Illyrian Movement' and champion of South Slav unity, based on the erroneous assumption of a common 'Illyrian' descent. These ideas appealed to Dimitriou, who evolved into an ardent Croat patriot. The ideal of a free Croatia would influence his entire literary work.[56]

From the 1830s onwards, Greek emigration to the northwestern Balkans began to ebb. First and foremost, there were economic reasons. Technological advance in the means of transportation dealt a fatal blow to caravans. Faster river boats propelled by steam engines needed no more to stop at intermediate little harbours along the way, where the Greek communities had flourished. Greek and indigenous merchants alike began to move their business elsewhere. Another factor was the establishment in 1830 of an independent Greek state, which eventually attracted part of the Greek diaspora in the Balkans. Moreover, Macedonian and other Greek immigrants were subject to gradual process of assimilation with the local, primarily Serbian, population. Intermarriages played no small part. In Habsburg lands, in particular, immigrants had to marry local women, usually Slav, in order to naturalize. Their spouses bound them to local

The great benefactress Eugenia N. Kiki.

customs, such as the family feast *slava*, while professional concerns and the social environment did the rest.[57]

All these reasons contributed to the eventual demise of the communities set up by Macedonian emigrants in the northwestern Balkans. The descendants of many Serbianized Greeks grew into ardent Serb patriots and some rose to top echelons. Among them, Kosta Stojanovic, Minister of Finance, whose family came from Milovista, near Monastir; Vladan Djodjević (Ippocratis Georgiadis), Prime Minister of Serbia during the rule of Milan Obrenovic; the physician and Minister of Finance Lazaros Patzou, from Monastir; the poet Ioannis Stergiou Popovic; Stephanos Hadjic, general and Minister of War; and Vasos Lazarevic from Moschopolis, Director of the Ministry of the Interior.[58]

IOANNIS PAPADRIANOS
`MACEDONIAN EMIGRANTS IN THE
BALKAN PENINSULA
NOTES

1. Apostolos E. Vacalopoulos, *Western Macedonian Emigrants during Turkish Domination* (in Greek), Thessaloniki 1958, pp. 3ff; same author, *History of Macedonia* (in Greek), Thessaloniki 1969, p. 349; Odön Füves, *The Greeks of Hungary* (in Greek), Thessaloniki 1965, pp. 11-13.

2. Ioakeim Martinianos, *Moschopolis 1330-1930* (in Greek), Thessaloniki 1957, p. 183ff.

3. Dušan J.Popović, *O Cincarima. Prilozi pitanju postanka naseg gradjanskog drustva* (On the Koutstovlachs. Contribution to the Question of the Creation of Our Middle Class), 2nd ed., Belgrade 1937, p.55.

4. Ioannis Papadrianos, *The Greek Settlers of Semlin, 18th-19th centuries* (in Greek), Thessaloniki 1988, pp. 30-31.

5. Vacalopoulos, *History of Macedonia*, pp. 355-356. V.Stajić: 'Cincari u Novom Sadu' (The Koutsovlachs of Novi Sad), *Glasnik Istoriskog drustva u Novom Sadu*, 9 (1936), 257.

6. Papadrianos, *op. cit.*, p. 32.

7. Vacalopoulos, *op. cit.*, p. 356, with related bibliography.

8. Popović, *op. cit.*, p. 164, 11; 'Siatistian Diaspora' in *Memory of Siatistians* (in Greek), Thessaloniki 1972, 148.

9. Popović, p. cit., p.19.

1O. 'Stiatistian Diaspora', 147; Popovic, *op. cit.*, p. 52.

11. *Ibid.*, pp. 53, 387; 'Siatistian Diaspora', 147

12. Popović, *op. cit.*, p. 51

13. Franz Sartori, *Historisch-ethnographische Übersicht der wissenschaftlichen Kultur, Geisterthätigkeit und Literatur des österreichischen Kaiserthums nach seinen mannigfaltigen Sprachen und deren Bildungsstufen*, Vienna 1830, p. 181; J. Schilling, *Adressen-Buch des Handlungs-Gremien und Fabriken der k.k. Haupt-und Residenzstadt Wien, dann mehrerer Provinzialstädte, für das Jahr 1834*, Vienna [1834], p. 581.

14. Papadrianos, *op. cit.*, pp. 72-73.

15. Popović, *op. cit.*, p. 54.

16. Stajić, *op. cit.*, p. 257; Eleutheria Nikolaidou, 'Contribution to the History of Four Greek Communities of Austria-Hungary (Zemun, Novi Sad, Orsova, Temesvar)' (in Greek), *Dodoni*, 9 (1980), 324, 327; Popović, *op. cit.*, p. 119.

17. Maria Symeon, 'The Greek Communities in Yugoslavia' (in Greek), *Makedoniki Zoi*, January 1967, no. 8, 22.

18. Emanuel Turczynski, *Die deutsch-griechischen Kulturbeziehun-*

gen bis zur Berufung König Ottos, Munich 1959, pp. 73-75; Vacalopoulos, *op. cit.*, pp. 359-360.

19. Füves, *op. cit.*, p. 14ff.

20. Papadrianos, *op. cit.*, p. 90.

21. A.E. Vacalopoulos, *History of Modern Hellenism* (in Greek), vol. 4, Thessaloniki 1973, p. 214.

22. Vacalopoulos, *History of Macedonia*, pp. 353-354.

23. Lj. Stojanović, *Stari sprski rodoslovi i letopisi* (Old Serbian Genealogical Lists and Chronicles), Belgrade - Sr. Karlovci 1927, pp. 343-344.

24. I. Papadrianos, 'Die Spirtas, eine Familie Klissuriotischer Auswanderer in der jugoslavischen Stadt Zemun während des 18. und 19. Jahrhunderts', *Balkan Studies*, 16 (1975), 120

25. However, in 19th century Zemun, there were usurers lending money at rates of 20%, 50%, or 100%, a fact that contributed to certain merchants' economic collapse. See *Društvene prilike u XIX stolecu u gradu Zemunu* (Social Conditions in the City of Zemun during the 19th century), pp. 3-4.

26. Tanasije Z. Ilić, 'Zemunski brodograditelji "Šuperi" krajem XVIII veka' (The 'Schopper'-Boat Builders of Zemun at the End of the 18th Century), *Matica Sprska. Zbornik za društvene nauke*, 51 (1968), 47-48.

27. Mita Kostić, 'O dunavsko-savskoj trgovini, ladjama, ladjarima i ladjarskim cehovima u XVIII i XIX veku do povjave željeznica' (On the Commerce in the Danube and Sava Rivers, the Boats, Crews and Shipowners' Guilds during the 18th and 19th Centuries to the Appearance of the Railway), *Istoriski Casopis*, 9-10 (1959), 271-272; Papadrianos, 'Die Spirtas', 120.

28. Popović, *op. cit.*, pp. 138, 145, 425.

29. Gustav Weigand: *Die Aromunen*, vol.1, Leipzig 1894, p. 303; Sreten L. Popović, *Putovanje po novoj Srbiji(1878 i 1880)* (A Tour of New Serbia, 1878 and 1880), Belgrade 1950, pp. 95, 213.

30. Ignaz Soppron, *Monographie von Semlin und Umgebung*, Semlin 1880, p. 381.

31. Popović, *op. cit.*, pp. 464-465.

32. Papadrianos, *op. cit.*, 99.

33. *Literary Telegraph* (Greek journal), Vienna 1820, no. 22.

34. *Istorijski Arhiv grada Beograda, Zemunski Magistrat* (Historical Archives of the City of Belgrade), Zemun City Council, 1793, F. 21, no. 4.

35. Papadrianos, *op. cit.*, 116ff.

36. Popović, *op. cit.*, pp. 208-210, 214.

37. I. Papadarianos, 'A Great Macedonian Migrant: Euphonios Raphael Papagiannousis-Popovic', in *Macedonian Intellectuals during the* Tourkokratia (in Greek), Thessaloniki 1972, 111ff.

38. Papadrianos, *The Greek Immigrants...*, pp. 121-123.

39. Despina Loukidou-Mavridou - I. Papadrianos, 'Dimitrios Darvaris: sa contribution à l' evolution littèraire bulgare', in *First Greek-Bulgarian Symposium, Proceedings*, Thessaloniki 1980, 211ff.

40. Todor Stevanović Vilvoski, 'Stari Beograd. Postanak i razvitak sprske varosi i Kulturne i društvene prilike u njemu (1820-1850)' (Old Belgrade. The Emergence and Growth of a Serbian City and its Cultural and Social Conditions (1820-1850)), *Sprski knjizevni Glasnik*, 26 (1911), 309

41. Papadrianos, *The Greek Settlers*, p. 153, with related bibliograhy.

42. Padadrianos, 'Euphronios Popović', 126-127.

43. Papadrianos, *The Greek Settlers*, pp. 177.

44. Popović, *op. cit.*, p. 222ff.

45. *Ibid.*, p. 228ff.

46. I. Papadrianos, 'Der griechische Gelehrte Panagiotis Papakostopoulos und die Serben, 1820-1827', in *Collection of Reports from the Second Greek-Serbian Symposium: Greek-Serbian Cooperation, 1830-1908*, Belgrade 1982, 117ff.

47. I. Papadrianos, 'Der griechische Gelehrte Georgios Zachariadis und sein Bietrag zum slawischen Schrifttum in 19. Jahrhundert.', *Balkan Studies*, 17 (1976), 83.

48. Popović, *op. cit.*, p. 241.

49. *Ibid.*, p. 161.

50. I. Papadrianos, 'An Epitaph of the Spirtas Family in the Yugoslav Town of Zemun', *Balkan Studies*, 16 (1975), 23-24.

51. Popović, *op. cit.*, pp. 165, 171; Vacalopoulos, *op. cit.*, p. 361.

52. Papadrianos, 'Georgios Zachariadis', 82, 85.

53. Popović *op. cit.*, pp. 174-175.

54. *Ibid.*, pp. 270-273.

55. For more details, see Papadrianos, *The Greek Settlers*, p. 92ff.

56. Sime Jurić, *The Greek Lyric Poems of Dimitri Dimitriou*, (in Greek, edited by Kleovoulos Tsourkas), Thessaloniki 1965, p. 15ff.

57. Papadrianos, *op. cit.*, p. 73, with related bibliography.

58. M. Symeon, *op. cit.*, 23.

Anti-Turkish Movements in Macedonia before the 1821 Greek Revolution

Ioannis K. Hassiotis

General Remarks

Most of what has been written about anti-Turkish movements in Macedonia during the long period between the consolidation of Ottoman rule in the first half of the 15th century and the outbreak of the 1821 Revolution is largely characterized by oversimplification. The enthusiasm with which idealist and even Marxist historians have projected revolutionary activities in the area has not been based on sufficient evidence. What is more, anachronisms have not always been avoided. Confusion further increases as a result of the geographical identification of present-day Macedonia —both Greek and 'Greater Macedonia', which stretches over parts of three neighbouring countries— with an area which, albeit known under the same name, had an entirely different geographical content during the period of Ottoman domination.

These phenomena should not be ascribed solely to political or ideological expediency influencing the writings of Greeks and foreigners on modern Macedonia alike; they are also due to the frustrating scantiness and ambiguity of the sources available. Even today, one has to rely on the relatively small collections of published Ottoman documents (mostly references to isolated often individual, outbreaks of disobedience against the Turkish authorities in Central and Western Macedonia, particularly during the 17th century); on latter local traditions, generally obscure, and undated folk songs about the activity of *klephts* and *armatoles* (usually of the 18th and early 19th centuries); on rare, often exaggerated, information given by foreign travellers (who recorded their general impression of local anti-Turkish feeling); and, finally, on rather laconic references in Western archives (which also present at least as many problems of accuracy and reliability.) Even data from the late 18th and early 19th centuries, although no longer as scanty as before, do not entirely cease to be of a fragmentary nature. A clear historical picture emerges only in the period following the outbreak of the Greek Revolution in 1821.[1]

Thus, in view of these limitations, it is not yet possible to cover here, however synoptically, the many *desiderata* of the subject. We shall, therefore, confine ourselves to listing only the most suggestive historical evidence —particularly that which refers to the so-called 'dark' period of the 16th and .17th centuries— which are derived from both published and unpublished archival cources. This listing will be combined with an initial, entirely schematic periodization, to the extent that this can be based on, at least, the obvious 'characteristics' of the internal and external factors which influenced the attitude of the inhabitants of Macedonia *vis-à-vis* the foreign ruler. Finally, we shall try on the basis of available evidence to draw whatever conclusions are possible at the present time.

The Early *Tourkokratia* and the First Challenges to Ottoman Domination

The information available on the earliest period of Turkish rule is particulary disappointing. There are a few vague references, in Bertrandon de la Broquière's account, to the readiness of the newly-converted *Sipahis* to collaborate with the Western powers against the Sultan in 1432; there are certain undocumented, later indications of widespread brigandage in Thessaly and Central Macedonia in 1458, carried out by irregulars operating from the region of Mt Agrapha; or late 15th century references to the secret protection offered by the monks of Mount Athos to Christian fugitives. Such facts are caracteristic of what has been so far brought to light by research into the attitude of the inhabitants of Macedonia towards the Ottomans during the 15th cen-

Travellers accounts mention insurrectionary movements in Macedonia as early as the 15th century. In this engraving from the early Ottoman period, the Macedonian capital is depicted in a much idealized form.

tury.[2] In that same period and during the first Turkish-Venetian war, there were some naval operations carried out by the Venetians in the territory of Macedonia, such as the two landings on Thasos and Chrysoupolis and on the Gulf of Thessaloniki in 1466 and 1469 respectively.[3] Yet, as related sources indicate, those raids, as it was the case with later such incidents, did not aim at some sort of cooperation between the Venetians and the local Christian population against the Ottomans; they served wholy tactical purposes with grave consequences for the inhabitants. All these facts merely reinforce the impression of general insecurity, typical of the Balkans under Turkish rule, particularly during the periods of military confrontation between the Ottomans and the Western powers; yet they remain generalizations: they do not adequately document the extent to which the new regime was disputed, especially in Macedonia.

The situation started to change at the beginning of the third decade of the 16th century. The reasons for this were both internal and external. On the one hand the transformation of the fairly lenient regime of land

The shores of Macedonia, like the rest of the Aegean, became targets of Venetian raids from the 15th century (contemporary map at the Royal Academy of History, Madrid).

*Emperor Charles V, who, in early 16th century, attracted the
enslaved Balkan Christians' hopes for liberation
(painting by Tizian).*

ownership provoked justifiable reactions, and spurred on some of the remaining Christian fief holders to spasmodic, last-ditch efforts before their inevitable conversion to Islam.[4] On the other the confrontation between the Habsburgs (of both the Austrian and Spanish branch) and the Ottomans in the northern Balkans, the Adriatic and Ionian seas and the Peloponnese fostered a general climate of hope and unrest among the enslaved population. With the help of anti-Turkish propaganda by interested Christian powers, chiefly Spain, this climate was to be maintained until the third decade of the 17th century. It began following rumours of Christian victories during Emperor Charles' V very first campaigns, when troops were continually being moved fron the garrisons in the sultan's Greek dominions to the battle-fronts of Hungary and the Central Mediterranean.

Various sources make mention of pro-Imperial demonstrations by a number of prelates, both named and anonymous, in the Balkans; among them are Prohoros, Archbishop of Achris, and, Ioasaph, Metropolitan of Thessaloniki. In the summer of 1532, in fact, rumour spread in Constantinople to the effect that the forces which the Emperor's admiral, Andrea Doria, had mustered at Messina were intended for use in a surprise capture of Thessaloniki. Needless to say, the goal of the Christian armada was not Thessaloniki, but Koroni, which was taken by Doria's forces without great difficulty in September of that year. Nevertheless, the rumours of a projected campaign against Thessaloniki, too, did subside, even after the Christian garrison's inglorious departure from the Emperor's advanced *presidio* in south-western Peloponnese in March 1534.[5]

In was within this climate that the brothers Alexakis (Lixicho) and Doukas Palaiologos, notables of Thessaloniki, decided in concert with the city's Metropolitan Ioasaph to come into contact with the Emperor, though not before securing the Ecumenical Patriarch's approval for their step. Thus on 21 August 1535 Angelos Palaiologos, the son of Alexakis, left Constantinople with a message to Charles from the Patriarch; and on 9 September he travelled onwards from Thessaloniki, heading for Messina or even Spain, with further messages from the Metropolitan and his uncle Doukas. Unfortunately, the documents themselves have not survived: Angelos was forced to throw them into the river Axios when in danger of being arrested on his way to Edessa. We are informed of their contents, however, by an Italian report on the statement which Angelos himself made to the military authorities in Messina, where he eventually arrived on 20 October. The writers, after lamenting over the terrible situation in Greece, assured Charles that "*tutti li poveri e desolati Greci, giorno e notte, così loro come li figlioli loro*" were ready, "*con tutto l'animo e cuore*" to rise against their oppressors and place themselves at the side of the Emperor, should he only decide to land with his army in order to liberate them from "all that captivity and servitude".[6]

The intentions of the Habsburg ruler were naturally far removed from the daring expectations of the Thessalonian notables. Their proposal, however, does not appear to have left his counselors unmoved. It is, perhaps, significant that during the deliberations in the Imperial Council in October 1538 —on the implementation of the terms of the treaty of alliance which had been signed about seven months earlier by the Spain,

In 1572, Metropolitan Timotheos of Grevena conceived a plan, according to which a Christian force from the plain of Thessaloniki on Constantinople (engraving).

the Holy See, Austria and Venice— the possibility was considered of a landing by Christian troops at Thessaloniki, along with ways of employing local support in the operations.[7]

The Decline of Ottoman Power and the Western 'Challenge'

A similar climate prevailed thirty years later. However, this time the causes should be considered in the light of new factors: the problems generated by the debilitation of the Ottoman administration, the chronic economic crisis and the concurrent exacerbation of anarchy and the arbitrary conduct of the sultan's representatives in the provinces, the violations of the —until then institutionalized— measure of autonomy and the particular 'privileges' of the Orthodox population and, in general, the drastic changes in the conditions that had secured to the Christian element a tolerable *modus vivendi* with the conqueror. To these, one should add the decline of Ottoman military power towards the end of the 16th and the begining of the 17th centuries, which then appeared more vulnerable to the prospect of a co-ordinated counter-attack of the Christian powers.[8] These conditions became more noticeable in periods of mobilization for war, as oppression and arbitrary rule intensified and, at the same time, hopes were generated among the enslaved population as if a foreign military intervention against the empire was about to take place.

As regards Macedonia, Greek and foreign sources from the years 1567-1570 refer to widespread seizures of Athonite lands and dependencies and, in general, to a systematic plundering of monastic estates, to the destruction of churches in Thessaloniki and Serres, and even to massacres of monks and clergy on Mount Athos and at the monastery of St John the Baptist.[9] These events were certainly connected with the extensive imposition of extraordinary taxation by the Ottomans on the lands from Macedonia to the Peloponnese and the forced conscription of oarsmen to meet the increased demands of the Ottoman fleet in view of the war with Venice for Cyprus in 1570-1573. The situation deteriorated still further when panic was caused among the Muslim population by persistent rumours that the fleet of the Holy League was about to start operations in various sensitive areas of the Greek Levant; the rumours and panic were reinforced by the Christian allies' impressive victory at the naval battle of Lepanto on 7 October 1571.[10] Some Greek prelates and notables were then accused of being in collusion with the Holy League's commander-in-chief Don Juan of Austria (1547-1578). Among them was the Metropolitan of Thessaloniki Ioasaph Argyropoulos, who finally managed to save himself by bribing high Ottoman officials in Adrianople and Constantinople, while other churchmen, such as the Metropolitan of Old Patras Germanos I, were put to death. The accusations against Argyropoulos were not unfounded. There is even evidence from more than one

During the 1570s there was an attempt to involve N. Epirus and W. Macedonia in an ambitians revolutionary plan. The engraving depicts the joint assault of Cheimariots and Venetians against the fort of Soppoto.

source to the effect that the Ecumenical Patriarch Mitrophanis III was involved, at least indirectly, in these secret deliberations.[11] On the other hand, information sent by the French envoy from Constantinople in spring 1572 should be regarded as exaggerated: his report refers to Turkish reprisals with thousands of victims in the areas of Thessaloniki, Mount Athos and the Aegean Islands.[12] Meanwhile, the Metropolitan of Grevena Timotheos conceived a strategic plan for ridding the Greek peninsula of the Ottomans, and sent it to Pope Pius V (1566-1672) from Warsaw in March 1572: his proposal was that two expeditionary forces should meet up with rebels on the plain of Thessaloniki; from there on, he predicted, the Christian troops would march victoriously, "God willing", all the way to Constantinople.[13]

Timotheos' claims about the readiness of the inhabitants of north-western Greece and southern Albania to take active part in the Holy League's enterprises against the Ottomans were not made arbitrarily; a noteworthy anti-Ottoman effort had begun at exactly that time in the prelate's own district, on the initiative of two notables of Argyrokastro, Manthos Papagiannis and Panos Kestolikos. This movement soon became known and provoked harsh reprisals by the Ottoman authorities not only against its two instigators but also against rural communities near Argyrokastro that were probably not involved. It nevertheless spread to include more local prelates: Archbishop Ioakeim of Achris, Metropolitans Photios of Velessa (Veleš) and Nektarios of Velegrades and the '*protothronos*' Metropolitan of Kastoria, Sophronios. Papagiannis persisted for a long time —up to January 1577 at least— with his attempts to persuade, either through personal contacts or in writing, first the commander-in-chief of the League, Don Juan of Austria, and, after its dissolution, King Philip II of Spain to give military support to the uprising which was being planned.[14]

The Christian powers, especially the Spaniards, did not reject in principle the more serious, at any rate, of

Insurrectionary movements were fomented by the frequent presence of Christian fleets on the shores of Macedonia, particularly of Mount Athos.

the proposals for armed intervention in mainland Greece. This fact made up for their procrastinations, and so, far from putting an end to the Greek tendency to seek foreign intervention in their country, did much to encourage it. The legality of the sultan's rule was all the more likely to be challenged in view of the desperate conditions brought about by institutional decay and maladministration, especially in Western Macedonia, Epirus and Albania. Another factor not to be ignored was the external 'challenge'. It is well-established that the unabating anti-Turkish activity in Cheimara and Mani was the result not only of special local conditions, but also of contacts with the West, particularly with the viceroys of Naples and Sicily. The latter were working systematically to foment unrest in these most restless parts of the empire; their purpose was diversionary in order to reduce the pressure which the Ottomans and their Northern African allies were applying upon them with naval raids and landings in Southern Italy.[15] In this context one should consider the setting up of a Spanish

network of espionage in the Greek regions[16] and the frequent presence of flotillas from Naples, Sicily and Malta off north Aegean islands and mainland harbours during the first decades of the 17th century. The available sources on these corsair raids —which on the whole still await scholarly attention and interest— often refer to assistance received from local Christians and the monks of Mount Athos.

The secret contacts with the lieutenants of the Spanish crown in the Italian peninsula mostly originated with the Greeks. The links were facilitated by the various persons who frequently travelled from Ottoman-dominated Macedonia to the West. Some of these people were fugitives, or janissaries who wanted to return to the Christian faith and sought refuge with the Greek communities in the West (such as the three Thessalonians Nikolaos and Dimitrios Palaiologos and Dimos, son of Panagiotis, who fled to Southern Italy between the end of the 16th and the beginning of the 17th centuries).[17] Others were clergymen, usually

Secret missions to the Western Courts usually set sail from the port of Thessaloniki (17th century engraving).

monks of Mount Athos, who set forth on alms-begging missions, or '*ziteies*', to raise funds for their monasteries (such were the occasional plenipotentiary of the Iviron Monastery, Ioasaph Atsalis, in 1606-1607[18], and the monks of the Philotheou Monastery, Ieremias and Parthenios, in 1613[19]). Others were the relations of prisoners-of-war, whose object was to collect the necessary ransom (for example, Nikolaos from Lemnos in 1624[20] and the priest Serapheim from Serres, in 1628[21]). Some were on their way to study at famous Spanish schools (as, for example, the monk Savvas from the Iviron Monastery, who, after studing at Salamanca in 1603, stayed at Escorial as a teacher of Greek.[22] More than a few were mercenaries, who joined as *stradioti* the Greek-Albanian companies in Southern Italy or as sailors the fleet of Napoli and Sicily.[23] Others were temporary or professional spies of Spain or of the Pope, whose task was to collect information on Ottoman troop movements in the Greek peninsula (as, for example, Michalakis Dimou from Thessaloniki in 1572-1577[24]). Finally, there were a number of adventurers, who went from one Western court to another canvassing ambitious and often completely unrealistic plans for military operations in the Turkish-occupied Levant. Among this last category one should certainly include the notorious pseudo-sultan Yahya (1585-1649), who claimed to be the son of Mehmed III and Eleni Komnini, a Greek woman from Serres, and was close to Metropolitan Kosmas of Thessaloniki and the monks of the nearby monastery of St Anastasia at Galatista.[25]

Many of these self-appointed agents were uncovered and had to pay for their activities. Around 1600, for example, with the help of lavish bribery, the monks of the Esphigmenou Monastery on Mount Athos narrowly escaped being collectively impaled when it was discovered that they had been supplying the galleys and feluccas of Naples and Sicily, as well as harbouring Christian escapees and helping them out, and that they had even passed military information on to the West. This episode led the monastery into bankruptcy, so that its hegumen Nikiphoros was forced to spend at least thirteen years (1602-1615) in Rome, Naples and Spain trying to collect the sum required to pay off the mortgage on the monastery's movable and immovable property. It is nevertheless worth noting that Nikiphoros was not thereby prevented from proposing to King Philip III of Spain in January 1605 —in order, perhaps, to present his financial requests in a more convincing manner— that he use the Esphigmenou Monastery as a base for anti-Ottoman operations in the Levant.[26] Nor is it impossible, it seems to us, that the plan formulated by the viceroy of Naples (1603-1610), Juan Alonso Pimentel de Herrera, Count of Benavente, in the following year for an audacious raid on Siderokausia and Mount Athos originated with Nikiphoros.[27]

The fact remains that an enterprise of this sort did occur in the Kitros area in March 1612, provoking Ottoman reprisals, which cost the lives of many local Christians. Bishop Ieremias of Kitros himself just managed to escape "by taking to flight", to use the

Athonite monks played an important part in the secret contacts between Greeks of Macedonia and Western powers. In the picture, the Byzantine double-headed eagle on the cistern of the Philotheou Monastery.

The St Anastasia Monastery at Galatista.

phrase of a Patriarchal document of 1617 which put an end to his vicissitudes.[28] Nor do we possess enough information to be able to specify what anti-Turkish actions of theirs forced a number of people to flee

The Esphigmenou Monastery (as sketched by Barsky in 18th century) was involved in deliberations with the Spaniards aiming at insurrectionary moves in Chalcidice and Mount Athos.

Macedonia in haste in the last years of the 16th century and the early decades of the 17th, abandoning kindred and estates, and seeking refuge in the West. The following people fled in this way: Bishop Kallistos of Moglena;[29] the much-wandering Metropolitan of Pelagonia Ieremias (a native of Serres);[30] Archbishop Gabriel of Achris, the well-known scholar from Jannina;[31] Konstantinos Palaiologos, the nobleman from Thessaloniki;[32] Archimandrite Anthimos of the Dochariou Monastery;[33] the monk Meletios, also of Mount Athos;[34] and a host of other people, both named and unnamed, whom we come across in the Venetian-ruled Ionian Islands and the Greek communities of Western Europe.

The anti-Ottoman initiatives in Macedonia were seldom of a purely local character. In May 1605 secret deliberations between the viceroy of Naples, on the one hand, and the Metropolitan of Thessaloniki, the city's notables and various other people from Kitros and Platamonas, on the other, took place in concert with similar approaches made by both churchmen and laity from almost every corner of mainland Greece.[35] It is

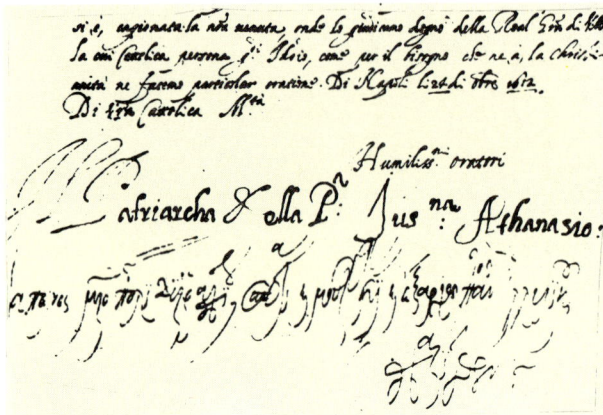

The most important insurrectionary attempt in the early 17th century was initiated by Athanasios, Archbishop of Achris, and Hariton, Metropolitan of Durazzo. This document is the italian translation of an appeal to King Philip of Spain, signed by the two prelates.

possible that those contacts were not unconnected with the Ottoman reprisals of 1612 at Kitros and the flight of the local bishop, as already mentioned. Nevertheless, an interesting brief chronicle of 1612 from the Olympiotissa Monastery links the episodes in Pieria, at least chronologically, to the second dramatic uprising led by (former) Metropolitan Dionysios of Larissa, known as the Philosopher, which took place at Jannina in 1611.[36] This corroborates the testimony of Spanish sources, which clearly imply that the anti-Turkish movement of 1605 in Macedonia began on the initiative of a few ardent Thessalians, who had been involved in the preparations for Dionysios' first bloody uprising in western Thessaly four years earlier.[37]

Almost contemporaneously with these events, another widespread anti-Turkish effort was beginning; this time it was to affect —more directly than before— almost the whole of Macedonia. Its instigator was the Peloponnesian Archbishop of Achris Athanasios Rizeas, already known for his active part in the bloody uprising of Cheimara in 1596-1597.[38] The failure of the Cheimara rebellion, and Athanasios' various experiences up to the time he was unexpectedly restored on the archiepiscopal throne, did not dishearten him from assuming the leadership once again in this new and more ambitious endeavour, which lasted for at least eight years. An important role in it also seems to have been played by Metropolitan Mitrophanis of Kastoria, who assumed the task of persuading Archduke Ferdinand of Austria to provide the necessary military support from the north. Meanwhile Athanasios and Metropolitan Hariton of Durazzo, a native of Arta, were responsible fot the negotiations with Spain. Another personality from Macedonia, Bishop Zacharias Tsigaras of Prespa, was also repeatedly employed in the search for support from among the Italian rulers and the Papacy. A significant contribution was made, too, by Athanasios' secretary, Alexandros Mouselas, who worked for the cause in both mainland Greece and the West. Mouselas made two secret tours of Epirus and Macedonia (all the way from Valona, Cheimara and Korytsa to Jannina and Arta; from Monastir and Florina to Grevena, Kastoria and Sisanio; from Stagoi and Servia to Verria; and from Edessa to Stromnitsa, Melenikon and Petritsi) with object, firstly, to register the strategic positions, fortified points and the numerical military strength of Christians and Muslims alike, and, secondly, to sound out the intentions of the inhabitants. He also travelled to Spain many times in order to communicate this information to the counsellors of Philip III and persuade them finally to make a military intervention in his country.[39]

It seems that the first secret meetings of the conspirators took place at Arta around 1601, at least according to account of Metropolitan Hariton of Durazzo some ten years later.[40] This initiative should probably be regarded in connection with the climate of uneasiness and hope generated throughout mainland Greece by the Christian victories against the Ottomans during the 'continuous war' in the nothern Balkans and the repeated raids of flotillas from Sicily, Naples, Malta and Tuscany upon the shores of the Eastern Mediterranean, from Cyprus to Patras and from Mani to the Dalmatian coast.[41] Furthermore, it was widely held that Ottoman military power had seriously declined, a view corroborated by the frequent mutinies amongst the Janissary units and, even more so, by the centrifugal tendencies of the uncontrollable Muslim lords in the provinces of the Empire; in some cases, the latter did not hesitate even to come to terms with representatives of Western powers, as in the case of the notorious rebel pasha of Bosnia, Deli Hasan, in 1604-1605.[42]

It was in those conditions that the first bloody uprising led by Metropolitan Dionysios of Larisa was organized. It might even have been the case that Athanasios Rizeas was not party to the initial deliberations but that he hastened to gain control of the movement when the conspirators were already in contact with the viceroy of Naples. Be that as it may, the first approach —through the Spanish agent in Naples, Iero-

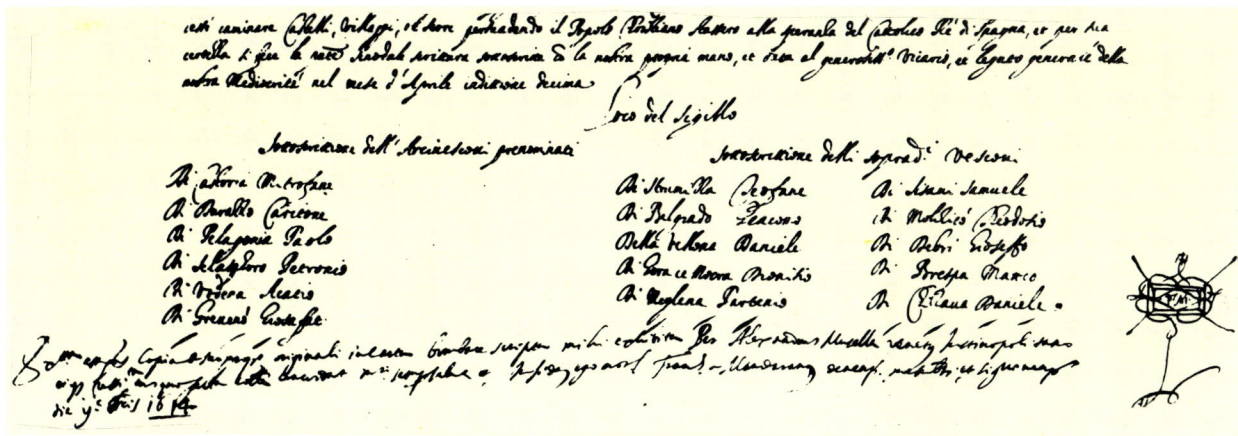

Nearly all prelates from Western Macedonia took part in Athanasios' of Achris initiative, as indicated by their signatures on this copy of an appeal to the Viceroy of Naples (1612).

nymos Combis from Cyprus— of the conspirates to Count Benavente met whith the usual encouragement, matched by an equally strong temporizing attitude. With the very recent failure of Dionysios' uprising in western Thessaly still fresh in mind, Benavente advised Athanasios to postpone his plans, while making vague promises of military support at a propitious moment. Benavente's successor, Pedro Fernández de Castro, Count of Lemos (1610-1616), did the same thing, now citting the tragic outcome of Dionysios' second attempt in Jannina in 1611. After this, Athanasios —who had refused to collaborate with Dionysios— decided, as he himself claimed, not to rouse the people unless he was certain that armed support would be forthcoming from Spain and the Holy See. This support should begin with the capture of Leukas and Preveza or Valona. Next, the Christian forces should advance into the heart of Macedonia, where —as Alexandros Mouselas promised— 12,000 guerrillas would be available from the mountains around Kastoria.[43] This exaggerated figure should probably be connected to the widespread brigandage and guerrilla activity in those years throughout northwestern Thessaly and Western Macedonia, which other contemporary sources ascribe to the presence there, over a number of years, of an almost legendary *klepht*, *kapetan* Vergos of Grevena.[44]

At all events, in the spring of 1612, there was an effort to rekindle older insurrectionary movements in north-western Greece. In April seventeen prelates, who were under the jurisdiction of the local archdiocese, met in Ochrida and decided to send Athanasios himself to

Naples and Spain accompanied by Metropolitan Hariton and Mouselas.[45] For the next six years or so, the persistent Greek prelate and his colleagues, in common with other envoys from Epirus, Western Macedonia, Thessaly, Mani, and even distant Cyprus, strived unsuccessfully to persuade the Pope, the Spaniards, the Venetians and certain ambitious rulers of small Northern Italian states, too, to provide, at last, some galleons, a few thousand soldiers and the necessary equipment for some kind of uprising in the Greek Levant.[46] In vain did the Greeks point at the various internal crises that were tearing the Sultan's realm apart: financial bankruptcy, the perceptible weakening of its military strength, the

The revolutionary plans of Athanasios of Achris provided for a landing of Christian forces at Preveza (16th century map).

Habsburg military operations in the Balkans intensified after the unsuccessful Ottoman attempt to take Vienna in 1683.

and other clerics from the same area.[49] The Holy See was in no position to urge the weak Italian principalities or the by now decadent Spain to military adventures; the latter, from the third decade of the 17th century onwards, ceased to encourage the creation of even temporary centres of agitation in the Greek Levant.

The Venetian and Habsburg Counter-Offensive and Macedonia

Other European powers which continued to clash with the Ottomans in the second half of the 17th century and almost throughout the 18th century, did not entirely abandon these tactics. They were mainly interested in creating diversionary fronts in the interior of the empire. At the time of their two final confrontations with the Ottomans, the Venetians first sought to take advantage of Greek collaboration, primarily in the Ionian sea, Crete, the Aegean and the Peloponnese. Austrian interest in the Christian peoples of the Ottoman Empire constituted a new factor to which the enslaved peoples might also turn. To be sure, it was not the first time that this interest became manifest. But the spectacular Habsburg advance to the south, particularly after the victorious campaigns of Prince Eugene of Savoy, created new prospects for their Balkan policy, which required more direct contacts with the Ottoman-dominated Christian world. Of even greater importance were the renewed relations between the enslaved Greek-Orthodox element and the Russians, who, already in the late 17th and particularly after the second half of the 18th century, entered the struggle for supremacy in southeastern Europe.

Macedonia, however, did not find itself near the theatre of war again. Consequently, it was only fleetingly and quite coincidentally associated with certain events. Yet the general climate of insecurity, fuelled by the military preparations of the rival powers, was bound to affect certain sensitive areas of Macedonia, especially the exposed to naval raids coastline, and the north-western regions, which suffered from chronic Ottoman maladministration. To this climate also contributed the preventive measures taken by the authorities, which were designed not only to repel Venetian surprise landings but also to discourage the Christian inhabitants from giving any sort of assistance to the invaders.

Ottoman fears were not entirely unfounded; it so appeared, at least, in the case of the Venetians' naval raids in the Northern Aegean during the Cretan War

centrifugal tendencies of the local Muslim overlords, the slackening discipline of the increasingly mutinous Janissaries. In vain did they try to prove that the Ottoman Empire was a ripe fruit ready to fall into the hands of any Christian ruler who would support militarily any of the uprisings that were taking place at that time in Cyprus, Mani, Albania, Dalmatia, Montenegro, Bosnia and other provinces of the Turkish-dominated Levant.[47] Also unheeded passed the impressive argument that certain Ottoman officials in Epirus and Macedonia were prepared to collaborate in the uprising —as did Osman Pasha of Jannina, known from Dionysios' movement insurrection, in 1607-1613, and Redjep Pasha of Verria.[48]

Equally dissapointing was the outcome of similar, though less ambitious, efforts by Athanasios' successors

In 1687 Christian notables of Thessaloniki sought Venetian intervention against their Ottoman rulers.

(1645-1669), and, to a rather greater extent, during their only victorious war with the Ottomans from 1684 to 1699.[50] It is also a fact that, despite the Venetians' extensive pillage during their landings on Thasos, Kavala and Kassandra in 1684, some inhabitants of the Macedonian littoral were rather disposed to collaborate with them. Thus, three years later, in November 1687, certain notables of Thessaloniki, apparently impressed by Francesco Morosini's successes in the Peloponnese and Central Greece, hurried to Euboea and Piraeus to assure the Venetians that they were willing to take part with 300 horsemen in a possible operation of the Christian forces inside the Thermaic Gulf. However, word of these deliberations reached Thessaloniki's governor, Ismail Pasha, in time for him to reinforce the city's defences. Thus, the Turks were not taken by surprise when, in early May of the following year, a Venetian naval squadron entered Thessaloniki's harbour and started bombarding the city. The operation did not go according to plan and produced only meager results: a few fires and temporary panic among the Muslim population of Thessaloniki.[51]

Although it is known that the other partner in the Christian alliance, Austria, had been urging the Balkan peoples to rise against the Turks at least since 1690, available evidence on deliberations between the Habsburg Empire and the Greeks are not earlier than

1716 and refer exclusively to Macedonia. At exactly that time, almost the whole of nothern Greece suffered from its comparative proximity to the Austro-Turkish war front. Serious reasons of distress were the violent behaviour of Turkish troops on their way to the front, pillage and acts of brigandage on the part of deserters and irregulars, and also the high-handed methods of the local *armatoles*. These conditions drove the population to despair and were at the roots of mass islamizations.[52] In some occasions, however, the despairing inhabitants reacted violently against the Ottoman authorities (as in the cases of the people of Liti, who refused to pay capital tax in 1702, and of Naousa, who took part in a short-lived but bloody revolt led by the local *armatole* Zisis Karadimos in April, 1705).[53]

Under these cirmumstances, a familiar dynamic personality from Siatista, Zosimas Roussis (1686-1746), former archbishop of Achris, who during this period 'presided' over the diocese of Sisanion, established contacts with the Austrians. In April 1716, he sent his compatriot Ioannis Gipropoulos, a merchant, to the Austrian camp in Transylvania, conveying messages to the effect that the inhabitants of Moschopolis, Kozani, Siatista, Naousa and other centres in Macedonia were determined to rise against the "common enemy" if only the Emperor's campaign extended to their land too. It is interesting to note that during these deliberations, the

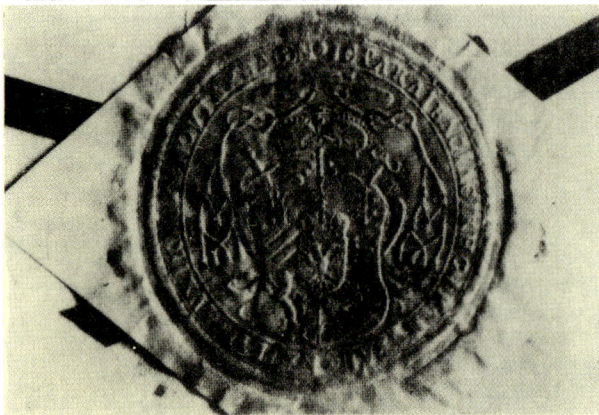

sacratissimo, Pijssimo, ac Potentissimo Prin-
cipi Carolo Sexto, in Christo Deo fideli Cæ-
sari, et Romanorum Imperatori, semper Au-
gusto, necnon Germaniæ, Hispaniæ, Hunga-
riæ, Bohemiæ, Sclavoniæ, Servia, Utriusqz
Siciliæ, etc. Regi, Archi = Duci Austriæ,
Duci Burgundiæ etc etc etc, Regi Duci,
Principi, ac Domino omnium Gratiosissimo ——

In early 18th century, the Metropolitan of Sisanion (Siatista)
Zosimas Roussis was in the forefront of attempts to
co-ordinate local anti-Turkish action with the Austrians.
Here, the frontispiece of his appeal to Emperor Charles
VI and the Metropolitan's seal.

Greeks —apparently taking advantage of the prevailing ideological atmosphere and the favourable conjunction resulting from the emergence of the Russian factor— demanded in advance that the Austrians pledge themselves in writing to respect Orthodoxy and freedom of religious practice; in other words, they put forward a condition which the previous archbishops of Achris had not dared to expressedly state in their talks with Western Catholic powers. Written guarantees were actually given by Prince Eugene of Savoy, although they eventually proved of no practical value —as did the promises of the victor of Zenta to advance into Western Macedonia: as Austria proceeded to conclude the Treaty of Passarowitz with the Ottomans in July 1718.[54]

All the same, Zosimas did not loose heart. In December 1736, no less than twenty years after his first attempt, he foresaw the coming Austro-Turkish conflict (1736-1739), and returned to his old proposals. This time they were conveyed to the Austrians by his colleague, the former Metropolitan of Old Patras Paisios II.[55] But the new initiative taken by Roussis, which the Austrians greeted with the same ineffectual response, was to be the Greeks' last appeal to the hesitant Habsburgs. Henceforth, they would turn to Russia, except for a brief interlude when their hopes would be pinned on revolutionary France.

The Shift to Russia

The Greek world had ancient and deeply rooted connections with Muscovy, with which it shared the same Christian Orthodox faith. Many of the monks and clerics who did the rounds of the Western courts with their anti-Turkish proposals also passed through or ended up in Muscovy, where they were equally fervent in expounding their plans for the expulsion of the Ottomans from the Greek Levant. However, towards the end of the 17th century, and increasingly as the 18th century went by, Greek-Russian contacts became more frequent and systematic, for they now accorded with the broader ambitions of the up-and-coming northern power in southeastern Europe.

The response of the inhabitants of Macedonia to the new historical challenge was commensurate with that of their compatriots in the other Greek regions, as, at least, is indicated by the actions of certain scholars and clerics associated with the area. I need mention here only a few examples, such as the appeals made to Peter the Great by Archimandrite Isaias of the Athonite Monastery of St Paul in 1688; the journeys and talks in Russia of the restless former Metropolitan of Thessaloniki, Methodios, in 1704; and the work *Vasilikon Theatron* by the Naousean monk Anastasios Michail written in 1709 in praise of the Russian victories. Such tendencies were limited in the initiatives of a few known personalities alone; they were also reflected in popular literature (mainly prophecies) or various anonymous expressions of similar ideological preference, a fact which Western observers (diplomats, missionaries, travellers, et al.) noted with concern.[56] The Ottomans, too, were aware of and increasingly alarmed by that ideological association of the *rayah* with the Muscovites as early as the beginning of the 18th century. In 1711 Thessaloniki's garrison commander, Hasan Pasha, was warning the Sublime Porte of the dangers which lurked in the by now open political relations of the Orthodox population with Muscovy, which were constantly renewed and expanded by clerics and merchants on their frequent journeys between Russia and Macedonia.[57] This was one reason why, during the successive Russo-Turkish wars and until the eve of the 1821 Revolution, the Ottoman

During the Russo-Turkish War in 1768-1774, the Thermaic Gulf (here in Rigas Velestinlis' map) and the island of Thasos became targets of Russian raids.

authorities took the greatest care to disarm the Christian population of Thrace and Macedonia.[58]

The Greek political problem was to be directly and fully linked with Russian policy at the time of the first Russo-Turkish War (1768-1774) waged by Catherine II, particularly during the operations of the Orlov brothers in the Peloponnese and the Aegean. It should be remembered that an important role in the secret preparations for the 1768 uprisings in many Greek regions from Cheimara to Mani was played by a Macedonian agent of the Czarina, the imperial guard officer from Siatista Georgios Papazolis. According to an as yet unconfirmed local tradition, Papazolis, apart from his other activities, had worked in Central and Western Macedonia initiating local leaders and clerics into the Russian plans.[59] It should also be noted that during the war a little known Moschopolitan, Athanasios Vainakis, served as secretary to the Orlov brothers.[60]

Although once again Macedonia remained outside the principal theatres of the Russo-Turkish confrontation and the pro-Russian uprisings in Greece, it nevertheless experienced the concecuences of the war. Northwestern Macedonia was particularly affected, as local Muslim little satraps taking advantage of the war plunged the region into chaos and anarchy. These developments caused fresh waves of mass islamization or mass expatriation, as in the case of Moschopolis in 1768-1769. Central Macedonia also suffered from the destruction wrought by the Ottoman armies on their way to rebellious Morea, the successive mobilizations of the Yuruks, the violent reprisals after the destruction of the Ottoman fleet at Çesme (July 1770). Moreover, the coast of the Thermaic Gulf often became the target of corsair assaults by the Russians and their Greek associates, a fact with far-reaching consequences for the security —both during the war and afterwards— of the Northern

Aegean. Finally, Thasos was briefly occupied by the Russians following the capture of its main port by their fleet in August, 1770.[61] Several Macedonians collaborated with the Russians by either forming small armed units or participating in the revolutionary effort in the Peloponnese or in the naval operations in the Aegean and the Eastern Mediterranean. Their role, however, has not been satisfactorily documented as yet; nor has historical research substantiated whatever information we owe to popular tradition concerning the activity of *klepht-armatole* clans of the Macedonian hinterland during the 1768 to 1774 war, such as the Ziakas in the region of Grevena, the Zidros, Lapas, Lazos and Blahavas families on Mts Olympus and Hasia.[62]

Regarding the attitude of the Macedonians during the next Russo-Turkish War (1787-1792), information is scanty. It should be remembered, however, that Greek patrication in this war —which, unlike the previous one, did not directly affect Greece— was definitely limited. The Russians, of course, once more tried to win the Greeks over to their side, with the aim to foment disturbances in the usual, sensitive spots of the Greek penincula. To this end, Czarina's Greek delegate, Louizis Sotiris, engaged in secret deliberations with clerics and band leaders of Central and Western Macedonia in summer 1789. However, these clandestine contacts proved fruitless owing to the Greeks' distrust of Catherine's true intentions, especially after the bitter experience with Russian behavior in the Peloponnese twenty years earlier. It was for this reason that no important revolutionary activity took place then both in Macedonia and in other Greek regions. The attacks in early 1790 of the Olympus *armatoles* against Turkish-Albanian bands are merely isolated exceptions. Even the broader political significance of these episodes depends on the reliability of the more general information on the understanding between Greek leaders with Lampros Katsonis and a few other occasional associates of the Russians in the Northern Aegean.[63]

Local *Klepht-Armatole* Activity and National Liberation Efforts

By the end of the 18th and even the beginning of the 19th century, the most pressing problem facing the inhabitants of Macedonia was the presence of thousands of Muslim Albanian irregulars who had been used to quash the uprising in the Peloponnese in 1770. Their uncontrolled mass movements and their acts of brigandage caused the destruction of whole villages and towns (such as the until then flourishing city of Moschopolis). Of course, the ruinous work of the Albanian irregulars had started thirty years earlier, with the malpractices and arbitrary rule of local governors and their tyrranical associates.[64] That activity —which was not effectively checked after Ali Pasha of Tepelene extended his rule towards Macedonia— plagued the Christian and the Muslim inhabitants alike.

Against this background one should proceed with the evaluation of the confrontation between the most famous *armatoles* and *klephts* of Olympus, Hasia and the Pindus Mountains and the rival Turkish-Albanian bands. In the general confusion which reigned and in view of the prevailing social and cultural conditions, which did not permit a distinction between the more general question of independence and the acute local problem of security, the activity of these leaders should be considered as largely the continuation of the peculiar tradition of armatolic activity or even brigandage that earlier circumstances had established. Clashes between the Greek-Orthodox irregulars and their Turkish-Albanian rivals were not only a matter of an unbridgeable religious chasm or their involvement into some sort of early ethnic rivalry; they were often the result of 'professional' competition between those pugnacious chieftains of the countryside. For this reason the anti-Turkish activity of the Christian irregulars was not invariably characterized by a selfless desire to defend their fellow Christians and even less so by a conscious pursuit of national independence. The Macedonians who were initiated (and were among the first to do so) to Rigas Velestinlis' revolutionary plans (such as Markides, the sons of Poulios, Konstantinos Doukas and Theocharis Tourountzias from Siatista and Georgios Theocharis, Panagiotis and Ioannis Emmanouil from Kastoria) had no ideological affinity with the illiterate highlanders of their native land whose exploits —however idealized by popular tradition— had not yet acquired the national character that was later ascribed to them.[65]

Even as late as the beginning of the 19th century, the motives of the Greek *kapetanioi* were not entirely clear. The contacts, however fortuitous, of Nikotsaras and Thymios Blahavas with the Russians during the 1806-1812 war (particularly at the time of the spectacular presence of Seniavin's fleet in the northern Aegean in 1807[66]) lend some political-ethnic dimension to their anti-Turkish activities. However, there is no evidence that the activity of these two Greek leaders was connected with the initiatives of those who were consciously promoting the cause of freedom on a national level. The participation, on the other hand, of Georgakis Olympios (and, perhaps, of Nikotsaras) in the Serbian uprising is a remarkable fact, which highlights the indisputable appeal of the 1803-1804 events among the Greek world.[67] However, it cannot be regarded as representing a clear realization of the need to face the national problem through a co-ordinated liberation effort of the Balkan peoples, as envisaged by Rigas in the 1790s[68], or by important initiates of the *Philiki Etaireia* from Macedonia some twenty-five years later.[69] However, by the second decade of the 19th century, in Macedonia, as indeed in the rest of Greece, the long and arduous process had begun that would lead on to a conscious struggle for national liberation: the Revolution of 1821.

The Macedonian hinterland suffered as a result of the activities of thousands of Albanian irregulars, which continued after Ali Pasha of Jannina extended his rule over part of Macedonia (here, Ali Pasha as depicted by a British traveller).

Conclusions

This study has been confined perforce to the most indicative instances of revolutionary behaviour in Macedonia before 1821, primarily focusing upon the less known period between the 16th and the early 18th century. Despite these limitations, however, it is still possible to put one's finger on certain features which apply more or less to almost the whole range of anti-Turkish activity in pre-revolutionary Macedonia.

As we have repeatedly stated, the evidence upon which this paper is based is inadequate in terms of both quantity and quality. But this paucity should, in our opinion, be considered in relation to the historical circumstances of the time, by which we mean the manifestly reduced intensity and extent of the insurrectionary movements in Macedonia, as compared with the considerably more dynamic manifestations in Epirus, the Peloponnese and Cyprus. The same was true of other parts of the Greek world too —such as the eastern Central Greece, eastern Thessaly, Thrace and Asia Minor— and it is due to geographical and historical factors. Macedonia in particular, cut off to the west and south by the mountain ranges of Pindus and Olympus, and off the usual routes from Western Europe to Constantinople and the Middle East, almost up until the beginning of the 18th century inevitably found itself out of the way of external influences which had familiarized other parts of the Greek-Orthodox world with the notion of replacing Ottoman rule with a more acceptable Chris-

tian regime. In other words Macedonia was for long deprived of those essential factors which, elsewhere, accelerated the ideological processes that would eventually lead to the national awakening of the Greeks. Even the peculiar political role of Mount Athos was not unrelated, as we have seen, to the Athonite links with the Christian rulers of the West. The revolutionary activity that went on in Western Macedonia should, of course, be correlated with the prevailing local circumstances, and particularly with the fact that it had easier connections with the West, via Epirus, western Thessaly and southern Albania. Furthermore, the territory of Macedonia was not a target of the European powers during their interventions in the Ottoman Empire almost up until the middle of the 19th century; and this explains why the Western 'challenges' eventually reached Macedonia in a considerably attenuated form.

Apart from external factors (though these continued to be a basic consideration in any anti-Turkish activity), the inhabitants' attitude was also negatively affected by the fact that they had long been immobilized in backward forms of economic and social life, with the exception, of course, of the few urban centres, and notably Thessaloniki. Consequently, as we have seen, the Chris-

An **Armatole**, *as presented in Pouqueville's* **Voyage de la Grèce (2nd ed., 1826-7)**.

compromise on religious matters; the despairing feudal lords and the *Sipahis* of the early period of the Ottoman rule, who had suffered from the structural changes in the system of land ownership; the declining *armatoles* and professional fighters of the Macedonian countryside, particularly after the end of the 17th century; the peasants who were reduced by poverty and under the frequent threat of conversion to Islam; and, finally, the various soldiers of fortune, who knew how to combine the anti-Turkish feeling prevalent in some Western courts with self-interest. Yet these initiatives in a way expressed the general inclinations of the Christian population, though admittedly these were deliberately —and occasionally misleadingly— overstated in reports to the West. Therefore, although the exaggerated picture of Macedonia's revolutionary fervour and dynamic insurrections (as depicted by an enthusiastic nationalistic historiography) should be viewed with scepticism, the idea —which one might form out of lack of sources— that the region was politically inert is no less of a distortion. A rational assessment of the extent and significanse of the anti-Turkish efforts in Macedonia in the period between the 15th and the early 19th centuries would certainly demand assiduous and systematic research, and this cannot be carried out in full as long as the Ottoman archives remain inaccessible, particularly to the Greek historians.

It is also clear that virtually the same internal and external factors which influenced the rest of the Greek world also provoked similar, though less vigorous, revolutionary initiatives in Macedonia: successive war crises and extraordinary conscription and taxation, violation of local privileges, outbreaks of internal anarchy and their traumatic effects particularly on the peasant population, and the, albeit temporary, presence of the Christian powers in the Greek Levant or of even a small Christian flotilla in the Greek seas...

Collaboration with the other Balkan peoples —the Serbs and particularly the Albanians— as the relevant sources indicate, was not ruled out; but it was normally of a tactical rather than an ideological nature. Despite religious affinity, certain important factors prevented a political rapprochement. Cooperation between the Christians of Macedonia and the Serbs, for instance, was hindered by their divided ecclesiastical loyalties. The Greeks rallied round the Orthodox dioceses of Macedonia or, often, the archbishopric of Achris which enjoyed primacy over many of these dioceses. The Serbs increasingly turned to their own national-religious

tians of Thessaloniki were frequently involved in anti-Turkish movements from as early as the 16th up until the 19th century. Matters appear quite different in the case of the Macedonians who lived in the Greek communities of Western urban centres. Significantly, those in the forefront of the national movement at the end of the 18th century came from relatively urbanized families of the diaspora, such as the Macedonian associates of Rigas and the first ardent members of the *Philiki Etaireia*. Finally, any kind of challenge to Ottoman authority in Macedonia, and particularly in its central and eastern parts, was unquestionably further discouraged by the presence of a compact Muslim population: a factor which, as we know, also had a negative effect on the outcome of the revolution of 1821-1822.

All the same, the Greek-Orthodox element in Macedonia was far from indifferent to the political problem of the Levant, as is indicated by the repeated anti-Turkish initiatives discussed above. The fact is, of course, that such activities involved a limited number of people or even constituted isolated cases. This is a general phenomenon, however: it inevitably characterized, as we know, most similar efforts in the rest of the Greek world. That was also the case with the social groups which, in Macedonia as in the rest of Greece, led the way in challenging the political *status quo*: scholars nurtured on Greece's ancient glory; ambitious prelates who maintained close ties with the West and who were prepared to accept, if only for tactical purposes, some

The Dionysiou Monastery.
Painting by Edward Lear (1862).

centre of the patriarchate of Peć, coordinating their efforts against the Turks with the Catholic Dalmatians who were familiar with the ways of the West. Cooperation between Greeks and Albanians was closer and more frequent; yet it was often held back by the Albanians' greater tolerance towards the Holy See and, even more so, by their closer links with the Catholics of northern Albania. Furthermore, after the late 17th and the first decades of the 18th century, when the islamized Albanians extended their brigand activity throughout Western Macedonia, the rift deepened. Despite of all these, at least until the mid-17th century, the Greek insurrectionary movements met with a response usually from the Orthodox Christians of southern Albania, and particularly those who were under the juristiction of Greek prelates. That rapprochement —which was facilitated by the regular participation of the Greeks of North Epirus, chiefly the Cheimariots, in anti-Turkish activities— occasionally resulted in a degree of identity which often made it hard for Western sources to distinguish between the *Greci* and the *Albanesi*, and, even more so, the *Greco-Albanesi*, a phenomenon which is common in the construction and ideological function of the Greek communities of Southern Italy as early as the beginning of the 16th century.

Finally, the instances of revolutionary activity discussed in this study indicate that the anti-Turkish movements in Macedonia were usually co-ordinated with similar efforts in the southern Greek provinces. Indeed, the same people frequently played a leading part or were at least informed about the same or parallel revolutionary movements. Even when this fact is evident only in the intentions, rather than in the final result, it is by no means isignificant: for it indicates the common perception that liberation from foreign rule was a shared problem, a matter that concerned the whole of the Greek world.

●

IOANNIS K. HASSIOTIS
ANTI-TURKISH MOVEMENTS IN
MACEDONIA BEFORE 1821
NOTES

1. For a more complete (even in view of these remarks) history of Macedonia during the period under study, see Apostolos E. Vacalopoulos, *History of Macedonia, 1354-1833* (in Greek), Thessaloniki 1979.

2. Vacalopoulos, *op. cit.*, pp. 96, 114-115, 158; cf. S. Aravantinos, *Annals of Epirus* (in Greek), vol. 1, Athens 1856, p.176; Vacalopoulos' reference to the rebellion of the inhabitants of Western Macedonia between 1444 and 1447 (*op. cit.*, pp. 109-111) is not convincingly documented.

3. I.K. Hassiotis, 'Military Conflicts in Greek Territories and the Greek Connection, 1453-1669', *History of the Greek Nation* (in Greek), vol. X, Athens 1974, pp. 269, 271.

4. I.K. Hassiotis, 'The European Powers and the Problem of the Greek Independence from the Mid-15th through the Early 19th Century', *Greece, History and Civilization* (in Greek), vol. 5, Thessaloniki 1981, pp. 66-69.

5. I.K. Hassiotis, 'The Peloponnese in Charles's V Mediterranean Policy' (in Greek), *Peloponnisiaka*, 15 (1984), 187ff., 192ff., 198, 202-208, 224-225.

6. Archivo General de Simancas, Section de Estado [hereafter cited as AGS-E], legajo (folder) 1311, no. 197. It appears that Angelos Palaiologos did not return to his native land; he probably stayed in Southern Italy where his name is to be found in an (undated) list of fugitives from Koroni (AGS-E 1024, no. 13); although the Metropolitan's name is not mentioned in these sources, it certainly is Ioasaph whose presence is acknowledged between 1527 and 1535: A. Glavinas, 'Some Metropolitans of Thessaloniki in XVI Century' (in Greek), *Yearbook of the School of Theology of the University of Thessaloniki*, 19 (1975), 285-289.

7. Hassiotis, 'The Peloponnese', 193-194.

8. Regarding the impact of those conditions on the ideological orientation of the Greeks, see: Hassiotis, 'The European Powers', pp. 79-88.

9. A.E. Vacalopoulos, *History of Modern Hellenism* (in Greek), vol. 3, Thessaloniki 1978, pp. 169-170.

10. I.K. Hassiotis, *The Greeks on the Eve of the Naval Battle of Lepanto, 1568-1571*, Thessaloniki 1970, pp. 21ff.

11. *Ibid.*, pp. 72 (note 2), 78-79, 102 (note 3).

12. Vacalopoulos, *op. cit.*, p. 269.

13. G.T. Kolias, 'Letter of the Metropolitan Timotheos to the Pope Pius V (1572)', *In Memoriam of K. Amantos* (in Greek), Athens 1960, pp. 391-411; regarding Timotheos' diocese (Grevena) and his Exarchic See in Southern Italy, see: Hassiotis, *op. cit.*, p.39 note 2.

14. I.K. Hassiotis, 'Archbishop Ioakeim of Achris and the Conspiratorial Movement in Northern Epirus (1572-1576)' (in Greek), *Makedonika*, 6 (1964-65), 237-256, 290-291. On the deliberations of Papagiannis with Martín de Acuña, secret envoy of Spain to the Balkans, in January 1577, see: AGS-E 1078, no 60.

15. Cf. Peter Bartl, *Der Westbalkan zwischen spanischer Monarchie und Osmanischen Reich. Zur Türkenkriegsproblematik an der Wende vom 16. zum 17. Jahrhundert*, Wiesbaden 1974. More specifically on the Greek anti-Turkish activities, see: I.K. Hassiotis, 'Spanish Policy towards the Greek Insurrectional Movements of the Early Seventeenth Century', *Actes du Ile Congrés Intern. des Etudes du Sud-Est Européen*, vol. 3, Athens 1978, 313-329.

16. Regarding the organization of the Spanish network of espionage in the Ottoman Empire, see: G. Hassiotis, 'Venezia e i domini veneziani tramite di informazioni sui turchi per gli spagnoli nel sec. XVI', *Venezia, centro di mediazione tra Oriente e Occidente (secoli XV-XVI)*, vol. 1, Florence 1977, pp. 117-136.

17. Information on Nikolaos in: AGS-E 1601, s.n. (Dec. 1604); E 1161, no. 124 (autumn 1604); E 1661, s.n. (1609); E 1662, s.n. (16 July 1611); E 1667, s.n. (1 Aug. 1615); E 1697, s.n. (26 Apr. 1604); E 1989, s.n. (7 Dec. 1604, 1618); about Dimitrios Palaiologos (who should probably be idenified as the Christianized former Janissary Dimitrios from Thessaloniki) see: AGS-E 1599, s.n. and E 1602, s.n. (1604); E 1661, s.n. (17 Sept. 1609); E 1696, s.n. (29 March 1604); E 1702, s.n. (9 Sept. 1598), and E 1964, s.n. (1604); regarding the activity of Dimos, son of Panagiotis, see: AGS-E 1691, s.n. (16 June, 1615).

18. AGS-Secretarías Provinciales, Nàpoles [hereafter cited as AGS-SP Nàp.], libro 168, ff. 88-89 (24 Feb. 1607); E 1608, s.n., and E 1699, s.n. (Aug.-Sept. 1606), where Ioasaph is characterized as "procurador general" of the Athonite "monasterio de Nuestra Señora de Portulana", a probable translation of the 'Panagia i Portaïtissa'. Regarding Atsalis' carrer in the Greek community of Palermo (1612-1613), consult Matteo Sciambra, 'Clero di rito greco nella comunità greco-albanese di Palermo', *Bolletino della Badia Greca di Grottaferrata*, 18 (1974), 11-18; cf. Z.N. Tsirpanlis, *The Greek College of*

Rome and its Scholars, 1576-1700 (in Greek), Thessaloniki 1980, pp. 311-313.

19. Archivio Segreto Vaticano, Nunziature di Spagna [hereafter cited as AS Vat-NS], vol. 337, f. 322, vol. 338, f. 379 (23 and 26 Jan. 1613), regarding the "procurador" of the Athonite monastery of "de Santa Maria de los Angeles', monk Jeremias, and his comrade Parthenios; cf. *loc. cit.*, vol. 333, f. 114 (13 Feb. 1606) for a similar *ziteia* of some unnamed representatives of an unspecified monastery of Mount Athos.

20. AGS-SP Nàp., vol. 189 (21 Nov. 1624).

21. AGS-SP Nàp., vol. 191, f. 184 (30 Aug. 1628).

22. Regarding this monk, AGS-E 1698, s.n.; E 1714, s.n.; E 1995, s.n. (1605-1607).

23. Regarding the role of the 'stradioti' of Southern Italy in the plans for a military intervention in Turkish-occupied Greece, see: Hassiotis, 'The European Powers', pp. 70-74.

24. AGS-E 1061, no. 47 (1572); E 1070, no. 27 (2 Dec. 1576); E 1506, no. 32 (1572), SP Nàp., libro 139, no. 89 (20 Dec. 1577).

25. Regarding Yahya's activities: Stephanos Papadopoulos, *Charles Gonzaga's, Duke of Nevers, Movement for the Liberation of the Balkan Peoples, 1603-1625* (in Greek), Thessaloniki 1966, pp. 220-230, with previous bibliography; more on his life in his own report to Emperor Rodolfo II: AGS-E 1949, no. 27 (4 Aug. 1609); regarding the connection of the pseudosultan's proposals with the plans of the Greeks of Naples for Spanish military intervention in Greece a few years later: AGS-E 1949, no. 235, 237 (28 Jan. 1614).

26. The Spanish bureaucracy has preserved several related documents, albeit of a frequently repetitive nature: AGS-E 1103, no. 209; E 1595, no. 716; E 1596, no. 16; E 1597, no. 7; E 1602, s.n., s.d.; E 1604, s.n. (Jan. 1605); E 1673, s.n. (21 Feb. 1615); E 1697, s.n. (5 March and 23 May 1602 and 23 Sept. 1604); E 1989, s.n. (17 Jan. 1605); E 1990, s.n. (1602).

27. The execution of the plan —in which Smyrna, Tenedos and certain other unspecified parts of the northern Aegean were included— would be entrusted to the experienced commander of the fleet of Naples, Alvaro de Bazán, second Marquis of Santa Cruz; that was, at least, Viceroy Benavente's suggestion to Philip III on 25 November 1606, which was eventually rejected: AGS-E 1103, no. 209.

28. A. Glavinas, 'Bishops of Kitros during the Ottoman Domination

according to the Sources' (in Greek), *Makedonika*, 18 (1978), 76-78.
29. AGS-E 1596, nos. 84 (22 Aug.), 152/176 (July); E 1707, s.n. (7 May), E 1989, s.n. (22 June and 20 July 1602), where vague reference to the adventures of Kallistos, bishop of Molisco. With respect to the diocese and its names: D. Zakynthinos, 'Contributions to the History of the Churches of Achris and Peć' (in Greek), *Makedonika*, 1 (1940), 443 and note 10.
30. AGS-E 1345, nos. 87, 109 (1593-1594); AS Vat.-NS, vol. 324, f. 66 (31 May 1597), with reference to Ieremias' adventure at an ecclesiastical court in Rome shortly before his departure for Spain; more on this interesting personality: B. Mystakidis, 'Two Archbishops of Achris in Tübingen' (in Greek), *Theology*, 9 (1931), 337, and *ibid.*, 10 (1932) 69, 73, 146.
31. On Gabriel see: I.D. Psaras, *The Archbishop Gabriel of Achris and His Wanderings through European Countries. A Biographical Sketch, 1527-1593*, M.A. dissertation (unpubl.), Thessaloniki 1976; for an "arcivescovo de Macedonia", who should be identified with Gabriel, cf. AGS-E 1693, s.n. (26 Sept 1605), and E 1699, s.n., s.d.
32. For his services to Castille and his vague, standard proposals to the Spaniards regarding the capture "del imperio de Constantinople": AGS-E 1673, s.n. (5 March 1614) .
33. AGS-E 1670, s.n. (27 April 1613), regarding the involvement of a representative of the Athonite monastery of the Archangels Michael and Gabriel (probably of Docheiarion), Anthimos, in "negocios secretos".
34. AGS-SP Nàp., libro 193, f. 231 (21 May 1632), where Meletios is described as the procurator of the monastery "de Nuestra Señora de la Gracia del Monte Santo".
35. There are numerous documents in this connection in AGS; by way of indication: AGS-E 1102, no. 149, s.d. (1605: 'Manuelo Greco's and 'Manuel de Giovanni's report to the Viceroy of Naples on their secret mission to Greece); no. 151 (May 1605: Italian copy of an appeal to Viceroy Benavente by the prelates and notables of Macedonia, Thessaly, Epirus, Central Greece and the western Peloponnese; the original had been signed, among others, by the Metropolitan of Thessaloniki —anonymously— and Timotheos of Servia.
36. Glavinas, *op. cit.*, 76-77.
37. Cf. José Manuel Floristàn Imizcoz, *Documentos neogriegos en el Archivo de Simancas*, Ph.D. thesis (unpubl.), Universidad Complutense, Madrid 1987.

38. For Athanasios' turbulent life, see: N.J. Milev, 'Ochridskijat patriarch Atanasij i skitanijata mu v cuzbina (1597-1616)', *Izvestija na istoriceskoto druzestvo v Sofija*, 5 (1922), 113-128; A.P. Péchayre, 'Les archevêques d'Ochrida et leurs relations avec l'Occident à la fin du XVIe siècle et au début du XVIIe', *Echos d'Orient*, XXXVI (1937), 409-422; M. Lacko 'Alcuni documenti riguardanti l' arcivescovo di Ochrida Atanasio', *Orientalia Christiana Periodica*, XXXIII(1977), 620-638; and Bartl, *Der Westbalkan*, pp. 124-131.
39. A full exposition of that ambitious attempt is, of course, beyond the scope of this general account. Floristán Imizcoz's work also relies on AGS sources on Athanasios (*op. cit.*, pp. 436ff.)
40. In a report to Philip III, dated 30 November 1612: AGS-E 1949, no. 85.
41. Alex. Randa, *Pro Rebublica Christiana. Die Walachei im 'langen Turkenkrieg' der katolischen Universalmächte (1593-1606)*, Munich 1964.
42. Hassiotis, 'Spanish policy', 318-319; Bartl, *Der Westbalkan*, pp. 153-155.
43. According to Athanasios' report, dated October 1614: AGS-E 495, s.n. (= E 1879, no. 339).
44. AGS *loc. cit.*; on Yahya's probable cooperation with Vergos, cf. Papadopoulos, *Charles Gonzaga's, Duke of Nevers, Movement*, p. 226; regarding the endemic brigandage in these regions, see: Vacalopoulos, *History of Macedonia*, pp. 188, 190.
45. The appeal written by Athanasios and the prelates associated with him on April 1612 (text in Italian translation), in: AGS-E 495, s.n.; also, briefing report by Ieronymos Combis, 17 July 1612, in: AGS-E 1949, no. 68; cf. AGS-E 1949, no. 72 (11 Sept 1612).
46. Floristàn Imizcoz, *p. cit.*, p. 446ff; Athanasios' proposals were being discussed by the *Consejo de Estado* as late as 14 March 1615, after the positive but rather lukewarm report of Viceroy de Lemos, submitted on 6 December 1614: AGS-E 495, s.n. In that period Athanasios was already involved in other insurrectionary plans, this time in his own native place, Mani, as demonstrated by M.T. Laskaris in his 'Appeals of the Bishop of Mani Neophytos to the Spaniards (1612-1613) for the Liberation of the Peloponnese' (in Greek), *Ellinika*, 15 (1957), 303-306. References to the activities of that restless prelate continue for a few more years: AGS-E 1881, no. 253 (18 Aug. 1618).
47. Papadopoulos, *op. cit.*, p. 53ff; I.K. Hassiotis, *Spanish Sources of the History of Cyprus, XVI-XVII Cent.* (in Greek), Nicosia 1972, p.

82ff; Bartl, *Der Westbalkan*, p. 156ff; cf. Alex. Matkovski, 'Hei-duckenaktionen in Mazedonia in der ersten Hälfte des 17. Jahrhunderts', *Südost-Forschungen*, 21 (1972), 394-402.

48. AGS-E 1949, nos. 199 (11 July 1613: Italian translation of a Greek appeal for intervention in Macedonia, sent to Ieronymos Combis by the Metropolitans of Kastoria, Pelagonia, Grevena and Ventson, Selasphoron and Korytsa, Valona and Kaninon, Sisanion and Anaselitsa, and Velessa), 202 (Italian translation of a confidential message to Combis from the Pasha of Verria, in Greek, dated 15 July 1613). Common messenger in both cases, the bishop of Prespa Zacharias: AGS-E 1949, nos. 163-165 (3 Aug. 1613), 187/2, 193 (10 Sept. 1613).

49. Péchayre, *op. cit.*, pp.435-439; cf. S.L. Varnalidis, *The Archbishop Zosimas of Achris (1686-1746) and his Ecclesiastical and Political Activities*, Thessaloniki 1974, pp. 72-76; for a related initiative, taken in 1699 by the Cretan Metropolitan of Durazzo, Symeon Lascaris, cf. I.K. Hassiotis, 'Crete and the Spaniards during the Venetian Domination' (in Greek), *Proceedings the 3rd International Conference on Crete*, vol. II, Athens 1974, pp. 368-370.

50. Hassiotis, 'Military Conflicts', *loc. cit.*, vol. X, p. 342; cf. B.J. Slot, *Archipelagus turbatus. Les Cyclades entre colonisation latine et occupation Ottomane, c. 1500-1718*, vol. I, Constantinople 1982, p. 232. No evidence has been hitherto found on *armatole* leader Meintanis' alleged cooperation with the Venetians during the 1684-1699 war (Vacalopoulos, *History of Macedonia*, p. 255). The acts of brigandage in northwestern Macedonia during the same period should rather be attributed to common problems of insecurity than to external provocations: Alex. Matkovski, 'Svedenija za hajduti v Makedonija prez vtorata polovina na XVIII vek', *Istoriceski Pregled*, XXII/3 (Sofia 1976), 67-82.

51. K.D. Mertzios, 'Fransesco Morosini and the Incursions on Kassandra, Kavala, and Thasos' (in Greek), *Makedonika*, 3 (1953-1955), 1-7; cf. Hassiotis, *op. cit.*, vol. 11, Athens 1975, pp. 33-34.

52. Vacalopoulos, *p. cit.*, pp. 317-329.

53. I.K. Vasdravellis, *Historical Archives of Macedonia. I. The Archive of Thessaloniki, 1695-1912*, Thessaloniki 1952, pp. 41-42, and *II. The Archive of Verria-Naousa, 1598-1886*, Thessaloniki 1954, pp. 113-115; cf. Vacalopoulos *p. cit.*, pp. 258-260 (all sources in Greek).

54. Varnalidis, *op. cit.*, pp. 78-92, where previous bibliography.

55. *Ibid.*, pp. 92-119.

56. Vacalopoulos, *History of Modern Hellenism*, vol. 4, Thessaloniki

1973, p. 67; cf. A. Tamborra, 'Pietro il Grande e la lotta per l' eretidà politica di Bizanzio (1696-1711)', *Atti dello VIII congresso intern. di studi bizantini*, vol. I, Rome 1953, 420-436; Vacalopoulos, 'Peter the Great and the Greeks in Late 17th and Early 18th Century' (in Greek), *Yearbook of the School of Philosophy of the University of Thessaloniki*, XI (1979), 247-259; A. Argyriou, 'Les exegèses grecques de l' Apocalypse à l'époque turque (1453-1821)', *Esquisse d' une histoire des courants ideologiques au sein du peuple grec asservi*, Thessaloniki 1982, pp. 88-90.

57. I.H. Uzunçarsili, *Osmanli tarihi*, vol. IV/1, Ankara 1956, pp. 70-71.

58. Vacalopoulos, *History of Macedonia*, pp. 260-261, 302-303.

59. Vacalopoulos, *History of Modern Hellenism*, vol. 4, pp. 377-380.

60. D.K. Mertzios, *Documents of Macedonian History*, Thessaloniki 1947, pp. 190.

61. Vacalopoulos, *History of Macedonia*, pp. 301-307.

62. I.K. Vasdravellis, *Armatoles and Klephts in Macedonia* (in Greek), Thessaloniki[2] 1970, pp. 51-56; Vacalopoulos, *op. cit.*, pp. 306-307.

63. N. Kasomoulis, *Military Memoirs of the Revolution of the Greeks, 1821-1833* (in Greek), vol. 1, Athens 1939, pp. 13, 67, 95; Mertzios, *Documents*, pp. 450 and 464-465, and *New Information about Lampros Katsonis and Androutsos* (in Greek), Athens 1959, p. 82; E.G. Protopsaltis, 'The Revolutionary Movement of the Greeks during the Second Russo-Turkish War under Catherine II, 1787-1792. Loudovikos Sotiris' (in Greek), *Bulletin of the Hist. Ethnol. Society of Greece*, 14 (1970), 73-76; cf. Vacalopoulos, *History of Modern Hellenism*, vol. 4, pp. 567-568.

64. Vacalopoulos, 'History of Macedonia', p. 307.

65. Vasdravelis, *op. cit.*, pp. 53-60; for bibliography on the Macedonian followers of Rigas, see: Vacalopoulos, *op. cit.*, pp. 429-431.

66. *Ibid.*, pp. 523-530, and Vasdravellis, *op. cit.*, pp. 61-74; cf. A. Vacalopoulos, 'New Documentation concerning the Greek *Armatoliks* and Thymios Blachavas' Revolt in Thessaly in 1808' in Greek, *Yearbook of the School of Philosophy of the University of Thessaloniki*, 9 (1965), 229-251 (in particular pp. 245-250).

67. For related bibliography, see: Vacalopoulos, *History of Modern Hellenism*, vol. 4, p. 699.

68. *Ibid.*, p. 595.

69. Vacalopoulos, *History of Macedonia*, pp. 544-545.

The Revolution of 1821 and Macedonia

Artemis Xanthopoulou - Kyriakou

Introduction

An examiner of events that occured in Macedonia during the National Uprising would realize immediately that this chapter of Modern Greek history appears understated both by historians of the Struggle and by memoir writers (with the exception of Kasomoulis).[1] Many question marks will arise, gaps or even controversial information and, therefore, one would be compelled to regard with scepticism some of the assessments that have been made from time to time (especially issues relating to the events in Chalcidice and Vermion). All of this is due to several reasons: first of all, a discounting –conscious or unconscious– of the significance of the struggle in Macedonia must be linked with the fact that results in this region were not as impressive as in other Greek regions. In addition, popular participation and details of the fight and the sacrifices of the people did not become widely known in Europe; this is why they did not attract the emotional response of, for example, the heroic resistance and the exodus from Messolongi, the slaughter of Chios and the holocaust of Psarra. There are no literary or artistic works by Western Europeans inspired by the heroism and sacrifices of those who fought in Macedonia. An almost solitary vibrant feature of the desperate struggle in Chalcidice was the heroic and tragic figure of Emmanouil Papas, complemented by the repetition of the Zalongo sacrifice at Arapitsa of Mt Vermion. Only the popular Muse, the popular art –and more recently, a handful of Modern Greek writers and artists– have been inspired by the dramatic events in Macedonia to a similar degree, perhaps, to the corresponding events that took place in the rest of Greece.

Despite all that, Macedonians claim a substantial share of the participation in almost all stages of the Struggle both through their activities within the Macedonian region or through their contribution in military encounters at other fronts, outside their native land. It should also be noted that Macedonia had been prepared psychologically and, to an extent, organizationally, for the impending National Uprising since the first decade of the 19th century. This is not the place to trace the methods of ideological preparation of the population –at least of certain leading sections of society. Nor is it necessary to highlight here the role of the Macedonian diaspora, especially those settled within the Habsburg empire, the Danubian Principalities and Russia.

In addition, Macedonia had undergone some form of revolutionary groundwork, especially amongst the old *armatoles* of the mountainous areas of Central and West Macedonia. This preparation had begun long before the first linking of the *Philiki Etaireia* (the secret 'Friendly Society') with Macedonia. At the time of the Russo-Turkish War of 1806-1812, the Christian population, the irregulars of the rural regions in particular, had already begun to be conditioned about a possible overthrow of the infidel tyrannical regime. Despite the brief duration of the Russian presence in Greek seas during that the course of that war (1806-1807), events had –in the fashion of previous Russo-Turkish conflicts– established contact between many *armatoles* and *klephts* from different parts of the Greek peninsula and Russians in the Ionian and the Aegean seas. Included amongst this group were Nikotsaras and the Lazos family. Indeed, it appears that the Thessalian and Macedonian band leaders co-ordinated their anti-Turkish activities with corresponding activities by leaders from other parts of Greece, such as with, for example, Kolokotronis.[2] Their stand, however, especially that of the Lazos and the Blahavas clans, should be examined from within the context of the special characteristics of the *armatoles* opposition in the northern Greek regions to the expansionist efforts of Jannina's Ali Pasha towards Thessaly and Macedonia.

To a degree only, an important role was played by

The dramatic end of the revolutionary movement of Prince Ypsilantis. Georgakis Olympios, the armatole from Macedonia, blows up the Secu Monastery, in Moldavia, to avoid surrendering to the Ottoman army. Painting by von tless.

the impression made on the Greek world by the Serbian uprising (1803-1804). The facts, of course, have not been satisfactorily proven yet. There is evidence, however, which reveals that some well-known Macedonian fighters (the case of Georgakis Olympios from Vlacholivado is the most prominent) co-operated closely with the Serbian revolutionaries.[3]

Whatever the real situation, this revolutionary mobilization constituted an important factor influencing the conditions which existed in Macedonia on the eve of the Revolution. It is also not coincidental that even in its early stages of activity, only a few years since its establishment in Odessa in 1814, the *Philiki Etaireia* indoctrinated some characteristic representatives of Macedonian armatolism: Georgios Pharmakis from Blatsi (at Odessa in 1817)[4]; Georgakis Olympios (at Chotin in

Bessarabia in 1816-17).[5] The Thessalonian merchant Nikolaos Ouzounidis was also initiated during this early period (in Moscow in 1816).[6]

Philiki Etaireia Activity in Macedonia

Despite the scarcity of relevant sources and the contradictions which characterize surviving information, we can make some preliminary observations about the work of the *Philiki Etaireia* within Macedonia itself. It must initially be emphasized that *Philiki Etaireia* members were generally confronted with great difficulties in recruiting supporters in Macedonia, compared with the relatively smaller problems encountered in southern Greece. These difficulties had various causes: firstly, the presence of the compact Muslim element which was settled in strategic parts of mainly Central Macedonia. Macedonia was also the permanent area for the passage and regrouping of armies continuously directed towards Epirus to put down the Ali Pasha mutiny. It was for this reason that the first Macedonian members were initiated

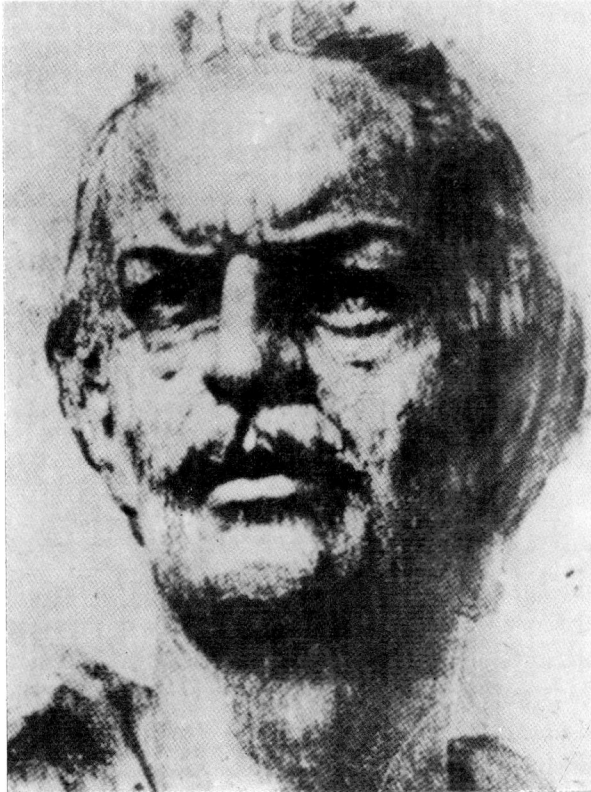

Emmanouil Papas, the leader of the uprising in Chalcidice in May 1821.

by the Apostles of the *Philiki Etaireia* (who were active there a short time) not in Macedonia but in Greek communities in Central and Eastern Europe, during trips to the Danubian Principalities, in Russia and even in Constantinople. The Macedonian members of the *Etaireia* (mostly merchants) then brought back their revolutionary ideas to the motherland.[7] During the summer of 1818, however, the move of the *Philiki Etaireia* headquarters from Odessa to Constantinople brought the revolutionary centre closer to the Greek peninsula, facilitating the expansion of the Society's activities to the entire Ottoman-dominated peninsula. It was then that Ioannis Pharmakis, seventh in the list of the Society's twelve 'Apostles' was dispatched to Macedonia, aiming to recruit the *armatoles* of Macedonia and Epirus. Pharmakis' mission received financial backing from a well-known banker from Constantipople and active member of the *Etaireia*, Panagiotis Sekeris; however, it was not completed as he was required to leave, as early as the beginning of 1819, for Bucharest in order to meet with the other members. However, as historian Ioannis Philimon tells us, during his brief stay in Macedonia he twice visited Serres, where his family had settled, as well as Mount Athos. During his stay, he initiated the dynamic Metropolitan of Serres Chrysanthos, Ignatios, the bishop of Ardameri who had withdrawn at Athos, as well as some monks. Attempts to instruct Gregory V, then exiled to Mount Athos, did not prove successful as the Patriarch was affraid of the consequences on his flock of a possible revelation of his participation in the conspiracy.[8] At any rate, Pharmakis' recruitment of senior Church officials at exactly this time has to be seen as part of a broadening of the horizons of the *Etaireia* and an effort to get close to the leading groups among the enslaved population.

The lack of reliable sources perhaps suggests that following Pharmakis' departure from Macedonia, there was a suspension of recruitment by the *Philiki Etaireia*. More than a year went by before any conspiratorial activity was to be observed. This activity was related to a new organizational initiative which had begun with the election of Alexandros Ypsilantis to the position of General Commissioner (April, 1820). It was in July 1820, therefore, that the member of the *Etaireia* Ioasaph Vyzantios arrived at Thessaloniki from Skopelos following an invitation from the Thessalonians who were "in need of preachers". Ioasaph became a guest of the *Etaireia* member Christodoulos Balanos, between July 1820 and January 1821 toured the churches of Thessaloniki and the Kassandra region preaching the ideals of the society. His activities are documented in reports he filed back to Ioannis Philimon.[9]

At the same time, in mid-December 1820, with Macedonia in a state of unrest as Ottoman armies moved to Epirus against the renegade Ali Pasha, two new apostles of the *Philiki Etaireia* appeared: Doctor Evangelos Mexikos who undertook to organize the Mount Athos monks, and Dimitrios Ipatros from Metsovo.[10] Ipatros, who had already been tried during his successful mission to Egypt (in the spring of 1819), arrived to continue Pharmakis' work in Macedonia. His objectives, as with all other members of the society who dispersed in almost the entire Turkish-occupied Greek regions, revolved around organizing *nuclei* of members in Macedonia and Epirus and co-ordinating their actions in view of the coming movement. His curious and tragic murder following his departure from Naousa and his meeting with Naousean elder Logothetis Zaphirakis, a sworn enemy of Ali Pasha, was justifiably considered by most contemporary sources as the work of men of the latter. Out of the various theories that have been advanced about the murder motives, however, at present the most likely one holds that Zaphirakis, uninitiated to the *Philiki Etaireia*, believed that Ipatros' sole objective was to convince the Epirot leaders to collaborate with Ali Pasha against the Turks. For that reason, he arranged not only to have him removed but also to surrender to the Ottoman authorities the confidential letters carried by Ipatros.[11]

What appears to have shaken the *Etaireia* was not so much the loss of one of its agents, even one with the skills of Ipatros, but the loss of the secret documents he carried with him. This incident was extremely dangerous because it coincided with another misfortune: the arrest, as a result of treachery, of one of the most diligent of the Society's officials, the Thessalian Aristidis Papas. This arrest was followed by his transfer and beheading in Constantinople. Papas was carrying confidential messages to the Serbs and these also fell in the hands of the Ottoman authorities.[12] These successive misfortunes fuelled mounting speculation in Constantinople that everything was known to the Turks and were responsible to a great degree for Ypsilantis' decision to hurry the revolution. So, on 21 February 1821, the Greek prince left his family home in Kisinev of Bessarabia, on the 22nd crossed the Pruth river to Moldavian territory, while on the 24th of the same month arrived at its capital, Iasi, and circulated his stirring proclamation "Fight for

The seal of the **Philiki Etaireia.**

Faith and the Fatherland".[13] Notable among his senior officials was the presence of a Macedonian patriot, the literary figure Georgios Lassanis from Kozani. Lassanis never left Alexandros, even following the failure of the movement in Moldavia-Wallachia and Ypsilantis' imprisonment by the Austrians at Hungary's Muncacs fort (1821-1823) and Bohemia's Theresienstadt (1823-1827); he was perhaps the only one to be at Alexandros Ypsilants' side at the moment of his death (Vienna, 31 January 1828).[14]

From Preparation to Action: The Revolution in Chalcidice

Apart from the negative geographical and military conditions which predetermined the fate of revolutionary activity in Macedonia, the course of events was influenced, as could be expected, by the initiatives of figures who, for various reasons, were required to assume responsible roles. It came to pass, therefore, that even at the beginning of the movement, the responsibility for crucial decisions in Macedonia fell on the not-so-strong shoulders of an ardent patriot, yet inexperienced in military matters, the big merchant from Dovista in Serres, Emmanouil Papas (1772-1821). Papas had fled to Constantinople in the autumn of 1817 to

The fighter Georgios Lassanis, Prince Ypsilantis' aide.

managed, in February or March of 1821, to buy, in Constantinople and with his own money, weapons and supplies to be used in a revolutionary effort in Macedonia. In fact, during this period, he left secretly for Mount Athos, after an order from Alexandros Ypsilantis.[15]

The choice of the Athos peninsula as the first launching pad for Macedonian revolutionaries was, of course, not accidental. In its favour was its natural fortifications, the absence of a Turkish garrison in the monastic community and the favourable climate cultivated by the presence of conscientious patriots amongst the monks. This peninsula could also be used –as was indeed the case– to spread the revolutionary flame to Chalcidice, an area inhabited by dense Greek populations and which included numerous natural coves facilitating access by Greek forces from the sea. Despite this, developments showed that Chalcidice was probably not the most suitable area on which to base a long revolutionary campaign in Macedonia. Its strategic geographical position was neutralized by its proximity to the great military centre in Thessaloniki which also isolated it from the mountain masses of Central-Western Macedonia. However, the basic reason for the unfortunate outcome of the uprising was the delay that took place at its outbreak because of organizational and other factors. The benefits of surprise and of timely co-ordination of anti-Turkish operations with those in the rest of Greece were therefore lost.

Indeed, things did not proceed according to the revolutionaries' optimistic predictions even at Mount Athos itself. Although the number of ready fighting force had been thought to be about 3,000, with the exception of a small nucleus of spirited monks versed in revolutionary ideas or who rushed, even at the last moment, to co-operate with the movement, the majority were unwilling to take the risks involved.[16] Reluctance was to be attributed further to the awkward organization of the uprising and the prospect of cruel reprisals of the occupier. Very quickly, then, as Emmanouil Papas was forced to appeal to the monasteries for financial help to cover even the most basic needs of the revolutionaries, reaction and displeasure mounted against him.[17]

There is no specific evidence regarding Emmanouil Papas' activities from the time of his arrival at Mount Athos to about mid-May 1821 when the revolutionary events took place in Chalcidice. Whatever the situation, the uprising began under the pressure of the wild ter-

escape persecution by the bey of Serres, Yusuf, who had blackmailed him out of substantial sums of money. In Constantinople, Papas sought and even managed to recover a part of Yusuf's debt. This was where he was indoctrinated to the *Philiki Etaireia* in December of 1819. Very little is known about his activities as a member of the *Etaireia* during his stay in the Ottoman capital. However, as it appears from surviving evidence, Papas, who had proved a generous sponsor for the society since his recruitment, had been appointed to a three-member committee, probably early in 1820. This committee registered subscribers to the so-called 'National Bank', i.e. members of the *Etaireia* whose duty was to "meet its debts and shavings". Despite his role as financial manager of the 'National Bank', Papas rorism perpetrated by Yusuf, the Pasha of Thessaloniki. These tactics of terror followed, of course, orders from the sultan. Indeed, through the series of sultanic decrees issued immediately following the outbreak of the uprising in the Danubian Principalities and, subsequently, in the Peloponnese, we are able to follow the series of initially preventive and then cracking down measures adopted by the Ottoman authorities to ensure that there were no further similar movements in other regions of the empire. In Constantinople, in fact, the imprisonment and executions of notable clergymen and Phanariots had already begun as early as March 1821, climaxing with the hanging of the Ecumenical Patriarch Gregory V on 10 April (Easter Sunday).[18] In the beginning of May, the Porte, conviced that "the entire criminal nation of the Greeks is in agreement and united in malice and treachery against the Muslim state..." ordered that it be known to all Muslims that "the coming struggle is one for faith, incomparable to any other".[19]

In this climate of rekindled religious fervour and escalating repression, Macedonia saw the start of pre-emptive arrests of hostages and persons suspected of links with the revolutionaries. In Serres, specifically, where some preparation had taken place following communications between the city's metropolitan Chrysanthos and Emmanouil Papas, no revolutionary moves took place. This was due to the news that arrived from Constantinople relating to the Ottomans' savage punitive measures. Hesitancy soon turned into paralysis when, on 8 May, the Turks arrested the metropolitan and Greek merchants of the city, looted their wares and began searching the area for hidden weapons.[20]

Much harsher steps were taken by Yusuf in Thessaloniki. When revealing letters about the coming movement in his region fell into the hands of the Ottoman official, he pre-emptively imprisoned a great number of hostages from various places at the governor's house (konak). Among these were included about one hundred monks of Athonite metohia. Half of these prisoners were, according to the testimony of Mullah Hayrullah, slaughtered as soon as the news arrived that the inhabitans of Polygyros had taken to arms (17 May), had invaded the konak of the local aga and had killed him and his men. This action virtually provided tha Pasha of Thessaloniki with the excuse he needed to massacre the Thessalonians. Mullah Hayrullah describes the tension and tragedy of those moments simply and synoptically in his 'travel diary'; he considers that the tragedy reached

Prince Alexandros Ypsilantis, a leading figure of the early revolutionary movements.

its climax with the lynching of Makarios, the bishop of Kitros and an aide of the metropolitan of Thessaloniki, with the axing to pieces of Father Giannis, the priest of St Minas, with the hanging of the city's elders and with the slaughter of the women and children who had sought refuge in the cathedral.[21]

In other instances, oral tradition preserved the memory of similar atrocities in many other regions of northern Greece and the coast of Asia Minor.[22] These, however, are not always in a position to be cross-referenced and confirmed and it is not one of the objectives of this work to discuss and resolve the host of problems and questions which derive both from the conflicting information of the sources and from the manner in which

The letter of the Mademochoria notables, informing E. Papas of their insurrection against Ottoman rule.

they were used by researchers of the history of the revolution in Macedonia.[23] Within this framework, therefore, we will attempt to define the conditions in which it developed, the positive factors which fuelled it and the negative which undermined it.

As outlined above, the outbreak of the revolution at Mount Athos and the rest of Chalcidice took place under the pressure of repression of Thessaloniki's Yusuf Pasha. The revolutionary plans, as can be gauged from the participants' correspondence, provided for simultaneous revolts by the inhabitants of Kassandra and surrounding villages and by those at Mount Athos. Their objective was to reach Mademochoria, clearing the area from Turks. From there, the revolutionary forces would proceed against Thessaloniki. A concurrent concern was to secure their cover from the sea, hiring boats which would assume responsibility for guarding the coast and for supplying them with munitions.[24] The plan was at least partially successful. The inhabitants of Kassandra rose towards the end of May, and carried with them the surrounding villages. At the same time, the people of Polygyros successfully repelled the attacks of a relatively small Turkish force from Thessaloniki. The revolutionary forces then united and managed to advance to within three hours of Thessaloniki (6 June 1821). The Mademochoria also rose at this time.

All of these haphazardly organized revolutionary groups, however, virtually acted arbitrarily and without co-ordination. There was also an obvious lack of weaponry and leadership experienced in war. Em-manouil Papas, the target of the calls for help, was in constant contact both with the elders of Hydra and Spetses and with Dimitrios Ypsilantis, from whom he expected weapon supplies to support the revolution in Chalcidice.[25] However, Ypsilantis was not in position to satisfy the Macedonian demands and responded to Papas' calls for help by emphasizing to him on 15 June 1821 the need "for eneryone to contribute what he can so that the boats bringing you food and war supplies not be a burden on the Islands".[26]

Under these circumstances, the revolutionary move-ment in Chalcidice bogged down dangerously. As the rebels were virtually in a state of indecisive inaction, the dynamic intervention of the strong forces of Bayram Pasha took place, aiming to clear all revolutionary pock-ets along their march from Thrace to the Peloponnese. Thus, by the end of June, the rebels were forced to retreat ingloriously towards the Kassandra peninsula while the women and children rushed *en masse* to Mount Athos to avoid being captured.[27] This development, apart from the dangers of reprisals and Ottoman raids, placed a heavy financial burden on the monasteries. It was with displeasure, therefore, that the Athonites were forced to assume the responsibility for housing, caring for and feeding thousands of civilians. Their reluctance to accept the new state of affairs prompted captain Rigas Manesis[28] to note angrily in a letter to Emmanouil Papas on 19 June that the monks, attached to "their views, which they approve and worship only, and care only for themselves and their security", abandoning the people to its fate. He also expressed fears about the consequen-ces of the grave plight of the civilians: "perhaps", he writes, "the people might be driven by hunger and other deprivations to rise against them and we might not be able to hold them back".[29] The Athonites, of course, foresaw such a development; repeatedly, almost daily, they called to Emmanouil Papas –who was in Kassandra with the remnants of the rebel forces– for cereal and other foodstuffs.[30]

Papas himself had to confront other, more immediate problems: effectively organizing his defence against the Turks by arranging a continuous supply of weaponry,

Dimitrios Ypsilantis.

food and rest for his troops. Several calls regarding the latter were sent to the leaders in Olympus asking for co-operation, communication and support; it appears that only Diamantis Nikolaou responded, sending some men and his lieutenants, Liakos and Binos.[31] Disappoint-ment came quickly, however, and it was caused not only by the lack of supplies and the diseases prevalent in the Papas camp, but also by the general inaction. Thus, Diamantis' men left Kassandra and returned to Olym-pus, without even awaiting their leader's approval.[32]

During the period between the summer of 1821 and the final, unequal encounter of the Chalcidice rebels with the forces of the new, powerful governor of Thessaloniki Mehmet Emin (also called Ebu Lubut) on 30 October, the Greek leadership showed interest in co-ordinating the various movements and encouraging others still being hatched. This was especially the case since the revolution appeared to be taking firm hold in the Peloponnese and to develop strong roots in Central Greece. It is in this context that we must view the invitation extended on 25 August 1821 to the Macedonian fighters and the Mount Athos monks by the organizers of the Eastern Central Greece Assembly which called upon them to send delegates to Salona on 14 September. In this invitation it was pointed out to them that "no Greek region, even if you were to slaughter myriads of tyrants, can be saved on its own. Only Greece as a whole can be saved..."[33]

Dimitrios Ypsilantis, on the other hand, was aware of the difficulties facing the Macedonian revolutionaries. Obviously trying to strengthen the somewhat

The fighter and chronicler of the Revolution, Nikolaos Kasomoulis from Siatista.

shaken standing of Emmanouil Papas as leader of the Chalcidice uprising, but not having the capacity to support him materially, he confined himself to appoint him "with a sealed letter" (on 11 September 1821) as "leader plenipotentiary and governor of Mount Athos, Kassandra and Thessaloniki". It seems, however, that Ypsilantis' first priority during this period was to secure supplies for the revolution in the Olympus region and the participation in it of other *kapetanioi* mainly from Western Macedonia.

Within the context of Macedonia's new revolutionary effort, great emphasis was placed on the participation of Naousa. The city was considered "essential because of its abundant guns and swords". To this end, the involvement of Emmanouil Papas was sought after once again. The courier for these orders was the *Philiki Etaireia* member and fighter Nikolaos Kasomoulis, envoy for both the Olympus *kapetanioi* and Papas to Dimitrios Ypsilantis in September 1821.

It concerned, in fact, the opening of a new front in Macedonia. Thus, this new strategic move meant that Chalcidice was once again abandoned undefended. In turn, the Athonite fathers were called upon to themselves contribute to the struggle in Olympus "to occupy Thessaly as soon as possible". Despite this, the leaders of the uprising in Chalcidice could not abandon the struggle and their followers in such an inglorious manner. In 'defiance' of Ypsilantis' orders, Emmanouil Papas did not leave the camp in Kassandra until its few defenders fell to the superior forces of Ebu Lubut.

There were also no prospects of maintaining the effort in Mount Athos. The tendency of the monks towards acceptance of capitulation was obvious and it was expressed in their effort to appease the Turks, releasing on 9 November the Ottoman governor of Mount Athos Haseki Halil Bey, who had been held at Karyes since the beginning of the movement. The first act of the now free administrator was to issue a warrant for the arrest of Emmanouil Papas and his loyal colleague Nikiphoros Iviritis, who had in the meantime sought refuge at the Esphigmenou monastery. It must be noted that Haseki Bey's order was accompanied by a document with similar content signed by the representatives of the remaining 19 major monasteries.[34]

Papas was not arrested, of course, as the leader of the Chalcidice uprising was able to reach a ship owned by Thracian Hatzi Visvizis with his son Giannakis and other lay and clerical colleagues. The ship was destined for Hydra but he was not able to set foot on free Greek soil:

he would die of a heart attack at the same time as the extinction of the revolutionary fire that this ardent patriot had lit with such expectations in Chalcidice.

The epilogue of the drama was completed with the inglorious and total subjugation of Mount Athos. The monks, as mentioned in the chapter on Athos in the present volume, were forced to accept military supervision of their monasteries by special Turkish guards which they were even required to pay and supply. This situation undoubtedly constituted a reversal of the long-standing regime of autonomy, which had survived through various means countless Ottoman efforts to undermine it. It also caused substantial damage (primarily financial) to the monasteries, some of which were deserted and others –the majority– went through a long period of poverty. However, the military presence of the Ottomans in the Mount Athos peninsula was obviously preferable to the threatened imposition of harsher reprisals for the, however grudging, collaboration of the monks with the Greek revolutionaries. Viewed from this perspective, it may be said that the occupation saved the

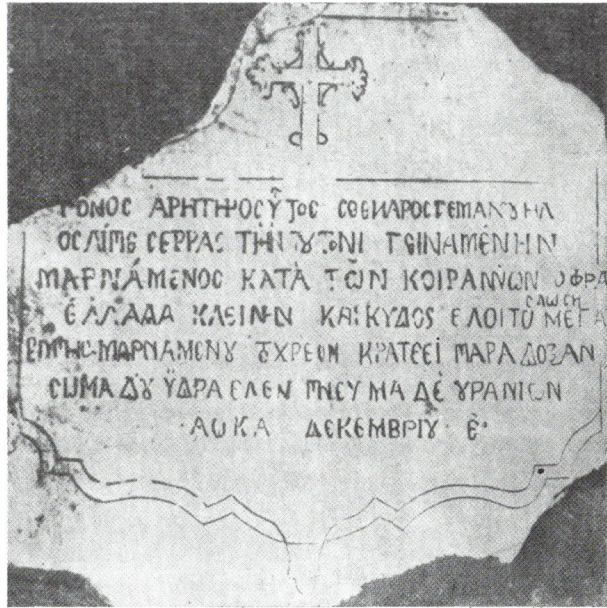

The grave of Emmanouil Papas on the island of Hydra.

Mount Athos was severely affected by the revolutionary events in Chalcidice. The Athonites were forced to accept the stationing of Turkish garrisons at their monasteries until 1830.

monastic region from total devastation.

In the meantime, Ebu Lubut, having totally crushed the revolt in Chalcidice, settled in Ierissos for the winter of 1821, imposing from there tough economic conditions on the entire region.[35] The revolt on Thasos which had taken place almost concurrently met with a similar fate. Unfortunately, there is not sufficient evidence about that revolutionary effort. According to oral tradition, in the summer of 1821, thirteens ships from Psarra, on patrol in the northern Aegean, caused some of the inhabitants to rise led by the island's notable, Hatzi-Giorgis Metaxas. Although they did not create a permanent revolutionary centre, they engaged the island's Muslims in a few skirmishes, compelling the Turkish voyvod to flee to the coast opposite. It was inevitable that the suppression of the Chalcidice uprising saw the Thasians also laying down their arms to Ebu Lubut, who made a triumphant return to Thessaloniki (February 1822).[36]

The Revolution in the Olympus and Vermion Regions

The delayed mobilizations in Western Macedonia and in the Vermion and Olympus regions, from which so much was expected by Emmanouil Papas and Dimitrios Ypsilantis (each for his own reasons), were due to inter-related external and internal factors. Firstly, Ali Pasha's mutiny caused the amassing of strong forces in Western Macedonia which, both in passing and during their stay, left no scope for seditious activity. These military movements, while on the one hand attracting the ire of the populace, on the other hand discouraged any thought of dynamic reaction. It must also be repeated that, apart from these negative factors, no serious organizational preparation by the *Philiki Etaireia* had taken place. Isolated instances of indoctrination of some *klephts - armatoles* and notable figures at Siatista, Kastoria, Kozani, Grevena and certain other Western Macedonian towns did not alter the disappointing picture (even these instances are recorded in fragmented fashion and are derived from mainly unconfirmed oral traditions).

In Central Macedonia, a widespread uprising presented much greater and more serious inherent difficulties. Most of the strategic positions –at Verria, Thessaloniki and in the Aliacmon river region– were well fortified and covered by strong Turkish forces. In addition, the population of some urban centres, as for example, in Verria, was to a great degree Muslim or at least unwilling to participate in dangerous and uncertain revolutionary activities. Moreover, the Sublime Porte did not intend to risk its sovereignty over that region. Repeated orders from Constantinople sought the imposition of harsh preventive measures against Christian subjects (*raya*) in order to stave off troublesome situations in exactly those regions through which the routes of communication of the centre with the Peloponnese and Central Greece passed.

Another serious shortcoming of the revolution concerned the lack of suitable leaders. The only men experience in warfare were the few *armatoles* and *klephts* of Pieria, Vermion and Olympus, and they actively supported the other rebels. Only Naousa could boast of some tradition in fighting from its record of resistance against Ali Pasha's attacks. Naousa also had guns and powder, derived from its flourishing industry. The Greek leadership, however, failed to exploit this element, nor did it formulate a systematic plan of operations. These weaknesses were not only due to a lack of interest, as many have contended, but to the spasmodic fashion in which the revolutionary mechanism operated during the first years of the Struggle. The revolutionaries, rank and file, just were not prepared for a continuous merciless and harsh war; there was no capacity to solve, in a prompt and orderly fashion, problems of supply, civilian transfers, military manoeuvering, training, etc.

The Olympus region, on the other hand, manifested some encouraging signs. The local band leaders –men with a long insurrectionary experience– were in more immediate contact with the Chalcidice revolutionaries, because of geographical and other reasons. This, at least, can be gauged by the admittedly brief collaboration between Emmanouil Papas and captain Diamantis Nikolaou, probably the most sensitive to the cause of the revolution. Despite this, Diamantis himself was not at all optimistic about the attitude of other Olympus leaders in case of an uprising within the areas of 'their jurisdiction'. "These captains", he wrote to Emmanouil Papas on 7 July 1821, "are not as you may think and their conduct is Turkish" or, neutral at best, as can be seen from the remainder of the same letter: "I sent a letter to Goulas and Mantzaris and they did not reply, either with a good or a bad answer".[37]

Despite this hesitancy, Diamantis appeared to have convinced at least some of the captains to follow him. Some months later, on 17 September 1821, in a joint letter to Papas, Diamantis Nikolaou and Goulas Draskou announced that discussions had already taken place regarding an uprising in the Olympus and Vermion regions and that they would presently be acting to secure the necessary military supplies from Ypsilantis before making any moves; to this purpose they sent Kasomoulis to the Peloponnese as "commissioner of those in Eastern/Central Macedonia".[38] Kasomoulis and his companions (among them Diamantis' brother, Kostas Nikolaou) arrived in the Peloponnese during the period in which the rebels were celebrating the fall of Tripolitsa but arguing over the spoils. In this climate of euphoria and of absurd competition, the Macedonian fighters did not find the response they were expecting. Ypsilantis, with his characteristic and unassuming enthusiasm, adopted the idea of an uprising in Olympus but was not then in a position to contribute either adequate economic or serious military help. Thus, after referring the Macedonian envoy to the powerful committees of Hydra and Spetses, he confined himself to appointing his deputy and former officer in the Russian army, Grigorios Salas, as commander-in-chief of the Macedonian revolutionary forces (and, following Papas' death, "General Commissioner of Macedonia").[39]

Despite his disappointing reception in southern Greece, Kasomoulis called upon Emmanouil Papas (on Ypsilantis' orders) to cross to Olympus and, in collaboration with the captains there, to devise strategic plans for the Macedonian uprising, to inform Siatista's Georgios Nioplios and the Metropolitan of Grevena Anthimos and to ensure the participation of Naousa at all costs.[40]

As we have seen, Papas did not, of course, follow these orders, preferring to stand by his companions in Kassandra. Despite this, plans for a revolt in Olympus and Vermion quickly got under way. In the beginning of 1822, the most important leaders of the region, met at Dovra monastery, near Verria. These leaders included Anastasios Karatasos, Angelis Gatsos, Naousa's notable Zaphirakis Logothetis, Panagiotis Naoum from Edessa, Georgios Noplios, Ioannis Papareskas from Kastoria, as well as other spokesmen from the villages of Vermion and the plains of Verria. It was first desiced to bring together Naousa's two warrying factions (those of Zaphirakis and Mamantis). The reconciliation took place in a formal manner, before the icons of Christ with mutual oath-taking and swearing among the former enemies. It was then decided to use Naousa as the centre of the revolutionary campaign with secondary centres at Kastania (on Mt Pieria) and presumably at Siatista.

Verria was ruled out –although identified as one of the first targets– because, as we have seen, it not only had a great number of Turkish-Albanians but was also guarded by strong Turkish forces.[41]

It should also be noted at the outset that the revolutionary effort in Olympus did not begin with favourable portents. Rebels in the region, without any substantial logistical support from the rest of the Greek world, had to depend on their own resources. There was no one in the region sufficiently idealistic and ready for sacrifices (such as Chalcidice had found in Emmanouil Papas) nor were there any special resources available (such as those sought by Chalcidice's rebels in Mount Athos). In addition, the local population had not been prepared adequately for an organized revolt and could not be mobilized when the time came. Thus, there was no pitching

Anastasios Karatasos, **armatole** *of Mt Vermion.*

into battle, as had originally been planned, during the uprising in Chalcidice and Athos, so as to create a diversion to Turkish pressure and to exploit the fragmentation of the Ottoman forces in Macedonia to two concurrent fronts. Nor were any serious military reinforcements dispatched to Olympus from the South: it was only towards the end of February 1822 that two briques from Psarra arrived at the small port of Elephtherochori (today's Nea Agathoupolis) carrying gun-powder, supplies and Kasomoulis, returning from southern Greece.

The arrival of the *Philiki Etaireia* member was quickly made known to the captains of Olympus and Pieria. Impatiently, Diamantis rushed to send a special envoy to inform the *armatoles* of Naousa and Edessa, in fact presenting the arrivals from southern Greece as strong reinforcements. Kasomoulis was more reserved and, fully aware of the difficulties of the task (especially the weaknesses amongst the Greeks in areas such as discipline, weaponry and supplies) was hesitant in sharing the captain's enthusiasm and sought the application of revolutionary plans with due caution. In this context, he made a timely appeal to the elders of Naousa to take precautions: "I wrote", he notes in his memoirs, "to Zaphirakis, Karatasos, Gatsos, to my father and the rest of them: to raise their families, those in that category, and to send them here so that we can put them on ships to transport them to islands where they can all be free. Let us not rouse the people in the cities, let us strike deftly in the straights until Odysseus (Androutsos) and his camp can advance to us; then we can rouse the people to revolt.[42]

On 13 March, spokesmen of Dimitrios Ypsilantis and some German Philhellenes arrived at Elephtherochori. On this occasion, the weaponry which was unloaded was greater in volume and more suitable. Indeed, the rebels managed to utilise them in a haphazardly organized attack against Kolindros, the first objective of Diamantis' attacks. Presently, the new General Commissioner of Macedonia, Grigorios Salas, also arrived in the Greek camp outside Kolindros. Salas, however, did not appear to realise the seriousness of the situation and the unique nature of the operations which he was to lead and guide. As Kasomoulis observed ironically –he knew him from southern Greece and had bitter experience of his lack of organization and his useless exhibitionism– "the commissioner arrived with all the desirable features: with deputies and deputy-deputies, with priests, with whatever one thought of". He was attired in bright

uniform and irritatingly demanded special respect for his office.[43]

In a conference that took place immediately following the congregation of the revolutionary leaders, it was decided to continue the siege of Kolindros –something which unnecessarily tested and occupied without result many revolutionary forces– and to send to Naousa the new envoy, Salas' deputy, Nikolaos Kanousis. Kanousis took with him to the Naouseans letters from the revolutionary government as well as new instructions. Flags were also sent to Kanousis, manufactured outside Kolindros on the basis of designs by Dimitrios Ypsilantis. The text of the revolutionary proclamation carried by Kanousis to the rebels of Vermion was composed by a prominent member of Salas' entourage, the eminent cleric and scholar Theophilos Kairis, composer also of an interesting, if laconic, diary of the operations.[44]

A valuable source of information about the events of the revolution in Olympus, despite the traps of subjectivity they contain, are the memoirs of one of its protagonists, Nikolaos Kasomoulis (1795-1872). The memoirs of the member of the *Philiki Etaireia* from Kozani are also the only one of the National Revolutionary period as well as one of our most important source of information, both regarding the *klepht-armatole* tradition in Macedonia and its short-lived revolutionary movements.

Thanks to this source and to some other uncovered by contemporary historical research, it is possible to follow, almost day by day, the development of military operations in Olympus, from the skirmishes that took place after Kasomoulis' arrival (22 February 1822) to the more serious combat from mid-March onwards at Kolindros, Kokkinoplos and Kastania (of Pieria). We also have information about the heroic resistance on Easter Sunday (2 April) of fighters who locked themselves with women and children inside the tower of the Lazos family at Milia, their tragic exodus and their despondent escape to safer places. There are also references to the destruction of Olympus villages, sometimes by Turks and other times by Diamantis' men. Through the same texts, one can easily discern the lack of communication and the suspicion which often characterized relations between the leaders of the revolution.

Thus, in the very first week of April of 1822, the fate of the revolution in Olympus had already been sealed. Out of the fragmented rebel forces, some took the south road to Greece while most Olympus captains, such as

Diamantis Nikolaou and his deputies, rushed to assist Naousa which had revolted. With a few men, Kasomoulis managed to reach the *armatole* band of Nikolas Stornaris at Aspropotamos after an adventurous journey which is described in every detail in his memoirs. The remaining survivors of Salas' band and some women and children also reached the same camp.[45]

In the meantime, the Turks did not confine themselves to overpowering the Olympus and Pieria rebels; they immediately acted to eliminate the revolutionary flame in the neighbouring regions. They completed their programme of disarming the Greeks, they appointed a metropolitan of the sultan's confidence in Verria and continued to methodically round up and detain the elders of the area. In March 1822, 74 elders of Verria were arrested and led in chains to Thessaloniki. Hostages were taken from Kozani, Siatista, Kleisoura, Blatsi, Kastoria and other small and major towns of Western Macedonia and even Epirus. Only Naousa refused to surrender hostages.[46] In this way it formally accepted the consequences of its stand and the inevitable results of its anti-Turkish activities.

There is no agreement as to the precise date of the outbreak of the revolution in Naousa. Disputes are fuelled by the contradictions in the few sources that we have at our disposal.[47] The most widely accepted view, however, is that, as agreed at Dovra monastery, Zaphirakis proclaimed the revolution on 19 February, a Festival Sunday of Orthodoxy, without waiting for the long-awaited arrival of the General Commissioner of Macedonia, Grigorios Salas. A few days earlier, on 13 February, Mehmet Emin had, as a preventive measure, provocatively replaced the *armatole* in charge of the Verria Pass with the "brave and experienced" Suleyman Kontos to supervise "the defence of this (Pass) against the rebelling Greek infidels".

Organized operations appear to have taken place during the last ten days of February, with the unsuccessful attempt (probably on 21 February) to occupy Verria, the strongest military centre in the region. The morale, however, of the revolutionaries was subsequently boosted when, some days later (12 March), a body headed by Karatasos and reinforced by Gatsos and Zaphirakis, confronted and overcame some 4,000 Turks at the Dovra monastery.

The final confrontation, however, was destined to take place within Naousa itself where there were concentrations of the main revolutionary forces as well as of unarmed civilians, those at least who were unable to seek further and safer places. The city, according to assessments by the Turks themselves, appeared capable of holding out against the attacks as its defenders "built really solid fortifications at the city's boundaries, affording it strong protection" and were not prepared to accede to repeated calls for for surrender by the enemy.

The actual siege of Naousa must have begun on 26-27 March, while from 6 April until its fall (12-13 April) Mehmet Emin himself had assumed direction of the operations. Oral tradition has preserved the information that the besiegers entered the city through treason from an unguarded thoroughfare. Irrespective of the soundness of this information, it was a fact that both within Naousa and at the governor's *konak* in Thessaloniki, where Zaphirakis' political opponents had taken refuge, a defeatist mood and pessimistic predictions were being cultivated, causing much confusion to the besieged.

Zaphirakis, however, put up brave resistance till the end: surrounded for three days in his impregnable tower, he attracted the invaders' attention to himself and provided the opportunity to many of the besieged to escape to the surrounding hills, himself following an heroic exodus. In his subsequent attempts to meet up with other leaders and to continue the struggle, he was surrounded by the mercenary Albanians of Suleyman Kontos and, during the skirmish that followed, he was killed along with his companion Giannakis, son of Karatasos.

Other captains, such as Nasios Kampitis, Giannis Katsaounis and Kostas Malamos, having made their escape to Vermion, continued to harass the Turks until the summer of 1822 when they too were vanquished. Our familiar Olympus captains, Diamantis Nikolaou and Tolios Lazos, as well as Anastasios Karatasos and Angelis Gatsos, having realized the futility of continuing the war in Macedonia, escaped to the rebelling southern Greece.[48]

Fighters who remained in the city, however, were dealt with "without mercy", as dictated by the sacred *fetvah*: on 21 April 1822, while still at Naousa camp, Mehmet Emin Pasha noted, in a review of the successful siege of the city, that the slain enemy casualties totalled above two thousand, that their families had been taken hostage, their property confiscated and their homes razed.[49] This cold, brief paragraph of the Turkish official's report epitomized the entire heroic and desperate resistance of the besieged, the acts of self-sacrifice and the tragic drowning in the waters of Arapitsa of thirteen girls who chose to avoid dishonour in this manner.

The villages surrounding Naousa also felt the brunt of Mehmet Emin's soldiers. Their inhabitants, at least those who had not been able to get away in time, were slaughtered and their homes pillaged. About fifty villages were deserted. It was then, according to a letter which has survived, that many people, mainly young, fled to the hills. However, the tragic epilogue of the history of the revolution in Macedonia was again written in Thessaloniki with the execution of about sixty revolutionaries, the auctioning of spoils and the bartering of prisoners.[50]

When order was restored by these means, efforts were made to restore Naousa and to attract those of its inhabitants who had fled. Measures were even taken to have confiscated land returned to them. It was also with land that had belonged to those who had been slaughtered that the new colonizers of the town, mainly Turks and Bulgarians, obtained their dowry.

Important neighbouring urban centres, such as Kozani, Siatista and Kastoria, managed to avert the danger of an invasion by Mehmet Emin's forces thanks to the mediation of powerful local beys and through payment of substantial sums of money. Nevertheless, they could not avoid completely the consequences of the continuing struggle in southern Greece: the prolonged upheaval which later saw an increase because of the Russo-Turkish war (1822-1829), enabled uncontrollable Albanian brigand bands to ravage the area. Especially damaging was the raid of Albanians Tafil Buzi and Aslan Bey upon Siatista itself (1827-1830). Kozani was occupied for about a month (May 1830) by the same brigand gangs, an event which caused the evacuation of its inhabitants. The same situation also existed in Eastern Macedonia, where Turkish-Albanian mercenaries headed by Saban Geka, together with various brigands, stalked the regions of Kilkis, Stromnitsa, Petritsi and Demir Hisar. Only after the end of the Russo-Turkish war did it become possible to partly control the anarchy in Macedonia, thanks to the engagement of some regular troops for that purpose.[52]

The situation appeared more complex in southwestern Macedonia where certain areas continued to be under the control of Olympus captains. Some of them had returned to their *armatole* camps while others could never relinquish the vision of a rekindling of the revolutionary flame in the area.

The Macedonian Refugees in Southern Greece

Following the failure of the revolutionary movements in Macedonia, a multitude of refugees, the exact number of which is not possible to ascertain, sought safer bases in southern Greece, in both the mainland and the islands. The Northern Sporades especially (Skiathos, Skopelos, Skyros) provided refuge to a great portion of the women and children who arrived from Kassandra and Mount Athos (end of 1821), as well as for other refugees from Thessaly-Magnesia and Psarra. It was there, also, that the Olympus captains and their men with their families escaped after the failure of their movement (April 1822).[53] However, the influx of all these homeless and destitute people upset the already sensitive (because of the war) balance on the islands. The lack of even the fundamental day-to-day means of subsistence as well as the shameless, on many occasions, exploitation by the local populace, caused a build-up of aggressiveness on the part of the Macedonian refugees, in particular, who comprised the most numerous and dynamic element. Indeed, in time, most of the Macedonian men either joined one of the Thessalo-Macedonian groups fighting the Turks or became a real scourge to the region because of their pirate activities. There are references to their raids in the Turkish-occupied regions of Chalcidice (1824), Olympus (1826) and Thasos (1827) and to acts of violence they perpetrated against the inhabitants. In addition, during their operations in their old areas of jurisdiction, these bases also became their refuge when search measures by the Ottoman authorities became tougher.

It was only after the arrival of Ioannis Kapodistrias to Greece (end of 1827) that systematic attempts were made to restore order in the area. Macedonian pirate-captains were compelled to surrender their ships to the government, to settle in a special area established for them at Atalanti under the name of 'Nea Pella' and to join regular military units (1828).[54]

Macedonian Participation in Operations in Southern Greece

Apart from the problems created by the refugee presence in the Northern Sporades, Macedonian fighters constituted a large revolutionary force, ready for war,

Mt Olympus, focal point of the revolutionary movement in Macedonia.

which contributed substantially to the struggle in southern Greece. Macedonian presence in fronts outside Macedonia was, of course, something that was not new. The revolution in Moldavia-Wallachia saw many Macedonians, obviously conscripted from the mainly northern-Greek communtities of the northern Balkans and Central Europe.[55] Isolated cases of Macedonian fighters can also be identified even in other small fronts and skirmishes in Central Greece and the Peloponnese.[56] However, following the collapse of the revolutionary movement in Macedonia, Macedonian refugees made up a first class source of manpower from which almost all fronts in southern Greece were able to draw since June 1822.[57] The Western Macedonian captains Karatasos and Gatsos, who had sought refuge at the Aspropotamos *armatole* camp after the suppression of the revolution at Naousa, went on to place themselves under the orders of Alexandros Mavrokordatos (Mesolongi, May 1822) and participated, together with their men, in the battle of Kompoti in Epirus (10 June 1822), of Peta (beginning of July 1822), collaborated with the Peloponnesians in the organization of the defence against the forces of Dramalis and responded to the call of the inhabitants of Trikkeri in repelling the Turks from southeastern Thes-

saly (May 1823). The inclusion, however, of the two dynamic guerrilla leaders in areas under the responsibility of Mavrokordatos inevitably embroiled them in internal feuds. With their men, they invaded the Peloponnese and fought with the Roumeli forces against the Peloponnesians (end of 1824) but did not follow their comrades in their rushed return to Central Greece which was threatened by strong Turkish forces. They chose to remain in the Peloponnese and to fight alongside Makrygiannis against the Egyptian invader Ibrahim Pasha. Indeed, they distinguished themselves for their bravery and discipline in battles at Schinolaka and Kremmydi (March 1825).[58] In his memoirs, Photakos, one of the fighters, compares the panic-striken retreat of the Greeks following their defeat at Kremmydi with the stand of Karatasos' men and observes: "In this battle, the Mace-donians with Karatasos fought bravely, killed a few Turks, captured a few weapons and saved our honour".[59]

In order to complete the picture of the dispersal of Macedonian fighters throughout the entire rebelling Greek territory, we have isolated two of the most tragic stages of the struggle: the Psarra holocaust (June 1824) where a body of some 1,000 Thessalo-Macedonians

Skopelos: retreat of Macedonian fighter during the Revolution.

deed, among the first to die from within the ranks of the "free besieged" was the gunner of the famous 'Franklin' cannon-station, Kostis Baltas from Serres (11 May 1825).[60]

It is also a fact that the resourse of Macedonian refugees was not exploited as much as it could have been in southern Greece, as was correctly highlighted in a letter to "Our Honourable Government" by the Olympus captain Diamantis Nikolaou on 3 November 1827: "Everyone knows the magnitude of the desire by the Olympian men to follow the orders of their leaders at different times, of Kolettis and others, according to the wishes of the Administration and how the various errors we have witnessed rendered our movements ineffective".[61] These observations by Diamantis were based on his personal experiences; however, they were fairly representative of the manner in which Macedonian captains were treated by the leaders of the revolution: it was to Diamantis that the *Areios Pagos* administration assigned the continuation of operations in rebelling Euboea in September 1822. This choice, however, was dictated not only by the appreciation of the fighting abilities of the Olympus men on the part of the 'sovereign' administrative body of Eastern 'Mainland' Greece but primarily by the desire to control the military forces under their command, directly and absolutely. Thus, an ambitious refugee military man (Diamantis), his lack of local support notwithstanding, was selected to be used as a counterbalance in the administration's dispute with Odysseus Androutsos. Diamantis' appointment was also aimed at eliminating the polyarchy in Euboea following the death of Apostolos Govginas and the recognition of Nikolaos Kriezotis as leader of Karystia by his companions. However, this move condemned to failure the operations at Euboea during the most crucial stage of the struggle.

This was because the rivalry between Kriezotis, who enjoyed the support of other local leaders, and Diamantis eliminated the likelihood of carrying through some temporary Greek successes to ultimate completion (1822-1823).[62] Finally, Diamantis, disappointed by the whole situation, withdrew initially to Skiathos where he was probably involved in pirate activities[63], and then returned to Olympus to arrange the rekindling of the revolution in the area.[64]

It is precisely these efforts by Diamantis that may be placed in a wider framework of an almost universal mobilization of the revolutionary forces following the

took part until the final fall, and the long siege and heroic exodus of Mesolongi (1825-1826). Many Macedonians took part in the organization of the city's defence. In-battle at Navarino (8 October 1827), in Thessaly, Euboea, Crete and Chios in order to ensure the inclusion of these regions within the boundaries of the Greek state about to be created. It is worth noting that many Macedonian captains participated in these operations with their men.

This new revolutionary effort in Olympus and the Pieria, however, was once again left to the local captains, the elders and the clergy of the region. The monastery of St Dionysios at Olympus was used as a meeting place for the conspirations. From there, on 3 November 1827, more than 30 captains, elders and clergy submitted two reports to the revolutionary government of Greece. The reports highlighted the need to mobilize at that time, given that the boundaries of the Greek state were about to be defined; sought the dispatch of war supplies as well as the appointment of a leader of standing to head their revolution such as, according to the reports, Dimitrios Ypsilantis or Bavarian Philhellene Colonel Heideck. In return for the interest to be shown by the government, they promised "to display deeds worthy of our illustrious ancestors and to extend the boundaries of the state with giant steps". As may be seen by the content of the reports, one of the main inspirations behind them must have been Diamantis Nikolaou, who, in fact signed ahead of all the others. The pleas from Olympus, however, –it appears that they continued even after the arrival of Kapodistrias and with greater intensity after the outbreak of the Russo-Turkish war (1828-1829)– elicited no response: the conditions that were prevalent in southern Greece combined with the perceived attitudes of the Great Powers did not favour the opening of a new Greek-Turkish front. For its part, the Sublime Porte acted quickly with systematic mopping-up operations. These operations, one of which destroyed the St Dionysios monastery in October 1828, eliminated the permanent troublesome areas of the Olympus region. In July 1829, when, during the proceedings of the 4th National Assembly, the Thessalo-Macedonians conferred upon Kapodistrias full rights to act on their behalf, they received his final answer that

their future fortunes depended entirely on the attitude of the Great Powers. For this reason he suggested that they should not, in the circumstances, endanger good relations with the Turks.[65]

Following the abandonment of their revolutionary ambitions, many Macedonian captains declared obedience to the Ottoman state in the hope of retrieving their appointments as *armatoles* or being able to return to their homeland. Others, Diamantis Nikolaou and Tolios Lazos among them, preferred to settle permanently in free Greece. Until the end of their life, however, they could not shake off the nostalgia they felt for their native land and the pain for its continuing subjugation. These sentiments are reflected very effectively in the final (?) letter written by perhaps the most conscientious Olympus *armatole*, Nikolaos Diamantis. On 30 December 1855 it was sent from Achladi, a settlement area for many Macedonian refugees, to Senator D. Hatziskos in Athens. The veteran leader wrote:

"Brother,

I write to you in my own hand. My chest condition has progressed to its ultimate and soon I will bid you farewell. Do not think that I am afraid of death; no, I am sixty-four years old. Yet I regret the following: firstly, I do not feel that much sadness for my wife and under age children; I place my hopes in the common father of the Greeks, the Honourable King Otto, and their defence by friends against misfortune. The second saddens me greatly: I will not see this great war to its conclusion. The third grieves me to my heart: I will not see the land of my birth free, the land where so much blood has been shed on my account when carrying the revolution,... I am not in a position to write more.

Your brother

Diamantis N. Olympios"

On 19 January 1856, twenty days after this letter was sent, Diamantis died[66], thereby closing, even in a symbolic sense, the circle of the life and action of the leaders who 'carried' the revolution in Macedonia.

ARTEMIS XANTHOPOULOU - KYRIAKOY
THE REVOLUTION OF 1821
AND MACEDONIA
NOTES

1. The member of the *Philiki Etaireia* and 1821 revolutionary, Nikolaos Kasomoulis from Kozani (1795-1872) left us copious memoirs which were published by Giannis Vlachogiannis under the title *Military Reminiscences of the Revolution of the Greeks 1821-1833*, vol. 1-3, Athens 1939-1942. For an extensive presentation of Kasomoulis' memoirs as well as details about his life, see: Thomas G. Kalodimos, *Nikolaos Kasomoulis (1795-1872)*, Athens 1977. For a brief critical presentation of his work, see: Tasos A. Gritsopoulos, 'Historiography of the Struggle', *Mnimosyni*, 3 (1970-1971), 123-39.

2. Theodoros K. Kolokotronis, *An Account of Events Concerning the Greek Race from 1770 to 1836*, reprint of the original edition; introduction - index - editing by Tasos A. Gritsopoulos, Athens 1981, p. 32 of the text.

3. About the revolutionary upheaval in Greece at the beginning of the 19th c., see Apostolos E. Vacalopoulos, *History of Modern Hellenism*, vol. 4, Thessaloniki 1973, p. 691; about the Serbian revolt specifically, see pp. 699-704.

4. Ioannis Philimon, *Historical Essay on the Greek Revolution*, vol. 1, Athens 1839, p. 374.

5. I. K. Vasdravellis, *The Macedonians during the 1821 Revolution*, 3rd edition, Thessaloniki 1967, p. 75, where the possible place and time of Olympios' initiation.

6. Philimon, *op. cit.*, p. 406, record 436.

7. Philimon, *op. cit.*, pp. 384-416 *passim*. Oral tradition has saved the names of many eminent Thessalonians and other Macedonians recruited into the *Philiki Etaireia* (see A. E. Vacalopoulos, *History of Macedonia 1354-1833*, Thessaloniki 1969, pp. 544-545. Cf. Dimitris Seremetis 'The *Philiki Etaireia* member Konstantinos P. Tattis (1787-1864)', *Makedonika*, 23 (1983), 67-8.

8. Vasdravellis, *op. cit.*, pp. 69-72 with related bibliography; see also: Stephanos I. Papadopoulos, *The Preparation of the Revolution in Macedonia*, Thessaloniki 1968, pp. 15-17; about the activity of the dynamic Bishop Ignatios, see: N.B. Tomadakis, 'Ignatios, Bishop of Ardameri (1769-1839) and his Ecclesiastical Work in Crete (1827-1830) during the Greek Revolution', *Mnimosyni*, 4 (1972-73), 117-142.

9. A. Archontidis, 'An *Philiki Etaireia* Apostle: Ioasaph Vyzantios (1773-1845) and his Pre-revolutionary Activity', *Makedonika*, 13 (1973), 200-202.

10. *Ibid.*, p. 202, and esp. pp. 209-210, for details about Mexikos' pre-revolutionary activity.

11. S. Papadopoulos, 'The *Philiki Etaireia* member Dimitrios Ipatros', *Ellinika*, 14 (1959), 149-165.

12. Vasdravellis, *op. cit.*, pp. 88-89. About the plan of the *Philiki Etaireia* to attract Serbian interst in the upcoming revolt, see: S. Papadopoulos, 'The General Plan of the *Philiki Etaireia* and the Contacts with the Serbs', *Makedonika*, 17 (1977), 40-53, where there are references to sources available.

13. Vacalopoulos, *History of Modern Hellenism*, vol. 5, Thessaloniki 1980, pp. 184-189.

14. K. A. Vacalopoulos, *Three Unpublished Historical Essays by the Philiki Etaireia* member Georgios Lassanis, Thessaloniki 1973, pp. 19-21; cf. S. Papadopoulos, *Georgios Lassanis, the Kozanite Fighter and Scholar (1773-1870)*, Thessaloniki 1977, pp. 6-7.

15. A. E. Vacalopoulos, *Emmanouil Papas, 'Leader and Defender of Macedonia': the History and Family Records*, Thessaloniki 1981, pp. 33-36 and 49-50.

16. Vacalopoulos, *History of Macedonia*, p. 548, with relevant bibliography.

17. I. Mamalakis, 'New Evidence on the Chalcidice Revolution of 1821', *Historical and Ethnological Society Bulletin*, 14 (1960), 490-504.

18. Vacalopoulos, *History of Modern Hellenism*, vol. 5, p. 494.

19. Vasdravellis, *op. cit.*, pp. 246-249, with a translation of the *firman* (decree) of 4 May 1821.

20. *Ibid.*, pp. 122-123; cf. Vacalopoulos *History of Macedonia*, pp. 549-551.

21. Avraam N. Papazoglou, 'Thessaloniki during May 1821', *Makedonika*, 1 (1940), pp. 551-553.

22. Vacalopoulos, *History of Modern Hellenism*, vol. 5, pp. 515.

23. Consider, for example, the questions posed by the Chalcidice Revolution researcher Mamalakis (*op. cit.*, pp. 407-433); most of them have not as yet been answered.

24. Vacalopoulos, *Papas*, pp. 57-58 (letter of 29 May 1821).

25. See related bibliography in Vacalopoulos, *op. cit.*, pp. 545-556, and Vasdravellis, *op. cit.*, pp. 130-132.

26. Vacalopoulos, *op. cit.*, p. 86.

27. Vasdravellis, *op. cit.*, pp. 253-255 for a translation of the *firman* of 2 July 1821, with which the outcome of Bayram Pasha's mopping up operations was announced. Also see pp. 133-135 for a detailed presentation of Bayram Pasha's operations in Thrace and Macedonia.

Cf. Vacalopoulos, *History of Macedonia*, pp. 565-566.

28. That is how he signs his letter of 19 July 1821 to Emmanouil Papas (Vacalopoulos, *Papas*, p. 111). Vasdravellis (*op. cit.*, pp. 139, 143), following the example of erlier researchers, refers to him as Rigas Manthos, while the Athonites in their correspondence refer to him simply as Captain Rigas (Mamalakis, *op. cit.*, pp. 439, 479).

29. Vacalopoulos, *op. cit.*, pp. 106-107.

30. *Ibid.*, pp. 114ff.

31. See the brief but especially interesting letter of July 7, 1821 sent by Diamantis Nikolaou to Emmanouil Papas in: Vacalopoulos *op. cit.*, pp. 98; cf. the same author, *History of Macedonia*, pp. 558; Mamalakis, *op. cit.*, p. 461.

32. Vacalopoulos, *op. cit.*, pp. 157; cf. evidence by Olympus leader Dimos Nikolaou or Psarodimos, that the Olympus men left the camp of Kassandra to assist in the rebellion of the villages in Mt Pelion, in: G. Hionidis, 'Unpublished Documents and Unknown Evidence about *klephts-armatoles* and the revolution in Macedonia (1821-1822) and especially in Olympus', *Makedonika*, 20 (1980), 108-109.

33. Vacalopoulos, *op. cit.*, pp. 133-134; a new invitation was sent on 5 September, *op. cit.*, pp. 141-142.

34. See the interesting documents by Vacalopoulos, *op. cit.*, p. 148; also, Mamalakis, *op. cit.*, pp. 520-523; regarding developments in Mount Athos and the fruitless efforts of Emmanouil Papas' friend and spokesman Nikiphoros Iviritis, see Vacalopoulos, *History of Macedonia*, pp. 570, 572-574; regarding the extensive revolutionary activity of Nikiphoros, former secretary to Gregory V, see: A. G. Geromichalis, 'The Member of the *Philiki Etaireia* record-keeper Nikiphoros Iviritis and his unpublished correspondence', in *Makedonika*, 8 (1968), 1-73, esp. 14-19.

35. Vasdravellis, *op. cit.*, pp. 155-158. Pages 159-163 contain a list of villages of Chalcidice absolved from tax obligations for 1821 because they had no revenue whatever: the land remained uncultivated, houses were burnt and the inhabitabts dispersed.

36. Vacalopoulos, *History of Macedonia*, pp. 556-559, 575. Details about the life and times of Hatzi-Giorgi Metaxas, see: K. Hionis, 'Biographies of Thasos Youth', *Thasiaka*, 3 (1986), 100-104.

37. Vacalopoulos, *Papas*, p. 98.

38. *Ibid.*, pp. 157-159.

39. Kasomoulis, *op. cit.*, pp. 149-159.

40. Vacalopoulos, *op. cit.*, pp. 161-164 (letter of 5 October 1821).

41. N. G. Philippidis, *The Revolution and Destruction of Naousa*, Athens 1881, pp. 39-44.

42. Kasomoulis, *op. cit.*, p. 186.

43. *Ibid.*, pp. 195.

44. I. Vogiatzidis, 'Modern Greek Unpublished Material 1812-1831', *Historical and Ethnological Society Bulletin*, 7 (1910-1918), 7-8, 26-40.

45. Kasomoulis, *op. cit.*, pp. 185-219; G. Hionidis, *The Campaign and Revolution in Olympus during 1821-1822 (with unpublished documents and new evidence about the Lazaioi family and Diamantis Nikolaou of Olympus'*, Thessaloniki 1975.

46. Vacalopoulos, *History of Macedonia, op. cit.*, pp. 585-586.

47. G. Hionidis, 'Events in the Naousa - Verria Region during the 1822 Revolution (Problems regarding dating)', *Makedonika*, 8 (1968), 211-220.

48. Vasdravellis, *op. cit.*, pp. 180-202, for an analytical account of events as they unfolded during the siege and occupation of Naousa. Much of the information desires from local oral tradition and must be checked. Cf. Vacalopoulos, *History of Macedonia*, pp. 591-597.

49. Vasdravellis, *op. cit.*, pp. 275.

50. Vacalopoulos, *op. cit.*, pp. 597-600 for reference to terrorist activities perpetrated by Ebu Lubut in Thessaloniki and his shameless economic repression of financially strong Greeks. The murder of the vice-consul of Denmark Manolis Kyriakou and the theft of his proper-

ty must be placed in this context; *op. cit.*, pp. 600-602; cf. A. Karathanasis, *Thessaloniki in 1822. Information and Reports of the French Consul Bottu: Essays on Macedonia*, Thessaloniki 1990, pp. 188-199.

51. Vasdravellis, *op. cit.*, pp. 202-204; see on pages 282-292 the situation of the Naouseans who were (a) killed or forced to flee leading to confiscation of their property (408 names), (b) those who returned and managed to recover their land (198 names) and (c) those who despite being granted an amnesty decided not to return (33 names).

52. Vacalopoulos, *op. cit.*, pp. 603-606, 617-623; also by the same author, 'The Liquidation of the Albanian Mercenaries of the Porte in Monastir (mid-1830), the Persecution of the Last Macedonian *Klepht-Armatoles* (1830-1834) and the Elimination of Their Institution', *Makedonika*, 19 (1979), 2-5.

53. It is worth presenting some of the data given in the work of G. Hionidis, 'The Macedonian Refugees on Skopelos, 1829', *Makedonika*, 17 (1977), 135-137: out of 545 families of settlers, 230 came from Macedonia. The overwhelming majority was from Chalcidice (over 190) followed by those from Olumpus (about 30).

54. A. Vacalopoulos, *Refugees and the Refugee Question during the Revolution of 1821*, Thessaloniki 1939, *passim*. Similar problems to those of the North Sporades were faced by the neighbouring Cyclades, to where many Cretan refuges had fled (see A. Drakakis, 'Piracy in the Cyclades during the 1821 Revolution', *Mnimosyni*, 5 (1974-75), 324-365).

55. N. Todorov, *The Balkan Dimension of the 1821 Revolution (The Bulgarian case). A List of Fighters in Moldavia-Wallachia (Odessa Records)*, Athens 1982, pp. 193-294, *passim*, for names of Macedonians, mainly Thessalonians, who took part in the revolution in Moldavia-Wallachia.

56. In view, however, of the absence of specialized research on the subject, we will restrict ourselves to gathering information scattered in sources related to the revolution.

57. Valuable data exist in the Records of Fighters, where notes by Macedonian soldiers are kept; see, for example, G. Hionidis, 'Macedonians Registered in the Veteran Records of 1821', *Makedonika*, 12 (1972), 34-64; also by the same author, 'Nine Unpublished Documents by Olympus fighters of 1821 by I. D. Manakopoulos and Mich. Dimitrakopoulos', *Makedonika*, 24 (1984), 197-207.

58. 'The Greek Revolution and the Creation of the Greek State, 1821-1832', *History of the Greek Nation*, vol. 12, *passim*; G. Hionidis, 'Sketch of Old-Karatasos and his Family', *Makedonika*, 9 (1969), 295-315.

59. Photios Chrysanthopoulos or Photakos, *Memoirs of the Greek Revolution*, reprinting of the original edition; introduction - index - editing by Tasos A. Gritsopoulos, vol. 2, Athens 1974, pp. 35-36.

60. Ioannis Iakovos Mayer, *Greek Chronicles. Diary of the 2nd Siege of Mesolongi*, in the series, *Memoirs of 1821 Fighters*, vol. 5, Athens 1956, p. 107 (recording of 11 May 1825). Detailed description of the siege and the heroic exodus of Mesolongi is contained in the memoirs of Nikolaos Kasomoulis, who fought there as a member of Nikolaos Stornaris' unit (*op. cit.*, vol. 2, pp. 88-301).

61. S. Papadopoulos, 'Macedonian Miscellanea: 3. Efforts of Macedonian Leaders to Rekindle the Revolutionary Struggle in Macedonia (1827-1828)', *Makedonika*, 6 (1964-1965), 159.

62. B. Sphyroeras, 'Consolidation of the Revolution, 1822-1823', *History of the Greek Nation*, vol. 12, pp. 260-262, 290.

63. K. A. Vacalopoulos, 'How the European Consuls in Thessaloniki Saw the Situation in Macedonia during the Previous Century', *Makedonika*, 20 (1980), 53-54.

64. Hionidis, *The Campaign and Revolution in Olympus*, p. 79.

65. Papadopoulos, 'Macedonian Miscellanea', 155-169.

66. Hionidis, *op. cit.*, pp. 86-87, note 2.

Liberation Movements in Macedonia, 1830-1870

Ioannis S. Koliopoulos

The revolutionary fervour and activities of the Greeks of Macedonia after the setting up of the independent Greek state in 1830 were a continuation of the liberation movements which had culminated in the outbreak of the War of Independence in 1821; only this time their manifestations were more frequent and more intensive than had previously been the case. The acquisition of a free national focal-point and the triumph of Western ideals and principles in connection with the nation-state and the self-determination of peoples seemed to inaugurate a new phase for the struggles for national liberation: the efforts of the Greeks in enslaved Macedonia were now directed towards unification with the free Greek motherland. The Kingdom of Greece of the period, though small and weak in comparison with the Ottoman Empire, exercised an irresistible appeal and heavy influence on unredeemed Greeks – an influence which became progressively stronger than that of the traditional centre of Orthodoxy and Hellenism, the Ecumenical Patriarchate.

The vigorous appearance of the new national centre on stage after 1830 decisively influenced the course of the liberation movements of the Greeks, both in the case of those still enslaved and of those of –liberated– southern Greece. The existence of the Greek state meant that activity in the cause of liberation had to take on new forms and contributed to a revision of the traditional ones. Gradually, the consulates of the Greek kingdom in Macedonia developed from agencies for the protection of the commercial interests of Greek subjects into dynamic centres of activity for the advancement of the national interests in those parts of the country still under the Ottoman yoke. Particularly after the pressing of Bulgarian claims on Macedonia, the Greek consulates became nerve centres for the guidance of the struggle for liberation.

Other important factors in determining the form taken by the liberation movement were the Church –the local bishoprics– especially towards the end of the period, the communities, the cultural associations, the patriotic societies and the armed bands that took part in the ever-intensifying revolutionary uprisings.

The bishoprics in Macedonia under Turkish rule gave expression to the traditional policy of the Orthodox Church, the objective of which was to manage affairs by placating the arbitrary secular power of the non-Christian ruler, so that, in the words of Veniamin, metropolitan of Servia and Kozani at the time of the 1821 Revolution, "none of our blessed Christians should suffer any evil, either to his [well-]being or to his honour and reputation".[1] However, the local prelates continued to be under pressure from the more restless elements in their flocks, who were agitating for action. The prelates, held responsible for the law-abiding behaviour of those in their charge and accountable to the Turkish authorities, but also as the undisputed leaders of the nation, were faced with a dilemma: should they openly favour the revolutionary movements of the enslaved Greeks and so compromise both themselves and their flocks, exposing them to the ire of the tyrant, or should they condemn and undermine such movements, thus calling down upon themselves the condemnation of those who constantly favoured such action? Unlike the laity who rose up against Turkish domination, the prelates were not in a position to play such a role, not so much because they were afraid of martyrdom, as much as because they had a duty to protect their flocks from the rage of the authorities in the event of the uprising ending in failure. The leaders, whether political or military, of such revolutions, could take flight if their enterprise failed, seeking refuge either in free Greece or in the mountains: the spiritual leaders had to stay where they were to "pick up the pieces" and protect their exposed charges.

Towards the end of this period, particularly after Bulgarian designs had become manifest, many prelates collaborated with the leaders of the revolutionary movements. The claims and activities of the Bulgarian Exarchate in Macedonia questioned and undermined the authority of the bishops in their dioceses and that of the Ecumenical Patriarchate in the Orthodox world. Thus the Bulgarian factor acted as a catalyst in the policies of the Church in Macedonia and contributed to its convergence with the representatives of the Greek state in this matter. The degree of deviation from the Church's traditional policy and of inclination towards that of the Kingdom of Greece was in direct proportion to the degree of awareness on the part of the Orthodox prelates of the leading role which the small Greek kingdom was destined to play in national affairs.

The Greek communities in Macedonia were called upon to play a similar role –and were thus forced to deal with the same dilemmas. Like the bishops, the community leaders were obliged to compromise. The authority which they exercised, although achieved by economic and social status among their own –fellow-Orthodox– people, was nevertheless conceded and revokable, at the discretion of the state representatives. The exercise of such authority in periods when the enslaved population was behaving provocatively towards the foreign overlord often proved an intolerable burden and required unusual abilities. Unlike the nation's military leaders, the *kapetanioi* of the *klephts* who operated in the mountain regions, the community leaders were as vulnerable in the face of the central authorities as the prelates; yet they lagged behind neither the *kapetanioi* nor the bishops in the difficult task of liberating the enslaved population. This required courage and self-sacrifice, as well as caution and prudence. Community leaders played their part in the uprisings too, usually in charge of the necessary local revolutionary authority, or in close contact with the Greek consulates and the agents of the patriotic societies –sometimes even as leaders of armed bands.

The cultural associations, which began to make their appearance mostly in the second half of the 19th century, played an important role in shaping and disseminating the new national ideology which stemmed from the free Greek national centre. Thus, they helped cultivate a climate which favoured the questioning of the legality of 'alien' rule and identification with the manifestos of the revolutionaries. Moreover, these associations rallied around themselves the most vigorous and progressive elements of the population, who were in the forefront of all the activities aimed at promoting the cultural development and political emancipation of the Greeks. Thus, these cultural associations, which were an adornment of the life of the Greek cities of Macedonia, were rallying-points for the cause of freedom and greatly contributed to the long and arduous progression of the enslaved Greeks to the desired goal.

A more direct part in preparing for and carrying out the revolutionary uprisings in Macedonia was played by the various patriotic societies which had been formed both in free Greece and in the as yet unredeemed Greek

The entrance of the Greek Consulate-General in Thessaloniki.

provinces of the Empire. It was usually soldiers, often refugees from those parts, but also politicians, university teachers and journalists, for example, who from time to time formed secret societies with the aim of liberating their enslaved compatriots. These secret societies, which had links with the representatives of the Greek government, acted in the stead of the official authorities, in an effort to circumvent the expressed opposition of the Great Powers of Europe, particularly Britain and France, to the fomenting of uprisings within the Sultan's domains and any disturbance of the territorial *status quo* in the Near East. From the time of the first irredentist societies set up immediately after the foundation of the independent Greek state, chiefly among refugee *klephts* and *armatoles* from Macedonia and the other unredeemed regions, down to that of the all-powerful societies which directed the revolutionary movements of 1878 and the operations of the bands of freedom-fighters in 1896-97, the part played by the state, though behind the scenes, constantly increased. This neat way of direct-

The interior of a hani (inn) in Macedonia (second half of the 19th century).

ing the aims and activities of the societies without compromising the official state was safeguarded by the participation of responsible individuals who were aware of the objectives of Greek policy, the attitudes of the Great Powers and the prospects of success of such revolutionary operations.

The fact that Athens was unable to undertake openly the liberation of the enslaved Greeks because of the opposition of the two Western states which were the country's protecting powers helped increase the importance and the role of a further factor in the progress of the nation's struggle for liberation: armed bands. For as long the state was precluded from using the regular army for fulfilling its irredentist programme, the role and importance of irregulars of every description who were called upon to man the revolutionary bands formed either in free Greece or in the unredeemed lands was progressively reinforced. Refugee *klephts* and *armatoles* from Macedonia and northern Greece in general, local *klephts* who were active in the mountain ranges of Macedonia, soldiers, gendarmes, mountain rangers and brigands from Greece hastened to join the armed bands

which were formed under the supervision of the patriotic societies and their agents in the enslaved regions. A basic feature of these armed bands was that their membership was drawn from all Greek lands, free and unredeemed. Local men naturally predominated among volunteers; nevertheless, these bands were veritable microcosms of the Greek nation. Macedonians, Epirots, Thracians, Thessalians, Roumeliots, Peloponnesians, islanders, men from Asia Minor, Cretans and Cypriots took part in the uprisings as leaders or members of irregular bands, with many sacrificing their lives. They were attracted by the spoils of war and by adventure, but also by the glory of the fight for the faith and the freedom of their fatherland. All these men constituted the unofficial army of the nation, which had been entrusted with the task of liberating the Greeks still under the Turkish yoke –a task which was shared by the whole of the Greek world. These bands of freedom-fighters did not, of course, succeed in liberating the enslaved regions, but by their presence they strengthened the morale and aspirations of the Greeks of the Ottoman Empire and the demands of the Greek government in the international level, and thus contributed to preventing Macedonia from being awarded to other claimants with strong protectors. Thus the material damage which normally resulted from the activities of the irregulars in the areas in revolt was not without a positive effect for the outcome of the liberation struggles.

Refugee *Klephts* and *Armatoles* in Free Greece

The settlement of the Greek question after the end of hostilities and the intervention of the Great Powers of Europe left many of Greece's national problems unresolved. Among these was that of the Greeks of Macedonia and of other areas who had fought in southern Greece after the collapse of the uprising in their own localities. The Greek *klephts* and *armatoles* of Macedonia who had fought in the Peloponnese, Roumeli, Euboea, and the Aegean islands remained in what was now free Greece, but never gave up the hope that they would return to their homes, still under the Turkish yoke, in order to liberate them. From Hasia, Olympus and Vermion, the best part of the northern Greek *klephts* and *armatoles* was found in various military camps in Central Greece or the Sporades Islands. Old Man Karatasos and his son Tsamis, Diamantis Nikolaou and his brothers Kostas and Harisis, Georgakis Koutoulas, Karatasos's second-in-command, Michalis Pitsavas, Dimos Tzachilas, Poulios Blachavas and his brother Athanasios, and Liolios Xiroleivaditis were among those who, after many fruitless attempts to open a front in Macedonia and after many wanderings –since they had lost all their landed property– were by 1830 destitute, homeless and vagrant. Many who had returned and patrolled their ancestral fiefs were the victims of a sudden assault by strong Turkish forces in December of 1830. In this many of the *kapetanioi* of Aspropotamos, Tzoumerka, Hasia and Olympus met their death, though the majority found safety in southern Greece.

Through the mediation of Ioannis Kapodistrias and of the Russian Consul in Thessaloniki, Angelos Moustoxydis, the families of many *kapetanioi* from Macedonia emigrated in late 1830 and early 1831. About two hundred wives and children of famous *kapetanioi* of the period took refuge in the Sporades, northern Euboea and Phthiotis, where they met up with their soldier husbands and fathers, who had already fled there or had been there since the beginning of the Struggle. In spring 1831, large numbers of *kapetanioi* settled with their families on Skopelos, but later moved, by government decision, to Atalanti, where they created their own settlement, known as 'Nea Pella'. Gradually others joined them. The government, in recognition of their services to the cause

of the liberation of Greece, granted the settlers building sites and farm land, in order to facilitate their rehabilitation. The Macedonians' settlement soon became a community in its own right, and later still, a municipality.[2]

The thinning-out of the traditional military aristocracy of Macedonia during the course of the Struggle and the departure of many *klephts* and *armatoles* to free Greece proved to be developments without serious effects on the ability of this military caste to reproduce itself. The gaps were quickly filled by the descendants of the slaughtered or expatriate *kapetanioi* The conditions which had produced the pre-revolutionary aristocracy of *klephts* and *armatoles* produced its new representatives, who continued the region's fighting tradition.

Greek expatriates from Macedonia who fled to Greece during the Revolution or immediately afterwards constituted the nucleus of a constantly increasing social element in 19th century Greece: the Macedonian 'refugees'. The uprisings which took place from time to time and the consequent reprisals and repressive measures of the Turks in Macedonia created new waves of refugees and fresh strata of immigrants in free Greece, at Nea Pella, in the Sporades and in northern Euboea, as well as in Lamia and Athens.

The areas where the refugees from Macedonia settled were, throughout the 19th century and down to the time of the liberation of Macedonia, the places *par excellence* for recruitment of volunteers to man the revolutionary bands which went over to the enslaved territories on the occasion of the various uprisings in order to support the struggle of the local people. It was also in these areas that the patriotic societies recruited members –even from the time of the *etaireies* formed during the last phase of the Struggle and in the time of the Kapodistrias down to the last quarter of the 19th century, when their tendrils embraced every aspect of public life in Greece.[3]

The Macedonian settlers in Greece, especially those who distinguished themselves in the army, in politics and in letters, formed a powerful pressure group and made an important contribution to the shaping not only of the country's irredentist policy but also of its national ideology. They were the links which bound together enslaved Macedonia and the national centre and, at the same time, the most sensitive audience for the appeals addressed by its inhabitants to the free homeland. They, perhaps more than anyone else, ensured by their activities –pressure, appeals, the collection of money and signatures, the recruitment of volunteers, the setting up of secret societies– that the struggles of the Greeks of Macedonia for liberation and union with Greece should be, from every aspect, a Panhellenic cause –particularly at a time when the official Greek state had not yet shaped or projected a clear position with regard to the northern boundaries of its national ambitions. Themselves the product of the special conditions which prevailed in their own localities, while taking full part in the national process building at a Panhellenic level too, the *heterochthones* (i.e. not native of the liberated part of Greece) from Macedonia, like those from the other unredeemed parts, greatly contributed to the clarification of the identity and the course of the nation.

Early Episodes in the Struggle for Liberation

Among the first efforts to promote the cause of liberation, after the putting down of the Revolution in Macedonia in 1822, were certain understandings on action between the Macedonian *kapetanioi* who were fighting in southern Greece and Makrygiannis, who maintained friendly relations with many of the Macedonian *leaders*, including Karatasos, Gatsos and Ilarion Karatzoglou, "a brave lad", as Makrygiannis himself describes him, from Kavala. Under Kapo-distrias, as Makrygiannis records: "He wanted to go as a *klepht*; I advised him to go into his own country so that he could have men under his leadership, and we would see: when the right time came, the Greeks, all of us, would undertake secretly to liberate the other parts of Turkey which were under the tyranny of the Sultan, and carry out the oath of the Society [i.e. the *Philiki Etaireia*]... We agreed on a password *phouseki* [i.e. cartridge] when he sent someone to me, so that I would know he was from him; my password was to be *doupheki* [i.e. rifle]. 'Larion went to Mount Athos and worked hard and went as a *kapetanios* to Mademochoria, and was a long time there. As we ourselves had taken the oath, he began to initiate the men there with great secrecy, and made great progress. I swore in Vasilis Athanasiou; he was leader of the cavalry in Crete and came to Argos and I was best man at his wedding; he was a Macedonian too".[4]

In 1834, Makrygiannis was again in touch with Ilarion. "He sent a monk to me", he notes, "and he told me that he had a large force there, but that he needed a force from here and concord and good command for [an expedition], so that we wouldn't have these men to answer for. I told him to instruct men there prudently and I would follow the same course. People came here, I took them into my house, we talked of the wretched state of the motherland and I prepared them to leave for action. And I instructed the whole state for when it was time for us to make a move". Among those initiated, according

to Makrygiannis, was Tsamis Karatasos, who visited Thessaloniki at that time in order to assess the situation.[5]

In Thessaloniki, Karatasos met with the Greek Consul, Theodoros Vallianos, the Consulate having just recently been set up. The tense situation in the region, caused by the activities of local pirates, aroused the suspicions of the Ottoman authorities as to Karatasos' visit. Despite the efforts of the Greek Consul to allay the fears of the authorities, the Turks had incontrovertible evidence of the role played by Karatasos: letters under his seal which had been found in the possession of local *klephts*, presumably containing instructions for the liberation enterprise which was being planned.[6]

The activities of Makrygiannis and Tsamis Karatasos were perhaps linked with a secret liberation society which had been set up in Phthiotis by *heterochthones*, principally from Macedonia and Thessaly, who were active at that period (1835) in the area. The centre of this society was Lamia, where at the same period rebellious movements were being fomented –which actually broke out at the beginning of 1836 in Phthiotis and the whole of Central Greece. Among those mentioned as being members of the society (or societies) were Karatasos, Tzachilas, Pitsavas and Theodoros Ziakas. The co-ordinator of the activities of at least one circle of *kapetanioi* from outside the Greek state was Christophoros Perraivos, himself a Macedonian.[7]

The disturbances which broke out in Central Greece in 1836 overshadowed the activities and movements of the Macedonians and their supporters. A large number of Macedonian *armatoles* served in the various bands of irregulars in the area, either with the revolutionaries or with the government forces, their basic motive being their desire to be incorporated into the country's army or gendarmerie. However, a much larger number remained active in Thessaly and Pieria and created grave problems for the Ottoman authorities, who saw in their activities the prelude to a revolution. Hundreds of Macedonian fighters, in small or larger groups, with differing short-term aims and their own *kapetanioi* as a rule, were active in the whole of Greece north of the Gulf of Corinth. Included in the lists of the various leaders of armed bands of the time are the names of the Macedonian fighters who were involved in the vortex of events, many of them cut off from their ancestral fiefs of Hasia, Olympus and Vermion. We are given their place of origin: Olympus, Chalcidice, Grevena, etc.[8]

The reverberations from these upheavals had hardly died down when the fighting men of Macedonia, both in free Greece and in Thessaly and Macedonia itself, found themselves again involved in the turmoil of irregular

Makrygiannis, a major figure of the Greek War of Iderpendence, whose memoirs provide rich information about his many Macedonian connections during and after the Revolution.

band activities –in this case an uprising in northern Central Greece and in Thessaly, under the leadership of the Thessalian Ioannis Velentzas, in the autumn of 1840 and the spring of 1841. Both Karatasos and Makrygiannis were privy to these moves. The latter tells us: "Then some of us agreed together to lay down our money, our efforts so that, hopefully, there should be an uprising in Thessaly and Macedonia. We made a host of preparations and came to an understanding with those outside; and we made new initiates everywhere. And we got people together: they sold their securities, whatever they had. We sent them to [Atalanti, Lamia, Xerochori and elsewhere, to be ready to issue forth one day. And the affair went forward secretly and was carried out in the fear of God and we spent an enormous amount of money. We also had Tzamis Karatasios [sic] in the secret".[9]

The various complexities and aspects of the part played by the Macedonian *kapetanioi* in the Velentzas insurrection are not known to us. A lack of co-ordination in the activities of various circles and societies resulted in the outbreak of uprisings which seemed to their contemporaries to be contradictory, and sometimes traitorous. It would seem that Karatasos was involved in more than one such move and, at the same time, was in close contact with government circles. Also involved was Ilarion in Chalcidice, but it was his last appearance on the stage of the liberation movement, since he was

Theodoros Vallianos, the first Greek Consul-General in Macedonia.

arrested by the Turks and imprisoned in Constantinople. Makrygiannis's 'Larion' was killed a little later in circumstances which remain obscure.[10]

The movements of Velentzas and of the other *kapetanioi* from outside the Greek state took place during the major crisis of the Eastern Question (1839-1841), which shook the Near East. Simultaneously with the uprisings of these *kapetanioi* in Central Greece, a revolution broke out in Crete, and among those who hastened to fight for the island's liberation were a large number of Macedonian settlers from southern Greece, following a fruitless attempt on the part of Karatasos and a band of volunteers to foment an uprising on Mount Athos. In the absence of any real preparation and co-ordination of the activities of the various circles in free Greece and Macedonia, the monastic community showed understandable reluctance. They had not forgotten the tribulations caused by the revolution in Chalcidice some twenty years earlier and the wounds had still not healed.[11]

The part played by Macedonian fighting men in the uprisings which broke out at that time in Central Greece and in Crete was the culmination of sporadic action in land and pirate raids on a considerable scale in 1835-36. The area of activity of the amphibious Macedonian rebels against the established order of law was that bounded by Mount Athos, the Sporades, northern Euboea, Mt Pelion, Pieria and Olympus. This was where during the 18th century in particular a peculiar form of brigandage, a kind of 'pirate-brigandage', had developed. The mountainous parts of the region and the uninhabited islets of the Sporades and Chalcidice served as the bases of these pirate-brigands. They used light, very fast craft, the sight of which struck terror into the crews of the merchant ships which plied in the northern Aegean. The pirate-brigandage of the region kept a considerable body of men on a war footing. Brigands from Olympus, Hasia, Ossa and Pelion and pirates active in the Sporades in peacetime, the outlaws of the region, were transformed into 'brigand freedom-fighters' and took part in uprisings such as that of Velentzas or more serious ones such as that of 1854, which will be described below.

Kapetan Karamitsos, *Kapetan* Pitsavas, *Kapetan* Harisis, *Kapetan* Biziotis, *Kapetan* Tsaras, *Kapetan* Koutouvas were the names of some of the pirate-brigands most frequently mentioned during that period. These were the offspring of famous families of *klephts* and *armatoles*, whose relatives (and in some cases, they themselves) had settled (or were attempting to settle) in

Vlach shepherds of Central Greece.

free Greece. They were the subject of strong *démarches* on the part of the Western European consuls in Thessaloniki to the Ottoman authorities –and to the Greek Consul, whom they had reason to believe as being aware of the movements of all these *kapetanioi* and their raids on Western European merchant vessels.[12]

Easier to trace are the links between the 'brigand-*kapitani*' or '*Turkokapitani*', as they are called in official documents of the period, and the Albanian *derven-aga*, those responsible, that is, for the guarding of the mountain passes and for the maintenance of order in the mountain regions in general. The former were in every sense the descendants of the old *klepht-armatoles* and continued to play the same role. When they were not robbing or blackmailing weak and strong alike, they were leading bands of *armatoles* in the forces of the *derven-aga*. Frequently rebels against law and order and equally frequently organs of that same law and order, the *kapetanioi* of the region with their men represented at one and the same time outlawry and legality, or, more correctly, the obscure line which lay between the two in the sultan's territories. They continued the time-honoured tactics of provocation with a view to striking deals, of intensifying illegal acts in order to legitimate the unlawful and to share in the spoils of office. The difference now was that this alternation of roles was interrupted by a new factor: participation in revolutionary movements aimed at toppling the regime which allowed and favoured relations of this kind between the representatives of authority and the outlaws. Participation in revolutionary uprisings with such aims lay outside the limits of traditional provocation, and the return of the revolutionaries to service as *armatoles* was very difficult, if not impossible. It was for this reason that the uprisings produced refugees –former *klepht-armatoles* who headed for free Greece, where the plans for many of these uprisings in Macedonia and other unredeemed territories ripened.

The 1821 Revolution had served as a catalyst throughout the Greek lands, both in those parts which had been liberated and in those which looked forward to their liberation. The Greek state which resulted from this struggle constantly infiltrated in a variety of manners into the enslaved Greek world (and the remote parts of free Greece itself) through the cracks caused by the struggle itself, as well as by the impact of the Enlightenment and the French Revolution. The revolutions in Macedonia and in other parts still under Turkish rule were manifestations of this infiltration. The fact that the protagonists had now been made refugees created the conditions for further penetration, which in turn

strengthened the bonds between the free and the enslaved Greeks.

The infiltration of the Greek state into Macedonia was helped at that period, and much more so later, by the Consulate of Greece in Thessaloniki, which was set up in 1835. The activity of the first Greek Consul in Thessaloniki, Theodoros Vallianos, in support of the national interests of the Greeks was invested with the prestige of the official representative of an independent country. He rapidly became the principal agent of national penetration into the traditional world of the enslaved country. It was to him that community representatives, teachers and leaders of armed bands turned for instructions and advice. The role of the Greek General Consulate in Thessaloniki was strengthened by the consulates which were subsequently set up in Monastir, Kavala and Serres, as well as by the consulates at Larissa and Volos, until the annexation of Thessaly in 1881, and subsequently that at Elassona.

The next appearance of the Macedonian freedom-fighters on the national stage, before the revolution of 1854, was in the disturbances of 1847-48 in Central Greece. In September 1847 we hear of a national guard unit in the area, commanded by Konstantinos Binos, a lieutenant-colonel of the *Phalanx* and a Macedonian refugee. This was the 'Corps of Macedonians' and it consisted of 23 officers of the *Phalanx* and 36 men. Most of the members of this corps came from Nea Pella. In October of the same year, the Corps of Macedonians was in Chalkis, "billetted in the homes of the citizens", as the Prefect of Euboea wrote. The men had not yet been paid for their services –they had been recruited in order to impose order in Euboea after the rebellion of Nikolaos Kriezotis– and had pawned their weapons in order to make ends meet. Macedonians also served in the units of the national guard recruited in order to impose order in the various provinces of Central Greece. At the same period we hear of a *kapetanioi* who was ready to mount a campaign at Grevena in order to claim back his ancestral fief in the region; his name was Theodoros Ziakas, and he was destined to play an important role later. We do not, however, know the outcome of these intentions.[13]

The Uprisings of 1854

The outbreak of the Crimean War (1853-56) gave fresh opportunities to the restless *kapetanios* from Grevena, and to many other renowned band leaders from Macedonia residing in free Greece. Since May 1853, on the occasion of the fourth centenary of the Fall of Constantinople, the daily and periodical Press in Greece, and particularly in Athens, had been preparing public opinion for the struggle for liberation which was to be undertaken the following year. The Greeks of the period found themselves in a maelstrom of national and religious fervour whose origins went back to the previous decade, to the multi-faceted ideological and political quest to formulate the content of national ideology. Belief in the Greeks' role as an 'elect' people with a mission to bring enlightenment to the East was widespread –a belief which was inextricably bound up with faith in the rights of the Greek Orthodox. The War of Independence was fresh in the memory of the generation still at the helm of the nation, and the national crusade of 1854 was projected as a continuation of that struggle. In the course of a series of articles entitled 'The Second Greek War' (the first had been in 1821), Neophytos Vamvas wrote on 3 February 1854 in the pro-Russian and pro-Orthodox newspaper *Aion*: "Bless, Lord, this betrothal, this small Kingdom of Greece, and crown him whom Thou hast ordained bridegroom with the diadem of the Greek empire. Amen".[14]

"The movement of our brothers without", one of the nation's apologists wrote a year after the revolutionary events, "was a continuation of the uprising of the nation in 1821, which had as its aim the restoration in the East of a strong civilized Christian state". The West should then say: "Behold, the peoples in Turkey have risen up and are seeking the formation of a Christian state; no cause for war exists for all of us any more; let us convene in a European conference, let us decide to place this Christian state under the protection of the Great Powers of Europe in order to safeguard it, and let us allow it to develop and reach there where the all-wise God has fore-ordained it". 'Liberty', 'the cross', 'union of the race', 'the Greek empire' were terms with a special charge at that period and as concepts moved the overwhelming majority of the nation –before they were whittled away for various reasons of expediency and by the slow but sure departure of the ruling circles from traditional popular beliefs. Similar ideas were expressed in the manifestos of the revolutionaries in the enslaved regions.[15]

The movements for the liberation of Macedonia in 1854 had, nevertheless, very little chance of success. The omens were unfavourable, largely because of extraneous factors. Macedonia was nearer to the centres of military power of the Ottoman Empire than the other unredeemed Greek territories. Turkey's Western allies, moreover, were in a position to use their fleets to neutralize Greek attempts to create the necessary bridgeheads on the

shores of Macedonia. The geographical distance of the region from free Greece and the presence in between of a region which had priority in the demand for liberation (Thessaly - Epirus) were additional negative factors. It is worth noting that many Macedonian expatriates took part in the movements in Thessaly and Epirus, reckoning that the struggle for the liberation of the enslaved regions of mainland Greece was one and the same and, as such, would follow a northerly direction.

Among the first to make a move were the Western Macedonians living in Phthiotis, led by Theodoros Ziakas. After a first fruitless effort in October 1853 to cross from Phthiotis into Thessaly, heading for Western Macedonia, Ziakas finally succeeded in crossing the frontier in February and in reaching, through Agrapha, the Grevena district. Ziakas's force increased considerably in size by the addition to his corps of expatriates of many local volunteers. A memo in a ledger from Libohovo (Vlachopanagia) states: "In 1854, in the month of May, there was a great uprising. The leader Ziakas came with 300 men from the Greek [territory]. From our own village the revolutionaries were the following: Nikolaos Kokolis, Kostas I. Katzou, Stergios K. Noulas, Georgis Noulas, Nikolaos Komporelas, the two brothers Dimitris and Vasileios Tzouphaios, Christos Tzouvalis, Kostas (father-in-law of Lampros) Kostavel and Kostas Z. Kostavel (the bandit). They came to Demenitza, a village in the province of Grevena and fought a great battle with the Albanians and *Kekides*. Of the revolutionaries, five were killed and 15 wounded. Of those from our village, Nikolaos Kokolis was wounded; they took him to the monastery nearby. It is called Zimnatzi. And Nikolaos Komporelas guarded the wounded. Then they came to Spilaion and fought for a month and then left. The women and children fled from the Vlach villages, and after a year these families returned. The leader of the Turks was Avdi Pasha".[16]

The note does not mention the outcome of the battle between the revolutionaries and the Albanian irregulars. The former put up a strong defence in the mountain village of Spilaio, where a large number of women and children from the surrounding villages had taken refuge. But they were finally obliged to withdraw, through the mediation of the British Consul at Monastir and his French colleague at Jannina. The revolutionaries and many non-combatants fled to Lamia, where they settled temporarily.

Also short-lived was the uprising on Olympus, which many Macedonian fighters from free Greece who had already taken part in the uprisings in Thessaly-Magnesia hastened to join. Many local *kapetanioi* and their men

The Karakalou Monastery, with Mount Athos in the background.

also joined the ranks of the rebels from southern Greece. As had been the case at Grevena, however, they met with strong Turkish forces and were obliged to withdraw.

More serious was the challenge to the sultan's authority in Chalcidice, where a corps of rebels under Karatasos landed at the beginning of April. Coming from northern Euboea via the Sporades, Karatasos and his men landed in Sithonia. There, the freedom-fighters, most of them Macedonians from free Greece, were joined by local men, rallying under the banner of the famous *kapetanios*, who was proclaimed 'Commander-in-Chief of Macedonia'. Karatasos also received reinforcements from Poligiros. The monks of Mount Athos, however, were slower to respond to the summons of the rebels to send reinforcements themselves. The monastic community hesitated to compromise itself with the Turkish authorities, surely since they knew better than the rebels the intentions and capabilities of both the Turks and their Western allies in putting down the revolutionary movement. Nor had they forgotten the tribulations suffered by their monastic community during the Struggle of 1821. Thus their reply to the rebels' invitation was in the negative.

In the meantime, the Turks had received reinforce-

ments in Chalcidice. At the end of April, strong forces of the army and of irregulars forced the Greek revolutionaries to abandon the villages which they had taken. Karatasos and many of his men fled secretly to Mount Athos, where they found shelter and supplies. The increasing pressure of the revolutionaries for the active involvement of the monks called forth appeals from the latter that Turkish sovereignty over Mount Athos should not be abrogated, thus provoking an invasion by Turkish forces, which the revolutionaries were not in a position to deal with. When, finally, Karatasos raised the flag of revolution, the Holy Synaxis sent to the commander of the Turkish forces a written declaration of allegiance, in order to avoid an invasion by the Turkish army.

In May, following clashes between Turkish forces and Karatasos's men on the borders of the Holy Community, the latter faced the danger of a Turkish invasion, with all the consequences which that entailed. The situation was saved as the revolutionaries were recalled by the new government which had been formed in Athens under pressure from Britain and France. A French steamship took Karatasos and his corps, more than 400 men, to Phthiotis and northern Euboea. The recall of the revolutionaries prevented a Turkish invasion of Mount Athos and its certain ruin.[17]

Thus ended the venture of 1854, without, of course, the national aspirations coming any nearer to fulfilment, but also without irreparable damage to the national interests in the unredeemed regions. What had been attempted was the liberation of the enslaved Greeks, not only contrary to the wishes of the country's protecting powers in the West, but in cooperation indirectly with the third of the protecting powers, Russia, with whom the first two were at the time in a state of war. Moreover, this liberation had been attempted at a time when Russia was unable to assist the Greek uprisings in the unredeemed regions and at a time when Britain and France were able to cause –as they did cause– serious problems for the movement of the volunteer corps at sea. In addition, this attempt at liberation was undertaken at a time when the Turks still had forces in the Balkans far stronger than those which the rebels could field, concentrated in effective fronts. In other words, the national liberation efforts in 1854 were premature and beyond the existing capabilities of the Greeks. This venture did, however, contribute to the tacit acceptance of the advice of the more level-headed elements in public life that the liberation of the enslaved populations should proceed by stages and should keep pace with the gradual decline and weakening of the Ottoman Empire.

The enterprise of 1854 also had this result: it promoted the nation's claims on the international level and proved useful in many ways in the furthering of those claims at a critical point in the Eastern Question at which, on the one hand, the traditional tendency for the Greeks to look to Russia for their liberation was on the decline and, on the other, the Russians were turning exclusively towards the Slavs and abandoning their old slogan which promised the liberation of all the Orthodox.[18]

The "Desperate Revolt" of Leonidas Voulgaris (1866)

The last 'pro-Orthodox' uprising was that led by Leonidas Voulgaris in spring 1866. It is worthy of attention since it reflected precisely the survival of the traditional national beliefs and also because it caused serious concern to the Turkish authorities when it was learnt that this romantic figure of a *kapetanios* was in Macedonia, obviously because of the sensation which he aroused in that region. "The news from our city", wrote the correspondent of an Athenian newspaper from Thessaloniki in 1866, "is still of the revolution which has

already been manifest in our region. Wherever you are, wherever you go, you hear no talk but of Leonidas Voulgaris and his men".[19]

Voulgaris and a band of 27 landed in April 1866 in Chalcidice, where he was joined by a local chieftain, *Kapetan* Georgakis from the Mademochoria, and his men. They were soon pursued by strong Turkish forces which captured Voulgaris and some of his companions, though Georgakis and the rest avoided arrest. While action was still being taken against them in Chalcidice, *Kapetan* Georgakis sent a message from Ormylia to the Greek Consul in Thessaloniki and sought "a helping hand and instructions as to what he should do, where he should head and where he should take refuge until the right time should come".[20]

The Greek Consul in Thessaloniki, like the other consuls of his country in the European territories of the sultan, had already received urgent instructions from the Greek Minister of Foreign Affairs, Spyridon Valaoritis, to assure the Turkish authorities that the Greek government "not only condemns with indignation such senseless and rash acts, but does everything and will do everything which lies within its power to check them...". According to Valaoritis, "this uprising has no source of any significance, but is the result of the levity and fever of certain brains without importance in Greece".[21]

Such was the official position of Greece. Nevertheless, such "rash" acts still, it seems, found a response among the masses, in the Greece of the prophecies of Agathangelos. It would appear that involved in the Voulgaris revolt was a certain Russian, by the name of Lazariev, who seems to have been responsible for the wording of a proclamation brought by Voulgaris to Macedonia with the title *The Future of the Byzantine Empire*. This pro-Orthodox outburst concludes: "Christians! How long shall this disgrace triumph over the virtue of the Christians? How long shall the sons of Ismael oppress and tyrannize the pious Orthodox Christians of the East, beloved in the Lord? Christians! Remember always that according to the prediction of the divinely-inspired prophet Agathangelos, the work of Divine Providence will be brought to pass in a miraculous manner and at a time when no one anticipates [it]".[22]

The representatives of the Greek state, however, and those who were in a position to follow developments in connection with irredentist matters, and particularly Macedonia, made a different assessment of the situation. A threat had already begun to appear on the Macedonian horizon, a threat which could not be seen by those who remained incurably attached to the ancient visions of the nation. The cases of Slavophones in Macedonia who were reported to be seeking from the local bishops and from the Ecumenical Patriarchate that services should be conducted in Bulgarian and that separate Bulgarian schools should function in the region were becoming increasingly numerous. Behind these incidents, the representatives of the Greek state were able to discern Bulgarian emissaries who roamed Macedonia, cultivating such attitudes and trends. The recruitment of the Slav-speakers to the Exarchate was the immediate aim to be promoted by separate Bulgarian churches and schools: the ultimate aim was, through the cultivation of the Bulgarian national identity, the creation of a Bulgarian national state. In the face of the danger of the ethnological composition of the population of Macedonia being transformed by the cultivation of Bul-

garian national consciousness among the Slavophones, the liberation of Macedonia took on special importance, certainly greater than it had had before when no such threat was visible. Now, however, liberation had to be undertaken at a time propitious for Greek claims in Macedonia. Appropriate international circumstances were essential for the promotion of Greek aims, particularly the balance between the great European powers and the attitude of the Porte, which would have to be deemed favourable to Greece's positions. Liberation movements would have to be an extension of the delicate manipulations of diplomacy, otherwise they would be detrimental and dangerous. Uncontrolled uprisings, such as that of Voulgaris, no longer had a place in the irredentist policy of Greece.

●

IOANNIS S. KOLIOPOULOS
LIBERATION MOVEMENTS IN
MACEDONIA, 1830-1870
NOTES

1. V.G.Sampanopoulos, *The Church and Liberation Movements in Kozani* (in Greek), Thessaloniki 1973, p. 36.
2. See the relevant documents in the Historical Archives of the Ministry of Foreign Affairs (henceforth AYE), 1831/45/1 and 1831/4/1 of the period January-June 1831. On the development of the settlement, see Grigorios Velkos, 'Unpublished Documents from the Archives of the Macedonians' Settlement at Nea Pella, (Atalanti) (in Greek), *Makedonika*, 19 (1979), 195-238. The settlement was completely destroyed by a severe earthquake which struck the area on the Saturday before Holy Week in 1894.
3. John S. Koliopoulos, *Brigands with a Cause: Brigandage and Irredentism in Modern Greece, 1821-1912*, Oxford 1987, p. 4.
4. Makrygiannis, *Memoirs* (in Greek), edited by I. Vlachogiannis, Athens 1907, vol. 2, pp. 108-109.
5. *Ibid.*, pp. 111-112.

6. Communication of the British Consul, dated 17 November 1835; see K. Vakalopoulos, 'The Trade of Thessaloniki, 1796-1840' (in Greek), *Makedonika*, 16 (1976), 130.
7. Dinos Konomos, 'Thessalian freedom-fighters of the National Uprising and Their Plans for the Liberation of Unredeemed Greece' (in Greek), *Thessalika Chronika*, 10 (1971), 53-58. In February 1836, Karatasos was at the head of 50 armed freedom-fighters, obviously Macedonians and Thessalians, in Phthiotis. See the newspaper *Athina*, 5 February 1836.
8. Ioannis Koliopoulos, 'Brigands and Brigand-rebels in Central Greece in 1835-1836' (in Greek), *Mnimon*, 7 (1979), 118-34.
9. Makrygiannis, *op. cit.*, vol. 2, p. 116.
10. *Ibid.*, p. 117.
11. *Ibid.*, pp. 117-118.
12. K. Vakalopoulos, *op. cit.*, 130-45.
13. Ioannis Koliopoulos, *Brigands of Central Greece in the Mid-19th century* (in Greek), Athens 1979, pp. 63ff.
14. *Ibid.*, pp. 48-52.
15. *Ibid.*, p. 80.
16. *Ibid.*, pp. 80-81.
17. A.E. Vacalopoulos, 'New Historical Evidence on the Revolutions of 1821 and 1854 in Macedonia' (in Greek), *Academic Yearbook of the Faculty of Arts of the Aristotle University of Thessaloniki*, 7 (1956), 72-3.
18. See reports from Thessaloniki, in the journals *Aion*, 1, 22, 26, 29 May and 2 June 1854 and *Athena*), 26 April 1854. See also A. Vacalopoulos, *op. cit.*, 74ff.
19. M.T. Laskaris,, *The Eastern Question, 1800-1923* (in Greek), Thessaloniki 1948, p. 127.
20. *Avgi*, 13 May 1866.
21. AYE, Embassy in Constantinople, consular authorities (1866), the Consul in Thessaloniki to the Minister of Foreign Affairs (copy), Thessaloniki, 15 May 1866.
22. *Loc. cit.*, the Minister of Foreign Affairs to consulates in Epirus, Thessaly, Macedonia and Albania, 16 April 1866, and the Minister of Foreign Affairs to the Greek Ambassador in Constantinople, 18 April 1866.
23. *Loc. cit.*, the Minister of Foreign Affairs to the Greek Ambassador in Constantinople, 18 April 1866, with proclamation annexed.

Macedonia at the Epicentre of Rival Balkan Nationalisms (1870-1897)

Ioannis S. Koliopoulos

The Establishment of the Bulgarian Exarchate

The projection of Macedonia as the focus of competing Balkan nationalisms and the concurrent involvement of the Great European Powers in the settlement of the Macedonian Question, as this important aspect of the Eastern Question became known at the time, are connected with the Bulgarian national 'awakening' and the crucial role played in that development by the Russian Panslavists. Until after the Crimean War, the Slavophile rivals of the pro-Western faction in Russia had shown little interest in the Slavs of the Balkans and the Habsburg Lands. In fact, Nicholas I and his associates hardly concealed their displeasure with expressions of solidarity for the Slavs of those areas which were bound to create problems for the multinational Habsburg Empire. Following the Crimean War, pro-Slav feeling and activity manifested themselves in new fields. In 1858, a 'Slav Philanthropic Committee' of eminent Slavophiles was founded in Moscow, which by 1867 had organized the 'Moscow Slav Ethnographic Exhibition' – an event hailed as the first manifestation of official Russian interest in the fate of the Slav peoples. The Moscow committee and other similar organizations which were later founded in St Petersburg, Odessa and Kiev constituted the champions of 'Panslavist' propaganda which found expression mainly after the subsequent crisis of the Eastern Question (1875-1878).[1]

Led by such figures as Ivan Axakov, Nikolai Danilevski and Konstantin Pobiedonoscev, the Russian Panslavists abandoned the theories of the old Slavophiles regarding the messianic mission of Russia and concentrated their interest in the Orthodox Slavs. Towards that direction, the subjugated Bulgars in particular, they tried to draw the attention of the Russian public and to attract the active interest of the Russian government. Such pressures and the consequent interest displayed by St Petersburg acted as a catalyst in the Balkans during the 1860s and, even more so, the following decade. This resulted in the national awakening of the Bulgarians which, in that period, found expression in the movement for the establishment of a separate Bulgarian Church.

Initially, the Bulgarian national awakening took the form of a cultural and religious reaction against the Greeks and the Ecumenical Patriarchate. It should be noted that an important contribution to this development was made by Greek education provided by Greek schools which had been established in parts of Bulgaria since the second decade of the 19th century. That the Bulgarians, as it was the case with the other Balkan peoples, received Greek education is not surprising: most new schools of note, not only in mainland Greece but also in every part of the Ottoman Empire where Greek populations lived and in the rest of Europe where Greek communities had established themselves, were Greek. Pioneers of the Bulgarian national awakening, such as Ilariy Stojanović, later bishop of the Bulgarian Church, Ivan Dobrovski, publisher of a Bulgarian journal in Vienna in 1850, Stojan Tsomakov, a physician at Philippopolis, Peter Berov, the author of the first Bulgarian primer, Georgi Rakovski *et al.*, had all attended Greek schools.[2]

The combination of education and national diffentiation produced, on the one hand, the tendency to use exclusively the Bulgarian language in schools and churches, and, on the other, frequent complaints and accusations against the Ecumenical Patriarchate and the Greek prelates in the predominantly Bulgarian provinces of the Empire. The charges of arbitrariness and abuse of authority against prelates were not always unfounded; similar accusations emanated not only from Bulgars but also from Greeks. They certainly reveal discontent against oppressive prelates, but they also came as an

Late 19th century Thessaloniki; a view from the sea.

expression of the spirit of self-assertion and disobedience towards the Ecumenical Patriarchate and its representatives, which was fanned by nationalism. Faithful to its ecumenical *status*, the Patriarchate of Constantinople attempted to maintain some balance between its supranational mission and the pressing demands of the awakening peoples for more ecclesiastical autonomy – first of the Greeks and later of the Bulgarians. Yet it was an effort which failed to satisfy either side, for the Patriarchate perceived in it a threat to its prerogatives and the Bulgarians considered it inadequate.

The *Hatt-i-Humayun* reforms of 1856 favoured the Bulgarian demand for a separate Church. During an assembly of prelates and lay representatives of the dioceses convened by the Patriarchate in Constantinople in 1858, the four Bulgarian delegates demanded the establishment of a Bulgarian hierarchy and the entry of Bulgarian prelates into the Holy Synod. These demands were rejected at the time. Subsequently, a claim for the reconstitution of the autocephalous Archbishopric of Achris or of the Patriarchate of Tirnovo as separate from the Ecumenical Patriarchate was put forward.

The Bulgarians of Ochrida stopped recognizing the Patriarch of Constaninople and their example was followed by other Bulgarian dioceses. In response, the Patriarchate deposed the provocative bishops. Although the Porte lent its support to the Patriarchate in that occasion (1860), the official rift between the Bulgarians and the Ecumenical Patriarchate seemed only a matter of time.

The appointment in 1864 of the Panslavist Count Ignatiev as ambassador of Russia in Constantinople rekindled the conflict. In 1866 the Bulgarians submitted to the Porte and the Patriarchate fresh proposals for solving the problem of the Bulgarian Church. They asked for an equal number of Bulgarian bishops to that of the Greeks sitting at the Holy Synod. They further asked that the hierarchs in dioceses of mixed population should belong to the prevailing national group. In short, the Bulgarians claimed 30 out of the 49 European dioceses of the Patriarchate, many of which had a predominantly Greek or Serbian population. Among the contested dioceses were those of Tirnovo, Philippopolis, Kyustendil, Samokov, Sofia, Vidin, Rustchuk, Varna, Dibra, Velessa, Moglena, Kastoria, Niš, Polyani, Raskoprisreni, Adrianople, Pelagonia, Prespa, Stromnitsa, Vodena, and Anchialos – many of which eventually came under the jurisdiction of the Exarchate established in 1870.

The following year (1867), Patriarch Gregory VI suggested to the Porte that the Bulgarian dioceses form a separate *thema* of the Ecumenical Patriarchate under a high-ranking Metropolitan as 'Exarch' and a local synod which would elect metropolitans and bishops. It was a conciliatory gesture on the part of the Patriarchate which gained Ignatiev's support to the extent that it virtually constituted, as the Patriarch said to the Russian ambassador, "a bridge to the political independence of the Bulgarians".[3] The Patriarch's proposal, however acceptable to the moderate Bulgarian patriots, failed to satisfy the hardliners since it did not guarantee complete independence; what was more, the proposed Bulgarian *thema* excluded some two-thirds of the dioceses claimed by the Bulgarians, particularly the mixed dioceses of Philippopolis, Pelagonia, Achris and Skopje.

The position of the intransingent Bulgarian patriots

Patriarch Gregory VI. During his tenure of office the Bulgarian Exarchate was set up (1870).

was favoured by the policy of the Porte, which chose to stand by and watch the Greek-Bulgarian dispute escalate and thus forestall a possible accommodation. It should be noted here that such a compromise was favoured by both the Patriarchate and the Russian government. The revolution in Crete, which had broken out in 1866 and still dragged on, contributed to the policy of the Porte which aimed at prolonging the conflict between Greeks and Bulgarians. This policy was reinforced after the break-up of diplomatic relations between Greece and Turkey as a result of the Cretan revolution. At this point, the Porte suggested that the Patriarchate consider the establishment of an independent Bulgarian Church, the Exarchate, under an Exarch seated at Constantinople. The Turkish proposal envisaged a Bulgarian Church encompassing not only the Bulgarian provinces lying between the Danube and Balkan mountain range but also Macedonia and Thrace, yet it failed to be specific about the number of the Bulgarian dioceses and the boundaries of the mixed ones, so as to perpetuate the Greek-Bulgarian conflict.

At this stage, in December 1868, the Patriarchate contemplated the convening of an Ecumenical Synod to consider the issue of the Bulgarian claims but ran against the opposition of both Russia and Turkey. This attitude encouraged the hard core of intransingent Bulgarians in Constantinople to call upon the Bulgarian prelates to set up their own synod at the imperial capital. Deposed Bulgarian hierarchs and others who hastened to resign their positions, such as Dorotei, Metropolitan of Sofia, Ilariy of Loftzou and the metropolitan of Vidin, pledged allegiance to the Bulgarian Church.

This provocative act of the Bulgarian prelates paved the way for the schism which became official a few years later. The Ottoman intervention in the Greek-Bulgarian dispute was officially manifested by an imperial decree (*firman*) issued on 27 February / 11 March 1870 without the knowledge of the Ecumenical Patriarchate, whereby the Bulgarian Exarchate was established. The decree provided for a permanent Bulgarian holy synod presided by the Exarch and seated at Tirnovo, but limited the dioceses of the Bulgarian Church to thirteen. However, it was possible for other dioceses to adhere to the Exarchate, provided that at least two-thirds of their Orthodox flock so wished. Regarding relations with the Patriarchate, the Exarchate was practically independent, since the Patriarch was merely requested to ratify the election of the Exarch.

This was a piece of arbitrary and unlawful legislation

which forced Gregory VI to resign his throne but not before denouncing the Ottoman gonernment of unlawfulness and the Bulgarians of acting in collusion with the Porte; he also reaffirmed the need for convening an ecumenical synod in order to solve the question of the Bulgarian Church – without, again, being able to secure Russian consent. By way of contrast, the Bulgarians, with permission of the Ottoman government, proceeded to convene an assembly of clerics and lay representatives in Constantinople which elaborated and ratified the constitution of the Exarchate before it dissolved itself in July 1871.

The new Ecumenical Patriarch Anthimos VI resumed his predecessor's efforts to negotiate with the Bulgarians. His attempt, however, foundered on the persistent Bulgarian claims to the mixed dioceses of Skopje, Dibra, Ochrida, Melenikon, Pelagonia, Moglena, Stromnitsa, Kastoria, Polyani, Drama, Vodena and Adrianople – as was indeed provided by the 1870 decree. The Bulgarian intransingence on the question of the jurisdiction of the Exarchate and the provocative presence of deposed prelates at the Epiphany liturgy of 1872 compelled the Patriarch to suspend all contacts and to protest to the Porte against its tolerating the humiliation of the Patriarchate.

All interested parties, the Patriarchate, the Bulgarian prelates and the Porte, each for its own reasons, considered that there existed no room for conciliation and concessions. Bulgarian provocations led the Patriarch to depose more prelates and to excommunicate the leading advocate of the separatist movement, the already deposed Ilariy. The Porte, for its part, authorized the implementation of the 1870 decree and the election of an Exarch. After the resignation of the first Exarch-elect, Ilariy of Loftzou, Antim of Vidin was elected and officially appointed by imperial warrant (*berat*) in April 1872.

In order to protect the prestige and dignity of the Patriarchate, the Ecumenical Patriarch proceeded then with the deposition and excommunication of the Bulgarian Exarch and hierarchy. He also convened a Grand Synod, which was attended by former Ecumenical Patriarchs Gregory VI and Joachim II, Patriarchs Sophronios of Alexandria and Ierotheos of Antiocheia, the Archbishop of Cyprus Sophronios and 25 prelates of the Ecumenical Patriarchate. The resolution of the Synod, which was read in the final session of 16 September 1872, castigated national feuds, 'racialism' in the affairs of the Church, and denounced those who had instigated such feuds, i.e. the Bulgarian clerics and laymen, as 'schismatic' and alien to the Orthodox Faith.

The Schism of 1872 (which was abrogated as late as February 1945) caused a deep breach in the bosom of Orthodoxy. The deterioration in the relations between the Bulgarian hierarchy and the Ecumenical Patriarchate had a grave impact on relations between Greeks and Bulgars, particularly in Macedonia and Thrace. Although, perhaps, an inevitable development, the establishment of an independent Bulgarian Church was weighted down with the ensuing controversy, which largely came about as a result of Bulgarian intransigence, the equivocal attitude of Russia and the opportunistic policy of the Porte.

The Eastern Crisis of 1875-1878

The establishment of the Bulgarian Exarchate and the Schism were the first steps of the Bulgarians towards statehood which was achieved by the end of the great Eastern Crisis that shook the Balkans during the second half of the 1870s. A local uprising in Herzegovina against the chronic Ottoman maladministration and oppressive taxation sparked off the crisis. To the pressures of the ambassadors of the Powers urging the immediate intoduction of reforms as an antidote to the uprising, the Porte reacted in its customary fashion: in October 1875 it announced a programme of sweeping reforms, as it always did in the face of co-ordinated Great Power pressure. Yet, as it turned out, the application of these reforms was neither as timely nor as extensive as the least pessimistic observers and the representatives of the Powers had wished. The announcement of the reforms failed to stem the revolutionary tide; far from that, Serbs and Montenegrins soon joined the uprising in Herzegovina.[4]

The situation in Herzegovina was a source of concern for Austria-Hungary in particular, because it had errupted near the South Slav provinces of the multinational Habsburg Empire. For this and military reasons, too, the High Command in Vienna favoured the annexation of Bosnia and Herzegovina. The Magyar foreign minister of the Empire, Count Julius Andrassy, although he was essentially opposed to annexation which would add to the numbers of the Slav subjects of the Dual Monarchy, also regarded with apprehension the prospect of Bosnia and Herzegovina being incorporated into Serbia and Montenegro, or even the granting of autonomy to these two provinces as presaging their incorporation. In order to avert such a prospect, Andrassy, in agreement with the rest of the Powers, addressed a *démarche* to the Porte demanding the immediate implementation of the reforms. The sultan once more hastened to comply with the suggestions of the Great Powers, issuing a new decree introducing the already promulgated measures.[5]

Before long an uprising broke out in Bulgaria instigated by Bulgarians residing in Romania. The Turks promptly dispatched army troops and irregulars to the rebellious provinces of Tirnovo and Rhodope. The atrocities which followed the suppression of the revolt, particularly the incidents at Batak of Rhodope in May 1876 (dubbed by the European press as the "Bulgarian massacres"), gave rise to a wave of indignation among the European public and strong protestations on the part of eminent liberals.

European opinion was roused by another event in the region, which was not directly connected with the revolutionary events in Herzegovina and Bulgaria: the slaying of the consuls of France and Germany at Thessaloniki on 6 May 1876 by the frenzied Turkish mob of the city. The killing was provoked after a young Slav-speaking woman from Bogdantsa, who had expressed the wish to be converted to Islam, was kidnapped by Greeks and hidden at the railway station of Thessaloniki. The kidnapping caused violent demonstrations of agitated Muslim crowds demanding that the young woman be handed over to them. In their effort to mediate in order to avert bloody clashes and casualties, the consuls of France and Germany fell victims to the rage of the mob.[6]

The continuing crisis in the Balkans led Russia, Austria-Hungary and Germany to agree on a fresh *démarche* to the Porte in May 1876. In this, the three Powers, while repeating Andrassy's suggestions, asked for a truce in Bosnia and Herzegovina in order to forestall the spreading of the hostilities and the intervention of the Great Powers. France and Italy supported the *démarche* but Britain failed to do so; British Prime Minister Benjamin Disraeli, who followed a pro-Turkish policy, interpreted the action of the three Powers as another Russian attempt to penetrate into the Ottoman Empire.

Eventually, the *démarche* was not delivered, because in the meantime a coup d'état broke out in Constantinople on 30 May 1876 leading to the replacement of sultan Abdul Aziz by his brother Murad V. It was a movement primarily directed against the pressures of the

Great Powers, Austria and Russia in particular. The new Ottoman leadership requested explanations from the ruler of Serbia for his country's armaments and the sending of volunteers to the provinces in revolt. Milan Obrenović for his part demanded the withdrawal of the Turkish troops from the frontier between Bosnia and Serbia and the entry of the Serbian army into the region. The acute tension between the two countries led Serbia, joined by Montenegro, to declare war on Turkey on 18/30 June.

The outbreak of the Serbian-Turkish war found Greece in a difficult position. Its treaty of alliance with Serbia (1867) had expired – that, at least, was the view of the Greek government when the Serbs invoked it. Following the last Cretan Revolution, the Greek government had sought to normalize relations with Turkey. This objective was considered more urgent during the ensuing period of the Ecclesiastical Question, when it became clear who would be the main rival of Hellenism thereafter. Moreover, the Greek government was anxious to secure the support of Germany and Austria-Hungary, on one hand, and of France and Britain, on the other, so as not to find itself isolated in case that the Great Powers were to decide the fate of the sultan's European territories. Conversely, Greek inactivity in the event of a Russian intervention in the crisis seemed detrimental to the national interests in the region. Finally, the Greek government tried to promote some sort of a compromise between the Patriarchate and the Exarchate. The aim was for the Bulgarians to recognize the limits of the Exarchate's jurisdiction as the future political boundaries of Bulgaria in return for the repealing of the Schism. The Patriarch, however, refused to take part in deliberations of a political nature; nor were the Bulgarians, in any case, prepared to limit their claims to the European provinces of Turkey.[7]

Greece was obliged to adopt a policy of neutrality *vis-à-vis* the armed struggle of the Slav peoples against Turkey. The unredeemed Greeks of European Turkey ought to remain calm and to avoid insurrectionary activities. The Greek government tried to persuade the Porte that it would be in its interest to support the Patriarchate and restrain the Exarchate, but without success given the reluctance of the Ottoman government to take any action which might provoke Russia. At the same time the Greek government engaged in an effort to bring back to the Patriarchal fold the Slav-speaking population of Macedonia and Thrace who had sided with the Exarchate – partly on account of the persecution to which the Greeks of these regions had been subjected under the pretext of the Cretan Revolution (1866-1869). In this field the Greek policy scored remarkable successes, as many mixed villages of the dioceses of Pelagonia, Stromnitsa and Serres returned to the Patriarchate. According to contemporary Greek consular reports, in the diocese of Kastoria only three villages did not abandon the Exarchate (the rest 150 villages remained loyal to the Patriarchate); in the diocese of Florina only seven villages had adhered to the Exarchate and remained loyal to it; in the diocese of Pelagonia of the 60 (out of the total 150) villages which had joined the Exarchate, only six returned to the fold. The situation was quite differnt in the northern parts of Macedonia, where the Exarchate appeared well entrenched, particularly in the countryside. Even there, however, the inhabitants did not appear inclined to follow the example of the Bulgarian provinces. In the southern dioceses of Macedonia, Kozani, Anaselitsa and Servia, the Exarchate's influence was non-existent.[8]

These data referred to the conditions prevailing in Macedonia at a time when the Shar and Rila mountains were projected as its northern boundaries. The Christian population of Greater Macedonia, which comprised two-thirds of the total, was roughly distributed in three zones, one Slav-speaking, one mixed and one Greek-speaking. This distribution of population will be examined more thoroughly later. Suffice to note here that the population of southern Macedonia and the littoral was almost wholy Greek-speaking with only a few Slav-speaking 'islets'. To the north of an imaginary line stretching from Drama to Kastoria there was a mixed zone of Greek-, Slav- and Vlach-speaking population. To the north of this zone, apart from a few Greek-speaking pockets, the population was Slav-speaking with Vlach-speaking and, to the west, Albanian-speaking admixtures.[9]

In view of the situation in Macedonia and the Balkans and the international developments already mentioned, the policy of the Greek government, a policy of caution and co-operation with the Great Powers, seemed to involve few risks for the Greek national interests. Yet this policy did not enjoy universal support in Greece, as some believed that caution ought to be supplemented by

Mt. Olympus, as depicted in a 19th century engracing.

a clandestine, if not open, effort to incite insurrectionary movements in the unredeemed regions. Such movements would help bring once more the Greek national claims to the forefront and would reinforce the bargaining position of Athens. Leonidas Voulgaris, who represented those in favour of a general uprising of the Empire's Christian subjects in order to drive the Turks out of Europe, had been in touch with politicians and army officers in Serbia and with Greek guerrilla leaders, such as Chronis Basdekis, Achilleas Velentzas and Theodoros Ziakas, who maintained close ties with the unredeemed Greek regions. The government of Alexandros Koumoundouros, however, although the prime minister himself was personally well disposed towards co-operation with the Slavs, was determined to follow a peaceful policy and to neutralize the activity of those who attempted to incite uprisings in the *irredenta*.[10]

However, the situation in the Balkans developed fast and the mounting tension in Russo-Turkish relations was grist to the mill of those who sought to involve Greece in the war of the Balkan Slavs against the Ottoman Empire. In December 1876 the ambassadors of the Great Powers met in Constantinople to examine the situation. Their proposals, though rejected, are worth mentioning because they prepared the ground for the settlement of the Bulgarian Question attempted by Russia a little later. The conference proposed the vertical division of Bulgaria into two parts, each one under a gonernor-general appointed by the Porte, with an elected local assembly consisting of Muslims and Christians, a local gendarmerie, Turkish military presence confined in a number of forts, an international commission of control with a one-year mandate and a special foreign police force to oversee the implementation of the commission's decisions. Eastern Bulgaria, with Tirnovo as its capital, was to include the *sanjaks* of Tirnovo, Rustchuk, Tulcea, Sliven, Philippopolis and the *kazas* of Kirk Kilisse, Mustafa-pasha, and Kizilagach. Western Bulgaria, with Sofia as its capital, was to include the *sanjaks* of Sofia, Vidin, Nis, Skopje (Uskub), Monastir, the *kazas* of Tikves, Veles and Kastoria, and three *kazas* of the *sanjak* of Serres.[11] In other words, the proposed two Bulgarias included the best part of Macedonia, leaving out only the regions of Kozani, Thessaloniki, Chalcidice and part of Serres.

The proposals of the ambassadors' conference proved fruitless largely because their presentation to the Porte coincided with the proclamation of a constitution by the Sultan. The 1876 constitution was the work of the precursors of the early-20th-century Young Turks and provided for a parliament, a cabinet accountable to the parliament and the protection of civil liberties.

The Ottoman constitution was hailed by the liberals in Europe and the subject populations of the Empire, but Sultan Abdul Hamid had no wish to implement it. Indeed, he dismissed the reform-minded Grand Vizier, Midhat Pasha, thus leaving no one in doubt as to the kind of authority he intended to exercise. The ambassadors of the Powers departed from Constantinople in protest against the sultan's inconsistency and the Porte seemed to be heading for a clash with Russia, the one Power which was not inclined to leave developments in the Ottoman Empire within Abdul Hamid's discretion.

Meanwhile, Russia had secured the neutrality of Austria-Hungary and Germany. Britain engaged in a strenuous effort to stave off the confrontation but without much hope for success. Following a cease-fire between Serbia and Turkey (February 1877), Czar Alexander II, using as a pretext the Sultan's refusal to implement both the 1876 reforms and the *Hatt-i Humayun* (1856), declared war on the Ottoman Empire. But for British sympathy, the Porte found itself isolated and practically at the mercy of Russia.

The situation had developed in an extremely uncomfortable way for the Greek government, too. The appeals of Alexander II for a co-ordinated effort on the part of all Orthodox peoples in the East against the Turks seemed to appeal to the Greek public opinion. Russian victories in the battlefield were in the headlines daily, thus creating a climate of anticipation and tension which was particularly ominous for govenrment stability. Britain, for its part, consistently advised Athens to steer clear of actions that might set off a general conflagration in the area and thus play into the hands of the Russians. What was more, the Greek government hesitated to enter the war being fearful of an attack by the powerful Turkish navy. At that point, in June 1877, King George I took the initiative to appoint an all-party cabinet under Konstantinos Kanaris, in which Harilaos Trikoupis served as Foreign Minister.

The Russian advance across Bulgaria complicated things further for the Greeks. In December, following the fall of Plevna and as the way to Constantinople seemed clear, Serbia resumed hostilities against the Porte. Greece, under British pressure and unprepared for war, stuck to neutrality. On 20 January the Russians entered Adrianople and eleven days later the Turks were forced into signing an armistice and accepting preliminary peace terms.

The San Stefano Treaty, which the Porte signed on 3 March 1878, caused serious concern throughout Europe. Turkey was to lose territories south of the Caucasus and Dobrudja, which Russia ceded to Romania in exchange for Bessarabia which it had lost after the treaty of Paris (1856). Serbia, Montenegro and Romania became independent and the former two countries were to expand at the expense of Ottoman territory in the Balkans.

The treaty made no mention of the Greek claims. On the contrary, it provided for the establishment of an antonomous Bulgarian principality which would include, in addition to the Bulgarian provinces between the Danube and the Balkan Mts, Eastern Rumelia, Western Thrace and Macedonia (with the exception of the provinces of Thessaloniki and Chalcidice). That was to be 'Great' Bulgaria to which the Bulgarians would aspire thereafter. Yet this proved a stillborn dream of Russian patent which was not to be resurrected. A conference was convened in Berlin in which all interested powers were invited. The treaty, which was concluded at the end of the conference on 13 July 1878, annulled many provisions of the San Stefano settlement, particularly those referring to Bulgaria. In place of Great Bulgaria, the following arrangement was reached: a) a Bulgarian principality was created as a tributary state to the Sultan, which included the area between the Danube and the Balkan Mts; b) Eastern Rumelia, that is the region between the Balkan and the Rhodope Mts, became an autonomous province of the Ottoman Empire under a Christian governor; c) Thrace and Macedonia remained provinces of the Empire. Only Thessaly was awarded to Greece but the danger of Macedonia and Thrace passing under Bulgarian rule was averted.

Revolutionary Movements in Macedonia in 1878

The impact of the Great Eastern Crisis was felt in Macedonia too, particularly in its southern regions, where insurrectionary movements broke out. During the early stage of the crisis the Greeks of Macedonia, while remaining calm, did not stop preparing for the moment when they would be called upon to defend their national interests with the assistance of free Greece. Metropolitans and the Greek consuls were there to provide discreet guidance to the more restless elements in

Stephanos Gragoumis, the politician of Macedonian descent who grealy contributed to the liberation movements of the land of his ancestors.

Macedonia. The ambassadors' conference in Constantinople provoked a storm of protest among the Greeks of many provinces, when it became known that the ambassadors were about to suggest the cession of their homelands to the prospective Bulgarian principality. Letters of protest signed by thousands were then addressed to the Patriarchate, stating the determination of the inhabitants not to submit to 'Bulgarism'. Undoubtedly, the Greek consuls (Konstantinos Vatikiotis in particular, the consul at Thessaloniki) contributed to the sending of these letters; this is hardly surprising in view of the paramount national interests involved. The acute threat of Bulgarian supremacy proved the determining factor, the catalyst for the rallying of national forces in the predominantly Greek provinces of Macedonia. The periodic appeals of the Greek irredentist circles for resort to force in order to liberate Macedonia found fertile ground among the most restive elements, especially the youth. The danger of passing under the rule of a Slav country, Bulgaria, particularly after the unbridgeable gap opened by the Schism deeply shocked the Greeks of Macedonia; they hardly needed outside inducement to express their protest.[12]

At the same time, the first armed groups made their appearance on the mountain ranges of Macedonia, Oly. pus, Pieria and Vermion in particular.[13] In free Greece numerous national committees were set up, most notably the 'National Defence' and the 'Brotherhood', with the aim to mobilize the necessary forces, in co-operation with the Greek authorities or independently, for action in the unredeemed areas. The government's inability to undertake similar action rendered the role of these committees all the more essential for the convincing projection of the Greek claims at the right moment.

Pivotal to these efforts was the activity of Stephanos Dragoumis, a lawyer by profession, and the 'Macedonian Committee' which was assigned with the task of organizing a revolutionary movement under the auspices of the 'National Defence' and the 'Brotherhood'. The Committee consisted of five eminent personalities of Macedonian origin; Ioannis Pantazidis, Professor of Ancient Greek Literature at the Athens University, Georgios Papazisis, officer of the Medical Corps, Professor Nikolaos Halkiopoulos, the lawyer Leonidas Paschalis and Stephanos Dragoumis.[14]

At about the same time (January 1878) the Greek government, under the pressure of both external developments and public agitation, sent troops to Thessaly and gave the patriotic committees the green light to foment uprisings in the unredeemed regions. Greece did not declare war but claimed that its military action in Thessaly was meant to protect the Greek population from the Turkish irregulars. It was an unfortunate, short-lived adventure, as the invasion of the Greek army coincided with the armistice which the defeated Turkey was forced to conclude with Russia. The army was immediately ordered back and the government sought the mediation of the ambassadors of the Powers in order to stave off a Turkish reaction.[15]

The only course left to Greece was that of revolutionary unrest in the *irredenta*: Crete, Thessaly, Epirus and Macedonia. Yet, in this field, too, there had been no systematic preparations on the part of the government. The patriotic societies, refugees from the Ottoman-dominated regions, and, of course, the unredeemed Greeks were summoned to save the day. The revolution in Macedonia started in February, following the outbreak of similar movements in Epirus and Thessaly the previous month.

The Macedonian Committee concentrated its efforts on forming volunteer units at the source of fighters of Macedonian origin in free Greece, New Pella. Captain Kosmas Doumpiotis was appointed leader of the "campaign to Olympus". Of course, most of the 1821 Revolution fighters had passed away, but those still alive offered to form and head guerrilla bands, as did Tolias Lazos, a member of the famous Lazos family from Livadi of Olympus, and Panos Tsaras, Nikotsaras' son, both aging but willing. Nikolaos Blachavas, another scion of a *klepht-armatole* family of Macedonia who had settled in Greece in 1854, also offered to head a guerrilla band. Other such representatives of the *klepht-armatole* aristocracy of Macedonia were Georgios Tzachilas, Giannakos Olympios, Diamantis' son, Mitros Gatsos, adopted son of the fighter Angelis Gatsos, Konstantinos Kasomoulis, Nikolaos Kasomoulis' nephew, and Anagnostis Pitsavas who had also taken part in the 1854 revolt.[16]

The register of the 505 men comprising Doumpiotis' guerrilla unit also mentions the occupation of each volunteer: there were several 'workers', 'servants', 'farmers', 'shepherds', 'hunters', 'stone-masons', 'soldiers', 'merchants', but also 'students' from all parts of Greece, free and unredeemed. They came from villages and towns of the Peloponnese, Central Greece, Thessaly, Epirus and Macedonia, most of them young men in their twenties, but also several older men between 30 and 50 years of age. Apart from New Pella, their places of origin included Kataphygi, Kozani, Kassandra, Vasilika, Kapudjilar (Pylaia of Thessaloniki), Polygyros, Olympus, Verria, Thessaloniki, Velvendos, Boufi (Megalochori of Florina), Vogatsiko, Kastoria, Bitola (Monastir), Smardesi (Krystallopigi), Krushevo, Florina, Vabeli (of Kastoria) and Blatsi.[17] It was a typical guerrilla unit of the period: a Greek microcosm dominated by those whose place of origin coincided with the unit's destination.

Doumpiotis' unit landed on the beach of Litochoro and tried to capture Katerini through negotiations with its Turkish garrison. Before long the entire region of Kolindros-Pieria was in revolt. Local leaders Evangelos Hostevas and Panagiotis Kalogirou joined the revolutionary ranks. The entire activity in the region was co-ordinated by Nikolaos, Bishop of Kitros, whose most difficult task was the arming of the local population: many villagers who came to join the guerrilla units were obliged to go back to their villages owing to the lack of arms. Despite some local gains in Pieria, Doumpiotis' delay coupled with the shortage of weapons to deprive the revolutionaries of an early decisive success, such as the capture of a city. During that early crucial stage the Turks managed to transfer strong army and irregular forces from Kosovo and Thessaly and to , press the revolution in a bloodbath. One after the other the villages of the area fell into Turkish hands, while many were set on fire, including Litochoro. Three new volunteer units, which the Macedonian Committee intended to send to Macedonia in March, were ordered to remain in Thessaly for the needs of the revolution there. Doumpio..s with the remnants of his for ce crossed into Thessaly, as did other figures of the uprising in Olympus, such as Nikolaos, Bishop of Kitros, and Evangelos Karovangos, president of the provisional government which had been set up in Pieria. Through the mediation of the British consuls in Athens and Adrianople, the leaders and volunteers of the Macedonian uprising together with many refugees were ʼ ʼe to make their way to Greece bringing along with them ihe sorrow and disappointment over the new setback in the uphill task of liberating their beloved country.[18]

At that time, a Greek revolt in Western Macedonia looked imminent, too. Local preparations had advanved to the point that a 'provisional government' was formed in February 1878 under Ioannis Govedaros, with Anastasios Pichion as its Secretary. In its proclamation, which was issued 'in the name of the Nation' from Mt Vourino on 18 February, the 'provisional government' declared:

"Our province, no longer able to withstand the un-
eakable Turkish yoke of slavery, the unheard-of atrocities of those oppressing the fatherland of Alexander the Great, the countless ills and the terrible pressures to which not only our possessions but also our very life and honour are exposed, and seeing that the remorseless diplomacy not only overlooked the calmness of the subject Greek provinces but also misinterpreted it, and that the Sublime Porte, having signed the preliminary peace terms with Russia, sold out most of Macedonia to Panslavism, took up the arms to a man in order to declare before God and men its liberation from the yoke of slavery and its union with Mother Greece under the sceptre of our divinely crowned and most constitutional King of the Hellenes, George I...".[19]

The 'provisional government' at Vourino had a force of 500 men at its disposal led by Iosiph Liatis. The number of armed men could increase as much as five times provided that weapons and volunteers from Greece to train the men became available. But neither were forthcoming – not even guerrilla groups from the Olympus region, as it might have been expected following the suppression of the uprising there. Little by little, local chieftains from several parts of Western Macedonia who had gathered their bands at Vourino, started returning to their regions for reasons of maintanance and in order to provide some protection to their fellow Christians against the roaming bands of Turkish and Albanian irregulars. The dispersion of the armed bands resulted in a sort of guerrilla warfare across an area extending over the provinces of Kozani, Anaselitsa, Kastoria, Florina and Monastir. From February, when the armed groups first assembled at Vourino, until summer, Western Macedonia was at the mercy of these armed bands, Christian and Muslim. It was a state of extensive brigandage and open confrontation between those armed Christians, who up until then had been in the service of the Ottoman government, and the authorities, which regarded this confrontation as a rebellion and dealt with it accordingly.[20]

After a long period of hesitation the Greek government finally gave its consent to revolutionary action in Macedonia, partly in order to keep up the pressure on the Ottoman government, at least as long as the latter refrained from ceding territories to Greece, and partly in order to strengthen its hand at the table of negotiations, where it was expected to be invited to present the Greek national claims. Another factor, which certainly influenced the Greek government's attitude, was public feeling which gave rise to frequent disturbances in Athens. The press kept clamouring against the government's inability to secure territorial concessions from the Porte like the other Balkan peoples had done. The following piece of satirical verse is quite indicative of the mood prevailing at the time:

To the wedding we were not invited,
We didn't savour the wedding cake,
We were left out of the ball,
And played the trumpet;
Stuffed with pap,
Jealous and grambling,
Out of spite
We broke the window panes in Athens.
The wedding is over,
And no one has wisned happiness to us.
And our poor mother-in-law

Has made other sons-in-law
Who relished the youth:
The Serb, Wallachian, Bulgarian
And the Montenegrin.[21]

With the moral support of the Greek consular authorities, the activity of the guerrilla bands intensified, particularly in August and September 1878. During autumn the activity of the Greek guerrillas was perceptibly reduced until, by winter, it was practically brought to a halt. Many local guerrilla leaders, mostly former chieftains of brigand bands, followed the nomads of the area who moved with their herds to the winter pastures of Thessaly, as it was the habit of the herd-track followers, nomads and brigands.

After the suppression of the 1878 uprising the activity of Greek guerrilla bands in North-Western Macedonia did not cease altogether. The co-ordination of such activity remained largely in the hands of Anastasios Pichion, a teacher who had settled at Kastoria since 1865, founder of the local Educational Association and a representative of the Athens-based Association for the Dissemination of Greek Letters. Between 1882 and 1887 Pichion, who was in close contact with the Greek Consulate at Monastir, in common with a committee of citizens of Kastoria systematically worked to improve the standards of Greek education for the local population and to neutralize the effects of various foreign propagandas. At the same time he was actively involved in arming and organizing the guerrilla groups of the region, which had undertaken to defend the villages against the raids of Turkish-Albanian bands and the oppression of the Turkish *agas*. At some point, the activity of the Greek patriots was denounced by pro-Romanian Vlachs to the Turkish authorities. A wave of arrests was launched which, after lengthy interrogations and trials, led to the protagonists of the Greek national activity in Western Macedonia being imprisoned or exiled. In 1888 Pichion himself was sentenced to five years imprisonment and was transferred to Palestine from where he managed to escape two years later.

Now that the deterrent of the Christian armed bands had all but eclipsed, the Turkish and Albanian irregulars set about their task of restoring the kind of 'order' —employing the sort of means that had outraged liberal public opinion in Europe a few years earlier. Europe, however, by then considered Near Eastern affairs— and public opinion its own conscience – as settled by the Berlin Congress. The rebels in Macedonia paid dearly

for rising against the "unspeakable Turkish yoke of slavery"; yet their acts not only bolstered up the position of the Greek state at the Congress of Berlin, but also helped project Macedonia in the international level as a land which had risen for liberty and its union with free Greece.

National Rivalries in Macedonia (1878-1897)

The period from the Congress of Berlin (1878) to the Greek-Turkish War of 1897 was one of intense national rivalries in Macedonia. These rivalries, which were to escalate further after 1897, crystallized during this period and propelled Macedonia to the forefront of international affairs and at the crossroads of competing spheres of influence. Moreover, national rivalries and the international interest that arose thereof greatly contributed to the definition of the extent of the geographic notion which has been identified as 'Greater Macedonia' ever since.

The fundamental features of this period may be summed up as follows: (a) the dynamic advance of the Bulgarian position in Macedonia both on the international level and within the contested land itself; (b) the simultaneous furtherance of other interests, especially of Serbia, Romania and the Uniate movement; (c) the retreat of the Greek presence in the northern provinces, particularly in the countryside; and (d) the co-operation of the Ottoman authorities with the Orthodox Metropolitans and the Greek element in general in order to check the Bulgarian penetration.

It has already been mentioned that the main agents of the rival national positions and interests included the domestic and foreign press, schools, churches, consulates, communities, associations and guerrilla bands. The importance of these agents increased during the period under discussion and so did the significance of the petitions to various recipients which sometimes thousands of inhabitants were invited to sign in order to declare their support to some or to denounce other. Influencing foreign public opinion and governments constituted a basic aim of the rivals. This effort bore fruit in many occasions; yet it primarily helped crystallize and consolidate the position of each side among its connationals and undermine or even eradicate other views which did not conform to the principle of unshakable unanimity which was postulated as the foundation of all national activity.

The sequence of events which influenced Macedonian affairs was as follows: (a) the Congress of Berlin, which had a lasting impact; (b) the annexation of Thessaly to Greece in 1881 following tough negotiations; (c) Bulgaria's forcible annexation of Eastern Rumelia in 1886 and the consequent Balkan crisis; (d) the dynamic appearance of two powerful national secret societies, the Bulgarian-Macedonian 'Internal Macedonian-Adrianople Organization' (which eventually became known simply as the Internal Macedonian Revolutionary Organization-IMRO) and the Greek *'Ethniki Etaireia'* (National Society).

Prolonged large scale disturbances were the legacy of the 1875-1878 uprisings in Macedonia. After 1878 the Bulgarian revolt evolved into guerrilla warfare with Bulgarian bands infiltrating Macedonia from time to time, in exactly the same fashion as Greek guerrilla bands had been penetrating into unredeemed Greek regions since the establishment of the Greek Kingdom in 1830. Such bands, sometimes numbering several hundred armed men of all sorts, frequently entered the northern parts of Macedonia, particularly Djuma, Melenikon and Nevrokopi. According to foreign observers, their aim was to instigate a new revolution. Yet the 'Bulgarian' (or 'Bulgarian-speaking', according to the representatives of Greece) peasants of the area, particularly the villages in the districts of Gevgeli and Demir Hisar, appeared reluctant to co-operate with the rebels coming from Bulgaria and their local associates. These 'Bulgarian-speaking' people remained loyal to the Patriarchate of Constantinople and had even struck some sort of a tacit understanding with their Muslim neighbours in order to protect themselves against the Bulgarians and the Bulgarian-Macedonian guerrillas.[22]

Similar, although on a smaller scale, was the course of the Greek insurrectionary movements in southern Macedonia. The Greek armed groups rarely constituted sizeable units. They moved and acted mostly as brigand bands. By way of contrast to the policy of Sofia, the Greek government did not favour the use of brigand band formations for insurrectionary purposes. Besides, the Greek bands did not extend their activity into the northern provinces of Macedonia, but, like traditional brigands, limited themselves to the familiar and friendly environment of the south. In one recorded case of Greek brigand bands joining forces after the revolutionary events of 1878, it becomes clear that their motives were related more to the customary pursuits of outlaws of this sort than to the objectives of the guerrilla formations

Greek mountain guards of the mid-19h century, whose part in contemporary insurrectionary movements was substantial.

which originated from or were directed by Bulgaria at the time. In February 1880, according to Konstantinos Vatikiotis, the Greek consul in Thessaloniki, 185 brigands led by 15 chieftains of the Olumpus area, "devotedly heard Mass said in the open by the Bishop of Kitros, and listened to his speech which moved them to tears, according to what the Holy Father of Kitros confidentially reports".[23]

In a letter to the military governor of the *vilayet* of Thessaloniki, the outlaws of Olympus wrote:

"We, the Kapetanioi (Chieftains) of Olympus, convey our sincere and profound respect to your Excellency and announce that we have received through Iωαννίκιος, Bishop of Kitros, the R[espected] Government's declaration of definite and full amnesty to us and have accepted Your fatherly advice to resign this dishonourable craft which the circumstances and need obliged us [to undertake] and submit to lay down our arms and to live as honest citizens henceforth..."

In order to lay down their arms, the *Kapetanioi* of Olympus asked to be employed by the sultan's government as mountain guards (*kir-sirdar* or *armatoles*). If appointed, these chieftains promised that "acts of brigandage would never be heard of again" in the area of their jurisdiction.[24]

Vatikiotis, one of the most ardent supporters of Greek national policy in Macedonia and authentic representative of the new national-state ideal which irresistibly infiltrated the traditional society of the contested land from north and south, did not trust the declarations of the *kapetanioi*, nor did he consider that they could be relied upon to further the national cause. Local band leaders and their companions could be used to man guerrilla units at times of crisis. At this time, however, new agents and means were required. Vatikiotis and those sharing his ideas had reconciled themselves to the situation in Macedonia and the ability of the Greeks to defend their national interests in the subjected land. This 'compromise' originated from a familiarity with the Macedonian Question. The delusions of the Greeks who seriously concerned themselves with national affairs that Macedonia would be rightfully assigned to Greece had been shaken in 1870 and all but vanished in 1878. The security, which the traditional identification of religion with nationality afforded to the Greeks, had been decisively undermined when rival national ideologies advanced similar arguments in support of their own position and claims. Insurrectionary movements relying on irregulars did not suffice for defending national interests. Nor was it enough to raise the historical rights of the Greeks to Macedonia. Macedonia constituted neither geographic nor national – not even administrative – entity. The limits of the contested land were those defined by the respective positions of the two basic contenders, the Greeks and the Bulgarians. More important than these 'external' boundaries were the limits of the spheres of influence which the two rivals and protagonists of the drama had been promoting within the country itself. The southern provinces of Macedonia did not pose any great problem: their character was Greek by any standard. By the same standards the northern provinces had acquired a Bulgarian identity: their Christian inhabitants were Slav-speaking, had sided with the Exarchate from the start and hardly concealed their pro-Bulgarian feelings. The problem was with the mid-

dle zone of Macedonia, the multilingual zone, in which the Slavophones predominated in the countryside, the population of urban and semi-urban centres was predominantly Greek- and Vlach-speaking, while Albanian-speaking pockets existed in the western parts of all three zones.[25]

The multilingual zone of Macedonia presented a challenge to all competing parties. The Greek- and Vlach-speaking populations had already accepted the national ideology emanating from Greece. An exception was a small part of the Vlach-speaking population, the so-called – then and later, too – 'Romanizing' Vlachs, who identified themselves with Romania. Far more limited was the appeal of the nationalist Albanian League among the Albanian-speaking Christians, who had largely made common cause with the Greek-speaking Christians. The Slavophones were a special case. Many, labelled by the Bulgarians as *Grecomans*, were fervently loyal to the Ecumenical Patriarchate and Greece. Others had sided with the Exarchate and Bulgaria from the outset. Yet in between these two sides there were many, the peasantry in particular, who lacked a clear ethnic character of their own. This multilingual mass, with or without clear national orientations, inhabited a region lacking clear geographical or administrative definition: it stretched south to a line beginning at lake Ochrida, crossing Krushevo, passing south of Prilep and north of Monastir and ending at river Nestos including Stromnitsa, Petrich, Melenikon, and Nevrokopi; its southern boundaries began at Mt Grammos, passed north of Thessaloniki and ended to the north of Serres and Drama. The northern boundaries of this zone marked the maximum of the Greek claims and, from that time onwards, were to become an objective for Greek foreign policy.[26]

Education and religion, which are given detailed study in the appropriate chapters of the present volume, were the basic means for advancing the national strategies of the rivals. The work done in the fields of education and religion was indispensable to diplomacy, the traditional method of furthering national interests, which, in turn, was often required to sustain and safeguard this kind of work. Among the great powers, Austria-Hungary and Russia had an immediate interest, the former to a greater extent than the latter. Bulgaria could rely on Russia insofar it was prepared to jeopardize co-operation with Austria-Hungary, which wished to avoid the emergence of a powerful Slav state in the Balkans that might deny Vienna access to Thessaloniki, the natural outlet of Central Europe on the Aegean. Britain, in particular, and, to a lesser extent, France were expected to support the Greek positions provided that the territorial integrity of the Ottoman Empire was not endangered – until, towards the end of the 19th century, Germany replaced the two Great Powers as the guarantor of the integrity of the sultan's Empire. Greece could count on the two Western Powers but not quite as much as Bulgaria could rely on Russia: the latter was in a position to threaten the Porte much more effectively than the other two Powers. An understanding between Greece and Bulgaria was out of the question insofar the Bulgarians persisted in their claims and the Ecumenical Patriarchate did not intend to repeal the Schism – nor did Greece wish it to do so as long as Bulgaria refused to curb its ambitions. A rapprochement between Greece and Serbia stumbled over both the latter's refusal to clearly define its objectives in Macedonia and the limited nature of its interest in this region, at a time when Serbian irredentism was primarily directed towards the South Slav provinces of the Habsburg Empire. An understanding with the Porte was excluded too, since it would mean that Greece would have to repudiate its irredentist goals; it was possible, however, to postpone irredentist activities for a more propitious time and to support the preservation of the sultan's rule over his European territories until international circumstances favoured a solution to the Macedonian Question not damaging for the Greek national interests. The prolongation of Ottoman rule, however intolerable to those enslaved and repugnant to the impatient 'irredentists' of free Greece, was preferable to a settlement of the San Stefano type: such a solution would signal the irrevocable loss of Macedonia since it was expected to lead to the uprooting of the Greek element from its ancestral hearths. By way of contrast, Ottoman domination as it had developed between the mid-19th century and the Young Turk Revolution (1908) did not present a threat to the ethnic composition of Macedonia.

The annexation of Eastern Rumelia to Bulgaria in 1885 complicated matters further. After a brief lull in armed band activity in the aftermath of the 1878-1879 crisis, the situation in Macedonia deteriorated once again: since the spring of 1885 sizable bands started penetrating deeply into the middle zone of Macedonia. Largely consisting of Bulgarian-Macedonians armed by Bulgarian patriotic societies, these bands were infiltrated from Bulgaria, where they retreated when pressed by the

Pavlos Melas, by Photis Kontoglou.

Ottoman army. According to a contemporary estimate (April 1885), 700-800 armed Bulgarian-Macedonians organized in large groups operated in Macedonia. Their numbers included convicts or persons awaiting trial who had been released for the purpose of participating in these incursions.[27] In this the Bulgarians followed the example of the Greeks[28], with a delay of half a century – as long it had taken them to establish their own free national state. Like their Greek counterparts, the Bulgarian governments were exposed to the influence of the Bulgarian-Macedonian refugees and of the various patriotic societies which exercised relentless pressure on them to go ahead with their irredentist pledges. Indeed, the Bulgarian governments at times seemed captive of the refugees and their societies.[29]

Macedonia had once again attracted the interest of European public opinion following a series of reports on local conditions which appeared in the *Pall Mall Gazette* in late 1884. Basic features of these accounts, which raised a storm of protest from the Greek side, were the following: (a) the presentation of population estimates favourable to the Bulgarian point of view; (b) the frequent allegations of malpractices and acts of violence on the part of the authorities against Bulgarians; and (c) the frequent reference to cases of banditry with victims primarily Bulgarians. The Greeks reacted by submitting letters of protest carrying thousands of signatures, in which the newspaper's biased journalism was condemned.

The case of the *Gazette*'s pro-Bulgarian journalism is worth mentioning as it illuminates certain aspects of the situation in Macedonia of the mid-1880s. The allegations of the newspaper were taken up by the British government, and, in December 1884, the military attaché to the British Embassy in Constantinople, Major Henry Trotter, was dispatched to Macedonia. After touring numerous towns and villages of Central and Western Macedonia for nearly two months, the British officer was able to confirm many cases of Ottoman malpractices, but he also ascertained that, in the most part, they had been exaggerated. He further found much of the information concerning the Greek-Bulgarian dispute to be of questionable validity – particularly in that it identified language with national identity. While in Vodena, Major Trotter, on his way to the local Metropolitan, came across a group of villagers from neighbouring Lefkovitsa. They had just visited the prelate in order to protest against the tyrannical conduct of the local *bey*. "These people", the British officer reported, "spoke only Bulgarian and a little Turkish. When I asked them their nationality, they answered to my surprise that they were Greeks. That was my first acquaintance with the Greek-Bulgarian Question".[30] In Monastir he was handed a petition signed by the Metropolitan, the elders, the clerics, members of six guilds, and over two hundred other Greeks, in which they protested against pro-Bulgarian press reports. He received a similar petition at Kastoria, "a completely Hellenised province", as he reported. Wherever he went, he was impressed by the vehement reaction of the Greeks against the distortion of the ethnological picture by journalists who had fallen victims to Bulgarian propaganda.[31]

The Greek reaction to the annexation of Eastern Rumelia and the infiltration of Bulgarian guerrilla bands into Macedonia was limited to a partial mobilization of the army and the preparation of volunteer units, most of which, however, never set foot in Macedonia. The lack of any serious preparation combined with the pressures of the Western Powers to prevent the Greek government from effectively claiming territorial compensation from the Porte to offset the unauthorized gains of Bulgaria. Students, in particular, and soldiers, who deserted their units, came to join guerrilla bands in Central Greece and Thessaly, but very few crossed the frontier. The winter season (1885-1886) was not suitable for adventures of this sort in Macedonia.

At about the same period, Serbian interest in Macedonia was manifested in the founding of the 'St Savva Educational Society' in Belgrade in 1886, and two further societies, the 'Solidarity' and the 'Serbian Brotherhood' a little later. Through their activities, Serbian education in Macedonia was reinforced as the number of Serbian schools increased. In the field of religion, too, the Serbs scored a few successes, particularly after 1896, when a Serbian bishop was appointed at Skopje.

The next and last phase in the contest for Macedonia before the onset of the armed struggle in early 20th century, began in 1893-1894 with the formation of a revolutionary organization of the Bulgarian-Macedonians at Thessaloniki which later came to include the Bulgarians of Thrace and was initially called Internal Macedonian-Adrianople Revolutionary Organization (later IMRO). Among the protagonists of this movement were Damian Gruev, Gotse Delchev, and Jane Sadanski. In 1895, representatives of the Bulgarian-Macedonian associations, among whom a prominent part was played by Boris Sarafov and Ivan Tsonchev, set up the 'Supreme Committee' (*Vrhoven Komitet*) in Sofia, while the IMRO retained its own Central Committee. After an initial period of close co-operation, the 'Centralists' (of the IMRO) and the '*Vrhovists*' clashed: the *Vrhovists* aimed at the incorporation of Macedonia into Bulgaria and accepted the leading role of the Bulgarian government in the direction of the struggle. The Centralists, whose membership included many socialists, without denying their Bulgarian ethnic identity, regarded the armed struggle for the annexation of Macedonia as an unrealistic objective. By way of contrast to the *Vrhovists*, they advanced socio-political slogans designed to win support from across national lines with the aim to set up an autonomous or independent Macedonia. Their slogan "Macedonia for the Macedonians" was directed to all the populations of Macedonia, at least in theory. The autonomy of Macedonia promoted by the Centralists was acceptable to the *Vrhovists* only as a transitional stage leading to incorporation into Bulgaria. The ideological and political divergence between the two committees was temporarily overshadowed by an outbreak of rebellious activity in Macedonia during that same year (1895).[32]

In summer 1895, largely on the *Vrhovists*' initiative, there was a co-ordinated effort to recruit and arm guerrilla bands mostly from among the Bulgarian-Macedonian refugees. The formation of these units and the necessary fund-raising was done almost in the open, as may be inferred from the detailed reports of the Ottoman authorities which watched these activities in Bulgaria with justifiable uneasiness.[33] When it finally took place, the guerrilla invasion failed to match expectations. The Ottoman army was ready to face the invaders successfully, while the populace did not seem to be moved by the pleas of the rebels to take up arms against the Turks. Sarafov, an officer of the Bulgarian army and a leader of the invasion, failed to hold his own at Melenikon and gave up the effort. The other units met with a similar fate. In many cases the rebels were still in Bulgarian army uniforms. Some who had been taken prisoners revealed that they had been recruited by Bulgarian-Macedonian committees. Many were brigands who had crossed into Bulgaria after being invited by the Bulgarian-Macedonian committees. The rebels operated from Kyustendil, the centre of activity of the Bulgarian-Macedonian committees and societies.[34]

The Greek *Ethniki Etaireia*, founded in 1894 by young army officers, was meant to play a role similar to that of the Bulgarian patriotic societies. In summer 1896 the *Ethniki Etaireia* organized and sent to southern Macedonia armed units, composed mainly of refugees or seasonal workers (mostly masons) from Macedonia. Among the most active *kapetanioi* during that summer the following may be listed: Athanasios Brouphas from Krimini of Voion, Papadimos, Alexis Beloulias, Zisis Vrakas, Kolousias Lachtaras, Panagiotis Alamanos, the brothers Christos and Panagiotis Ververa, Goulas Groutas, Naoum Spanos, Leloudas, Zarkadas, Georgios

Athanasios Brouphas, a mason from Krimini of Western Macedonia who took part in the irredentist moves of 1896-97.

Katarrachias, Davelis and others. Moving either overland or by sea, the guerrilla units of the *Ethniki Etaireia* made their presence felt throughout Macedonia, at times penetrating as deeply as Morihovo and other northern areas. At that point, their appearance did not particularly disturb the Ottoman authorities as it constituted a rather spasmodic initiative of the *Ethniki Etaireia*. The venture was repeated in the spring of 1897 in a more organized form. This time, however, the provocation, in connection with the continuing revolt in Crete, was not left unanswered and led the Porte to break off diplomatic relations with Greece. The war that broke out in April of that year, resulted not only in the ignominious defeat of the Greek army but also to a temporary relaxation of Greek vigilance in Macedonia. The opportunity was seized upon by the Bulgarians who attempted to advance and consolidate their own positions. Yet out of the defeat and humiliation of 1897 the leaders of the new phase of the Greek national effort sprang up, men such as Pavlos Melas, Konstantinos Mazarakis, Georgios Tsontos and others.

IOANNIS S. KOLIOPOULOS
MACEDONIA AT THE EPICENTRE OF
RIVAL BALKAN NATIONALISMS
(1870-1897)
NOTES

1. Laskaris, *The Eastern Question, 1800-1923* (in Greek), pp. 240-242.

2. *Ibid.*, pp. 246-255.

3. *Ibid.*, p. 266.

4. Evangelos Kofos, *Greece and the Eastern Crisis, 1875-1878*, Thessaloniki 1975, pp. 42-43.

5. Laskaris, *op. cit.*, p. 275.

6. A. Vacalopoulos, 'The Dramatic Events at Thessaloniki in May 1876 and Their Impact on the Eastern Question', in *Pankarpia Makedonikis Gis: Studies of Apostolos E. Vacalopoulos* (in Greek), Thessaloniki 1980, pp. 101-169. See also Public Record Office (henceforth PRO), FO 195/1107, British consular reports from Thessaloniki for May 1876.

7. Kofos, *op. cit.*, pp. 45-47.

8. Evangelos Kofos, *The Revolution in Macedonia in 1878* (in Greek), Thessaloniki 1969, p. 14, note 2.

9. Kofos, *Greece and the Eastern Crisis*, pp. 35-36.

10. Kofos, *The Revolution in Macedonia*, pp. 16-18.

11. Laskaris, *op. cit.*, p. 283.

12. Kofos, *op. cit.*, pp. 16-18.

13. PRO, FO 195/1149, British consular reports from Thessaloniki for February 1877.

14. *Stephanos Dragoumis Papers: Unpublished Documents on the 1878 Revolution in Macedonia*, edited by I.S. Notaris (in Greek), Thessaloniki 1969, pp. 13ff.

15. Kofos, *Greece and the Eastern Crisis*, pp. 147ff.

16. *Stephanos Dragoumis Papers*, pp. 79ff.

17. *Ibid.*, pp. 111ff.

18. Kofos, *The Revolution in Macedonia*, pp. 33-35. See also British consular reports for that period (Jan.-March 1878), PRO, FO 195/1196.

19. *Stephanos Dragoumis Papers*, p. 302; Sampanopoulos, *Church and Revotutionary Movements at Kozani* (in Greek), pp. 40-43.

20. PRO, FO 195/1196, British consular reports from Thessaloniki for the period from January to July 1878.

21. Koliopoulos, *Brigands with a Cause*, p. 195, note 16.

22. PRO, FO 195/1198, British consular report from Larisa, 14 Nov. 1878, and PRO, FO 195/1255, consular report from Thessaloniki, 27 April 1879.

23. Historical Archives of the Ministry of Foreign Affairs, 1880/4/1, report for 5/17 March 1880.

24. *Loc. cit.*, attached letter dated 21 Feb./4 March 1880.

25. Evangelos Kofos, 'Dilemmas and Orientation of the Greek Policy in Macedonia, 1878-1886', *Balkan Studies*, 21 (1980), 45-48.

26. *Ibid.*, pp. 48-49.

27. PRO, FO 195/1515, British consular reports from Thessaloniki for the period between April and June, 1885, particularly the reports of 17 April, 15 and 29 May, and 9 June 1885.

28. Regarding the organizing of Greek irredentist incursions, immediately after the establishment of the Greek Kingdom, see Koliopoulos, *Brigands of Central Greece*, pp. 63ff.

29. PRO, FO 195/515, Foreign Office communication to the Turkish Ambassador in London, 13 Feb. 1885.

30. P.G. Tsailis, *The Glorious Monastir*, Thessaloniki 1932 (reprint, 1982), pp. 40-41.

31. See Henry Trotter's lengthy report dated 2 Feb. 1885 and attached reports of the Greek communities of Kastoria, Monastir, Prilep and Koprulu and of the 'Romanizing' inhabitants of Prilep in PRO, FO 297/1807.

32. Evangelos Kofos, 'The Macedonian Struggle in Yugoslav Historiography', *The Macedonian Struggle* (in Greek), Thessaloniki 1987, pp. 21-23.

33. Papers of the Turkish Embassy in London, File 306, where the telegrams from the Sublime Porte to the ambassador and attached reports from Macedonia, June-Dec. 1895.

34. *Loc. cit.*, Turhan Pasha, Minister for Foreign Affairs, to Rustem Pasha, Ambassador in London, 20 July 1895, and attached telegrams and letters, incl. a telegram from Zihni Pasha, governor of Thessaloniki, 7 July 1895; PRO, FO 195/1877, British consular reports from Thessaloniki for July 1895, where details on the movements and strength of the guerrilla forces.

Pavlos Melas, the heroic figure of the Greek Struggle in Macedonia, as glorified in a popular lithograph.

The Macedonian Struggle 1903-1912. Paving the Way for the Liberation

Basil K. Gounaris

1. From the 1897 Catastrophe to the Ilinden Uprising

The Greek defeat in 1897 inevitably marked a turning point in the evolution of the Macedonian Question. The shattering military defeat, the overwhelming economic problems, the imposition of international economic control, coupled with the devastating blow to the morale of the whole nation (and especially the army), provoked a severe domestic crisis and a revision of Greek foreign policy. The shock waves generated by this national disaster were naturally felt in Macedonia. It was deemed necessary to put an end to the activities of the *Ethniki Etaireia* (which was considered, and not unreasonably, to be partially responsible for the country's premature entanglement in military operations) until spirits could be pacified at home and abroad. In response to powerful pressure from the Theotokis government the Society was dissolved in 1900, although its members remained in close terms.[1]

The departure of the Greek armed bands, which had only made their first serious appearance in 1896, at the behest of the *Ethniki Etaireia*, tilted the balance in favour of Bulgarian, Serbian and Romanian propaganda, which moved swiftly to fill the gap left by the Greek withdrawal. Thus the Greek communities in Macedonia were once again exposed to an onerous situation, having been deprived of not only the minimal protection of the Greek state, but also the slightest solicitude on the part of the Ottoman authorities. The greatest danger, of course, came from Bulgaria, which proceeded to adopt a policy of undisguised aggression. The favourable (for Greece) progress of the Cretan Question suggested to the leaders of the Bulgarian Principality that Macedonia was a logical territorial adjunct. In fact, as we have already seen, Bulgarian penetration had already made significant gains in northern Macedonia during this decade, so that Bulgaria's hopes of eventually prevailing were not unfounded.

Although irredentism in Greece had somewhat subsided, in Bulgaria in 1897 the various Macedonian committees were more active than ever. The Supreme Macedonian Committee (*Vrhoven Komitet*) even issued patriotic bonds in support of Bulgarian efforts in Macedonia, payable when the revolution achieved its aims. The issue was widely advertised, and purchase of the bonds was compulsory, even for the Greeks in the Principality. By the following year, under the dynamic leadership of Boris Sarafov and with the full support of the Bulgarian government, the influx of armed bands into Macedonia redoubled. Usually consisting of ten men, these bands were largely formed of Bulgarians of Macedonian descent, some soldiers, some civilians, who had recently settled in the Principality and belonged for the most part to the Internal Macedonian Revolutionary Organization, or IMRO. The aim of these guerrilla bands was on the one hand to organize local revolutionary committees and armed cells, and on the other to prepare the economic and psychological groundwork for the revolution.[2]

In practice, however, things were not as easy as the instigators of this plan wished to believe. The initial idea of the founders of IMRO, Gruev and Tatarchev, that is, the enlistment in their movement of anyone of any nationality who desired to take part in a quasi-socialist revolt against the Turks, gradually proved impracticable. The overwhelming majority of the Greeks had been suspicious of the Bulgarian movements right from the outset. Moreover, the mini-uprising of 1895 had already shown that in the eyes of the Bulgarian *komitadjis* (i.e. members of the *Komitet* bands) there was very little

A 1904 photograph of the first nationalist organization of the Macedonian Struggle, the "Fraternity of the Friends of the Poor of Gevgeli".

difference between Greek and Turkish aims.[3] Inevitably, then, IMRO's struggle served to foment the by now traditional conflict between Exarchists and Patriarchists, and the movement naturally sought support solely from the former party. The movement was further reinforced by means of acts of terrorism against the leading figures of the Greek community in Macedonia, support for Exarchist schools and churches, forced levies from the Slav-speaking Patriarchists, and the conversion of some of the traditional *klephts*, who offered their considerable experience to this unorthodox war.[4]

Eventually, and despite Greek resistance, the balance-sheet at the end of the two-year period 1898-1900 was probably in favour of the Bulgarians. They had two very capable leaders, Poptraikov and Pavel Christov, who helped organize armed cells in the Kastoria region; and the murder of several tax collectors and tax farmers established the movement's credentials as a tyrannicide. Internal strife within the Greek communities, as well as the questionable practices of some of the ecclesiastical representatives of the Patriarchate, also helped push some of the oppressed residents of the middle zone into the Exarchist camp.[5]

The formation of these cells continued into the early years of the 20th century, while the simultaneous arming of Exarchist peasants was accelerated. Some of these arms had been purchased in Athens with Bulgarian funds, and had been dispatched into the Turkish-held provinces by way of Larisa and Trikkala, via a carefully organized network whose chief agents were Vlachs. The authorities on the Greek and Turkish borders were alerted, however, and this traffic was stopped before it

could become a serious problem. Furthermore, the Bulgarian units had by now grown to such an extent that they could openly challenge the Turkish army, which indeed gradually began to take action, the most significant battle between the two forces taking place in February 1902. In addition, the constant representations of the European states to the Bulgarian government constrained it to refuse IMRO its open support; they were, however, unable to impose its dissolution.[6]

The Bulgarian organization would certainly have been able to accomplish even more if it had not been torn by internal strife. First of all, there was serious friction between local Slav-speaking chieftains and IMRO officials. To a great extent this was a reflection of the refusal of the Slav-speaking Kota Christou from Rulia (Kota) to fight against the Greeks under the command of the Bulgarian Markov, who was a newcomer to Western Macedonia (1900), and his subsequent gradual estrangement from the Bulgarian committee.

Just when open conflict between Kota and IMRO seemed inevitable (August 1902), Major Jagov arrived with an armed unit at Zagoritsani (Vasileiada), in Western Macedonia, as the principal agent of the Supreme Macedonian Committee and personal representative of the President, Ivan Tsonchev. His goal was to instigate an uprising as soon as possible, with the promise of open Bulgarian and Russian support. The local chieftains, Tsakalarov, Kliasev, Mitros Vlachos, and others, were opposed to this idea, contending that the region was unprepared. The supply of arms, for example, and despite all Tsakalarov's efforts, had shrunk as a result of the Turkish army's intensive searches in 1901-02. Jagov did not abandon his plans, but threatened to turn to Kota instead; he also accused Tsakalarov of embezzling IMRO funds. Tsakalarov's reaction was spirited: he flung the accusations back at Jagov, and even tried to collect some of the arms that had been distributed to the peasants. The tide seemed to have turned against Jagov, but he did not give up.

However, in spite of these leadership clashes, the activity of the Bulgarian bands all over Macedonia, with every imaginable sort of pressure and violence against the Greek population, continued relentlessly throughout 1902, raising the spectre of imminent revolution and provoking redoubled activity on the part of the Turkish army. The possibility of the complete disintegration of the revolutionary infrastructure was now a daily reality, and there were certainly Bulgarian chieftains who were ready to lay down their arms at a moment's notice; it is also true that there was a general absence of co-ordination.

These were the circumstances that Tsonchev and Jagov were attempting to exploit, in prosecution of the wishes of the Supreme Macedonian Committee. Towards the end of 1902 the former appeared in the Razlog-Djumaja area at the head of a band of 300 men, and with the help of local units tried to incite an uprising against the Turks. Jagov, for his part, was proclaiming the revolution in Western Macedonia. These efforts were doomed from the outset, of course, since they did not have the approval of Sarafov and Gruev. This did not worry their perpetrators, however, whose sole concern was to create as many nests of revolution as possible in order to provoke violent Turkish intervention, and to promote the concept of Macedonian autonomy on the international scene. In reality, very few villages in the Djuma-Bala-Melenikon and Edessa-Gevgeli areas joined the movement, and none voluntarily. The critical battle was fought at the Kresna Pass. In spite of heavy losses, the Turkish army managed to capture the *komitadji* positions and force their defenders to withdraw. The Turkish advance was accompanied by atrocities on the part of certain Albanian units and some Bashibazuks, who indulged their predilection for rapine and arson. These incidents, suitably inflated by the Bulgarian and foreign press, succeeded in attracting the attention of European public opinion; and from this point of view, which was what really interested the Bulgarian Principality, the uprising can be considered a success.[7]

In order to make the European position comprehen-sible, a brief outline of the balance of power connected with the Eastern Question at the end of the 19th century is necessary. In 1897 Austria-Hungary, Russia and Italy had concluded a two-fold treaty defining their spheres of influence in the Balkans and upholding the *status quo*. This of course did not mean that they had abandoned their designs in the area, and so while Austria-Hungary intensified its pursuit of economic penetration in the eastern side of the peninsula, towards Thessaloniki, Russia seized the opportunity to present itself as the just and natural protector of Serbia and Bulgaria. Mean-while, although British interest in preserving the Ot-toman Empire was waning, the Sublime Porte had found a new ally in Germany, which was beginning to play a more dynamic role on the international scene.[8]

Such being the situation, then, the first sequels to the internationalization of the Macedonian Question were not long in appearing. The IMRO had already paved the way with a memorandum to the Great Powers in January 1899 demanding a settlement of the Macedonian Ques-tion along the lines of that applied to the Cretan Question (1898). Four years after the refusal of the powers to accept the memorandum, the Bulgarian government was able to claim outright that Turkish brutality was sending streams of emigrants to the Principality, resuscitating irredentism and endangering peace in the Balkans. The curbing of the Bulgarian revolutionary committees, so imperiously demanded by the Europeans, was impos-sible without some reform in the Balkan provinces. Late in November 1902 the Porte, in a combination of deference to international pressure and pursuit of its own dilatory policy. Appointed Hilmi Husein Pasha Gover-nor-General of the European *vilayets*, with a mandate to restore normalcy to Macedonia.[9]

By the end of the year it was obvious that the new measures were no improvement on existing legislation, and that the situation demanded the direct intervention of the Great Powers. In a joint declaration from Vienna in December 1902, the Russian Minister of Foreign Affairs, Count Lambsdorff, and his Austrian counter-part, Count Goluchowski, suggested the introduction of a specific programme of reforms on the *vilayets* of Thessaloniki, Monastir and Kosovo. These measures, known as the 'Vienna Programme', included the ap-pointment of an Inspector-General to the Macedonian *vilayets* for a period of three years, with military as well as administrative authority, the reorganization of the gendarmerie under foreign officers, the admission of

Christians to the gendarmerie and the rural guard, and amnesty for political offences. Financial stipulations included separate budgets for each *vilayet*, tithe collection by village rather than by region, and honest management of revenues. By February 1903 this programme had been approved by all the Great Powers; for the Porte, objection was neither possible nor desirable. Actual application of the measures, however, was another matter. Despite initial enthusiasm from the Porte and the co-operative attitude of the Inspector-General (Hilmi), the overwhelming technical difficulties, combined with growing anarchy, soon put an end to any attempt at reform.[10]

Indeed, as 1902 approached its close, the Turkish army's mopping-up operations slowed down, while the great majority of released political detainees moved straight from the jails to the mountains. Pressures on Patriarchists increased, especially in the northern areas. Forced levies and violence were once again a daily reality, while the ever-growing armed bands of Bulgarians made their presence felt constantly. In Western Macedonia the number of armed revolutionaries jumped from 700 to 1,200. In the spring of 1903, there were some 2,700 armed *komitadjis* in Macedonia, organized into about 90 bands. Arms-gathering and other material preparations were once again proceeding rapidly and everything seemed to indicate that Macedonia was on the brink of yet another revolutionary explosion. The bombings of railway stations and telegraph lines that occurred in late March and early April convinced the Turkish authorities that something serious was in the wind.[11]

Their suspicions were confirmed when Thessaloniki was hit by a wave of bombings at the end of April. The perpetrators were members of a small group of anarchists which maintained casual links with IMRO, and their goal was to focus European attention on the future of Macedonia. This was why their targets were shops and services with direct or indirect European connections, such as the Ottoman Bank, the steamship *Guadalquivir*, the Turkish Post Office, and selected coffee shops, clubs and hotels. Although at the time the Bulgarian organization was blamed for the bombings, in fact these were completely unrelated to the spate of incidents in the countryside. In any case, the rapid intervention of the foreign consuls shielded the citizens of Thessaloniki from brutal reprisals.

In the Macedonian countryside the Bulgarian bands

A demonstration in Thessaloniki in 1903, in protest against Bulgarian actions.

continued their active and varied campaign, seeking to stir up revolutionary fervour against the Turks; this time, however, they insisted more on the social aspect of the movement, telling the peasants that when the revolution was successful the *chiflik* lands would be redistributed. While Thessaloniki was rocking from the bomb explosions, the Bulgarian leaders were gathered at Smilevo, near Prespes. The meeting was attended by the secretary general of the Supreme Macedonian Committee, Damien Gruev, and Boris Sarafov, who was very critical of the Committee's strategy –immediate revolution– in view of the actual state of preparations. He also pointed out, though, that the independent and ill-considered bomb attacks in Thessaloniki had alerted the Turkish army, and that what preparations they had already made might well be discovered if the insurrection were not speedily organized and carefully carried out. This point of view was supported by other leaders, who realised that they must act while the initiative still lay with them. The views of the Committee, then, which was acting in close liaison with the Bulgarian Ministry for

War, were adopted, and preparations for the revolution were set in hand. Nevertheless, the decisive influence of the Vrhovists and the overt support of Bulgaria not-withstanding, the revolutionary machine was still in the hands of IMRO, which continued to mislead the local population by brandishing the slogan "Macedonia to the Macedonians".

In the meanwhile, the Turkish army had commenced a new round of mopping-up operations, of which the most important took place at Smardesi (Krystallopigi). A band of Bulgarians under Antonov were trapped in the village when a sizable Turkish force of both regular and irregular soldiers encircled it; they did in the end manage to escape, but the village was almost completely destroyed: 85 dead, 50 wounded, 230 houses out of a total of 300 burned, and almost all the animals lost. This incident was not unique; nor were its corollaries slow to appear. By now the consequences of any abortive insur-rection were perfectly clear, and the peasants had every reason to be wary of IMRO. The latter, however, was not about to let any such obstacles impede its course: it had long since developed quite effective methods for ensur-ing the support of the peasants –willing or otherwise.

Frequent skirmishes with the Turkish army did not slow down the steady growth of the Bulgarian guerrilla bands, which were constantly being reinforced by ar-rivals from the Principality. IMRO's battle to amass sufficient men, food, money and equipment led to an orgy of blackmail, forced levies and violence against the Patriarchist population which neither the local Greek leaders nor the Turkish authorities were able to stop. Early in July, when preparations were well under way, the date of the insurrection known as the Ilinden Upris-ing was fixed for July 20, the feast day of Prophet Elijah.

The events which followed, over the rest of that year, do not really merit the title of revolution. The principal aim of the Bulgarian guerrilla bands was to drive as much of the population as possible into the mountains in order to create the impression of a broadly-based movement with adherents from various classes and nationalities. Military action was restricted to Western and Northern Macedonia. The relentless searches for arms and the undiminished presence of the army in the rest of the territory made diversionary action impossible, while absolutely no revolutionary activity took place in the southern, Greek-speaking zone. The insurrection had two operational goals: on the one hand to prevent Turkish reinforcements from reaching the main theatre of operations in time, and on the other to seize certain secondary administrative centres, such as Krushevo (Krousovon), Kleisoura, and Neveska (Nymphaion), which did in fact fall to the insurgents and were endowed with 'revolutionary committees'. No attacks were made on urban centres like Monastir, Florina or Amyntaion. A number of bridges were destroyed and railroad tracks bombed. The bands also laid waste certain *chifliks* and murdered a number of Turkish landowners and govern-ment officials. Several of the Greek notables also fell victim to the insurgents, while others were obliged to seek refuge in the cities.

Despite the damage to roads and railways, the Turks quickly assembled sufficient forces to put down the rebellion. The troops they used were levied from the Albanian territories, and their ranks included many of the second reserves who were renowned for their lack of discipline, as well as a fair number of Bashibazuks. Krushevo was retaken in mid-August and consigned to the flames. The Greek quarter suffered the most damage, and many Greeks lost their lives. Similar scenes were repeated in most of the villages in the 'insurgent' ter-ritories. By the end of August the rebellion had col-lapsed, although scattered skirmishes occurred throughout September and more rarely in October. In fact, towards the end of September the Vrhovists under Tsonchev and Jagov attempted to spark a new revolt in the area around Razlog, in Eastern Macedonia, using Bulgarian troops exclusively. IMRO, however, refused to support them; and the Turks, after defeating the insurgents in Western Macedonia were easily able to detach troops for the new front. Within a week the Bulgarian units had retreated into Bulgaria.

In that summer of 1903, a total of 22 villages were completely destroyed and many more suffered serious damage, leaving 40,000 people homeless. The bulk of the damage was to the Greek and Vlach Patriarchist communities in the areas around Florina, Monastir and Kastoria. For the Bulgarian side, the balance-sheet at first glance appeared negative. The revolutionary machine which had been built up with such difficulty had been severely damaged and never really managed to recover. Nevertheless, once again there had been significant gains on the diplomatic front. Although the movement had failed to persuade the Great Powers to agree on an immediate solution for the Macedonian Question, much less its preferred option of autonomy, nonetheless Turkish violence had been sufficiently widely publicized in the press to give new urgency to plans for reform in Macedonia.[12]

During this period (1897-1903) the Greek government, unable to intervene openly on behalf of the Greeks in Macedonia, engaged in an unrewarding effort to improve its diplomatic position on the international scene as well as within the Balkans in order to counteract Bulgarian headway. One such attempt was a series of negotiations with Serbia in 1899 in an attempt to establish spheres of influence in Macedonia. Unfortunately the intervention of Russia, which stepped in to settle Serbia's differences with Bulgaria, upset this plan, although a Greek-Serbian rapprochement seems unlikely to have succeeded in any case. Generally speaking, Greek-Serbian co-habitation in northern Macedonia was anything but comfortable in the period 1898-1903, but conflict was restricted to religious and educational matters. Also unsuccessful was the attempt to approach Romania, despite a meeting between Kings George I of the Hellenes and Carol I of Romania. Although the Romanian government had accepted in 1898 that the likelihood of converting the Koutsovlachs was not great, and although the conclusion of a trade pact in 1900 set the stage for closer co-operation, nonetheless the two governments could not agree on explicit terms for a common position on Macedonia. Conversely, Greek-Turkish relations improved after 1900. Despite their enormous differences, Athens and the Porte did share one common interest: preservation of the *status quo* in Macedonia. For Greece, Turkish sovereignty in Macedonia was the only guarantee against the Slav danger. This realisation soon led Greece to a rapprochement with Germany, which was also anxious to see the Ottoman Empire remain intact. For Turkey, on the other hand, friendly relations with Greece were indispensable to guard against a Balkan coalition.[13]

Although the Greek state was unable actively to promote and defend its positions on Macedonia, it was ably seconded at this critical juncture by private initiatives. After the dissolution of the *Ethniki Etaireia*, a number of uneasy patriots, not only of Macedonian origin, swelled the ranks of a variety of associations. Their role was to alert and enlighten public opinion in Greece, and to co-ordinate the defence of Greek Macedonia. Some of these societies were: Theocharis Gerogiannis' 'Central Macedonian Society', Stephanos Dra-goumis' 'Macedonian Society', Neoklis Kazazis' 'Hellenism Society', and later, in 1903, the Archbishop

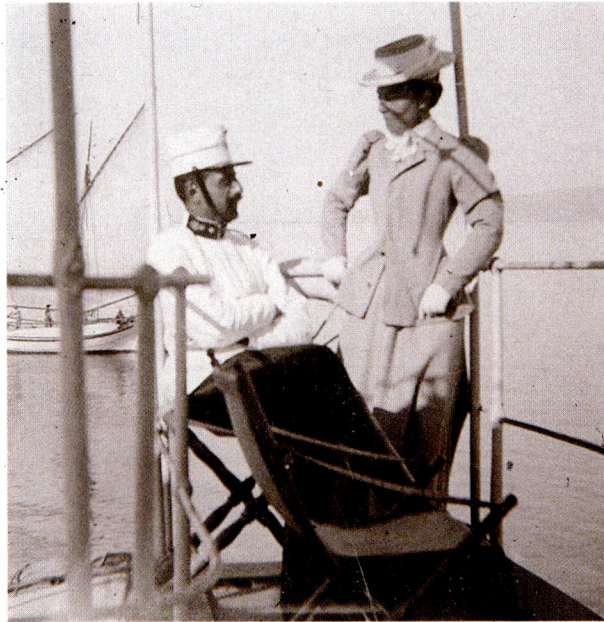

Pavlos Melas and his wife.

of Athens' 'Committee for Succour for the Macedonians'. Of similar outlook was the 'Committee for the Support of Greek Church and Education', which functioned under the aegis of the Foreign Ministry. Its most active members were Dimitrios Vikelas, Georgios Streit and Georgios Baltatzis, and it essentially replaced the 'Society for the Dissemination of Greek Letters' in educational activity in Macedonia. Especially in the period immediately after 1900 this committee's financial support increased dramatically. Significant work in education was also performed by the 'Greek Literary Society' and the 'Macedonian Educational Fraternity of Constantinople'. Moreover, the numerous societies and fraternities which had sprung up during the 1870s in virtually all urban and semi-urban centres in Macedonia continued their efforts for the improvement and the spread of education, It is worth noting that at the beginning of the 20th century the Greek population of Macedonia boasted more than 1,000 schools with approximately 70,000 pupils.[14]

Significant work was also undertaken in the period after 1900 by the Church, that is, by the Patriarchate of Constantinople, which abandoned its defensive strategy in favour of a policy of re-conquest. In order to achieve this it was essential to replace certain metropolitans who, whether from lack of enthusiasm or from excessive devotion to the ideal of the 'Great Church' (which after

Germanos Karavangelis.

these troops rarely came into open conflict with IMRO (except during the Ilinden uprising when some units directly confronted the revolutionary forces) they nevertheless served to guard the Patriarchist villages, and did succeed in causing some people to turn away from the Exarchists.[16]

In November 1902 Karavangelis acquired a worthy adjutant in the person of Ion Dragoumis, the son of Stephanos, who at his own request was posted to Monastir as vice-consul, where his activities far exceeded his sphere of competence. In Monastir the young diplomat founded an association called *'Amyna'* (Defence), which quickly became active in most of the principal towns and villages in Western Macedonia. Its purpose was to set up an information network and to intimidate the Bulgarians. Similar defensive organizations were established in Gevgeli, Yenitsa, Naousa, Thessaloniki and elsewhere. At this time veterans of the *Ethniki Etaireia* were beginning to pour arms into Macedonia through the good offices of certain officers in the Army Cartographic Service in Thessaly. Indeed, in response to Kara-

Georgios Dikonymos-Makris.

the catastrophe of 1897 was completely unrealistic), were unable to cope with the demands of the national struggle. They were replaced by active young prelates who were in their prime during the period of armed struggle, among them Metropolitans Germanos Karavangelis of Kastoria, Chrysostomos Kalaphatis of Drama, and Ioakeim Phoropoulos of Melenikon.[15]

But the activities of paedagogues and churchmen, the guarded diplomatic efforts of the Greek government and the less than remarkable abilities of many of those in the diplomatic service were unlikely to alter the balance of power in the Balkans, which was so unfavourable to Greece, unless they adopted some more energetic forms of action. The ambassador to Constantinople, Nikolaos Mavrokordatos, had indicated to the Foreign Ministry as early as January 1900 that the use of force was a matter of unassailable urgency; but the initiative behind the application of such measures was taken by Germanos Karavangelis, in the very year he was elevated to the metropolitan throne of Kastoria. Karavangelis soon inclined towards the formation of an armed corps, and more specifically towards making use of Kota, who had already quarrelled with IMRO. He also turned to other guerrilla leaders, such as Vangelis of Strebeno (Aspro-geia), Karalivanos and Georgis of Negovani (Phlam-pouron), and his irresistible personality ensured that his efforts were crowned with success. Although the first of

vangelis' constant pleas for more substantial aid, the first armed band was sent to Macedonia in May 1903 by colleagues of Stephanos Dragoumis. It consisted of eleven Cretans, including Euthymios Kaoudis and Georgios Dikonymos-Makris, and it saw action against IMRO forces on the very first day of the Ilinden Uprising. Its eventual escape to Greece was only accomplished by the personal intervention of Karavangelis.[17]

2. From the Mürzteg Agreement to the Young Turk Revolution

As we have seen, the bloodshed which followed the suppression of the Ilinden Uprising once again focused international attention on the Macedonian Question. By the end of August 1903, it had become obvious that the Vienna reform programme had failed. Great Britain had early proposed a series of modifications, but the substantial revision of the programme was the result of a joint Russo-Austro-Hungarian initiative. In September 1903 the two emperors met at the Styrian city of Mürzteg. The new schedule of reforms drawn up by their Foreign Ministers was submitted to the Porte at the end of October, and one month later had been agreed in full, despite the initial reservations of the other Great Powers and Turkish attempts to reach an understanding with the Bulgarian Principality. The Porte was left with no alternative but to accept the proposals, reserving only the right to negotiate the manner of their implementation.

The principal aims of the Mürzteg agreement were the restoration of order, the reparation of damages resulting from the insurrection, and the application of the reforms agreed in the Vienna programme. Particular importance was also assigned to reinforcing the European presence in Macedonia, which was deemed of fundamental importance for its eventual success. Provision was thus made for: 1) two political advisors and liaison officers, one Russian and one Austrian, with appropriate staff, to assist Hilmi Pasha; 2) reorganization of the gendarmerie with officers and NCOs supplied by the Great Powers; 3) re-drawing the borders of the administrative districts to reflect as far as possible ethnographic distribution; 4) reorganization of the administration and justice systems with a view to decentralization and the employment of Christians; 5) the appointment of joint commissions of investigation for political and other crimes; 6) financial aid to the ravaged areas and repatriation of refugees from Bulgaria; 7) annual tax relief for the devastated villages; 8)

Lambros Koromilas.

immediate implementation of the Vienna reform programme, and 9) the disbanding of all irregular military units.[18]

While the Great Powers were working for peace in Macedonia, the Greek government was beginning to give serious attention to the question of more dynamic and vigorous intervention in that region. The demonstration organized by the Macedonian societies on 15 August in protest against the brutality of the Turkish army had aroused public opinion and awakened the government to a sense of its tremendous responsibilities. The first decision was to proceed to a survey of Macedonia in order to ascertain whether an armed defence system could be installed. For this purpose a committee of army officers was dispatched to Western Macedonia in February 1904 (Anastasios Papoulas, Alexandros Kontoulis, Georgios Kolo-kotronis and Pavlos Melas), while the preparatory work for the other regions was undertaken by the interpreter at the Embassy in Constantinople, Georgios Tsorbatzoglou. By the summer of 1904 their work had been completed, but their

Dimitrios Kalapothakis, editor of "Embros"
and president of the Macedonian Committee

reports and proposals did not concur in any detail.

Although action had to be delayed, the machinery had nevertheless been set in motion. During the spring of 1904 the Foreign Ministry had begun to reorganize its consular representation in Macedonia. Dimitrios Kallergis was named consul in Monastir, and Lampros Koromilas was sent to Thessaloniki as Consul General; while at the same time the Foreign Ministry dispatched a group of officers to serve in the Greek consulates and vice-consulates in Macedonia. Further, in May 1904 some former members of the *Ethniki Etaireia* founded the 'Macedonian Committee', with the editor of the newspaper *Empros*, Dimitrios Kalapothakis, as its chairman. Its purpose was "...the defence of Hellenism in Macedonia, Thrace, Epirus and Albania against any attempt to diminish it, and the restoration to its bosom of however many villages and individuals have against their will been severed from us and against their will remain severed". Its charter indicates that right from the beginning the Committee undertook a wide range of activities, not only in reconnaissance and propaganda

but also in the funding, initiating, recruiting and initial organization of various bodies.

Barely four years after the dissolution of the *Ethniki Etaireia* the Greek government greeted with relief the resurgence of private initiative, which both satisfied the need for immediate action and served as cover to the state. It was obvious from the beginning, however, that complications were bound to ensue if activities were carried on by both the state and private persons at the same time. The Committee was assigned the *vilayet* of Monastir as its sphere of activity, while the Foreign Ministry assumed responsibility for the *vilayet* of Thessaloniki. In practice, however, the interests and the ambitions of the two bodies ranged far beyond the borders of their respective provinces, and in the years that followed the co-ordination of the struggle and the allotment of men and material were anything but smooth.[19]

While Greece was about this preparatory ground-work, the Bulgarian bands were not wasting their time either. The IMRO had, despite the disasters, managed to save a large part of its arms and explosives, although it was, of course, much less active than it had been in 1903. Although Hilmi Pasha wanted to believe that this was due to the implementation of the reform programme, a more correct interpretation would probably be that IMRO did not wish openly to undermine the reform and thus provoke the displeasure of the Great Powers. Indeed, the gendarmerie was still in the process of reorganization and so did not constitute a serious threat; it was merely serving as a sort of *locum tenens* for the interests of the Great Powers, while the work of suppressing the activity of the bands remained the responsibility of the army. Furthermore, the calm which had prevailed since the Bulgaro-Turkish rapprochement in April 1904 (and which had been condemned by the Bulgarian committees) was if anything favourable to IMRO, for it provided for a general amnesty for those arrested after the Ilinden uprising and the repatriation of refugees.

In any case, the IMRO units were by now chiefly devoted to seeking to convert the Slavophones to the Exarchate; skirmishes with the army were rare. It was this new atmosphere that inspired the ambush which resulted in the assassination of Kapetan Vangelis of Strebeno in May 1904. A few months later, a series of misunderstandings culminated in the betrayal of Kota to the Turks; he was tried, sentenced and executed in the autumn of 1905. The void left by the loss of these two traditional chieftains, who had been the leaders of the struggle in Western Macedonia, a renewal of activity on the part of certain Serbian guerrilla bands in the north, and the new dangers arising out of Bulgaro-Romanian collaboration, that is, the adherence to the Exarchate of a significant number of villages in the median and northern zones, all contributed to render the dispatch north of Greek troops a matter of urgency.[20]

By the end of July 1904 Athens had been convinced that the dispatch of armed men to Macedonia could no longer be delayed. In mid August three units made ready (under Georgios Bolas, Pantelis Kokkinos, and Euthymios Kaoudis) and crossed the border, but only the last was able to take any effective action. Towards the end of the month it was reinforced by the unit led by Pavlos Melas (Zezas), but it achieved little. Melas was a polite and obliging person, an idealistic and easily moved patriot; but, although perfectly willing to adopt the forms of the invaluable klephtic traditions, he was essentially unable to accept the savage rules of this unorthodox form of warfare, and so it was not long before he became a tragic hero. The letter he wrote to his wife ten days before his fatal encounter with the Turks is typical of him: "I

Pavlos Melas' tomb in a contemporary photograph.

Kapetan Kotas.

had hoped for much, but the people here are terrified of the murdering *komitadjis* and for that reason do not help us as much as they should... They are willing and full of good intentions, and they come to me and enthusiastically propose all sorts of fine schemes. Poor me! I make my plans, I set off –cold, wet, hungry– and when the moment arrives either they do not come or they trick me in every possible way or they warn the Bulgarians to hide... I could have punished them, but I preferred to speak to them logically, sternly, movingly".[21]

Melas' death led to a redoubling of activity in Athens. A few days later the unit led by Georgios Katechakis (Rouvas) crossed the border, followed in mid November by that of Georgios Tsontos (Vardas). These two groups, together with Kaoudis' men, struck the first major blows at IMRO, thus restoring Greek prestige in the eyes of the people of Western Macedonia. Progress was also made in the *vilayet* of Thessaloniki under the systematic leadership of Lampros Koromilas and a group of officers who had at intervals been assigned to the Consulate in Thessaloniki (Georgios Kakoulidis, Michail Moraitis, Konstantinos Mazarakis, Athanasios Exadaktylos, Spyros Spyromilios, Dimitrios Kakkavos, and Ioannis Avrasoglou). Before the end of 1904 several units, formed mainly of local men and Cretans, had already made their presence felt both in Central and in Eastern Macedonia.[22]

Winter put a temporary halt to hostilities, but preparations for the spring campaign began early in 1905 when Konstantinos Mazarakis journeyed to Athens on behalf of Koromilas. He pressed for unification of leadership under the Consul General in Thessaloniki, arguing the weaknesses of the Macedonian Committee, its spasmodic bouts of activity and problems of co-ordination. But by now the Committee enjoyed too much political patronage and sufficiently high prestige to suffer any restrictions to its activities, and it thus continued to control the course of the Struggle in the *vilayet* of Monastir.[23]

*Georgios Katechakis
(Kapetan Rouvas).*

Mazarakis was more successful in recruiting fresh forces. Indeed, on the Greek side 1905 was marked by intensive military activity. By May there were around nine major units campaigning in the *vilayet* of Thessaloniki, more than twelve in that of Monastir, and a host of smaller bands, mostly recruited locally, which carried out secondary missions. They had also managed to collect an impressive supply of arms and ammunition.

The most significant military event of that year was the assault on March 25 (April 7, New Style) on the overwhelmingly Exarchist village of Zagoritsani (Vasileiada), by a force of 300 men under Georgios Tsontos. The plan to encircle the village worked perfectly; and not only did Tsontos' men crush all resistance (some 79 villagers were killed), but they also repulsed a Turkish attack at the same time. One month later the units led by Georgios Katechakis, Petros Manou (Vergas), and Pavlos Gyparis successfully repulsed a massive Turkish attack near Blatsi (Oxyes). Less fortunate were the men of Nikostratos Kalo-menopoulos (Nidas) and Christos Tsolakopoulos (Rebelos), who at about the same period were entrapped by Turkish forces at Belkameni (Drosopigi) and suffered heavy losses. But in general the weight of the campaign in Western Macedonia was shouldered by Konstantinos Mazarakis (Akritas), Spyros Spyromilios (Bouas), and Manolis Katsigaris and their men; and despite betrayals from pro-Romanian Vlachs and many reverses, they were extremely success-

ful in increasing support for the Greeks in the areas around Prilep, Monastir, Kastoria and Edessa. IMRO activity had in the meantime slackened, both because of the organization's differences with the Supreme Macedonian Committee and because the Bulgarian government was trying to suppress any activity which might endanger its good relations with the Porte.

In Central Macedonia there was less actual fighting, but tremendous efforts were made (and seconded by the local guerrilla leaders) to organize the defence of the villages and to create bases in the marshes around Giannitsa. In Eastern Macedonia the struggle was less successful. After Turkish forces had exterminated Ioannis Daphotis' band, Greek resistance was left entirely in the hands of local units, and unfortunately their opponent was the extremely capable Sadanski. In northern Macedonia the Serbian bands were continuing to preach their cause and to fight their battles, whether with Bulgarian or Turco-Albanian bands or with the Turkish army.[24]

The Greek, Bulgarian and Serbian guerrilla bands usually avoided frontal attacks, which were counterproductive for two reasons: they wasted men, and they generally provoked the intervention of the Turkish army, usually with unpleasant consequences. All the parties were principally interested in converting to their cause any person or village that may have displayed a certain fickleness of national attachment. Their methods, of course, were anything but peaceful. The tragic death of Pavlos Melas and the frequent betrayals and denunciations had put an end to the era of peaceful propaganda. The only guaranteed method of shaking or altering people's beliefs was systematic terrorism: arson, assassination of priests and civil leaders, blackmail and brutality of every kind were now commonplace. Other strategically important targets were the adversary's communication networks and support systems; this was a major source of conflict between the Greek bands and pro-Romanian Koutsovlachs throughout 1905. Indicative of the savagery of the struggle, especially in Western Macedonia, was the flood of emigration which began after the Ilinden uprising, although economic conditions should not be discounted. In 1905 alone some 5,500 men emigrated to America from the Monastir area, mainly from the Slav-speaking villages which were the object of heavy pressure from both sides.

The situation, meanwhile, had not escaped the attention of the Great Powers, which flooded Sofia, Athens and Belgrade with complaints of the guerrilla activity which was impeding implementation of the reform programme. The British government was particularly active throughout 1905: in its attempts to prevent Austria and Russia from being sole masters of developments in Macedonia it pressed for sterner measures and increased European presence in the European provinces of the Ottoman Empire. The combination of the opposition of the other powers and the opportunism of the Porte sufficed to modify and delay British plans, but nonetheless, between May and November 1905 a certain number of additions and modifications to the reform programme helped considerably to curtail Ottoman sovereignty in Macedonia.[25]

Generally speaking the military situation throughout 1906 was much what it had been the previous year. In Western Macedonia Antonios Vlachakis (Litsas) and Konstantinos Poulos (Platanos) with their men, along with a local band under Loukas Kokkinos, kept the front open through the winter months. The most significant battle of the year took place on New Year's Day, when Vlachakis and his men successfully attacked Mitros Vlachos and his band at Ezerets (Petropoulaki). In May reinforcements began to arrive for the summer campaign: Zacharias Papadas (Phouphas), Georgios Dikonymos-Makris, Georgios Volanis, Pavlos Gyparis,

Georgios Kanellopoulos, Vasileios Pappas (Vrontas), Grigorios Phalireas (Ziagas) etc., with fairly large numbers of men. Once again the Greek forces found themselves fighting mainly against Turkish troops. Early in May Vlachakis attacked the Exarchist village of Osnitsani (Kastanophyton), but he was counter-attacked by a Turkish battalion and forced to retreat, with severe losses. Towards the end of the month the bands led by Volanis, Gyparis and Kanellopoulos suffered heavy losses in an extremely bloody battle with à large Turkish force at Strebeno (Asprogeia); the same fate awaited Tsontos' band at Zelovo (Antartikon) in June, and those under Ioannis Karavitis and Evangelos Nikoloudis at Gornitsovo (Kelli) in July.

It is true that the massive presence of Turkish troops in Western Macedonia severely restricted the activities of the Greek guerrilla fighters, and to a certain extent inhibited the local population from supporting them. Nevertheless, such reverses are in no way indicative of what they actually accomplished in the *vilayet* of Monastir. The initiative now lay with the Greeks, who kept up their heavy pressure on the Bulgarian bands and attacked the principal *komitadjis* relentlessly. Severe damage was inflicted on the Romanian propaganda and espionage networks and on several bands of brigands. The attacks on Exarchist villages were continued, two of the most significant being those carried out by Konstantinos

Grigorios Phalireas and his band.

Goutas on Smilevo and Phalireas on Holista (Melis-sotopon). In other words, despite certain reverses the Greek position in Western Macedonia was strengthened, both in the countryside and in the town of Monastir.

It is however undeniable that the situation in Western Macedonia could have been even better for the Greeks if they had had a unified command. In principle, responsibility for this area belonged to the Macedonian Committee under Dimitrios Kala-pothakis, but in practice there was constant government interference, via the consulate in Monastir, both in funding and in campaign decisions. The problems caused by this dual leadership were extremely serious. A fierce battle for supremacy raged between the consular officials and the senior members of the Committee. The civil leaders of the Committee were opposed to responsibility for the Struggle being exclusively in the hands of the military; while as far as the officers were concerned, it was obvious that, given the tremendous problem of communications, operations over a constantly changing front could not possibly be conducted from Athens. Since neither side would yield, the result was that contradictory orders were issued, and that several undesirable local chieftains whose brigand activity could only embarrass the Committee, were drawn into the struggle, which then served to widen the abyss between the two sides.

The activity of the armed bands in Central and Eastern Macedonia under the aegis of the Consulate in Thessaloniki was more effective. Between May and November of 1906 about 30 raids were carried out on Exarchist villages, which enhanced Greek prestige immensely. Generally speaking, the conduct of the struggle was irreproachable, the flow of arms, men and money unimpeded, the selection of officers appropriate, discipline adequate and outrages infrequent. The systematic labours of Lampros Koromilas, who since the middle of the year had only occasionally appeared in his consulate in Thessaloniki, were bearing fruit. One of the most notable bands was that under Konstantinos Garephis, which in June 1906 completely annihilated the band led by voivode Danev, and early in August those of Karatasos and voyvod Luka. In this last battle Garephis was wounded, and he succumbed to his injuries soon afterwards. Meanwhile, the bands led by Nikolaos Rokas (Kolios) and Michail Anagnostakos (Matapas) were active against the brigands on Mt Olympus and Romanian propaganda in the area surrounding Edessa, Goumenissa and Mt Paiko, and progress was being made

in Eastern Macedonia under the guidance of the consulate in Serres. Three units patrolled the area, and civil guards were formed in various villages. Invaluable organizational assistance was provided by the Metropolitan of Drama, Chrysostomos. It should be remembered that in this region the Bulgarian party had to cope not only with Greek attacks but with the 'civil war' raging between the bands supported by the Supreme Committee and those of IMRO, while the only problem the Greeks faced in Central and Eastern Macedonia was that caused by the undisciplined behaviour of the men under Giaglis, a brigand chief enlisted by a Macedonian association in Athens called 'Alexander the Great'.

One of the most heroic pages in the story of the struggle for Macedonia was written in the marshes around Giannitsa. This area was traditionally the headquarters for the Bulgarian bands which roamed the territories of Edessa and Almopeia as well as the marsh villages. At the beginning of 1906 the Greek leaders in the marshes were Stavros Rigas (Kavodoros) and Michail Anagnostakos, who were reinforced in April by Panagiotis Papatzaneteas and Ioannis Sakellaropoulos (Zirias). Throughout the summer the Greeks tried unavailingly to dislodge the Bulgarians. When it was realized just how ideally the marsh was situated for controlling communications and the flow of arms, and in general for commanding all of Central Macedonia, fresh forces were sent out in September 1906 in order to redouble activity in this area. The bands led by Telos Agapinos (Agras), Konstantinos Sarros (Kalas) and Ioannis Demestichas (Nikiphoros) did indeed reinforce the Greek positions, but despite repeated attempts they fell short of dealing a decisive blow on the Bulgarian forces. It should be noted that besides the unwillingness of the Bulgarians to fight when they were outnumbered, operations in the marshes were further hindered by the frequent changes in leadership occasioned by malaria.

Within the city of Thessaloniki the Greek counter-attack was identified with the organizational efforts of second lieutenant Athanasios Souliotis (Nikolaidis). Souliotis was posted to Thessaloniki in March 1906, where, under the cover of a commercial agency, he very soon set up an extremely efficient network called the Organization of Thessaloniki. Its purpose was to collect information on Exarchist activity in the city, but his own activities did not end there. Between 1906 and 1908 he managed to reinforce the Greek presence in the city,

Kapetans *Kalas, Agras and Nikiphoros in the marshes of Giannitsa.*

strengthen the solidarity of the Greek community, organize a small scale economic war and terrorize the Exarchists to the greatest possible degree.[26]

An overall evaluation of military operations shows that in 1906 the situation in Macedonia had begun to favour the Greeks. The great number of active bands (more than 80 bands and 1500 men are mentioned during the summer of 1906) restored a significant number of schismatic villages to the Patriarchate. Also important is the fact that Greek losses to the Turks were far less than those of the Bulgarians, who were the Turkish army's chief target. This period also saw renewed efforts in the field of education, with the creation of nursery and primary schools in the villages which had recently been recovered. The work of the Foreign Ministry and the Committee for the Support of Greek Education and the Greek Church was supported by the Society for the Dissemination of Greek Letters and the Melas Nursery Trust.[27]

As was only to be expected, the growth of the Greek bands and their frequent clashes with the Turkish armed forces caused the Great Powers to redouble their protests to the Greek government. Incessant strife in Macedonia was hindering the implementation of the reform programme, in spite of all the efforts being made. The flow of emigration continued, and the large landowners were unable to pay their taxes, just when the local budget had to meet the extra expense incurred by the reorganization of the gendarmerie. The Porte requested that import duties be increased from 8% to 11% in order to offset the additional costs; this was nothing less than an attempt to blackmail the Great Powers into sharing the cost of

the reforms. It was quite predictable, then, that pressure would next be put on the Greek government. The latter tried to draw the attention of the powers to Bulgarian atrocities in Macedonia, but was in the end obliged to agree to impose restraints and to check the formation of armed bands and the sale of arms. These measures were never implemented, of course, because it was obvious that the Porte did not want an open confrontation with Greece which essentially would be of benefit only to the Bulgarian Principality. On the contrary, the fact that Greek and Serbian forces were occupied with the Bulgarian rebels, at a time when their activities were becoming steadily more alarming, was all to the Turks' advantage. Meanwhile, relations between Bulgaria and the Great Powers had improved. Despite unremitting protestations from the Porte, the Europeans were nevertheless convinced that the Bulgarian government was doing all it could to control and direct the bands. Prince Ferdinand of Bulgaria, in an attempt to exploit the friendly climate, went so far as to propose including in the discussions on the Cretan Question a similar settlement for Macedonia.[28]

After the inevitable halt over the winter months, in the spring of 1907 guerrilla activity resumed on all fronts, once again drawing out the Turkish forces. In the Morihovo region the bands led by Vasileios Pappas (Vrontas), Georgios Kondylis (Zagas), Philolaos Pichion (Philotas), Dimitrios Papavierou (Gouras) and Manolis Katsigaris continued to organize the defence of the villages and harry the Bulgarian bands. In the Kastoria-Kastanochoria region Phalireas and Zacharias Papadas (Phouphas) were very active; the latter unfor-

Officers Al. Mazarakis, Kyr. Tavoularis, Kourvelis, Kourkoulis and Exadaktylos in the garden of the Greek Consulate in Thessaloniki.

tunately was killed in April of that year in an unsuccessful raid on Palaiochori (Phoupha). Tsontas was fighting in the sector comprising Florina, Monastir, Prespes and Korestia; his attacks on the villages of Kalenik (Kalliniki) in April and Ostima (Trigonon) in June were successful, while in July, at Grentsi (Phtelia), Georgios Tompras (Roupakias) destroyed the band led by voyvod Karsakov.

Action in Central Macedonia was co-ordinated from Thessaloniki by Athanasios Exadaktylos, Dimitrios Kakkavos and Kyriakos Tavoularis (Katsanos), and later Andreas Kourouklis (Kolyvas) and Alexandros Othonaios (Palmidis). The struggle in the marshes of Giannitsa continued relentlessly all winter, despite the exceptionally severe weather. In the spring Demestichas and his band undertook impressive campaigns in the surrounding area, including important raids on Bozets (Athyra) and Kouphalia in March. Fighting in this region came to an end the following month, however, when Turkish operations drove both the Greeks and the Bulgarians out of the marshes. Meanwhile, Dimitris Kosmopoulos (Kourbesis) managed to keep the Bulgarians in check in Chalcidice.

The progress of the Greek national forces was less spectacular in Eastern Macedonia. The imprisonment of cavalry lieutenant Dimitrios Vardis, the removal of the metropolitan of Drama, Chrysostomos and the vice-consul of Kavala, the restrictions placed on the free movement of the metropolitan of Serres, Grigorios, and the consul, Antonios Sachtouris, were so many checks; some local units did nonetheless continue their raids on a small scale, and a remarkable number of villages were recovered for the Patriarchate.

Of course, as happened every year, there were clashes with Turkish troops which were usually catastrophic for the Greeks. In June the bands led by Phalireas, Tompras and Papavierou encountered a large Turkish force outside Lehovo, but they managed to avoid encirclement and to inflict serious losses. Phalireas was less fortunate one month later when his band, along with that led by Nikolaos Tsotakos (Germas), was trapped in the Kalogeriko gorge near Losnitsa (Germa) and decimated: only eight men (including Phalireas) managed to escape. That same month the band led by Andreas Makoulis (a chieftain from Stenimachos) was annihilated at Dovista, and in August another chieftain, Pantelis Papaioannou, or Graikos, was killed in a skirmish with a strong Turkish detachment near Stromnitsa.

Nor were things were easier for the Bulgarians that year. Not only were they being incessantly and severely pounded by Greek and Serbian units, but there was no respite in the friction between IMRO and the Supreme Macedonian Committee, friction which often flared into open conflict and to which Sarafov himself fell a victim. After the death of Gruev, however, the influence of the Supreme Committee within IMRO increased sharply.

Large numbers of local chieftains, dismayed at IMRO's collapse, began to attach themselves to the Greek party, while continued emigration to the New World curtailed recruitment from among the peasants. In the course of such negotiations Agras fell into an ambush, and was hanged near Edessa. Then too, especially in Western Macedonia, a considerable number of the leading *komitadjis* were eliminated, whether by Greek or by Turkish forces, leaving a gap which was very hard to fill.

These developments in Macedonia were anything but encouraging for Bulgaria's foreign policy, which slowly began to become more conciliatory. The Greek government, on the other hand, continued all through 1907 to be swamped by protests from Turkey and the Great Powers, especially Great Britain. Despite all the nimble manoeuvring by Foreign Minister Alexandros Skouzes, it was evident that Greece had neither the desire nor the power to check the activities of the various bodies in Macedonia. In the summer of 1907 the Theotokis government tried to deflect the menace of diplomatic isolation which was hanging over his country by proposing an alliance with Great Britain and France, but his efforts came to nothing. When in September 1907 Russia and Austria-Hungary joined Britain and Turkey in their league against Greece, it was no longer possible to ignore the pressure, and the Theotokis government proclaimed abatement of Greek efforts in Macedonia a matter of necessity. The Foreign Ministry, on the other hand, began to pay more serious attention to identifying and solving chronic problems in education, such as subject matter, curriculum, teachers' qualifications, inspection, etc.[29]

Curtailing military activity, however, was only one aspect of the problem. The divergence between the Committee and the consulate in Thessaloniki had developed into an open breach. The final removal of Koromilas, in response to Turkish pressures, and his posting to the United States, did facilitate matters, as he had been the Committee's principal vindicator. It appears that the Theotokis government even considered conceding direct responsibility in both *vilayets* to the Committee, which would certainly have improved its position *vis-à-vis* the Great Powers. The officers attached to the consulate in Thessaloniki, however, had a different point of view. Besides their objections to certain plans of action and their solid scorn for politicians and journalists who gave orders from afar, these officers felt embittered by the partiality displayed by the Com-

Theodoros Askitis, interpreter at the Greek Consulate in Thessaloniki. He was assassinated in 1908.

mittee, which had often led to able officers being passed over. The officers attached to the centre in Thessaloniki did not want to oppose the government's wishes completely, and so an alternative solution was proposed: that Colonel Panagiotis Daglis be named head of this new section.

Indeed, in mid February 1908, Daglis was summoned to assume the direction of the eastern division, with full powers and with the mandate to reconcile the Committee and the officers. In the meanwhile, during the course of the winter, the dwindling away of the Greek guerrillas and the increased activity of the Bulgarians had created serious problems. Bulgarian enterprise reached its climax with the murder on February 22 of Theodoros Askitis, the interpreter attached to the consulate in Thessaloniki. With the arrival of Greek reinforcements in the early weeks of the spring and their resumption of the offensive, the losses were no longer so one-sided; and in any case, with the exception of the Serres region, the fighting was not as frequent as it had been in previous years. Despite all the problems he had to face and his repeated requests to resign his post, Daglis was able to maintain Greek support in Macedonia unabated at a very critical juncture. Because of the pressure exerted by the Committee, however, and despite the support of the officers attached to his sector, he was unable to establish a paramilitary service answerable only to the government and the Army High Command; for this reason he refused all responsibility for the actions of the Committee and ceased to attend its meetings.[30]

3. From the Young Turks to the First Balkan War

The success of the Young Turk Revolution created a whole new situation in Macedonia. After the rebellion of the 3rd and the 2nd Army Corps and the complete ascendancy of the paramilitary Committee of Union and Progress, Sultan Abdul Hamid II was forced on 11 July 1908 to promise a constitution and grant an amnesty. The result was that the vast majority of the amnestied rebels moved into the cities, and the Bulgarian and Greek bands disintegrated. By the end of the month 26 Greek bands with a total of 217 men, 55 Bulgarian bands (707 men), and 340 Albanian brigand fugitives had definitively laid down their arms.[31]

This new state of affairs coupled with the imminence of elections for the Ottoman parliament quickly transformed the former guerrilla chiefs into party leaders. Vlahov, Sadanski and Panicha's short-lived Federal People's Party held its constituent assembly on August 15 1908 in Thessaloniki. Although Sadanski wanted Macedonia to rebel and declare its independence immediately, the party eventually adopted a more conciliatory stance, though one still befitting the radical socialism which distinguished it. Its demands included: administrative decentralization and autonomy, no discrimination against religious minorities, nationalization of mines and railways, compulsory education, universal franchise, and the redistribution of large estates. It proved more difficult for the remaining members of IMRO to agree on a common platform. After extensive discussions on the local level, a congress met in September in Thessaloniki which proposed the following: revision of the constitution based on the primacy of national rights, freedom of conscience, press and educa-

tion, provincial parliaments, preservation of religious privileges, changes to the electoral law, reform of the justice system, etc. The Greek party presented a united front. In its memorandum the Greek community in Thessaloniki urged a variety of economic, administrative and legal reforms, and stressed the necessity both for the Greek community to remain a distinct society and for the Patriarchate to retain its prerogatives untouched. It was evident that neither the Greeks nor the Bulgarians were disposed to forget the religious aspect of their struggle and allow themselves to be swallowed up in the racial equality proclaimed by the Young Turks.[32]

For the Greek government, the establishment of a strong constitutional regime in Turkey signalled the end of the immediate threat of a premature collapse which might have found the Greek army unprepared to take advantage of the opportunity thus presented. On the other hand, however, it was by no means certain that the gains in Macedonia would be pre-served once the Greek bands were no longer there. On the contrary, it was extremely doubtful that the Greek population could survive guarded only by peaceful means. Moreover, it soon appeared that IMRO was determined to exploit the situation to its own advantage. In August it began to re-arm the Exarchist peasants and to step up propaganda; meanwhile, many of the *komitadjis* who had been held in Turkish prisons were released. By October the local bands had resumed their activities.

By now the creation of an organization in the European provinces of the Ottoman Empire, at least in those where Greece had vital interests, was a matter of considerable urgency. Agents such as Ion Dragoumis, Athanasios Souliotis and Panagiotis Daglis were sounding the alarm, and eventually they convinced the Foreign Minister Georgios Baltatzis of the necessity of this step. And so was founded the Panhellenic Organization, a paramilitary service under the direction of Daglis which set up special offices to furnish arms and economic support to the Greek population and to undertake nationalist propaganda. Some 75 officers and NCOs, all reliable veterans of the Struggle, joined its ranks and offered their services either as consular employees and agents or military leaders.

The work of the organization, however, did not proceed unimpeded. In the Epirus sector the parallel activity of the Epirotic Society caused serious misunderstandings. In Constantinople the Constantinople Society, founded by Dragoumis and Souliotis, did what it could to preserve its autonomy. Finally, in Macedonia, Kalapothakis' Committee continued unremittingly to undermine Daglis and his work in an attempt to avenge its supersession. Additional problems were created by the dissatisfaction of many members at the unfair and limited rewards offered to the veterans. The major obstacle, however, was the steady pressure from the Young Turks for the removal of all Greek officers, pressure which, after the publication of certain compromising letters about Greek activity in Macedonia, became an unveiled threat of war. Early in the summer the Theotokis government, anxious to avoid an inopportune clash with the new regime, pushed forward a scheme to strip all the special offices of the Organization in the Monastir area. A few weeks later the government of Dimitrios Rallis, in an attempt to defuse a new crisis of the Cretan Question, ordered and effected the removal of all officers and NCOs from Macedonia. The return of all these disgruntled soldiers, who had seen their activities curtailed and all they had fought for years thrown away, accelerated the process which culminated in the coup at Goudi and the fall of the Rallis government. The Panhellenic Organization was itself formally dissolved in November 1909.[33]

In the meanwhile, the situation in Macedonia had changed after the disappointment of the elections and the sultan's coup in March 1909. While the Greek officers were being withdrawn, the Young Turks were hardening their stand. In July 1909 a parliamentary resolution put an end to the activity of the civilian nationalist societies. As the interventions of the Great Powers lessened, the high-handedness of the Young Turks increased. The intensification of Turkish nationalism provoked IMRO to fresh activity, in order to excite European interest. In the autumn of 1910, in their attempt to bring IMRO to heel, the Turks even made use of Sadanski and his men, who at that time were preaching autonomy for Macedonia within the Ottoman Empire. The battles between IMRO and the army continued all through 1911 and 1912. It seems too that Austria-Hungary took a hand in the game at this point, with support for the Bulgarian bands. The situation worsened sharply after the Albanian rebellion in 1912 and Albanian collaboration with the Bulgarian bands in the Monastir area. In view of this generalization of the fighting, armed bands began to assemble in Greece in August 1912, and, under the command of Anagnostakis, Papatzaneteas, Alexandros Zannas and others, they crossed into Macedonia late in

September. These new arrivals not only facilitated the operations of the regular army but also conducted operations of their own in several areas around Chalcidice, Nigrita and Pravi (Eleutheroupolis).[34]

In conclusion one could say that the military activities of both the Greeks and the Bulgarians in Macedonia were organized to the same pattern, adapted to the current political necessity and the demands of a peculiar and unorthodox war. Fear of an unexpected martial confrontation with the Ottoman Empire in an exceptionally uncertain diplomatic context induced both countries to pursue a fairly discreet policy, if one overlooks the situation in Macedonia. This policy, of course, favoured the formation of patriotic committees, which took over the irredentist campaigns of both countries. Although the activity of these committees certainly served the long term interests of both the Bulgarians and the Greeks, co-operation between government and individual nevertheless proved exceptionally difficult and often imperilled the outcome of the national enterprise. The soaring prestige of irredentism in the young Balkan states and its corresponding political support lent the committees such power and prestige that the legitimate governments hesitated to curb them, even though they held their purse strings.

Irredentism without the support of the military was of course impossible. Both the Bulgarian Principality and the Kingdom of Greece had a surfeit of officers eager to abandon the inactivity of the barracks and seek glory, honours and dignities, to write pages of heroism and self-sacrifice, and at the same time to seek to advance their own future. Their bands were composed not only of Macedonian refugees and seasonal labourers, but also of volunteers from many places, often fellow villagers from their own villages. Greece also had an exceptionally effective militia in its border guards, who were always ready for a raid on their neighbour.

Even more important than the contribution of the officers was that made by the local chieftains, brigands and nomads. Survival in an unfamiliar mountain area, in exceptionally severe weather conditions, and at the same time to prosecute the struggle on many fronts was impossible for any corps, Bulgarian or Greek. First the Bulgarians and then the Greeks realized that the affiliation of local brigand bands would confer an enormous advantage. Thus, a considerable number of brigand bands were enlisted in this national conflict, reinforcing the units with men in fine fighting condition, passing on

Celebrations in the streets of Thessaloniki
on the occasion of the Young Turks' proclamation
of the Constitution in 1909.

their invaluable experience of guerrilla warfare, and keeping the front open throughout the winter. Of course, the engagement of these traditional rejecters of law and order could often get out of hand. Many of them were unable to abandon their old habits: they robbed, they made deals with the enemy, and their activities often jeopardized the efforts of the Greek and Bulgarian nationalists in the eyes of the local population. This also explains the frequent clashes between the brigands and the guerrillas. In any event, the importance of the brigands became particularly obvious when they began gradually to abandon IMRO in its decay and adhere to the Greek party.

Equally important was the employment of the nomads. Their assistance was essential for bivouacking, succouring the wounded, marching, provisioning, and helping whatever units had the courage to brave the severe Western Macedonian winter to see it through. They were also invaluable in collecting and passing on information in a struggle where early information and precise knowledge of the ground could be decisive. This was why raids on nomad camps were not infrequent: their perpetrators were assured of supplies at no cost while at the same time paralysing their opponents' support system.

As far as operations were concerned, Greek and Bulgarian methods were identical. They relied on eliminating their opponents' informers, organizing civil guards to defend their villages, severe reprisals against villages, terrorism against individuals, especially local notables, teachers and priests, betrayal of enemy bands to the Turkish authorities and blockading certain sensitive areas. Open battles between Greek and Bulgarian bands were rare all during the struggle, much rarer than those with Turkish forces.[35]

Despite all the similarities between the conduct of the Greek and Bulgarian bands, there was one essential difference which effectively decided the struggle for supremacy in Macedonia. The Greek side had the overwhelming majority of the local population behind them, and an extremely vigorous system of education. This essentially was what enabled the Greeks, within a short space of time, to organize their defences, consolidate their support, neutralize Bulgarian operations over a lengthy period, and counter-attack decisively and victoriously.

BASIL K. GOUNARIS
THE MACEDONIAN STRUGGLE
1903-1912 PAVING THE WAY
FOR LIBERATION
NOTES

1. K. I. Mazarakis-Ainian, 'The Macedonian Struggle, Reminiscences', in *The Macedonian Struggle, Memoirs* (in Greek), Thessaloniki 1984, pp. 175-176; Pavlos L. Tsamis, *The Macedonian Struggle* (in Greek), Thessaloniki 1975, p. 69.

2. Douglas Dakin, *The Greek Struggle in Macedonia, 1897-1913*, Thessaloniki 1966, pp. 48-49, 55.

3. Konstantinos A. Vakalopoulos, *Macedonia on the Eve of the Macedonian Struggle, 1894-1904* (in Greek), Thessaloniki 1986, pp. 56-58.

4. Vakalopoulos, *op. cit.*, pp. 135-146; Dakin *op. cit.*, pp. 61-62.

5. Vakalopoulos, *op. cit.*, p. 151; Dakin, *op. cit.*, pp. 62-63.

6. Nikolaos Vlachos, *The Macedonian Struggle as a Phase of the Eastern Question, 1878-1908* (in Greek), Athens 1935, p. 161.

7. Dakin, *op. cit.*, pp. 65-81.

8. Vlachos, *op. cit.*, pp. 77-86.

9. *Ibid.*, pp. 146-152, 240.

10. *Ibid.*, pp. 253-261; Dakin, *op. cit.*, pp. 86-91.

11. Dakin, *op. cit.*, pp. 92-94; Vakalopoulos, *op. cit.*, pp. 197-208.

12. Dakin, *op. cit.*, pp. 92-106; Vakalopoulos, *op. cit.*, pp. 208-214; E. Kofos, 'Liberation Struggles', in *Macedonia: 4000 Years of Greek History and Civilization* (in Greek), Athens 1982, pp. 471-472.

13. Dakin, *op. cit.*, pp. 83-85; Vakalopoulos, *op. cit.*, pp. 239-256; Vlachos, *op. cit.*, pp. 186-190, 198-201.

14. Army General Staff/Army History Directorate (AGS/AHD), *The Macedonian Struggle and Events in Thrace* (in Greek), Athens 1979, pp. 125-126; Kofos, 'Struggles', p. 471; K.Th. Dimaras, 'Spiritual Life', from *Macedonia: 4000 Years of History and Civilization*, p. 493; Eleni Belia, 'The Educational Policy of the Greek State in Macedonia and the Macedonian Struggle', in *Proceedings of the Symposium on the Macedonian Struggle* (in Greek), pp. 32-33; Dakin, *op. cit.*, p. 19.

15. Vlachos, *op. cit.*, p. 229; Haralampos K. Papastathis, 'The Church and the Macedonian Struggle', in *Proceedings of the Symposium on the The Macedonian Struggle*, pp. 69-70.

16. K. Svolopoulos, 'The Decision to Organize the Armed Struggle', in *Proceedings of the Symposium on the Macedonian Struggle*, Thessaloniki 1987, p. 53; Dakin, *op. cit.*, pp. 119-133.

17. Dakin, *op. cit.*, pp. 142-145; Kofos, 'Struggles', pp. 470-471; Tsamis, *op. cit.*, pp. 152-159; AGS/AHD, *op. cit.*, pp. 116-117.

18. Dakin, *op. cit.*, pp. 112-115; Vlachos, *op. cit.*, pp. 294-297.

19. AGS/AHD, *op. cit.*, pp. 130-138, 346-348.

20. AGS/AHD, *op. cit.*, pp. 138-146; Dakin, *op. cit.*, pp. 162-183; Vlachos, *op. cit.*, pp. 326-343.

21. Anonymous, *Pavlos Melas. Biography* (in Greek), Athens 1931, p. 440.

22. Konstantinos A. Vakalopoulos, *The Macedonian Struggle (1904-1908). The Armed Phase* (in Greek), Thessaloniki 1987, pp. 69-97.

23. Mazarakis, *op. cit.*, pp. 208-210.

24. Dakin, *op. cit.*, pp. 221-242.

25. Vlachos, *op. cit.*, pp. 339-411.

26. Athanasios Souliotis-Nikolaidis, 'The Macedonian Struggle. The Organization of Thessaloniki.1908-1908', from *Memoirs*, Thessaloniki 1959, pp. 31-49.

27. AGS/AHD, *op. cit.*, pp. 207-234; Dakin, *op. cit.*, pp. 250-279; Belia, 'Educational policy', p. 36.

28. Vlachos, *op. cit.*, pp. 455-470; Dakin, *op. cit.*, pp. 288-294, 301-305.

29. Dakin, *op. cit.*, pp. 306-339; AGS/AHD, *op. cit.*, pp. 243-280; Belia, 'Educational policy', p. 35.

30. Vasileios Gounaris, 'From Macedonia to Goudi. Activities of the Officers-Fighters of the Macedonian Struggle(1908-1909)' (in Greek), *Bulletin of the Historical and Ethnological Society of Greece*, 29 (1986), 181-189.

31. AGS/AHD, *op. cit.*, p. 300

32. Dakin, *op. cit.*, pp. 385-392; Kostis Moskov, *Thessaloniki. Profile of the Trading City* (in Greek), Athens 1978, pp. 145-146; Centre for Marxist Research, *The Socialist Organization* Federation *in Thessaloniki 1909-1918* (in Greek), Athens 1989, p. 40 and footnote 3.

33. Gounaris, 'From Macedonia to Goudi', 189-225; Konstantinos A. Vakalopoulos, *Young Turks and Macedonia 1908-1912* (in Greek), Thessaloniki 1988, pp. 218-247.

34. Dakin, *op. cit.*, pp. 392-396; Ioannis Koliopoulos, 'The Situation in Macedonia from 1909-1912', from *History of the Greek Nation* (in Greek), vol. 14, Athens 1977, pp. 279-280; Vakalopoulos, *Young Turks*, pp. 261-350, 371-379, 382-395.

35. John S. Koliopoulos, *Brigands with a Cause. Brigandage and Irredentism in Modern Greece 1821-1912*, Oxford 1987, pp. 215-236.

END OF VOLUME II